2016 • UNITED STATES OLYMPIC TEAM TRIALS
57 KG CHAMPIONSHIP SEMIFINAL
RAMOS FLEXES AFTER HIS VICTORY OVER SCOTT
PHOTOGRAPH COURTESY • UNIVERSITY OF IOWA ATHLETICS

The Official Biography
Wrestling with Ramos
Behind the Stare
• TC LiFonti

One Forty-Two Productions, LLC
Illinois

©2017 • TC LIFONTI • ONE FORTY-TWO PRODUCTIONS, LLC

Any reproduction of this work, whether it be scanning and posting or distributing or imaging or reworking this story for any use of any kind, without the expressed written consent of TC LiFonti and One Forty-Two Productions, LLC, is strictly prohibited.

ISBN • 978-0692508626 • TC LIFONTI
ISBN • 0692508627

Editor • Peter Giaquinta

Photographs • Glenbard North Photographs / Courtesy: Ramos Family • Courtesy: Glenbard North Wrestling

Photographs / Some photographs from Glenbard North High School produced and purchased from Marlon Brooks Photography • Photographs also courtesy of Jeff Eldridge • TC LiFonti • Glenbard North Yearbook

Photographs • University of Iowa and Olympic Team Trials Photographs / Courtesy: University of Iowa Athletics

Front Cover Photograph / Courtesy: University of Iowa Athletics
Back Cover Photograph / Courtesy: University of Iowa Athletics

Photographs • The remainder of the photographs purchased or taken by the Ramos family or family member; however, for some of the pictures, the photographer and/or company or where the photograph was taken is unknown. Some of photographs are courtesy of Tony and Megan Ramos.

Logos • All logos have been used with a consent from Tony Ramos, Glenbard North High School Wrestling, the University of Iowa, and the Tar Heel Wrestling Club.

Printed in the United States of America • Self Publication through www.createspace.com
Title • Set in Times New Roman
Text • Set in Times New Roman

While the author has made every effort to provide accurate information, such as matches and scores, records, numbers, names, Internet addresses, and other contact information at the time of publication, neither the author, TC LiFonti, nor the publishing company, nor production company, nor Anthony Ramos assumes any responsibility for errors or for changes that occur after publication. Further, the author or publishing company or Anthony Ramos does not have any control over and does not assume any responsibility for third-party websites or their content and representation/s. All photographs used were either taken by or purchased by the Ramos family or used with permission of the University of Iowa Athletic Department or Glenbard North High School Wrestling or Yearbook. Any photograph not credited is unknown or uncertain as to the photographer; however, photos were purchased or taken by a member of the Ramos family and thus their permission was given for use. Any logo used is with consent.

WWW.TEAMRAMOS.CO

ABOUT THE AUTHOR
TC LiFonti

TC LiFonti is an English teacher and coach at Glenbard North High School in Carol Stream, Illinois, where he has been employed since 1999. Prior to, he spent one year at Galesburg High School, Illinois, where he also taught English and coached.

Since, he has been a published poet and children's book author; at North he coaches both wrestling and football.

LiFonti earned his bachelor's in creative writing and literature, as well as received a master's degree, from North Central College in Naperville, Illinois, where he wrestled and played football for the Cardinals. Additionally, he intermittently wrote for the college's paper.

Currently, LiFonti is hoping to put together a series of biographies or stories on wrestlers and coaches to help grow the sport by bringing attention to great moments—triumphs as well as defeats. Through those publications, he hopes to bring about and uncover how people have grown and worked through obstacles or successes and make them available to the ever-growing and deserving wrestling community.

For a sport that is so rich in history, not enough has been shared. LiFonti's hope is to collect and share stories and allow younger wrestlers to learn and grow through their heroes' lives, as well as allow older fans to look back in appreciation to what they were able to witness or be a part of in that moment.

Grow wrestling.

OTHER WORKS BY TC LIFONTI
TCLIFONTI.COM

Each of TC LiFonti's five children's books are co-authored with Charles "Peanut" Tillman, a former All-Pro cornerback for the Chicago Bears and the Carolina Panthers. Tillman, who heads the Charles Tillman Cornerstone Foundation and who is a very strong philanthropic figure throughout the states of Illinois and North Carolina, works tirelessly to help enrich the lives of those around him and those in need. Since 2005, Charles Tillman's charitable efforts have impacted the lives of over one million children.

One Forty-Two Productions, LLC, in partnership with the Charles Tillman Cornerstone Foundation, is donating a portion of all earnings from each of the five children's books to the foundation and its efforts to continually help those in need.

For more information or ways to donate • charlestillman.org

ALL BOOKS CAN BE PURCHASED • amazon.com

ALL TITLES ARE ALSO AVAILABLE IN SPANISH

TABLE OF CONTENTS

11 • 17	INTRODUCTION	• BY TC LiFONTI	
18 • 19	FOREWORD	• BY ANTHONY RAMOS	

SECTION I • IZZY STYLE • GLENBARD NORTH HIGH SCHOOL

22 • 29	CHAPTER 1	• NINE DAYS OUT
30 • 38	CHAPTER 2	• LEARNING HOW TO WRESTLE AND WALK
39 • 41	CHAPTER 3	• THE GREATEST MATCH EVER WRESTLED
42 • 57	CHAPTER 4	• DOIN' IT IZZY STYLE
60 • 79	CHAPTER 5	• THE PROGRAM
80 • 87	CHAPTER 6	• MAKING GOOD ON AN OLD PROMISE
88 • 92	CHAPTER 7	• GOING BACKWARD TO MOVE FORWARD
93 • 98	CHAPTER 8	• GROWING PAINS
99 • 109	CHAPTER 9	• CUTTING TO THE CHASE
110 • 116	CHAPTER 10	• MAKING HIMSELF KNOWN
117 • 121	CHAPTER 11	• BEING DIFFERENT
122 • 134	CHAPTER 12	• JUST ANOTHER TOURNAMENT
135 • 159	CHAPTER 13	• FIGHTING FOR THE OPPORTUNITY
160 • 162	CHAPTER 14	• AFTER HOURS
163 • 173	CHAPTER 15	• INCENTIVE-BASED WRESTLING
174 • 182	CHAPTER 16	• WORKING WITH THE WEIGHT
183 • 185	CHAPTER 17	• THE LONGEST LESSON EVER LEARNED
186 • 193	CHAPTER 18	• BOOED AND SNUBBED
194 • 198	CHAPTER 19	• THE NEXT CHALLENGE
199 • 203	CHAPTER 20	• A BUMP AND A MOHAWK
204 • 209	CHAPTER 21	• TAKING DOWN THE RECORD
210 • 217	CHAPTER 22	• ONE FOR THE FAMILY
218 • 224	CHAPTER 23	• THE HEATED FIRST ROUND
225 • 229	CHAPTER 24	• FARGO
230 • 243	CHAPTER 25	• MURDERERS' ROW
244 • 249	CHAPTER 26	• THE TWO SEED
250 • 261	CHAPTER 27	• CHASING TITLES
262 • 272	CHAPTER 28	• BUCKING WITH THE BRONCOS
273 • 275	CHAPTER 29	• A NEW LEADER
276 • 280	CHAPTER 30	• THREE PERCENT
281 • 291	CHAPTER 31	• ONE LAST TIME THROUGH
292 • 300	CHAPTER 32	• THREE OUT OF FOUR
301 • 305	CHAPTER 33	• LAST CHANCE
306 • 309	CHAPTER 34	• SURPRISING EVERYONE ELSE

2016 • UNITED STATES OLYMPIC TEAM TRIALS
57 KG CHAMPIONSHIP SEMIFINAL
RAMOS CELEBRATES AFTER HIS VICTORY OVER SCOTT
PHOTOGRAPH COURTESY • UNIVERSITY OF IOWA ATHLETICS

SECTION II • THE UNIVERSITY OF IOWA

312 • 326	CHAPTER 35	• THE PROGRAM
327 • 339	CHAPTER 36	• BUILDING RELATIONSHIPS
340 • 344	CHAPTER 37	• A SIX-HOUR DRIVE FOR A THIRTY-TWO MINUTE CONVERSATION
345 • 351	CHAPTER 38	• ON HIS WAY OUT THE DOOR
352 • 363	CHAPTER 39	• STEPPING ON THE MAT
364 • 377	CHAPTER 40	• TAKING OVER THE WEIGHT
378 • 387	CHAPTER 41	• COMING UP SHORT
388 • 392	CHAPTER 42	• COMING INTO HIS OWN
393 • 403	CHAPTER 43	• THE MAGIC OF CARVER-HAWKEYE ARENA
404 • 418	CHAPTER 44	• LET IT BEGIN
419 • 425	CHAPTER 45	• OFF TO A FAST START
426 • 435	CHAPTER 46	• CARVER'S LOUDEST MOMENT
436 • 441	CHAPTER 47	• SEPARATING THE FIELD
442 • 459	CHAPTER 48	• THE MONSTER IN HIS CLOSET
460 • 465	CHAPTER 49	• SAYING GOODBYE AND MOVING FORWARD
466 • 475	CHAPTER 50	• THE UNEXPECTED
476 • 483	CHAPTER 51	• UNDEFEATED IN CARVER
484 • 493	CHAPTER 52	• CHASING THAT B1G TITLE
494 • 500	CHAPTER 53	• KEEPING IT CLOSE
501 • 505	CHAPTER 54	• FIGHTING THE SCOT
506 • 517	CHAPTER 55	• THE KING'S HAT

SECTION III • THE HAWKEYE WRESTLING CLUB

520 • 531	CHAPTER 56	• THE TIME IS NOW
532 • 539	CHAPTER 57	• BRANDING THE MODERN WRESTLER
540 • 555	CHAPTER 58	• MAKING A STATEMENT
556 • 564	CHAPTER 59	• THE FOURTH OF JULY IN CANADA
565 • 580	CHAPTER 60	• ADJUSTING TO THE WORLD
581 • 611	CHAPTER 61	• MAKING IT ALL FIT THE SCHEDULE
612 • 623	CHAPTER 62	• THE ELEPHANT IN THE ROOM
624 • 626	CHAPTER 63	• QUALIFYING THE WEIGHT
627 • 629	CHAPTER 64	• EXCITED AND AGITATED
630 • 653	CHAPTER 65	• THE TRIALS' TRIALS
654 • 658	CHAPTER 66	• OUT TO DINNER
659 • 669	CHAPTER 67	• IT TOOK A HAWKEYE TO BEAT A HAWKEYE
670 • 675	CHAPTER 68	• THE BLOWOUT
676 • 688	CHAPTER 69	• THE BETRAYAL
689 • 692	CHAPTER 70	• OUT FOR BLOOD, OUT FOR A BURRITO
693 • 697	CHAPTER 71	• MONDAY MORNING
700 • 716	BIBLIOGRAPHY	

2008 • IHSA REGIONAL CHAMPIONSHIPS
RAMOS TAKING VIDEO OF HIS BROTHER VINCE'S CHAMPIONSHIP MATCH.
PHOTOGRAPH COURTESY • GLENBARD NORTH WRESTLING • JEFF ELDRIDGE

INTRODUCTION
BY TC LiFONTI

WHEN I HAD FIRST MET TONY RAMOS, HE WAS about eleven years old. We were holding an open mat at Glenbard North High School in Carol Stream, Illinois, and Frankie Defilippis, Tony's eldest brother, brought both of his younger brothers, Tony and Vince, into the room to work out because he was looking after them for the day; Frankie taking the boys was nothing out of the ordinary.

At that point, I had known Frankie for about two years and he was always bragging about how talented his brothers were and that they would also be coming to North just as he had done—Frankie wrestled for North from 1995 through 1998.

Anyway, while practice was going on it was very difficult to not peek over every now and then and watch this little kid just wrestling as hard as he could against his older, bigger, heavier, and more talented brother. His tenacity caught my eye more than anything else. No matter what position he was in, he just kept fighting.

Now, when I say that Tony and Vince were going at it, I mean they were coming at each other with heavy forearms in the back of the other's head and then yanking the other with strong tugs, constant motion, fakes and levels, and just a relentless pursuit of trying beat up and score on one another while not being scored on.

For about the first five minutes of the live session, the little brother, Tony, was abusing the older, Vince. Tony would get in on Vince's leg and circle, come out or draw Vince in before blasting him with a double-leg. This is not to say that Vince was not abusing Tony back, physically, because Tony was taking his share of the punishment—Tony was just fighting to earn his takedowns. Tony would snap Vince into a front headlock and then circle and pull until he could find a way around him. He was unrelenting.

The hand posts to the head may as well have been jabs. There were slaps to the face, cupping of the ears on ties, and more fighting hands than hand fighting. Getting up after a takedown required pushing off the other brother's head or back or shoving him into the wall with a palm to the face while bracing himself as he was shoved back in the face or chest or the back. There was no out of bounds—the walls and the doors were in—and Frankie allowed no water breaks for these two. He told them, "You're here to wrestle. I don't want to see you stopping or bitching or not working. If I see that, I'm sending you back home tonight."

As the wrestling continued, I walked up to my friend, another assistant coach, Chris Edwards, and we took a look and started commenting on the boys. It was easy to see that Vince was the more gifted; however, it was just as easy to see that Tony was the fighter. Even though Vince would put Tony in bad positions, Tony was determined not to allow a score and battled out of each situation. Until it happened.

As Chris and I were watching, Tony took a hard shot on Vince, drove him to the mat—shoulder in his chest—pushed on Vince's face to get up, and then started taunting him with his body language.

Vince worked to his feet, took a shot in on Tony, lifted him up, and drove him down to the mat where the mat and the wall joined—it was the first takedown I had seen Vince score, and he asserted his own toughness in that moment. From there, Vince wrapped up a tight waist and chopped Tony's arm sending Tony's face into the mat before Vince pressured into him with his forearm and drove his younger brother's head into the west wall of the wrestling room.

Tony, not happy with the pressure, grabbed one of Vince's fingers and started bending it backward, not letting it go until he had found a way to his feet. When Tony finally circled out and found himself in the neutral position, Vince stopped and looked at his finger—but Tony moved forward. As Vince looked up to say something to Tony for bending it back, Tony just wound up and threw a right hook and landed it on his brother's jaw. All Tony said as Vince looked at him, confused about the punch, was, "You made me look bad in front of Coach Hahn," and then Tony took a hard double-leg and Vince began to defend it—the two continued their live wrestling.

FROM THERE, I WOULD SEE TONY WHEN I WAS

over by Frankie's house to go out or hang out or go up to their lake house for boating or whatever. However, no matter when it was that I saw Tony, I was always reminded of that first moment—that first impression.

When Vince came to North, a year ahead of Tony in school, Vince and I became really close. I had the pleasure of being mat side for Vince and helped coach him through the state series. His senior season, when he won his first state championship, I was lucky enough to be in his corner with Frankie and share in his success—he had finally claimed what could have been a second or third state title.

Throughout high school, once Tony entered, Frankie and I still hung out, and Vince and I would have some good conversations at the house or have some playful banter—Tony would try to jump into the conversations or give a side comment, but nothing more.

One day in the practice room, Tony's sophomore year, I was working with Vince and made a comment to Tony about his technique. He was dead set on chasing the ankle on his slide-by even on taller opponents who could step out of or over it due to Tony's shorter reach. I told him to attack the knee and close the gap quicker.

Tony was not open for critiques; in fact, he was pissed.

"Don't talk to me!" Tony screamed. "You don't talk to me." Then he waved me off with the back of his hand. "You like Vince better than me anyway. Talk to him! Coach him!"

I looked up at Frankie and smiled with a laugh and said, "What a little prick." Frankie smiled back and told Tony, "Eh, do as Coach LiFonti says." Then, begrudgingly, Tony practiced it until Frankie told him that he could get working on something else.

After practice Tony stomped around and gave me two stares with no words: When I checked him in on the scale for his weight, and when he walked past the coaches' office upon leaving the locker room.

That same night, when I saw Tony at Frankie's house, he came up and pushed me in the back without saying anything—I knew that was his apology and I knew, even well before that push, that was Tony. I loved the kid.

WHEN TONY WAS IN EIGHTH GRADE, HE CREATED

a book for a project at Stratford Middle School in Ms. Campbell's Language Arts class. The title of Tony's book was, *My Book about Me*.

Inside of the book Tony had artwork that accented his name, Anthony Joseph, going vertically on the page, and small pieces of clip art that represented his personality. On top of the 'A' in Anthony, he had placed a king's crown. For the 'T' it was TONY, for the 'H' it was HELPFUL, and for the 'N' and the 'Y' he spelled out NEW YORK. Above the 'J' in Joseph, Tony placed a storm cloud with two thunderbolts of lightening, and inside of the 'O' there was an old man cradling a baby. Much of what was placed on this opening page symbolizes a great deal about Tony even early on. His desire to be successful or sustain a type of wealth. His ability to want to state who he is, but also be helpful to others. As for New York, there is no greater stage to perform on—and Tony is a performer.

For his middle name, the clouds and lightening may have represented what he felt he was in store for his opponents. The man cradling the baby shows his compassion or need for support; it may represent him most at the end of the day.

The next page had a poem about where Tony was from:

"Where I'm From"

I'm from the windy city and a car speeding by
while I am crossing the street.
I'm from the tires screeching and the blood gushing.
I'm from the ambulance coming and
the life-threatening accident.

I'm from the smell of bleach coming off the mats.
The crowd screaming as I win the match.
I'm from the "Go to your room" and the "You're grounded."

I'm from the green and tan park with the sand
getting in your shoes.
I'm from the "not its" and the game I love the most:
Freeze Tag.

What followed next was a timeline of his life up to that point. His first holidays and when he started wrestling. The dates of his stitches and when he was hit by a car. When he started playing football, won his state championships, and his first New Year's Eve party. Behind the timeline was a picture of the Olympic rings.

There would then be another poem that followed:

"I Am"

I am caring, thoughtful, and athletic.
I wonder about what happens after death.
I hear people honking as I walk through city streets.
I see my opponent across from me on the mat.
I want my family to love me.
I am caring, thoughtful, and athletic.

I pretend to be standing on the top of the Olympic podium.
I feel the love from my family.
I touch the leather pigskin football before I throw it.
I think about how people starve every day.
I understand not enough
I am caring, thoughtful, and athletic.

I believe in family and myself.
I say many things before I want to.
I dream of winning a gold medal.

INTRODUCTION • BY TC LiFONTI

> I try my hardest every day.
> I hope for my dreams to come true.
> I am caring, thoughtful, and athletic.

The final pieces of his book dealt with his favorite things and a comparison of someone or something else to whom he felt that he was. Here are Tony's favorite basics in 2005:

FOOD	I love steak because it is very good for me and it is high in protein.
MUSIC	Techno or dance is my favorite music because it gets me pumped up for when I have tough matches.
SPORT	Wrestling is my favorite sport because I love it and have been around it since I was a very little kid.
ACTIVITIES	My favorite activity is cooking. I love to cook and I think I might be a chef someday.
CLASS	I love science. It is so interesting to me because I like dissecting things and mixing chemicals. I also like learning about the universe and how there could be more people out there.
PLACE TO GO	Somewhere by the ocean. The ocean makes me relax because the sound of the waves coming in and the beautiful fish just make it so easy to have fun.
COLOR	Pink is my favorite color because it is so bright. If I could, I would have a pink room so in the morning I am not so tired.
MOVIE	I love any type of action movie. I like always having to predict what will happen next or being on the edge of my seat. Also, I like when things blow up.
TV SHOW	My favorite TV show is *Lizzie McGuire* because it is about kids our age and things that go on our age.
THINGS TO DO	My favorite thing to do is be with my friends or girlfriend. I hate being alone because it is just so boring. I like being active.

In regard to who or what he saw himself close to, he chose to write about Kermit the Frog. He discussed how Kermit was green and the color green brightened his day. Tony also described how Kermit was "loving and caring for his family and friends, just like me." Kermit "would always try to help out his friends if anything was wrong, just like me." Finally, "Kermit is optimistic. He always thinks for the good in things and not the bad. He always tries to cheer people up no matter what is wrong. I try to do that, but I am not the best at it, but I try."

Now, all of those pieces are from a fourteen-year-old and maybe some of those ideals still hold true to who he still is. I believe the best part about that project is having something to connect and reflect on and see where one was at, what his dreams and goals were, and then how he went about, even at an early age, trying to chase those dreams. Just as important, even if he knew who he was and what was ahead of him, how sometimes one changes and sometimes remains the same.

WHEN I APPROACHED TONY ABOUT WRITING THIS biography in 2015, we were in agreement: be open and honest—no secrets—and let us see this through no matter what happens.

As Tony has grown as a wrestler and a young man, I have been fortunate enough to have known him through it all. And, in those years, there have been some changes, and there have been some things about him that will never change.

Tony's pursuit of greatness is nothing less than willing himself to be great. His work ethic and his desire to be great are the cornerstone of what has pushed him to where he is. He has never been shy or one to hold back his feelings—if he feels it, he says it. If he is wrong, he owns it. If he is right, he echoes it. And if he is not sorry, he will not apologize. In this, Tony has either made people love him or made people hate him. But, to Tony, he is not going to change to appease the masses or be someone that he is not. Tony is Tony. I learned that very early on. This is not to say that he does not reflect back and right his wrongs—like all people, some aspects in life take longer than others.

As we started going through his life and talking and sharing stories, it became more and more apparent that Tony was someone who was determined at an early age and someone who always found a way to be successful or win in the end—no matter what the drawback was. Nothing ever came easy to Tony and he fought for what he has been able to accomplish; he has always been very willful.

This biography covers Tony's childhood years as a kids' club wrestler, into his high school and college years, and then into his international competition. There are moments where his life is personal and other moments where it is very open. But the story is about Tony and those who have impacted him and how he has responded—good or bad. The biography stretches all the way through the 2016 Olympic Trials in Iowa City, Iowa. Much of the focus will be on Tony's growth, successes, failures, and reflections that have made him who he is and placed him where he is currently at. There are moments of triumph, defeat, laughter,

INTRODUCTION • BY TC LiFONTI

and sadness. I do hope people enjoy the following pages and have a better understanding or appreciation for Tony Ramos—not only as a wrestler, but also as a person. I hope this provides a deeper look into Tony's life and provides people with a better sense of who he truly is.

I know there will be critics and I know there will be those who question why I wrote a book on Tony Ramos. The critics will say what they will; however, as to why Tony Ramos: he has had a profound impact on the sport of wrestling. Some of it is hard work and talent. Some of it is timing. Some of it is his brash outspokenness. Some of it is how he is villainized by others. Regardless, Tony Ramos is a very relevant person in the world of wrestling. Not only is he one of the best in America, but he, like many, has a story to tell. In that, I hope you enjoy the following pages.

FOREWORD
BY ANTHONY RAMOS

WHEN COACH LIFONTI FIRST APPROACHED ME about releasing a biography about my story, the first question I asked myself was: *Why? Why would someone want to know more about me?* Then it hit me. *Do people really know who I am?* Yes, they know Tony Ramos the wrestler, but do they know what makes him up? What was my upbringing, my social life, my family life? I thought this was a great opportunity to allow people in on a more personal side—what makes me me and what makes up the man behind the stare.

As I read through the book, it was like going through a time capsule of emotions. It brought back many great childhood times and many great accomplishments. It also brought back setbacks and difficult times. One thing that always stayed constant throughout was the support of the people surrounding me that I always was able to fall back on. I am very grateful to have made amazing relationships and friends along this journey.

People always ask, "If you could do it over, what would you change?" For me: nothing. Even though everything was not always sunshine and rainbows, as you read in the book you will see that I always learned something from each situation.

Coach Mark Hahn may have been the least-credentialed coach I had, but he was the best. Not in terms of technique and skill, but he was the man who taught me about work ethic and life lessons that I have used and will use forever. Izzy Martinez showed me how tough I really was and what I was capable of doing. Tom and Terry Brands helped guide me to that next level. Yes, with all the coaches I listed above, there were times we bumped heads or had falling outs—but I can truly say they have each molded me into the man, athlete, and coach I am today. I don't regret any time with any of them because of what it has made me become.

Along with these coaches, there were many other people who had a great impact on my life, starting with my mom and dad. They drove hours on end and spent countless amounts of money. They also let my brother and me out of their homes and lives at a very young age. Looking back now and reading some of these stories, you guys were crazy. And, Frankie, you were even crazier. I don't know how a twenty-four-year-old in his prime just out of college could even think about moving in two teenage boys, but you had the fortitude to make it happen for the better of us. There have been many sacrifices made for my success and one of the biggest that goes unnoticed, even in this book, is my sister Brandi. Thank you.

There are things that are in this book that people may never fully understand, and one of those is the time lost with my family. I have missed milestones in my children's lives and even with my wife that I can never have back. I just hope one day that when my children understand what their dad was doing, they can be proud. I can never have their first Thanksgiving or Halloween back, but I hope I have created memories with my family and boys that will mean much more. One day, when they grow up and read this book, I hope that they will understand who their dad was—not just as Dad, but as a competitor, coach, and person.

The goal of this book was to give people an inside look at myself and who I really am. Through the stories and events, I hope my fans, the wrestling community, and anyone else out there can truly see there is more to me than just the stare. There is a compassionate, fierce competitor and person. Thank you to everyone who has made me who I am today and that has been along for the ride.

For my wife and children.
Thank you for allowing me the time to pursue my other passions.

CHAPTER 1
NINE DAYS OUT

"Four years ago I sat right here with my brother as I watched the Trials unfold. I told him and myself that the next time this came around, I would be out there not just competing, but claiming my spot on the Olympic team."

• *Tony Ramos*

MARCH 27, 2016

TWO WEEKS FROM TODAY, 22 YEARS OF HARD work, dedication and sacrifice from myself, my family, my coaches, and my team will be put on the line to represent the greatest country in the world at the Olympic Games! #HWC #Rio2016

• • •

That was Tony Ramos' first Instagram post in a countdown leading up to the 2016 United States Olympic Team Trials in Iowa City, Iowa; the Trials would be held at Carver-Hawkeye Arena. At that point in Tony's career, he had already been a two-time United States World Team Member, undefeated domestically on the senior level, and had yet to be defeated inside of Carver-Hawkeye Arena on any level.

The rise of Tony Ramos through the senior circuit came immediately after his exit from the University of Iowa where he was a Big Ten and NCAA champion at 133 pounds. A few months later, he stepped onto the mat as a member of the Hawkeye Wrestling Club at 57 kg; once on the senior scene, Tony never looked back.

Headed into the 2016 Olympic Trials, Tony had put himself in the best position possible to be an Olympian. He was the number-one ranked wrestler in America at his weight, and he had proven his merit state side and overseas—he was ranked number fourteen in the world, and he was confident. However, even with his successes, there were many critics who always picked against him—up to that point, Tony had always proven them wrong. Therefore, as the Olympic Team Trials neared, it was one more tournament where Tony would have to prove his critics wrong and, if he did, he would represent the United States of America at 57 kg in the 2016 Rio de Janeiro Olympic Games.

Nine days out, leading up to the Trials, Tony used his Instagram account to countdown the days and thank the people closest to him before everything that he had ever worked for would be on the line in a one-day tournament. Here was his countdown:

• • •

APRIL 1, 2016

#9Days #IowaCityToRio • Doing a

countdown of some of the most important people on my journey as we countdown the days until I compete in Iowa City to cement my spot in Rio! #9 is one man who is behind the scenes and will never get the credit he deserves, but is a huge part in my success! My buddy @Pilcher_Mania10 is there no matter the situation. If we need a house/dog/ babysitter, he drops what he has to make it happen. If I need a workout partner at night so I don't need to do it alone, he finds a way to drive up to 30 minutes to make it happen. He tries to make sure I am as comfortable as possible in the process leading up to go time—whether it's driving me or picking up whatever I need. Go give my man a follow, and I will

TONY RAMOS' INSTAGRAM ACCOUNT
COURTESY • TONY AND MEGAN RAMOS

never be able to thank you enough! Stay tuned to see who is featured tomorrow! #USA #OlympicTrials

• • •

APRIL 2, 2016

#8DAYS #IOWACITYTORIO • TODAY'S FEATURE

goes out to all of my partners over my career that have helped me prepare for battle, but a few special ones that have been put in roles they may not have chosen. These guys have helped me at some of the most crucial times to prepare for the biggest moments in my career. Thanks @JakeKadel, Nick Trizzino, @PhillyCheeseSteakao1 for even when you were not competing, still coming back to make sure I got what I needed!

APRIL 2, 2016

Today we're getting some gymnastics in, but getting very excited to see Carver transformed for the OTT. Can't wait to hear the roars of the Hawkeye faithful when welcoming me back to for my first match! Let's sell it out!

• • •

APRIL 3, 2016

#7DAYS #IOWACITYTORIO • TODAY IS GOING

out to all the coaches that have helped me grow into the wrestler I am today. Starting all the way from the coaching staff at the Villa-Lombard Cougars, Stateline Wildcats, Jr. Golden Eagles, Wrestling Factory, and Martinez Elite. Then to my high school wrestling staff at Glenbard North. @IzzyStyleWrestling who really started to get me going towards my Olympic Dream. The Iowa coaching staff and especially Tom and Terry Brands who have taught me how to make myself the best athlete and man I can be!

PHOTOGRAPHS COURTESY • TONY RAMOS

APRIL 3, 2016

A.J. and Mom had a great day at the park out in the ☀ today while dad was at practice and at home resting!

APRIL 4, 2016

#6DAYS #IOWACITYTORIO • TODAY I WANT TO

say thank you to all my fans over the years! Your support does not go unnoticed. Also, a big thank you to the Hawkeye faithful who welcomed me to Iowa City seven years ago with open arms. I cannot wait to compete in this beautiful environment again and look forward to a sold out crowd April 9th and 10th! Let's blow the roof off Carver on Sunday.

APRIL 5, 2016

#5DAYS #IOWACITYTORIO • TODAY GOES OUT

to all the teammates I have had over my career who have been there during the good times and the bad. There are way too many people to name and it could take all day, but you guys know who you are and thanks for pushing one another and lifting each other up when we were down!

APRIL 6, 2016

#4DAYS #IOWACITYTORIO • TODAY GOES OUT

to all my sponsors they make it possible for me to put all my efforts into becoming my best while supporting my family with no worries. You guys are a huge part in my success by making life outside of wrestling worry free! Thank you @FlipsWrestling @DanmarWarrior @AsicsWrestling @PristineHydro @HookSweep @TitanMercuryWrestling #HawkeyeWrestlingClub

APRIL 6, 2016

Four years ago I sat right here with my brother as I watched the Trials unfold. I told him and myself that the next time this came around, I would be out there not just competing, but claiming my spot on the Olympic team. Four years and two World Teams later I have put myself in position to make this happen; now I need to show up on Sunday! #IowaCityToRio @TeamUSA

TONY RAMOS' INSTAGRAM ACCOUNT
PHOTOGRAPH COURTESY • TONY RAMOS

APRIL 7, 2016
#3DAYS #IOWACITYTORIO • TODAY IS GOING TO

be a long one, so here is your warning. This one is to my family. Not just my immediate family, but everyone who I consider my family. Thank you for all your support Mom and Dad through the years and always believing in me. To Frankie and @BeatriceDefil28 who has put up with him watching hours of film and letting him travel the world with me. To my sister @Brandi_Alexis21 who was always in the shadows growing up, but you stood and supported me through it all. One the biggest ones, @VinceRamos1989 who has been through more than 90% of this journey right by my side putting in the same work! You made me work harder every day and made me as tough as I am today. Now onto my family that travels everywhere and I can always count on when in need. The Hensley family: @DeliaPadilla, @MelHens, @JHens89, Jerry, Brandon, @BrittMariex26 and Matt I know with your support I always have the biggest crowd! Vinny and @MamaMaria15, thanks for letting Vinny have unlimited knowledge of all wrestling by watching Flo all day long. Geno, Gregrow, Rader, Smith, Timmy D, Timmy W, and many more I am forgetting right now, I know I have the toughest group around! Thank you everyone for all your support not just these past years but from the moment we met!

TONY RAMOS' INSTAGRAM ACCOUNT
PHOTOGRAPH COURTESY • TONY AND MEGAN RAMOS

APRIL 8, 2016

#2DAYS #IOWACITYTORIO • THIS LITTLE MAN

may be the smallest fan of mine, but is the one of the biggest also. My son has been put on the back burner a little bit these past few weeks and hasn't gotten the attention he has deserved from dad, but he has been great and the happiest baby. He motivates me even more every day and has made me a better person. Little man, I love you and can't wait to celebrate with you on Sunday!

TONY RAMOS' INSTAGRAM ACCOUNT PHOTOGRAPH COURTESY • TONY AND MEGAN RAMOS

APRIL 9, 2016

#1DAY #IOWACITYTORIO • THIS LAST ONE IS FOR MY BEAUTIFUL WIFE

@Megan_Ramos who, no matter what happens, will always be proud of me and by my side. She makes me a better person and a better athlete. Let's go finish this journey we've been on for the past few years together tomorrow and start planning our trip to Rio!

TONY RAMOS' INSTAGRAM ACCOUNT
PHOTOGRAPH COURTESY • TONY AND MEGAN RAMOS

• • •

ON APRIL 9, 2016, WHEN IT WAS TIME FOR WEIGH-ins, Tony first stepped on the scale, and then, as he stepped off, he began building his body back up—he would be on the mat competing for his dream of being an Olympian in less than twenty-four hours. A lifetime of work would come to a head and, at the end of the Trials, Tony believed that his next stop was Rio de Janeiro, Brazil, for the 2016 Olympic Games.

Tony would leave Carver-Hawkeye Arena, return home, relax, and then, a few hours later, he would head out for a family dinner with the people closest to him. Over the course of his ten-day countdown, Tony had a great deal of time to reflect on those who had made a profound impact on him and his journey as both a person and a wrestler; however, Tony's journey to become an Olympian started long before he was one of the best wrestlers coming out of Illinois, and well before he was the face of Iowa wrestling. It began as a three-year-old in Carol Stream, Illinois, when he was trying to mimic the same wrestling moves he saw his oldest brother learning while at his club's practice. From that point forward, Tony would always wrestle.

TONY RAMOS' INSTAGRAM ACCOUNT
PHOTOGRAPH COURTESY • TONY AND MEGAN RAMOS

2017 • THE RAMOS "WOLF PACK"
TONY RAMOS • LINCOLN RAMOS • AJ RAMOS
PHOTOGRAPH COURTESY • TONY AND MEGAN RAMOS

1994 • VILLA-LOMBARD COUGAR PICTURE DAY
RAMOS GROWLS FOR THE CAMERA IN HIS FIRST WRESTLING PICTURE
PHOTOGRAPH COURTESY • TONY RAMOS

CHAPTER 2
LEARNING HOW TO WRESTLE AND WALK

"He was always into everything. He had so much energy and was always just so determined and curious."

• *Deb Ramos*
Mother

IN 1994, AT THE AGE OF THREE, TONY RAMOS first consciously stepped on a wrestling mat working moves and actually wrestling. Since his eldest brother Frank Defilippis was in the Villa-Lombard Cougars kids' club, and Tony and Vince looked up to him, it was only natural that they would follow as wrestlers—if Frank was doing something, the boys also wanted to do it. And, if Tony wanted to do it, he wanted to do it better than Vince or Frank—even at an early age everything was always a competition to Tony.

Coincidentally, as Frank was entering his final year with the Cougars—he was in eighth-grade and would be attending Glenbard North High School the next year—their mom, Deb, thought it was important and wanted the boys to all be on the same team for one year. It would be the only chance all three boys would ever have to compete together as brothers.

The only catch was the ages of the boys, but it did not bother Deb or her husband, Al, and it did not seem to bother the boys either.

"At first," Deb remembered, "we would just take Vince and Tony into the [wrestling] room to watch Frankie and Dana [Holland]. But, as soon as we got home, Tony would start doing the moves on Vince that they were doing at practice."

Unfortunately, Vince would take the worst of it as Tony did not necessarily know everything that he was doing, but he was doing it in a fierce manner. "Vince would have scratches all over his face," Deb said. "If Tony didn't like something Vince did or if Vince got the best of Tony, Tony would scratch his face and rip his skin. But that was just the way Tony was."

Then, as the boys came and watched more practices and started trying to practice with the older boys along the side where they were supposed to be watching, it was obvious they wanted to wrestle.

Frank remembered, "At an early age, Tony wanted to wrestle more than Vince. But if Tony was doing it, Vince was doing it."

"It was Tony who asked me to be on the team," Deb remembered. "And I told him I would have to speak with the coaches." From there, Deb spoke with [Head Coach] Jim Considine and asked if she and Al could coach a little kids' room.

Considine loved the idea and now Vince and Tony would have a room where they could learn the sport at a pace that was beneficial to them.

Fortunately, that room also opened the opportunity for other children to come in and be exposed to the sport in a positive way at an early age. But, do not for one second think that just because there was a "little kids' room" that there was full compassion when the boys struggled. There was not. True to the family, when one of the boys was on his back, and early on it was usually Tony, the others let him know about it. There would a number of days where Vince would beat up Tony in the room—the sport just came much more naturally to Vince—and Deb and Al would walk past Tony and say, "How many lights can you count on the ceiling, Tone?"

Even at an early age, Tony knew what that meant—being on his back meant being ridiculed. Deb said, "He knew we were picking on him and he understood why. He knew he wasn't supposed to be on his back and, if he was, he was going to hear about from us. He had to learn to fight—and he always fought. He was relentless and always tried as hard as he could. But he was smaller and he had to take his beatings—but he never backed down."

Little did Vince and Tony know that they would start their wrestling careers in the very same room that would close out their high school careers—the Glenbard North varsity wrestling room.

For Tony and Vince, walking into those Villa-Lombard practices was special. Not only did the Cougars have a rich tradition and established history of success, but the boys became very comfortable with the coaches, the practices, and the surroundings. The Cougars had already won team state championships and had numerous place-winners and individual state champions. The boys were around the best in the state in those early years.

Even though there were separate rooms for the age groups, the practices began with the entire club warming up as one. The younger wrestlers would warm up with the older boys; the warm-up run and routine would be led by the leaders of the program and, to many of the younger wrestlers, this made those warm-ups very special—they were actually running around and interacting with the boys they looked up to.

However, even though some of the older boys were being looked up to, Tony had his own ideas on what he wanted even at a young age, and he walked around that way. Even though imagining a three-year-old as walking around with a confident stride seems almost impossible, no matter what his age was, or what he was doing, he was always aggressive and relentless, and he simply walked around that way. In fact, it was not just on the mat. Sometimes, at home, Tony would simply attack Vince out of the blue for no apparent reason.

Vince told how, "I had to put vitamin E oil on my face because he would just run up and claw at my face. He was a pain in the ass and a brat. But even when he was in trouble, and even when he wasn't, he always walked around with that swagger. He never cared what anyone thought or said; he was basically going to do what he wanted and what made him happy."

Even when it came time for the Cougars to take their season pictures as a team and as individuals, Tony would poise himself in the manner he wanted to be seen.

Vince recalls how Tony had "put Power Ranger tattoos up and down his arms for his pictures. He got in his stance and just started growling at the camera. Growling at the camera, what kid does that? He was asked to smile by the cameraman, but he stayed put, stared into that camera, and kept growling."

Maybe this moment was the unconscious beginning of Tony's stare. However, regardless of the picture, Tony would have to put his tenacity on the mat. And he did.

"He was the tough one," Vince recalls. "We would go to tournaments and he just started pinning kids at a young age."

But, in the wrestling room, Tony would have his share of frustrations. "We always had to put him with bigger kids," Deb said. "And he would get so pissed because he was the smallest one in there at thirty-two pounds and he was just beat up. But he never gave up. He had a great deal of energy and was determined to find a way to win."

TONY, EVEN AS A SMALL CHILD, HAD A GREAT

deal of energy and he had his own agenda—consequences did not matter to him. "He was always into everything," Deb said. "He had so much energy and was always just so determined and curious."

Early on, as Deb was working a day care out of her own home, she would receive telephone calls about her naked baby on the driveway. Of course, a few feet from naked Tony, was the diaper that he had pulled off.

"He hated being in a diaper," Deb remembered. "If there was a way, he had the will to figure it out. He was potty-trained well before he was two years old. He was not going to be in something his brother was out of. And if he didn't like something, he found a way to take care of it."

Of course, this same determination grew in everything that Tony wanted to attempt as a child and, sometimes, his inquisitiveness would be damaging and cost money to replace or repair.

One day he was in the garage all by himself and he cut the cable on the lawnmower because he wanted to see how it worked. When it was time to cut the lawn, Deb went to start the mower and nothing seemed out of the ordinary—Tony had funneled the cord back into the starter. And as she pulled hard to start the machine, she punched herself in the face because there was no resistance. When she asked him if he knew anything about it, he said, "I wanted to see what it did, so I cut it," and went about playing.

Another time he took the neighbor's bicycle and cut up the seat with a knife because he wanted to see what was inside of it. When the boy asked Deb what happened, she turned to her son. Tony simply said, "I wanted to see what was inside of it," and turned around, walked away, and went about his day.

Even though Tony did things that a normal child would consider *bad* or *wrong*, he did not see it that way. "He was always honest about what he did," Deb said. "If you asked him something, the first thing out of his mouth was going to be the truth. He doesn't think of consequences or anything. He believes in what he does and what he says and he moves on—he has always been that way."

For one birthday, he was given a remote control wave runner with a truck to pull it, and he accidentally drove the truck into the pool. Quickly, Tony took the truck and brought it into the garage. On the floor, piece by piece, he took it apart, laid each of the pieces in a way he understood, and dried them out.

Of course, when his father returned home from work and saw his son in the garage, he questioned his wife on what had happened. Deb simply explained to him that Tony drove his truck into the pool and wanted to fix it. Al looked at his wife and said, "He's not going to be able to put this thing back together." Moments later, Al took the truck, and its pieces, and threw them in the garbage can.

Outraged and not to be denied by what his father had done, Tony went into the garbage can, retrieved all of the parts, laid them out, and began putting his vehicle back together.

To his father's surprise, hours later there was Tony and his remote control truck moving around the house.

BUT JUST AS TONY HAD STARTED WORKING ON

how to wrestle and defeat other kids his age, or battle against those who were older and bigger, his life would take a momentary setback at a very young age.

One weekend, when he was four years old, Tony was staying at his aunt's apartment in Chicago just off Grace and Central for the night. His grandmother, who was living with his aunt at the time, had taken him to the store the day before and allowed him to pick out a toy—he chose a Thunder Cats action figure. Being close with his brother, he asked his grandmother if he could pick one out for Vince as well; of course, she obliged.

The next morning, after Tony and his grandmother had gone to the park and then stopped for some ice cream, they returned to the apartment because Deb was coming to pick Tony up and head to the zoo for the day with Vince.

When they returned, his mom and brother were already there—the parking lot was across the street from the apartment, and everyone was standing around and talking.

Tony, with his mouth stained blue from his ice cream, showed Vince his new Thunder Cats action figure that he was playing with, and, Tony remembered, "Vince thought it was pretty cool. I told him that we had bought one for him and I would run over to the apartment and grab it for him."

Almost instantly, excited to give his brother his new toy, Tony started to run across the street at the crosswalk; at the same time, there was a car darting down the road that saw neither Tony nor the stop sign because the driver was looking back at his baby in the backseat. Unfortunately, Tony would never make it across the street for Vince's toy.

With Vince watching, the car struck his younger brother in the stomach and pulled him under, dragging him before the car came to a tire-screeching stop.

Tony's mother and grandmother heard the tires and that was attention-getting enough to make them turn, but Vince's yelling made it clear what had just happened. Running over, Deb was frantically looking for her son. Within moments, Tony was crawling out from underneath the car.

"I was immediately in shock," Deb remembered. "I couldn't see him and all of a sudden I saw him crawl out from under that car, hurting, and he came right to me."

Quickly, as family raced to check on Tony, his cousin, Dyan, ran and grabbed a towel to wrap him up to help stop all of the bleeding.

Luckily, a police officer just happened to be passing by as all of this occurred, and he did not hesitate to pick up Tony and take him to Resurrection Hospital, not wanting to wait for an ambulance.

As the nurses took Tony into the hospital, and Al had already been called and was on his way, Deb noticed that the driver showed up to the hospital to check on her son; however, Deb asked him to leave as that was not a good time for him to be around her family.

The young four-year-old did not remember much, but he recalled how he was going to be have a body scan to check for internal bleeding, and the nurse told him to drink some apple juice. "I remember that it tasted so sour," Ramos said. "It must have been rotten for days, but they forced me to drink all of it."

The drink, of course, was not apple juice. It was a contrast that the doctors needed inside of Tony's body for the body scan they needed to take to work accordingly.

As the doctors checked and treated him, he was lucky to have no internal bleeding, but he did have third degree burns on the same foot that had also been crushed. The burns were so bad that his foot could not be placed into a cast, so the healing process would be longer and much more difficult.

"I do not remember much; it is a bit foggy," Ramos reflected on being in the hospital. But, he did remember "my father coming in yelling and throwing things and crying—scared me more than anything I think—and going crazy once he saw me lying in that hospital bed. He was hurting and he punched a few cabinets."

"It was tough on all of us," Deb reflected, "but Al didn't get to really see Tony. All he saw was Tony wrapped like a mummy by the time he got there." The family would have to wait for the hospital's results.

After being at one of Resurrection's smaller units for a few days, Tony was transferred to Children's Memorial Hospital in Chicago, to the burn unit.

Upon arrival, he immediately panicked when he saw a young girl in a body cast and asked his parents, "What happened? Why is she like that?"

He would spend a one week at Children's Memorial and, each day, as they were teaching him to learn to walk with a walker, the dressing on his foot had to be changed to make sure he was healing and there were no further complications.

For Tony, the worst part of the entire situation was when he left the hospital—he had to learn how to walk all over again.

However, when Tony followed up with Dr. Lopez, his mother's orthopedic in Elk Grove, he was not certain if Tony would be able to walk the same as he had before. Because of this, Deb ordered her son a wheelchair to get him around as he learned to walk again. In that time, Tony was confined to that very wheelchair.

"Going through the rehab process was the worst time I remember in my childhood," Ramos said. "Seeing all of the other kids up and running around, playing, it was rough for me in that wheelchair. I wanted to be outside, to walk, to run around—I wanted to just be able to play again."

But the rehab process was a process, and it took an emotional toll on the family. At home, Deb had to change the dressings on the foot and no one really wanted to be around for that—she did it alone. Also, knowing that her son wanted to be outside with his friends and playing, but was unable, made the situation difficult for her to stomach. And that was already added to the thought of her son not being able to possibly walk normally again and that thought, all by itself, brought tears to her eyes. But Deb, always resilient, maintained a strong front in Tony's presence.

"During the day, when it was nice out," Deb said, "I would put him out on a blanket so he could be outside and at least be around his friends who were playing. And when the wheelchair came, I would seat him in that [outside]."

Over the matter of a few days, she could tell that her son could not handle being in that chair while everyone else was running around. Deb said, "It was maybe the second day he was in that wheelchair, and I looked out the window to check on him and he was out of it and dragging his foot behind him. He was so determined to be out playing with his friends and he didn't care how."

Looking back on the accident, Tony believed that "not being able to run around and play is what motivated me to get back on my feet. I was not going to be stuck in that wheelchair. I was going to force myself to get better as quickly as possible—and I did."

The doctors told Al and Deb that their son would be back to walking normally in about six to seven months—Tony was back to walking around with his swagger in about four months.

The adversity of that moment, even at a very early age, was the first indication of Tony's toughness and ability to endure and overcome. It was also the first time that he remembered having a difficult goal that he wanted to attain that he had to work at in order to accomplish. But his family was not surprised. He was always that way.

Even at the Cougars' end-of-the-season banquet, Head Coach Jim

Considine commented on Tony's toughness. In introducing him for his award, he said, "This kid thinks he's so big and tough that he tried to take on a car."

Obstacles never seemed to bother Tony, even at a young age. He saw each as an opportunity or a curiosity to figure out and then go about doing something else. Even throughout his rehabilitation process, his mom said, "He was never discouraged or afraid—or never showed it. He just did what he was asked to do and what he wanted to do and, soon enough, he was back to being himself as if nothing had happened."

CHAPTER 3
THE GREATEST MATCH EVER WRESTLED

"He took a lot of losses, but he always came back fighting for more."

• *Frank Defilippis*
Ramos' brother

AS TIME WOULD PASS AND TONY WOULD GROW older, his competitive nature and tenacity would also mature—but at a much quicker rate than most children his age. Now, even though he looked up to both of his brothers, Tony was and always wanted to be himself. He was closest to Vince in age, but he was closer to Frank in attitude.

"To say he wanted to be like anyone," Defilippis said, "would be a discredit to Tony. He was [messed up] in the head from an early age. He was ultra-competitive. You knew that when he did things that he wanted it, but he never voiced it in that way. He was all about actions."

As soon as Tony physically moved past his accident and completed his rehabilitation, he was back to running around and putting himself on the mat—he was full-go.

When Frank was a freshman at North, he would go to school, head to wrestling practice, and then come home to Tony who wanted to wrestle him.

"As a freshman in high school," Defilippis commented, "I was close to my brothers. Tony was five, Vince was seven, and we always did family things together. But, don't get me wrong, there were times when I just wanted to come home, do my homework, hang out with my girlfriend, and go to bed. They were sometimes happier to see me than

I was to see them. They had so much energy—but Tony was the worst. This kid was non-stop."

What Tony wanted more than family time with Frank when it came to doing things, was wrestling matches. Even though Frank would give him attention, and wrestle around with him here and there, it became a mission of Tony's to defeat Frank.

Tony wanted matches when Frank walked into the house or when there was a commercial on or at half time of a Bears game— Tony did not care. He wanted to wrestle and he wanted to win—and he wanted them with Frank at all costs and with no care for anyone's time or lack of patience or injury. He was relentless.

"Every single day when I came home," Defilippis recalled, "we had to have a match. Had to. I was a freshman in high school and like one-hundred pounds heavier, and he was waiting for me. He is five and just waiting for me to enter the house. I would play around with him and he just wouldn't stop. It didn't matter what I did to him—he didn't stop."

And in each of these matches, and in his own mind, Tony believed that he had a legitimate chance to defeat his oldest and much heavier and stronger brother.

Frank continued, "He would fight tooth and nail to take me down and, when he did, he didn't realize that I was letting him. If he did, he would get pissed and punch me in the face. He took a lot of losses, but he always came back fighting for more."

However, through all of the battles and losses that Tony took from Frank, he would have his one victory.

"My girlfriend was coming over and he was non-stop," Defilippis remembered. "He kept wanting to wrestle. So I was like, whatever. So, before she got there, we wrestled. The match was something like 17-17 and it was going into overtime. Tired of everything, I let him take me down. Immediately, he got up and started screaming as loud as he possible could and was running around the house, 'I beat you! I beat you!'"

Tony would take his victory with him for about the next eight years and always reminded his brother that he had defeated him. In front of family or friends or coaches, even strangers—it did not matter. Tony was proud of his over-time win and even at ten and eleven-years-old, he would make it known.

If they were in a fight or argument or match, Tony was always quick to walk away fuming, but added, "I don't care. I beat you before 19-17— I'll beat you again."

"He truly believed that he won that match," Defilippis laughed. "I do not think it really set into him until he was like thirteen-years-old. No matter how many more matches we had, he would always come back with, 'I beat you when I was five-years-old, 19-17 in overtime.'"

"Beating Frankie," Tony reflected with laughter, "was the highlight of my childhood. It may have taken me a long time to realize that he *let* me win, or maybe it's still taking him a long time to come to the realization that on that day, in that room, I was just better than he was."

CHAPTER 4
DOIN' IT IZZY STYLE

"When I watched him, I got to see how he was as a competitor—and that's what I fell in love with. I saw him as a competitor, not the skill set, and that's when I knew I could work with him."

• Israel Martinez
Head Coach, Montini Catholic High School
Owner, Izzy Style Wrestling

AS TONY WOULD HOLD ONTO HIS MOST STORIED victory, carry it around with him, and as he gloated about his impressive win in overtime any chance that he had, he would be making a few wrestling changes that would alter his path.

After wrestling for five years in the Villa-Lombard Cougars kids' club, Tony would be leaving the program as the family would move to Johnsburg, Illinois, after Frank graduated from North.

With the move, however, the Ramos family would struggle greatly trying to find another club, in their area, that would offer the boys the same opportunities that they had just left.

The problem was, the Villa-Lombard Cougars had such a rich tradition and set way of coaching the kids and helping them grow and learn through discipline and hard work and current techniques; any new club the boys went to would be held to that same standard.

"We were having such a difficult time finding another team that was up to the level of the Cougars," Deb said. "We knew how the Cougars won and how good those coaches were with their techniques and the kids. So when it came time to search for that same fit, it was much more difficult when we were exposed to what else was out there. It was more difficult than we thought it was going to be.

"We went through about five different clubs for one reason or another.

At one place, one of the coaches was giving Tony a horsey back ride when I went to pick him up. I said, 'What the hell are you doing? He's not here for horsey back rides. He's here to practice.'

"Another time, I didn't like how the coaches treated their wrestlers. With some of those places, the more I saw, the less I liked. At one club, a coach was just too over-the-top with the boys, especially with his own son. The father grabbed his son by the throat and pushed him into a wall—I couldn't believe it. He would even make his son, after he would lose a match, run outside in the snow as punishment. That was too much."

Fortunately, their search would end with a family Al and Deb had known for a long time. "For us," Deb said, "we needed a place where the boys would not be babied and where they would be pushed; but we also wanted them somewhere they would not be in any danger either. We had known Jose [Martinez] for many years; he'd be good for the boys."

The club was Martinez Elite, and the drive would be down to the Fox Valley area in Aurora, Illinois, some days, and to Montini Catholic in Lombard, Illinois, most other days—depending on where Jose was at the time. Since the Ramos family lived in Johnsburg, Illinois—about forty-five minutes to an hour away, depending on traffic—they would sacrifice the drive for a top-notch club in order for the boys to get the best their parents could provide.

"That drive was rough," Deb said. "But that was the sacrifice we had to make for what we knew the boys needed."

At the time they joined, Tony was now in third grade and his wrestling path was about to change his life path.

The club's head coach, Jose Martinez, had a number of reputations. The criticism on the club was that the parents partied too much and the coaches were over the top and yelled too often. However, if one could put all of that aside, there were positives in the practices and competitions and in the coaching.

For one, even though Jose was verbally very tough on his wrestlers, he cared about each one of them greatly as individuals. Some commented on how he was, at times, a loose cannon, but not one person could refute his desire and passion to pull all that he could out of each wrestler in his club.

And, more than anything, Jose had phenomenal technique and the wrestlers in his club benefitted greatly from his desire to stay ahead of other coaches through his knowledge and understanding of the sport.

In regard to what Jose offered that Deb felt was not offered elsewhere was "his firmness with the club and how he was tough on the boys. But he was not just tough on them, he cared. And he was great at explaining what he wanted and what they needed to do—and the kids always responded because they respected him."

However, what most people looked to, when speaking about Jose's long-term impact on his wrestlers, was the success of his two sons, Nathan and Israel. Nathan was an Illinois high school two-time state champion and Israel was a three-time high school state champion—and they were both extremely dominant wrestlers.

Therefore, when people began to put aside Jose's crass outer shell, they saw how his push and passion, in connection with his technique and care, helped wrestlers become better wrestlers; they took the good with the not-so good.

To Deb, "Jose not treating the boys like babies and making them earn everything that they wanted is how I wanted my boys raised as wrestlers and people."

Additionally, to enrich an already strong formula of hard work and cutting edge technique, Jose was able to collect a very strong group of kids in his club's room to partner up with each other at each practice. These higher-level partners being paired up bred daily competition where no wrestler wanted to back down or be caught not working hard—and this was where he was making the committed and strong-willed wrestlers become great ones.

Also around that time, the club wrestling scene was changing dramatically in Illinois. By 1999, a select few had started to open specialized wrestling clubs. Each was opened by a reputable coach who had previous success in high school, and some at the collegiate and world levels. But, most of these clubs, or schools of wrestling, were deemed as *invite only* and very much a financial and time commitment on the part of the wrestlers and the parents.

"When I got into Martinez Elite," Ramos said, "it was the best kids' club out there. The coaches were great, the workouts were hard, and most of the best partners were in that room. They were always competing for a state championship and we knew that was where we needed to be at that time."

As a result, as a fifth-grader, Tony would transition very well. When everything was added together—the commitment of time and travel by his parents, and the partners and the practices—Tony placed fifth in the Illinois Kids' Wrestling Federation (IKWF) state championships. But he was not satisfied.

"After I placed fifth," Tony remembered, "I never wanted anything less than first again. I hated seeing someone else higher on the podium than me and I promised myself that it would not happen again."

But even though Tony was having success as a wrestler on a number of levels, and he was extremely tough on the mat, each time he did lose it brought out an emotional anger that he had difficulty controlling—and he cried uncontrollably as a way to release and try to deal with those feelings.

Those tears, however, were tears of self-disappointment and a reflection of how mad he was at himself for, what he felt was, allowing himself to be beat. To defeat that opponent—himself—his parents had both boys attend a prominent sports' psychologist in the Chicagoland area.

"Tony was so hard on himself," Deb said. "And we felt he needed to balance the physical as well as the mental and emotional aspects of the sport better."

For Tony, the losses hurt more than anything. He just struggled with losing because he felt that he worked hard and did everything right—so he never understood losing because he never considered it as a possibility.

WITHIN A FEW SHORT YEARS AFTER THE TIME

Tony entered Martinez Elite in 2003, another former Illinois wrestler with great success would be helping out at the club; he was also the son of Jose.

Israel Martinez had won three Illinois High School Association (IHSA) individual state championships at West Aurora High School. Prior to that, he was only the second wrestler in the history of the state of Illinois to win five IKWF state championships—Tony Davis was the first.

In his four years at West Aurora High School, he was one of the most dominant and dynamic wrestlers the state had seen; however, he fell short of a coveted fourth state title when he was dismissed from the team during his senior campaign. To that point, he had won 118-straight matches and was also a four-time Fargo All-American in freestyle and Greco-Roman; likewise, he had already won six Northern Plains National Championships. His resume was impressive; however, when it came to rules and boundaries, Israel struggled.

"My senior year was intense," Israel remembered. "After I was without my brother my junior year, it was to a point where my senior year was a free-for-all. I loved to go out and party and have fun and I didn't want to cut the weight—even though I told my coach I didn't mind cutting the weight. It was a lot more about a young guy wanting to do the things the way he wanted to do them. Unfortunately, it came to the point where they had to set rules and guidelines and, if I broke them, I'd be off the team."

Even with those new rules and guidelines, Israel still had some trouble attending some of the practices and not making weight. His coaches continually tried to work with him; however, he was asked to leave the team.

"I never thought it would happen," Israel said. "It was a crazy time. But, looking back, it was the best thing that could've happened to me because it set me up for the next part of my life."

The next part of his life would now be taking a break from wrestling and relaxing and watching the sport more intently than he did as a competitor.

"I think I learned a lot when I was dismissed from the team," Israel reflected. "It gave me a chance to relax and when I stepped on the mat the next time, it was pure fun."

The next time he would step on the mat would be at the national championships in Fargo, North Dakota. "I went to Fargo and took third and it was the coolest thing ever," Israel remembered. "I just went out there and had fun. Along the way, some coaches came up to me and asked if I'd ever been to North Idaho. I hadn't, but I needed to get out of Illinois."

Upon arrival, Israel had what he needed—a fresh start. No one up there knew him and he did not know anyone; however, this also caused a few problems as he still put himself in positions to get into trouble, but since he was not under anyone's microscope, he was able to get away with more than at home; he liked the freedom and anonymity.

Wrestling-wise, in 2002, Israel compiled a forty-one-match win streak and won the National Junior College Athletic Association (NJCAA) national championship at 158 pounds. From there, he was recruited by then University of Iowa Head Coach Jim Zalesky on his way to the airport; Israel wanted nothing more than to be a Hawkeye.

To take the next step, he would move to Iowa City, Iowa, and attend Kirkwood Junior College. Since the school did not have a wrestling team, Israel would train with the Hawkeye Wrestling Club and thrive in his first semester.

With just one semester away from having his grades where they needed to be prior to entering the university, Israel was not only working out in arguably the most competitive club at the time, but he was also falling in love with the Iowa idea of wrestling.

Unfortunately, for Israel, that second semester did not end the way he would have liked. He remembered, "It just didn't work out. I was working out and loving it, but things happened and I had to come home."

From there, Israel found himself back in Aurora with no real skills for a steady job and no idea with where or what he wanted to do—and he had no real direction.

"When I got home," Israel said, "wrestling was really the only work skill that I had to apply to the real world. But my dad had his club and when I walked in, I had heard that a friend's little brothers started training with the club."

Frank Defilippis and Israel Martinez had been close friends in high school; however, they attended different schools in very different communities. But, they each wrestled in all of the big off-season tournaments and hung out outside of school because their focus was the same—it was wrestling and only wrestling.

"All we did was wrestle," Israel said. "And the only people that we hung out with were wrestlers who won and who also only wrestled. So when I heard that Frankie's brothers were training at my dad's, I wanted to see this kid that Frankie kept bragging about."

Of course, Frank was bragging about Tony and how good he was going to be—but, make no mistake about it, Vince was the better wrestler of the two.

As Israel walked into his father's club, there was an elite few that he would focus his attention on. "When I went in," Israel recalled, "I was just working with a few guys. Almost immediately, Deb Ramos approached me and told me that I needed to start training Tony."

When Deb approached Israel, it was not as if she had approached a stranger. Again, the families and the boys had known each other for quite some time—and Israel and Tony were familiar with each other just from Tony being around the house and bothering him and Frank when they would get together.

The difference now, though, was that Israel would be looking at Tony as a wrestler and not Frank's little brother.

Therefore, as Israel came into practice, after Deb had spoken to him, he had heard how good Tony was from Frank and Deb and everyone else. "But, what's crazy," Israel explained, "was that even though everyone was saying how good he was, it was my dad who told me that he wasn't [very good]. He said that Tony was hungry and mean and tough and he likes to wrestle hard—and he doesn't give up many points. But his offense was limited and my dad was working on some shots with him. But I needed to see him wrestle live to know what he had and didn't have."

That weekend, at a tournament in Lombard, Israel would see what he needed to see in Tony. "When I watched him," Israel said, "I got to see how he was as a competitor—and that's what I fell in love with. I saw him as a competitor, not the skill set, and that's when I knew I could work with him."

Israel felt that Tony had the internal drive that could not be coached or taught. "Most kids," Israel said, "have a certain toughness about them or they do not—Tony had it." Once Israel saw Tony's determination and fight, he was all in.

"I knew that I could make an immediate impact with him," Israel commented. "Sometimes he was last in the sprints and dogging it every chance he could. He was pushed hard at a young age and I knew I could also be that buffer he needed from his brother and his mom and everyone else. Because of this, I got to spend a lot of time with him, and this is where our relationship started."

Over the next spring and summer, Israel would focus on Tony's weaknesses and work further on his strengths. "When I spoke with my dad and then saw Tony wrestle, it was clear that he had to work on his attacks more," Israel commented. "Which is why they came to my dad's program—they were coming to pick up the offense and attack more."

One of the keys, Israel remembered, was "how awesome Vince was, and how brutally and fundamentally challenged Tony was. But Tony would win and Vince would lose. Vince was much more skilled than Tony, but Tony just had the fight to win."

By the time the fall season came around, Tony, now under Israel's guidance, would dominate the practice room. And, when the season began, between the dual meets wrestled and the tournaments entered, Tony dominated and started to quickly make a name for himself. His aggressive style and unrelenting nature was rather uncommon to almost all of the opponents in his age group.

However, he would struggle with his diet at times and that, in some matches, caught up with him—but he always found a way to turn it on in the end and win. Also at this time, he and Israel's relationship was growing closer and even stronger.

"Going into the summer of seventh grade," Ramos remembered, "I started to work with Israel one-on-one, more than anyone else. All of a sudden, I am not working with the club, but I am doing one-on-one trainings and practices with Israel."

What Israel saw in Tony was what Tony saw in Israel: attitude. Each had a swagger about him that was natural—neither was capable of faking who they were.

"What I liked the most about [Israel]," Ramos said, "was his 'I-don't-care' attitude. He didn't care what it took and how hard he had to push me. He made me believe that I was going to win, and I believed that I was going to win no matter what. It didn't matter what it took, I would find a way to win every match. And I did."

For Israel, it was more than just the coaching that helped Tony improve, it was more that Tony and his family were committed to wrestling four, five, and six days a week that was making the difference. The young boy was maturing and growing quickly in the sport because it was all that he was doing—and he was being pushed the entire time by someone he trusted and respected.

"I really jumped in and started training him at a good time," Israel said. "We got to work while he was growing in the sport and we didn't lose much together. It was strange because I saw a lot of myself in how Tony was competing and how I used to compete. You see, Tony hated giving up points and refused to do so—he was so stubborn and tough in all positions, and that's how I was."

And then, along the way, as the groundwork for the offense and the attacks were put in place, it was time to open up Tony's offense. "It was a fun time," Israel remembered, "because Tony wanted to try new moves and I had a huge bag of tricks that I could pull from. What made it exciting was that Tony had no fear in trying the moves—if I told him it would work, he would train, try it, and he just believed it. Trust is big with Tony, and he trusted me."

However, there would still be losses and there would still be those uncontrollable tears. The problem was more or less how to find Tony's breaking point and teach him how to control his emotions in a more healthy way.

"At first, we would just tease him about crying all the time," Israel said. "But, nothing would piss him off except losing. So, we would make him lose sometimes—not wrestling—but sports in general or sprints or put him in situations where he was trailing by seven points with 00:45 left in a live go to try and figure it out. We would start him late on sprints or make him wrestle heavier guys in the room just to get him to lose and not cry—but it never worked and the concept was impossible to break. He cried when he lost at wrestling a real match, that was it.

"You could call him names, kick his ass, work him out for hours to try and break him—we tried everything—but the only time he was affected was when he lost. You can usually see when a kid is breaking by backing down or looking depleted, but Tony wrestled until the whistle blew. And, if he lost, he snapped. And then he cried—a lot."

Therefore, along with the techniques and set-ups and offense, there would also be the mental aspect of the sport that Tony would have to learn to overcome at a young age. Israel remembered, "That part of the deal with working with Tony was teaching him how to respond to losing or being down by points. Since he wasn't used to being behind in matches, he would hear his brother and mother and father screaming at him and it was crazy. But he got used to coming back, but we had to fix the mindset."

As that process unfolded, Israel tried subtle tricks to work with Tony's mental approach. "I would tell him that no girl is going to want be with a crybaby," Israel said. "Or, one day your kids are going to watch this video and see you acting this way. In the end, it was all about having Tony see the bigger picture and learning how to cope with the trigger. We tried to throw a number of analogies at him and try to put him in situations where he had to bounce back. But nothing worked. When he won, he smiled. When he lost, he cried."

ALONG WITH TRAINING WITH ISRAEL FULL TIME,
Tony also had his brother Frank, recently out of college, around to help him in any fashion that he could.

"Frank was at everything on the weekends," Tony said. He would scout my next opponent and keep his eyes on wrestlers that he thought I might face. It was comforting having him there too because I trusted him and I knew he knew what he was talking about."

As for why Tony trusted Israel, initially, it more or less came down to his family telling him to trust him. Tony trusted Frank, and Frank trusted Israel; therefore, Tony did what he was told. This is not to say that he always wanted to listen, but he did.

"I think Tony trusted me because I was able to show him a different style of wrestling and I would stand up for him," Israel commented. "Anytime someone said something negative about Tony, I was ready to fight. I think he liked the concept of fighting because he was a fighter, and he liked that he wasn't liked and that I wasn't liked and together we could prove them all wrong. If there is one thing about Tony, he loves to prove people wrong."

According to Tony, he trusted Israel based on how his coach handled him and how similar they were. "I trusted [Israel] because his coaching style meshed perfectly with me," Ramos said. "He was blunt and didn't beat around the bush. When I was a jack-ass, he told me so. When I lost, he made it clear why I lost—there was no time to get over it because I had to move forward. He never held back on me and I needed that. I didn't always like it and we argued, but that was who we were. It wasn't about making me feel good, it was about making me better. He brought my wrestling to a new level and, early on, he started to help me set goals that I had never thought about."

In addition to his training, Tony would have further help from Frank—and this made a major difference in his tournament wrestling. "With having Frankie scouting," Tony commented, "and training with Israel, I was never going to go into a match unprepared, and I was never going to get hit with a move by surprise. Frankie helped me train and he pushed me and Vince to go that extra mile at practice, on the mat, and at home in our workouts."

With a full off-season of working with Israel and now living with Frank as a seventh-grader in 2004, Tony would win his second IKWF State Championship in grand style. Some people liked Tony. Some people hated Tony. But, no matter which, people knew Tony, and, even at an early age, Tony liked that people talked about him.

As Tony was on the rise, and Israel had found his direction, a bold move—a leap of faith—was about to take place as Israel's relationship with his father, in regard to the club, would soon be a source of contention.

SINCE MARTINEZ ELITE STARTED WORKING

solely out of Montini Catholic High School, Montini's program was on the rise and head coach Mike Bukowski was reaping the benefits of his relationship with Jose.

Within a few years, the Broncos were the elite of Illinois' Class A division—there were only two classifications in Illinois at this time—and Montini was winning multiple team and individual state championships with a number of wrestlers who had come out of the Martinez Elite kids' club. However, there was a change of the guard slowly occurring and everybody saw it coming except Jose—until it was too late.

As soon as parents were paying closer attention to what was happening at Martinez Elite, a slow tide began swinging in Israel's favor; however, this was not Israel's intention.

Tony was maturing quickly in the sport and having immediate success that everyone else was aware of. Soon, other parents wanted that same growth and were pushing for one-on-one time with Israel as well. In this, parents and kids alike wanted Israel to take more of an active interest and role in the practices; so, Israel tried to work it out with his father.

Unfortunately, Jose was not ready to relinquish control of his club and wanted to continue to run his practices his way.

"What really started the turn," Israel said, "was Deb Ramos. She would tell parents that it was five dollars to come to Izzy's practice today before Jose's. It started off with Tony and then two and then five and the next thing I knew I was making one to two hundred dollars a night coaching wrestling—it was awesome."

All of a sudden, Israel had found his niche and he was not going to be going to work for his father anymore—whether it was cutting trees or coaching wrestling.

"Figuring it out was tough," Israel admitted. "Basically, on my dad's off days, I started Izzy Style Wrestling. My dad would work out on Monday, Wednesday, and Thursday, and he would start at 6:30 p.m.; so, on those days, I would run a practice from 5:00 to 6:30 p.m. Then, on his off days, we would also practice at night and the room was filled."

Israel knew that having Tony made the move possible because he had a face to his style and a proven formula. The overwhelming disagreement between Jose and Israel came with how each wanted to teach fundamentals. According to Israel, he felt that even Tony, as well as the other wrestlers, needed much more fundamental work and, since the father disagreed with the son and his ideas and coaching concepts, Israel started the transition to his own club.

Also, at this time, Israel was an assistant coach at Montini, so he was taking his coaching stipend and putting it toward his new business.

Jose was not fond of this move by his son—presumably because he may have felt that it undermined him, and Israel remembers how his father "Would walk in at the end of my practice, right before the beginning of his, and I would have forty guys and his practice would start and he only had twenty. He was not happy, but the shift had already occurred."

As for head coach Mike Bukowski, he was torn because he had a great relationship with Jose, but he saw the masses and momentum turning; he liked what Israel was doing with all wrestlers regardless of their own ability.

Soon thereafter, Jose would leave and the floodgates opened as more and more wrestlers started coming to what would become known as Izzy Style Wrestling.

Of course, what started the team was having Tony—privileged with being named the first Izzy Style wrestler.

Israel recalled, "When I broke off, I knew I could build a team around Tony—the problem was going to be which wrestlers that I recruited would be able to put up with Tony. I knew what I wanted—Vince was talented and Tony was Tony. So I built the team by recruiting guys bigger than Tony. This way, I would have someone close to Vince's weight and Tony was tough enough to go with this wrestler as well. I would go to tournaments and watch kids who took bad shots and brought them in so Tony had kids who were fearless at taking shots. The biggest thing was watching the kids and seeing what kind of competitor they are—you can see it in boys at a young age. You can see who's a fighter and who's a competitor. All I needed them to do was come in and be able to put up with Tony. I knew they might not win right away, but if they could get through the practices, they would win down the road."

As more and more wrestlers started coming Israel's way, his style and beliefs on fundamentals was beginning to take off. "You see," Israel said, "my dad grew up with that flashy John Smith style of wrestling with open shots and fake-fake-duck or arm-drag him and not really two or three set-ups. So what I noticed as I got older and the gap was closing talent-wise in matches, it was because guys could counter leg attacks better. I had to learn more set-ups and better penetration steps. Basically, I had to work on the core fundamentals and I knew that is what I wanted to teach because I wanted my kids to be better earlier."

The problem was, as more wrestlers were coming in, not many wanted to work with Tony. "He was an asshole," Israel commented on Tony's inability to be a good workout partner. "He was a guy that loved being number one and someone that loved being the guy; he was a dick to them. He would not let his partners work their moves—he was a terrible partner."

However, outside of the room, Tony was the calmest and nicest kid. "He was the cool kid," Israel said. "He had the fun pool parties and his mom was the team mom—he was great outside of the room, but inside he was just a vicious animal."

But soon, as with all practice partners, some of the wrestlers were finding ways to get in on Tony's legs and finding other ways to frustrate him. Early on, none of the club wrestlers liked Tony; however, over time, and as they interacted with him more and more outside of the room, they saw that was just how he was and they accepted him and embraced the opportunity to wrestle with him. They knew that if they could score on him or get close, they could score and get in on anyone.

"One practice," Israel recalled, "one of the kids got in and sat the corner on Tony and Tony just got so pissed that he choked him out. The kid got back up and got back to the line to wrestle, but he didn't like it. In the end, Tony helped toughen up some of those kids without purposely doing it."

As matches would happen throughout practice, Israel and his coaches looked for ways to frustrate Tony and put him in awkward positions to keep him focused and motivated. Any chance that they had to knock him down a peg, they took.

"Even at a young age, Tony's attitude needed to be put in check," Israel said. "One day Colton Rache snuck a takedown in on Tony and I announced it to the room. It would echo: 'TWO...TAKEDOWN, RACHE!' And, true to Tony, he would get up and head-butt him and just beat the shit out of him. The guys hated it, but they knew that was just Tony."

But as they wrestled with each other more and more, they saw Tony as a teammate and they all shared in his successes and had their own successes as well. "In the end," Israel commented, "they all loved him—or they *hated* him."

ONE WEEKEND, WRESTLING AT THE OHIO
Tournament of Champions, Tony would have a breakdown and find himself in an argument with his coach.

"We fought all the time," Israel remembered. "But it was never anything serious. Most of time it was trying to get Tony to change—Tony didn't like that. Getting him to change his style was hard at times. He argued with me, but he did it."

"Israel was really trying to get me to hand fight," Ramos remembered. "He wanted me to learn how to attack and stay in my opponent's face because, in college, that is what I would have to be able to do."

Tony relented because he liked space between himself and his opponents. He had been very successful with his double-leg attack the past three seasons; his defense was pretty good, and he felt that these aspects of his style was enough. Because he could defend so well, he would move, change levels, create space, his opponent would step, and Tony would have a takedown. He had, for an eighth-grader, really figured out how to make his opponents make a mistake by putting them where he wanted them, and he knew how take advantage of those mistakes almost immediately.

But, Israel wanted more out of him. And when his coach challenged him to hand fight and stay inside to battle, Tony did not know how to handle it right away. But, begrudgingly, he listened and did as he was being coached.

"Things did not go my way at that tournament," Ramos said. "I was upset. I was pissed. I yelled at Israel and blamed him for changing my style. I said, 'You made me change my style and now I suck.' Of course, Israel stood his ground and argued back with me about how he knows better and I need to change to be better later on."

While this argument ensued, and Tony's emotions were running higher and higher, his mother came up and Tony turned to her for support. He received none. She grabbed her son, spoke to him, and calmed him down; she explained that he needed to listen to Israel.

When he finally settled, Tony and Israel sat down and Israel explained the importance in what he was trying to do. "He knew that I was upset with my performance and he stood there and took me yelling at him,"

Tony said. "But he knew what I needed to improve on to make me a better wrestler for high school and college. In the end, I listened to him because I trusted him."

It was not long after that when Deb decided that it might be a good idea to have Tony and Vince see a sports' psychologist to help prepare them better for greater competitions and learn how to focus better.

"The reason we decided to take the boys," Deb commented, "was because Vince never thought he was good enough and Tony would have the outbursts of crying after a loss. We knew the boys were talented, but they needed that mental edge and needed to balance their physical training as well as discover mental training."

The man the boys would go to was the Mental Skills Coach for the Chicago Blackhawks, Doctor James F. Gary.

Through multiple sessions, Dr. Gary would give the boys small tricks and practices to help them handle any of the stresses or uncertainties or jitters or, in Tony's case, moments where he would lose control of his emotions during or after a match, and work to help him solve his issues on his own.

"He really helped us," Ramos recalled. "We learned how to prepare for our matches by using visualization and self-talk. Before matches I would tell myself that I am faster and stronger and quicker and, at the same time, visualize my match and my opponent and my moves. Putting myself into all types of positions and finishing my moves and getting out of them in my mind. I would even visualize getting my hand raised."

From those sessions, Tony learned how to take a few steps back in order to move forward, and focused on not becoming so worked up before his matches. He would visualize his matches, wrestle his matches, and then actually go out and physically wrestle.

"The focus is what helped me the most," Tony revealed. "It was more of a laser focus and that is kind of where my stare came from. I was focused and in there and ready to go because of what I had done beforehand. I knew that all of the preparation and all of the work and struggle was done—there was no reason to be nervous or afraid because I would be prepared for whatever happened."

IN THE END, TONY WAS GROWING AS A MORE

mature adolescent. In the practice room, as a partner, Tony would still be Tony and refuse to give up points and struggle with being a good partner—he did not want anyone to score on him, even if it was just technique. However, he was maturing and learning about himself and working to correct areas where he knew that he could grow.

His arguments with Israel were not as frequent, but they existed, but his hustle and focus was stronger. He started looking toward larger goals and working to improve on areas Israel and Frank told him he needed to perform better in, and his goals were set.

"The biggest thing to understand about Tony," Israel said, "was he was a good kid who just wanted to win. As we got closer and our relationship grew, he grew and started to see the bigger picture that I was trying to show him. He was not always the best at doing everything for everyone else, but he got better. He was on his path and he was focused and he was relentless in working toward his vision."

2004 • IKWF STATE CHAMPIONSHIPS • 84 LB NOVICE DIVISION
RAMOS CELEBRATES AFTER WINNING HIS SECOND IKWF STATE CHAMPIONSHIP
RAMOS WON A 5-3 OVERTIME DECISION
PHOTOGRAPH COURTESY • THE RAMOS FAMILY

GLENBARD NORTH HIGH SCHOOL

CHAPTER 5
THE PROGRAM

"When it comes to wrestling, wrestling is a battle. In fighting for the sport, every battle, like every point in a wrestling match, is worth fighting for early on to secure things."

• Bob Fulk
Former Head Coach, Glenbard North High School

CAROL STREAM • ILLINOIS • BECAME THE HOME of Glenbard North High School in 1968. Months before the school opened its doors, the administration had neither filled all of its teaching positions, nor had it filled all of its coaching positions.

During the same time that North was still trying to staff its school, a new coach, by the name of Bob Fulk was just promoted to take over the football program at Proviso West High School in Hillside, Illinois.

Fulk had played football and wrestled at Eastern Illinois University. However, even though he wrestled at the collegiate level, Fulk had never wrestled in high school. The first match that he ever wrestled was at Eastern Illinois as a sophomore.

After Fulk accepted the head football position that spring, he was having difficulty with the Proviso administration, particularly the athletic director, letting him run the football program the way he wanted; due to this, he was uncertain if the Proviso job allowed him to pursue his vision for success.

One of the pieces of Fulk's vision was bringing in new coaches. He knew that he needed to clean house with some of the older coaches and bring in new and more like-minded individuals. However, as he was promised one thing and shown another, Fulk grew more displeased, but at that time, he received new opportunity: a teaching and coaching position at Glenbard North.

Neil Hudson, the future athletic director of Glenbard North, had phoned Fulk for an interview. Now, North was still under construction, but the salary would be the same. By the end of that interview, the soon-to-be principal, Raymond Livingston, had offered Fulk a contract. Fulk, not signing the contract, took it home to discuss the offer with his wife, Janet—and then Fulk received another phone call.

This time, it was the athletic director at Proviso West; he had found out his new football coach had just been offered a contract to teach physical education, drivers' education, and be the first head wrestling coach at Glenbard North.

"He told me that I had to make a decision in forty-eight hours," Fulk said. "I went home and thought about it and I had one goal in mind: To build a top wrestling program. And I figured, *Why not do it at Glenbard North?*"

Fulk remembers how he and his wife "stayed up late discussing what we should do. Well, in the end, I was going to take this opportunity and work toward my goals and what I knew I had to do to have a successful program."

Once Fulk accepted the physical education and driver's education position, as well as being the head wrestling coach, he could start building. Unfortunately, there would be some obstacles that he would have to overcome.

A few weeks before the school was about to open, Fulk was taking a tour of it with administrators. He recalled how, "The school was the most beautifully decorated school I had ever seen. All of the hallways were painted black and gold—mostly gold. Every restroom, boys and girls, painted and designed well. And then I walked into my wrestling room—it was bare concrete block. It was like they just got done with it and the mortar people left it."

"Immediately," Fulk continued, "I showed some disgust with that. They told me, 'Well, it's just a wrestling room. Why should it be painted?' So, that was my first challenge. But by the start of the next season, it was painted like the rest of the building."

The battles would continue, and Fulk would never choose big battles with the administration—everything was a fight. He spoke about how, "When it comes to wrestling, wrestling is a battle. In fighting for the sport, every battle, like every point in a wrestling match, was worth fighting for early on to secure things."

In fact, he had to fight for equity in his sport to receive the same treatments that was given to the football, basketball, and baseball programs. As time wore on, Fulk never backed down. The more Fulk knew about what other programs were getting, the more he went after those same entitlements for his wrestling program.

For example, when the district purchased new cleats for the entire football program in North's inaugural season, Fulk made them purchase new wrestling shoes for the wrestling program.

"I walked right into the A.D.'s office with all of the shoe sizes and refused to leave until he put the order in," Fulk remembered. "I sat through him calling the district office and talking to the superintendent. The way I saw it, if one sport was going to be given something, we were going to be given something in return." The following year no shoes would be purchased by the district for any program.

Former Athletic Director Neal Hudson made it very clear how Bob approached his job. On one of Bob's evaluations, there was a question that asked: *Does this coach promote his sport?* Neal's response was: "Bob makes damn sure that everybody at Glenbard North knows Glenbard North has a wrestling team."

Most of the administrators and teachers were retired football, basketball, and baseball coaches. "None of them knew anything about wrestling," Fulk explained. "Good people, but they had no clue that the wrestlers were the hardest working and most dedicated kids in the school. I made sure they knew."

In addition to fighting for the team's basic needs, he was relentless in building the wrestling program and putting Glenbard North on the map as a wrestling school. His practices were difficult, and he pushed his wrestlers past what they believed to be their breaking points.

To Fulk, who grew up a farmer in a small southern Illinois town, Moweaqua, hard work was the answer to any problem, and the surrounding communities, as well as the state, grew to know him and the program and how they worked and performed.

Other schools feared wrestling Glenbard North, wearing their black and gold singlets, because they knew they were in for a six-minute fight, and they would have to earn each and every point.

From 1979 through 1983, Fulk's teams went on a 68-0 dual-meet win streak, and he only experienced one losing season throughout his career.

It was not until 1984 that the state of Illinois began its Dual Team State Championships, and in that inaugural year the Panthers were the State Runner-Up at season's end. Therefore, previous to Fulk's final team state trophy in 1984, every other team finish was earned at the Individual State Championships held, early on, at Horton Field House on the campus of

Illinois State University in Bloomington, or at Assembly Hall at the University of Illinois in Champaign.

Fulk retired with a final record of 288-86-5, with five Top 20 finishes in Illinois, not including one Eleventh, one Seventh, one Third, and two Runner-Up team finishes.

Additionally, in his 19 years, Fulk's teams won eight of nineteen conference championships and were 72-11-3 in conference duals. Furthermore, he had coached 45 conference champions, 39 state qualifiers, 20 state place-winners, and two state champions.

What Fulk was able to accomplish for the program at an early stage, and then into the later years of his tenure, was truly remarkable. Wrestling was still growing at the high school level, and Glenbard North was well known and well respected within Carol Stream and the wrestling community.

In fact, as soon as he took over the program, Fulk brought wrestling into the Carol Stream community through a kids' club that he began through the park district.

Fulk taught physical education and driver's education during the day, coached wrestling after school, and then ran the park district club in the evening. He believed that "to be successful you have to work hard and sacrifice—no matter how long the day gets."

Through his work ethic and desire to succeed, and then surrounding himself with like-minded individuals on his coaching staff, wrestling in Carol Stream became competitive and a consistent winner each year. Due to the winning tradition Fulk had created, the team and its duals were always a must-see event during the winter season.

• • •

When Fulk retired in 1988, he would leave the program to another farmer, a former park district and Glenbard North wrestler with the same ideals, named Mark Hahn.

In 1988, the first year of Mark Hahn's tenure, his team would win the DuPage Valley Conference, the Regional championship, and defeat Villa Park Willowbrook 33-22 to win the Dual Team Sectional championship and advance to the Dual Team State Championships.

Once down state, the Panthers would first defeat Lane Technical 45-18 before falling to Oak Park River Forest 18-37 in the semifinal match. Hahn's team would square off against DeKalb, losing 39-3, ending with a fourth place finish in Illinois and his first trophy as head coach of the program.

Unfortunately, it would not be until 2001 when each of these feats, in succession, would occur again. However, before 2001, the groundwork was being laid by Hahn as he was working to bring the program back to its dominant form.

In truth, it was not until Frank Defilippis' sophomore season, in 1996, when the team would once again have enough fire-power to trophy and even possibly win a dual team state championship.

In the early 1990s, Naperville North was the powerhouse of the DuPage Valley Conference; however, on their heels each season was Glenbard North. The dual meets were as heated between the wrestlers as they were between the coaches and the fans.

Intensity surrounded these match-ups and the two communities would come together to cheer on their own and verbally attack the other. Car loads of fans would travel to each town as they would square off in duals, conference championships, and even Regional competitions. In Illinois, at this time, the top two Regional finishers would have a dual for the Regional Championship and the winner of the dual would advance into the team state competition.

Wresting fans knew that when Glenbard North and Naperville North wrestled, something was going to happen—and being there, anticipating it, only ignited everyone in the crowd.

The rivalry was heated, and not always healthy. There were stories of mothers throwing shoes at officials and fans being separated and moved to opposite sides of the gymnasium as certain sections had to be dedicated to specific colors and guarded off to lessen unforeseeable problems. Additionally, men and students, even mothers or general fans pointed at one another, yelling, gesturing, and coaches had words of hate thrown at them from behind as they coached their wrestlers. The duals were intense and made into events that few in the community missed and many in the surrounding area made sure to attend.

For Hahn, even though the varsity was not consistently winning the conference and qualifying for the Dual Team State Championships each year, his teams were very competitive. However, in those early years, something was missing in the program—the fear that opponents felt going against North had subsided a bit since Fulk left, and the program needed it back.

But, make no mistake about it, Hahn and his staff were solely dedicated to bringing not only the fear back in the black and gold, but restoring the glory of Glenbard North wrestling as well.

Hahn, like Fulk, took on a number of responsibilities outside of his education duties. Aside from being a physical education teacher, Hahn coached freshman football, ran the park district club that Fulk had started, and continued running Illinois' longest standing wrestling club, Mat Rats. He remained active in the community where he had grown up and farmed to promote wrestling at the youth and high school level and, slowly, momentum was gaining.

And then, in the midst of everything coming together, Hahn received a call from Jim Considine, the head coach of the Villa-Lombard Cougars, which would change everything for the better.

IN THE WINTER OF 1983, JIM CONSIDINE'S ELDEST

son, Auggie, was convinced to give wrestling a try by one of his friends, Dennis Donovan. At the time, Donovan wrestled for a club located in the back of the Veterans of Foreign War (VFW) post on the north side of Lombard. It was a relatively new club, but it was growing.

For Illinois, particularly DuPage County, there were few wrestling opportunities for young children. The surrounding high school programs had wrestling, but that was generally all that there was.

In regard to actual wrestling clubs in the general area for kids, there were two. There was a park district club in Carol Stream, and Donovan's club, the Villa-Lombard Cougars, in Villa Park. Unfortunately, until Auggie came home with the news, Considine was unaware of both because there was no wrestling at the junior highs, so he had never researched it. Besides, these clubs were generally promoted through word of mouth and nothing more; therefore, had Auggie not heard of it, odds are that Considine would not have either.

Considine had been a four-year wrestler at Willowbrook High School in Villa Park, lived in Villa Park with his wife, Alicia, but, even though he wrestled and loved it, he did not want to push the sport on his sons. Auggie coming home and telling his dad that he was interested was all that Considine needed to take the next step; he immediately signed him up.

Of course, when Considine arrived at the VFW, the setting was not a very safe place for the kids to be practicing. The club had started in a church and the parents had fundraised to purchase mats through a car wash. The club had now moved, after a few years, to the VFW.

"When I walked in," Considine recalled, "there was a glass trophy case hanging off the wall. During practice, three or four kids had to stand in front of it so no group wrestled into it. To make it worse, the door that separated the back room and the bar was warped. So as the veterans were up front drinking and smoking and telling stories, their smoke would creep into the back room where practice was. As bad as it was, it was all they had at the time."

After five practices, Auggie was about to compete in a tournament at St. Lawrence High School in Chicago. Considine recognized Mike Donovan, Dennis' father, from little league baseball, so he walked over, sat, and began speaking with him. However, as he watched his son's first meet, he was a bit confused. The coaches who ran the club just sat in the corner and wrote on their clipboards and never spoke to the kids.

Concerned by this, he turned to Donovan and asked him why the coaches did not coach. Jean Gagne, a mother who was sitting in same area, turned and told Jim that, "[The coach] said that he coaches them during the week. So when they get out there, they are supposed to know what to do."

At that, Considine's mouth dropped open. Being a wrestling fan, he would follow the papers and go watch the top high school duals each week. So, aside from experiencing the sport as an athlete, he was a spectator and watched how other coaches coached—all of them coached their wrestlers during their matches.

As he turned to Donovan and Jean Gagne, he said, "That's ridiculous. Even college coaches yell at their kids."

Immediately, Jean Gagne turned and asked the question that started it all: "Do you know a lot about wrestling?"

At that very moment, when she asked, every one of the Villa-Lombard parents looked at him. He knew that if he replied with a "No," then he would look like a fool for criticizing the coach. But if he said "Yes," he might find himself in a position where only God knows what would happen.

To this, Considine replied, "I know enough."

Another parent jumped into the conversation, "You go coach our kids."

Now Considine had to come clean. He told them, "I know wrestling, but I am not in the room. I don't know the terminology they are using or what they have been taught. The room is crowded, all I've done is try to help Auggie when I can."

Then Jean Gagne said, "Well, you tell me what to say and I will tell it to Bobby."

A bit shocked, Considine turned to Jean's husband, Bill, and asked if she was serious. It was confirmed: she was very serious.

Over the next few competitions, true to her word, Jean Gagne sat next to Considine and yelled to her son. However, as the season was coming to an end, Considine had come up with a less obvious way to coach his son, Auggie.

Determined to help his son figure out the sport, Considine took a camera, sat mat side as if he was taking pictures, and verbally coached Auggie through his matches. Soon enough, when the Regionals came around, hosted at Waubonsie Valley High School, he was "taking pictures" of Dennis Donovan and Bobby Gagne as well.

At the season's end, neither of the two club coaches were coming back, and the parents had talked Considine into taking it over. His first order of business was to relocate the club. Since the club was located in Lombard, and Considine and his family had moved into that district, he went to speak to the head wrestling coach at Glenbard East High School, Rich Kruse.

All Kruse had to do was agree to hand Considine a contract to practice at the high school, and East would inherit experienced wrestlers.

Two years later, in 1986, ten of the starting twelve wrestlers at East had been through the Villa-Lombard program. However, that same season, Kruse was fired and a new coach took over.

Add another two years, now 1988, and there was a strong presence of Villa-Lombard wrestlers at East with high expectations. Unfortunately, these seasoned seniors, now coached by someone the parents and wrestlers were not too fond of, would lose by 1.5 points at the Regional championship to their sister school rival, Glenbard North. That season, Glenbard North placed fourth in the Dual Team State Championships under first-year head coach, Mark Hahn.

After a difference of opinions with the new head coach at East, Considine moved the club to Glenbard West High School in Glen Ellyn and worked with head coach Bernie Botheroyd.

While at West, Considine was approached by Mark Hahn to see if he had an interest in taking over the Carol Stream Park District club. But Considine was loyal to Villa-Lombard, the club he kept alive and had now grown into a kids' club that people knew and respected. He told Hahn that he would not go anywhere without it and the conversation ended there.

But then, two years into their relationship with West, the Villa-Lombard Cougars were involved in an unfortunate disagreement with the administration at West.

About two weeks after a large tournament the club hosted at West, Considine received a critical letter from the assistant principal with a $1,500 bill attached from the high school that the gymnasium had been left a mess, and that he and his club did not know how to handle their kids. The bill covered the overtime pay the custodians needed to make sure everything was ready for the school day on Monday.

Considine was beside himself. "We wrestled in the field house across the street from the school," he said. "There was one custodian there, and he was down in the basement drinking, watching television. We told him all he had to do was make sure there was toilet paper and that the bathrooms were clean—we would do the rest."

When the tournament concluded, Considine said, "We cleaned up everything. We carried all of the tables and chairs back up the hill to the school, through the snow, and back into the cafeteria. We cleaned the halls, the gymnasium, we took the garbage out—we did everything."

Unfortunately, as Considine approached Botheroyd about the situation, and also spoke with the assistant principal, Considine said, "They made it very clear that [the school was] not going to fight the union on the issue of truth and overtime pay for the event."

The following year the Cougars hosted the same tournament, cleaned up as well as they had the previous year, brought the janitor a six-pack of beer in case he was the one who took issue with them, and, unfortunately, received another bill claiming the same unruly behavior as the year before.

However, this time, Considine was a step ahead of the school and custodians' union—he had his wife take out her camera, at 3:58 p.m., faced a clock, and took a picture of the clean gymnasium and had it dated and timed.

Considine first called Botheroyd, whom he now felt he could not trust because he would not back the club. Then, he went to the assistant principal and had to sit through a lecture on how poorly he ran his club and the trouble that it had caused.

At this, Considine reached into his pocket, pulled out a picture of the gymnasium, and told him, "You don't know jack-shit!" Considine explained. "I had that picture blown up and made sure the clock was able to be seen. It was timed and dated and we even put the bleachers up. I told him we were not going to pay this; it's bullshit. And if he wanted to take legal action, I would make sure that there was a reporter there to explain how their janitors enjoy screwing a non-profit out of money."

When Considine spoke with Botheroyd again, a comment was made that he has never forgotten. "He told me," Considine remembered, "that his program was not seeing any results from having the club there anyway."

Three important events happened after this moment in the span of a few months: 1. Considine decided that the Cougars were not going back to West, but West had no idea; 2. Glenbard West, with experienced Villa-Lombard club kids in their line-up, defeated Glenbard North in the Regional championship; and, 3. Mark Hahn contacted Considine and told him that he was welcome to bring his club over to North and run it out of their varsity wrestling room.

AFTER THE CAROL STREAM COMMUNITY OPENED

its doors to the Villa-Lombard Cougar program in 1991, wrestling would change at Glenbard North—and on February 12 of that same year, Tony Ramos would also be born.

With North now having a kids' club in-house, Considine was coaching both the park district wrestlers combined with his club wrestlers and, almost immediately, the Cougars became the top kids' club in Illinois—their numbers were growing and North would be benefitting from this relationship.

The Cougars would win the Illinois Kids' Wrestling Federation State Championship three years in a row—1992, 1993, and 1994. On that 1994 team were a couple of wrestlers that Considine knew would be impact wrestlers in high school: Frank Defilippis and Dana Holland.

Considine recalled, "Dana and Frankie always practiced together—they were into it and they were inseparable. Dana was naturally gifted and Frankie was just a hard worker who brawled. Where Dana could outslick kids, Frankie would just outwork them."

At the same time that Frank was helping his club win its third-consecutive IKWF State Championship, his younger brothers, Vince and Tony, were being introduced to wrestling and the Glenbard North varsity wrestling room.

"Vince was five and Tony was three when they started," Considine recalled. "Tony was so young and small that he had to wrestle five and six-year-olds. Obviously, he did not win very often in the practice room. But I knew right then and I told Hahn, 'Frankie's little brothers are freakin' tough. You have to see these kids.'"

In fact, even though Tony lost a great deal, he was never discouraged. "He never gave up," Considine remembered. "He never cried about getting his ass kicked. All he did was get back up and work to get better every day. He was a tough little son-of-a-bitch. He never missed practice; he never whined no matter if he was wrestling older kids or heavier kids. All that mattered to Vince and Tony was that they were wrestling."

And as Frank went into high school and was pushed into the varsity room as a freshman, Vince and Tony remained Cougars and both were excelling. At the time, Vince was the better technician—it just came natural to him. Tony had to work at it—he was more of a brawler who would walk on the mat and battle every opponent for every point. In that, they were both excelling at the sport, winning, and now part of the future for Glenbard North wrestling.

ALSO IN 1994, THE PARK DISTRICT WRESTLERS

that Hahn had coached were now juniors and seniors. It would be this group that would start the rotation of power back into Glenbard North's favor.

Unfortunately, Hahn would be unable to attend the DuPage Valley

Conference championship tournament this year as he was standing up in a wedding for one of his closest friends that day.

Rather, it would be his other two close friends and assistant coaches, Jeff Cherry and Kent Garrett, who would witness the team's resurgence and keep Hahn informed throughout the tournament on a car phone.

Since Naperville North had swept the conference in duals, and was looking for its sixth-consecutive title, it would take a team effort and some additional help to make the improbable probable. Naperville North had defeated Glenbard 37-18 just four weeks earlier in their dual.

As needed, North's two high-powered studs, Rob Serio, 145, and Al Licka, heavyweight, would take their number-one seeds and have to maximize points throughout the DVC tournament.

That week, Hahn recalled, "We knew we needed some upsets and we had to win head-to-head match-ups. But we also knew we needed [Naperville North] to drop a match here and there. The DVC is not very forgiving, so every match and every point counts."

As the tournament ended, Naperville North Head Coach Tom Arlis commented in a *Daily Herald* interview how, "Two of my top point-getters, Nate Patrick (119) and Ryan Hanson (171), happened to fall in a bracket with two state place-winners. In any other conference, away from those guys, we're going to get big points. In here, we run into a brick wall. At 145 and heavyweight, there was nobody here to stop their two studs."

The two Glenbard standouts would do their jobs. Rob Serio claimed his second DuPage Valley Conference Championship with a 00:48 fall, and Al Licka, the heavyweight and nephew to Hahn, would claim his first title. But the tournament was not won in these two weight classes alone; those points were expected.

Freshman 103-pounder Sol Rigitano would reach the championship match, as would Keith Gall (125), Brian Smith (152), and Mike Burlack (160)—each would place second. In the consolations, big points were earned as Ken Biala (119) and Dave Carlin (171)—each wrestled back and placed third.

However, the match where the fans realized the team championship would be won, was the 189 third-place match.

Glenbard's Dave Singleton would be matched up against Naperville North's Mike Jelinek. At that point, heavyweight had not been wrestled, but the outcome favored Glenbard, and all eyes were focused on the mat to the right of the championships mat.

In a tightly contested match, Singleton would find himself on top of Jelinek from a scramble and then turned him to earn the fall and secure the team championship. Glenbard would go on to win by a 225 to 215 margin, and this would be the springboard to ignite Glenbard.

Watching all of the drama of the tournament and each win, loss, wrestle-back and championship match, were the seventh and eighth-graders of the Glenbard North kids' club, the Villa-Lombard Cougars.

In this group would be Frank Defilippis, his best friend, Dana Holland, and a number of their teammates who would keep the Glenbard wrestling tradition alive. Witnessing that tournament unfold was the motivation that they needed for their group of young wrestlers to know the importance of coming together as a team. Considine would echo the lesson to those young Cougars.

"After that championship," Considine said, "I told them that if they could come together as a group, and wrestle for one another, that they could accomplish anything. In wrestling, on any given day, someone could defeat someone or some team they are not supposed to on paper. It was a great day."

THE FOLLOWING SEASON, 1995, FRANK ENTERED

Glenbard North and bypassed the freshman room, going directly into the varsity room. Even though he did not start on the varsity team, he and Dana Holland would wrestle junior varsity and be initiated into the structure and demands of the program.

On the varsity mat, even though Glenbard would go undefeated in duals, Naperville North would seize control over the DuPage Valley and defeat Glenbard in the conference tournament by a team score of 255.5 to 232.5.

Then, in 1996, when Frank was a sophomore, Glenbard North would earn a conference championship, Frank's first, and he and his teammates believed that they were now in position to go on a DuPage Valley Conference championship run as juniors and seniors, and bring a dual team state trophy back to North.

What had slowly been happening in the past few years was largely due to the success of the Villa-Lombard Cougars kids' club and exposing children in the community to wrestling at an early age. The club was affordable, it was accessible since it was in the varsity room at the high school, and it was successful.

The word had spread. Since 1992, Villa-Lombard was the best kids' club in the state and they were producing some of the best high school wrestlers in the area.

Practicing in North's varsity wrestling room, these young wresters were surrounded by North's history and some of the wrestlers before them on the Wall of Fame had once been Cougars. Each day as they they walked in, they could see pictures of North's most successful wrestlers, hear stories about those wrestlers, and have their own dreams of their faces being added to that wall one day. Vince and Tony Ramos were no different in their thoughts when they walked into that room and looked up at that wall.

All of a sudden, as wrestlers came into the program, freshmen were seasoned freshmen—but there were still those who came out for the team who had never wrestled before—and their experience and excitement to be wrestling for not only Glenbard North, but also for Mark Hahn, was seemingly alive in everything that they did.

The North mantra had remained the same from the Fulk era: *Hard work will solve all of your problems.* And Hahn and his staff were true believers in that philosophy, as well as adding a few wrinkles of their own. An in-season weight lifting program and morning conditioning was instituted, as well as some creative and hard-nosed practices and conditioning in the afternoon.

Hahn's wrestlers would never be out of shape. He believed, "If a wrestler is out of shape, then he was out-worked before he even stepped on the mat. Our goal is to outwork our opponents each day. This way, whoever we face will never be prepared when they step across from us."

So, as the 1996 season came along, a number of these wrestlers who had come up through the Cougars were now sophomores and juniors and seniors and primed to restore the Glenbard glory of old; Frank, who was one of them, was looking to make his first run into the state championships. But first, there would be a DuPage Valley Conference championship to win and a Regional title to lock up for the team.

Team-wise, "There was no better dual team in the state that year," Hahn recalled. "But, we did have some seniors on that team that were not really dedicated, and that came to bite us in the ass at the end of the season."

When the end of the season arrived, and the Panthers found themselves in the Dual Team Sectional championship match against LaGrange Lyons Township, those same seniors who had been cutting corners throughout the season, were now about to be called upon to secure the Sectional championship.

Frank would step on the mat against another sophomore, Matt Sandburg, and defeated him 10-1. "When I stepped off the mat," Defilippis said, "we were up 24-0 with five matches left and I had no doubt in my mind that we were going down state as a team. But little did I know what was about to happen."

Then, as senior after senior stepped on the mat for North, Lyons was winning, scoring big bonus points, and the lead had disappeared.

Frank then recalled, "All of a sudden, we were getting steamrolled.

One guy was up by a point with a few seconds left, then he gets taken down. Another guy gets body-locked to his back and stuck. We just kept getting pinned; they had kids with no business being out there pinning us. Senior after senior went down. It was unbelievable. I couldn't believe what was happening."

North would lose 27-29, earning only one more win, but the loss would stick with Hahn and those wrestlers who were coming back the following season.

Moving forward, there would have to be a tightening of the reigns from the coaching staff and the team captains if something like this was going to be prevented in the future.

IN 1997, THE TEAM WOULD HAVE A DIFFERENT

look with mostly juniors wrestling in the lineup, but the ability to qualify for the Dual Team State Championships would still be a struggle. By the time the DuPage Valley Conference championships came around, Glenbard North was simply dominating. They were 17-1 on the season and, at the conference tournament, the Panthers would boast eight individual champions out of fourteen possible weight classes, claim two more all-conference selections, and amass a then conference record 300 team points. This team was real and they were ready.

"In 1997," Defilippis remembered, "we were really good. But we were not ready for what was going to happen on the night of the Sectional championship."

After winning the Regional dual, and qualifying five wrestlers for the Individual State Championships, and walking away with three individual medals, the team was primed for overcoming the Dual Team Sectional hump.

When Tuesday came, North was pretty surprised to see that Maine West's entire team had cut one full weight class to match up better against them.

In 1997, Maine West had one individual state champion, a state runner-up, and a third-place finisher—Miguel Garcia who defeated North's Dana Holland 7-4 for third place that previous Saturday—and three additional state qualifiers with a combined season record of 115-10. That meant that during and after the grind of the Individual State Championships, these wrestlers, along with their teammates, were cutting weight and still competing at a high level.

On North's side, they would have five state qualifiers—one state runner-up, a fourth, and a fifth; Frank would not place as a junior. And, even though North felt very confident about their line-up, some of North's studs would be met by some of Maine West's studs.

As the match unfolded, and even though Maine West had made an unprecedented gamble with their weight cutting, they had won the big matches they needed to win and led going into the final two matches of the dual. In that, North still had the opportunity to close out the first round match of the Sectional Championships when Frank stepped onto the mat with the team losing by four points. He would wrestle Miguel Garcia, a 135-pound All-State wrestler who had cut to 130.

The match-up for Frank meant he would be followed by Dana Holland, a two-year fourth-place state medalist. Most likely, Holland would be wrestling a sub-par opponent compared to Garcia and, in all considerations, earn a win that would clinch a team state appearance.

Frank controlled the match and was winning by one point with 00:13 left when he was called for stalling while defending a shot. As he came back to the center of the mat, Frank took a quick shot off the whistle and got in on Garcia's leg—he would then be called for a second stalling warning, for not finishing the move, and that cost him one match-point.

So now, with no time remaining, the match would go into overtime where Garcia would score a late takedown. Maine West would forfeit to Dana Holland and win the dual by one point, advance to the Sectional championship match, and eliminate North, this time, with its possible strongest team and greatest opportunity to trophy since 1988.

"I feel like I cost us that dual," Defilippis said. "That should never have happened. Going into my off-season and my senior season, I would use that match as my motivation."

COMING INTO THE 1998 SEASON, THE CORE OF THE

team was not only seniors, but wrestlers that were experienced and had seen two deserving teams come up short on qualifying for the Dual Team State Championships.

This group of seniors would be led by captains Frank Defilippis, Dana Holland and Gino Rigitano. More importantly, this group was very close and had grown up and competed together since they were ten years old—and almost all of them came through the club together. The only real question would be: What would make them different from the more talented teams that had come before them that could not qualify for the team championships after the ten-year absence?

When asked about the ten-year drought, Hahn commented, "In 1988, it was too easy. I didn't appreciate it. It was basically Fulk's team and I took over what he had already laid the groundwork for—I didn't really know what went into it. After having teams that came close and teams that were deserving and better than a lot of teams not make it, I never really knew if it would happen again. But we kept at it, and I felt the 1998 team had a chance to do it because of how close they were."

After the Maine West Sectional loss, it would be a few weeks before the identity in the following year's team would be seen. After spring break, it was time for the spring season to begin, and the team responded. North's club, Mat Rat Wrestling Club, was filled with upper and lower classmen each week, and wrestlers were competing. The captains made sure the word was out: "Be there. No excuses." And everybody was listening.

Every weekend, the captains and the team were gaining experience, hanging out with each other and simply laughing and having fun while they wrestled. Gone was some of the selfishness, the smoking and drinking—the distractions—from some the graduated seniors. These new seniors felt that they owed it to each other to do right, and just being together as a team was enough.

So, when the season began that November, the work had been put in during the offseason; the leadership was in place, and the team's goals had been laid out and planned for everyone to work toward. Everyone was on the same page.

Now, even though North started their season with strong out-of-conference victories in their season opener, the Fulk Quad the night before Thanksgiving, there was still work to do. Their conference schedule, in addition to a dual against Willowbrook of, who upset them the previous season, would prove to be the true barometer on the strength of the team and how they might fair at the season's end.

That team, the 1998 squad, had nowhere near the natural talent of the 1997 team. However, what they lacked in natural ability, they made up in toughness. "What made our team special," Defilippis reflected, "was that we wrestled for each other—this is what made us competitive. We were not going to let each other down."

After the team's three opening dual meet victories, they entered the Hoffman Estates Conant Tournament that same Friday and Saturday. Also competing in that tournament would be Catholic school powerhouse New Lenox Providence and DuPage Valley Conference rival Naperville North.

When the championship matches came around, North would have senior captain Dana Holland ending on mat one at 140 pounds, and senior captain Frank DeFilippis ending on mat two. The way Conant ran their championships was by running two first-place matches at one time. The 103-pound championship began on one mat and moved up the weight classes before ending at 140 pounds. And, conversely, the other mat began at heavyweight and worked down to 145 pounds.

For Mark Hahn, he could not have ended with two stronger weight classes for his team. Dana was a two-time place-winner as a sophomore and a junior, fourth place each season, and Frank was a returning state qualifier. Both wrestlers opened the season ranked in the top two and three of their weight classes.

By the time Dana and Frank stepped on the mat, Naperville had not only closed the gap, they had taken the lead by four points. That meant Dana and Frank not only had to win, but they would need bonus points to guarantee a third team title in the past four years.

Dana would take his talents and leadership to the mat first. He would defeat DeLaSalle's Andy Bugajski 13-4. This would win Dana the title at 140 and add bonus points to North's total.

The final match of the night could not have shined a larger spotlight on both Frank and the Panthers. He would be facing Providence Catholic's Mark Alessio. A win would secure the championship for both himself and his team—and Frank did not disappoint. He would go on and win by a major decision and North would claim a 186.5 to 181.5 victory over Naperville North.

From there, Glenbard would roll through three dual meet victories giving up a total of nine team points before its dual with the Huskies—and Naperville North had not forgotten about Conant.

As it had been in the past, this was a highly touted dual between two of the three DuPage Valley Conference's powerhouses. The stands were full; the tensions were high, and, in the end, Naperville North would walk away with a 31-19 victory.

During the meet and exiting the gymnasium, Naperville fans made sure to remind the Glenbard faithful that wrestling in a tournament was different from wrestling in a dual. And, on that night, Naperville had Glenbard's number. They proved that they were still the team to beat and, if it was not difficult enough, Glenbard left that dual a bit disappointed with a shot to their pride.

"The most difficult part of that night was knowing we were better than we performed," Hahn said. "Our team was not as talented as the teams we had in the past. So getting the guys to believe in themselves was the biggest obstacle."

The Panthers would bounce back and rack up three more dual meet wins before their next conference foe, Wheaton North. Again, the stands would be packed and the voices were loud and obnoxious on both ends of the gymnasium.

Unfortunately, and for a second time on the season, Glenbard would Fall; this time, a 29-32 loss.

Four weeks would pass and North would take down four more programs in duals before their third test of the season against last year's perfect dual season dream crusher, Villa Park Willowbrook.

The week in the room was focused and the team had put in a full effort, always reminded of their two losses on the season and their season ender; however, in the end, and unfortunately for the third time, Hahn's team would fall. Willowbrook would win in fine fashion with a commanding 30-22 dual meet victory.

"I was so disgusted after that loss," Hahn recalled. "When we got back to school, I just dropped them off at the door and left. The captains took the guys in and talked to them. They stayed as a team, ran, and came in with a renewed focus."

When Hahn walked away, the captains took over and the renewed focused came in the form of a team meeting and a self-punishing. The team ran for forty minutes and pushed themselves, exhausting themselves as they did not want to lose again. There would be teammates throwing up and feeling weakened by the day's events, but no one stopped and no one walked away until the team was satisfied.

Heading back into the room on Monday, Hahn knew that he would have to fine tune his team with only two weeks before the DuPage Valley Conference championships.

As the Saturday of the conference tournament came, and the Panther wrestlers dyed their hair gold to show a united front and made their goals known, they battled and would win five of the fourteen weight classes. But even though Glenbard had a strong showing, it looked as if Naperville North, in the consolations, was racking up win after win and scoring a great deal of bonus points.

When the tournament ended, Naperville North escaped with a team score of 244 to 240.5 and a team championship.

"We wrestled probably as best we could that day," Defilippis said. "We did not have the fire power for a tournament—we were better in duals, but even there we weren't always that strong. We were always moving guys around trying to get the best match-ups."

During that week of practice, Hahn worked his guys hard. "I knew that I could push them," Hahn said. "They worked hard and wanted to work—they were not afraid of hard work—they welcomed challenges. Getting them to all perform on the same day was where I was concerned after we had given away a few duals that season."

Coming into the week of the Regional, Glenbard was favored to win the team championship over Wheaton North since they scored higher at the conference meet the week before; however, Wheaton North was riding on their dual meet win earlier in the season and was very confident.

Regardless of who won the tournament on Saturday, as both teams knew, the top two teams in the Regional would wrestle off in a separate dual for the championship that following Tuesday.

As fate would have it, Glenbard would lose the Regional to Wheaton North and watch them celebrate.

After the Regional ended, Hahn remembered Wheaton North's celebration. "They were celebrating as if they already beat us," Hahn said, "—taking pictures and parents and fans shouting in our direction. I walked up to [Head Coach] Steve Holland and said, 'Well, I guess we don't even need to wrestle the dual.' Steve apologized for the team, but I think seeing all that helped us dial in for the practices and motivation that we needed."

When Tuesday came and the dual began, there was no doubt who came to wrestle and who just came to wrestle. Glenbard would defeat Wheaton North in a very hostile environment by a score of 34-16, avenging its conference loss, and putting an end to the celebratory pictures taken just three days before.

However, heading into the first round of the Sectional Championships, in a few weeks, would be the Naperville North team that defeated the Panthers in their conference dual and at the DuPage Valley Conference Championships.

When the Tuesday of the Dual Team Sectional Championships came, hosted by Wheaton-Warrenville South, Glenbard and Naperville squared off with a strong fan following for each school.

Glenbard would end up stunning the reigning DuPage Valley Conference champions with a 26-25 win.

Still riding the high of knocking off Naperville, Glenbard would now have a chance to right a loss from Willowbrook both from earlier in the season, and from the 1996 Sectional championship.

Glenbard would start out by winning the first seven weight classes and opening a 24-0 lead before hitting the power of Willowbrook's line-up in the lower weights—Frank opened the dual with a fall. Along with Frank's win, his teammates won some tight decisions and even some upsets in overtime.

As was known by the North coaching staff, in a dual meet situation, some heroes had to emerge. These heroes were usually not the team's studs; but rather, dedicated wrestlers who were all in and waited and seized their opportunity when they could contribute.

In fact, one wrestler, Brian Fogle, had been out all season and came back for that dual and defeated state qualifier Rich Behnke, 10-8, in a hotly contested overtime match.

North would go on to pull out a 33-22 victory and qualify for the Dual Team State Championships with a team that was less talented than the previous two, but more determined and more united.

"Why were we so good?" Defilippis said. "We worked hard and had a lot of fun. I mean, we all believed in what the coaching staff was telling us and teaching us. We had good leadership on and off the mat and everyone wanted to wrestle for everyone else. No one wanted to let the guy next to him down."

Down state, Glenbard would lose to East Moline United Township 41-18 in their first Elite Eight appearance in ten years.

And, just as Frank had watched a team succeed in 1994, others were now watching him and looking forward to their time wrestling at North and being coached by Hahn.

In fact, two young wrestlers in the stands taking it all in were Vince and Tony. The younger brothers had seen the ups and downs and the commitment by friends and teammates to each other. Whether they were fully aware of it or not, they experienced what their brother was working for and, they too, would soon be working for those same goals in a few short years.

The 1998 season held a great many landmarks in the Glenbard North program. The team was back in the Dual Team State Championship series, and they were wrestling well in duals and tournaments when it mattered most. They were qualifying multiple wrestlers to the Individual State Championships, and those wrestlers were bringing home medals.

Additionally, North would crown its fourth state champion in Dana Holland, Frank's best friend and the program's first since 1989. Dana would also shatter the program's record for Most Takedowns in One Season (248) and Most Takedowns in a Career (594). He had now set new standards on the mat and in the program.

All along the way, Vince and Tony would be watching these duals and matches and rivalries, taking it all in, and learning from each experience as they were inadvertently being prepared for their high school careers.

CHAPTER 6
MAKING GOOD ON AN OLD PROMISE

"I didn't think I needed another year to grow and mature for an athletic advantage—I saw it as a copout. I knew I was ready to compete in high school."

• *Tony Ramos*

AFTER TONY'S SIXTH GRADE SEASON, IT WAS time for the family to make a decision on where the boys would be going to high school.

Frank had been adamant about the boys making the move with him to Carol Stream to attend his alma mater, Glenbard North. In the past few years, North wrestling was back on top and they had no intention of leaving. In 2001, Glenbard wrestled to a state runner-up finish in the Dual Team State Championships. They would place third in 2002, 2003, and 2004, each time losing to the eventual state champion in the semifinals.

The program was back to being a state and national powerhouse, and it ran like a well-oiled machine. The coaching staff was set and in rhythm, each level out performed its competition, and the wrestling and the wrestlers coming out of Glenbard North were some of the state's best. Additionally, since Frank wrestled for North, he knew the value of the coaches in the room and what they would bring to his brothers as mentors. Frank also knew what the school offered academically and how the exposure of being in such a well-known program would only benefit the boys as they were college bound and wanted to wrestle at the next level.

As both Tony and Vince had been growing up and competing at a high level, Frank had made it clear to Glenbard's head coach, Mark Hahn, that his brothers would be wrestling for him when the time came for them to enter high school. Of course, Hahn was skeptical, and he commented, "A lot of people talk, Tiger. We will see."

However, in the end, Hahn was not the person Frank had to convince; it was not even his mom. It was his step-father, Al Ramos.

As Tony was about to enter seventh grade, and brother Vince was headed into high school, the family had already been relocated up to Johnsburg, Illinois, from Carol Stream—Al's work dictated where the family would live. Frank recalled, "The first thing I asked was what everybody already knew was an issue, 'Where are the boys going to be going to school and wrestling?'"

Johnsburg High School did have a wrestling program, but, as Frank reflected on the issue, he felt, "That wasn't the right fit and the whole family knew that. Up to that point, I am not even sure if they had had a state qualifier. North was where they needed to be."

When Frank presented his plan to his parents, he told them point blank, "If you really want them to succeed, this is what is best for them."

Immediately, Deb Ramos, the boys' mom, said, "I know. We can make this work." However, her husband needed more convincing. To Al, these were his boys and he wanted to be around them.

As for the rest of the conversation, Frank just refused to take no for an answer and, in the process, cited success after success in North's program arguing that the only other option was purchasing a new home in Fox Lake for the boys to attend Grant High School. Of course, this was also not an option, and Frank knew it.

Frank had since taken on a new job and was looking for a place to settle down—he knew his home would be in or near Carol Stream because his home had to be in North's boundaries; he had big plans for his younger brothers and he also had a promise to keep with his former coach. But, it was not just Frank who knew where the boys should be—Tony and Vince also knew that Glenbard North was where they would excel—not just for their high school years, but in college, Fargo, anywhere. "We were supposed to go to Johnsburg once my parents moved out of Carol Stream," Ramos said. "But, there wasn't much of a tradition there, not like North. North offered a better room and a better group of coaches, and that was where we knew we would get what we needed."

However, for all of that to happen, Frank he was going to have to commit the next six years of his life to the boys—and he did. In the end, Frank won the consent of his parents and, in 2003, he took custody of the boys. Now, for Frank to put his words into action, he would have to make a commitment and a lifestyle change in order for that to happen.

"Once [the boys were] registered at Stratford Middle School,"

Defilippis said, "Hahn knew it was real."

Additionally, like many parents were doing with their children, Vince would ultimately be held back one year in school to gain one more year of maturity. This would put Tony in seventh grade and Vince in eighth—making the boys one year apart in school and a handful at home. Only twenty-three years old and right out of college, Frank committed himself by taking on the guardianship of his brothers so they could attend and wrestle for the same program that he did.

"Looking back on what Frankie did," Ramos reflected, "taking on two teenagers like that, at twenty-three, was crazy. And with the hours he worked, getting home around 10:00 p.m., we had all of the freedom in the world. So there wasn't much of him watching over us—we had a lot of leeway. But, we knew what he was doing for us, we never abused it—if we had, he would have kicked our asses."

Early on, both Tony and Vince had to make a number of adjustments living with their older brother. Frank had three rules that were non-negotiable: 1. They were not allowed to get into trouble with the police; 2. They each had to get good grades and keep them up; and, 3. They had to train hard and win. There were no misunderstandings about any of the rules and they were not up for negotiation; everything was made very clear to boys early on and repeated often.

"To tell you the truth," Ramos admitted, "I think living this way early on helped me grow as a person and into a man quicker than most kids. Most kids our age had their mother waking them up, cooking for them, doing their laundry—it was pretty much all on us. If we did not do it, it was not going to get done. At the start, I struggled with the cooking; however, as I did it more and more, I fell in love with it."

Aside from the early adjustments and botches with cooking, Tony also struggled with laundry and, even worse, waking up for school. For a thirteen-year-old, there was no surprise that these would be major adjustments.

"Laundry ended up being something that I found to be too time consuming," Ramos said. "First I had to separate everything, wash it, dry it, and then wait to fold it all. I could not believe how much time it took to do this. The more and more I did, I found that I needed a routine to get it all done. I would do my homework while I did it—or run on the treadmill between loads."

Therefore, as he grew up, his mom was around less and less and there was not much to take for granted. When he lived with his parents, his mom woke them up for school and made their lunches. "I think it was the first two weeks of school that every few days I had to be called in by someone because I was waking up late," Ramos remembered.

Of course, to follow the rules set by his brother, he needed to make it to school and attend his classes. "I knew that if I did not discipline myself to wake up," Ramos commented, "my grades would have fallen and then there would have been no club wrestling or wrestling in high school or college. I had to live up to my end, no matter how tough it was."

IN 2004, AS VINCE WAS ENTERING GLENBARD

North High School as a freshman, Tony would be left to his own devices in middle school with no older brother around. Also, Tony's parents, as they had done with Vince, wanted Tony to repeat a grade so he could gain another year of maturity. The Ramos family saw the benefit of Vince having grown mentally and physically during that extra school year, and it had become commonplace for a number of parents to be entering their boys into high school around 15 and 16 depending on their birthdays. However, Tony did not see it that way.

"When my parents told me that they wanted to hold me back another year," Ramos said, "I was not happy with it and I let them know how I felt. I didn't think I needed another year to grow and mature for an athletic advantage—I saw it as a cop-out. I knew I was ready to compete in high school."

In fact, when Tony and Vince would get into a fight, Tony would sometimes throw it in Vince's face that he was held back—it did not matter that it had nothing to do with grades or intelligence. Tony did not care. He would call Vince derogatory names and question his toughness and remark why Vince was held back—even though none of it was true and Tony knew why. True to form, Vince would just brush it off, but Tony would always take whatever jab or free shot he could take since his brother was bigger than him and held back.

Therefore, when Tony was sent off to Stratford Middle School for a second first day of seventh grade, he was not going to be denied moving into eighth. Frank's story was that he would "bet anything that for the entire first week of school, Tony walked into the principal's office and told him, 'I did this already. I don't want to be here—I should be in eighth grade. Get me out of here.'"

Tony, however, holds that he "didn't do anything about it except I focused more on my school. Soon, my teachers saw the grades I was getting and didn't understand why I was being held back."

And then, at the end of that first week, Frank received a phone call from his mom. "Tony has to go to eighth," Deb said.

Frank was floored when he heard this. He inquired as to why, why now after a week of school. Deb simply said, "They said Tony's got to go to eighth. He did this last year."

"I was very excited," Ramos said. "Now I could go to high school without being held back and my parents didn't have a choice. I was also happy because I would be one year behind my brother and most of our friends."

Again, Tony's willingness to live on his own terms was obvious. He did not care about his size or what challenges he was going to face. All he knew was that it was time for him to move forward and no one, not even his family, even with good intentions, was going to hold him back.

Now, as a fairly undersized eighth-grader, Tony, who wrestled 84 pounds in season and was closer to 90 pounds out of season, had a certain chip on his shoulder that everyone could see—and Tony did not care.

"It didn't matter what we were doing," Vince said of Tony's antics. "Even when we played video games, if Tony lost, he would go nuts. One time he even reset the game after he threw the controller at my face. He was ultra-competitive. It was not normal. He was not normal. But that was Tony."

Tony did not just act out against Vince and the friends he had around his own age, he was never scared of anyone—regardless—and would act out via pure emotion or as he felt was appropriate regardless of age or size or anything.

One night after Frank had purchased a brand new plasma television, Tony had to make sure Frank knew how unimpressed he was. With one of Frank's friends over at the house, as he was in the living room showing his buddy his new purchase and just talking, Tony saw this as the perfect opportunity to share his opinion about the purchase with his brother.

The two talked back and forth until Tony threatened Frank and told him, "I'll come right over there and slap you in the face."

And Tony did not do this from a distance, he walked right up to Frank and said it face-to-face, as close as he could get, while he looked up at him.

Frank just laughed, "Oh really? You're going to slap me? Get out of here," and then continued his conversation with his friend.

As for some of Frank's more dominant traits, he was not one to mince words or actions. He was just as blunt, if not more than Tony. He was recently out of college and college wrestling, and he was still in good shape. On top of that, Frank had his own chip resting on his own shoulder, and it may have been bigger than Tony altogether. Therefore, the last thing that he was going to do was take grief from 90-pound kid in his own home and in front of a friend.

Regardless of anything that Frank said, Tony kept coming back to his threat of slapping him. "I couldn't believe the set of balls on that kid,"

Defilippis remembered. "He just kept stepping closer to me, sticking out his little chest and chin—it was funny—but I was getting tired of it. Sometimes, even with me, Tony took things too far."

So, at that, Frank egged Tony on, "Okay, I dare you to slap me and just see what happens."

Fearless and confident, as Tony stepped up closer and inflated his chest further with his head raised and his eyes locked on Frank's eyes, Tony reached back and slapped Frank straight across the face and just stood there staring at him and nodding his head, proud, as if he had just proven himself. And then, before anything else happened, Frank extended his hand and grabbed Tony by the hair, lifted him up off the floor, laughed with a tone of bewildered amazement, "You little shit. You're out of here."

Not to be outdone, Tony fought back. He began swinging and kicking—but he was too small to even come close to making contact with his brother as he was elevated off the floor. His heightened tantrum was useless.

From there, Frank carried Tony to the door and threw him out into the cold and locked the door behind him. Of course, this would be another instance where Frank would threaten to call their mother and tell her to take her children back. But, in his heart, he loved the fire and fight and fearlessness in his youngest brother.

True to his form, even in that instance, Tony was pounding on the door demanding to be allowed back into the house and casting new threats about what would happen to Frank if he did not concede to his demands. But, Tony would have to wait outside until his mother showed up and, again, had to talk to her about appropriate behavior—it was not her first trip down from Johnsburg in regard to such instances, and it was certainly not her last.

Frank had moments where the boys were difficult to handle, and where he would have to threaten them, but he loved them and he tolerated it all because he knew what was best for them in the end—no matter how out of hand they became at times.

But, even though there were rules the boys struggled with, when it came to wrestling, they listened. Frank purchased videos and magazines and Tony would immerse himself in them, watching and reading about techniques and anything he could get his hands on.

During Vince's freshman campaign at North, the Ramos family as always around supporting both Vince and the program. Vince would earn All-DuPage Valley Conference honors, a Regional championship, qualify for the Individual State championships, and become an All-State wrestler by placing fifth—at the time, he was only the third Glenbard wrestler to ever place as a freshman.

So, for Tony, when he was not wrestling and defending his IKWF state championship, he had a front row seat and first-hand introduction to the DuPage Valley Conference, the Regional and Sectional Championships, the Individual State Championship, the Dual Team Sectional Championship, and the Dual Team State Championship.

Just as his oldest brother Frank had seen teams perform and excel and experience Assembly Hall with the Grand March and the finals, Tony was able to do the same right before entering high school. True, he had experienced the moments during Frank's junior and senior seasons, but now he was much more conscious of the future and the relevance of it all more than ever—it was, in reality, all one year away. But there was a new problem that had to be resolved before anything else moved forward.

AFTER TONY GRADUATED FROM EIGHTH GRADE,
the plan was for him to attend Glenbard North; however, an issue came up. Tony now wanted to attend Montini Catholic, where Israel was an assistant coach, so he could keep working with him more and more. This would split up the boys and put Frank in a position he refused to be in.

"After eighth grade," Ramos remembered, "Israel and I talked and I wanted to go to Montini so we could work together every day. I was all in and I remember my parents telling me that it was my choice. Things had changed from when I was younger."

To make his decision more real, Tony went to Montini and took the entrance exam. He felt, truly, that while his brother was growing and furthering his wrestling career at North, he would do the same for himself at Montini.

At this time, Montini and Glenbard North were two of the powerhouses in each of their divisions. Montini had already won a string of state championships, and North was close many times and always knocking on the door, but had always come up short. That following season, Montini would be bumped up to the AA Division, and a heated rivalry was destined to follow.

Now, if Tony was to attend Montini, they already had a senior captain at the 103-pound weight class, and Tony's entrance would cause a possible controversy if coaches were not sticking by their seniors and bringing in new guys to replace them. That issue, if it had become a real issue, may have caused a potential nightmare for Montini's recruiting in the future.

"We knew the family," Israel said, "and we knew Montini was an option because of Tony living with Frankie. But, we also knew Glenbard was probably where Tony was going to go because their family had the ultimate respect for Coach Hahn and his program."

However, even though Israel knew where Tony might end up, he did like to tease him about the choice in front of him. "One of the things I used to say to Tony to get him to Montini when he was confused about us and North," Israel remembered, "was, I would tell him, 'They don't have any team titles over there, Tony.' He loved the banter and he loved the idea of people talking about him. I would joke about how he would win individual titles over there, but not a team title."

Of course, as Tony approached Frank about the idea, Frank was not going to allow it—he shut the idea down immediately.

"I flat out told Tony," Defilippis said, "Montini is not an option. You're going to North. We didn't do all this to go to Montini. I'm not paying for it."

Allegedly, to cover costs if Tony wanted to attend Montini, Frank was told that everything would be taken care of and not to worry about anything. Frank recalled, "They offered to pay for everything—even offered my dad a work truck. They were going to get Tony a car, pay for both their tuitions—this is all they were telling me. But I told them, 'They're going to Glenbard, so none of this is an option.'"

As Tony remembered it, he said, "Frankie told me that he wasn't going to have it. He told me, 'You will not live with me and attend that school.'"

With that, Tony, along with Deb, Al, Frank, and Israel, all sat down to talk; the decision was final: Tony would attend North but still train with Izzy Style in the fall, spring, and summer.

CHAPTER 7
GOING BACKWARD TO MOVE FORWARD

"After college I now knew how to train and how to go about setting goals and just more about the sport in general. I was not going to let my brothers make those same mistakes that I did."

• *Frank Defilippis*
Ramos' brother

AS A SENIOR WRESTLER FOR NORTH, FRANK Defilippis was ranked number one in the state of Illinois by the midpoint of the 1998 season. However, his first trip to Assembly Hall on the campus of the University of Illinois, where the Illinois high school state championships were held, was not when he qualified for the state championships as a junior, or when he was picked to win state as a senior.

When Frank was an eighth-grader, his kids' club coach, Jim Considine, head coach of the Villa-Lombard Cougars, took all of his captains, as he had done each season, to the finals of the high school state championships at Assembly Hall to experience the Grand March, and the state finals matches. Considine did this to motivate the boys for their high school years talking to them about what it took to be on that stage and be able to wrestle at that level. The captains always looked forward to that trip.

"When I walked into Assembly Hall for the first time," Defilippis remembered, "my eyes popped out of my head. That was when there were two classes and the brackets were big and in that bright orange with thirty-two guys per weight class—I wanted to be walking out of that tunnel and in that Grand March. And I wanted one of those brackets for my wall."

Entering his senior campaign, Frank would dominate all of his opponents. He would claim his first DuPage Valley Conference championship and earn his second individual Regional championship. Then, when he entered the Individual Sectional Championships, he would wrestle his way to the finals and face Justin Becker of Elgin, a senior with a record of 32-02. Becker had placed fifth as a junior and, as a sophomore, was two matches away from the podium—Frank defeated him by a major decision.

That week, however, as the Individual State Championships came around, and Frank was ready to take his 43-0 record into the tournament with his dreams of walking in the Grand March, standing atop that podium, and seeing his name forever engraved on his own bright orange bracket board, he and his family experienced a set back and some family hardships.

"That week was a hard one," Defilippis remembered. "We found out some terrible news that Sunday after the Sectional. We don't even talk about it in the family. My little sister was having a surgery at five-years-old from something that happened in gymnastics. I had to be with my family and I missed a workout. Walking in the room, I wasn't all there. But this is where I was and where I wanted to be—so I had to figure it out."

When the tournament began, Frank received an opening round forfeit since he was a Sectional champion. Because of that, he watched the Preliminary Round that would feed into his second round match—Erik Skoczylas of Chicago Mather, a senior with a 27-5 record, was wrestling Russ Withaeger, a 31-10 junior from Hoffman Estates Conant. Withaeger would win with a convincing 6-2 decision and Frank would have Withaeger for his first match.

As Frank stepped onto the mat for his first match, he would take little time in disposing of the Conant junior with a fall in 2:56.

Now in the state's top eight, Frank faced another senior. He would have to win this match in order to secure all-state honors, and have a chance to wrestle in the semifinals for an opportunity to wrestle in the state championship match on Saturday night.

His opponent was Quincy senior Sam Smith, who had brought his 37-1 record into the tournament and his 39-1 record into that match.

Smith had to wrestle in the Preliminaries due to his Sectional championship loss, his first on the season.

Almost immediately, Frank took Smith down and cut him. From there, Frank would work a few more positions and carry a 2-1 lead into the second period. However, as he chose the bottom position and took a 3-1 lead after his escape, his next offensive attack, where he was hoping to close out the match, was used against him.

"I was running a knee-pick," Defilippis recalled, "and I stepped and stepped—and he was pretty long—and by my second step I was a bit off balance, and Smith fell into a headlock. He got five points and, from there, he just ran and ran and ran. I tried everything to catch up, but it never happened."

The match would end with Smith as the winner by a 10-3 score. Now in the wrestle-backs, Frank had to make a decision; but first, he would sit in the very tunnel he had hoped to walk out of with the hopes of winning a state championship and try to come to terms with how he ended up in that position.

"I went into the tunnel and [Coach] Hahn just sat there with me," Defilippis said. "—it felt like forever. I think the lights were on and I felt like we were the only ones in there. But, for me, there were no wrestle-backs—I was there to win."

On Frank's shoulders were his goals and his family's hopes of crowning a state champion. And even though he had overcome some adversities from the beginning of the week, he refused to make any excuses. "I had a rough week, but I make no excuses," Defilippis said. "It was my responsibility to win that day and I didn't."

So as Frank sat in that tunnel, he simply sat and pondered why.

"In my mind," Defilippis continued, "it didn't matter if I missed a whole week of practice; I still should've won. I did everything right all year long. Since I walked into Assembly Hall as an eighth-grader, this is where I was supposed to be and it got away from me. I think maybe the pressure got to me a little, but I still should have won."

As he sat there in the tunnel, still sweating with his singlet on, his back was against the wall with his sweats piled between his legs. He raised his head to the ceiling, confused. Looking back down, shaking, and rocking back-and-forth against the cement wall, he turned to his coach and asked, "Why me?"

His coach, Mark Hahn, would talk to his senior captain about life and not wrestling in that moment as he tried to help him make sense of it all. He said, "Frankie, look, if this is the worst thing that ever happens to you in your life, you did pretty good."

From there they would sit together until Frank was ready to move. They remained there, on that floor together, until the next round began. Smith would go on and be a state runner-up that weekend. Frank would win his first wrestle-back by a major decision, 9-1, over Brad Schrader of Hononegah before falling, 3-1, to Matt Sandburg of LaGrange Lyons. That loss to Sandburg would eliminate Frank from the tournament.

Watching all of the drama unfold and all of the unexplainable take place—Frank was supposed to win—were Frank's younger brothers, Vince and Tony Ramos. However, Frank had to quickly collect himself and his thoughts and be prepared to wrestle in the Dual Team Sectional Championships that Tuesday—just four days away.

"It was a devastating loss for Frankie," Hahn remembered, "and it was a devastating loss for me as well. I felt like Frankie should have been in the finals, or at least place. I know how much it hurt me, so I knew it hurt Frankie even more. But we still had to wrestle on Tuesday and the team needed him to be ready, so that was where I needed to get him focused—no matter how tough it was."

About a month after his loss at Assembly Hall, Frank would wrestle at the High School National Championships in Ohio and win the tournament—he recorded either a major decision, a technical fall, or a fall over each of his opponents. When the referee in the finals raised his hand, and approached Jim Considine, Frank's coach that weekend, he asked him, "Hey, how many state titles did he win in Illinois? That kid is phenomenal."

Considine smiled and simply replied, "None. Never even placed." And then Considine just grabbed Frank's gear and walked away.

Even though Frank never medaled in Illinois, he knew the sport of wrestling, loved it dearly, and would take his talents to Eastern Illinois University.

At Eastern, as a junior, he was passed over on a coaches' bid as he was not a conference champion; he was the runner-up. He did not do enough to be voted into the national championships by the coaches. But, as a senior, he would win the conference and become a DI National Qualifier. Unfortunately, his chase at All-American status would end as he went 2-2 ending his career.

"I know what I did wrong," Defilippis said. "I went to a program that I thought was good because I saw that they were 12-2 the year before. But I got caught up in the wrong things early on—I never even had a beer until college. It wasn't until my junior year when I started figuring it all out. But, by then, and by the time it was all over, I realized that maybe I set my goals too low."

And by too low, he realized that by setting minimum goals, he was never going to reach them. "I would have been content placing eighth and being an All-American," Defilippis admitted, "but not shooting for anything higher is why I never even reached my goals."

After graduation, Frank would use his experiences, both his successes and failures, to help coach his brothers and give them the opportunity to do what he was unable to finish.

"When I graduated and looked back on it all," Defilippis reflected, "I realized that one of the things that I didn't do right was I didn't make it fun. For something that is so hard, if you're not having fun along the way, there is just something wrong. I put too much emphasis on some of the wrong things. After college I now knew how to train and how to go about setting goals and just more about the sport in general. I was not going to let my brothers make those same mistakes that I did."

• • •

So, at 23-years-old, Frank had now convinced his parents to give him custody of his brothers, but he would only have three weeks to find a house within the school's boundaries—and even the cheapest house was well more than he could afford.

In the end, it was the Ramos family working as one unit to give Tony and Vince the best opportunity possible—they found a way to purchase a home. "It was crazy," Defilippis said. "I was working thirteen and fourteen-hour days and my mom was coming over and doing our laundry and buying groceries and keeping the house running. Al was working seven days a week and providing whatever he had to in order to make this work. We couldn't have done it without each other."

Frank paused, "People who don't know the story behind how the boys ended up with me think that the boys' home life must have been terrible. People say, 'What? Were your parents junkies or something?' But that wasn't the case at all. We knew that if Vince and Tony were going to reach their potential, this is what had to be done. Coach Hahn and [Coaches] Garrett and Cherry and Edwards and Considine all knew me and my family. We knew the boys would be in good hands and have people watching and looking after them. At North, they'd thrive."

CHAPTER 8
GROWING PAINS

"I gave those two everything they needed. I expected them to get good grades, train hard, and win. I wanted them to put themselves in a position to go to college."

* *Frank Defilippis*
Ramos' brother

BEFORE ENTERING HIGH SCHOOL, THE BOYS HAD already learned how to be more self-sufficient and survive with Frank at work. However, sometimes their mode of survival, even when they tried to do a little extra around the house to help, backfired on them.

Even as they entered high school, they were not perfect. They had their faults, and sometimes just not knowing—being young—mistakes were made. Big mistakes.

Before leaving for school one morning, Frank made it clear that the dishes had to be cleaned and put away before he came home.

That night, upon returning from their workout, Tony took the dishes, put them into the dishwasher, but saw that there was no more dishwasher soap left. He figured nothing of it—and thinking that soap was soap—he grabbed a liquid soap bottle, squeezed what he felt was a good amount, ran it, and went to get ready for bed.

Once he was all ready for bed, Tony came back downstairs to make sure the house was closed up for the night since Frank was still at work. Suddenly, as he walked into the kitchen, he yelled, "Vince! Vince! Get down here!"—there were bubbles everywhere pouring out of the dishwasher.

Immediately, they shut off the dishwasher, opened it, and began to frantically clean. They grabbed piles of towels and the shop vacuum and went to work.

They started with the furthest bubbles on the linoleum floor, trying to stop them from reaching the carpet in the living room and the hardwood floors in the dining room.

"As we were cleaning," Ramos recalled, "all we could think about how we were going to have our asses kicked for this."

By the end of the clean-up, the boys headed to bed, believing it was clean and covered up. However, Tony remembered being woken up later that night. "It had to be 2:00 a.m. when Frankie walked in the house," Ramos said. "He came up into our rooms and said, 'What the fuck were you two doing? There are bubbles everywhere downstairs—unbelievable! Get your asses out of bed and clean that mess up right now. Every week it's something with you guys. Every week.'"

UNFORTUNATELY, AS MUCH AS TONY AND VINCE followed the rules, and did their best to do their best, they were teenager boys and things happened.

Frank was out of the house most days and some nights. Therefore, when the boys were not in season, Frank did not want to have to be handing out cash every few days; he had to figure something out. Since he had established himself fairly quickly in his career, and he was finally making money, in order to make more money, Frank could not be home as often—his hours were fluctuating more and more and his dedication to his career was very time consuming.

Due to that, Frank decided that giving the boys a credit card would help them buy what they needed when they needed it; however, neither of the boys truly understood the value of a dollar and how quickly swiping a card's magnetic strip added up.

"I sat down with the boys and explained to them what the card was for," Defilippis remembered. "But when I got that first bill, Tony had spent $1,800 in the first month."

When asked what Tony could have possibly purchased, Frank laughed, "You name it. Lunch. Dinner. Dunkin Donuts. Sports Authority. I was furious. I pulled the boys in. There was no conversation—I was screaming!"

Unfortunately, as the boys were being yelled at, Frank's message was not getting through to them. The boys just truly had no concept of their actions in relation to money. Because they could not see the total amount added up—and the card was never declined—the idea of money and how fast everything added up was just not real to them.

"Vince started to learn and understand," Defilippis said. "But Tony, Tony could not grasp it. But I don't think he cared either. I can't tell you how many times I yelled at that kid about money."

THE OVERLL DYNAMICS OF THE HOUSE WERE
based on trust. "We never drank," Ramos said, "and there was a refrigerator filled with beer for Frankie and his friends. He was just out of college, young, a few years into his job, had money, and was having fun—but we respected the house and Frankie, and he made it so we never had anything to worry about."

"I gave those two everything they needed," Defilippis said. There was always food in the house for them and their friends when they came over. I made it so they didn't have to go out to have fun—the house was filled with all they needed. I didn't require them to work or pay their own way. I expected them to get good grades, train hard, and win. I wanted them to put themselves in a position to go to college. If they couldn't do that, I told them I was signing them back over to mom and Al."

But, regardless of house rules and the respect they did have for their brother, boys would be boys.

Since Vince was bigger, he would pick on Tony. And, since Tony was Tony, he would always fight back. Sometimes he would fight back immediately, and sometimes he would store it all inside of himself and concoct some scheme of revenge for later on.

In the epic battles between Vince and Tony, there were very few wins for Tony; most times he lost, but he always got even and, in the end, Tony felt, "it just made me tougher. I was not going to take his shit—I didn't care how much bigger he was."

The boys usually watched television in the finished basement; that was where they could lounge around and have their friends over to just unwind. There would also be the days where wrestling matches or even full-out fights took place down there as one brother would simply snicker at the other as he released a crude comment. Other times, there would be a slap to the other's face, a smack to the back of the neck in passing, a push here or a shoulder there, a look, or just bringing up something old and personal and unsettled to ignite the other's pride.

In one act that began very innocently, Vince tried a UFC move on Tony and it ultimately escalated quickly when the move went too far—Tony did not find it as funny as Vince.

"We started off watching UFC," Tony remembered, "and Vince wanted to try a move. I let him, but then he started getting rough with me—so I got rough right back. Neither of us know how it all transpired, really, but a fight broke out. And as we were fighting, Vince took me and picked me up and threw me into the bannister by the stairs. The fight immediately stopped when the wooden spindles broke and we saw what had just happened."

Vince recalled how the boys "looked at one another and, shaking our heads, we said, 'Oh shit!' at the same time. We knew Frankie was going to kill us and we had to figure something out before he came home."

Just as before and with each instance after, the boys always found a way to clean or hide their destructive ways—they always came up with a solution, even if it was temporary.

Having a number of family members and family friends in the trades, the boys immediately called their cousin D.J. whom was a painter. He came over and the boys were already gluing the spindles together and trying to put them in their place—but woodworking was not necessarily one of their fortes.

When D.J. showed up, he was laughing as the boys told him what happened. He sanded the spindles down and painted them to match. It was not a great job because the damage was so severe, but it was a job that would buy the boys some time.

Of course, there was still the issue of retaliation inside of Tony for being thrown around—and he was not one to forget as he was not one to allow someone bigger to have the upper hand for too long.

Two weeks later the boys had a sleepover at the house. Jaime Warczynski was Vince's friend who was spending the night, and Alec Pineda was whom Tony chose to have over. All of the boys were friends—they only hung around with their closest friends; Frank never allowed an outsider, someone he did not know, into the house and the boys knew that. Even when Frank was not home, the boys never crossed that understood rule—there were never outsiders.

As the night wore on, Vince had been picking on Tony and Tony was not very happy about it; besides, he still owed Vince from the UFC night a few weeks back.

Throughout the night, the boys hung out together, watched television, joked and laughed; however, as soon as Vince and Jaime went to sleep, Tony explained to Alec what had happened and that he wanted to get back at Vince. Tony was always scheming and waiting for the most opportune time to get back at his brother or anyone whom he felt had crossed him.

Here was Tony's plan: "I told Alec that when Vince fell asleep, we would sneak into his room and dump a huge bucket of ice water on his head. But first, we needed to put a chair in my bedroom to barricade the door for when Vince comes at us."

So they waited, and waited, and waited until Vince and Jaime fell asleep. Once they did, Tony went into the kitchen for a chair, and then into basement to fill up the mop bucket with cold water and ice.

As Tony and Alec were sneaking back upstairs to Tony's room, they had to walk past Vince's room. In that moment, Vince was tossing and Tony froze. Suddenly and slowly, all at the same time, Vince woke up in an uncertain-groggy-tired-dream-like state.

"Tony?" Vince asked. "What are you guys doing?"

Not really expecting Vince to wake up, Tony had a moment of pause. But he was able to come up with something, "We are breakdancing," he told Vince.

Overly tired, Vince responded, "Oh, okay," and put his head back down on the pillow.

About five minutes later, Tony and Alec returned with the bucket and did not hesitate. Tony came in the room and immediately dumped the ice-cold water on Vince. Unfortunately, for Jaime, he was hit with most of the water, so he was not that happy about the retaliation either.

As fast as they could, Tony and Alec bolted back to Tony's room, shut the door, and barricaded it with the kitchen chair.

Vince came storming out of his room and began pounding on and kicking at Tony's door while yelling at him. "And as he was yelling at me," Tony said, "I was just laughing. But all of that came to an end when Vince kicked a hole through my door trying to get to me. At that point I knew I had to just face this because he was going to break the door down and we were going to get into more trouble with Frankie."

When Tony opened the door, a fist fight immediately broke out in the hallway. For the boys and the hallway, nothing was spared in the fight. It was a disaster area when it was all over.

From what Tony remembered, "It didn't go too well for me. But I was never going to take his shit—I was going to stick up for myself regardless [of the outcome]."

Of course, before Frank came home, the boys had tried to cover up their night. They were asleep when Frank walked upstairs, but he noticed something was different. "All of a sudden there were wrestling posters up and down the door," Defilippis said. "I was like, *Now what the hell did they do?* So I ripped down the posters and saw all the holes."

To say that he was not happy about the door would be an understatement. But, through all of the fights, he never gave the boys grief for standing up for themselves—he just would have rather the house had not suffered.

THAT NEXT SUNDAY, WHILE FRANK WAS WITH

the boys downstairs watching a Bears game and hanging out, he reached out to lean on one of the bannister's spindles. Of course, as he did this, the glued spindle could not support his weight and he went crashing through the spindles and onto the staircase and then onto the floor.

Bringing himself to his feet, he could see the glue and cracks in the wood. He looked right at the boys, "You [little] pricks, when did you do this?"

The boys came clean with the truth, and Frank just could not believe there was something else in the house that was broken. He knew there were probably more secret damage in the house, but only time would reveal it.

CHAPTER 9
CUTTING TO THE CHASE

"I was going to dominate and I wasn't going to leave any doubt that I was the best; this is mine, and if you want to wrestle, it won't be at this weight."

• *Tony Ramos*

COMING INTO GLENBARD NORTH HIGH SCHOOL, Tony had set his individual goals high. He had set out to be undefeated all four years, a four-time state champion, and he wanted to break every individual record at North, specifically, the Career Takedown record and the Most Falls in a Career record.

Likewise, Tony also stated that he "wanted to be known and remembered as the greatest wrestler to come out of Glenbard North and out of the state of Illinois. When people mention Illinois wrestling, I want them to start [their conversation] with me."

AS THE 2005-2006 HIGH SCHOOL SEASON BEGAN, Tony entered his freshman year and walked into a varsity room that was very young and very talented. However, there were still a number upperclassmen who were tough-nosed, successful, Glenbard raised and trained, and who cared solely about the program's success as a whole, and not the individual.

The previous season, the team had just finished second to Carl Sandburg High School in the IHSA Dual Team State Championships. Add that to a program that had just won their seventh-consecutive DuPage Valley Conference team championship, their fifth-straight IHSA Regional championship, and were coming off five-consecutive

Dual Team Sectional championships with five-consecutive trophies; the team Tony was walking into was primed for a strong season and North was closer and closer to a team state championship.

So, not unlike any other wrestler who went from his youth program's wrestling room into one of the premier wrestling rooms in the state, Tony was going to have to make some adjustments.

Tony fit right in when it came to hard work; however, there were some upper-classmen who were not so welcoming of his attitude and over-confidence because, just like when he was a child, if he had something to say, he would say it—and it did not matter how big or how old the person was that he was speaking to. Regardless of his attitude, there were still adjustments.

Of course, having Vince and a few friends around did make this transition easier. Vince had already established himself and had been voted in and named as a team co-captain for that, his sophomore season.

"Having Vince around," Ramos recalled, "did make walking into the room easier. Knowing that I had my brother with me to train with and fight with and cut weight with—for both of us—made it fun and pushed us. When I would see him working hard, it pushed me to work harder. Besides, I knew he always had my back—right or wrong. But I was usually right."

"I knew that when Tony came into that room," Vince admitted, "he would have to take some beatings from the older guys—we all do. But he held his own and owned his circle. His attitude was that he could step in and win a state championship. He was confident and never thought that anyone—in or out of the room—was better than him and it showed."

As for some of the others on the team, especially some of the upper-classmen, Tony rubbed them the wrong way early on. "Coming out of middle school," Ramos said, "I came into that room and I wanted to be the big man on campus. And some of those guys wanted to be the big guys on campus. There would be times where we butted heads with each other, but it always got worked out. We're all family and sometimes family has to fight with each other."

Needless to say, Coach Hahn always had the final word, and the team always came together for the benefit of the program and its overall team goals.

ALL OF THAT BEING SAID, THE EXPECTATIONS

were very high for the team and the returning 103-pound state qualifier for North was back for her senior season—she was coming off a record-setting campaign in Illinois and had just won her third consecutive freestyle national championship in Fargo.

Caitlyn Chase, as a junior in 2005, was well-known throughout the state of Illinois. She started for the Panthers intermittently as a freshman and sophomore, but made her mark on the state as a junior.

During her sophomore campaign, what put everything in motion was that boys began to be timid when having to wrestle her for one simple reason: she was beating them. Caitlyn was fearless, aggressive, and could hit a headlock out of nowhere from anywhere. She was not as strong as some of the boys, but her technique was solid. Her experience was vast, and she was aggressive from whistle-to-whistle—these were her true strengths.

In fact, during Caitlyn's sophomore season at the 2004 IHSA Dual Team State Championships in Moline, Illinois, in the third place dual against Carpentersville Dundee Crown, the match came down to her at 103 pounds versus Josh Pasek.

Glenbard was winning the dual 27-25 headed into that final match and, whichever wrestler won, his or her team would take home the third place trophy.

Immediately into the match, Caitlyn was taken down and being over-powered by Pasek. However, as the match wore on, and Pasek wore down, she slowly worked her way back and, by the end of regulation, she had tied the score 9-9 on a fireman's carry with seconds remaining.

In overtime, Caitlyn became more aggressive and Pasek became more and more nervous—he could lose to this girl wrestler and everyone would know about it. To Caitlyn, though, she never saw wrestling in terms of her wrestling boys—she was just wrestling to win. Moreover, that match was not about her, it was about the opportunity to help North win and take home a third place trophy.

Overtime started with Caitlyn and Pasek were hand fighting and vying for position—Caitlyn was working to her fireman's carry, but Pasek was blocking her off with good position. With time running out, Pasek changed levels and came in on a shot. Caitlyn, almost immediately, defended it and dropped directly into her carry. Locked on Pasek's arm, under and through, she scored the winning takedown to secure the third place trophy for Glenbard North.

With that match as her springboard, when she entered her junior season, her expectations were high and fans had something else to come see. Add to her lore that she was already a two-time Fargo freestyle national champion and she was known in every gym she entered, Caitlyn was primed to make the most of her junior season.

Throughout her junior campaign, Caitlyn was winning. She more or less had a .500 record, but her wins were wins and her only losses came from the upper-tier wrestlers in the state. At the DuPage Valley Conference championships, she placed third, by fall, helping the Panthers collect their seventh-consecutive team championship.

One week later, Caitlyn would continue her success at the IHSA Regional championships, hosted by Glenbard North.

Caitlyn, who had earned the three seed, defeated Andrew Mott of Marmion Academy by fall in 1:26 in the quarterfinals, and then, in the semifinals, she defeated the two seed, Nathan Fitzenreider of Wheaton North by fall in 2:53. Just the week before, Fitzenreider had defeated Caitlyn in the DVC semifinals.

With that win over Fitzenreider, and now already a Sectional qualifier by reaching the finals, Caitlyn continued her streak and won a tight 3-1 decision over the one seed, Ricky Krauze of Wheaton-Warrenville South—the DVC champion a week earlier.

By defeating Krauze, Caitlyn became the first female wrestler in Illinois to win a Regional championship and qualify for the Sectional championships through any means of placing.

A week later, in order to keep her season alive, at the IHSA Sectional championships, Caitlyn defeated Mike Walls of Lyons Township, 15-4, before she defeated Naperville Neuqua Valley freshman standout Chris Spangler, 6-4, in the semifinals.

With the defeat of Spangler, and making it into the championship match, where she would eventually lose to Hinsdale Central's Matt Tolbert, 16-5, she had secured a trip down to Champaign, Illinois, for the IHSA Individual State Championships.

Additionally, when she defeated Spangler, she became the first female wrestler in the state's history to qualify for the IHSA Individual State Wrestling Championships.

Now, even though she would lose in the first round to Proviso East's Lavell Miller by fall, there was a great deal of interest in her match even before it even started. For an opening round match at 103 pounds for two wrestlers with average records, the crowd poured in anticipating a possible upset and wanting to witness what they had been hearing about Caitlyn—it was possibly historic.

Although she would never see the wrestle-backs with a chance to earn an individual medal, she would step onto the mat in the finals of the IHSA Dual Team State Championships one week later.

In the championship dual, she squared off against Orland Park Carl Sandburg's Mike McAuliffe who had just won the 103-pound individual state championship a week earlier.

McAuliffe was up 5-0 headed into the second period, and Caitlyn had choice—her choice was neutral.

When the whistle blew, McAuliffe was dancing around and making a bit of a mockery of the match when he locked up with Caitlyn. In his jest and tie on Caitlyn's head, he suddenly found himself on his back bridging in a panic—she had headlocked him.

His eyes widened and fear was immediate as he was trying to find a way to his belly or somehow bridge and get out of bounds. But he did not know where he was as Caitlyn had him turned toward the middle of the mat. He would have to fight.

As she squeezed and lowered her head, lifting his, she watched his panicked shoulder blades slowly sinking to the mat. She was confident he was not going to escape—everyone knew he was not going to escape until the whistle blew and the mat was slapped.

And as both of his shoulder blades where finally in unison and looked to be flat on the mat, the referee blew his whistle. However, he did not slap the mat for the fall; but rather, the whistle was blown because Caitlyn had a small cut on her lip and she had a speck of blood forming. The second referee, not the head referee, felt the blood warranted clean-up; thus, allowing McAuliffe off his back and a chance to breathe a sigh of relief.

"When I hit that headlock," Caitlyn remembered, "I felt my braces go through my lip. The second referee stopped the match because he saw a small amount of blood—I got screwed."

Head Coach Mark Hahn recalled it as, "Had she been a boy, the referee would have called the pin and never had stopped the match in that position. But a girl throwing the state champion to his back and having him pinned; they were not having it. The cut was so small, I couldn't believe they stopped the match. No one could. Carl Sandburg knew it and everyone else knew it—he was stuck."

For the remainder of the match, McAuliffe ran backwards in fear of locking up—he was warned for stalling, but came out with a 9-6 decision.

The Panthers would lose the state championship by a score of 26-23, and Illinois had to now take an even more serious look at Caitlyn.

Therefore, coming into her senior season, with a freshman coming into the room, she was not just going to stand aside and give up her weight class—she was going to work hard and fight to keep her spot on the team.

Also coming into the wrestling room that season with Tony would be another freshman that the program would put a great deal of stock into by the name of Jimmy Chase—Caitlyn's younger brother.

• • •

During the fall of the 2005-2006 season, Tony and Vince, along with one of their closest friends, Geno Capezio, would be linked to a strength and conditioning coach by the name of Alex Ponds—Caitlyn and Jimmy Chase also worked with Ponds.

Ponds was a former member of the Cuban National Wrestling Team before he left and came to America. With Ponds, the wrestlers would lift and condition, and he would bring them down as well as build them back up. "Ponds had us doing things I had never seen or heard of," Capezio said. "He was tough on us and his workouts were difficult, but he helped us get better."

Most of these training sessions would happen at the local gym where Ponds was a trainer; however, he would sometimes meet the kids at clubs or in various wrestling rooms when required.

Since Tony and Caitlyn were training with Ponds, they saw much of each other; however, they had known each other prior to high school through their IKWF days.

"I have known Tony since he was wrestling in the midget division," Caitlyn said. "And what I remember most about him was he was a perfectionist—even at a young age. He did not take losing well and sometimes his mom would ask me to talk with him. Tony would always go hide under the bleachers, so I would follow him and talk to him."

Of course, times were changing for both Tony and Caitlyn. Both had moved on in their own way and had great accomplishments for their ages, and now, years later, they were reunited and competing against one another.

Ponds' workouts usually ended with some type of hard conditioning. After one of the workouts, Caitlyn and Jimmy were walking away, down the hallway, when Jimmy told his sister, "Tony was talking to his brother and Geno, and I heard him saying that he could beat you."

With that, Caitlyn saw Tony and Vince and Geno headed upstairs. She looked up and yelled, "Hey Tony, if you think you can beat me, say it to my face!"

At this, Tony stopped on the stairs and there was a moment of silence as each looked at the other. Nothing more was said and, ultimately, everyone left. "There were never hard feelings," Capezio said. "It was just two competitors holding their ground early on."

But, early on was about to end as the season would ultimately begin. In that, there would be a final standoff for the starting spot at 103 pounds on the varsity team, and both appeared to be ready for it.

AT THE SEASON'S OPENING, TONY AND JIMMY

would be competing for the same weight class at 112 pounds. The idea was for Tony to wrestle at 112 until he dropped to 103; Jimmy would wrestle at 119 until the drop occurred and he moved to 112. As for the team, North was a much stronger dual team with Caitlyn, Tony, and Jimmy all in a row. However, there was one question: As soon as the drop happened: What would happen to Caitlyn?

Originally, even though some of the coaches wanted the drop, Tony was not in agreement. "Tony hated cutting weight," Defilippis said. "If we weren't on him to do it, he would've stayed at 112 just to prove that he could win it there."

Not in agreement with the drop was also head coach Mark Hahn. "When Tony came in," Hahn said, "I thought it was going to be exactly what it became: a mess. We had Caitlyn coming off being a state qualifier and was our starting [103] pounder. And then Tony is wrestling twelve and wants to go down and challenge her. I can't really complain. We had flip-flopped this thing a lot over the years, but I had a hard time not allowing someone who could win the state going down to win the state. I had a hard time with it all; it was just messy."

Since Caitlyn and Tony knew that they would eventually be competing for the 103 slot, and Jimmy was going to wrestle 112, the three would go at it when Caitlyn was healthy—and when allowed.

Assistant varsity coach Chris Edwards recalled Tony and Caitlyn's relationship as them both "having a great deal of respect for one another. However, there was a lot of tension—and it wasn't talked about in the room. When they would go live, I don't think it was totally unintentional. If Tony or Cait could work an extra shot in, they took it."

"Originally," Caitlyn said, "I drilled with Jimmy—but that stopped because we just talked too much." I never drilled with Tony when Frankie was in the room; he didn't like it. I usually worked with Ray Varella or Mike DiVito or some of the other lightweights."

Unfortunately, as the season was underway, Caitlyn suffered an injury that kept her out of practice and competitions for a bit. And, as she began to make her way back and the drop had already taken place, Tony had control of the 103-pound weight class even though there was never an official wrestle off; the coaches dictated the weights due to Caitlyn's injury.

As Caitlyn was slowly working her shoulder back to health, she wrestled with some of the junior varsity wrestlers in order to drill and get her strength and timing back, as well as build some confidence.

And then, it happened.

Vince remembered wrestling with senior Mark Schultz when, all of a sudden, Coach Hahn allowed Caitlyn to step into the live group with Tony and Jimmy as she was feeling better and needed to get back on the mat and competing. The way Hahn saw it, "It had to happen sometime."

Suddenly, the room focused in on one circle.

"Coach Hahn really never let the two wrestle because Caitlyn had not been healthy" Vince said. "But, when she walked into the circle that day, everyone was curious.

"Being in the front of the room, I was going to watch. Schultz and I pretended to be wrestling, locking on each other with a head tie, but we were just looking and watching. I am pretty sure there was no circle wrestling because everyone just wanted to know."

Tony remembered how "Caitlyn said that she wanted to be treated just like one of the guys. And if another guy wanted to try and take my spot, any chance that I had I was going to prove that the weight class belonged to me. I was going to dominate and I wasn't going to leave any doubt that I was the best. This is mine. If you want to wrestle, it won't be at this weight."

"When I wrestled Tony," Caitlyn said, "I had to be physical. He hated it when people would close the gap on him and hand fight. Faking to a re-shot was a daily occurrence," but so was the physicality of the live goes.

As the first few live goes went, Tony dominated immediately. He took Caitlyn down with double-leg after double-leg and, true to her competitive nature, she went right back into the middle of the circle and attacked again.

Unfortunately, it was never going to get easier or better. In fact, as Caitlyn would tie up or get taken down, she was taking small shots at Tony. An elbow here or a pulling of his hair or a head-butt inside on a tie, and even a small punch to the side against the wall of the room. She was frustrated, not fully healthy, and just not ready to relinquish control. In most other wrestling rooms she was the starter.

But make no mistake about it, Tony did not allow these shots on him to go on for long.

"That day was an irritating day," Caitlyn said. "Tony and Jimmy had gone live and Jimmy had taken him down a few times. Tony could give a beating, but had trouble taking one. After one of the goes, Tony punched Jimmy in the face—Jimmy just smiled and I think that frustrated Tony." And as Caitlyn looked to hold her ground, she was going to stick up for her brother as well.

The goes became more heated and more competitive, and ties on the head were like hammers being dropped on each other's neck. Set ups or shots to the forehead were more of a boxer's jab, and finishes were ended with driving shoulders or sharp elbows or swift knees or heavy forearms followed by a heavy push as one braced himself on the other to get up.

"The hand fighting became more intense," Caitlyn continued. "There may have been a few head butts. Tony swung, I shoved. He shot, I punched the back of his head," it continued on and on.

As he watched, "I couldn't believe how patient he was at first." Vince recalled. "Of course, everyone was watching and knew something was going to happen. But it had to be about the fifth go that Tony had enough. He took her down straight into the wall and Caitlyn took another small shot at him. Immediately, Tony took a step back and just punched her straight in the face. We all froze and the room went dead silent."

"There were punches," Caitlyn said of the live goes. "But I don't remember him landing one. What I do remember is his brother Frankie telling me, 'If you can't handle the heat, get out of the fucking kitchen!'" At this, Caitlyn got up and shouted back, "The only reason you're in this God damn room is for them!"

The battle of words, of course, broke through all of the silence and shock of many. Tony just adjusted his headgear and stomped his way back to the circle and rested in his stance waiting for Caitlyn to step back on the line. Caitlyn turned from Frank and met Tony on the other side of that line.

"The way I saw it," Ramos said, "that was a wrestler entering my circle and trying to take my spot—not a girl. And I wasn't having any of it. If someone is going to hit me and get aggressive with me, I'm not going to sit there and take it—I don't care who it is. Did it get out of hand? Maybe. But, you had two wrestlers who wanted the same thing and wanted to prove it to the room. In the end, it was still my circle."

In the moment after the exchanged words, in the stillness of the room, Vince recalled, "Hahn just yelled at us to put on our shoes and get on the track for three-lappers. As we ran, it had to be the quietest conditioning we ever had. No one wanted to say anything or even knew what to say." Once the team changed shoes and took their feet to the line on the indoor track to run, Tony was running just as hard as he always did, as did everyone on the team.

When the conditioning concluded, the only voices heard were in the final team breakdown before everyone headed back into the locker room.

"Walking off the indoor track, when we were done and we were in the locker room changing," Vince said, "I looked at Schultz and said, 'Did that just really happen?'"

Mark Schultz looked to Vince, "I think it did."

But, to Tony, this was a wrestler taking shots at him. Caitlyn was a good wrestler and she was going to assert herself—she wanted the starting spot, and there was no custom on the mat when it came to one's weight class other than proving to whom it belonged. If any wrestler stepped on that line across from Tony, and then came after him being physical, he was going to be just as physical and prove himself as well.

"And that's just Tony," Vince shrugged. "He has that I-don't-give-a-shit attitude. The way he saw it was, 'Okay, you want to wrestle hard and play this game, let's go.'"

There would be more battles throughout the remainder of the season between Tony and Caitlyn; however, none were as intense as those first few. In the end, Tony, Caitlyn, and Jimmy played a vital role for the team in duals, but the individual tournaments would be filled by Tony, focused and taking the steps he believed that he needed to accomplish his goals.

2006 • DUAL MEET VERSUS GLENBARD EAST
RAMOS DEFEATS BADSING BY TECHNICAL FALL
PHOTOGRAPH COURTESY • GLENBARD NORTH WRESTLING

CHAPTER 10
MAKING HIMSELF KNOWN

"Going into the first Clash tournament, I wanted to be undefeated and make the all-tournament team. I knew the teams were good, but I didn't care. That was my goal—I wanted to stand out."

• *Tony Ramos*

THE SEASON WOULD OPEN AS THE PREVIOUS eighteen did under head coach Mark Hahn, with the Fulk Quad on the Wednesday of Thanksgiving in Neal Hudson Gymnasium at Glenbard North High School in Carol Stream.

Tony would immediately make his presence known with an opening night 3-0 record—all at 112 pounds. He would earn his first high school win against Minooka's Joe Ruettiger by fall in 4:34. He would then move through Batavia's Adam Hernandez by fall in 1:58, and Lincoln-Way's Kevin Ryan by fall in 3:30.

The next day the team was off for Thanksgiving, but Tony, along with a few other teammates, would take in a late optional workout as a group, practice Thursday as a team, and then, that Friday, Glenbard would wrestle in their first tournament and first real challenge of the season, the C.O. Feutz Wrestling Classic hosted by James B. Conant High School in Hoffman Estates.

The tournament was known for its top-tier in-state competition, as well as some of the stronger out-of-state teams that would wrestle there. According to Hahn, "It's nice to see where we're at in comparison to some of the other teams in the state right away. But it's a long season and even though it's great to do well [at Conant], there's a lot of work to be done."

As for Tony, he would receive an opening round match against one of the premier high school wrestling programs at that time, New Lenox Providence Catholic. In the first round of his first high school tournament, Tony would defeat the Celtics' Jake Wojak by a 4-2 decision. He would then go on to handle Conant's Steve Barnett with a 12-4 major decision, and Normal Community's Tyler Winland in similar fashion, 14-3.

This would set up a clash of styles for Tony in the finals. He would have to face Proviso East's Lavell Miller—the same wrestler who defeated Caitlyn in the first round of the state championships the season before. Miller, as many of the Proviso East wrestlers, was more upper body than a leg attacker. He was tall and lengthy, which contrasted greatly with Tony's stouter frame and more open style.

The length would give Tony some trouble early, as did the real weight of Miller after having some hours to pile his weight back on, but Tony would circle and hand fight out of a number of ties and use underhooks and overhooks to work into his leg attacks. Early on in the season it was noticeable that taller opponents who knew how to keep their distance caused some trouble for Tony. However, in the end, Tony would earn an 8-6 decision for the championship and help North claim a runner-up finish at the tournament.

From there, the season would be more dual meets instead of tournaments for a period of time. The schedule for the DuPage Valley Conference was about to start, and big duals against Neuqua Valley and Wheaton North were coming up, as well as the esteemed Clash High School National Duals in Rochester, Minnesota.

As the Neuqua dual neared, the question was raised at one of North's coaches' meeting whether Tony was going to drop to 103 pounds to wrestle Chris Spangler. But the answer was a no. The non-match would give Tony more time to make the weight and give the staff and Tony a look at Spangler.

When the night arrived, Caitlyn was out again with a nagging injury and back-up, Billy Heyduk, would square off against Spangler. To that point, Heyduk had only lost a few matches. He lost in the C.O. Feutz Wrestling Classic finals to the highly-touted Ellis Coleman of Oak Park-River Forest, 5-2, and dropped two other dual losses; so, Heyduk was a solid wrestler and he looked to compete every match.

Unfortunately, for Heyduk, his time on the mat would not last long as Spangler defeated him by a technical fall in 3:00.

Next up at 112 pounds, Tony faced Matt Walters. The only difference now was that Walters, also a freshman and with only four loses on the season to that point, would be able to give Tony a much better match and give Spangler a much better look than Heyduk was able to do for Tony.

In the end, Tony would win by a 3-1 decision, and both Spangler and Tony would have their first look at the other's style.

The last time that Tony would wrestle at 112 pounds would be in a DuPage Valley Conference dual against the previous season's 103-pound DVC champion, Ricky Krauze from Wheaton-Warrenville South. The match would be close in score, a 5-2 decision, but Tony clearly dominated.

From there, a decision was finally reached at home between Frank and Tony. Frank recalled, "I kept telling him that he had to cut the weight to win the state and there would be a national audience at the Clash at the end of the month. But, he didn't want to hear about it. Tony hated cutting weight and would rather prove a point by winning close matches and battle to show he could do it. But after his matches started getting closer and kids were sucking down now for the final stretch, and he could feel their strength, he agreed to make the move. It was the best decision."

This decision would occur in a dual meet against conference rival Wheaton North. "We knew he needed and the team needed to make the weight before the Clash," Hahn said. "If it was going to happen, it had to happen early so they could be used to the cut and drop before we went up to Minnesota."

In mid-December, wrestling at 103 pounds for the first time, Tony won by fall in 5:17 over Wheaton North's Adrian Laskero. The team would go on to win the dual, 40-22, and it was time for everyone to take a serious look into the second half of the season in order to make good on the program's goals.

THE CLASH HIGH SCHOOL NATIONAL DUALS

began in 2003—Glenbard North was the inaugural champions defeating state and national powerhouse Apple Valley, Minnesota, in the finals, 33-25, and ending Valley's 81-match win streak.

To some people in Minnesota, it was simply a great dual and they were happy to see the Valley fall. However, to others, they saw it as a slap in the face that an Illinois school came up to Minnesota and knocked off their best program.

Either way, ever since 2003, Minnesota fans either loved to watch Glenbard North wrestle and cheer for them, or they despised the program and rooted against them.

Walking into that same tournament three years later, after having finished ninth the year before after losing to Apple Valley 30-35 in a controversial dual in the pool's semi-final match—a North wrestler was pinning a Valley wrestler in a cradle, and the official called the fall in Valley's favor—the Panthers were young and motivated and looked to wrestle their way back into that esteemed championship pool.

Also entered in the Clash IV for the second consecutive season, after winning the Clash III the previous year, would be Orland Park Carl Sandburg—the state of Illinois' number-one rated team and the defending Illinois Class AA State Champions.

North would open up their tournament with the Cardinals of Coon Rapids, Minnesota, and the starting weight drawn at weigh-ins was the 160-pound weight class. This gave Tony some time to settle in and prepare for his first opportunity to make a national impression.

"Going into that first Clash tournament, I wanted to be undefeated and make the all-tournament team," Ramos said. "I knew the teams were good, but I didn't care. That was my goal—I wanted to stand out."

The Panthers would only drop two matches in that opening dual; one by decision and one by forfeit at the end of the dual. North easily won by a 56-8 score—the Cardinals were penalized one team point. As for Tony, by the time he stepped on the mat, his team was up 20-0, and he would be noticed. In his first match, he put on a takedown clinic and defeated Kyle Anderson by a major decision, 22-9.

For the championship semi-final match-up of their pool, North would now wrestle the Bombers of Midwest City, Oklahoma, who, in the coaches' poll, were rated number-two in Oklahoma's Class 5A. Again, North would have little trouble working through the dual and advanced into the pool's championship dual with a commanding 44-15 win.

In Tony's match, however, he would have a much stronger opponent in Willie Gunter. Gunter, a sophomore who was ranked number one in Oklahoma, gave Tony more of a fight. However, in the end, Tony would top the eventual Oklahoma three-time state champion and two-time All-American by a score of 5-3.

For the final dual of the pool, to see which team moved on into the championship pool and who entered the runner-up pool, North would have to go against another Minnesota powerhouse, St. Michael-Albertville (STMA). STMA was currently rated number one in Minnesota's Class AA and had been in the team state championship dual eight of the past ten years. They were, again, coming off a state championship from the previous season. On paper, the dual was to be close as STMA had eleven senior varsity starters, two juniors, and one freshman; the freshman was David Thorn at 103 pounds.

Thorn, though a freshman, had already been ranked as the number-one wrestler in his weight class; he came into the dual with a 29-1 record.

For Tony to remain on track of his goal for making the all-tournament team, this match would end his first day and leave an impression on the Minnesota fans and voters in the tournament—Tony would not disappoint.

Almost immediately, Tony would score on his feet and in the top position and never relinquish his lead. The final ended with Tony scoring a 9-4 decision, and a 3-0 record, taking down two number-one ranked wrestlers.

As for North, they would dominate the dual and defeat the defending state champions and soon-to-be-crowned two-time state champions by a score of 31-19.

The young Panthers were wrestling well and would now be tested. "The second day of the Clash," Hahn explained, "especially that championship round with the top four teams, really shows how tough your team is. There are no easy matches as an individual or as a team. We always look forward to being in that pool."

When the pairings were posted, North found itself paired up with Carl Sandburg, Illinois, in the opening round. It did not take long for the coaches or the team to focus in on their opponent. Both staffs knew each other well, knew the wrestlers well, and much would be riding on the dual. At that point in the season, Carl Sandburg was rated number-one in Illinois and North was rated number-three. However, every time these two teams wrestled, the rankings had to be taken out of the equation as the match-ups were just that tight.

The starting weight class on Day Two would be the 215-pound weight class. Sandburg would end up with a tight 3-0 decision to lead off the dual. From here, Sandburg would win again by decision and lead 6-0 before Tony would step on the mat at 103 pounds; this is where the team came into the youth and strength of their line-up.

For Sandburg, they would send out their freshman, Jon Morrison, who was the number-three ranked wrestler in Illinois and highly touted in many wrestling circles.

"Jon entered high school as a very polished wrestler from a technical standpoint," Sandburg Head Coach Eric Siebert said. "Jon's strength was his technique, particularly his short offense. This was something that set him apart. He definitely did not have a glaring weakness other than his size. There was a slight concern of getting away on bottom and I remember thinking that Jon was definitely outsized. Tony was big and strong, not to mention very skilled, so it was certainly an uphill battle."

That match-up had been anticipated by both wrestlers and schools and now, on a national stage, each wrestler would have the opportunity to show off his merit as each came into the center of the circle as two of the top freshman in Illinois and in the country.

Tony, as he stepped onto the mat, was undefeated. Morrison had but one loss on the season thus far and that was at Illinois' most prestigious holiday tournament, the Al Dvorak Memorial; he was topped in the semifinals by Chris Spangler of Neuqua Valley in a dominating performance that ended with a 10-0 major decision.

Up to that point in the season, Tony was ranked as the number-four wrestler in Illinois at 112 pounds. There had not yet been a confirmed updated ranking; however, this match-up would prove the two and three in the standings.

The match would open with a great deal of head ties and level changes and fakes with the wrestlers feeling the other out as position was vied for; the first period ended up scoreless. Morrison would have the choice in the second period and chose down—he would escape early into the period and more hand fighting would commence.

As Tony would pull and snap and try to work into his front headlock, Morrison was being moved around and circling to prevent a leg attack. However, with the period coming to an end, Tony finally got in on Morrison's legs and scored a takedown to end the period and take the lead, 2-1.

For the third period, Tony chose down and was out quickly; he now led 3-1. From here, there would be some shot attempts and hard head ties, but the match ended with Tony having a 3-1 decision victory over Morrison.

Morrison exited the match with his second loss; however, his team gave North their first dual loss on the season by an 35-18 final score. Sandburg would advance and face Jackson, New Jersey, next, while North would wrestle another Minnesota powerhouse in Hastings.

Hastings, like most of the teams at the Clash to that point, was currently one of their state's best teams and was rated number-six in Minnesota's Class AAA Division. They also had lost in their first round of the championship pool to Jackson by a score of 39-16.

Tony would be the second match of the dual and he would be facing Luke Vaith who was currently ranked number three at 112 pounds in Minnesota. Like Tony, Vaith, also a freshman, had made the cut for the tournament and would remain at that weight for the duration of the season.

When the match began, Tony began quickly and made it very clear who the better wrestler was. Scoring four takedowns and relinquishing four escapes, Tony won the match on his feet, scoring an 8-4 decision.

Vaith only had two losses on his record that season at 103 pounds— one of those to Tony, and one to the eventual Minnesota state champion, Destin McCaulry, from Apple Valley; Vaith placed third in his state's tournament at season's end.

As for the team, North defeated Hastings 44-19 and would now be wrestling Jackson, who had just lost to Sandburg 40-16. This dual determined who would finish up as either the runner-up or the third-place finisher.

For the final dual, Tony's weight class would start the dual—this was a perfect way for Tony to end his first Clash tournament and put on a show. He would be wrestling Jackson's freshman back-up instead of their starter, Sean Cook. And even though Tony would put on display his arsenal of takedowns and grind down his opponent to win the match by a 14-5 major decision, North would fall 33-17 for their second dual loss of the season and place third at the national duals.

At the tournament's conclusion, Tony was awarded All-Clash tournament honors and he was ready to move forward into the second half of his freshman season.

HOWEVER, THE GREATEST OBSTACLE FOR TONY

was still cutting the weight because his greatest challenge was his diet. "Tony's downfall with cutting weight," Israel said, "was that he eats so poorly. Tony likes pizza. Tony likes burgers. And, Tony does not like to cut weight. Most of his suffering came from not dieting the right way—but, really, what 15-year-old does?"

Fortunately, like everything else in his life that was difficult for Tony, or where he had trouble adjusting, he always found comfort and support in his brothers.

"Having Vince in the room and with me at extra workouts was a big help," Ramos admitted. He was not cutting as hard, but he would run with me, hand fight with me—he was the energy that I needed and I think that he needed to work off those final pounds. He would stay late—I could not have done it without him."

And when it was not Vince, it was Frank who was by Tony's side. "We had [this] little room where Frank put a treadmill. He would sit in there with me talking to me about my matches or whatever, motivating me, or pushing me. He never took it easy on me. When I wanted to stop or would slow down, he put the treadmill on an incline, made me go faster, and upped the time."

"I got to hand it to him that freshman year," Defilippis said. "What I put him through, I could never had done. If he bitched, it got worse—so he learned to just shut his mouth and do it. He would grind his teeth and you could see the anger in his eyes, but he just did it."

CHAPTER 11
BEING DIFFERENT

"The best wrestlers struggle with that type of schedule—that's just another example of how different Tony was."

• Israel Martinez
Head Coach, Montini Catholic High School
Owner, Izzy Style Wrestling

THE SECOND HALF OF THE SEASON WAS WHEN North's strength and conditioning program was either going to be fought or embraced by each wrestler—which position he took determined his season's fate as the physical and mental challenges were put in place to have the team and its wrestlers peak at the right time.

Additionally, once New Year's hit, the competitions would be a steady ebb and flow of competitions: some conference duals, a trip to number-one rated Wisconsin Rapids, Wisconsin, for a triple dual, a varied quad, a highlighted and marquee match-up with Carl Sandburg and Jon Morrison. The regular season would end with a feel good Leyden Invitational tournament before the grind of the DuPage Valley Conference Championships concluded the regular season, and before moving into the Illinois state series.

In conference duals, Tony would make little work of his remaining opponents; he would receive two forfeits and score a fall and technical fall. He would finish his DVC season 7-0 and he guaranteed himself a number-one seed at the tournament.

However, before this would occur, Tony would have to get through a dual with Wisconsin Rapids. Each season Coach Hahn liked to travel north to wrestle them. "It's good for us," Hahn said. "The kids get to see what it's like to have the cards stacked against them and get no calls from the officials. The rules are different in that gymnasium; it's good for the team to be exposed to that. It makes us wrestle and avoid keeping the score close enough for an official to have an impact on their match."

North would open with Ellsworth, Wisconsin, a traditionally strong team in their state's Division II. The Panthers would stockpile an early lead and never relinquish it, winning 43-12. At 103 pounds, Tony would wrestle Chance Kinneman, a sophomore and an Honorable Mention wrestler in his state.

As soon as the whistle blew, Tony became aggressive on his ties, always moving forward, and began wearing Kinneman down—the sophomore trailed 4-1 before he knew what was happening. When it was over, Tony earned an 8-3 victory.

Next up would be Minnesota's Totino-Grace. Tony and North would make it through unscathed against them as well. Tony would score a 10-2 major decision, and North would close out the dual with 57-8 win.

The final dual was the highlighted match-up. Each year, Rapids pushed the start time back in order to give the community time to come in and pack the gymnasium with staunch supporters—all dressed appropriately in their red and black Red Raider gear. In the short series wrestled between these two programs, North trailed by a three wins to four total.

Dating back from the start of the Glenbard North at Rapids duals, Rapids had won the Wisconsin Class A team state championship six out of those seven years and earned a runner-up finish once. Ironically, in those past seven years, three of their fourteen losses would come from Glenbard who had yet to win a state championship, even though they were able to string together solid teams and strong seasons.

These duals were great match-ups for wrestling fans—both Rapids and Glenbard had a strong following. The duals were especially helpful for the growth of the wrestlers and the teams and, no matter how heated the matches and the duals became, the wrestling and the atmosphere never disappointed.

Also, since both schools attended the Clash, there was much jesting between the coaches back in Rochester about scouting and match-ups and quick, in-passing banter about styles and match-ups and where wrestlers may shift in the line-up.

So, on an overly windy and cold snowy Saturday in the middle of January in the middle of Wisconsin, the bleachers were full, and the radio station was tuned in with the announcers setting the possible matches and dictating possible outcomes. Both officials had been chosen and were checking in with the head table, and the crowd was getting louder and more raucous as the music was turned on just as the Rapids wrestlers ran out from their locker room and warmed up in front of their home crowd. As they ran, they circled the mat around North before each school lined up for introductions.

The dual went back and forth and, as Tony stepped on the mat against state-ranked Jeremy Clark, he would again have a chance to compete at a high level and shine. Off the whistle, Tony came out banging and Rapids had done a good enough job scouting to coach Clark into staying in good position—but Tony would ultimately have none of it. After the first push out of bounds, Tony went on a scoring frenzy. Takedown, let him go. Takedown, let him go. Takedown, let him go. Takedown, near fall. And on and on it went. The final score was a major decision in Tony' favor, 17-7.

When Tony became overly aggressive, the Rapids faithful would boo and hiss at him. And when a Red Raider scored or returned the aggressive favor, the red and black section stood and cheered and shouted at North's wrestlers, coaches, and fans.

Through all of the hisses and cheers, the meet swung in North's favor, 28-20, and the series was now tied at four wins apiece in the eight years of the rivalry.

Clark would end his season losing in the opening round of the state championships to the eventual champion, Chad Leviner of Mukwonago, before winning out and placing fifth—any loss outside of the semifinals was not allowed a wrestle-back to third. Rapids, on the other hand, would go on to win the team state championship for a fourth-consecutive season and end with a 29-2 record. The Red Raiders' only two losses would be Hastings, Minnesota, at the Clash, and Glenbard North.

Upon the return home, Hahn spoke to the team about the upcoming week and the importance of that following Saturday—this would be the second match-up against Carl Sandburg. For Tony, it would be his second run-in with Jon Morrison.

THE POSITIVE OF GOING FROM A WISCONSIN

Rapids dual into a Carl Sandburg dual that following week simply meant that the week of practice was going to be focused. For Tony, since the season began, he was doing his morning and after school workout at North and then going to Izzy Style three days a week, depending on competitions, or having another workout with his brother Frank at night. Unfortunately, for Tony, North's program, combined with Israel's workouts, were wearing on him.

"When Tony and I started working out," Israel said, "I was a young coach and had no idea about what kind of program Coach Hahn ran over there at Glenbard North. Tony would come in and get an hour and a half hard from me after going through two Glenbard practices. It was tough on him. He went through his whole freshman year that way. The best wrestlers would struggle with that type of schedule—that's just another example of how different Tony was."

However, this was not to say that Tony was not slipping every now and then at North's practices due to the workouts. "Tony would dog it sometimes or refuse to do the techniques we were showing," Hahn said. "Early on with him, everything was a contradiction about how a move should be done or why it is done this way and not that way. He was yet to fully buy into the program."

Having his brother Frank in the room as a coach helped because of the respect and admiration Frank had for Hahn. Also, Frank understood the program and how it built the guys up and brought them along. As for Tony, he was focused on Tony and he was not yet mature enough to see how the team dynamic came together at North. In this, Frank put to rest most of Tony's questions and contradictions, and sometimes the combative nature, and then Tony did as he was coached.

In fairness, all of the contradictions were not about Tony purposely being vindictive; it was more that here was a wrestler who had really had so much one-on-one work and little team concept that being in an atmosphere that was about the whole, and not just about the one, was an adjustment. It would take Tony time to realize this and to fully understand and commit to the team concept instilled at North.

As the week wore on, and Saturday approached, Frank made it clear to both of the boys what was expected of them. For Vince, he would be going against the number-one ranked wrestler in the state, Conrad Polz—Vince was the number-two rated wrestler and Polz had defeated him at the Clash by a 2-1 decision. When it came to Tony, Frank was harsher. "I told both of them what had to happen," Frank said. "Vince had to get a win because he could beat Polz, and I told Tony that he needed to blow [Morrison] out to shut everyone up who was talking."

When the day of the meet came, just as it was the week before, the gymnasium was packed with Sandburg's Golden Eagle blue and gold covering one half of the bleachers and North's black and gold covering the other half.

The dynamics of each community were very different, but their style of wrestling and grit were very similar. The parents were into the match, alumni came, and shouts and arguments ran rapid throughout the meet.

Vince would defeat Polz in the dual by a 3-2 score. He had done his job. Tony would now be matched, once again, against Morrison. At the Clash, Morrison was able to keep it close and would be looking to do the same—Tony had a different idea.

"After I beat him the first time," Ramos said, "I saw what he did and where I could take advantage [of him]. Once he was exposed, I knew I could dominate."

That was exactly what Tony did. By the end of the match it was clear who the more dominant wrestler was—Tony had run up a 7-2 decision that was even more lopsided than the score indicated. Unfortunately, again, when the dual meet was over, Sandburg had now defeated North three out of the last three meetings—this time the dual score would be a 34-21 loss for the Panthers.

The next stop for Tony and the team would be a quad that they would sweep through, the Leyden Invitational, where thirteen wrestlers made the finals, ten were crowned champions, and one wrestler placed third, and two more duals that were dominated by a combined team score of 145-10.

It was time for the week of conference and North would be the heavy favorites as they were looking to win their eighth-consecutive DuPage Valley Conference team championship.

CHAPTER 12
JUST ANOTHER TOURNAMENT

"I knew I would win it; that wasn't my concern. But I wanted to make sure I dominated because everyone was against [North] and that motivated me."

• *Tony Ramos*

THE WEEK OF THE DVC CHAMPIONSHIPS WAS always a very special week for North's program, the alumni, the coaches, and, of course, the wrestlers. It marked the first time that all of the coaches were in the varsity room together—all of the other levels' seasons were over and they hung out to wrestle and help the varsity—and the only focus was winning the conference. After that week, the only focus was winning the Regional; then the focus shifted to qualifying as many wrestlers into the Individual State Championships as possible. Immediately after the individual state, the focus was winning the Dual Team Sectional, and, finally, the sole focus was winning a Dual Team State Championship. The weeks were different, but the ultimate focus of improving never changed.

Headed into his first DVC Championships, Tony knew that all of the other schools would be gunning for North.

Up to this point, North had won eight-consecutive conference championships and had not lost a conference dual since halfway through the 1997 season—Frank's junior season.

When the coaches' meeting took place two days before the tournament, there was no contest when Tony was put up by Hahn for the number-one seed. Tony would receive an opening round forfeit and his second match, against Glenbard East's Zach Badsing, would be worth double points on the win.

Even though North had come in as the heavy favorite, Hahn always emphasized the importance of the conference tournament and how it helped set the tone for the Regional the following week. Each wrestler had to perform well to solidify a positive seed the following week and give himself the best chance to make a run in the state series.

For Tony, he knew this was where his individual goals would begin, but not where they ended. "I didn't see the conference tournament so much as a big deal to stress over," Ramos said. "We were too good and the other schools knew it. I knew I would win it; that wasn't my concern. But I wanted to make sure I dominated because everyone was against [North] and that motivated me."

Two years earlier, West Aurora almost knocked off North as the conference champions—and they were walking around halfway through the finals letting North know it. However, in the fifth-place match, North's Geno Heredia won by fall at heavyweight to give North a 239.5-238.5 advantage and the DVC championship.

Last season, Vince's freshman year, Wheaton North had a very talented line-up and was on Glenbard's heels, but Glenbard pulled away in the finals securing the title 274.5-226.5 when the tournament ended.

What soon became the norm at the DVC tournament, the other schools in the conference were doing all they could against North—both at the coaches' meetings for seeding votes and during their matches. However, to date, nothing had worked on slowing down North's momentum. Unfortunately for the other schools, the youth movement at North was very confident, talented, and ready for any challenge.

For Tony, in his semi-final bout, he would score a technical fall over Badsing in 2:42. Takedown after takedown demoralized his opponent until he just broke. That win placed Tony in his first DVC championship match—he would face Eric Concha of West Aurora; Concha was not in the line-up at the conference dual.

As the tournament would be scored, before the finals even began, North had already captured the DVC crown by having nine finalists—six of those finalists would be the first six weight classes in a row and underclassmen.

Of the six champions, Tony would be the first. Concha would do his best to stall and move away from Tony, but the final decision would be a well-controlled and dominated 9-2 victory and his first conference championship.

Next week would be the IHSA Regional Championships and, from there, Tony's journey to the state championship and the first step in his goal of being a four-time Illinois state champion would begin.

IN 2006, THE REGIONAL CHAMPIONSHIPS WERE held at Bartlett High School, merely a few miles away from North, and Wheaton North would be the team that would be looking to knock the Panthers off.

"We knew it would be a two-horse race," said Hahn. "Wheaton North was a good team and it would come down to team points."

The importance of winning the Regional was that, in Illinois, the Regional champion would qualify as a team into the Dual Team Sectional Championships. Therefore, the only way to win the state championship, or even trophy, started with winning the Regional.

As the 103 bracket began, it was a no-contest. Tony would once again open with a forfeit, and then win by fall in 1:18 over Mitch Godfrey of South Elgin in the semifinals, before steamrolling Wheaton North's freshman standout Adrian Laskero by fall in 1:22.

The Panthers would also claim the Regional championship for the sixth-straight season. They would place eleven wrestlers in the finals, earning nine championships, and qualify thirteen out of the fourteen weight classes to the Sectionals. With the Regional title, North was now in the Sectional duals with a chance to earn a team state berth—this would all occur after the individual state championship weekend.

Also, with a Regional championship, Tony, the now number-two ranked wrestler in the state, would head into the Sectional Championships with an opening round bye, and sit across the bracket from the number-one ranked wrestler in Illinois at 103 pounds, Naperville Neuqua Valley sophomore Chris Spangler.

THE NAPERVILLE NORTH SECTIONAL WOULD BE A grind on the individual wrestlers, as it was regarded as the most competitive and most difficult of the eight state Class AA Sectionals. Qualifying for the IHSA Individual State Championships the following week in Champaign, Illinois, would be overly demanding on each wrestler in each weight class.

The 103-pound weight class was loaded with talent and at least one of the top-ranked wrestlers in the state would be watching the state championships from the stands—at the time, a wrestler had to place in the top three to advance.

Each of the four Regional champions received a first-round bye. This meant that they were able to sit back and watch their next opponent—a third-place wrestler would be matched up against a runner-up wrestler, and the winner advanced into the quarterfinal round.

Tony's match would ultimately be Blake Tirewold, a freshman from

Sandwich, who would win by fall over Hinsdale South senior Fawwaz Qayyum in 5:53. In that quarterfinal bout, Tony would make very quick work of Tirewold with a fall in 1:21.

For his semi-final match-up, he would either face senior captain and 2005 state qualifier Joe Norton from Montini Catholic—the wrestler whose spot he may have taken had he been allowed to attend Montini, and someone he had trained with. His other possible opponent was Bolingbrook sophomore Brian Rodgers. As fate would have it, Tony would be matched up against Norton.

The senior captain from Montini had been around Tony for a few years. Obviously, since Israel was running his club out of Montini and practices were together, Norton knew Tony's style, as Tony would know his, and thus create the potential for a competitive match, if not an upset.

This would also be the first time that Israel would be coaching against Tony—the two were usually paired together.

"When Tony had to wrestle Norton," Israel explained, "Tony knew he could beat him, so he was really having fun with me about it—but he was nervous, too."

In regard to being in opposite corners, "It was what I had to do and what Tony had to do," Israel said. "I had trained my guy to win, coached my guy to win, and that's all it was—nothing personal. But it was interesting."

As the match began, Tony would continue his aggressive style of wrestling and put together some takedowns and choosing not to ride from the top position; Tony stayed on his feet to wrestle.

When the six minutes concluded, Tony earned a 7-3 decision, had a guaranteed qualification into next week's individual state championships, and now had the opportunity to wrestle the number-one ranked wrestler in Illinois at his weight class: Chris Spangler.

Over the session break, Tony had an opportunity to speak with his coaches about his finals match-up. He first talked with his brother Frank—Frank had already spoken to Hahn—and then he would receive some input from Israel.

What Tony did know was that Spangler was strong and stayed in good position. The message communicated by each of Tony's coaches was that in order to win, he was going to have to open up his offensive attacks. In doing that, Tony would then force Spangler to open up and make the match uncomfortable for him. Spangler was a position wrestler, and Tony would have to work him out of position to be successful.

THE PREVIOUS SEASON, CHRIS SPANGLER WAS regarded as one of the top freshman in Illinois. He came into Naperville Neuqua Valley High School having already won two IKWF State Championships, and Head Coach Mick Ruettiger knew he was special coming into his program.

"Coming in, it was easy to see that he had a will to work hard and a desire to win," Ruettiger said. "He knew both of those had to go together to be successful. I think he realized that just because he was successful in the IKWF, that didn't automatically mean he would be successful in high school. He worked hard and pushed himself every day in the practice room."

Unfortunately, what Spangler had in mat-time and tenacity, he lacked in size. "He was a small [103 pounder]," Ruettiger said. "But he never backed down. He would go out there, fearless, and fight and claw through every match."

Early on, Spangler would see the fruits of his labor and focus. In the beginning of December, he won the traditionally tough Barrington High School tournament. He would receive a bye in the opening round and then win his next two matches by fall in a total time of 3:17. In the semifinals, he would face and defeat Wheeling High School's freshman standout Max Nowry by an 18-2 technical fall. Once in the finals, he defeated Prospect's Johnny Brennan, another freshman on the rise and his closest match of the tournament, a 5-4 decision.

The momentum was swinging in his favor; however, he had yet to be challenged by an older and more experienced wrestler with some real weight behind him. Walking into the state's largest and most recognized holiday tournament, the Al Dvorak Memorial, Spangler knew that he would be tested—and he was prepared.

With a 17-1 record, Spangler would earn the number-two seed of the tournament. In his opening match, this after receiving a bye, he wrestled Oak Park's Lil'Lashawn Coleman and won by fall in a time of 3:24. He would then have to wrestle, arguably, his toughest opponent to date, Montini junior Joe Norton.

In the end, Spangler would prove himself against the older and more seasoned Norton by a 10-2 major decision.

Next up, in the semifinals, Spangler wrestled Chicago Marist Catholic sophomore Ryan Blake. Blake, coming in as the three seed, and into the match with an 11-3 record, would be quickly extinguished. Spangler defeated him 7-1 and earned an opportunity to win a Dvorak title. Standing in his way would be the physically stronger and experienced Oak Lawn undefeated senior, Matt McNaughton.

Earlier in the season, and Spangler's only loss coming into the holiday tournament, was McNaughton—he defeated Spangler in the finals of the Park Forest Rich East tournament. And, just as he had done the first time, McNaughton would do in the finals. He would defeat Spangler by decision, 12-5.

"Chris wrestled a strong tournament and beat some really tough wrestlers," Ruettiger said. "However, when he had to compete with the older and more experienced wrestlers, the ones cutting real weight and just physically bigger, he was simply out-matched—and there was no shame in those losses."

McNaughton, who was ranked anywhere from one, two, or three in the state, depending on the publication, would win the Dvorak title and Spangler would have to regroup.

"Chris was really good about understanding the sport and knowing that he was just out-matched in those losses," Ruettiger said. "He was never discouraged and when we talked, he knew he would have to wrestle smarter in those matches to keep the score close and give himself a chance to win."

Spangler would not lose for the remainder of the regular season.

As the state series began, Neuqua Valley, who was young and talented and ready to compete for an opportunity to qualify for the state series as a team, would first have to win the Bolingbrook Regional.

At the 103-pound weight class, Spangler earned the number-two seed to Hinsdale Central sophomore Matt Tolbert. When the two would meet for the finals match, Tolbert would injury default, which gave Spangler the Regional championship, and both would walk away with a 30-3 record.

Neuqua Valley won the Regional championship as a team, but they were now headed to arguably the state's toughest Sectional that season, hosted by Downers Grove North High School, that following week.

There would be no seeding in this tournament in Illinois other than the Regional champions receiving a blind schematic opening round bye, while the second and third place finishers from pre-arranged and non-similar regionals wrestled it out. Also, the format was simple: If a wrestler lost, his opponent had to make it to the semifinals in order for that wrestler to receive a wrestle-back.

Spangler would sit and watch his first opponent—he would then defeat him. This would pit the freshman against Glenbard North junior Caitlyn Chase in the semifinals. Chase would defeat Spangler in a 6-4 decision; thus, automatically qualifying Chase to the Individual State Championships and knocking Spangler into the wrestle-backs.

If Spangler was going to have an opportunity to qualify for the IHSA

Individual State Championships, he would have to win his next match, and then his third-place match. However, and he knew it, the next match was crucial.

After being beaten by Chase, the regrouping would be difficult, but necessary. "Getting beat by Chase," Ruettiger remembered, "a girl—albeit, a very good girl—he showed a lot of pride and a lot of toughness to put it behind him and finish strong by taking third."

In the qualifying match, Spangler defeated sophomore Josh Thompson of Summit Argo High School by a 3-1 overtime decision. That win qualified Spangler for the state championships and, in having done so, he became Neuqua's second freshman to ever qualify for the tournament—the first came earlier that day when freshman Jimmy Duffy won his semi-final match.

Now qualified, and with his ticket punched to Assembly Hall, Spangler would have one benefit and one downfall. He would have the luxury of wrestling, in the opening round, an opponent he had already defeated, Lillashawn Coleman from Oak Park. Again, and this time with more dominance, Spangler would crush the Huskie by an 18-7 performance. This, however, would lead him to his kryptonite—Oak Lawn's Matt McNaughton; and the senior had yet to lose on the season.

Unfortunately, the senior would come out aggressive and win by fall over the freshman in a time of 1:06. Just as was true at the sectional a week earlier, Spangler would have to hope that his opponent, McNaughton, would make the semifinals in order for him to receive a wrestle-back opportunity.

McNaughton would next defeat the highly touted and controversial Kaz Hashimoto from LaSalle Peru High School by a 21-4 technical fall in 3:04 and, thus, put him in the semi-final match. Since McNaughton advanced, Spangler would receive a wrestle-back, and this wrestle-back would come in the form of Hashimoto. The winner of this match would automatically place in the state's top six and earn all-state honors.

In the end, it would be the older and more physical wrestler, Hashimoto, with the win—a fall in 1:28.

In his next match, Hashimoto would lose by previous decision to McNaughton, who had lost a heart-breaking 10-8 overtime thriller to Josh Kratovoil of New Lenox Lincoln Way Central High School. Kratovoil would end up as the state's runner-up to Carl Sandburg's Michael McAuliffe—McNaughton would dominate Tolbert 10-0 and earn all-state honors by placing third.

Spangler would sit back and watch the tournament unfold. However, to his credit, it did not have an adverse effect on him. "It wasn't easy coming in with all of those expectations," Ruettiger explained. "There was a lot of pressure there and he handled it really well for a freshman. I think what helped Chris was that he was a smart kid with common sense and a good understanding of everything that happened. Having been [at the state tournament], he now had a sense of what he needed to do."

That next Tuesday, Spangler would defeat Caitlyn Chase in Dual Team Sectional; however, Glenbard North would advance to the Dual Team State Championships and Spangler and Neuqua would prepare for the offseason and look forward to their next season.

• • •

When Spangler entered his sophomore campaign, he was the number-one ranked wrestler in the state. He would once again win the Barrington tournament in early December—leaving no doubt in any match, winning by fall or major decision as he worked himself into the finals. In the championship match, he had his closest match, a 7-1 win over Grant's Danny Deligio.

Near the end of the month, he once again found himself in the Al Dvorak Memorial holiday tournament; this time, the number-one seed.

The tournament bracket at 103 pounds included the top-ranked wrestlers in the weight class, minus state-ranked number-four Tony Ramos. The seeding was based on the previous year Dvorak finishes and then it broke down into prior accomplishments. In the Dvorak seeding criteria, state rankings had little to nothing to do with how the tournament and match-ups were decided.

As predicted, due to his runner-up finish last season, Spangler was seeded first and, coincidentally, ranked number one in the state. Montini senior Joe Norton was the second seed—he lost to Spangler in the quarterfinals of the Dvorak the previous year—and had currently been ranked number-five in the state. Chicago Mt. Carmel sophomore sensation, B.J. Futrell, was the third seed in the tournament and the number-two ranked wrestler in Illinois. Finally, freshman Jon Morrison of Orland Park Carl Sandburg was seeded fourth, and he was the number-three ranked wrestler in the state.

Throughout the tournament, it would all wrestle itself out. In the quarterfinals, Spangler would leave little doubt who the more dominant and experienced wrestler was as he handled Morrison by a 10-0 major decision. In the bracket's lower half, Futrell would defeat Norton, 3-1, setting up a one-versus-two finals match. And, when the smoke cleared, Spangler would leave little doubt who number-one was—he earned his first Dvorak championship with a 12-6 performance against Futrell.

Exiting the Dvorak, Spangler now carried the unblemished 21-0 record into the New Year and solidified his number-one ranking before the season's second half was underway.

By the time the Bolingbrook Regional Championships came around on the fourth of February, Spangler would still be undefeated, now 32-0. As the day progressed, he would extend his mark to 35-0 and end his tournament with a dominant performance against Brian Rogers of Bolingbrook, winning by fall in 3:57, and claiming a Regional championship. More importantly, he would earn a first-round bye at the Sectional the following week.

In his first match at the Sectional Championships, Spangler had to wrestle Elmhurst York sophomore Sean Conell in the championship quarterfinals—he defeated Conell with a technical fall in 4:44. Now in the semifinals, he faced a West Aurora junior, Eric Concha, with a number-six ranking in the state. Concha only had one loss on the season coming into the Sectional, and that came to Tony Ramos in the DuPage Valley Conference championships; however, to his credit, Concha had earned twenty-five victories, as well as a reputation as one of the toughest wrestlers at the weight.

Unfortunately, for Concha, Spangler would defeat him, pushing him into the wrestle-backs. He would win his next match before losing to Montini's Norton in the third place match by way of a 12-4 major decision. Concha, one of the state's finest wrestlers in his weight class, would not qualify for the state championships.

Conversely, Spangler, with the win, automatically qualified for the trip to the University of Illinois; however, he would have one more match on the day—he would finally face off in the Sectional championship with the number-two ranked wrestler at the weight, Tony Ramos.

WHEN THE FINAL SESSION BEGAN, IT WOULD open with the most anticipated match in the state—Ramos versus Spangler for the Sectional championship and the claim of who is number-one at 103 pounds. It had been debated on the message boards and through the hundreds of threads about what each wrestler offered, who really was the best, and on and on and on the two were compared. The anticipation had been so heightened since the season began and, now, none of that mattered. After the playing of the national anthem and finalist introductions, all of the debates would come to an end because it would be proven in the opening match of the final session.

For Spangler, he would have to contain Tony's strength and find a way to counter his offense. "We knew that we had to control Tony's aggressiveness," Neuqua Valley Head Coach Mick Ruettiger said. "We knew we had to slow him down and then, through that pace, get to our shots. Chris had a nice single, but we didn't want to rush anything early."

While the upper-weight class wrestlers kept their sweat bottoms and tops on and continued to play their music and warm-up, both Tony and Spangler, in their assigned mat corners, had received their final words from their coaches and headed to check in at Mat One—not even the official was as ready as the two wrestlers were.

Before Spangler made his way to check in at the table, Tony was in his traditional black and gold North singlet and stomped in place at the top of the circle behind his starting line—he had already checked in. When Spangler reached the middle of the mat, the official would follow, and the match to determine the best wrestler in the weight was about to unfold.

Much was debated on offense and the high scoring of Tony and the slick attacks of Spangler; however, when the match began, it was about defense. Each wrestler was being tactically aggressive and was not willing to be too far out of position and take a chance.

In the hand fight of the first period, Tony did most of the forward moving and shots on the edge of the mat. Spangler, using his length and experience, knew how to keep Tony at bay and kept himself in position to attack—he was just not opening up for his attacks.

At the end of the first period, the score would be a 0-0 tie. Tony would win the flip and escape in the second for a 1-0 lead. To Tony, the quick escape was imperative as Spangler was a strong top wrestler and his length, provided the position, could have posed a problem for the freshman.

The hand fighting and edge of the mat shots, head snaps, level changes and fakes, and referee's invitation for action would take up the second period.

When the third period began, Spangler chose down—this would be a critical moment for Tony. If he could ride him out, he could win the match 1-0. Of course, the assignment would be difficult as Spangler was seasoned and skilled in all three positions.

Initially, Tony looked to his corner to cut Spangler and defeat him on his feet; however, he was signaled to ride tough from the top position and look to win it there.

As the third period began, there would be efforts by Spangler to get to his feet and escape, and by Tony to return him to the mat and continue his ride. In the end, Spangler escaped; however, Tony would be the aggressor and, as the period wore on, there were no full-fledged attempts made to score. Spangler would be hit for a stalling warning; however, it would not matter. The score would remain 1-1 at the end of regulation.

The first overtime was no different from the previous three periods—hand fighting, half shots in the middle, full shots on the edge. And, even though Tony was the more aggressive of the two throughout the match, it would come to the first overtime period. Since Tony had scored first, he was given the option of top, bottom, or defer. Tony would choose bottom and have thirty seconds to escape. Then, Spangler would have his choice of position, be given his thirty seconds there, and the score would declare a winner, or a sudden victory period would take place.

In Tony's time on bottom, it was short-lived. He escaped and earned his one point with about 00:12 into the overtime. He now led 2-1 and the first thirty-second period ended with him in the lead. As the next overtime began, Spangler would be given his choice and he would choose down. He knew he needed at least one point, via an escape or penalty on Tony, to keep the match even.

Spangler set himself in the referee position; Tony covered, and the whistle was blown. The flurry for Spangler's point began instantaneously. Spangler was long and sat out and worked to a stand or to create separation, but Tony followed and chopped his arm and rode his wrist as he covered Spangler's hips and continued to control the position.

With 00:15 remaining in the period, coaches in both corners were yelling opposite instructions and working to help their wrestler anticipate his opponent's next move. At 00:10 Spangler would free his hip and, just as he would look to hip-hoist free, Tony stepped, captured his arm, drove his shoulder into the mat, and rode out a one-point victory. Tony had his hand raised, earned the number-one ranking in Illinois, and remained perfect on his season.

Afterward, the question that echoed around Spangler was if the stage was just too big for him against the top opponents. "I don't think the stage was too big for him," Ruettiger contended. "We knew that Ramos could score points and I don't think it was Chris getting tight as much as it was him getting more conservative to where he didn't want to make mistakes."

Even with the loss, Ruettiger knew that a Sectional championship was not the state championship, and the goal for Spangler was still in play. Since they met in the Sectional championship match, they would automatically be placed on opposite sides of the bracket next weekend at the state championships.

"I've seen a lot of kids lose at the Sectional," Ruettiger said, "and then come back and win the state the following weekend. This match was good for us because now we had a baseline on Tony and where we needed to go from there. We knew we would be on opposite sides and we couldn't worry about Ramos until we saw him. And if we saw him, it would be in the finals. Even though we would have to prepare for him, we were not going to over-compensate for one kid—we still had to beat the guys on our side of the bracket first.

"Anything can happen at the state tournament," Ruettiger continued. "I know that; I think Chris knew that from his experiences as a freshman and in IKWF. We had some tough guys to beat, but we knew, if everything went as planned, we'd probably see Ramos in the finals."

2006 • IHSA SECTIONAL CHAMPIONSHIPS
103 LB CHAMPIONSHIP MATCH
RAMOS IN A SINGLE-LEG ON CHRIS SPANGLER OF NEUQUA VALLEY HIGH SCHOOL
PHOTOGRAPH COURTESY • THE RAMOS FAMILY • MARLON BROOKS PHOTOGRAPHY

CHAPTER 13
FIGHTING FOR THE OPPORTUNITY

"If I was to reach my goals, head-butts or not, I had to win."

• *Tony Ramos*

QUALIFYING FOR THE STATE CHAMPIONSHIPS and being on the floor wrestling at the University of Illinois' Assembly Hall was all part of the plan. Likewise, Tony's road to the finals was nothing less than calculated when the first whistle blew.

He opened with a first round bye since he was a Sectional champion. In the championship round, he defeated sophomore Max Nowry of Wheeling, 7-5, before having to face the very tall and lengthy Ellis Coleman of Oak Park-River Forest.

When Coleman entered the tournament, he was 32-2. And now, in the quarter-final round against Tony, he would look to use his tall and slender frame to his advantage over his shorter opponent.

Before the match started, Tony stood to the circle's edge out of the center of the mat and paced, waiting for his opponent to put his foot on the line first. As Coleman stepped in, the green ankle-banded Tony stomped forward to his line.

Both wrestlers were very similar in style—they took open shots and battled through another's defense to earn takedowns. Each had his own style of fakes; Tony was more level and head and Coleman more with his hands and long leg stutters. Similarly, however, when each tied on the head, they came hammering down with authority.

About 00:20 into the match, Tony faked and shot an open double—

he would fight in that position for the next sixteen seconds as Coleman posted and crashed his hip into Tony with all he had. But, 00:36 into the match, Tony would score, Coleman would escape, and Tony was up 2-1 very early in the match.

From there, Coleman took three open doubles on Tony—all defended—before ending up in a double underhook position. Using his length, Coleman tried to lift Tony off the mat for a more favorable position, but Tony blocked and worked free.

Once separated, Coleman took an unadvised and overly frustrated shot that Tony defended, worked into a front head position, and then scored another takedown for a 4-1 lead. With a tight waist on his left, and a scarf ride on Coleman's right arm, Tony rode out the period.

In the second period, Tony had choice and chose down. Off the whistle, Coleman was looking to jump into his cradle. He had Tony's leg hooked as he draped his long slender body over the top of him trying to lock his hands from neck to knee. With his body smothered over Tony, Tony was able to peel the top hand, control it, and keep fighting until an eventual stalemate was called with 00:54 left in the period.

Upon the fresh start, Coleman would go to a spiral ride—he would work it up high on Tony's back, keeping the pressure forward. However, being so long, when Tony blocked his leg, Coleman was able to slide his head underneath and crate a scramble position—this favored the smaller Ramos. With Coleman trying to hang onto Tony's leg, Tony found the backdoor and posted, turned, and covered for a reversal and a 6-1 lead. The period ended this way.

Headed into the third period, Coleman chose down and escaped within six seconds—Tony did not even contend the position; he wanted to be on his feet. The score was now 6-2 in Tony's favor and both were now in the neutral position. Coleman would start hammering down aggressively on Tony's head with major right-handed windup ties that were pounding down on Tony's neck—Tony, however, kept his distance and circled and stayed in a good stance. Then, as they each broke free, both changed levels and dropped to open double-leg attacks at the same time—their heads would collide. Tony would be lower in position and finish the takedown and, in the process, capture Coleman's arm and put him on his back.

When the official was finished counting the back points, the match was quickly stopped as Tony's left eye had been split open and was bleeding. Upon removing himself from Coleman, in the middle of the circle, Tony flexed downwardly in excitement as he stomped back toward his corner for bandaging. Unfortunately, this break in the action gave Coleman an opportunity to recover and regroup. The score was now 11-

2, Tony, and Coleman would need an escape and a big move to put himself back in the match.

In the referee's position for the restart, Coleman stood up and Tony dropped to a single, changed off to a double, popped his hips, and lifted and dropped Coleman to his back for a second set of back points—Coleman would ultimately fight over to his belly. Again, Tony's eye was bleeding and the match was stopped to cover the cut, but he had extended his lead 16-2 over the Oak Park freshman.

Once Tony was bandaged up, the match ensued. Coleman would escape and, while on his feet, tried to raise Tony off the mat with double underhooks. Tony blocked and, as he motioned back, Coleman shot a double that Tony would pass by as time expired.

This win now placed Tony in the semifinals where he would face a very tough opponent from LaSalle-Peru, Kaz Hashimoto.

THE SEMIFINAL MATCH-UP DREW A LOT OF

attention because the fans were looking forward to watching two physical wrestlers go after one another. Hashimoto was the favorite to win the state that year even though Tony had been dominating. Regardless, no matter what Tony had done, many saw him as an underdog in this match due to the physicality and experience of the LaSalle-Peru senior.

Hashimoto, who had placed fifth the previous year and was now a senior, entered the state championships with a 30-3 record. Two of his three losses had occurred earlier in the season at 112 pounds while he was still in the process of cutting down to 103—the third loss came the previous week at the Sectional Championships.

Still, even with those three loses, and two of those losses to senior Tyler Winland of Normal Community, whom Tony defeated at 112 pounds by a score of 15-3, Hashimoto was still favored as a finalist on his side of the bracket over Tony.

Hashimoto and Winland had wrestled three times throughout the 2006 season. Hashimoto won one of those matches, a 1-0 decision at 103 pounds in the championship match at the Springfield Invitational. Winland, however, defeated Hashimoto twice, once at 112 pounds, earlier in the season by a score of 4-3, and at 103 pounds in the Sectional championship semifinals with an overtime fall at 6:41.

Additionally, in the Sectional championship match, Winland placed second to Tyler Johnson of Bloomington 4-1, and Hashimoto wrestled back and placed third with a technical fall in 3:59 over Minooka's Brian Bokoski to earn his trip to Champaign.

Haven taken third the week before, that put Hashimoto in the preliminary round of wrestling at the Assembly Hall; there, he defeated

Anthony Magaruh of Rockton-Hononegah, 14-5. That win led him into the championship round to square off against B.J. Futrell of Chicago Mt. Carmel.

Futrell, a sophomore, was 36-3 on the season entering the state championships, and one of those losses was a 12-6 decision to Chris Spangler that happened in the championship match at Al Dvorak Memorial Holiday Tournament.

Regardless, Hashimoto and Futrell was a highly anticipated match-up between those who rank the weight classes and the fans and those who just like contrasting styles and good, physical wrestling.

Some experts had ranked Futrell as the number-two wrestler behind Spangler, and in front of Hashimoto and Tony all season long. Others had Hashimoto rated number one, followed by Futrell, Spangler, and Tony.

Therefore, as the weight class began to wrestle out, there was much excitement and anticipation as to how the talented 103-pound class would unfold as it was the state's most difficult bracket.

The previous season, both Hashimoto, then a junior, and Futrell, then a freshman, lost in the quarterfinals and found themselves pushed into the consolations. Similarly, Spangler, then a freshman, lost in the first round of the championship bracket and found himself having to wrestle his way back if he was to earn a medal.

In the first round of the wrestle-backs, Hashimoto and Spangler met. As many figured, the upperclassman, with his unfamiliar style and strength, won the match by fall in 1:28. Spangler was eliminated from the tournament with that loss. Hashimoto, however, would go on and win his next match, 8-2, for his first state medal.

Therefore, after Hashimoto's 2005 state finish, along with Dan Fickel of *Wrestling USA* magazine having named Hashimoto the number-four best high school 103 pounder in the country, it was easy to see how any big-name match-up was a focus of the tournament.

So, as wrestlers advanced and match-ups matched, both experts and fans alike were anticipating the first round of the championship bracket between Hashimoto and Futrell.

Additionally, it was easy to see how the rankings had been formed early in the season as many of the top-tier wrestlers did not wrestle, but names had to be placed in the some sort of order.

As the match began, to the dismay of some and delight of others, there was a clear-cut winner and, even though the match was exciting in shots attempted and scrambles scrambled and pure athleticism of each wrestler, it was not close. Hashimoto would win each period, only giving up an escape, and won the match handily, 6-1.

The next match-up that would also carry much interest was the first round match that would ultimately feed into Hashimoto. The wrestlers on this mat would feature a freshman Sectional champion and the number-seven ranked wrestler by the name of Jon Morrison of Orland Park Carl Sandburg, and an unranked sophomore named Daryl Thomas of Edwardsville.

Unlike Morrison, Thomas had to wrestle in the preliminary round because he had placed third at his Sectional.

Now, Morrison had already faced Tony twice earlier that season, losing 3-1 and 7-2, and Morrison had also lost to Spangler as well, by the score of 10-0. However, in order for Morrison to have a third shot at Tony, this time for a great deal more at the state championships, he would have to first defeat Thomas and then work through Hashimoto, whom he had not yet faced throughout the entire season.

As the whistle blew, and the points started mounting, Thomas would win an exciting and tight 8-7 overtime decision that would place Morrison's wrestle-back fate into the hands of Thomas. Since Illinois did not offer a true consolation bracket, and wrestlers had to follow the leader, for Morrison to have an opportunity now to medal, Thomas would have to defeat Hashimoto.

But as Hashimoto and Thomas entered the circle and the match began, Morrison would quickly see his individual season end as Hashimoto took control from the start and defeated Daryl Thomas 10-3 to set up Tony's semifinal match with Hashimoto.

IN ADDITION TO HIS STRENGTH AND QUICKNESS, many said that Hashimoto's style, even though he came straight at his opponent, was too difficult to figure out and too awkward for a technical wrestler to defeat; they also concluded that his strength was far too much for younger wrestlers to handle, while his experience gave him the mental edge in the spotlight.

On the Glenbard North side of this match, Tony and his coaches felt it was a match-up that favored Tony—it would be physical and Tony had been able to, thus far, fight through frustration. If nothing else, North's coaches believed that if the match stayed physical for the entire six minutes, then it favored Tony because Tony's conditioning was above and beyond all of those he had wrestled.

There was also one more piece of Hashimoto's style that many argued was dirty—his notorious head-butts. He was a short and very stocky wrestler with quick-twitch muscles and hammering forearms. Similarly, when he shot, he would first take a quick back step to draw his opponent's step forward as he would simultaneously shoot a hard double where his knees would change levels and his head, forehead high, would hit either his opponent's chest or head. In that, Hashimoto would follow through for the takedown. And when he was not shooting his blast double, he was aiming for his high-crotch. Additionally, when on defense, he used his head to defend another's offense.

The truth of it was simple. In wrestling, a wrestler's first line of defense was his head and then his hands; however, many parents whose wrestlers lost to Hashimoto shouted foul and dirty wrestling and wanted him penalized or forced to forfeit those matches. Unfortunately, for them, the officials never saw the head-butting that way or penalized his style to dictate the outcome of any match. Of course, there were matches where the physicality was noted, but it never cost him.

Therefore, throughout the past two seasons, there was a cloud of scrutiny that followed Hashimoto around as matches would be stopped for heavy contact with the head and opponents' bleeding.

In light of it all, the good wrestlers knew how to position themselves and, yes, heads still collided accidently and purposely, but that was all part of the sport.

To some, that was just good, hard-nosed wrestling. To others, it was a cheap way to earn an advantage. Either way, the reality was that a match was going to be wrestled, and any advantage a wrestler gained over his opponent, he was going to gain. A wrestler's style was not going to be dictated by an upset mom, a furious father, or a penalty point.

For Tony, he knew what to expect and all that mattered, bleeding or not, was having his hand raised when it was over.

"I had heard from other wrestlers about the head-butting," Ramos said, "but I didn't care—that's wrestling. I had my head split open at the conference championships three weeks prior and I had to just keep wrestling. All I knew was that I had to remain aggressive and wrestle my match, get to my offense. If I was to reach my goals, head-butts or not, I had to win."

As both Tony and Hashimoto stepped onto the mat, Tony stood back from the center circle, just inside the outer rim of the circle and paced back and forth until his opponent stood on his line across from him. Now in the semifinals, Tony, in the green ankle bands, paced and waited and jumped up and down, paced, waited, and as soon as the official stepped into the mat's center and Hashimoto put his red ankle-banded foot on the line, Tony moved forward to the line and then the whistle blew.

Additionally, Tony's head was bandaged up even more now. The cut on his head continued to open, even though the trainers had placed a small pad over it. His eye was cut and, through it all, he kept true to his style; he wrestled hard and kept winning. That match, with Hashimoto's style, would test those bandages, the pad, and the athletic tape used to keep it all together.

Each wrestler started into his own fakes and quick footwork, dancing forward and backward and from side to side; however, there were no ties—it was all open at the onset of the match. And then, about 00:20 into the first period, it happened—Hashimoto took a quick step back and then came in for an open double. Immediately, Tony dropped his head to block the shot, but his face was up and he had it bashed in the process. Fortunately, Tony fought the position and found an underhook with his left hand to lift Hashimoto up and control the pace of the match. As the hand fight took them to the edge of the mat, Tony took a double-leg of his own and ran the both of them out of bounds.

The open style and shots to ties became a constant throughout the match—and then, in one moment, everything changed.

With 00:19 remaining in the first period, Tony would take a hard double, get in, and started to run his feet looking for a takedown—the pressure had Hashimoto going backward on his heels. Then, suddenly, while falling backward, Hashimoto desperately stepped, lifted hard on his whizzer, and fired his hip into Tony. With Tony's leverage being worked against him, he was thrown to his back on the edge of the circle. However, as both landed, and since Hashimoto was off balance and momentum was too strong to stop, he never settled his hips and he lost his whizzer. In that moment, Tony hit his back, arched on his neck, and rolled away. In his process of rolling, he caught hold of Hashimoto's arm and found his head—he locked up a headlock and rolled him over. Hashimoto, with everything he had, fought to keep his hips flat while Tony squeezed and lifted and the two struggled—Tony struggled to put him on his back, and Hashimoto did all he could do to keep his hips flat and not relinquish any type of control.

With the head referee positioning himself to make a call, the assistant referee was facing the clock as he counted down the final seconds. As soon as the count stopped and the buzzer sounded, the period ended with fans yelling opposed interpretations of what call should be made and how the points should be awarded.

Immediately, both coaches were out of their chairs, yelling, pointing, and trying to take the advantage. However, before the coaches could make their way to the table to confer or argue their claim, the two referees met off to the far side of the mat where the action took place and went through the sequence, in private, to determine the outcome.

Once it was determined, the head official gave the signal—arms crossed at waist high with the words, "No takedown either wrestler."

Fans on both sides of the call were shouting their disdain; regardless, the match would be 0-0 headed into the second period and Tony would choose down. Four seconds later, Tony escaped and led, 1-0.

As expected, the match became more than physical and the two worked from open shots and ended up in ties. Tony, as any traditional North wrestler, was working into his two-on-one series and found an underhook on the far side as he looked to open Hashimoto up as a possible path to his legs.

After the third consecutive hard open double by Hashimoto, Tony's head started bleeding through the pad and the white athletic tape. Due to the blood, blood time was given and that would give Hashimoto a quick break. With a newfound energy, as the match commenced, Hashimoto came out hard and heavy with his hands and even harder on his double-leg attempts. Both wrestlers would have their heads collide with the other, their forearms had met the back of the other's necks, and re-shots came up short as points were at a premium. The match was going to come down to remaining in impeccable position and someone not making a mistake if the other took a chance.

With about 1:00 left in the period, the snapping and head ties became more violent as foreheads were continually colliding like rams each time they came together. As Tony shot in on a double-leg, he was lifted up by Hashimoto and was, once again, in an underhook. But, as Tony's head worked up, the official saw more blood coming through the tape and the match was again stopped.

After more tape was used to make the old tape look clean and covered over the blood-stained white athletic tape, the match continued. As Hashimoto came out with another new burst of energy and a double-leg of his own, Tony down blocked and found himself into a re-shot before Hashimoto's defense responded. Once it did, Tony found himself being hit with a front quarter; Tony backed away until the period ended.

As they entered the third and final period, Hashimoto would choose down. About 00:10 into the period, Tony would cut Hashimoto loose knowing that the match would have to be won on his feet. Once he as awarded his escape, and the score was tied at 1-1, Hashimoto knew he had to find a way to Tony's legs and score. The two would exchange double-legs, strong defense, body position, and further ties on the head.

With 00:45 left in the match, Tony's head ties had finally begun to pay off—Hashimoto looked weakened and worn down as Tony was now pushing him around. Hashimoto was moving backward and that was making it difficult for Tony to work back to his underhook. And, as Tony was finally in the position he wanted, the two went out of bounds and Hashimoto's back step led the way.

Now, with 00:15 left in the match, overtime looked inevitable and everyone was anticipating at least one more minute of hard wrestling.

Once the official blew the whistle to resume wrestling, Hashimoto took a hard step at Tony and reached to lock onto his head; however, instead of feeling a re-tie from Tony, he found the freshman in on a low double-leg driving him backward as he tried to find some way to gather his feet defend a shot that he was not expecting with time ticking down.

As Tony drove, he was able to knock Hashimoto down to his hip and Tony just kept running his feet and driving until he ran Hashimoto over and was awarded the takedown.

Immediately, Hashimoto stood up with time remaining and Tony cut him loose to avoid a scramble. And, as Hashimoto took one last ditch effort at a takedown, Tony ducked under his arm along the edge of the mat, and time would expire. Tony fell backward, rejoiced, and found his way to his feet through a back roll into a hand stand—then he stomped his way, chest high, back to the mat's center.

Hashimoto, with a look of bewilderment on his face, shook Tony's hand and walked back to the center of the mat, still uncertain as how the last 00:15 just changed his fate; his dream of being a state champion was no longer possible.

When the referee grabbed Tony's wrist, and Tony looked to his corner under his overly bandaged head and cotton-plugged nose, he and Hashimoto exchanged a quick hug before his hand was lifted as the victor. In that moment, Tony would raise his index finger to the number-one position as he pointed it high and proud to the crowd.

On the adjoining mat, Chris Spangler would be the victor over Bloomington High School's senior, Tyler Johnson, by fall in 5:48.

As some of the crowd had hoped, there would be a rematch of last weekend's Sectional championship; however, this time, the winner would claim the state championship and the coveted bracket board. For Spangler, it would not only be an opportunity to right his only loss of the season, but to be able to do so on the state's greatest stage.

"We knew how we were going to wrestle Tony," Neuqua Valley Head Coach Mick Ruettiger said. "We didn't spend hours on this, but we touched base on a few points to control the tempo, like we did at the Sectional, slowing him down, riding and getting out—the basics. But we needed to score more points. So, Chris would have to be less conservative and open up to his shot sooner. And Chris was a mature kid who knew what was at stake, so he was going into the match with a good psyche and attitude. He felt he could beat Tony and he knew the match could go either way, but he felt the match was just as much his as it was Ramos' match."

For Tony, it was an opportunity to accomplish his first step in becoming an Illinois high school four-time individual state champion, just as he set out to do.

"I knew Spangler would be tough," Ramos said. "He was tough the week before. But, I had already beaten him and that had to be on his mind. As for strategy, I needed to score more points. He neutralized me a bit and, even though I was aggressive the whole match, I needed to put him in more dangerous positions and use my aggressiveness to open up my shots and score. I knew I could get out of bottom and that I could ride on top, but I wanted to be able to score more and make it clear who the better wrestler was—and that was me."

AFTER THE SEMI-FINAL MATCH HAD ENDED, AND

Tony had a chance to take off his tape helmet, both he and his coaches and family could see that the stitches reopened and they would need to be tended to immediately; in fact, the trainers were even questioning if he should be allowed to wrestle. Frank put a quick end to that notion. "I told them to fuck off," Defilippis remembered. "I know they weren't too happy with [our decision], but I told them to get away from Tony and that we will go get it stitched up. It's not their problem. It's the state finals—he's wrestling."

Fortunately, since he was now a finalist, he would only have to weigh in Saturday morning and he would not have to wrestle until after 6:00 p.m. So, after his match, Tony showered up and headed to the hospital for a re-stitch.

That night, Tony knew that they had now reached the next step to earning their family's first individual state championship. With Frank, they had watched their hopes, just eight years earlier, ripped away from them in the form of a headlock.

In regard to Vince, he had placed fifth the previous season, his freshman season, and now, this sophomore season, he would lose in the state semifinals to Carl Sandburg's Conrad Polz. Vince and Polz had split the season series, 1-1; however, Vince's hopes of a Grand March and possible three-time state championship run ended in a 3-2 overtime loss.

This left the family's wrestling hopes and dreams of crowning a champion that season solely on Tony's shoulders.

That next morning, Tony woke up, weighed in, and headed to breakfast. He would come to Assembly Hall to watch his brother place third, and then he mentally prepared for the finals.

The problem with the late time finals was that Tony would have all day, as would each competitor in the championship match, to think and over-think his match. Up to that point, the stage could never be big enough for Tony; in fact, the bigger the stage, the greater the performance.

Tony, all season long, had delivered. Always confident. Always focused. Always ready.

• • •

As the wrestlers were called into the tunnel on the floor of the Assembly Hall, they would be lined up for the Grand March. Each wrestler would walk out with one coach; appropriately, Tony and Frank would walk out together.

When the lights were turned out, and the low bass pedal of the introduction of the march delivered, it brought the excitement as Grand Marshals, officials, wrestlers, and coaches began their forward march. Fans stood and took pictures as the wrestlers and their coaches circled the championship mats. Sporadic lights flashed from all heights of Assembly Hall with no pattern and captured individual moments. Just as the song led into the trumpet's horn and then joined the strings and other horns and low woodwinds of John Williams' "Bugler's Dream and Olympic Fanfare Medley," the march was into full procession and there was excitement and anticipation by everyone in attendance.

Once the mats were circled, and the wrestlers were finally stopped at the edge of their division's mat, spectators waited as introductions were about to be given.

For the wrestlers, the anthem marked the moments before dreams were crowned. When one had the opportunity to take it all in, the sensation of the moment, mixed with the music and the echoing cheers that filled each competitor with an excitement unlike anything else, he knew he was one win away from immortality. The significance of it all, together, represented the culmination of, for many of the wrestlers, a young lifetime of sacrifice, dedication, and training. For a coach, it marked an achievement that was difficult to attain and a special moment that marked the time, dedication, and sacrifice given and made. Additionally, it marked the moment before an entire program received high praise and recognition based on that one wrestler's hand being raised.

For fans, it represented the excitement of witnessing the best wrestling in the state that was about to commence. And, for current wrestlers not participating, it represented hope, disappointment, and even envy.

As Tony circled the mat with his brother Frank, a first for each of them, it represented another goal accomplished before having to step onto the mat for the family's opportunity to win an individual state championship.

When Tony was introduced, he walked out into the spotlight and shook hands with Chris Spangler; he then went directly back into the tunnel, undressed from his warm-up, regrouped and refocused, and got ready—his weight class would be the first state championship match wrestled.

WHEN THE LIGHTS TURNED BACK ON INSIDE

Assembly Hall, the Grand March, along with the fantasy and dreamlike state, was over—it was time to wrestle. In a matter of six minutes, sometimes more and sometimes less, champions were crowned. While one was left to be revered and applauded, a lone wrestler, in defeat, would exit in a slow motion walk of uncertain sadness that would never leave his soul.

Once Tony stepped onto the mat for the finals—well before the referees were set and ready with the table workers, and well before Spangler had his singlet up and was ready from his corner—he paced at the top of the circle, green ankle bands velcroed to both legs, a fresh white-taped cap under his headgear with only a little hair spot showing where middle-aged men go bald, and a focused look of one ready to win.

In his corner were his coaches from the entire tournament, assistant varsity coach Chris Edwards and his brother, Frank.

Once the referee came to the center and Spangler stepped to his line, Tony walked forward in his standard stomp, shook hands, the whistle blew, and the match was underway.

Both wrestlers backed up, moved forward, backed up and, five seconds into the match, Spangler, who had circled back left, drew Tony in and was quickly in on a low single to his right leg. Immediately, Tony moved his leg out through a sprawl and countered with a front headlock position—he pulled on Spangler's left arm and torqued on his head by grasping the chin with his right hand—the official blew his whistle and a stalemate was called.

The next forty seconds would be open fakes and motion before Tony would take his first shot attempt. It would be thwarted by Spangler with a front headlock defense. Once again, both wrestlers would hold their position until the referee would call a stalemate.

It would take about twenty seconds more until Tony worked into a second attack; however, it would come while Spangler circled back toward the edge of the mat. As Spangler circled away, Tony attempted another open double and ended up locked onto Spangler's right leg—they fought for position until they were called out of bounds.

There would be 00:30 left in the period as a new start began, once again, Spangler circled back and to Tony's right side. In that sequence, Spangler's left leg would be back as he worked his fakes and changed his levels, ready to strike if the opening was there. Both would fake and move; however, they would end tied up and pulling on each other's heads and, as the period came to a close, Tony would snap Spangler's head down after the whistle was blown. Spangler would come up and walk directly into Tony, shouldering past him.

While each wrestler looked over to his corner, the referee pulled his two-colored disk out of his pocket and flipped it in the air. It would fall, green side up; however, the weight of the fall against the firmness of the mat would bounce it high enough to flip over one more time and fall green side down. Spangler, in the red ankle bands, would have his choice and he chose down to start the second period.

As Spangler was set and Tony covered the right side, the whistle blew and Tony went right into his cross-collar ride. Spangler defended the ride via a sit out and, as Spangler worked to maintain his head and chest up and Tony applied as much pressure forward as he could, the position battle continued. This fight would last 00:33 before Spangler found his way out and earned a 1-0 lead.

Once back on their feet, Tony saw the strategy by Spangler to circle away and back, and he began to chase and push and pressure forward even more. Then, at the 1:05 mark in the period, Tony would have a tight two-on-one hold and work forward as Spangler fought for position, backward and out of bounds. Spangler would be hit for his first stall warning of the match. Also in that moment, it was apparent that Tony seemed a bit frustrated and off his match; he did not look his normal comfortable, calm, and collected self.

As the two came back for the restart, Spangler would take a low single to Tony's right leg and he then felt a tight whizzer defend his offensive attack. This fight for position and control would last fifteen seconds before another stalemate was called. The remainder of the period would consist of head snaps, taps, eventual ties and snaps before the period would end with both wrestlers locked together, battling for position.

Without a turn to his corner, and before the referee even asked him his choice for the period, Tony was pointing down and already setting himself in the referee's position before the time on the clock was set. When everyone was set and the whistle was blown, it would take Tony eight seconds to defeat Spangler's spiral ride and work to his feet, escape, and tie the match up at 1-1; blood was starting to seep through Tony's bandaged head.

Again, Spangler found himself in on a single-leg and Tony found a way out of it; once again, Tony worked to a front head and cranked on Spangler's head and arm.

At the halfway point of the period, the two wrestlers would find themselves in very familiar positions with no real gain—shots and front headlocks and then stalemates called leading to a new start.

The ties and the circling and level changes and the pulls and the shots and the defending were all part of the technical match; however, the physicality of the match was now more apparent as regulation was coming to a close. Each wrestler was working to stay in good position—there were no chances being taken and it looked as if both were content taking it into overtime.

Working into another tie with 00:22 left, Spangler took a heavy-handed snap on Tony's head and pushed him off; Tony would reciprocate with a push of his own and the match would be stopped—not for the physicality of the match; but rather, for the blood coming through the tape and Tony's right eye was now also bleeding.

The period ended and, as the referee walked to the table to check the score, Tony and Spangler stood in the middle of the circle, staring at one another, in their stance, and ready to wrestle.

The moment the referee returned and overtime began, much was the same as far as fakes and levels and heavy-handed ties. This went on for the first thirty-seconds. Then, as the halfway point hit, suddenly, Tony was in on a double-leg and drove Spangler backward. Tony would scoot his hip and find his position, knocking Spangler down to his hip, but they would be called out of bounds. Tony's confidence in that moment seemed to be growing and Spangler appeared to now be wearing down.

With fifteen seconds left in the period, Spangler knew he had to make a move—he would circle left, back, and come forward on a shot. As he did this, Tony was also moving into a shot—Spangler would be lower and Tony would lock him down into a front head position, circling and looking to score. But Spangler blocked and time expired in the first overtime.

The next overtime would consist of two thirty-second periods. Each wrestler would have his choice and the total score would determine a winner.

Spangler would have first choice and choose down. Tony would cover his right side and, nine seconds later, Spangler would escape and lead 2-1. As each wrestler quickly gathered himself, Tony would take a hard shot that Spangler would defend and then counter with a reshot that shot Tony off the mat. Once back to the center, Spangler would take another shot and Tony would find his front head position off a down block and continued his position until time expired.

For the next thirty-second period, Tony chose down. Spangler covered his left side and as the whistle blew, Tony was tall and into his inside leg standup. However, as he came to his feet, Spangler tied up Tony's head and arm and pulled backward to whip Tony down to the mat and expose his back. Once they came back, it appeared as if Spangler would regain control in the top position, but Tony worked himself free and escaped ten seconds into the period. At 00:12, Tony's taped helmet came off and injury time was started.

There would be eighteen seconds left in the second overtime when the match resumed, and there would still be enough time for one of the wrestlers to score. Also, with the quick break, both wrestlers had a moment to collect himself with his coaches. If this second overtime period ended in a tie, the next period would simply consist of one wrestler having his choice and, thirty seconds later, the match would have a decisive winner and a decisive loser.

In those remaining seconds of overtime, Tony, who knew Spangler would have the final choice in sudden victory, moved forward with many open fakes and ended with Spangler having his back to the edge of the mat.

When the period ended in a 2-2 tie, the choice came to Spangler for the final overtime and, to no surprise, he chose the bottom position. It would now be up to Tony to ride him out for the entire period in order to claim the state championship. If Spangler escaped, he would be crowned as the state champion. An entire season now came down to thirty seconds.

While Spangler was getting set in the bottom position, Tony hovered, straddled anxiously over his back half with his hands on his own knees and his eyes on the referee as he anticipated the signal to cover.

Once granted, Tony covered the right side and, off the whistle, slid immediately into his cross-collar ride. For Spangler, he would circle up and Tony would leave his ride and drop to a single-leg—Assembly Hall could be felt taking in a deep breath. Spangler would battle and work to separate himself, moving backward and pushing forward, and Tony tried to changeover from his single-leg to a double-leg, and the fans could be heard and felt cheering and hollering and scoring the match the way they were seeing it in that moment. Some were already yelling, "ONE! Escape!" and others had clenched their own hands, "No loss of control! No loss! No loss! Keep 'em locked!"

On the mat, the fight continued and consisted of a position battle until Spangler was able square himself up with Tony, work his hip down heavy to the mat, and free himself as Tony crawled forward on his knees, after him, and tried to keep his hands locked on Spangler's leg. Spangler, who continued to keep his leg back while he extended his arms to create enough space, would earn the escape with Tony in a desperate chase that ended with eight seconds remaining on the clock.

Once the referee yelled and signaled, simultaneously, "One point. Escape," and the match was concluded by the sound of his whistle, Assembly Hall erupted.

Spangler would pump his fists into the air in excitement and, behind him on the mat, with his chest hunched over his knees, and paused for about two seconds, Tony would be seen gathering himself and slowly working himself to his feet. He would walk to the center, remove his green ankle bands and shake Spangler's hand. Spangler would give a brief hug to Tony before his hand was raised. When Spangler's hand was vaulted to the ceiling, Tony was in disbelief that his hand was being held down by the referee at his side—that had not happened all season.

Spangler continued to celebrate as he reached his corner. "For Chris," Ruettiger said, "it was pure excitement. Anytime you win a championship, it is a statement. And it wasn't a statement against Tony, it was just a statement that he was now a champion and he earned that right to be called one after wrestling a great match and pulling it out."

As Tony walked back to his corner, he was dejected. From the center of the circle all the way to his coaches, his head was down and he was in disbelief—he had lost for the first time in his high school career, lost the state championship, and now could never become an undefeated four-time Illinois state champion.

Once he reached his corner, he, again, fell to his knees and began to cry. Coach Chris Edwards consoled him with words and wrapped his arm around him. Frank was grabbing Tony's belongings and the three would exit the match and disappear into the tunnel.

About halfway into the tunnel, Tony stopped, dropped, and propped himself up against the wall; Frank would be found sitting right next to him.

Tony remembered, "Sitting there I was thinking and asking Frankie, 'Why? Why me? I do everything right. How did this happen?'"

For Frank, he knew that feeling—and knew that moment all too well. However, when it came time to speak to his youngest brother, he could only reflect on what he knew was right to say—what was told to him eight years earlier by his coach. "Tony looked to me like I looked to Hahn," Defilippis said. "I told him the only thing I knew to say. It was what Hahn had told me when I was in that tunnel my senior year. I told Tony, 'Hey, if this is the worst thing that happens to you in your lifetime, it's not going to be so bad.'"

Unfortunately, there would be little time to sulk as Tony would have to make his way to the award stand—the most difficult journey for a wrestler after losing in the finals.

On the award stand, there would be a stark contrast in emotions—Spangler was lit up with a celestial smile and color to his face as he accepted his medal and state championship bracket and, just one step below him, Tony would have his head down, saddened, and still working the match through in his mind as he tried to piece together what was actually happening in that moment.

Once the award ceremony concluded, Tony disappeared into the tunnel.

When he looked back at the match, he admitted, "I let the nerves get to me. I let the stage get to me. I was right where I needed to be to accomplish my goals, and I put a ton of pressure on myself and it pretty much came down to that. I didn't create enough offense and I didn't create opportunity, and then it came down to having to hang on for eight more seconds and I didn't. In high school, every day, it haunted me."

Even though those final seconds haunted him, they seemed to amaze him more when he talked about it: "Eight seconds and you can't hold a guy down and you're in on a single-leg?" he questioned to himself. "And then you let go of the single to switch off to a double—that's not smart. I wasn't thinking. I was not…it was not happening that day."

When Tony reflected a little more, he resigned himself to how "It made me smarter as a wrestler," Ramos said. "And it helped me understand situations better in those situations with eight seconds to go. All I had to do was just drop to the leg and hang on—you don't have to do much; you just have to hang in there and ride him."

For others, the loss was just as difficult to take. "Tony was in position to win that match," Hahn said. "But he had a moment of being in bad position and, in those moments, those mistakes can't be made. He knows not to switch off—it was hard to watch because I think Tony wins nine out of ten matches against Spangler and that one day happened to be in the state championship match."

"I didn't say anything to him in that moment. I knew Frankie and Chris [Edwards] were with him and that I would talk to him after he had time to cool down."

Israel, young and fiery, commented, "I was pissed. I yelled at him and told him, 'Why would you switch off to a double in double overtime?' You would think that a guy like Tony would know that position, until you realize that he has been so dominant that he doesn't get into those double overtime positions."

But then, after the anger subsided, Israel spoke how, "I was frustrated at first, but then I realized how bad it hurt him. And I just told him that he's got to use it as a motivation—and I just kept reminding him and that he could never feel like this again. Let's not talk about it, let's get his ass together and he was going to have to work harder."

Even the family took the loss very hard. Vince looked back on that moment of his brother walking off the mat, crying, all bandaged up from the match and said that he believed "Tony realized how close he was to a goal that the family had been chasing for a while."

And, make no mistake about it, the family goal for finally crowning an individual state champion had now eluded all three of the brothers. The tempers and frustration were high; however, the season was not over and a quick transition needed to be made—Tony had to turn around Sunday and Monday to practice, and then wrestle Tuesday night.

"The key, I think," Israel explained, "is to be in a good program because if you lose downstate, you can get your swag back right away on Tuesday night. Losing is bad, but he had to learn how to lose and that was one of the greatest lessons he walked away with."

Coach Hahn's approach focused on how Tony responded determined how he would be perceived. "He wrestled and he lost," Hahn said, "—it's not the end of the world. What would determine his character was how he responded that Tuesday. And, that Tuesday we needed him on weight—the team goal was still the same. After his finals match, win or lose, it was now about the team and we needed Tony ready to go for our team to be successful."

The motivation for Tuesday night would be easy for Tony. At the time of the Dual Team State series, a team would have to win two matches on Tuesday to qualify for the Team State Championships that Saturday. For North, they figured they would be facing Montini Catholic in the championship round to earn top eight honors in the state and qualify as a team for an opportunity to accomplish their goal of a state championship; however, before they would wrestle the Broncos, and before they could make the finals, they would again have to defeat Neuqua Valley—and Tony would have another shot at Spangler.

THE EXCITEMENT LEADING TO TUESDAY NIGHT

on the message boards from fans was pure excitement and emotion. It was not too common to have such a high profile match-up back-to-back weeks, and it was even more uncommon to have three high-profile matches of the same two wrestlers meeting in a matter of nine days; but, the dual was set and that specific match-up would bring out the fans and wrestling enthusiasts alike. It was expected to be something special.

Out of the four teams that were competing at Bolingbrook High School on this night in the Team Sectional, Montini was rated second in Illinois and, all season long, Neuqua Valley and Glenbard North would go back and forth on the number-three and number-four rated team. Number-one was last year's defending state champion, Carl Sandburg; however, they were not competing at the Bolingbrook Dual Team Sectional. Therefore, at the conclusion of the night, two of the top four rated teams in the state would not have the opportunity to earn a state trophy.

In the Sectional semifinals, Glenbard wrestled Neuqua Valley for the third straight season. In that, Neuqua felt they had an advantage over the young Panthers as they had a strong line-up of veterans, while North had younger wrestlers. Aside from the match-up of the teams and the intensity brought into the stands by each town, the Ramos versus Spangler match was the buzz of the gymnasium.

However, all of the excitement would cease once weigh-ins came and wrestlers were aligned in their weight classes. Neuqua would not weigh-in a 103-pound wrestler, and Spangler would bump up and wrestle at 112 pounds.

Neuqua's 112-pound freshman Sectional champion and state qualifier, Matt Walters, would not wrestle for undisclosed reasons. At the Sectional, he had defeated North's Jimmy Chase in the title match by a 6-5 score. But, on that night, he was not with his team and that would hurt Neuqua Valley's match-ups because that was a key member of their team and they needed his points in what was anticipated to be a very close dual.

"We had a very unfortunate situation come up," Ruettiger said. "So we had to move a few guys around and Chris going 112 for us was part of that move. We were not looking to dodge Tony, we were looking to win the dual and qualify for the team state championship. It was a tough decision, but we needed to creatively put our best team out there and that was one of our few moves."

Of course, Tony wanted to bump up and his brother Frank and family wanted the same; however, Coach Hahn saw it differently. Tony would walk out and claim his forfeit at 103 pounds and earn six team points for his team. Jimmy Chase would end up defeating Spangler by a 3-1 decision for another three team points, and North advanced to the Championship match with a 44-22 victory.

"Once the dual series begins," Hahn said, "it is about the team and not the individual. Tony would have to take his forfeit and Jimmy Chase would have the match. We didn't have room to bump a good wrestler out for one match and we were not going to start then. I know Tony wanted the match, but we needed the points and we took them. In the end, it worked—we won the dual and moved on to face Montini in the Sectional championship."

• • •

Montini Catholic was rated higher than the Panthers all season; however, both programs knew that that dual, with the match-ups, was not an on-paper dual—it would come down to bonus points, which guys wanted it more, and heroes.

Since the semifinals opened at 103 pounds, the finals would end at

2006 • IHSA STATE CHAMPIONSHIPS
103 LB CHAMPIONSHIP MATCH
RAMOS ATTACKS SPANGLER OF NEUQUA VALLEY HIGH SCHOOL
PHOTOGRAPH COURTESY • THE RAMOS FAMILY • MARLON BROOKS PHOTOGRAHPY

the 103-pound weight class. This would pit Tony, for a third time, against senior Joe Norton and everything could be on the line when that match came around for the final bout of the dual.

The last time Tony competed on a wrestling mat, he had lost. Norton, who placed fifth at the Individual State Championships, had won his last match at Assembly Hall, and had won his first match at the Sectional—he would be plus two on his last two matches.

There was no mistake that the match-up between Glenbard and Montini would be a high profile dual. Montini had just moved up to Class AA in Illinois, and they had dominated the Class A for the past four years with four-consecutive Team State championships.

Aside from that, many of the wrestlers not only knew each other and knew each other well, but they had been teammates on Team Illinois' national team, and some even worked out with and competed against each other in the spring and summer seasons. So, in addition to the team who won advancing to the Dual Team State Championships in four days, there was also bragging rights and the pride of public school versus the private school on the line.

The opening match would feature state qualifier Jimmy Chase—who lost a tough 3-2 match in the individual state opening round and was not granted a wrestle-back that past weekend—and All-State wrestler Connor Beebe. Chase would win by an 11-4 decision. Glenbard would add four more points to their team lead when sophomore state qualifier Geno Capezio won by a 15-4 major decision over Brandon Hensley at 119 pounds.

With the team score now 8-0, Montini would post its first win. All-State wrestler, Vince Hannon, would defeat sophomore state qualifier Danny Monaco with a 5-1 decision—Hannon had defeated Monaco in the Sectional finals two weeks prior as well. At 130 pounds, Glenbard sent out its first upper classman and team captain, Mark Schultz. Schultz, who had missed placing down state by one match, would have a lesser opponent in Montini's Dan Stelter and open up an 8-0 lead before earning a second period fall. The Panthers now led the team score, 13-3.

The next match would prove to be a wild display of talent and aggressive wrestling. For North, it would be Tony's brother, Vince, who had just placed third in the state. For Montini, Brian Martin would step onto the mat at 135 pounds. Martin, who was one match away from placing the week before, would be looking for validation. The two would exchange takedowns and escapes, as well as hard defense, shoves, and much emotion—they would also go into the third period tied at 3-3.

Martin would choose down for the period and Vince would cut him immediately and look for a takedown and the win. After three crazy flurries, Vince would come up short and lose a 4-3 heartbreaker; Montini would close the gap. North now led 13-6 with the experience of Montini's line-up slowly coming up.

At 140 pounds, Montini's Jered Hensley came up against senior Carlos Lopez and Hensley led the entire way. With less than 00:35 in the match, Lopez would shoot and score to earn a late takedown for the win; that pushed North's lead, 16-6. The black and gold erupted in cheers and some taunted the Bronco fans; in response, small retaliations were made and, at times, security had come over to calm the parents and fans of each school down.

The atmosphere was loud and alive and the voices in the gymnasium were colliding with other voices as they each tried to top one another.

Senior captain John Malizzio at 145 pounds was next up for North and he would face Isaiah Gonzalez. Malizzio, who had returned to the line-up after a torn ACL late in the season, made an individual run only to lose in the quarterfinals and then in the first round of the wrestle-backs down state—he was two matches away from placing. Gonzalez, cousin to the Ramos brothers, was a strong wrestler, but had failed to qualify. He would step on the mat against a proven senior while trying to pull Montini back into the dual.

Unfortunately for Gonzalez, Malizzio would pull through as he had done all season when he stepped on the mat for his team; Malizzio would win a 5-4 decision and give his team a 19-6 lead. However, Montini would be sending its state champion, Mike Benefiel, onto the mat at 152 pounds where he would close the gap and push Montini right back into the dual with his fall. He brought the Broncos to within seven points in one match. Montini now trailed 19-12 and the stomping of the bleachers was getting louder and more consistent by the fans as the cheers became more intense with the Benefiel fall. Additionally, the mat side demeanor of the wrestlers and coaches was greatly intensified in support through each person's voice and his body language.

Even though Benefiel earned the fall at 152, Montini did not get the match-up they wanted there. One of North's moves was to bump their 152-pound junior, Bryan O'Connor, up one weight class and go one-for-one instead of possibly dropping two matches. Since Benefiel had to report to the table first, Glenbard was able to play their hand and they did.

O'Connor, who placed third at the state championships, would face senior state qualifier Chuck Pieritz at 160 instead. Both O'Connor and Pieritz would exchange takedowns and the match would be wild and exciting and 5-5 at the end of regulation. In the first overtime, O'Connor, who struggled getting to his doubles, settled for a single-leg and won a 7-

5 overtime decision that was imperative to the dual score. North's gamble paid off and Glenbard now led 22-12. Next up would be another junior state qualifier for North in Roy Feltson.

In the stands the fans were loud and excited. The other teams had all stuck around to witness the outcome, and all was slowly coming to a close—anything was possible.

The match at 171 would go the full six minutes, but Feltson would never be in danger. He won a 6-1 decision over Dan Grimes, put his team in front by a 25-12 score, and this, just in time for three of Montini's hammers to take the mat. In the bleachers and on the bench, the Montini fans were letting the Glenbard fans know that they knew the dual was still up for grabs as their next three weights could push Montini right past the Panthers.

At 189, All-State Ethan Winel would place Montini another five points closer with a technical fall. In the 215-pound match, a tossup, All-State Garrett Goebel would take a 3-1 decision over North senior Rich Guidolin who missed qualifying for the state championships when he placed fourth at the Sectional.

These two wins by Montini, totaling eight points, closed the gap to 25-20 with two matches remaining. And when Montini heavyweight David Lembas stepped onto the mat for Montini and scored a fall for the Broncos, Montini would take the lead for the first time in the dual, 26-25, and the dual and the opportunity to wrestle in the Dual Team State Championships was on the line and left to the 103 pound weight class.

The final match would feature state runner-up Tony Ramos and senior All-State wrestler Joe Norton for Montini.

Since the 189-pound match, not one fan had sat down in his seat and the naturally large Bolingbrook High School gymnasium suddenly seemed cramped and crowded and almost unfit to host the dual.

The wrestlers from other schools had pushed and enclosed the far side of the mat and gossiped and cheered while North's and Montini's wrestlers were off the bench, on their feet, and intensely focused on the dual. Bodies were pressed toward the mat as close as they would be allowed, voices hollered and echoed inside of the gymnasium, and every person had a favorite and let it be known. Throughout the dual, each hand fight and snap and level change and shot and point led to some type of response from every wrestler and fan and coach. And now, it came down to two very familiar opponents, two intense teams, six minutes, and one winner.

Norton, seasoned and already part of three Dual Team State championships, knew the magnitude of the match and the quality of his opponent. Tony, a freshman, but no stranger to big matches—now his second in a matter of four days—wanted to and needed to go out and win.

"Of course I knew the dual and the chance to go down state as a team was riding on the match," Ramos said. "But I needed to come back and win because of what happened the last time I stepped onto the mat in the state finals."

This would also be the second time that Tony was wrestling and Israel Martinez was in the other corner as his opponent's coach.

"It wasn't different because I knew what the situation was," Ramos said. "I knew that if I went to Glenbard North, and we wrestled Montini, Izzy would have to coach Montini—that's his commitment as a coach, he has to coach his guy. Even though I was Izzy's guy, at this point in time Coach Hahn, Frankie, [Chris Edwards] were the guys coaching me because the situation was they were my coaches and I was at Glenbard North and Izzy was coaching at Montini. We knew that it was something that could happen. I don't know if he was comfortable with it, I don't know if I was comfortable with it, but it was something we had to do because it was the commitment we made."

The match would be close and tight and very calculated between the two wrestlers. Each knew where the other was strong, and each was trying to expose the other's weakness—Tony scored first on a late first period takedown and Norton would escape; Tony would lead early, 2-1.

In the second, Tony would defer, Norton would choose down and escape, and the two would remain in good position and for the remainder of the second the score would be tied, 2-2.

As Tony chose down, Norton knew he would have to try and turn him in the third. But the freshman would escape, go up 3-2, and as the match ticked down in time, and fans stomped and yelled and cheered and booed and directed the referee to the correct calls. The time on the clock would be closing out and the Glenbard faithful would start a countdown with five seconds left in the match. In the end, Tony would win a 3-2 decision and North would be victorious.

When Tony's hand was raised, and shouts between parents and fans from both schools intensified louder and with more angst; security came over to calm the tensions and excitement and made certain that nothing was out of control. Additionally, Tony had bounced back from his loss just three days prior, defeated a strong opponent for the second time that season, and helped his team qualify for the Dual Team State Championships that weekend.

The 28-26 victory would end Montini's perfect dual meet season, state championship streak at four in a row, and push Glenbard to their sixth team state berth in as many years.

In Illinois, there was no seeding for just about anything wrestling-related after the Regional. Therefore, when it came to the team series, any two teams could wrestle at any moment.

For the Panthers, they would have to face Carl Sandburg in the opening round of the state championships. Sandburg had defeated North at the Clash, in the duals, and was rated number-one to North's number-three rating at the season's end. Now, when it mattered most, in the state duals, and with Montini out of the picture, it would be a winner-take-all scenario as the two best teams would face off in the first round.

• • •

No other team matched up better with Sandburg than North, and both teams knew that. Therefore, when it came time to wrestle, there was much anticipation regarding this dual. Even though the entire tournament would have to be wrestled, it was understood that whichever team won this dual would end up, with the odds heavily in their favor, of winning the team championship at the end of that Saturday night.

The opening dual would begin at 135 pounds with Vince Ramos being given an opportunity to wrestle the current state champion, Conrad Polz, who had defeated him in the semifinals of the state championships. Vince would win a 3-0 decision and gave the Panthers a 3-0 team lead. After Vince, senior captain John Malizzio, who continued to wrestle on a torn ACL, pulled out a gutsy 3-2 decision over John Doyle. This gave the team momentum and a 6-0 lead heading into Sandburg's strength—the upper-weights. Unfortunately, in the next five matches, Sandburg would outperform North and take a 19-6 team score lead before the Golden Eagle heavyweight pinned North's Alex Hansen and gave Sandburg a 25-6 lead headed into the 103 pound match. North's opportunities were slowly fading away.

In another move by North, however, Tony would not face Morrison for a third time; instead, he would wrestle up at 112 pounds in an effort to put Caitlyn Chase in the line-up and try to allow the senior to sneak out a win. Unfortunately, the move would not be as fortuitous as planned. Morrison would defeat Caitlyn 5-2 and Tony would fall to the 112-pound state runner-up, Mike McAuliffe, by a 7-1 decision in his final bout of the season. The coaches would wrestle out their full lineups for the entire dual and Sandburg would not only win the match-up by a 35-14 margin, they would go on uncontested to claim the team state championship for the second year in a row.

Tony would end his season with a final match loss. He would be back to work that Monday in order to prepare for his offseason, his sophomore campaign, and construct a new set of goals that would put him in position to not fail.

CHAPTER 14
AFTER HOURS

"This is what the team voted, and this is what it's going to be. You're just going to have to move on from it."

• *Mark Hahn*
Head Coach, Glenbard North High School

AFTER EACH SEASON ENDED, NORTH HAD ITS annual awards night where it recognized its successes as a team and as individuals. As was tradition, some awards were based on coaches' votes, and others were predicated on the team's votes.

The standard awards were given to seniors and specialty awards were given out as well. Tony would take home the award for least amount of down time in a match and the second award Tony received was co-Most Valuable Wrestler—a recognition voted on by the team; both Tony and senior John Malizzio were granted the co-Most Valuable honor.

Malizzio had made his own sacrifices over the season for the team due to his knee injury. In fact, he pulled himself out of some meets and individual tournaments to stay as healthy as he could for the team state series. It was clear that when the team needed him, he was in the line-up and he performed. He was the physical, vocal, and emotional leader for the team—he was a Glenbard North senior who embraced the program for four years and would do anything for it, his coaches, and his teammates.

Tony's choice as a co-Most Valuable Wrestler was obvious as well. He had won and scored the team a number of points—no matter who he faced. He was hard-nosed, a hard worker, and the team rewarded his individual efforts and his state runner-up finish, the highest on the team with that recognition.

However, the one award that Tony was waiting for would come at the end of the night when Coach Hahn announced next year's team captains—an honor that was strictly voted on by the team.

When Hahn came to the final recognition of the night, there would be great anticipation on Tony's part.

Once a wrestler was chosen as a captain, he retained his captainship throughout his career. Returning captains would be junior Vince Ramos and senior Bryan O'Connor. Hahn would then announce that, "In addition to this past season's captains, the team has voted in senior Roy Feltson and junior Geno Capezio."

These four wrestlers would stand and receive their applause—but Tony, he would remain in his seat confused and hurt. As Tony remembered sitting there, "I was devastated."

HOWEVER, TONY WOULD NOT WAIT TOO LONG

to talk to Coach Hahn about what had just happened and why he was not named a team captain.

"I walked right into his office as soon as Awards Night ended," Ramos said. "I sat down and asked him, 'What did I do wrong to not be named a captain? I was the highest placer on the team. I only lost two matches. I worked hard in the room...why not me?'"

Coach Hahn sat in his chair behind his desk and looked Tony right in the eyes and was honest with him. "Don't worry," Hahn said, "everything is going to be all right. This is what the team voted, and this is what it's going to be. You're just going to have to move on from it. Things don't always go your way and this is one of those times."

But Tony, even though he heard his coach's words, and did not like the decision, was better when he stepped out of the office.

"After I talked to Hahn," Ramos said, "I was fine. I didn't necessarily like it, but he was straight with me and he was right—I had to accept it and move on. Those were the captains and those were the guys I would have to follow and, if I wanted to be one, I was going to have to earn it."

As he looked back, he reflected on maybe what hurt his chance at a captainship. "Maybe I was too selfish," he said. "Maybe I wasn't always a great teammate because I was more worried about myself. Maybe I needed to get guys to come together and work more my way instead of them going the other way. And maybe that's why he let the vote stand. Maybe he left it to teach me how to be a better teammate and asset to the team and not just a guy focused on myself."

But as Tony considered more, he considered why it hurt so much. "I think it was because Vince was named a captain after his freshman year," Ramos said. "And since we were always in a competition, and he was one up on me; I didn't like that."

From Coach Hahn's perspective, "Tony didn't fully buy into the program yet and I think the other guys on the team saw that. He needed to do some growing and this lesson may have served him well at that point. He was used to having the accolades, but with the guys on the team, particularly the older guys, this one had to also be earned."

Regardless, Tony would have to move into his spring season and focus on a few new aspects of himself as a wrestler and himself as a person and teammate. The motivation was already in place by not achieving his goal of winning a state championship—the next step was training.

CHAPTER 15
INCENTIVE-BASED WRESTLING

"I'll tell you what: I'm going to let you do this so you lose and understand that I am right."

• *Frank Defilippis*
Ramos' brother

EVEN THOUGH TONY ENJOYED WINNING, HE also enjoyed making outrageous bets with his brother Frank. They made these bets to add some further incentive to Tony's wrestling and have something to hold over the other's head. Frank liked talking, and Tony liked to prove people wrong—especially Frank.

"Any bet we made," Defilippis smirked, "no matter how ridiculous, that little bastard won."

The whole idea started when Tony was a freshman at North and he wanted a set of golf clubs—and he wanted Frank to purchase them for him.

"For some reason," Defilippis said, "Tony thought he was going to be a great golfer—he was terrible. We would go out and the kid sucked. Awful. But I think us laughing at him only encouraged him."

As for the bet, it all started when Tony and Frank were talking about what weight Tony should wrestle that season, and they disagreed greatly on what Tony should do.

"He was talking shit to me his freshman year about going undefeated through Christmas at 112 [pounds] because I wanted him at 103," Defilippis said. "I told him, 'Tone, you know there's some tough guys at 112. Heck, there's tough guys at 103. What do you mean you want to go 112?'"

But, true to himself, Tony did not care about his brother's opinion and, in that moment, their first bet originated. Tony said, "If I go undefeated at 112 through Christmas, then you have to buy me those Nike [golf] clubs I want."

Frank smiled at his brother, "I'll tell you what: I'm going to let you do this so you lose and understand that I am right."

When Christmas came, and Tony was still undefeated, Frank would have to make good on the bet—and Tony knew he would.

"Oh yeah, he reminded me," Defilippis said. "I had to buy him a set of Nike golf clubs. It cost me something like $1,200—I was so pissed. But, he did it."

THE SECOND BET WOULD PROVE EVEN MORE

costly than a set of golf clubs to Frank if Tony was able accomplish the task, but it would be more than one task.

The original incentive started as both Tony and Vince entered high school. "Frank flat out told us," Ramos said, 'If either of you win state, I will buy you a car.'" However, both Tony and Vince had come up short on winning that first family state championship —Tony had just placed second and Vince had now placed fifth and third. Due to that, Frank upped the ante coming home from the team state loss to Sandburg. And it was on this ride where the largest wager between Tony and Frank would take place.

After Tony's loss in the finals to Spangler, and how well he had wrestled that freshman season, Tony had reminded his brother of his promise about the car; unfortunately, Frank was also aware of his youngest brother's ability and would place some added stipulations on the agreement.

"Frank knew that I had a pretty good shot to win the state," Ramos said, "and he was going to make me earn it."

The wager was for a new Hummer, and Frank was going to push the limits. "The Hummer was the *in* vehicle at the time," Ramos said, "and I wanted one. So, I threw it out there."

But, according to Frank, the bet was not going to work in his youngest brother's favor; especially since Frank was burned on the golf clubs for not giving Tony either enough credit or enough of a task. The challenge in the value for a new truck would be significant, and Frank would work to stack the deck in his favor.

Frank recalled how, "Tony would have to win the Western Regional. Then, he would have to win the FILA Cadets where he would have to wrestle a number of nationally ranked guys, tough guys—he would have [Eric] Grajales [from] Florida, and [Boris] Novachkov from California, and then Josh Kindig [from Pennsylvania]—it was a loaded bracket.

"On top of that, to move up to 112 from 103 was not going to help him—he was too small—no way could he do it. I told him, 'Tony, you are too small and you are going to run into guys that you won't be able to handle.' But he told me, 'You don't know what you're talking about.' So, we would find out and he would see that he would have to go 103 if he wanted to win. He would have to make the sacrifice."

"For me," Ramos said, "getting down to 103 pounds seemed impossible. Having to cut that weight freshman year was just something that I didn't want to do again. I knew I could win at 112 and I didn't think it was such a big deal to go up in weight. I wouldn't say the sacrifice, but I didn't want to go through all of that running and extra work to make 103 when I could go 112 and just focus on my techniques and get better. It wouldn't be easy—at 112 I'd still have to make the weight, but it was a better fit for me."

Additionally, Frank declared that, "He would also have to place in Fargo, win the Iron Man, go undefeated at the Clash, and then win the state championship. He was going to lose and lose bad and I was going to tell him, 'I told you so.' But, Tony still took the bet—he always took the bet."

In regard to what Tony would wager against the Hummer, he said, "Nothing. I either got it or I didn't get it. It was that simple. Well, it sounds simple, but it's not; actually, it's pretty hard."

Frank knew that those wagers with his brother motivated Tony. "These were all things that I wanted," Ramos said. "They're all luxury things and things that you don't come by every day. So, to have the opportunity to get something like that or something of that caliber of a gift motivated me even more because it would be something cool that I could show off to people or friends. At that age, that was the kind of thing that drives you. You know, the *Who's got the better this* or *Who's got the better that* and you always want to have the best—at least I did."

The first mountain that Tony had to climb was that April to win the Western Regional. If he did not win the tournament, his first tournament, the bet was off and Frank would win. Frank would win and Tony would lose.

THE 2006 WESTERN REGIONAL FOR JUNIOR
freestyle was held in Las Vegas, Nevada, in the middle of April. Tony and family, along with his coach, Israel, made the trip to compete; the field of competition was very deep in talent.

In the opening round of the tournament, Tony wrestled and defeated Anthony Alvarez of California, 6-0, 7-0.

In the second round, he continued his winning ways with another shutout, this time a 6-0, 3-0, win over Oregon's Tyler Lander. The size of his opponents did not seem to influence the outcome of his matches—a great contrast to what Frank had expected. Tony was wrestling well, he looked strong, and he was dominating.

Nick Flores of Utah would be next and he would score the first points on Tony thus far throughout the tournament; they came after Tony took the first period, 1-0. In the second, Flores earned a 1-1 win on criteria, but then, to close out the match, Tony left no question who the victor was with a 5-0 decision and advancement. That win moved Tony into a bye round before having to wrestle Arizona's John Garza. Garza would go down in defeat, 7-0, 5-0.

In the final round before the round-robin finals, Tony had to defeat Max Ortega from New Mexico—he took down and defeated his opponent from the Land of Enchantment by a 1-0, 3-1 score.

Now in the round-robin, Tony had to face Eric Grajales of Florida. Grajales, who attended Brandon High School, was already a two-time state finalist—he took second as an eighth-grader and won the state that past season as an undefeated freshman. Additionally, he had already won a Fargo Greco-Roman national championship as well as a FILA Cadet national championship. Tony would be tested, and he was excited for the match-up.

"[That] was the first time that me and him would wrestle," Ramos said of his match-up with Grajales. "There was a bunch of talk about Eric Grajales and how he was supposed to be the next big thing because he would always wrestle folkstyle and in the junior division and all the other divisions they had out in Vegas. There would be a lot of people who followed him and I knew that I could beat him and that I could compete with anyone, so I was looking forward to it."

To an outsider, the physical-ness of Grajales could have posed a problem in that match-up for Tony due not only to Grajales' size, but also his upper-body strength and ability to throw.

However, from Tony's coaches' view, Israel and Frank, "They told me," Ramos said, "I can beat any one of these guys. I can compete with any of these guys. Frankie was very good at breaking my opponents down and had some strategy for me as well. But the biggest thing I got from them was the confidence to go out and compete against these guys that were older than me and had more success and accolades than I did."

In a well-balanced first period, Tony lost by a 3-2 score. Grajales controlled the ties and put Tony in unfavorable positions—Tony learned in that period that hanging on the head and being in an upper-body match did not favor him.

As the second was underway, Tony would be in on single-leg attacks, but he kept giving up crotch-lifts for points in the process of trying to score. However, with time about to run out on him in the third period, and trailing 4-3, Tony found his way into another shot and finished it for a 4-4 criteria victory.

That pitted the two into a final period for a winner-take-all scenario. In a tightly contested bout, Tony found himself trailing in the final seconds. "With short time left," Ramos remembered, "he ended up taking me down for the second time and going up 2-0. When I got up, I had to score. I got a takedown and had to force him over with a gut. I stepped over and forced it and got it and got the points that I needed for the match."

In the end, Tony took the victory from his Sunshine State opponent with a 3-2 win that pushed him into the finals and now put Tony on the national radar.

"That was a big win for me in my career," Ramos said. "It really spring-boarded me in getting noticed by these top-level college coaches and growing my confidence as my future moved on."

In his immediate future was his finals match against California's finest, Boris Novachkov.

Novachkov, who was two years older than Tony and attended Freemont High School in Sunnyvale, California, was already a state champion. He was born and raised in Radnevo, Bulgaria, before moving to the United States, and he had an older brother, Filip, whom he wrestled and trained with. Aside from his folkstyle credentials, he was a seasoned and accomplished Greco-Roman wrestler as well. This would pit Tony against another upper-body wrestler where, again, his smaller size may have worked against him.

"Going into the finals match I had heard of Boris," Ramos said. "He was the only one to beat Grajales, and he beat him good. He also beat [Jon] Morrison and had won Fargo—I hadn't even wrestled in Fargo yet. I knew he was really good at freestyle and I knew I had to be ready for anything from him."

In the first period, Tony would outlast the offensive and powerful Novachkov by a 1-0 score. What Tony had learned in regard to staying out of the upper body fight in his last match was paying dividends in this one. However, Novachkov would not be shutout and shut down two periods in a row.

In the second period, Novachkov would show his worth with a dominant 4-0 lashing of Tony. Tony would find himself in position to score offensively, but his position was used against him in the form of a crotch-lift. That shift in momentum favored the older and more electric wrestler; however, Tony had already proven that he could shut Novachkov down, and he needed to do it again in order to walk away with the championship.

Headed into the third period, Tony knew he could not allow Novachkov to open up and control the ties or catch him in poor position while in on his legs—again, he would have to keep the match close and work to score one time, without putting himself in danger.

As the match progressed and positions changed and favored each wrestler at different points and at different moments, Tony found a safe path to Novachkov's legs and scored a takedown. He would ride out the 1-0 lead and claim the Western Regional championship with that decision.

"Once I had my takedown," Ramos said, "I felt good about the period. I focused on staying in good position and not forcing anything. That takedown ended up being enough to win."

With that win, Tony not only stood atop the podium, but he also earned Outstanding Wrestler of the tournament honors due to the depth of talent in his weight class.

"That win was even bigger than the Grajales match," Ramos continued. "I don't think anyone expected me to win those two matches or the bracket or be in the finals. I think everyone expected it to be Grajales and Boris in a rematch of the Fargo finals. So it was good for me to go out there and get that tournament won and move on."

For Tony, it was not just his wrestling that made the difference that day, but also his coaches. "Frankie and Izzy made all the difference for me," Ramos stated. "For me, the people in my corner are huge. I have to know that they will fight for me because those are the guys I believe in and trust and they got me to this spot at this point. And not that I could always hear them, but being able to look over and see those guys is a reminder of the work that I have been putting in and believing that what they have been doing with me is what I need to win. That helped me with my confidence in those matches."

When Tony came off the podium, even though nothing was said between the two brothers other than a congratulations and what needs to be improved upon, both Tony and Frank knew that Tony was one-for-one on their bet.

NEXT UP WAS THE FILA CADET FREESTYLE National Championships where Tony entered the 50 kg (110-pound) weight class. The event was held at Northwestern University in Evanston, Illinois, close to home, and at the end of April—just two weeks after the Western Regional.

In the first round, Tony defeated Missouri's Mac Bailey by decision in the first two periods, 4-1, 3-0, before, in the second round, having to face, once again, one of his brother's greatest concerns, Eric Grajales.

Now, Tony had defeated him a few weeks ago, but surely Grajales would be ready and more prepared this time around.

"I had a lot of confidence going into that match," Ramos recalled, "because I had beat him beforehand. But, I knew that he wanted to prove something. But it was a really fast match."

In the first period, Grajales won by decision and shut Tony out on the scoreboard with a 2-0 decision.

As he came into the second period, Tony stormed back with a variety of scoring attacks and he took a decisive 5-3 victory.

When the break ended, and the third period was to begin, it would be another winner-take-all period and Tony knew he would have to stay offensive and on the attack to put himself in position to win. His only concern, of course, would be making sure his positions were secure when the opportunities presented themselves.

At the 00:53 mark of the third period "I shot in on a double-leg," Ramos said. "I picked him up and put him to the mat and got the touch fall." Tony would raise himself from Grajales and flex his muscles a bit in excitement for another big win against a very strong and top competitor.

"That win," Ramos said, "really got the ball rolling for me. That was the second round of the tournament and I started feeling really good from there."

For the third round, Tony took on Lee Munster—another native of Illinois. Had Tony stayed in the Fox Lake area, he and Munster may have been teammates at Grant High School.

"We did train together at one point," Ramos said. "So I kind of knew what to expect from him—he would be a strong and tough opponent who would be hard to get to and when I had my opportunities to get to my offense, I needed to score."

Tony was able to put the match away quickly and dismiss Munster in two periods, 3-2, 6-3.

In order for Tony to make the championship pool, however, he would first have to overcome Arizona's John Estrada, a freshman state runner-up and current sophomore state champion from Hayden High School. Estrada also trained with the Sunkist Wrestling Club outside of his high school's club—so Tony had another seasoned wrestler with a variety of skills that he would have to contend with.

Once the match began, however, it was all Tony as far as control. At the 1:38 point in the first period, Tony caught Estrada and won by fall.

Tony was now in the finals pool and would have to win his first match to have a shot at the Cadet championship.

First up was a Pennsylvania standout, Josh Kindig. Similar to two of the three previous opponents, Munster excluded, Kindig was bigger, physically, than Tony. Kindig, coached by his father, attended Blue Mountain High School in Schuylkill Haven and was a seasoned freestyle and Greco-Roman wrestler. Just that past season he had been a state qualifier, but did not place.

"This match is what would start me and Kindig's rivalry," Ramos said. "He was a tough competitor from Pennsylvania and Frankie knew his coach."

For the first period, Kindig outscored Tony by earning a takedown and scoring off Tony's shot with a crotch-lift. Kindig won a 3-0 decision at the first period's conclusion.

In the second, Tony worked into his positions and responded with two takedowns of his own and a two-point turn for the 4-0 shutout. With one period left, Tony needed a strong performance to push himself into the finals. When the match had ended, Tony had scored two more takedowns and another shutout for a 2-0 decision and an opportunity to win a FILA national championship.

"I think what helped is that, against Kindig, I was able to get to my offense better than others against him," Ramos said. "Maybe I had a little more power, I don't know, but I always felt that I could get in on his legs and did that match. He was a guy who liked to wrestle on the outside and maybe struggled with more technical guys. I think maybe I pressured him a little bit and made him uncomfortable."

In the opening round of the round-robin, Tony would have to wrestle fellow Illinoisan, Ellis Coleman. It would take but two periods to extinguish the Oak Park native by decision, 1-0, 1-1.

"Me and Ellis always battled," Ramos said, "and those close scores showed it. He is a kid that I was very familiar with and who was very familiar with me, but I was always able to find a way to win those matches—and this was the closest match I think we ever had. He was so tough as a competitor and had a lot of confidence in himself like I did, so it was about going out there and finding ways to win. I wasn't going to go out there and try to intimidate this guy because he believed that he could win. I had to wrestle smart and hard and I did."

That win gave Tony a walkover with Grajales from his previous win by fall and launched him into the championship match against Iowa's Dylan Carew.

Having come off a standout freshman campaign that ended with Carew wining the Iowa state championship at 103 pounds for Iowa City West

High School, and he had already won the FILA Cadet Greco-Roman championship a few days earlier, he was now looking to add a second title to his week in Evanston. His coach, a former University of Iowa Hawkeye and 1991 NCAA National Champion, two-time All-American, Mark Reiland, would have him ready for the always forward and aggressive Tony Ramos.

"Me and Carew grew up competing against each other and I knew he was good on the upper-body and had headlocks," Ramos said. "So we talked about staying on the legs. He could explode at any time and score points. The game plan was to stay out of his tie-ups and stay out of the upper-body stuff and make sure that I stay on his legs and finish with high-percentage finishes."

What made this match-up a greater challenge for Tony was that he and Israel had been working on his hand fighting and this match-up would put his practice into reality.

"At this time," Ramos said, "me and Izzy had been working on a lot of hand fighting. I had been good from the outside, but it was about being able to get to the inside to create openings and get to my angles. And that was what I had to do with Carew in order to beat him."

In the championship match, Tony defeated Carew, 2-0, in the first period by way of two takedowns where Tony had to fight to keep his position for more high-percentage finishes.

Unfortunately, in the second period, the tide turned in Carew's favor and he got the best of Tony and earned a 2-1 decision. This left, yet again, Tony having to find a way to win in the third in order to capture the FILA Cadet national championship.

In the third period, with the spotlight on him, the pressure high, and everything on the line, Tony was relaxed and calm and himself—he was aggressive and on the offensive. By the conclusion of the period and the match, Tony claimed a dominant 3-0 decision and the FILA Cadet national championship.

Tony had now, in just about a span of fifteen days, wrestled the top competitors in the country, one weight class above his brother's liking, as he was undefeated.

"This tournament was such a grind," Ramos said. "I think I had at least a state champion or someone pretty highly ranked or regarded every single round."

And, with that tournament won—that was two.

The next goal would be in Fargo, North Dakota, in July. Until then, Tony trained with Israel four days a week and attended North's club, Mat Rats, on Monday and Wednesday nights as well.

When it was time for the Illinois Freestyle State Championships, it was more of a formality than anything else for Tony. He had already qualified through the FILA Cadet national championship, but he wanted to be with his team and help the other guys through the tournament. He had not forgotten what he and Coach Hahn had spoken about in regard to him being a leader—so he did his part by winning, spending time with and being closer to his teammates.

WHEN THE FARGO NATIONAL CHAMPIONSHIPS
finally came, Tony was ready. He had a new swagger about himself and he was confident and relaxed in his wrestling. He had already seen everyone in his bracket and felt as if he should, if he wrestled as he had, be in the finals and win. Unfortunately, Tony's win streak would be halted in the Fargo Dome against Pennsylvania's Jordan Oliver.

"It was a real close match," Ramos remembered. "Oliver hit me with a slide-by—he's pretty good at shucking guys past him. We knew it was coming, we knew how he wrestled, but I got out of position. He got the takedown and won that period, 2-0. In the second period, he won 1-1 on, I think, a push-out. But I didn't do enough to open him up and score points. But that's where me and Oliver started to learn about each other and realized that we're both really tough competitors. He was no slouch. I think it was a tough and respected match between the two of us."

In the wrestle-backs to determine if Tony wrestled for third or fifth place, he had to wrestle New York's Ian Paddock. In the end, Tony earned a fifth place finish and All-American honors.

However, placing above Tony in Fargo would be wrestlers that he had already beaten, and this did not sit well with him.

"I was upset," Ramos commented. "The year before I took second and I had pretty high expectations on going in there and winning a Fargo title—that was the goal. It's frustrating that guys that I had placed higher than or beat in other pools now placed higher here, so I didn't have a good taste in my mouth after that. I needed to improve."

In his desire to further develop, Tony had to reflect and listen to what Israel and Frank and Coach Hahn were telling him. "I think the biggest thing I learned was that when things go bad, I can't whine or pout; I have to pick my head up and go out there and finish what I started. Fifth was the best I that I could do after losing those two matches, so I had to go out there and compete—even if it wasn't what I wanted or what I was expecting to do."

Of course, after he had placed fifth, Frank was quick to point out and give him grief about how had he listened to him about the weight, he would have won it. Also, Frank twisted the knife in Tony's back when he pointed out that one year prior Vince was in the national championship match. This only infuriated Tony—and Tony would not be outdone.

Unfortunately, all Tony had in his arsenal was a set of golf clubs that he had won in a bet earlier that winter—and he had no problem throwing those back in Frank's face. But, by now, it did not matter and Tony knew that—all of that was well behind him. In Frank's eyes, Tony had not listened and failed and Frank did exactly what he said he would do. "I told him," Defilippis said, "you were wrong. Now just tell me I was right." But Tony refused. Instead, he verbally pushed at Frank and tried to find a way, some way, to irritate him—but nothing worked.

I'm glad I wrestled up," Ramos said. "Had I gone down just to win, I wouldn't have faced the top competition like I did. I wanted to go where the toughest competition was and really make my name stand out. If I could do that, then I could prove to people that I was as good as I thought I was. In the end, it was what I needed. But at the time, it was not what I wanted."

Tony took his spring season very seriously. He had wrestled in the four top tournaments, won three of them, and placed in the other—"I wanted four championships," Ramos said, "but now it was time to train and get ready for the upcoming season, my sophomore season."

CHAPTER 16
WORKING WITH THE WEIGHT

"To see all the effort that I had been putting in all summer long really pay off so early, and to prove to all the critics and all of the country that I was the best guy and you better watch out."

• *Tony Ramos*

TONY'S SOPHOMORE SEASON OPENED IN THE same fashion as his freshman campaign. He would wrestle in Glenbard North's gymnasium on opening night in the Fulk Quad, and then take his 3-0 record into the Conant tournament that Friday and Saturday in Hoffmann Estates.

Additionally, as he had done the previous season, he was fighting with Frank in regard to his weight. When the season opened, Tony was happy and healthy and all smiles at 119. He had proven himself that past spring and summer and wanted to once again prove everyone wrong, especially Frank—he wanted to prove that he was big and strong enough to wrestle with heavier and stronger opponents. When he had wrestled that past spring, he was walking around a little over 125 pounds; therefore, as he wrestled at 119, he was not truly cutting weight and he was eating whatever he wanted and he felt good. But on that, he and Frank disagreed fantastically and both were very vocal about their stance.

"I never wanted to cut weight," Ramos laughed. "I hated it. I felt 119 was tougher and I wanted to wrestle tougher competition. But, for the team, it was best for me to go down to 112, and it was truly best for me, so that would eventually happen. But I was never a fan of cutting weight and I just didn't want to do it."

To Frank, Tony was just too small at 119; however, to Tony, his size had nothing to do with it. "Strength never bothered me," Ramos said. "I think through my whole career I've never felt overpowered or outmanned. I've been working out since I was young—around sixth grade I started on a weight plan—so I kind of had a jump start on some of the these kids who don't start until they get into high school. So, I never really felt overpowered and never looked at that being something I had to worry about. Coach Hahn always said that 'Strength is the great equalizer in wrestling,' and he was right. I felt strong, so it would come down to technique and want."

In addition to Tony, the team was coming off a great run from last season and all of their sophomores were now seasoned juniors. The Chicago Sun-Times High School Wrestling Preview had Glenbard North as the preseason favorite for winning the state championship. Carl Sandburg sat at number three and Montini would be listed as the four. Once again, Neuqua Valley would hold a five rating; Glenbard North also had six wrestlers ranked in the state's top ten in their respective weight class.

Therefore, Tony wrestling at 112 really did solidify the team throughout the season and his drop would be part of other wrestlers dropping a weight for a stronger team. But, as the season opened, Tony, and a few others, were not quite ready for the weight cut.

Therefore, regardless of the banter with Frank, Tony would stay at 119 pounds and enter his first tournament, the C.O. Feutz Wrestling Classic. The tournament was said to have no seeds and was a blind draw; however, as should have been done and was, Tony was opposite of the wrestler that he wanted to face: Oak Park-River Forest standout, Ellis Coleman.

Last year in the Individual State Championships, Tony and Coleman had wrestled in the quarterfinals. Tony dominated that match by a 16-3 major decision. And, when that season's tournament opened, Tony did what he did best; he dominated matches and scored points. After he received an opening round bye, he would defeat Jacob Bugajski of DeLaSalle by fall in 2:47 and then, in the semifinals, he wore down and ultimately pinned Providence Catholic's Jake Wojcik in 5:59.

Now in the finals, Tony would face Coleman for the championship. For Coleman, he had advanced through the bottom half of the bracket by fall, major decision, and another fall. He was a seasoned wrestler, and he wanted the match-up with Tony to showcase his talents.

When the finals began, Tony dominated Coleman all around. He would score seemingly at will and, in the end, he would walk away with a 9-2 decision and his first tournament championship of the new season.

As a team, Glenbard won the tournament with 285 points. They had seven finalists, four champions, five thirds, and two fourth place finishers. The runner-up team, Oak Park-River Forest, scored 174 points and had four finalists and one champion. In the preseason rankings, OPRF was rated number nine. Providence Catholic placed third at Conant, but a number of their wrestlers were still playing football—their preseason rank was number six.

With a 6-0 record for Tony, and the season young but very much well underway, Glenbard North was thriving in the practice room and on the competition mat. And, as the Walsh Jesuit Ironman was slowly becoming closer and closer, Frank sat his brother down one more time and explained to him the importance of that tournament, and he would also throw into the conversation a reminder about the bet that they had made; the Ironman would have to be won.

"Well, there was never really a discussion on what I was going to do," Ramos said. "It was pretty much Frankie sitting me down and saying this is what you're going to do. I wish there had been more talking, but every time I said, 'Okay, but I think…,' Frankie would cut me off and say, 'Yeah, but this is what's best for you. This is what you're going to do.'"

For Tony, he knew that he would eventually drop to 112 pounds and the Ironman would be the perfect time. He knew that at the big tournaments wrestlers wrestle their weight and he would be no different, but he still wanted more of a voice in the discussions.

THE LAST TIME GLENBARD NORTH ENTERED THE

prestigious Walsh Jesuit Ironman tournament, in Ohio, it was 1998, Frank's senior year. Since then, the Panthers had not returned; specifically, it was a very costly tournament to enter in addition to the team and tournament commitments North already had on their schedule. Unfortunately, it had not fit the budget or the schedule.

Since Vince's freshman year, Frank had been trying to convince head coach Mark Hahn to re-enter the tournament. Hahn's response was simple, "If you can raise the money, then we can make the trip."

Frank would do one better, he would front the money needed for the tournament that Glenbard could not afford. Once the money issue was no longer an issue, North requested entrance and received their invitation for the second week of December.

Of course, North's national rating had been slowly moving up and, that season, they had a mid-season national rating in W.I.N. magazine at number-sixteen. The only other Illinois schools ahead of them nationally were number-three Orland Park Carl Sandburg, number-eleven Montini Catholic, and number-fourteen Chicago St. Rita. Therefore, performing well at the Ironman would give more national exposure to an already credible program, but it would also give positive exposure to North's wrestlers as well.

Aside from his normal morning and afternoon practice at North, Tony was getting some extra mat time with his club coach, Israel. "It was hard going from our practices and then going over by Izzy," Ramos admitted. "But we did a few extra sessions to make sure I was doing some of the little things in the little areas to make sure I was fine-tuned and ready."

At North, the wrestling room was extremely intense for the beginning of December. "For me," Ramos said, "I was more amped up that week than any other week, aside from the state tournament, because this was like the state tournament—this was huge. The best guys and the best teams in the country were all coming to one tournament to see who really was the number-one guy—and I believed that I was the number-one guy at 112 pounds, and now I was given the opportunity to show it."

Even with the Ironman being Tony's first real cut to 112 pounds, he was weighing in around 116 and 117 pounds when he was wrestling 119. The only difference would be the mental aspect of the cut and adjusting a few phases of his eating habits.

"In regard to the weight cut," Ramos said, "it was probably one of the best weight cuts I ever had in high school. My weight was fine all week long, and even after weigh-ins I felt really good."

Intermatwrestle.com had published a weight class by weight class breakdown of the entire tournament that was written by OhioWrestlingSite.com. Their insight was rather enlightening in relationship to how the tournament had concluded. Here was the analysis of the 112-pound bracket:

This is easily the most wide-open weight class of the tournament. Consider that the #13 seed (Neibert) actually defeated the #1 (Sergent) seed less than two weeks ago.

The top ranked Ohio wrestler in Division I, Bo Touris, will face the equivalent of the state tournament in December on his side of the bracket. He'll be pitted against the dangerous Kyle Lang in the quarterfinals and most likely against state champ Steve Mitcheff in the semis (in theory—there are no sure things at this tournament). Mitcheff defeated Touris at state last year, avenging a prior loss at Brecksville.

It's my belief that Tony Ramos of Glenbard North, IL, is the best wrestler in this weight class. Ramos placed only 5th at Cadet National freestyle last year—but that is very deceptive, as he was the third best in his weight but in the far tougher pool. However, Ramos looks to have the toughest draw of the tournament—he'll have to beat a Cadet National Finalist (Villalonga) just to reach the quarterfinals!

There are a number of wrestlers in this wide-open weight who could "shake up" the bracket. The first is #13 seed Zach Neibert of Graham. Ironically, Neibert actually defeated the #1 seeded Sergent in an All-Star match last weekend, but earned the #13 seed. Neibert (who placed 6th at state) was a very light 103 this year, but is now a full 112. The transfer to Graham has helped him gain David Taylor as a workout partner among others. Neibert's 2nd round match with state runner-up Danny Genetin of Masssillon Perry on Friday night should be one of the highlights of Friday night.

Look for Chris Villalonga of Blair Academy to far outperform his #12 seed; in fact, he is a threat to beat anyone at this weight. Villalonga dominated his pool in reaching the finals of Cadet Nationals—where he was Stieber's final victim. Unseeded freshman Nick Sulzer of St. Edward had a nice showing in Fargo, could be a surprise place-winner.

OWS Projection: Tony Ramos over Bo Touris.

Dark Horse Picks: Zach Neibert, Chris Villalonga, Nick Sulzer.

After weigh-ins, and after some brackets had to be re-drawn and configured, North's coaches gathered, checked the final brackets, conversed, and then went through their tournament warm-up with their wrestlers. For Tony, his bracket changed a little; however, he would earn the number-five seed in his weight class and be the twenty-first bout called on the day. In his corner would be Frank and varsity assistant head coach, Chris Edwards, Tony's standard cornering duo.

In the opening round, Tony defeated freshman Kyle Bratke of Parkersburg, West Virginia, by fall in 1:49. As he advanced into his next match against the number-thirteen seed, sophomore Zach Neibert of Graham, Ohio, Tony would again dominate the match, this time by an 8-4 decision.

Now into the quarterfinal round, Tony had to wrestle a junior out of Perry, Ohio, named Danny Genetin. Tony would rack up a variety of points and advanced with a 12-4 major decision. He was now only two matches away from an Ironman championship.

Cody Kelly, a sophomore from Reynolds, Pennsylvania, would be the only person between Tony and him reaching the finals. In the quarterfinals, Kelly defeated the tournament's number-one seed and now looked to be again be thinking upset with Tony. But, Tony knew the time and the work that he had put in, and he was not going to be denied. By the time the match was concluded, Tony had left no doubt and defeated Kelly by an 11-5 decision that displayed an array of takedowns from a variety of positions.

Now in the finals, Tony would have to square off against a freshman wrestler from one of the top programs in the country and, at that time, Blair Academy, New Jersey, had been rated the number-two high school team in the United States. The match-up did not surprise many of the more knowledgeable fans who followed and knew the sport well. But Chris Villalonga, the number-twelve seed, had wrestled tight matches in his quarterfinal and semifinal victories—comparably, Tony who had separated himself from his opponents. However, Villalonga's ability to keep matches close had helped him reach the finals in Fargo and now at the Ironman. For Tony, who had not allowed a close match, it was going to be an interesting match-up to see if Villalonga could keep the score close enough to pull off a win at the end. Or, if Tony would be able to open the match up and create too much of a separation.

As for Tony, both he and Villalonga were no strangers to one another. "I knew him from when we were younger," Ramos said. "I think one of those preseason nationals in Kansas or something, but I used to beat him up pretty good. I knew that on top he was a good leg rider and he was a tough competitor. He's a Blair kid, so he's tough, and I knew what I was in for—but I knew that I could beat him because I beat him up [before], so I wasn't too concerned about it."

In regard to the match strategy, Tony and his coaches talked about whether or not they would go into the down position knowing how strong Villalonga was on top. "Frankie told me that if I do end up on the bottom or choose down, then I need to get up right away and not let him cling on and have opportunities from there," Ramos remembered. "But we were going to let the match dictate the position depending on where things were at. I felt good in any position, so I wasn't worried about where things would end up."

Upon introductions and the opening whistle, Tony was poised and confident and quickly into his stance and motion. Villalonga, long in stature, opened in a low stance, down on his left knee to protect himself, and was looking to use his length by staying in a square stance as Tony faked with level changes and head slaps.

Villalonga, at the start, seemed more passive, and Tony, throughout, appeared to be the same aggressive forward wrestler he had been all tournament. When the two finally locked up, Tony attempted to hit a left-handed elbow slide, which Villalonga would circle away from. After he circled back, Villalonga reached the edge of the mat and, about thirty seconds into the period, he took his first shot. It would be low ankle attempt at Tony's right foot, but Tony blocked with a lower shot. Here, Villalonga had Tony on the edge of the mat with his own back out of bounds with an underhook on his left side. Tony, aggressive, continued to drive into his opponent and, once Villalonga went to a right-armed whizzer on Tony's left arm, his left foot came up and Tony dropped down on an ankle pick. Unfortunately, for Tony, they would be out of bounds and head back to the center of the mat with no points awarded.

Again, as the whistle blew, Tony would motion and level change and Villalonga would attempt that low ankle snatch to Tony's right leg again—to no avail. Tony would continue his left-handed tie on the head and each would hand fight for position with the other hand—Tony's right, Villalonga's left.

Then, suddenly, as Tony felt Villalonga pressuring into him, he would hit his elbow slide from his left side tie and be in on Villalonga's right leg. As Villalonga fell to his hands, he tried to kick out, but Tony secured the ankle and, as the much longer Villalonga found his way to his feet, Tony switched over, dropped to a double-leg and drove across the body to his left as Villalonga circled to defend him. Tony would end up with Villalonga's left leg in a single-leg position as he pulled it in with his right hand and Villalonga fought to control Tony's left hand.

Tony, who remained patient, did not rush or force the takedown; on the contrary, the sophomore showed his physicality and persistence as he pulled the leg in and calmly fought the position. Patiently, Tony secured the leg between his own legs, changed his levels and freed his left hand before he tackled Villalonga on the edge of the mat to solidify his takedown and 2-0 advantage in the championship match.

In the top position, Tony conceded the escape point and the match was now 2-1. Immediately, Tony continued to stalk the taller freshman and, as they came to the edge of the mat, again, Tony attempted his elbow slide—but he was unable to secure anything that time around.

Forward motion and forward pressure continued from Tony and he seemingly became anxious and fired in on an open double-leg. Villalonga would sprawl and circle and, while on the edge of the mat, tried to secure a takedown by underhooking Tony and dragging his feet; however, Tony was able to square up his body and position himself to where no control was given and no score was awarded.

The first period ended with physical ties as the Illinoisan stalked his Jersey opponent and attempted a shot as time expired.

Villalonga chose down, escaped, and the second period would not be anything more than a hand fight and position battle. However, with fifteen seconds left in the period, Villalonga would be hit with his first stalling warning of the match.

In the third, now with a 2-2 score, Tony chose the down position and, when the whistle blew, the longer Villalonga would go to his cross-collar ride and work to ride Tony out. And as Tony moved to create space and tried to work to his feet, Villalonga worked his leg in with a right-hand half and rolled Tony while he looked for back points on top. As the two came over through the roll, Villalonga had Tony in danger; however, Tony was able to fight to keep his back at ninety-degrees and not force the referee's count for back points. In that, Tony used his right hand to peel the half and go flat, back to his stomach. Without delay, Tony needed an escape to take control of the match and remove himself from any further danger. But the younger and longer freshman was posing great problems for the sophomore in the referee's position.

Now with his right leg in, Villalonga worked a half on Tony's left side as he fought to force his left leg in as well. Tony fought and found his way to the edge of the circle and, with 1:15 left, they wrestled out of bounds and returned to the center for a restart.

From Tony's corner, Frank was shouting, "First move and you're out! Don't wait for him!"

The referee motioned to put Tony back in the down position, but Tony's nose was bleeding; he was sent to his corner for clean-up. In his corner, Edwards and Frank instructed Tony on how he needed to move off the bottom while his nose was being worked on. The way that period was going, Tony's bloody nose happened at a very opportune time for Tony to gather himself, receive some technical advice, and then come back with a more focused start off the whistle.

As the match resumed, Villalonga covered the left side and, as Tony stood up, Villalonga could not return or stay behind him; Tony would cut through and receive his escape point. The two wrestlers then found themselves in an over-under position. The score would be a 3-2 advantage for Tony and, as he blocked in the crotch not wanting to be in that position, Villalonga drove him out of bounds.

"One I got that fresh start," Ramos said, "I wasn't going to let that happen again. I saw what he did—how he wanted to [ride]—and I just came up quicker and in better position and scored my one."

With one minute remaining, Villalonga was going to have to open up and, off the restart, his levels and motions became more offensive as he needed to score. Tony, who had attacked the entire match, had gone to a more defensive style and looked to hand fight and allow his defense to now win him the match.

Unfortunately for Villalonga, Tony kept his position in the center of the mat and invited the longer wrestler to find a way to get underneath him—a very difficult task. Villalonga motioned and tried to bait Tony to step toward him, but it never happened. The sophomore, disciplined to his strategy, knew that he did not have to force anything and, if he stayed low and in a strong position in the center of them mat, he knew Villalonga had to take all of the risks in the final thirty-five seconds.

When Villalonga finally shot in for an open double, Tony defended; but, Villalonga now positioned himself into an over-under and Tony immediately began to block in the crotch just as he had done earlier in the period. Tony did not want to allow the longer freshman an opportunity to open him up and put him in danger, so the position battle ensued.

At the twenty-second mark, Tony, being draped over by Villalonga when Tony went to his two-on-one, had Villalonga's left arm over his head, weighing down, and in control of the position. Soon, however, Villalonga had to release Tony's head with his left hand if he was going to attack. What looked to be an unfavorable position seconds before became very favorable for Tony in those final moments.

Suddenly, as match reached its final ten seconds, Villalonga attempted an ankle sweep and Tony, caught off balance, stumbled backward. Fortunately, for Tony, he was able to regroup and regain his balance as the two ended up in the center of the mat. And, as Villalonga pressured forward, Tony, backing up, hit an elbow slide, and circled. When Villalonga came back toward him, Villalonga took another open double and got in deep on Tony with time about to expire.

Tony sprawled his hips and fought the position as they were neutral and time expired. Tony won a 3-2 decision and stomped back to the mat's center to have his hand raised as he claimed his first Ironman championship.

"I was freakin' excited when I won," Ramos said. "To see all the effort that I had been putting in all summer long really pay off so early, and to prove to all the critics and all of the country that I was the best guy and you better watch out. All of the best guys were there and that put me in position for the ASICS All-American Team that year. But there was still much to improve on. I only won the match 3-2, so I obviously needed bottom work and leg defense as well as getting into more opportunities to score."

But, overall, Tony knew, though short-lived, the importance of the tournament and what he had accomplished. "I wrestled some big-time kids and put up some big scores against them," Ramos said. "I mean, other than Fargo for high school, the Ironman is the premier tournament to win."

With that win, Tony became Glenbard North's first Ironman champion in the program's storied history, and he now was one step closer to winning his bet with Frank.

CHAPTER 17
THE LONGEST LESSON EVER LEARNED

"If he said you're going to have to run for being a fat ass, you're going to have to run."

• *Frank Defilippis*
Ramos' brother

AS THE SECOND HALF OF THE SEASON WAS underway, and each wrestler had to maintain his declared weight class, some of the wrestlers were coming in really heavy on Mondays and everything suffered because of it. To no surprise, since those wrestlers were more concerned about cutting weight, their technique and overall practices were impacted greatly. The coaching staff knew that something had to change and it had to change fast if each workout was going to be beneficial for the team.

For Tony, he was now wrestling at 112, but he was coming in on a Monday between 125 and 130—much heavier than when he was wrestling 119. Obviously, this was too much weight and not enough weekend discipline to make his workouts in the wrestling room matter.

Therefore, when Monday weigh-ins after practice started to worsen, a plan was implemented by Hahn and the coaching staff. The plan was simple:

> There would be an allowance of five pounds over scratch for each wrestler—it would go down one pound per day. But, for each ounce a wrestler was over the allowance, he had one lap on the indoor track. Therefore, if an athlete was one pound over the allowance, then he had ten laps—that was equivalent to one mile. And all weigh-ins occurred before practice each day.

The first day there were more than a few wrestlers on the track as the coaches, clipboards in hand, counted each lap assigned to each wrestler. It was not an ideal situation for the coaches, but the plan was put into effect and the staff was going to be committed to it no matter what.

As each day brought runners, some new and some the same, Tony's final lesson would be the one that stuck with him years after.

Almost immediately after the allowance was *gifted* to the team, and those overweight had been reprimanded, including Tony, Tony decided one Thursday night to just balloon up. The team was off that weekend and Tony just decided to indulge himself.

"I didn't care," Tony admitted. "I was struggling bad holding my weight because I hated cutting weight and I hadn't committed to a diet, so I was like, *I'm a sophomore, there's no way [Hahn is] going to have me run all these laps.*"

Of course, as Vince walked by and saw Tony at the table eating late that night, he told him, "You better not get too heavy. You know you'll have to run for being over."

"Shut up," was Tony's reply. Then he brushed his hand in the air, which was still holding some food, as if to say, "Just keep moving along." Arrogantly, Tony continued while chewing, "Get out of here. I'll be fine. Just worry about yourself."

Soon after Vince saw Tony, Frank came downstairs and saw Tony eating. He did a few minor chores around the kitchen and then the laundry room and then looked back and saw Tony was still eating. Frank walked past Tony a second time and told him, "You know Coach Hahn don't fuck around. If he said you're going to have to run for being a fat ass, you're going to have to run."

To Frank, Tony did not say much. He just stared at him and took another bite and just kept chewing and staring until Frank turned around, laughed and went back upstairs.

As Friday and the weight check came, Tony had to step on the scale in front of Hahn—he was 8.8 pounds over the five-pound allowance. He looked up and smiled and tried to make a joke of it; however, Hahn was not amused. Hahn looked at Tony in a disgusted manner and said, "Really, Tone? Really? That's 88 laps."

"My heart dropped," Ramos recalled. "I looked at Hahn and said, 'That's like a half marathon.'"

The only response Hahn had was, "You're going to run all those laps after tomorrow's morning workout." Then Hahn turned around and walked up to practice.

When Saturday morning came, and Tony had the night to let it all sink in, he still believed that there was no way he was going to be expected to run all those laps. Tony believed that nobody, no sane individual, would make him do that. He just figured he would have do a few laps to be taught a lesson, and then Hahn would allow him to go home. There was, after all, still an afternoon practice for the team.

"When we ended our morning circuit," Ramos said, "we went out to the fieldhouse for a two-lap cooldown. When [the team] finished, Hahn looked at me and told me to just keep running. He sat against the wall, in the dark, with his clipboard, and counted every single lap. I was thinking that if I ran slow enough, he'd just get so irritated with me that he'd let me go after a few. But all he said to me was, 'I got all day, Tiger.'"

Hahn's stance was simple: "There was no way [Tony] was not going to run all those laps—the whole weight program would've been thrown out the window because no one would've taken it seriously. Besides, I wasn't going to let that little pain in the ass get away with it. He needed to learn a lesson and be made an example of."

"Eventually," Ramos remembered, "I started to realize that I wasn't leaving, so I picked it up a bit. I knew I just better get this done and over with. As I got half-way through I thought he would just let me go—but he didn't. When I was getting toward the end, I started seeing the guys coming back for the afternoon workout, and then I had to go through that too."

Obviously, Hahn's position was one of discipline and that Tony better find a way to control himself and control his weight—there would be no shortcuts for anyone, Hahn included.

"That day," Tony said, "Hahn had to make a tough choice because he had to sit there with me. He not only showed me who the boss was, but he showed me that he was invested and if I didn't discipline myself, there would be consequences—and the worse consequences might be on the mat and not [on] the track. That lesson has always stuck with me and reminded me of my choices and where they can take me, both good and bad."

CHAPTER 18
BOOED AND SNUBBED

"I knew the flexing cost me, and I was really pissed about it."

• *Tony Ramos*

BY THE TIME TONY HAD "LEARNED" HOW TO control his weight in a more manageable way, the team was headed up to the Clash High School National Duals where he would take his number-one ranking, and it would be tested against some of the best wrestlers from some of the best teams in the country. True to his character, Tony welcomed the challenge and looked forward to the competition. The Ironman took place at the beginning of December, and now the Clash closed out the month, the first half of the season, and brought the season into the New Year.

Tony's practice time was sharp and focused and, more than others knew, he was beginning to come out of his shell and into his personality. Tony was generally relaxed off the mat and he enjoyed joking around, but he had a new air about him—and a much more comfortable and goofy side was becoming more apparent to the coaches and the rest of the team.

Unfortunately, in that stage, Tony made a mistake that almost cost him dearly. He decided that he would play a prank on one of the program's largest coaches, and the one with the smallest tolerance for stupidity.

Jeff Cherry was a Glenbard North graduate and best friends with head coach Mark Hahn. The two had been joined at the hip since they were children and their friendship had only grown stronger over the years. When Hahn accepted the head wrestling job in 1988, Cherry was already coaching in the school's football program—he coached the varsity linebackers and was the defensive coordinator—and that winter he agreed to coach the Junior Varsity II team for Hahn.

Over time, Cherry had developed a reputation that was very tough love and, mostly, just tough. He did not smile very often, but he was one of the funniest coaches on staff. When he did smile, everyone laughed.

He was educated in the sport and had a simple philosophy from the top position: "If the head is down: half. If the head is up: cross-face." To Cherry, that solved all problems for the top man. He was not one for flashy wrestling and he held to the tenet that the best way to wrestle was to just pin the opponent and get off the mat.

Knowing all of this, and for whatever reason, Tony chose to pick a moment with Cherry for a prank. That moment involved Cherry, a chair, and Cherry's attempt to sit down—Tony saw this as the opportune time for a good laugh. The prank was one of the oldest in the books: pull the chair out from underneath the person who tried to sit on it and, when he fell down to the ground on his back side, point and laugh. A classic.

However, as the prank was unfolding, Frank watched in amazement from a distance—he had no idea why or what his youngest brother was doing. Then he saw it all unfold.

"It was like it was all in slow motion," Defilippis said, "and there was nothing I could do about it. I thought [Cherry] was going to kill him."

When Cherry, who had already had a heart attack and wore a pacemaker, hit the floor, Tony pointed and laughed. Then, it all set in and Tony slowly backed away when he realized how not funny it was to Cherry. Frank ran to Tony's rescue.

Cherry was not amused. As for the wrestlers on the team that were there, they were not only astonished by the move, but they felt that it crossed a line. It was one thing to play a prank in the confines of the wrestling room where it was only the team, but it was another thing to openly embarrass a coach in public. Tony's actions were frowned upon by a number of the older wrestlers.

When Cherry got up and saw that it was Tony, he had some very brief and very choice words for him. Frank, when he finally arrived at the scene, was immediately apologizing and telling his brother to do the same. With a smile, Tony appeased Frank, but Cherry was not accepting of his words and he was not amused with the humor.

For Tony, he saw it as a small innocent prank and that was just who he was and what he did. When he came into the coaches' office to again apologize, Cherry just looked at him and listened, said nothing, and just motioned his head up to let Tony know that he heard him.

"We almost had one less state champion," Cherry said in response to the situation—and that was the extent of his comments.

ONCE UP IN MINNESOTA, TONY WOULD HAVE THE
attention he enjoyed and a prank-free focus as the Clash was always a business trip for the team. "I knew that every time that we were heading to the Clash," Ramos said, "I had to be focused that week on working and doing the right things."

The fans would be asking, "Where is that Ramos kid?" and his name would be highlighted by the announcer during introductions as one of the wrestlers to watch.

North was given the number-four seed by the organizers of the tournament and occupied the top half of the bracket that saw Apple Valley, Minnesota, at the bottom and the number-five seed.

What most Clash-goers wanted to see was the battle between the two programs and the intensity of the coaches. Since the inception of the tournament, the duals between these two schools had been nothing less than a street fight that had two officials who tried to maintain as much control as possible—there was a rivalry and everyone, the coaches, the fans, the wrestlers, they all loved it and they all looked forward to it. There would be two matches prior to the finals of the pool, so Tony and the team had to be focused.

Glenbard opened up with the number-six 1A team in North Dakota, Minot High School. The Panthers wasted little time as they beat up the Magicians 55-15; Tony defeated Mark Pierson by a 14-6 major decision.

Advancing into the championship semifinals, Glenbard had Sedro-Woolley, Washington. Sedro-Woolley was the number-one rated team in Washington's class 3A and, at the time, North was the number-two rated team in Illinois' class 2A. Therefore, as anticipated, Tony had a much stronger opponent in Derek Crouter.

Crouter, the number-one ranked wrestler in Washington, already a two-time state champion, came out strong against the nation's number-one wrestler. Tony, as had been his modus operandi with more high profile wrestlers, was score, concede the escape, escape on his own, give away another escape, and the score would show a 3-2 victory for him. Of course, in the process, Tony would never relinquish his physicality and pace of the match and, thus, he was well in control of those matches from the start.

As for the team, Glenbard would take down the Cubs by a 46-20 score and set up the anticipated finals match-up in the pool. North would now face Minnesota's most dominant program and number-one rated team, the Apple Valley Eagles.

When the match came, fans scooted over in the bleachers to watch the center mats and have prime seating. For Apple Valley, being a Minnesota team, they were allowed to have seventh and eighth-graders on their team as per their state's bylaws and regulations. For Tony, at 112 pounds, he would have the returning Minnesota state champion, Destin McCauley, who had posted a 43-3 record in that same season as a seventh-grader. Now in eighth grade, and a nationally ranked wrestler—a top twenty-five candidate—the match-up was one that held the interest of all in attendance.

There were no pleasantries when both teams met in the middle of the mat to shake hands; the tone of the dual was set early. The same was true in the match-up between Tony and McCauley.

"That match was big for me," Ramos remembered. "There was so much talk about McCauley and how he was going to be a six-time Minnesota state champion, and we had a good relationship as family friends—so I knew him and he knew me. But I wanted to go out there, in his home state, and with a very pro-McCauley crowd, and against a school like Apple Valley, I wanted to win. I was very excited to have that opportunity."

The first period of the match would be an aggressive and strategic play by each wrestler; in essence, feeling out the other's style and strengths while trying to wear the other down. When the second period came, McCauley chose down and escaped; the period ended with him leading, 1-0. When the third period began, Tony chose down, escaped, and the match was where it was seemingly expected to be at by that point, a 1-1 tie.

Additionally, the Minnesota crowd had their overwhelming favorite in McCauley and wanted Tony hit for unnecessary roughness for his strong head ties, or when they went out of bounds and it ended in an extra shove or snap. McCauley, however, did not seem to mind, nor did he back down. The tensions were rising and third period was slowly reaching the halfway point.

As the one-minute mark in the final period passed, the intensity and willingness to open up and take chances by both wrestlers began in a much stronger and wildly exciting fashion.

With about fifteen seconds left before overtime, McCauley saw an opening and took a strong shot in on Tony. He would get to Tony's left leg and the scramble was immediately on. The crowd, motioning excitement in their repositioning of heads and eyes, made it very apparent that something was going to happen. Their cheers slowly raised as their bodies methodically rose from their seats in anticipation of a takedown.

While Tony defended, McCauley was able to drop him to his left hip, momentarily, and, as McCauley reached with his left arm to secure the right hip, he soon found Tony's leg stretching over him, as well as trapping his arm.

McCauley, almost trapped as he was positioned awkwardly under Tony, was now being stepped over. In the process of the step over, Tony slid and sunk his right foot over McCauley's back and into a leg-rider position that stretched McCauley out once Tony began cranking on a pry-half with his hips pressuring down. In fear of being turned to his back, and with little option, McCauley had to release his hold. Tony would hear the referee declare, "Two! Takedown!" McCauley would belly out and, on top of him with the leg in, Tony would finish the match, cranking and forcefully pushing McCauley's head into the mat as he smiled and celebrated on top in the final few seconds as time expired.

"Yeah, I was celebrating," Ramos said, "that was the biggest match of the tournament. I was super excited."

When the match ended, the Minnesota hisses and boos came from the stands over the cheers like a tidal wave across the arena, and Tony loved every second of it. He stood up and faced the Apple Valley bench and had something for them.

"I remember throwing that leg in over the top and scoring the takedown," Ramos said, "and then getting up, looking at the Apple Valley bench and flexing. For me it was a statement. I was saying, 'Hey, you're soon to be six-time state champion will carry another loss on his record. He will not go undefeated—it's over, stop talking about it. There's other guys out here that are big dogs, too.'"

With that flex, the first time in his high school career, the booing came in even louder. Some fans even motioned their hands in a pushing away manner, as in disgust, and others had some words under their breath, and some even more outwardly vocal for Tony. But Tony, who could sense the displeasure of his actions, did not mind the attention. And as the voices and boos became louder and louder, Tony, as his hand was raised, slowly basked in the resentment and took his time walking off the mat as he took it all in. As fans became more boisterous, Tony was seemingly looking back into the Apple Valley fans' eyes and smiling at each of them individually.

When he reached North's bench, Tony slapped Frank's hand hard and shook Hahn's hand—the dual continued and the Apple Valley and Glenbard North rivalry would grow.

"It felt good hearing the booing," Ramos said, "because I was doing the right things, beating the guy in his home state and they weren't happy about it. So, that moment and those boos were something that I embraced."

The Eagles would go on to defeat the Panthers by a 31-25 score and

Glenbard had to settle for the opportunity to win the Runner-up Pool—the best possible overall finish would be fifth.

• • •

For the first match of the second day, Glenbard wrestled Albert Lea, Minnesota, and Tony won by fall in 3:22 over Tim Aldrich. North advanced with a 38-15 win.

In the second round, Arch Bishop Moener of Ohio would take Glenbard down to the wire. They would also try to make a move to steal a weight class, but North was ready. Tony was to receive a forfeit at 112 pounds, but the North coaches had their backup wrestler, Dan Rios, step on the mat and accept those six points. They ended up bumping Tony up to 119 pounds where he faced and defeated Drew Hammer by fall in 2:48.

As Tony had been going for takedowns and points, and the coaches were demanding falls and for Tony to fight for the falls, it was time for Tony to score for the team—and he came through. Up to that point, a number of the older wrestlers on the team were not too certain of Tony's team commitment to winning.

"Coach Hahn needed to bump me to give us a better chance to win," Ramos said. "He was comfortable with me up there for a win. In situations where I knew we needed to get the points, that's what I was going to do. Other times, I felt like, yeah, they wanted me to get six points, but was it something that we really needed? So, I guess I went for what I felt I needed to do to get the takedowns and chase that record when I knew the team score was in hand."

With the final match of the pool, Glenbard wrestled Hastings, Minnesota, and closed them out, 45-17, to exit their day with a 3-0 record and a fifth place finish at the national duals. In that match, Tony won by a 26-8 technical fall over currently undefeated Tyler Rohr. Tony had dominated both days of the Clash and the team, still very young, had picked up some great matches and some valuable individual and team experience.

When it came time for the tournament to hand out its awards for the most outstanding wrestler at each weight class, Tony, as was his team, expected Tony to earn his second All-Clash team award as he had proven himself to be the best 112 pounder in the field. As the name was called at 103 pounds, Tony waited. When they announced, "At 112 pounds, this year's Clash all-tournament team member, from South Plainfield, New Jersey, Patrick Hunter."

Immediately, as the Minnesota fans heard "South" announced, the cheers of gracious and joyous surprise nearly drowned out the rest of the school and wrestler name being spoken.

There had been no more dominant wrestler in the field than Tony, and

Tony, his team, and some others knew that. South Plainfield had finished eleventh overall—third in the Third Place Pool and, even though Hunter dominated his competition with four technical falls and two falls, he had faced nowhere near the competition that Tony had wrestled.

Tony felt snubbed. He believed that this was his penance for showboating as time expired in the match against McCauley and for flexing at the Apple Valley bench. He also thought that the voters had felt he made a mockery of a Minnesota school and their wrestler and they were not going to award him for that.

"I knew the flexing cost me," Ramos said, "and I was really pissed about it. You know, even though I did flex, the Minnesota committee that they had up there should not have held it against me because I beat their top dog. Not to give me that award was just selfish on their part and them being immature."

As Tony walked away from the Clash, he was aware of his level of wrestling, and where he needed to improve.

"I was aware how well I was wrestling," Ramos said. "I knew that I had a few close matches, but not many were close and I wanted to keep the momentum going. [My accomplishments] were not something I wanted to sit and focus on. It was more like: *Okay, good job let's move on now.* The season started off really good and I wanted to keep it moving good.

"As far as improving, I am sure [the coaches] were still on me about pinning people and I probably should have been working harder on that. But, there were little things, positioning-wise and dealing with situations that I'm sure I was adjusting. I know that Hahn and the coaches always had a new area for me to improve upon, so I needed to listen, practice, adjust, and improve."

Additionally, Tony's wins pushed him in the all-grade ranking by W.I.N. magazine; Tony was considered the fifth best wrestler now at 112 pounds. W.I.N. Magazine's Dan Fickel ranked the weight classes by Senior-Junior, Sophomore-Freshman, and as an All-Class ranking.

Here was his breakdown with classification and rankings:

ALL-CLASS RANKING • 112 POUNDS
NOVEMBER 24, 2006

01.	Connor McDonald	12	Sussex Central, DE
02.	Jordan Oliver	11	Easton, PA
03.	Eric Grajales	10	Brandon, FL
04.	Donte Butler	12	Summer, MO
05.	Tony Ramos	10	Glenbard North, IL
06.	Chris Villalonga	9	Blair Academy, NJ
07.	Andrew Long	11	Creston, IA
08.	Josh Kindig	9	Blue Mountain, PA
09.	Steve Mitcheff	11	Elyria, OH
10.	Justin Forrest	11	Raymore-Peculiar, MO
23.	Patrick Hunter	11	South Plainfield, NJ
24.	David Thorn	10	St. Michael-Albertville, MN
29.	Destin McCauley	8	Apple Valley, MN

SOPHOMORE AND FRESHMAN RANKING • 112 POUNDS
JANUARY 15, 2007

01.	Tony Ramos	10	Glenbard North, IL
02.	Eric Grajales	10	Brandon, FL
03.	Chris Villalonga	9	Blair Academy, NJ
04.	Kyle Lang	10	Brecksville, OH
05.	Michael Garofalo	10	Colonial Forge, VA
06.	Kyle Dake	10	Lansing, NY
07.	David Thorn	10	St. Michael-Albertville, MN
08.	Paul Liquori	10	Wantagh, NY
09.	Trent Cox	10	Andale, KS
10.	David Klingsheim	10	Liberty Brent, CA

CHAPTER 19
THE NEXT CHALLENGE

"I was fine with it because he was their best wrestler. I didn't care about bumping up a weight class; I wanted to face him. I wanted to challenge myself. This is what it's all about."

• *Tony Ramos*

THE NEXT STOP FOR NORTH'S WRESTLERS would be up to Wisconsin Rapids, Wisconsin, for a dual with the always difficult Red Raiders. Glenbard fans knew they had to travel well because the red and white would be in full support across the gymnasium floor from them as their dual was always the highlight of the quadrangular.

Glenbard rolled past their two first two teams in fine fashion. They defeated Ellsworth, Wisconsin, 42-13, and Totino-Grace, Minnesota, 63-3. Along the way, Tony did the same with a 20-9 and 14-5 major decision over each opponent. When the time came for the dual against Rapids, the gymnasium was packed; he radio station was broadcasting, and the setting was just as head coach Mark Hahn wanted it: hostile and uninviting.

"One of the biggest reasons we went up to Rapids," Hahn said, "was because of the competition. But, it is not a comfortable trip, the weather is bad, and the climate in the gymnasium is something our team can learn from. Aside from that, the refs are never in our favor and we really have to earn it when we go up there because things aren't always going to go our way. We need to be in those types of duals so we can respond when they matter back home."

The dual featured Glenbard North, Illinois' second-rated team, and Wisconsin Rapids, the defending Division I four-time state champions.

When the dual opened, North took the advantage at 103 pounds as

Jaime Warczynski defeated Rapids' Carl DeLuca by an 11-4 decision. At 112, Rapids was expecting Tony to step on the mat; instead, Hahn and his staff knew they could possibly steal a win with their back-up, Ray Varella, and pit Tony against Rapids' captain and returning state champion Josh Chappa who was currently special mention in the country at 119 pounds. This would also bump the line-up for North.

"I remember Coach Hahn telling me he would be bumping me for the dual," Ramos said, "and I was fine with it because he was their best wrestler. I didn't care about bumping up a weight class; I wanted to face him. I wanted to challenge myself. This is what it's all about."

With the two high-profile wrestlers to face one another, this gave everyone in the stands the excitement of the marquee match-up as soon as Varella checked into the head table at 112. When he did, a Rapids coach went to the warm-up area to let Chappa know he had Tony.

Of course, before this happened, Varella would have to do his part for the Panthers and he did. Varella defeated Colton Brehm by a 7-6 decision. This gave Glenbard the 6-0 team score lead headed into what was now the match of the afternoon.

As both wrestlers reported to the table, and the fans on both sides were cheering and excited. The radio announcer had been building up the match during the 112-pound bout, and now it was time. Tony came into the dual undefeated and Chappa's only loss on the season was at the Clash at 119 pounds in a 2-0 decision against Derek Schreiner from Wayzata, Minnesota—a returning state and national champion who was ranked thirtieth in the country at 125 pounds.

When Tony and Chappa were finally brought to the middle and shook hands, the longer Chappa worked to use his height and length over his shorter opponent by immediately going to a right-handed underhook and a left-handed overhook for leverage. In defense, Tony locked his arm down on the underhook and used his head to block, positioning it in Chappa's right clavicle.

The two would fight that position to the circle's edge and as Chappa attempted an inside trip—Tony defended and bent him back. In the fight, both wrestlers could not keep their position and each would find himself out of bounds.

In the next sequence, the offense consisted of a fake open shot by Chappa with Tony moving forward and controlling his left wrist while tying up on Chappa's right. As Tony worked into a two-on-one to close the gap, Chappa, again, much taller, came over the top with a front headlock. The two would stubbornly battle in that position until they were out of bounds.

At the match's continuation, off the referee's whistle, both wrestlers took an immediate shot—with no advantage to either. However, Chappa did work into his right-side underhook and Tony buried his head and worked to control the opposite side. Tony would shoot him off the mat and the strategy from Chappa appeared to be for him to tie Tony up in order to score and do not allow the distance for the open attacks.

When the first period ended, the match was tied, 0-0, but even though there was no scoring, the excitement and energy in the gymnasium and on the mat was very high.

In the second period, Tony chose down and Chappa, tough on the spiral ride and near arm chop, held him there for about one minute before Tony could secure his stand-up and earn a 1-0 lead. The remainder of the period was much like the first—two wrestlers vying for position as Tony tried working to an open shot.

In the third, Chappa chose down and, from a sit out, Tony was positioned directly behind him with a double-crab ride and a hand fight for inside position under Chappa's arms. As Chappa was pressuring back into Tony, he was able to elevate his hips above Tony's and hip-hoist through. In this moment, Tony tried to grab Chappa's foot to regain position, but he found himself working to fight off his back as the longer Chappa stepped over and through for a reversal and a 2-1 lead. Then the scramble began.

With the turn, Chappa was also able to secure an arm-bar on Tony's left side and, as he worked a turn, Tony saw an opening and bucked up to roll through. In the roll through, the referee, on the opposite side of the action, motioned a two nearfall count; thus, giving Chappa a now 4-1 lead with the near fall points—the Rapids' fans were out-of-their-minds excited. As soon as the count occurred, the red and white uproar echoed throughout the gymnasium. When Tony's roll finally came through, with no break in the process, he found himself under Chappa and posted up, but the score had widened and the scramble was still on.

On the post up, Chappa clenched his legs together—not a scissors as his legs never touched, but tight pressure—and Chappa found himself hanging over the top of Tony as Tony worked to find an arm to pull down on and expose Chappa's back. Instead, the longer Chappa locked around Tony's waist and trapped one of his arms as Tony tried to cut through. In that moment, Chappa leaned Tony over and caught him for another three count and, while the Rapids' roar was mightier than the first and stomps on the bleachers were deafening, Chappa extended his lead, 6-1, with five seconds left in the match.

Tony would find a way off his back and out of the hold and, once on his feet, he attempted a headlock; it would fail.

Chappa jumped up and punched his fists to the ceiling as the Red

Raider faithful were standing tall on their feet, punching the air, pointing, and wildly celebrating.

The final was a 6-2 decision in favor of Chappa and now a 6-3 dual meet lead for North. As Tony came off the mat there was a storm of anger from his father and mother in the stands. His father was not happy with Coach Hahn's decision to bump his son up and was pointing and yelling at the staff and even at his own son, Frank—Frank motioned for his father to calm his yells and sit down. It was a pure emotional reaction from the family.

When Tony exited the mat and saw his mother and father, as they worked themselves to the floor, he turned to them and said, "It's one match. It's not a big deal. It's not the state championship."

With those words, his parents appeared to collect themselves as everything about their son's statement was true. It was one match. It was not the state championship. And their son was able to have a clear mind and understanding in regard to his loss in conjunction with the bigger picture as he exited the mat. He would come back to the bench to support his team moments after he gathered himself and put his warm-ups back on.

"My parents weren't happy about me [wrestling up a weight class]," Ramos said, "but it was probably more because they wanted to see me go undefeated and they knew the guy was pretty tough. But I don't think they really understood that it was a decision that I wanted. I was pissed about it—they didn't need to be pissed about it too. I wanted the challenge; I thought I could beat him. It wasn't the end of the world."

From his coach's point of view, "Tony did what the team needed him to do," Hahn said. "He never questioned or backed away from any match-up that we needed. When I told him what we wanted to do, he was as confident as he always was. Any time one of our wrestlers loses it hurts, but Tony handled it well and being able to make that move helped win us the dual. And that was what that trip and that weekend was about."

Though the match was a loss, the growth in that moment with Tony was major in terms of his maturation and understanding of his overall goal—even though he had lost the opportunity to accomplish one of his own personal goals of being undefeated.

"Even though the match was just a match," Ramos said, "it was still a little devastating because there went my undefeated season, and that was something that I was shooting for and really wanted. But, even though I knew this, I had to be reminded that the loss and this would all go away if I won the state championship at the end of the year—that loss would be forgotten. For me, though, I wanted to do it all. I wanted the unblemished record with our difficult schedule—I wanted to be perfect. But, we all can't be perfect; it's hard to be perfect."

As the dual would play out, the bump worked to North's favor and they won the dual, 26-22, and, for the second season in a row, defeat the eventual Wisconsin state champions.

CHAPTER 20
A BUMP AND A MOHAWK

"I always wanted to be a little bit different. I wanted to do the team stuff, like dying my hair, but, at the same time, I wanted to have a bit of my own personality."

• *Tony Ramos*

AFTER RAPIDS, NORTH HAD A FEW MORE DUALS, mostly conference match-ups before heading into their conference tournament and then into the state series. Tony knew that he had to close out the last quarter of the season strong and, after his loss in Wisconsin, his time in the room was even more focused. Tony now had a better sense of where his efforts needed to be directed in order to win the state championship. He knew he had to continue to be strong on his feet and find ways to attack taller wrestlers, and he began working a little bit more down position for when he had to face those longer opponents and counter leg attacks.

For the final dual of the season, Glenbard squared off against the number-two rated team in the state, Carl Sandburg. And, although all of the match-ups would be strong for both sides, and Tony earned another win, the Golden Eagles defeated the Panthers, 34-21.

The following week, as the end of the regular season came along, Glenbard North was on track to win its tenth-consecutive DuPage Valley Conference championship after sweeping the season duals. In order to do so, there had to be some sacrifices made by certain wrestlers to put the program in the best possible position to win. Therefore, some wrestlers were asked to bump weights for the tournament as West Aurora and Wheaton North would be looking to knock Glenbard off its conference streak and take over the conference crown.

One of the North traditions that had become a mainstay was, the week of conference, all of the varsity wrestlers would dye their hair gold as a sign of unity and to signify what they were wrestling for. Tony, being Tony, did dye his hair gold; however, he went with a different look. When he walked into the school that week, he had a gold Mohawk instead of his entire head being gold.

"I always wanted to be a little bit different," Ramos explained. "I wanted to do the team stuff, like dying my hair and stuff, but, at the same time, I wanted to have a bit of my own personality. Being sixteen, I felt the Mohawk would look cool and give me a bit of a more fierce competitor look, and that's what I decided to go with."

While the wrestlers would do their thing, the coaching staff would do its evaluation of how they would match up and put themselves in position for championship number ten in a row. Hahn and his staff talked and, "We decided to put Ray Varella in at 112 pounds," varsity assistant Chris Edwards said, "and bump Tony [to 119] and Jimmy [Chase to 125]. That would move Geno [Capezio] to 130, Corey Hope to 135, Danny [Monaco] to 140, and Vince [Ramos] to 145. No one was going to beat Bryan [O'Connor] at 152, and [Eric] Wahrman and [Roy] Feltson and Mike [Eldridge] would make the finals and all could win it. We expected [heavyweight Alex] Hansen to be in the finals, so the move looked good to us. By getting Ray in the line-up, we were tougher and we knew it. Going into the seeding meeting, we would show our hand really quickly."

For Varella, he predominately wrestled 112 pounds when Tony bumped to 119 for duals. His record as the team headed into the tournament had been 8-4, and the junior's losses were to quality opponents and varsity starters—he was undefeated on the Junior Varsity level.

At the meeting, Varella had a record worthy of a seed; however, the coaches felt it did not matter as he only had eight wins in twelve matches. They believed that just because Varella worked out with Tony that did not mean that he had the talent to win the conference championship at that weight. He would go into the blind draw and Varella would feed into the second seed, Wheaton North's Adrian Laskero; a sophomore with a 23-7 record. When the North coaches saw their wrestler's seed, "We loved it," Edwards laughed. "We knew Ray was capable of a big win there—Wheaton North would see it as an upset—and Ray would block points for them, give us bonus points, and move on. He was good enough to beat everyone there."

The following day, as the tournament started, Varella would be the eighth match called and, when he reported to the mat, he was confident and ready to wrestle. As for Laskero, he may have seen the record and not thought much of it at the time, but when the match started, Varella made himself known.

With his team watching, and the team's bump being tested in the second weight class of the day, Varella did not disappoint. In fact, he surprised everyone as he not only defeated Laskero, but he won by fall in 1:50. He earned the two bonus points for the team, blocked a Falcon wrestler, advanced into the semifinals, and had a major confidence boost as the team started to roll.

Overall in the first round, the Panthers earned bonus points in ten out of their fourteen weight classes—seven by fall, one technical fall, and two major decisions. The strategy was working as the semifinals began.

At 103 pounds, Jaime Warczynski won by a technical fall and advanced to the finals. Now it was Varella's turn. He would have the number-three seed, Mike McDonnell from Naperville North, a 22-9 senior. During the match, Varella would not earn the fall, but he would earn the victory in fine fashion—a 9-2 decision and a chance at a conference championship. In the finals, he would face the number-one seed from West Aurora, 24-10 senior Eric Concha.

For Tony, he earned the number-one seed for the second season in a row, won by fall in the opening round at 119 pounds over Wheaton North's Jake Dore, and then, in the semifinals, added to his takedown total with an 18-7 major decision over Naperville North's four seed, Adam Hankin. Tony now had a second opportunity at a conference championship in as many years.

At 125 pounds, Chase reached the finals by a fall and decision, and at 130 pounds, Capezio reached the finals by fall and then a decision.

The 135 and the 215-pound weight class would score team points, but not reach the finals—Hope would place fifth and Chris Van Gundy placed seventh. But 140, 145, 152, 160, 171, 189, and 285 would all make the championship match, and five would score bonus points in the process.

When the championships round came, Glenbard had pretty much wrapped up the tournament, but there were still matches to be won.

Warczynski opened up the finals by winning his first DVC championship. And when Varella's match was concluded, the back-up upended the number-one seed with a strong 12-7 decision and his first conference crown.

Having known that, mathematically, the tournament was won, Tony wanted to add to his takedown chase—he would win his second title by an 18-7 major decision over West Aurora sophomore Josh Zinzer. Zinzer was now 29-7 on the season; Tony's record moved to 33-1.

The rest of the team, by scoring and making the finals would do their part; however, for Chase and Capezio, they were just out-manned and earned runner-up finishes. Monaco, Vince Ramos, and Bryan O'Connor would take the next three championships with a 7-5 decision and two falls.

At 160, Wahrman, and at 285, Alex Hanson, would earn runner-up finishes as well, and Feltson and Eldridge at 171 and 189 pounds, would be crowned champions—both by decision.

"Coach Hahn had talked to all of us," Ramos said, "and he felt the bump was the best way to win the conference and that was always one of our goals. On top of that, the streak was at ten if we won and that was a big thing because [Coach] Hahn would always talk about how when Iowa was going for ten national championships and put the 'X' on the singlets and lost—how that 'ten' can be kind of a devastating number. But it was something we, as wrestlers, thought we could do. It was something the coaches thought we could do, and he talked to all of us, made the adjustments, and we were all okay with it. After that, we all went out there and accomplished what we set out to accomplish, regardless of moving up in weight.

"Getting that tenth." Ramos continued, "was big for the program and the high school, and for us—not everybody is put in those types of positions with pressures to win and I think, with Coach Hahn, we embraced those moments. It was also special because it made a statement to the other schools [in the conference] that we did it, and we did it up a weight class."

The tenth-consecutive DuPage Valley Conference championship was won by 53 points over West Aurora and, the following week, North dominated their Regional with another team championship. North would score 325 points and the next closest team, St. Charles East, would score 239. For the Panthers, ten wrestlers were crowned champions, four were runner-ups, and all fourteen had advanced to the Individual Sectional.

In addition to the wrestlers advancing, a team Regional championship meant that the team qualified for the Dual Team Sectional championship; however, that would take place after the state championships, and North would be matched up against a very familiar opponent and current rival.

As for Tony, who was again a Regional champion, he was now in striking distance of Dana Holland's one-season takedown record. He would have the opportunity to take it over in Hudson Gymnasium at Glenbard North that weekend during the Individual Sectional Championships in front of his home crowd.

WHEN THE SECTIONALS ARRIVED, TONY SAW HIS matches as opportunities to break the record he so desperately wanted. Since Tony was a Regional champion, he had a bye in the opening round and waited to see who he would wrestle. When the match ended, he would face Nick Herling, a junior from Hersey. Tony would utilize everything in his arsenal and won by a technical fall in 5:16. In that match, he added fourteen more takedowns to his season's total.

In the semifinals, Tony had to wrestle someone very close to home, his training partner at Izzy Style, Montini's Benny Marti. Marti, who also knew Tony's style very well, did pose some troubles for him as he was taller and knew how to use his length and leverage and scramble very well against his opponents.

"Benny and me trained at Izzy's," Ramos said, "and I knew he was a real funky kid who liked to scramble, so I had to make sure I finished solid and stayed out of the scrambles that he is good at putting guys in. But, he was a kid that I could always beat pretty handily as long as I stayed sharp—he could give guys fits if he got to his positions."

Tony would stay out of the scrambles and win a 9-2 decision. In that match, Tony added four more takedowns and, as he headed into his finals' match, he was now just seven takedowns away from Holland's record, eight away from breaking it.

CHAPTER 21
TAKING DOWN THE RECORD

"I was looking to get seven, eight, nine takedowns a match. You throw three forfeits in there, that's at least 21 takedowns that I don't have a chance to add to my total."

• *Tony Ramos*

WHEN TONY WALKED INTO THE GLENBARD North restling room as a freshman, he wanted to replace every name on the record board with his. Some records he knew were more likely than others; however, he knew he wanted to leave his mark on the program by the time he graduated. However, of all the records up on that wall, there was one that stood out to him. One record that he vowed, no matter what happened, he would own.

"From day one," Ramos said, "I wanted to break the Most Takedowns in One Season record and I said it. It was something everyone knew I was going after; everyone was behind me. It became my biggest emphasis—the most important to me—because it shows that you are dominating guys. You take a guy down fifteen times in a match and win 30-15, he knows, and everyone knows, who the more dominating wrestling was."

Of course, in order to break that record, which was owned by one of his brother Frank's closest friends, Dana Holland, Tony had to be strategic from his very first match. As a freshman, Tony dominated his matches; however, his takedown total was 158 on the season—the current record for one season was 248. It would take a great deal more than one or two match differences to topple that total. In that, Tony entered his sophomore season with a plan.

"I guess the best way that I approached it," Ramos explained, "was going into every match trying to score as many points as I could without putting myself in crazy danger. I was trying to dominate my opponents by breaking their will to the point where they would just kind of give up, put their head on the mat, and let me run behind them."

And as takedowns started to add up, the conversations between Tony and Holland became lively, but were positive.

Since Frank and Holland were so close, Holland had known Tony since he was born. Also, at this time, Holland was on staff as a volunteer assistant at North; therefore, he was able to see Tony each day as well as at meets and tournaments.

Before Holland held the record, it was owned by Tony Rigitano who set it in 1990 with 171 takedowns. Before Rigitano, state champion Mike Palazzo held the record in 1989 with 139 takedowns—Mike took the record over from his brother Jim who set the total in 1987 with 130 takedowns.

"Originally," Holland explained, "when I was a sophomore, all of my losses came from me trying to ride after a takedown and getting ridden out or turned. So, immediately, as this was happening, I would just hear [Coach Kent] Garret and Hahn yell, 'Just let him up! Cut him!' And this kept me out of those situations because I could build my lead on my feet and not have those tight matches.

"As soon as I started cutting guys, I was majoring and tech-ing guys. While I was racking up these takedowns, Tony Rigitano said to me, 'Hey, you should go after my record.' But sophomore year, I would only come close. My junior year I told Coach Hahn I wanted to break the record and he was excited. He was glad I had a goal; he made sure I had a plan. At season's end, I had 193—22 more than Rigitano."

Holland's total his junior season set the record and that would become the new standard; however, in the end, he felt he made one mistake. "I wish I would have known where I was at each week," Holland admitted. "I had an idea, but I should have been more adamant about having the stat girls tell me my total. I thought I was doing a good job keeping it, but I wasn't—I should have tracked it. I mean, I had 193, so I beat it, but I think I would've challenged myself more for 200 or 250 had I known where I was at.

"Since I had the takedown record, my senior year my goal was to break the Most Falls in One Season record. Coach Hahn always made a big deal about the pin record because he said that if we wanted to show dominance, then that was the record to have. Me and Frank and a few others took the challenge, but Frank and someone else was ahead of me at the halfway point. And the more I tried to turn guys, the closer my scores were. I wasn't a pinner, I wanted to be, I just wasn't; I was better on my feet. At that point, I figured I would just stick to beating the record that I set the year before. My thought process at that point in the season was that if I could get three or four takedowns a period, or at least five or six in the first when I was fresh, I would be able to do it. If I was getting eight or nine on average guys, then I knew I needed three or four on state caliber wrestlers.

"Had I focused on takedowns all season," Holland laughed, "and not just taking it seriously in January, it would've been amazing to see what that number could've been. I mean, I was ranked number one and I was pushing the record against guys ranked second, third and fourth. I could've won those matches 5-1 and no one would've said anything. But I was majoring those guys chasing that record."

The mindset to accomplish such a record was simple: "Mental toughness," Holland said. "To me, the best defense is a strong offense. You have to score, score, score, score; break him, and then keep scoring."

Holland would end his senior campaign with an Illinois state championship and rewrite the takedown record for one season; the new record now stood at 248 takedowns.

When Tony opened his sophomore season, he made it clear what he was doing and he scored his takedowns well before he even thought about going for the fall—even if it was there. "Tony was going for the record," Hahn said, "and I was glad that he was. But there were matches where he should have pinned the guy or got the pin for [the team] instead of the tech. You want your guys to set goals and break records—it makes them better and hopefully the team feeds off of it. But, sometimes a fall is needed in a team race and you can get off the mat after scoring ten takedowns."

All along the way, Frank gave his former teammate and friend grief about his record that would not last the season. "Frank would say," Holland remembered, "'You know Tony's going to smash your record, right?' and then laugh. But I wanted Tony to break it; both me and Frank did—and so did Tony."

Whether it was in the wrestling room, at a competition, or at the house, there would always be some playful banter between Tony and Holland as well. "Me and Dana talked about it all the time," Ramos laughed. "I would tell him every week, 'Hey, I'm going to break that record,' and he would say, 'Good. I hope you do. Shoot for it. I want you to do it.' But he would always remind me, with a nudge and a laugh, 'You know, that's a lot of takedowns.'"

But, where Holland had made the mistake of not knowing his totals, Tony was on top of it every match. "After every dual or quad or tournament," Ramos said, "I would ask the stat girls how many takedowns I had. They were great about having that number and my total ready. It became fun because when I was close to breaking it, everybody knew—and there would be a countdown going on in the stands. I remember hearing, 'Nine. Eight. Seven...' It was fun. We all knew exactly what the number was."

The Glenbard North record for Most Takedowns in One Season fell in North's Hudson Gymnasium on February 10, 2007, during the Sectional Championships in the finals match against Prospect's Tyler Rossdeutcher.

In the crowd, Tony's friends and family were chanting a countdown with each takedown. In that match, seven takedowns were needed to tie it, and eight to break the record. With each takedown, one could hear, "Six more, Tony! Five! Four! Three more! Two! One more! He tied it."

"I remember getting the takedown to tie [the record]," Ramos said, "and then letting him go and getting the takedown to break it and hearing our fans cheer and then getting another takedown and another takedown—I broke him immediately. It was great."

In that finals match, Tony needed eight takedowns for the record—he scored 15 and won by a technical fall in 3:21 over Rossdeutcher. Each point that was scored for Tony was on a takedown. After the match, Tony and Holland shared a small moment of celebration.

"I wanted the record to be broken," Holland said. "But it would've been nice if I still owned it—it's always great to have that. But now I hope someone beats Tony's record. Not because it's Tony's record and he beat my record, but because that means someone else is trying to do something special."

"Deep down," Ramos said, "I think he would've liked to keep that record. But I know he was happy I broke it. I would feel the same way. I hope someone breaks it—but deep down I hope my name stays up there forever."

For Tony, the record stood for two qualities he wanted people to see in his wrestling: The ability to score points and to put fear into his opponents due to his ability to score points.

"This record was important to me because, for college coaches, and even just for me, I wanted to show that I could score points, take people down, and that's what they're looking for. College coaches want to know, *Can he score? How does he score?* They don't want someone who's going to be defensive the whole time, and I just wanted to showcase that I could score from different areas and that I could put a lot of points on the board.

"The other thing was," Ramos continued, "[my] opponents are seeing these scores, and those numbers put fear into them and they start saying, 'He put up 15 to 20 points last match, I know I'm going to be in for a go when I have to wrestle him and I don't know if I'm ready for that.' In the end, I wish I could've scored 300."

Of course, the greatest frustration for any high-level wrestler was when he received a forfeit. In those types of situations, the takedown record became a more difficult task to achieve.

"I hated it when coaches [forfeited] to me," Ramos said. "First, let your kid compete. Second, that just cost me takedowns. I was looking to get seven, eight, nine takedowns a match. You throw three forfeits in there, that's at least 21 takedowns that I don't have a chance to add to my total. If I get those matches, there's my 300 takedowns."

Even as he looked back at his sophomore season and the record, he felt the same. "It's special," Ramos said. "It's a big deal because I set my goals to do something and I accomplished it—and it wasn't an easy task. To score six, seven, eight takedowns a match, that's a lot of points. And that was against good guys too, we wrestled a tough schedule. It's also something that follows me around. When I walk into rooms or when you talk to other guys, the first records you look at are takedowns and falls, then you kind of browse the rest. A guy can go 44-0 and win his matches 1-0, 2-1, but not a lot of people can score six or seven or eight takedowns in every single match they wrestle."

Tony ended with 288 takedowns in the 44 matches that he wrestled; therefore, he averaged 6.6 takedowns per match. However, what was more impressive was that Tony had recorded 248 takedowns by the end of the Sectional championship match. That means that he scored forty more takedowns in the next two weeks against the best wrestlers and teams in the state of Illinois. To be precise, Tony scored 40 takedowns against five opponents—that is eight takedowns per opponent.

In addition to Tony's record and season dominance, Frank conceded the week of conference that Tony had pretty much won the wager that they had made the year before. Tony had won the Junior Western Regional, the FILA Cadet National Championship, he was a Freestyle All-American in Fargo, was a Conant and an Ironman champion, and he went on to win a DVC and Regional and Sectional championship—and all that was left was the individual state championship.

When Frank made the bet, he really and truly believed that to accomplish all of those goals was just too much; he knew the competition. Likewise, early on, Frank knew that wrestling up a weight put Tony at a disadvantage because he would be outmanned in those matches. In the end, Frank felt the bet, and the reality of having to accomplish it all, would just be too much. He would be proved wrong. Tony not only accepted the challenge and completed all but the final step, but he did it on his own terms in regard to the weight class that he wanted to wrestle.

"He did it," Defilippis admitted with pride, "and I had to buy him a truck. It was actually in the driveway before he even had his license. Every time I looked at that truck I smiled and laughed—I still can't believe he did it."

CHAPTER 22
ONE FOR THE FAMILY

"Hey, I'm freakin' out. I know that I'm supposed to win this tournament, but you know how many times I've seen the guy who's supposed to win get headlocked and pinned like Frankie? I've seen it firsthand and I don't want to be that guy."

• Tony Ramos

TONY'S TRAINING DURING THE WEEK OF THE state championships was even more focused than the week of the Ironman. Aside from remaining undefeated, he had accomplished all of his goals but one—the family's and his own individual state championship.

Heading into that week, Tony had all of the confidence that he needed; his season had proven that he was the best wrestler at the weight in Illinois. Now, he just had to go out there, wrestle, and prove it that particular weekend.

When it came time to wrestle, Tony opened up his tournament in Assembly Hall with a fall in 3:21 over Oak Forest sophomore, Ryan Burton. However, even though he made the match appear simple, he found himself in a moment with Coach Hahn in the tunnel after that very win.

"I don't think a lot of people know the story," Ramos said. "But after that first match I went to Coach Hahn and told him, 'Hey, I'm feakin' out.' He looked at me and asked why. I told him, 'I know that I'm supposed to win this tournament, but you know how many times I've seen the guy who's supposed to win get headlocked and pinned like Frankie? I've seen it firsthand and I don't want to be that guy.' He sat me down and told me, 'Look. That only happens when you're tentative. You got to go out there and keep wrestling like you've been wrestling all year. Score a lot of points and dominate your positions on your feet and then that's not going to happen—don't worry about it.' And once he told me that it kind of all went away and I felt relaxed again."

In his quarterfinal match, "I did exactly what Coach Hahn told me to do," Ramos said. "I went out there and scored a lot of points." That match featured a 13-5 major decision over 38-2 senior Tyler Winland of Normal Community.

For Tony's semifinal bout, he faced Dale Jarosz of Palatine who came into the match with a 45-0 record. In the quarterfinals, Jarosz had won a tight 5-4 decision over Oak Park-River Forest's Ellis Coleman. And, although many were anticipating a Ramos-Coleman match-up, the Palatine junior was now making people question if he could be the one to defeat Tony.

However, as soon as the match began, Tony quickly dispelled any possible hope of an upset. Takedown after takedown after takedown Tony scored. When the final whistle blew, and he was headed to his second Grand March and state finals appearance; Tony had won a 12-5 decision.

"That was the only match that I didn't at least major someone," Ramos said, "and I was mad about it because I had dominated everyone throughout the whole tournament. But it was on to the finals. I felt like everything I was doing was unstoppable and that I was going to win."

When Saturday night came around, and the Grand March ended, Tony was ready for his opponent and for what could be his family's first state championship. Earlier that afternoon, Vince had, like the year before, lost his semi-final match against the eventual state champion; Vince placed third for the second year in a row.

For Tony, he had to wrestle Geneseo sophomore Adam Sheley. Sheley was not only 43-1 when he entered the finals, but he had a number-fourteen ranking in the country. The match-up would not be between two wrestlers who had the tournament of their lives, it would be between the number-one and number-two ranked wrestlers in the state, as well as two of the nation's finest and most accomplished wrestlers.

As a freshman, the stage was possibly too big for Tony's eyes and it affected him. His sophomore year was much different.

"I'd been there before," Ramos said of not having had the nerves like he did a year earlier. "I was prepared and more mature mentally because of the tournaments I had already competed in like the Western Regional, the FILA Cadets, the Ironman—those huge-big tournaments where I had big moments—and now nothing bothered me. I just wanted to take it as another match and go out there and wrestle it as hard as I could."

In a pre-match interview, Tony commented, "It's great to be in the finals, I have a little of unfinished business from last year. [I] lost in double overtime [and I] have a picture in my room about it when I was walking off the mat crying last year. I felt awful after that and I don't want to feel like that ever again. So my strategy this year is I'm going to go out there—it's going to be in the back of my head the whole time—and I'm just going to go out there and wrestle how I can and I don't care what anyone else does."

In his own pre-match interview, Sheley talked about what he needed to do to win the match. "[I need to] limit Ramos' takedowns and try to turn him on the mat. My go-to moves are my power double and my tilts."

However, when the match opened up, Sheley would feel the force of Tony, as Tony immediately attacked Sheley's head, snapped and controlled him, and moved forward and shot his own double that took Sheley off the mat within the first seven seconds. Tony raced back to the center and was ready when Sheley stepped back on the line.

This time, Sheley went directly to his left-handed underhook to tie Tony up, and Tony would look to defend and ultimately circle and snap free of the tie. As they separated, Tony went to work back on the head and forced Sheley backward. As soon as Sheley resisted, Tony hit an elbow slide and, as Sheley stepped to defend it and keep his balance, Tony was in on a single-leg near the mat's edge. Tony pulled the single in on his knee and tackled the other leg for a takedown and a 2-0 advantage; all of that was merely thirty seconds into the championship match.

Having no ambition to ride, Tony wanted to open up the match very early and went to an optional start and conceded the one-point escape. Once neutral, Tony would go back to work on Sheley's head and again shoot him off the mat.

Tony worked back to his head ties and snaps and took Sheley to the edge again and forced him out. This time, Sheley was hit with his first stalling warning as he continued to struggle to keep Tony at bay and in a position for him to open up his offense and get to his leg attacks.

Off the restart, Tony took a quick shot off the whistle, fought inside for the position, lifted Sheley up and drove him into the mat for his second takedown of the period and a 4-1 advantage. In the process, however, Tony's head appeared to have hit Sheley's nose and the referee stopped the match for blood time and clean up.

As Sheley was being tended to, Tony headed to his corner where Edwards and Defilippis told him to keep the pressure on. In the break, the Geneseo coaches contested the takedown stating that the contact did not allow Sheley to defend himself and the points, as well as the takedown, should be taken away. The referees discussed and agreed with

2007 • IHSA STATE CHAMPIONSHIPS
112 LB CHAMPIONSHIP MATCH
RAMOS SCORES ON A DOUBLE-LEG TAKEDOWN AGAINST GENESEO'S SHELEY
PHOTOGRAPH COURTESY • THE RAMOS FAMILY • MARLON BROOKS PHOTOGRAPHY

the challenge; the score was put back to 2-1. This reversed call enraged Frank back in the corner and Edwards went to the table to contest the contested call, but the call stood.

"That was a horrible call," Edwards laughed. "It was almost as if they were punishing Tony for being aggressive. It was a clean double and the two should have stood."

Not happy with the decision, Tony stomped to the middle of the mat and, just as he had done moments before, he did again—another quick double off the whistle and a takedown on the mat's edge. This time, the call was not reversed. The match, although only in the first period, seemed to be Tony's match as he had already dominated. Sheley, it appeared, was at a loss with how to handle the number-one sophomore in the land and the first period ended with a 4-1 lead for Tony.

Off the disc flip, Tony choose neutral and went right back to work on his feet where he was strongest. Off the whistle this time, it would be Sheley driving into Tony; however, with a quick snap and circle, Tony was back in and driving him off the mat on yet another shot.

Tony went back to work on Sheley's head, and Sheley would look to two-on-one Tony to slow him down. Tony, accustomed to the position from the Glenbard room, grabbed the bicep hand, circled out of it, snapped Sheley to the mat, grabbed Sheley's right leg with his right arm, and tried to beat the corner and score his third takedown of the championship match. Instead, Sheley would circle and Tony would shoot him off the mat. Sheley's nose was tended to again.

When the match continued, two more times, Tony worked his head snaps and elbow passes and shot Sheley off the mat—the second time resulted in another stall warning and a point for Tony who now led 5-1. Sheley gave a look of disbelief, but the referee told him he had to wrestle forward. As that brief conversation happened, the trainer came out again to work Sheley's nose. Tony's relentless nature continued as the match resumed and, as Tony extended himself too far on a snap, Sheley finally found himself in on Tony's legs for the first time, and that with about thirty seconds left in the second period.

As Sheley looked to bring Tony's leg in, Tony sprawled and worked a whizzer tough to his right side and made the hold difficult for Sheley. The fight traveled to the circle and Tony would ultimately be able to break the hands and square up his hips to Sheley. As they faced one another, Tony circled in and, as he had been doing, pushed Sheley off the mat and beat him back to the center for another restart with fifteen seconds left in the period.

Off the whistle, Tony pounded the head, got to his elbow slide, and forced an open double-leg. Sheley would hip in hard, but Tony fought and fought for it, lifted Sheley off the mat, and scored another takedown as time expired. The lead now grew to 7-1 and Sheley's hope at a state championship was fading; he was slow to get up after the referee called them off the mat after the takedown. For Tony, his family and team were cheering enthusiastically on what seemed to be an inevitable win just two minutes away.

For the final period, Sheley went to his strength and an area where Tony had struggled—top position. Sheley was known for his ability to tilt his opponents and it was now time to see if Tony's recent work had helped him enough to avoid a third-period letdown.

Immediately off the whistle, Tony executed a standup, turned out, and escaped. The score was now an 8-1 advantage, and it appeared that Tony had broken Sheley's will as well—Tony continued attacking.

After he drove Sheley off the mat and a restart took place, Tony hit his elbow slide and scored another takedown. As Tony was getting off Sheley, Sheley was just lying there and slowly worked his way to his feet. In the process, Tony attacked and snapped his opponent's head as a sign of sheer dominance.

Once back on their feet, and the score now 10-2, Sheley took a half-hearted shot and Tony worked him to mat's edge. From Tony's corner, the words, "Keep the intensity up and score," would be shouted by Frank. Edwards would instruct, "Keep your composure. Be smart on your attacks."

The intensity would continue and, as Tony drove into Sheley, Sheley countered and threw a headlock—Tony's greatest fear was now a possible reality. The lock was tight and all of Assembly Hall's voices grew into a wave of excitement and shock as Sheley pinched and hipped and Tony defended. All came to their feet and repositioned their heads to see the outcome. After a quick fight, Tony was able to slip his head free and take Sheley down one last time. When his head popped out there was a mix of relief and disappointment echoing in Champaign.

For the remainder of the match, Tony rode out his defeated opponent, who did nothing to rise and escape—Sheley was simply exhausted and content with time expiring.

When the whistle blew, and the 12-2 major decision became the final score, Tony pushed off Sheley and put both arms in the air with the number one pointing high into the lights as he circled half the mat, stomping, as his celebration—Sheley still remained on both knees, defeated and worn.

Both wrestlers removed their ankle bands, shook hands, and, while Tony had his hand raised and Sheley walked off dejected, Tony once again raised both number-one fingers into the air to display himself as the victor to all of Assembly Hall.

In his post-match interview, Tony was asked to comment on the different offensive attacks and styles in comparison to last year's loss. Tony responded, "Being able to [compete] in the Ironman and the Clash really prepared me for these types of matches," he said. "And I approach six minutes, no matter how tired [I] am or how bad [my] legs hurt, [I] had to push it."

And that was what Tony did—he controlled and dominated and pushed his opponent and himself the entire match.

"I had planned over and over what I would do if I won a state title," Ramos said, "but all I did was raise my hands because I was so excited that I think my emotions just took over and that was how it came out. Once it happened and I won, I was so freakin' excited. Everything that I had been working for—the defeat that I had the year prior—it was all gone and I didn't have to think about it anymore. It was out of my mind, it was out of my head. It was a huge relief to finally get that done."

Now, one year later, Tony entered the tunnel of Assembly Hall with clarity instead of confusion, joy instead of pain, and his head held high instead of low—a complete turnaround from what he had felt at the end of the previous season when he exited in defeat.

"It isn't the easiest thing to describe," Ramos said, "but when you put so much effort into something and want something and you finally do it, there's so much satisfaction and excitement that you want to jump up and down and scream from the top of your lungs—anything that you can do to celebrate, that's what you want to do.

"And I remember walking into that back locker room," Ramos remembered, "and I looked at Frankie and said, 'We did it. We finally did it.'"

CHAPTER 23
THE HEATED FIRST ROUND

"The gym was hot, the crowd was hostile—literally hostile as people wanted to fight each other in the stands. It wasn't like people were hostile toward just the wrestlers, the parents hated each other, the fans didn't like the look of the other fans. It was a beautiful disaster waiting to erupt."

• Tony Ramos

THE SUNDAY AFTER THE INDIVIDUAL STATE championships was still a workday for Tony as the team had a first round Dual Team Sectional match-up against newly rivaled Montini Catholic High School. The match would take place on Tuesday, and it would be held in the Montini gymnasium located in Lombard.

Just as in previous years, the state of Illinois High School Athletic Association administrators, under heavy protest and with a strong urgency and even suggestions from the coaches and fans and wrestling-oriented principals, still refused to seed any of the state wrestling tournaments. In that, one of the strongest programs in the state, like the number-one ranked Montini Broncos, or the number-three Glenbard North Panthers, would not even qualify for the Dual Team State Championships. That meant that seniors who had worked hard for four years, would graduate without the same equitable opportunity to compete in the state championships that was given for other sports where their state tournament was seeded.

Coaches, fans, and wrestlers had a very strong dislike for the system in Illinois wrestling—but the only ones who could do anything about it, the administrators, continually refused and argued that regional representation was what was most important, not seeding tournaments—and the small school principals voted to make sure it remained that way.

But, even worse still, this dual was a merely a first-round match-up for an opportunity to go to the state championships. Therefore, the loser would not even make the Sectional championship match for the opportunity to wrestle as a top-eight team.

"The system is bullshit," Defilippis commented. "Do you think they would [have a system of no seeding] in football or basketball or baseball? No way. Wrestling is the best high school product coming out the state—look at all of the national titles—and they refuse to do the state series the right way. It's horrible. And the kids are ones who get screwed because the adults will not do what's right. But, that was the system—like it or not."

Therefore, regardless of the system, it was what it was and the winner of the dual would be favored to win their side of the state bracket and, ceremoniously, end up in the state finals against Carl Sandburg. The loser would not even be remembered outside of its own team's history.

THE MONTINI GYMNASIUM WAS SMALL AND already crowded forty-five minutes prior to the start time. Additionally, the limited bleacher space provided left an overflow of the crowd using standing room only to lean against the one wall where the mat could be viewed. Even closer, fans sat three rows deep in front of the bleachers on both sides and along those in front of the wall closest to the mat. It was loud and the energy filled the seemingly elementary-sized gymnasium that was about to possess a colossal-sized dual. It was the perfect atmosphere for a high-staked and high-profiled dual.

As the teams warmed up on the same mat, tensions were high as wrestlers did not want to move out of their opponents' way. Warm-ups consisted of wrestlers finishing shots into each other, drilling into one another, pushing and pulling and falling on one another—there were some words, there were some looks; there was no giving in by either team.

"The atmosphere was crazy," Ramos remembered. "The gym was hot, the crowd was hostile—literally hostile as people wanted to fight each other in the stands. It wasn't like people were hostile toward just the wrestlers, the parents hated each other, and the fans didn't like the look of the other fans. It was a beautiful disaster waiting to erupt."

Geno Capezio recalled a similar atmosphere. "When we came running out for warm-ups," Capezio recalled, "there were people stacked on top of one another on the floor. When we got on the mat the boo's just came out from the Montini side, and then the Glenbard fans tried to out-do them. Police officers lined the gym, security was everywhere; it was loud—I remember warming up and stopping and looking around and smiling and thought, *This is what a dual meet should look like.* And then

I went back to warming up. It was hands down the best dual environment I was ever in."

Tony, who agreed with Capezio, did have one addition to the drama that would only unfold on the mat. "See, with the wrestlers," Ramos clarified, "there was a level of respect aside from some of the antics. I trained with a lot of those guys at Montini, so it was hard because we wanted to beat them so badly. But, at the same time, we had relationships with them. Izzy was one of their coaches and he was one of my coaches."

Each program was rich in its own tradition and prideful in its own way. The two head coaches, Mark Hahn and Mike Bukowski, were both well-respected and well-accomplished; likewise, both coaching staffs were knowledgeable and intense. And the two teams, talented and young and ready for a winner-take-all scenario. Last year Glenbard won; however, last year was not this year—whomever won would have earned it and that was all that mattered on that Tuesday night in Lombard.

Glenbard had their moves, though there were only a few they could make. Montini, however, made a major move: They dropped five of their upper-weights down one weight class in order to match up better with Glenbard. When the dual opened at 103 pounds, junior Jaime Warczynski, who was ranked tenth, stepped onto the mat for the Panthers against Montini's Colton Rasche. Rasche, ranked sixth and who was one match away from placing in the state tournament, won by a 6-2 decision. That gave the Broncos an early 3-0 lead.

At 112 pounds, Glenbard was hoping for the coin flip so they could pit Tony against the tougher opponent; however, with Glenbard having to report first to the table, they had to play their hand with Varella and move Tony to 119. Varella, as he had done in the conference tournament, came up big for the team. He won a 7-2 decision over state qualifier Benny Marti, but he did not earn any bonus points. The team score was knotted at 3-3 with Tony up next.

When Tony took the mat, he was told that he needed a fall. He would work his takedowns against Donnie Quattrocchi, but was unable to put him to his back. He kept working on his feet as he tried to go feet-to-back and then worked for some turns. As time was running out, Tony needed to grab the extra team point, so the coaches instructed him to score a technical fall. He would oblige with a 22-7 win in 5:47. But, even though Quattrocchi lost, he saved his team an extra point by not giving up the fall to the state champion. North now took the lead, 8-3 and the North fans were cheering in full excitement.

The next five weight classes would be considered swing matches. The better wrestler on the night would win them and each team knew going into those match-ups, that the dual could be decided within them.

At 125 pounds, Jimmy Chase wrestled the same opponent from Montini that he had defeated the previous year in the dual; coincidentally, Chase also lost to his Montini opponent that previous Saturday, 5-1, in the state finals third-place match at 119 pounds. North knew it was a difficult match-up, but was counting on a turnaround win and some team points. However, Chase would lose to Carson Beebe by a 3-0 decision; Montini would close the gap, trailing by two points as another key match-up was to follow, and the Montini fans were now growing in volume as they felt a possible turn coming their way.

North's 125-pound All-State wrestler, Geno Capezio, now wrestling at 130 pounds, wrestled and lost a decision to Andrew Saunders, 8-6, and Montini now took a 9-8 lead in the team race. Saunders was one match away from placing at 130 and was ranked eleventh all season. The Montini momentum in the stands was growing louder and North's Matt Ranck would give up a fall for the Panthers against the Broncos' All-State wrestler Jared Hensley in 3:54. Ranck who was put into the lineup over Corey Hope, only had one assignment: do not give up the fall. Unfortunately, that loss gave Montini a 15-8 lead and emotions on both sides of the gymnasium where growing and the chants and retaliated words expressed that clearly.

At 140, in a barnburner of a match that was really anyone's to take, Glenbard's Danny Monaco, who placed fifth at the state tournament, stopped North's bleeding with a 12-10 decision over state qualifier Isaiah Gonzalez who was ranked tenth.

When Vince Ramos stepped on the mat, after having placed third a few days prior, he would wrestle against one of his training partners from the club, Danny Stelter. Stelter, a state qualifier and ranked sixth at 145, would be defeated by Vince in a 7-5 decision. With those two decisions, North trailed by one point, 15-14, as Glenbard's senior state champion, Bryan O'Connor, stepped on the mat against Carl Foreside. And this is where the atmosphere in the stands began to grow into something no one expected.

O'Connor, who was the 160-pound state champion wrestled 152 pounds for many of North's duals; he bumped up for the state series. Foreside, an honorable mention wrestler in the state, and a sophomore, wrestled at the Sectional but not qualify for the state tournament. In fact, he and O'Connor were set to wrestle in the semifinals, but Foreside disqualified himself from the bout and ended up placing fourth. Even still, Foreside was a strong wrestler with good upper body throws and both O'Conner and the Glenbard coaches knew it.

When the two stepped on the mat at 152, a Montini father, from the Glenbard side of the stands, was yelling, "Play the piano. Play the white keys. Play those white keys, Carl."

These final words enraged a few of the Glenbard supporters and hollers of, "Racist!" and, "Sit down and shut up!" as well as, "Go to your own side!" would be extended into that person's direction. There was now a new dynamic to the dual in that gymnasium.

When the match began, the seasoned Panther was just too good for the young Bronco. O'Connor continued to work his leg attacks and acquire points off of his tilts and rides. But, with time running down in the match, and O'Connor holding a steady 7-0 lead, he would push and go for the extra team point.

As O'Connor came in and forced a position from a neutral start, Foreside defended it into an over-under position and threw the state champion to his back. The Montini crowd erupted in cheers on their end and Glenbard fans gasped from their side of the bleachers. In that moment, that same Montini father jumped up and screamed at the Glenbard's fans, "That's how you play those white keys, Carl!"

The hollers ended and fans went after the Montini father who was making comments that they felt were uncalled for as he pointed at the Glenbard fans. Four rows of fans became a scrum and some coaches and security had to get in the middle, as well as some other fans, to pull people away from one another.

That particular Montini father was quick to interact, but held that he did not do anything wrong while other fans fantastically disagreed with him and continued to call him a racist. They yelled for him to go to the other side of the gymnasium and words would go back and forth and, on the mat, O'Connor would still win, but only by a decision. This gave the Panthers an advantage—but no bonus points. Foreside would exit the mat to congratulations from his coaches and teammates, and that father would be escorted to Montini's side of the gymnasium, proud of his actions and the match result.

With the dual headed into 160, North held the dual lead: 17-15. The final five matches would now dictate the dual meet, and Montini's four-time state champion, Mike Benefiel, who would also cut a weight class, was going against North's Eric Wahrman. Benefiel would win an 8-4 decision swinging the team lead back to Montini's favor, 18-17, but Wahrman gave him all he could handle.

Next up for Glenbard was Alec Pineda—and North was counting on his win. In fact, North was so confident that they bumped their 171-pound starter and state qualifier to 189, and their 189 starter up to 215 pounds, to take a possible three weight classes in the dual. However, the stage had appeared to be too much for Pineda and, during the match, he figuratively froze and was seemingly in slow motion. He would lose a 4-

3 decision that Glenbard desperately needed to state qualifier Dan Grimes.

"We had some line-up changes and made some moves where we needed guys to step up and win some big matches," Ramos said. "Guys like Alec Pineda wrestled like he forgot how to wrestle and lost a key match-up for us, as well as a team-point, I think. But some guys lost as well that we needed to win those close matches."

At 189, two-time state qualifier at 171 and fifth-ranked Roy Feltson would have an opportunity to keep Glenbard in the dual; however, in a close match, he would fall in a 9-7 decision to state qualifier and fifth-ranked Ethan Winel. Montini was now at a 24-16 advantage.

Senior honorable mention wrestler, Mike Eldridge, was next up for Glenbard and he would bring the dual to a one-match race when he defeated David Lembas, 3-2, to bring the team score to 24-19 in favor of Montini.

Last up for Glenbard was senior Alex Hansen at heavyweight. Up for Montini would be the reigning state champion, Garrett Goebel.

Before the match fans were stomping the bleachers, yelling as loud as they could, voices and noises echoed throughout the undersized gymnasium, and the two heavyweights took to the mat.

Goebel would wrestle tight and nervous—all he had to do was not lose by a fall—and Hanson, just not as talented, did all he could to create a monstrous upset. Unfortunately, for Glenbard, the score would end in a 3-2 decision in favor of Goebel, and Montini won win the dual 27-19.

The win was redemption for Montini—they had now returned the favor to Glenbard from the season before. Glenbard's season ended and the number-three team in the state would shake hands with Montini, and, as they exited, Montini fans hollered in their direction. As they did this, even though the match was over, the tensions increased and now wrestlers from both teams were finding themselves involved in non-wrestling activities.

"Afterwards, fans were flipping each other off, fans were saying things on both sides to the other wrestlers and wrestlers and fans were flipping each other off and exchanging words," Ramos said. "It was crazy. The whole dual was just nuts."

When Glenbard returned home, Coach Hahn met with his guys and talked to them about next year's possibilities. The team, aside from the six upper-weights, were returning and the 2008 season had the potential to be North's strongest team to date. Of course, there was an off-season and Coach Hahn would rally his team around improving. For Tony, he would report back to Izzy and Mat Rats in the spring.

At the season's end, when the awards were handed out, Tony would finally earn the team's respect and he would be voted in as a captain.

However, he did not earn the Most Valuable Wrestler Award, or even a share in the award. It would go to senior state champion Bryan O'Connor.

"Coach Hahn did bring me in to talk to me before Awards' Night," Ramos said. "He told me what the situation was and had an award for me because he said I should also be recognized for my accomplishments. It was something that the coaches picked; the Most Valuable was something the team picked.

"I still talked to Coach Hahn because I felt I should have been a co-Most Valuable Wrestler," Ramos said. "I won everything and only lost one match—so it was frustrating. I did everything I could do in one season. But the guys didn't vote for me. I don't know if it was a little jealousy thing or what, but O'Connor ended up winning it—and he won a state title that year as a senior—but at the time it meant a lot because I wanted to win everything."

Hahn was very candid with Tony. "I explained to Tony that, overall, Bryan was a better leader and did everything we asked him to do and Tony didn't do everything that we asked of him," Hahn said. "Being Most Valuable is more than credentials—in my opinion. Tony had a great season and he did things a lot of guys can't do. But, he needed to be a leader and a better example in the room. O'Connor was the team's leader that year and he was more deserving—that's how the team voted, and that's how the award was awarded."

Even though Tony did not fully understand or agree with everything that Hahn was speaking about to him at the time, and he did not see it all happen that way, he accepted the rationale and walked out of the office and moved into the off-season.

CHAPTER 24
FARGO

"It was 3-1, 3-1. But I wouldn't say it was a close 3-1, 3-1. I pretty much dominated the match. I got my takedowns—back then it was one point per takedown, so that's six takedowns in a match. I pretty much just went out there, went to work, did my job, and won..."

• *Tony Ramos*

"MY FOCUS GOING INTO THE OFF-SEASON AND into my junior year," Ramos said, "was to win another state championship. Win Fargo—I hadn't won Fargo yet. I wanted to repeat as an Ironman champion—we were going back there—I really wanted to be a back-to-back Ironman champion. So there were still some big, big things that I needed to win, and it wasn't going to be a cakewalk just because I did it last year."

Tony's first off-season tournament took place in the first week of April in Las Vegas, Nevada, at the Western Regional. Again, he focused more on his wrestling than cutting weight—he entered the tournament at 119 pounds. And, as he done the previous year, he found himself in the finals. This time, he would face one of Iowa's best in Andrew Long.

"He was a tough kid from Iowa," Ramos remembered. "He was a Fargo champ and when he was in the finals and they did the introductions, he was flexing behind that screen that shadowed the wrestlers before he came out. When I saw that, I was like, *Man, I've got to beat this kid. I can't let this kid beat me.* He was cocky and I knew that if I didn't beat him, I was going to hear about it from him and his dad—even his dad was a talker."

The match was in hand from the start and Tony walked away with the championship, 3-1, 3-1.

"It was 3-1, 3-1," Ramos said. "But I wouldn't say it was a close 3-1, 3-1. I pretty much dominated the match. I got my takedowns—back then it was one point per takedown, so that's six takedowns in a match. I pretty much just went out there, went to work, did my job, and won another Junior Western Regional title."

At the end of the month, Tony headed out to Akron, Ohio, for the FILA Cadet National Championships. As he had done the year before, he dominated his competition. He defeated Josh Kindig of Pennsylvania in the semifinals and then faced, in a rematch of the Ironman finals from the previous season, Chris Villalonga of Blair Academy. Tony won in two periods: 1-0, and then by fall in 00:58.

"When I won that title, I was really excited about that," Ramos commented. "I think I caught Villalonga on his back after a double, like Grajales, but I don't remember. But I wrestled two really good kids in the semifinals and finals, but there was nowhere to go after that title. I wish they would have had Cadet World Championships at that time—I think it really would have helped my development because I would have been on three World Teams."

Tony's progress and growth was a continued escalation—he dominated on all levels and at a fairly natural weight for himself. In response to his development, he simply brought it back to his training.

"Every year I think my training got better, my training got harder—I felt that it was going great," Ramos said. "I had great workout partners, we were all state champs in [Class] A, [Class] AA, whatever, but we were always battling with each other and every time I went in the room, I knew I was going to be in a good fight."

And now Tony would once again be competing in Fargo and chasing a title that had eluded him the past two seasons. To Tony, and to many people, Fargo was the ultimate title.

"Fargo was so big to me as a wrestler," Ramos said, "because that's where all of the college coaches were at—it's where they all went. You know, if you won Fargo, you were the man. You're the best guy in the country at that weight class.

"Fargo is special for a lot of reasons. It's not one of those tournaments that anyone can just sign up for—there is a process. You have to win or place top three in your freestyle state tournament or win or place at a regional, or those types of things. So, a kid that makes it to Fargo is the one who has been training all spring and summer long and really wants to be successful and have some longevity in this thing—for college or for an international career. Fargo is the best of the best—the kids that are putting in the time and the effort."

Once Fargo wrestlers had earned their place at the tournament, whether they wrestled for a national championship or an All-American place, there was always more to learn and techniques and positioning to walk away with and grow from.

"Fargo always made me a better wrestler," Ramos said. "It always made me strive to be better because I had never been a top dog. So there's always me leaving there with a bad taste in my mouth which always motivated me going into the next year and going forward."

Aside from the wrestling, the other special part about Fargo was the teammates and the relationships each wrestler made. Most of these guys knew of each other or had competed against one another, but now they were pulling for the same cause and were helping each other get better. This was also well before the big social media bang. Facebook was vaguely around, but there was no use of Twitter or other social media outlets like Instagram and Snap Chat to bring Illinois' elite wrestlers together. It was all about the camp.

"Meeting the guys and also heading to camp with our own teammates and other guys was always fun," Ramos said. "We would go together as teams, but everyone was very close. We would live in the dorms together, and just have a great time together. For North it was like Geno, me, Monaco, Chase, Vince, and Billy Heyduk. One year Monaco had to get stitches by his ribs because we were having too much fun running around.

"But, really, having all of those guys and all of those teams come together is really special and, more than anything, it was preparing us for the future for college and national and world teams. Teaching us how to put little things aside and come together as Team U.S.A. and work as one. Fargo is the same thing. A bunch of rivals come together and work to make Team Illinois the best that it can be."

As Tony entered camp, he was targeted right away by a few of the college coaches and some of the more high-end wrestlers. He was known throughout the state, and being on Team Illinois made him more *Tony* than just *Ramos* when he was off the mat.

When the tournament opened, Tony was excited as he was expected to win it and welcomed the challenge and the pressure and the hype that surrounded it.

"That year I was already in the running," Ramos remembered. "I had won first-team ASICS All-American honors, so I wanted to go out there and win and prove that that was no fluke and that there was a reason why I was number one in the country. And I was excited to go out there and win it."

When wrestling began, Tony dominated all of his opponents and found himself in the finals against an opponent he had always beat. In fact, he just beat him in the semifinals of the FILA Cadet National Championships earlier that spring. That would be Josh Kindig of Team Pennsylvania.

For Team Illinois, there had been a tradition that Tony was excited about earning with a Fargo championship: The championship belt. "The Belt," as it was referred to, was a plastic "Professional Wrestling" children's belt that could be purchased at any box or toy store. Team Illinois wrestlers would have them in the stands and, upon winning a Fargo title, their wrestler would be awarded it and wear it around.

"When I made the finals," Ramos commented, "I was anticipating getting one of those belts. It's something that Team Illinois did and it was pretty cool and it was something that you wanted—you wanted the belt."

As the spotlight came for the finals match, Tony was ready. "In that first period," Ramos remembered, "I scored take down after takedown after takedown and I was cruising and won 3-0 against Kindig, a guy that I had dominated and never lost to.

"Heading into that second period, I was still scoring. Jeremy Hunter and Carl Perry were my coaches and they were confident and they were excited and I was winning 3-0 in the second period; so now I have six takedowns. With about 00:30 left I am in a front headlock hanging on, and Kindig does this little move where he reaches over the back and falls to his butt and whips you over, and he hit me for three. So he had criteria and won that period 3-3 and I was like, *Shit. I was just a few seconds away from winning a Fargo championship and now I got to go another period—okay, let's go and do this.*"

As Tony headed into the third and final period, he knew, since he dominated on his feet, that he had to keep the match there in order to win his first Fargo title.

"In the third period I knew I just had to keep it on my feet," Ramos said. "So I go out there and get a takedown. Then I get another takedown and another. I am up 3-0 and I get in for another takedown, and I got crotch-lifted for two. Now it's 3-2. I get in for another takedown and he crotch-lifts me again. Now it's 3-4. He gets a takedown and now it's 3-5. I get in and score a two-point move, but he wins 5-5 on criteria because he had more two-point moves.

"So, it was pretty frustrating for me because I feel I dominated the match but I still lost. I had like eight or nine takedowns and a two-pointer and he has one big move, twice, and I lose. That was it. It was a hard pill for me to swallow. It was a hard thing for me to walk off that mat knowing that I just whooped his butt and still lost the match, how is that possible?"

Tony, who was used to scoring and being the guy who had won the big matches that season when it all ended, had now lost one. It was not that Tony could not score. It was not that the scoring system was faulty—it was the system at the time. It was just being out of position and being exposed for those counters.

"What I walked away with," Ramos said, "was not to be giving up the big points, especially in freestyle. I have to go out there and, when I had the opportunity to score, I have to score and not let him get to those three-point moves. I have to make it happen—no excuses. It's on me. And after that match, that was when I really started to focus in on not giving up those points. You know, scoring points and not giving up points—not giving anything up. That made me a better wrestler.

"That year I was supposed to win it and I didn't. But, life goes on and you have to move forward. I left Fargo with a bad taste in my mouth and that motivated me going into the next year and moving forward."

• • •

As the 2007-2008 school year began, Tony and a few of his friends decided to join the newly developed pep club at North—the school sponsor was a new teacher that the boys thought to be very attractive and this was all the motivation that they needed to show up and join.

"Some of the focuses were on how to get more fans and students to sporting events," Ramos said of the club's purpose, "and that's when we came up with themes [for each of the home football games] and the idea of 'Super Fans' that the school has had since."

However, the club also had the idea to bring back a school spirit staple of old. "We also thought about bringing back the Panther [mascot] and it being a part of sporting events at school." And once the idea came to be a reality, and the old mascot suit was found and cleaned, all it needed was someone to wear it.

"We were trying to find someone [to be the Panther]," Ramos remembered, "and I figured, *Why not do it and actually make it fun?* So, I got to dress up and be crazy and no one knew it was me. It was a lot of fun at the games and pep rallies."

Tony would become North's Panther mascot for his junior and senior year and he had a great deal of fun in his costumed role. However, the Panther would have one drawback with Tony in charge: it was never seen or able to make an appearance at a basketball game.

CHAPTER 25
MURDERERS' ROW

"There was no partying, there was no screwing around; all we did was wrestle. I don't know what we did, but we wrestled a lot and had a lot of fun doing that and just being around each other."

• Geno Capezio
Teammate, Glenbard North High School

BEFORE THE 2008 SEASON EVEN BEGAN, THE TEAM captains were holding voluntary workouts for their teammates who were not in a fall sport. These five captains: junior Tony Ramos, ranked number-one at 125 pounds; junior Jimmy Chase, ranked third at 130; senior 135-pounder Geno Capezio, ranked second; senior Danny Monaco, ranked number-three at 140; and, senior Vince Ramos, ranked number-one at 145 pounds, came to be known as "Murderers' Row." They occupied the middle of the Glenbard line-up and any team the Panthers went up against were looking at about a twenty-five-point deficit from just those five weight classes.

In calmer circles, they were more affectionately known as "The Big Five"; however, "Murderers' Row" was the nickname that stuck before the season opened and, in most other conversations, it seemed more appropriate,

For the first time since 2003, North would have one of the premier powerhouse wrestling teams in the state and in the country. North had been recognized in the 1970s and 1980s and known widely throughout Illinois as one of the best programs around. In the 1990s, it would not be until the later end of the decade that North had re-established a full fear in the black and gold. But, in the 2000s, that was when national attention to the program was more wide-spread as more wrestlers were wrestling at Fargo and North was traveling out of Illinois and dominating.

The 2008 team was loaded with senior talent, tough juniors, and sprinkled with a strong freshman and versatile sophomores. But, there was no mistake to be made, this team was filled with a group of matured seniors who were looking to claim the program's first state championship. They were poised for great individual success.

However, what made this team special, was they were all friends and they cared about each other's successes and failures. When they had to wrestle, they wrestled for each other, their head coach, and their program. "That was one of the best seasons for me being on a team," Ramos said, "because I had so many friends on the team that I wanted to see succeed."

There was a great deal of pride in that team and, as optional captain workouts began, it showed. "That summer," Ramos remembered, "we worked hard and we went and did all of our workouts together. Everyone wanted the same thing—we all wanted to win a team state championship and we all wanted to be individual state champs. We did everything that I think we could've done to make that happen."

Senior captain and friend, Geno Capezio, also reflected on that season very fondly. "We wanted to win that team state championship so badly," Capezio said. "That group, our team, was really close. We all hung out and we were running our own little pre-season workouts like three days a week at 5:30 a.m. It would be Tony coming up with a workout one day and then I would come up with one the next day, then Vince and everyone—we all traded off and we had good numbers there too, like fifteen to twenty guys would show up. That doesn't happen very often. We were all out to win it that year."

During those workouts, "We would just train together as a group and get some morning workouts in running bleachers, do a track workout—miles, sprints—things like that," Ramos recalled. "And it wasn't coaches pushing us through it; we were doing it on our own because we wanted to be the best. We had the devastating loss from the year before to Montini at the Team Sectional and we didn't want that to happen again. We had a chance to get Coach Hahn his first team state title and that's what we wanted to go and do—we put as much effort as we possibly could into doing it."

That would also be Tony's first season as a team captain and, now that he was voted in, he felt more ownership and responsibility to the team as a whole. "Because these were the guys that voted me as a captain and wanted me to step up and be vocal and lead," Ramos said, "I think that made it easier for me. The year before I felt that maybe there was a reason why they didn't think I deserved to be a captain, so I was discouraged and pretty much stayed to myself which was selfish by me, but now I felt like they all believed in me and trusted me with that leadership role, and I didn't want to let them down."

With Tony would be his closest friends, the seniors, as those were the individuals he had wrestled with and trained with more than his own class. He had been a varsity starter since his freshman year and, his classmates, aside from Chase, had gone through the program's under levels and gained and grew at their own pace.

"It wasn't just the varsity starters that were coming in to work," Vince Ramos said, "it was juniors, too. We all pushed each other. We would train together, go wrestle together, go up to the [Ramos'] lake house together—we were doing so much together it was to the point where we were all like brothers hanging out all of the time."

Since Tony was now an upper-classman, and now on a team with more teammates that he felt knew him better, that relaxed him.

"I think, for Tony," Capezio commented, "since he was more like a senior, he was able to open up more than in previous years. Since we all hung out and were friends with Vince, and Tony always tagged along, he just became one of us—one of the group. And when we wrestled, we always wrestled together at tournaments, traveling, clubs; it was always our group. We all had the same goals and the same mindset, so it never seemed like he was younger—he was just Vince's little brother who happened to be Tony Ramos the stud wrestler.

"There was no partying, there was no screwing around; all we did was wrestle. I don't know what we did, but we wrestled a lot and had a lot of fun doing that and just being around each other. We wrestled fifty off-season matches and, even if we were off, we would go up to the Ramos' lake house and we'd be working out there. Whether it was Frankie or Mrs. Ramos making us run or do some kind of workout before we could go on the boats and be on the water, it didn't matter. We were all on the same page. We were all committed to each other."

For Tony, the time that he put in with his friends was additional to the time he was putting in away from them, and sometimes in the same day merely hours after leaving them.

"I think what people don't get is that Tony wasn't flashy or overpowering on the mat," Capezio explained, "he was just a hard working kid who grinded out matches and outlasted his opponents. He was just always wrestling and working at wrestling. People don't realize the hours he put into just wrestling and position wrestling and mat wrestling each day—that was all he did. He may have looked slick, but that was because he was in better shape and would just wear guys down to where he looked stronger and faster than he really was. He was tough to score on and just outworked people in the room, in the offseason, out of the room, and on the mat."

That 2008 season would also prove to be a statement season for Tony as well. "People weren't necessarily giving Tony the credit he deserved," Vince Ramos commented. "People had said, 'You won a title at 112 [pounds], he didn't have to deal with the big boys in the middle weights.' I think that gave Tony something else to focus on. He had the takedown record, he was a state champion, but I think this was the motivation he needed to focus in on something new."

So, regardless of all of Tony's successes, he was still receiving scrutiny from the outside, and it bothered him. "When Tony had heard all of this," Vince Ramos said, "he wanted to come out and prove a point that season. He went from 112 to 125 pounds, and he wanted to show everyone that it didn't matter where he wrestled, he was the best guy. I also think this was his maturity year because he was able to handle a heavier weight—I know he could have gone 119—and he handled the team aspect better. I think this team was easier for him to blend in on because we were all so close and that allowed him to be more of a leader by example."

As the season opened, the team was not only having a great deal of fun together, they were wrestling as hard as they could for each other. And they needed to be wrestling hard for one another because everyone was up one or two weight classes; additionally, Chase ended up tearing his ACL that summer and looked to be out for the remainder of the season. Chase's injury was a major loss to the team. In addition, there were a number of starters on the team still competing in the football state playoffs as they had a strong run going; due to that, the team had no viable heavyweight and was forfeiting that weight.

Regardless of all the drawbacks, the team was winning and all of the workouts that were put in were paying off for the younger wrestlers who stepped onto the mat. Even with their little varsity experience, they had a positive impact in each tournament and dual. Additionally, the veterans were not just winning matches, they were scoring bonus points and falls to keep the team's unblemished record intact.

Once the team was as strong as it was going to be for some time, their first real test would be at the Ironman. Tony was looking to repeat as a champion, and the team was looking to put their imprint on the national rankings and a team and as individuals.

THERE WAS A GREAT DEAL OF EXCITEMENT THE week North was headed to the Ironman because they had the talent and the depth to have a number of wrestlers place, if not be finalists, and possibly earn a top-three team finish.

"That year was different than the previous year," Ramos explained, "because we had a lot of guys who could make a run [at a title]. Last year, we had maybe two guys that could have been finalists, but I was excited to defend my title and the team's attitude and expectations were high going in. We were planning on a great weekend."

When Glenbard walked in, they were healthy and ready to prove their team's worth to the country. In regard to Tony, he too was healthy and excited and prepared to wrestle and prove himself as the best 125-pound wrestler in the field.

Entering the venue, Glenbard had quite the swagger and the team's aura was one of confidence; that also lifted Tony's spirits. Up until that point, Glenbard had not been challenged, but they all knew the Ironman would not only challenge them, it might even humble a few of them. The team's focus was high and wrestling would reveal where they were at up to that point in the season.

For his opening match, Tony, the number-one seed, faced senior Michael Baxter of Perkins High School in Sandusky, Ohio, and Tony won a very unusually tight 5-4 match. Though he would advance, Tony did not move forward unscathed.

"In that first match," Ramos explained, "I kind of landed on my head and shoulder and I didn't know what was wrong with it—I had shooting pains going down my arm."

Tony continued wrestling, but did not say anything to anyone. "No matter what," Ramos said, "I always try to compete to the best of my abilities healthy or hurt. I don't like to make excuses so when I had that second match against Benny Marti of Montini, I went out to wrestle it."

When the match with the unseeded Marti came up, Tony was again opposite of Israel Martinez who was in Marti's corner. As the match began to unfold, Tony struggled with his positions.

Within seconds, Tony was able to get into his single-leg attack while penetrating on Marti; however, after a sprawl and scoot by Marti as he worked into a scramble position, Tony fought to hold his position with his head inside, but his head came to the outside as Marti climbed and scooted behind him for a first period takedown and a 2-0 lead.

Tony worked to his feet and claimed an escape point, but the first period ended with Marti in the lead, 2-1. From Tony's corner, his brother and coach, Frank, would be yelling to him, "Keep scoring from your shot! Double-legs, Tony! Keep position." From the other chair, Edwards instructed Tony, "Finish clean. Avoid the scramble."

Across the mat, in Marti's corner, Israel would be telling his assistant coach, Tony Marti, "He's got to keep the pressure on Tony."

When the first period came to an end, Tony was frustrated; however, he was able to collect himself as he chose down. Then, what had never happened to Tony became a reality; when the whistle blew, he was being ridden in such a way with the legs that he could not break free and get to his feet. Each time he found himself in a position for an advantage, the much longer Marti found a way to throw another leg in or elongate Tony and brought him back, flat, to the mat.

As the second period came to a close, Frank and Edwards had exhausted themselves trying to coach Tony out of Marti's positions.

In Marti's corner, his coaches told him to choose down—Tony had to cut him and concede another point. When Marti chose down, Tony did just that. He let Marti go and worked to win the match on his feet. For Tony, this was where he wanted to be anyway. He was known for his takedowns and his array of moves. Marti, who had trained with him, also knew this—as did Israel—as did Tony Marti.

With the match now a 3-1 lead in favor of Marti, Tony would work back into a single-leg as he was unable to keep position on his double-leg attack. Once again, as he found position in on Marti with that single-leg, Marti was able to scramble. This time, Marti would not only score a takedown, but he caught and earned near fall points in the process. With about one minute left in the match, Israel turned to Tony Marti and tell him, "Upset of the tournament, right here."

Tony Marti would scream out to his brother who was in the top position with his legs in, "Stay with the pry." At the 00:25 second mark, both corners were yelling opposite instructions. From Frank and Edwards, they were hollering for Tony to get up and out. From Marti's corner, he was hearing, "Just ride him out!"

When the match came to an end, Tony lost to a wrestler he had never lost to in the practice room or on the mat until now. It was an 8-4 decision and Tony was now in the wrestle-backs.

"I was getting to my shots and getting to my offense," Ramos said. "I just didn't finish. I would get caught up in his scrambling positions and he would beat me on the corners scoring points and I would end up losing that match."

For Marti, he wrestled the perfect match against his shorter opponent. He kept position, worked into his scrambles, and rode him out on top. Marti would lose his next two matches and be eliminated from the tournament.

"It was rough because I wanted to repeat," Ramos said, "and it was also rough because I didn't go to the Ironman to go lose to a guy from Illinois where I knew I would never hear the end of it. It would be the highlight of his season, if not his career in wrestling."

For his next match, Tony tried to wrestle; however, after warm-ups, he would injury default out of the tournament. The undefeated season was over, and he would have to regroup.

The rest of the team would fumble along through the remainder of the tournament as well. There would be some matches won, but not enough to appease the team's aspirations for making an impact on the country. North fell to the middle of the pack and only two wrestlers medaled; Danny Monaco placed sixth at 140 pounds, and Vince Ramos placed third at 145 pounds.

The team finished in an unexpected twenty-seventh place and headed back home with some injuries and egos to heal, as well as some specific working points for each to focus on before the Clash High School National Duals in a few weeks.

THE WEEKS LEADING TO THE CLASH WERE filled with hard work and recovery for the team. Since the school was on break for the Christmas holiday, the focus was simple: wrestle, recover, and repeat. The break was always the perfect time for the team to spend more time with each other and, as they headed up to Rochester, Minnesota, it was also a time for bonds to grow stronger and for the top wrestlers to showcase their talents, as well as some of the more unknown wrestlers to make names for themselves.

"For me," Ramos said, "all of my goals were still attainable except the undefeated season. I went back to work in the room and I could still go undefeated the rest of the season. I could still earn All-Clash honors and win the state championship as an individual, and the main goal was to win the team state championship and be the first team to do that for Coach Hahn and the program.

"When we left for the Clash, I wanted to go up there and make it known that I was the best wrestler in my weight class and that they would have no choice but to vote me as an All-Clash wrestler."

Tony and the entire team had chosen to dye their hair gold; however, he and his brother would, again, be different and run a thin black stripe through the right side and stand out a bit from the others.

"Yep, me and Vince sat there and dyed our heads like everyone on the team," Ramos laughed. "But we were like, 'Last year we had Mohawks where the Mohawks were only gold; why don't we do everything but a black stripe this year?' Of course, we thought it was a great idea so we just went with it and that's what we did."

Tony would enter the duals ranked number one in Illinois at 125 pounds and number six in the country. He was again featured as a wrestler to watch and, after feeling snubbed last year as an All-Clash wrestler, he wanted to prove himself to the Minnesota crowd.

First up for the North was the number-one rated team in Hawaii, Punahou. They raised the funds and made the trek to Rochester; however, they were unprepared for the Midwest winter and were not dressed accordingly. They had purchased coats and jeans; however, the weather that weekend was a frigid 8° with a light snowfall and a twenty-four mile per hour max wind speed out of the south; a stark contrast from the average 80° weather in Hawaii—it was cold.

Aside from the harsh weather that welcomed the Buff 'n Blue, their first taste of the Clash would come against the number-nine rated team in the country in Glenbard North. Tony had the number-one ranked wrestler from Hawaii, Reid Oshiro, to open his day. Oshiro, in addition to a large number of his teammates, was ranked in the top three of his weight class, was a retuning state champion, had qualified for Fargo, and had each experienced very few folkstyle defeats in his career.

As the dual began, Punahou dropped its first nine matches to North, the first three by decision, the following three by fall, a major decision at 103 pounds, and two more falls before it was Tony's turn.

When he took the mat, he was just as dominant as his team had been to that point. He put on a show and won by an 11-0 major decision. The team would blank the Buff 'n Blue by a 68-0 score.

"While I don't like the result, this is what we came here for," Head Coach Matt Oney of Punahou said in an interview with a local Rochester paper after the dual. "That's as physical of a team as we'll see. My kids were able to see that you can wrestle that physical and keep your technique. They were flawless; they're a great team. And we came here to see that type of team."

That season, Punahou won the Hawaii state championship and sent four finalists into the championship match, crowned three state champions, and medaled an additional eight wrestlers. At the Clash, they ended up in thirty-first place out of thirty-two teams.

Next up for Glenbard would be Simley, Minnesota, the number-four rated team in Minnesota's class 2A. Tony cruised through his match, winning by fall in 4:32, and the team rolled into the finals of their pool with a 46-19 performance.

Once in the finals, Glenbard faced the number-two team in the pool, Jackson County Central, who was rated number-five in Minnesota's class 1A. The dual featured two teams that knew the swing matches would be the difference in determining the final score.

Jackson opened the dual with two falls in a matter of four minutes before adding a major decision to their 16-0 lead. At heavyweight, North senior Jeff Jones stopped the bleeding and won a 4-0 decision as the dual turned to 103 pounds and the strength of North's line-up about to take the mat.

When it was time for freshman Joey Gosinski to wrestle, Glenbard was down 16-3; however, after he won by decision, along with falls by Warczynski and Varela at 112 and 119 pounds, Tony walked onto the mat with the team score now in North's favor, 18-16.

"Even though I had already won my first two matches, I wanted to end strong," Ramos said. "In my head, I was still trying to work through the loss at the Ironman and that terrible tournament, so I wanted and needed to win big. If I had to beat a guy up, I was going to beat a guy up—that's what I would have to do. I was going to be physical and get back on track and I didn't care if the fans or the coaches or the parents or the voters didn't think it was nice, or if the kid was going to go cry to his parents—they could take it or just get tough."

Just as Tony had opened up his first two matches in a very physical style, he wanted to end his day with a statement match; he faced sophomore Taylor Menke, a 2007 Minnesota and U.S.A. Wrestling Cadet Folkstyle champion at 125 pounds. And, as the match opened, Tony was on the attack and he was going to force Menke to either take it or get tough—and at the start, Menke was just going to take it. After Tony scored his first takedown and cut him loose, Tony would score his second and go up 4-1 almost immediately.

Once on the mat, Tony popped Menke's elbow forward and struck him with a cross-face as he looked for a cradle. The referee stopped the match and Tony lost a point for unnecessary roughness. From the Jackson County fans, hisses were heard and shouts of, "Throw him out! Give me a break!" came in unison. But Tony did not care; in fact, it only encouraged him.

Headed into the second period, Tony continued to control the match and the Jackson County fans were not pleased with the physical style imposed on Menke. Tony came down hard on Menke's head, he snapped him to the mat with great force, and pushed him around; Menke was simply trying to keep it close. When Tony was able to work in close enough to penetrate in on a double-leg, he lifted Menke, drove his feet, and brought the Jackson County wrestler down hard into the mat. The referee signaled and called out "Two" for the takedown and a Jackson County parent, yelled, "You gonna let him slam him?"

When the third period came, Menke was in position to still do right by his team—he only trailed 7-2 with 00:25 left in the match and he was in the bottom position. If he could remain in good position, he would lose by a decision and save his team a bonus point; thus keeping Jackson County in the dual and giving them a moral boost.

From North's bench, Frank barked orders for Tony to earn the major via a turn on top or through a big move. Hahn instructed Tony to cut Menke and win it on his feet. Unfortunately, Menke had been able to keep Tony and any big move at bay, so Tony had to really work in the closing seconds to make the extra team point a reality.

Once Menke was given the escape point, and a 7-3 score showed on the scoreboard, Tony had to chase and force a move, as well as execute it. Menke, as he hand fought, had about 00:12 to go for a moral victory. However, with 00:10 remaining, Tony found his way into a throw as Menke tried to take a shot. Tony caught him midway, lifted, and threw him to his back for a takedown, two near-fall points, and an 11-3 major decision. The Jackson County crowd ranted and raved about the previous calls and, when Tony got up, he looked over to them as his hand was raised and smiled at the booing Jackson County section.

"I could not believe he shot on me," Ramos said. "I was looking for the throw and he fed right into it. As for their fans, I loved it. Keep booing—your guy couldn't handle the match and neither could you."

More importantly, "That was a big match for Tony and the team," Hahn said. "It was a turning point for how some of the guys saw him and how he was wrestling—he was scoring for the team now. He was growing up at the right time."

After that match, the dual was in hand—North would only lose one match out of the final six weights. They would win their bracket with a 45-22 score and advance into the Championship Pool on Day Two.

That night, Hahn met with his team and they, along with in-state rival Montini Catholic, would be in the final pool—as would Apple Valley, Minnesota, and Waverly-Shell Rock, Iowa. When the pairings came out that night, North drew Waverly first, then Montini, and ended their day with Apple Valley. Glenbard knew that all three of the match-ups were important; however, their dual with number-two Montini would be the first time they would meet until the first round of the Dual Team state championships. Both teams were eager to wrestle, but there would be one dual prior for both.

Against Waverly, the Go-Hawks would outscore Glenbard with three falls, a major decision, and a regular decision in the five of the six upper-weight matches. And, even though the lighter-weights tried to keep Glenbard in the dual, it was simply too much to overcome against a strong team. Tony won with a 12-4 major decision over Matt Kittleson; however, Glenbard lost the dual, 38-28.

Next up was Montini—Illinois' top-two rated wrestling programs going at it. At the time, Glenbard had a number-two rating in Illinois, and Montini who, had defeated North last season at the Sectional and had a better showing at the Ironman, held onto the number-one rating. Of course, in the end, the dual would settle it for good.

For the dual, Hahn decided to tamper with his line-up a bit. They were looking to find some better match-ups, and they knew Montini knew where they were strong and might make some moves—it would be a chess match and a hard-fought dual, just as in the past two years.

Unfortunately for North, Montini would, as Waverly did, exploit their upper-weights and win five of the six bouts from 152 through 285 pounds. North would only win five of the fourteen weight classes, and Montini would walk away with a 35-17 victory.

Tony, who was bumped to wrestle 130, defeated Frank Bear, 10-4. However, North would only score bonus points in one match while Montini scored bonus points in five. Additionally, North's Jimmy Chase was still out—if he could make it back in time for the season's end, that would help strengthen the Panthers' line-up. But, there would still need to be ground gained in the upper weights.

In Glenbard's final match, they were paired up with Clash rival Apple Valley. Valley would be 1-1 coming into the match and needed a win to keep pace with the other two teams in the pool; Glenbard was 0-2 and needed a strong dual to walk away with some positives.

The dual started at 285 pounds and North took an early 3-0 lead. However, the next three weights were all Valley via two decisions and a fall. For Valley, leading by a 12-3 score, the match-up with Tony was an important one for the dual and for each individual wrestler. Valley's Tom Kelliher was a three-time Minnesota state finalist, ranked number one in Minnesota, and number eight in the nation; Tony was number one in Illinois and number six in the country. The match-up would be highlighted by the announcer and the Glenbard and Valley fans had prime seating for what was to be a great match. Of course, as Tony was called, he was booed again as the Valley fans remembered him from last season's antics.

"I remember the match vaguely," Ramos admitted. "I do know that I knew Kelliher because he was an Illinois kid out of the Crystal Lake Wizards growing up, but I also knew it would be a tough match because he had improved a lot and grew in his wrestling being at Apple Valley. Also, it was a big team match because the dual was close at that point, so I knew I needed to go out there and do my job."

In the stands, a Valley parent recalled last year's end to his match and screamed, "This ain't last year. Ramos is about to go from number six to number nine right here."

But the words never bothered Tony. "There was a lot of talk going into that match," Ramos recalled. "I was still looking to make a statement to the Minnesota people; my goal was to dominate and be All-Clash. Kelliher was not going to get in the way of that. I went into that match confident and I went right after him."

In fact, as soon as the opening whistle blew, Tony moved forward and was heavy on Kelliher. Kelliher, in that opening, would take a shot, but on the sprawl he hurt his head and an injury timeout had to be used. Once they went back to the center, Tony again came forward and started pushing Kelliher around, pressuring him and firing in on open doubles. The first period ended 0-0, but Tony had taken control of the match's tempo and was the aggressor.

In the second period, Tony chose down, escaped, and took a 1-0 lead. Throughout the remainder of the period, Tony continually pushed and shot on Kelliher until the referee hit him for stalling. The period ended 1-0 in Tony's favor and, for the third period, Kelliher chose down. Tony cut him to wrestle the match on his feet. Kelliher knew that he would have to open up. Kelliher would take a shot and Tony defended it, took a reshot, and scored. The score was now a 3-1 advantage for Tony and he was on top in a very tough butt-wrist ride.

As Tony continued to apply pressure on Kelliher, Kelliher was again hit with stalling and Tony now led, 4-1. With little time left, Tony cut Kelliher and, with seconds on the clock, the referee hit Tony for stalling, but the score would end 4-2. North and Tony would earn the victory, but they could not comprehend the stall call. "That stall call was garbage," Ramos said. "I controlled the match and applied all the pressure. The Minnesota referee must have just felt bad for Kelliher and felt he needed to give him something to walk away with."

Regardless of the call, North closed the gap momentarily, but Valley opened up and won five of the next nine matches. Glenbard would lose its third dual of the day, this time by a 36-18 margin.

"Some of us fell short," Ramos said, "but I don't think any of them have regrets because we gave it our all. We wrestled hard, we worked hard, and we wrestled our butts off. And it was exciting to see, not just me, everyone was putting points up and putting forth the effort. But, it was back to Illinois and back to work."

Tony left Rochester with an 18-0 combined record at the Clash and his second All-Clash award in three years.

2008 • CAPTAINS' PICTURE • "MURDERERS' ROW"
STANDING • L TO R • GENO CAPEZIO • DANNY MONACO • VINCE RAMOS
KNEELING • L TO R • JIMMY CHASE • TONY RAMOS
PHOTOGRAPH COURTESY • GLENBARD NORTH WRESTLING
MARLON BROOKS PHOTOGRAPHY

CHAPTER 26
THE TWO SEED

"In any case, it was going to be resolved on the mat. In my mind, it was a win-win for everybody. Tony would be pissed, and ready to wrestle. My guy would have the confidence of his undefeated DVC record being recognized."

• *Steve Holland*
Former Head Coach, Wheaton North High School

TONY NOW HAD A SEASON RECORD OF 26-1 AS THE team headed into their conference tournament and then into the state series. Jimmy Chase was back for the DuPage Valley Conference tournament and the individual and team state series, but his practice time had been limited and his conditioning was subpar. His return was an astounding six months after his ACL surgery.

With Chase back in the line-up, the lower and middle weights were really solidified. Tony would be at 125 pounds, then Chase, Capezio, Monaco, and finally Vince Ramos would cap off Murderers' Row at 145. The team was now at full strength.

It had not been since Frank's junior season, midway through in 1997, that the Glenbard program had lost a DVC dual, and the Panthers had also won the past nine-consecutive DVC team championships—and none of those records sat well with the other schools in the conference.

Wheaton North and Naperville North had given Glenbard some tight duals and close finishes, but they could never grab the win. With the entrance of West Aurora, there had been some strong duals and tight finishes with them as well. However, in the end, North always found a way to pull out a victory and the title.

During that 2008 season, it was West Aurora and then Wheaton North that was looking to dethrone Glenbard in their dual meets and at the DVC tournament; however, it would take a collective effort by the conference for that to happen as North had a great deal of talent throughout their line-up.

"When it came to West Aurora," Ramos said, "I always wrestled [Josh] Zinzer and those were big matches. A lot of people, especially their coaches, thought that maybe he could catch me in a headlock—he was kind of one of those guys like Ellis Coleman who was explosive and could get you from all different angles. We always battled with West Aurora, it was a big rivalry. We never lost to them because it was a big deal to us as a team to not let those matches slip away.

"The other team we battled with was Wheaton North. That year Wheaton North and West Aurora thought that they had a shot at beating us, which would have been their year—like they say every year—but we shut that down right away in our duals. [Wheaton North Head] Coach [Steve] Holland and Frankie were friends and I had a good relationship with him too, but those duals were great duals. I would wrestle Fitzenreider a couple of times, Vince did, too, so it was kind of a family affair going on as well. I wouldn't say that we hung out on the weekends—we did not have a pretty good friendship. I think they felt second best to us because they could never beat us. I think they thought they could, but they never did and they talked it up a lot—but it never happened. All we kept doing was widening the gap."

However, even though the conference duals were close, as a whole, Tony did want to make sure that everyone knew he was well above every other wrestler in the conference.

"When I went out there," Ramos said, "I wanted to and I was going to show the conference that, yeah, these guys are pretty good, but I'm on a whole different level. That was my mindset. And when it came time for the conference tournament, it always seemed like it was North against the entire conference, and that year was the worst of all with how it all played out—at least it was for them."

On the Wednesday night on the week of the conference championships, the coaches gathered and seeded the tournament.

For North, freshman Joey Gosinski earned the number-one seed. At 112 pounds, senior Jaime Warczynski earned the number-two seed with a 25-10 record and loss to Wheaton North's Adrian Laskero in the dual. Returning DVC Champion, Ray Varella, was voted into the number-four seed at 119, and then Tony's weight class was called for seeding.

The host school, who ran the seeding meeting, called out for which coach wanted to put his wrestler up for the number-one seed. Hahn raised his hand and no one else followed. However, as Tony's name and record went onto the board, Wheaton North Head Coach Steve Holland responded, "Who was his one loss to?"

Hahn would reply, "It was at the Ironman. Montini. Benny Marti."

Holland smiled, "I want to put my wrestler up for the one seed. Jake Denhof. He was 5-0 in conference duals."

Hahn turned to Holland, "He beat Marti? When did you guys wrestle Montini?"

"At the Dvorak," Holland said. "Our guy was undefeated in conference duals. He has criteria to be up there for consideration."

The DuPage Valley Conference rules did not follow traditional seeding rules. Normally, a one-loss returning state champion and two-time finalist, Fargo All-American, among other accolades, would be a shoo-in for the number-one seed. However, in the DVC, the first criteria was head-to-head—both were undefeated in conference and they did not wrestle each other; Tony wrestled 130 in that dual.

For the second criteria, it came down to common opponent. Denhof had beaten Marti who had beaten Tony. At the Dvorak, Denhof would lose in the quarterfinals to Iowa City West's Nate Moore, 14-9. Also in the quarterfinals, Marti would lose to Mark Augle of Providence Catholic, 4-3. In the wrestle-backs, when the two met, Denhof defeated Marti, 12-2.

With the common opponent, the seeding would not come down to the third criteria: a coaches' vote. However, there was some objection by the North staff based on Tony's body of work and Hahn wanted a coaches' vote.

"Let me tell you the real criteria for conference voting," Hahn said. "The first criteria is screw Glenbard North. Then it is head-to-head, then it's common opponent, and then it's a coaches' vote—which is also screw Glenbard North."

At the time of the conference meet, North was looking to win its tenth title in a row, and all of the other schools wanted to be the ones to break that streak. With Denhof at the one seed, it gave Wheaton North a strong opportunity to score more team points on the way to the championship match. Tony would not be contested as the number-two seed and would fill that spot in the bracket.

"That was ridiculous," assistant coach Chris Edwards said. "At that point, every team and every coach was looking for an advantage on [North], and that just showed how desperate some of those teams were. You have the returning state champion, an All-American, two-time conference champ, All-Clash, the list goes on, against this other kid who really hasn't done anything—he did not even wrestle Tony in our dual. Sitting in that room Mark and I just shook our heads—it was laughable. But, Frankie, Frankie was out of his mind."

"What did I see?" Defilippis reacted. "I saw a bullshit vote. There was no way that kid should have been in front of Tony—never, no way and under no circumstances—they all knew it. Steve [Holland] knew it, too."

The viewpoint from Holland was simple: it was a new year. "We didn't take the number-one seed from Tony, our wrestler had earned that spot by his performance up to that point in the season," Holland calmly protested. "I'm sure Glenbard North had challenge matches before the season and Tony had to earn his spot again for that season—that's wrestling.

"Jake Denhof was undefeated in the conference, went 5-1 at the Clash, and was a very solid wrestler as a senior. And, he beat someone Tony had lost to that year. Jake was one of those kids that responded to us being upbeat and positive with him all the time. My job at the seeding meeting wasn't to just give the position away. According to the conference rules, Jake had criteria to be the number-one seed at the tournament.

"The situation was eventually resolved through a coaches' vote," Holland concluded. "I assumed something might [happen] with us and the Tony Ramos seeding issue. The other coaches made the decision to follow the criteria. In any case, it was going to be resolved on the mat. In my mind, it was a win-win for everybody. Tony would be pissed, and ready to wrestle. My guy would have the confidence of his undefeated DVC record being recognized."

When Tony heard about the seeding, he did not know what to think. "I thought it had to be a joke," he said. "But it wasn't. I was like, 'This can't be. I dominated all year long. I dominated the whole state tournament last year. I won conference two years in a row and you're going to put me in the two seed?'

"I couldn't believe it! Coach Holland knew that it never should've happened. Yeah, I lost to Benny Marti in one of the biggest flukes ever, probably in Illinois wrestling, but he did his job as a coach and got his guy the number-one seed. I felt so disrespected by it as a competitor and an athlete. So I was going to make a point to Coach Holland about it when I met up with Denhof in that match. He knew it, I knew it, and Denhof had to know it—I was coming for both of them."

When the tournament opened, the team scores varied right away based on big wins and match-ups. However, by the end of the first round, North had taken hold of the team race.

"Any chance that West Aurora or Wheaton North thought they had in beating us went out the window right away," Ramos commented. "We had guys pinning and scoring big points—West Aurora and Wheaton

North couldn't keep up."

Tony won his first match by fall in 1:10 over Wheaton-Warrenville South junior, Robert Stewart. Next up was a grudge match, at least from West Aurora's point of view. Tony and Zinzer would wrestle in the semifinals. However, when the semifinals came, Zinzer defaulted.

"I think he probably thought that we would wrestle down the road and he probably didn't want to give me another opportunity to get my hands on him," Ramos said. "I had already beat up on him earlier in the year and a couple of other times. So, I'm sure they were just waiting and trying to catch me in the one match that really mattered, and they wanted me to have the least amount of opportunities against him to have him figured out even more."

Tony, along with nine other Panthers, would be in the finals. The championship was pretty much in hand for the team; however, Tony had some business to attend to.

Glenbard had gone into the finals dressed in their gold championship singlets to match their gold-dyed heads. Similarly, Wheaton North wore their gold Falcon championship singlets as well. However, when Tony came to the mat for his championship match against the number-one seed, Denhof, it was no contest. Tony would go up early and often on Denhof and Denhof had no real answer for the junior number-two seed.

When it ended, Tony earned his third DVC title in a 10-3 thrashing of the senior from Wheaton. But Tony was not satisfied.

"I was not happy with that 10-3 final score," Ramos laughed. "I wanted to pin him. I wanted to hurt him. I remember getting up and looking right over to Coach Holland and pointing with my finger and saying, 'One? Did you say that was the one seed? That was one? Are you kidding me? Him? The one seed?' But Coach Holland smiled; he knew. He knew I was going to say something and he knew I wasn't happy about it. But, we had a pretty good relationship, so he knew what to expect."

When the tournament ended, North claimed seven individual champions, two thirds, a fourth, one fifth, and one sixth, and also claimed their tenth-consecutive DVC championship.

2008 • DUPAGE VALLEY CONFERENCE CHAMPIONSHIPS
125 LB CHAMPIONSHIP MATCH
RAMOS HAS HIS HAND RAISED AFTER HE DEFEATS DENHOF OF WHEATON NORTH
PHOTOGRAPH COURTESY • THE RAMOS FAMILY • MARLON BROOKS PHOTOGRAPHY

CHAPTER 27
CHASING TITLES

"After three weeks of beating him up, he broke. And he broke hard."

• *Tony Ramos*

THE WEEK AFTER NORTH WON ITS TENTH-consecutive conference crown, the team headed into the Illinois state series. First up was the Regional Championship at Roselle Lake Park High School, and North would once again see conference foe Wheaton North. On the line was a team advancement—only the championship team moved onto the Dual Team Sectional Championships; additionally, each individual wrestler had to place in the top three to advance into the Individual Sectional Championships. In that, there was a great deal riding on the opening tournament of the state series.

Tony, who was already a two-time Regional champion, continued his dominance. As was true the week before, all points mattered as Wheaton North and Glenbard North were the two premier teams on a collision course for the Regional crown. Of course, this time, Tony would have the number-one seed; Wheaton's Denhof was the number-two seed.

When the two met in the finals, after North had already won titles at 103 and 112 pounds, while Wheaton won one at 119, the match was to be nothing like the week before. This time, Tony won a 16-3 major decision but, even though he dominated the match, he was still not satisfied.

"It was a major decision and I controlled everything about that match, but I still wanted that fall," Ramos said. "I knew I was going to win, but I wanted to put that stamp on the match that I wasn't able to do the week before. So, yeah, I was still upset about that number-two seed."

After Tony won, the rest of Murderers' Row was lined up as well. Chase and Capezio won titles at 130 and 135 pounds. At 140, Monaco would be upset in the semifinals and wrestle to a third place finish—Wheaton North's Eric Terrazas, who upset Monaco at the conference championships, won the weight class. Vince Ramos captured his third Regional title at 145, and North had three more wrestlers in the championship match—one of the three would win, and the remaining three in the consolations earned third place finishes to qualify for the Sectional.

When the tournament ended, North advanced all 14 wrestlers advancing to the Sectional and dominated the Regional with 240.5 points scored—Wheaton North would place second with 162.5 points.

This gave North its ninth-consecutive Regional crown and a team berth at the Dual Team Sectional Championships in three weeks. But now, the season was all individually focused for the next two weeks. North, now in position for a special season, would work to place as many individuals as possible, and then focus on a team championship.

THE NAPERVILLE NORTH SECTIONAL WOULD

prove to be as difficult a Sectional as there was in the state. Also that year, the state had shifted Montini into a different Sectional. Since Montini moved up in school classification, being with the DuPage Valley schools the past two seasons crowded that Sectional with more talented wrestlers than the other Sectional. However, even though Montini was removed, it still pitted a number of top-tier wrestlers against one another—it just provided a bit more breathing room than before. Wheaton North was still a very strong team with tough individuals and they were gunning for revenge matches with Glenbard wrestlers. Add the Naperville schools, Batavia, Aurora, Schaumburg, Geneva, and Lockport, and it was a fight for a top-three individual finish and a state qualification for each individual.

As the Sectional opened, it was clear that Glenbard and Wheaton North were the strongest programs, particularly in the middle weights.

Glenbard freshman Joey Gosinski placed second and earned a state berth at 103, and senior Jamie Warczynski placed third at 112 and did the same; Varella would take fourth and be in an alternate role.

For Tony, he had dominated the entire tournament. He first faced Cody Crawford of St. Charles East, a junior with a 35-5 record, and defeated him by a 13-2 major decision. Next, he faced West Aurora's Josh Zinzer, the 29-4 junior who had defaulted to him in the conference semifinals—he had to wrestle Tony this time around.

"I didn't care that he defaulted to me," Ramos said. "In fact, I think that hurt him more than it helped him. He didn't get that extra feel and when it was over, it was over."

The final would be an 11-5 thrashing of the Blackhawk by Tony. Then, in the finals, for the third week in a row, Tony faced Wheaton North's Denhof once again. And, as had been true in the past two meetings, this outcome would also be different.

From the opening whistle, Tony was relentless on the Falcon's 40-7 senior. Tony continually punished and pushed Denhof around the mat until it happened. "After three weeks of me beating him up," Ramos remembered, "he broke. And he broke hard."

When the match was in its final minute, and Tony had already gained an insurmountable lead, Denhof looked frustrated and paused—in that moment of pause, Tony capitalized. The match ended with Tony winning by fall in 5:28, an exclamation point as he headed into the state championships.

At 130, Chase claimed a Sectional title, now 9-0 on the season, with a fall in 1:35. Up next was Capezio at 135; he too would claim a Sectional crown, his first, against Wheaton North's Ryan Early, a 5-3 overtime decision. Capezio was now four for four on the season against Early.

Monaco would be up next and he and Eric Terrazas took their match, a heated rivalry, into the spotlight. Terrazas, who defeated Monaco in the conference finals, was, after that win, shouldered by Monaco when his hand was raised and told, "That will be the last time you ever fucking beat me. Enjoy it." Terrazas did, and then won the Regional crown when Monaco was upset in the semifinals. Now, in the finals of the Sectional, Monaco and Terrazas would be in another battle that ended in a 1-1 tie as the match headed to overtime.

In overtime, Monaco won on a Granby roll off an Abas roll. He would defeat Terrazas and Murderers' Row was now four for four in the finals with Vince Ramos up next on the championship mat.

As a freshman, Vince had placed third at the Sectional and then fifth in the state. During his sophomore campaign, he would lose in his Sectional semifinal match and struggle, emotionally, to bounce back in his wrestle-back match. He fought through it all and placed third at the Sectional, and then earned a third-place finish in the state. His junior season, Vince was on a mission and won the Sectional over Montini's Isaiah Gonzalez with an 11-7 decision—he would again place third in the state losing for the second-consecutive year to eventual state champion

Conrad Polz of Orland Park Carl Sandburg in the semifinals.

In that, the 2008 season, Vince was focused and nothing was going to stand in his way of the state championship. In the Sectional finals, he would put his own exclamation point on his name with a fall in 2:38 over Nick Proctor of Naperville Neuqua Valley.

No other wrestlers would qualify for the Panthers; however, their role in training and preparing for the team duals was of extreme importance. They all knew it and prepared accordingly.

For the qualifiers, they had one more week of being an individual and one weekend to accomplish their individual goals. For Tony, he was looking to repeat and dominate the state tournament as he had done the previous year. But he had another interest. "That was a special season because those were the guys I was closest to the most," Ramos said. "The five of us, plus Joey and Jamie, had a chance to make history in the program. It was also Vince's last chance to win a title and I wanted that for him. Heading into the championship weekend, we were all excited and relaxed and ready."

WHEN THE STATE CHAMPIONSHIP WEEKEND HAD

arrived, so did Glenbard. Freshman Joey Gosinski wrestled a strong tournament and earned All-State honors. Senior Jamie Warczynski went 1-1 and was eliminated early.

Tony opened with a first round bye and awaited the winner of the Deerfield versus LaSalle-Peru match-up. When that match ended, Tony had the 34-7 junior, Brad Gapinski, from LaSalle-Peru. The match would be handled in typical Tony fashion: a number of takedowns were scored and a 15-3 major decision was the final result—the pace was too much for Gapinski to handle. Next up for Tony would be the highly touted Chris Dardanes of Fenwick Catholic. This would be their first encounter, and Tony made it known who the better wrestler was from that first match.

"I think the score was a decision," Ramos said, "but I know I beat him up pretty good. I controlled the match and moved on."

The final score was a 7-2 decision with both of Dardanes' points coming off escapes that Tony gave him after takedowns. Tony moved onto the semifinals for the third year in a row.

This time, though, Tony entered the semifinals with many of his closest friends—each of the other four from Murderers' Row also made the semifinals.

"Going into that round was awesome," Capezio said. "I remember being in the tunnel, all of us, warming up and then watching everyone going out there one at a time. We all had our headphones in, walking past each other, doing our own thing, then they called Tony. I remember thinking, *Okay, here we go*."

For Tony, he wrestled Providence Catholic's Mark Augle, a senior with a 39-6 record.

"Augle cut down from 130 [pounds]," Ramos remembered. "It was his last year, his senior year, and he really thought dropping [down] to 125 was his best chance. When the brackets came out, that was the match everyone was talking about. If he could beat me, if he could give me a go."

When the match opened, it was a fan favorite for two types of fans, those pro-Ramos and those anti-Ramos—there were generally no casual observers. The match ended in regulation with a 1-1 tie. The first overtime saw the same style of wrestling. Tony, working hard to find position and score, and Augle, working hard for position and looking to capitalize on Tony's aggressive nature.

"They had a great game plan," Ramos said. "They kept me off my attacks a bit, but, more importantly, they kept me off my finishes. Going into overtime, no one scored, and then going into double overtime I rode him out for the first thirty seconds. Then, going into his turn on top, he chose to cut me and go on our feet. I was pretty confident that he wasn't going to score."

However, as the two tangled into a scramble, and the crowd rose to their feet as if to get even a few inches closer as Tony took a shot and found himself in danger of giving up a takedown and back points.

"We got into a little bit of a scramble and I was in on the leg and he almost spladled me," Ramos remembered.

While fans were cheering and the noise level rose, Tony found his way out of danger. "Somehow I got out of it," Ramos said. "I got my hand raised with a 2-1 win and I remember going into the tunnel and Vince was telling Frankie, 'I don't know how he does it, but he just finds ways to win every match. He was dead to rights in that position.' But, I found a way to make it happen and that put me into the state championship match."

With Tony's win, he would be the first of the five to make the finals. Every other member of Glenbard's Murderer's Row now had the opportunity to follow suit.

"In the tunnel, while we were still warming up," Capezio said, "You could hear the roars during the match. We would all move up to the front of the tunnel and watch. We would see Tony's hand get raised. Jimmy was next."

Chase, who was still trying to fight through his conditioning as well as his matches, would not keep the score as close as Tony. Chase reached the finals on an 11-2 win. The Panthers were two for two.

"Once I saw Jimmy's hand get raised," Capezio said, "I could hear the cheers and I knew it was my turn. I remember [Coach] Eddie and [Coach Tony] LiFonti were in my corner and LiFonti turned to me and was like, 'Now it's your turn. Let's go.'"

When Capezio walked to his mat, the experience was one he never forgot. "There's Tony and Jimmy, who already won, waiting to watch me," Capezio said. "There were cameras going off everywhere, the place was loud—it was a great atmosphere."

Capezio would face the 42-0 senior from Mt. Prospect, Matt Boggess. Capezio, a workhorse, would fall in a 3-2 decision as he was unable to score in the closing moments of the match. He was resigned to the consolations, placed fourth, and was utterly heartbroken that his dream ended one match shy of his goal. Everything he had been dreaming about since last season ended.

"Losing that match, that loss, that was the worst loss of my life—that hurt," Capezio said. "It hurt more than anything. It still hurts. I gathered myself and came out for Danny's match. I still wanted those guys to do well; I was hurting."

At 140, Danny Monaco rode out a 7-4 decision over Rockton-Hononegah's Rob Fenicle. That now made it three out of four in the finals with Vince Ramos coming up next.

Vince had been close to the finals as a sophomore and a junior, losing both times to the eventual state champion; however, Vince was certain that this year was his year.

When the match was started, Vince took control of Quincy's Lamor Hickman. Vince scored on his feet and rode Hickman out. Then Vince escaped, took Hickman down, gave up an escape, and went on to win a 5-1 decision. He entered the Grand March for the first time in his career. No one was happier than Vince; however, in a close second was Tony and Frank.

"When I saw Vince win his semifinal match," Ramos said, "I was so excited for him. He had worked so hard and come so close and now he had his chance."

Vince's win was the final match of the evening for the team. Regardless of how it all played out, North ended with six All-State wrestlers and four finalists.

"Watching Vince's hand get raised was exciting," Capezio said. "He had worked so hard and [he] deserved it. But, not being there with them hurt me more than anything. It was supposed to be the Big Five, not the Big Four, you know—it was supposed to be all five of us there. All I ever thought about was being in those finals, and I didn't make it. I still have nightmares about that. But, all of us together, in that moment, that was still so special."

Tony felt the same as Capezio about that run of five-straight weight classes. "When you looked at those five guys that we had in there, we were frickin' tough," Ramos said. "You throw a few others in there, especially Jamie and Joey, and it was a great line-up. We put five guys in a row in the semifinals and four in the finals. When we were going through that Grand March and we are all in the tunnel and I'm talking to all of them, I was like, 'Guys, the first time that I was here I blew it up into something that it wasn't and it hurt me. Don't do that to yourself, just go out there, wrestle your match—don't let the stage bother you.'"

After the Grand March, it would be Tony out of the four finalists to be the first one to have his chance on the state's biggest stage—his third time in as many years. Tony entered the finals match in a North throwback singlet from the 1970s—a two-tone black and gold cloth singlet that represented the tradition and fun-style the wrestlers were having that year. In fact, each North wrestler in the state tournament was able to wear whichever singlet he wanted. It became a tradition at North just a few years before, for the individual state tournament, where each wrestler could choose his own singlets from the program's history and be an individual for that one weekend.

As per the match-up, Tony faced Grant's Izzy Montemayor—they had a history and a friendship. Montemayor showed up in a black Grant lycra singlet with a giant white 'G' on the front of it. That match also marked the second time the two wrestled that season. In their first match, Tony defeated him in a dual meet format near the season's end.

"I remember wrestling him earlier in the year in our dual," Ramos said. "The takedown I got was off his shot. He came in and I kind of moved off it and shucked him by—I hit a little go-behind. Me and Izzy knew a lot about each other. We grew up together and wrestled together at Wrestling Factory where we were wrestling partners, and we were really good family friends. Those relationships make it tough and there's a lot of emotions, but when it's time to step on the mat, I've got to do what's best for me and that was going out there and getting the win."

Montemayor's road was nothing easy. He would win in his opening round with an 11-4 decision over Chicago Shepard's Mike Grice. He would then, in the quarterfinals, have the wrestler everyone believed would be in the finals on that side of the bracket, Oak Park-River Forest junior Ellis Coleman.

Coleman was currently 44-1 on the season and had just come off a 17-2 technical fall in 5:57. The match featured two very different styles of wrestling and, in the end, Montemayor took an 8-7 victory into the finals against Tony. Coleman went on and placed third.

"I had a ton of respect for Izzy," Ramos said. "He was a tough competitor—he was a strong kid—and I knew that going into the match. I was going to be in for a fight because he always battled tough. He gutted out a tough match against Coleman right before in the quarters. So, I knew it wasn't going to be an easy match, but I felt that it would be a good match for me because I was confident and felt the match was in my favor."

In the finals, Tony earned his standard takedown and escape; Montemayor earned one escape and looked to tie the match on his feet. In the end, Tony won his second state championship with a 3-1 decision. When the whistle blew, Tony threw up the program's symbol, a Gold Dot signified by his circled two hands, to the North section of the stands, then he paraded around with two fingers raised on each hand, once for each state championship.

After his victory, Tony watched his remaining three teammates who were to step onto the mat. "Chase goes out there and he wins," Ramos remembered. "Monaco goes out there and he competes hard; he doesn't win it, but he wrestled hard and took second place. We had two titles going into Vince's match, and I had all the confidence in the world in him."

Vince's match-up would be another close relationship, even more-so than Tony's with Montemayor. In the finals, Vince had one of his partners from Izzy Style in Isaiah Gonzalez. But, more than wrestling, Gonzalez was cousin to the Ramos family on their father's side. Watching from the tunnel would be Tony, hoping his brother finally claimed what was his.

"The whole time I'm just saying, 'Vince, please just win this one. It's your last shot. Just go out there and do it, you know you can beat this kid. You beat him every day in the practice room. He can't touch you; just don't mess it up.' The worry for me was not the opponent, but that he was going to put so much pressure on himself that somehow he was not going to get the job done. I did that when I was a freshman, I put so much pressure on myself and if I'd just gone out there and wrestled, I felt like it would've been a different story."

As the match began, Vince knew that if he scored a takedown, there was no way he was going to lose—he was too strong on top. He knew it, Isaiah knew it, and both sets of coaches knew it. Vince wrestled it safe— he was the ultra-conservative and in full control the entire match. "He just rode him out," Ramos laughed. "He didn't give a shit. He was content with a 3-1 win because he just wanted to win the state title—he didn't care how it looked."

When time expired, Vince had a state championship and he pointed to the Glenbard section and raised up his Gold Dot before falling to the mat in joyful tears. He walked to the center of the mat and had his hand raised. Once that ended, Vince would point to his two coaches and run directly to Tony standing off the mat's edge.

"I remember standing right next to the mat after he won" Ramos said, "He ran off and picked me up and gives me a big bear hug—I was so happy for him. I told him how great it was and how no one deserved it more. It was a great moment. That [state championship] was more special for me because it was the first time that I had won a state title and Vince had won one in the same year. The year before, I won and he lost and the family was happy for me, but, at the same time, they were really down for him. This was the first time that we were able to celebrate together. We had talked about winning a state title together for the past month and years before that. We also talked about the first person that we wanted to see afterwards and it was each other. That was a special moment."

Aside from spending that individual moment with Vince, there was also a moment that all three brothers shared in the back tunnel as well. Frank, who had done a great deal for both of his brothers, was now going to see Vince move on; the trio would be separated. "Frankie was very happy to share that final moment with us as individuals, but I think he was sad to see that we would be splitting up," Ramos said. "I know he was happy because he told us that he went into the back of the tunnel and cried. He told us he was so happy for both of us—he even cried a little then, too. And that he was proud that we accomplished one of our biggest goals."

That Saturday night, after Glenbard crowned three state champions, a runner-up, two All-State wrestlers, and a qualifier, it went down as the most decorated day in Glenbard's wrestling history. The *Chicago Sun-Times* headline read, "Glenbard North steals the show," as it recapped the championship results in Sunday's paper.

The celebration was lived, but it was short-lived. The boys and the team had a quick turnaround as Tuesday night was the Dual Team Sectional Championship.

**2008 • IHSA STATE CHAMPIONSHIPS • 125 LB CHAMPIONSHIP MATCH
RAMOS THROWS UP THE GOLD DOT TO THE GLENBARD SECTION IN ASSEMBLY HALL
PHOTOGRAPH COURTESY • THE RAMOS FAMILY • MARLON BROOKS PHOTOGRAPHY**

2008 • IHSA INDIVIDUAL STATE CHAMPIONSHIPS QUALIFIER AND PLACE-WINNER PHOTO
BACK ROW • COACH P. HARRIS • COACH K. GARRETT • COACH J. CHERRY •
COACH F. DEFILIPPIS • COACH C. EDWARDS • COACH J. CONSIDINE • HEAD COACH M. HAHN •
FRONT ROW • JOEY GOSINSKI • TONY RAMOS • JAIME WARCZYNSKI • JIMMY CHASE •
DANNY MONACO • VINCE RAMOS • RAY VARELLA • GENO CAPEZIO
PHOTOGRAPH COURTESY • GLENBARD NORTH WRESTLING
MARLON BROOKS PHOTOGRAPHY

CHAPTER 28
BUCKING WITH THE BRONCOS

"I would never have Frankie in my corner or Tony as a teammate or my best friends all around me doing what we loved ever again. The whole thing, it was surreal. It didn't feel like it was over, but it was."

• *Vince Ramos*
Brother

AS SATURDAY ENDED AND SUNDAY BEGAN, IT WAS all team for the next week. The Sectional championship would happen, but it was never in doubt. North won its two duals that Tuesday night. Glenbard fully controlled Carpentersville Dundee Crown, 58-13, and then, again, ended Naperville Neuqua Valley's season by a 33-22 score.

This was all expected by Tony, the team, and the coaching staff. Next up was the first round of the Dual Team State Championships and the rotation that year moved Glenbard and Montini from the Dual Team Sectional championship, to the Dual Team State Championship, Round One.

Montini, who was currently rated number six in the country and number one in Illinois, had already proven at the Clash to be a great challenge for North, who was number seven in the country and number two in the state. Both teams knew the dual would be more competitive and much closer than the first time that they wrestled—this one would come down to wire.

After weigh-ins, the 145-pound weight was drawn as the starting weight class. On the surface, this was to be a rematch of the state championship match: Vince Ramos versus Isaiah Gonzalez. However, both North and Montini would be making moves and, until the wrestlers were checked in at the table, any type of exchange was possible.

The crowd at Moline High School's fieldhouse could not have been any louder or more packed with Montini fans on one side and Glenbard fans on the other. The mats were lower than the seating, so it was like wrestling in a pit where the noise surrounded and echoed down on top the mats and the wrestlers. Additionally, the hype behind the opening round match-up also sent some shouts toward the direction of the IHSA directors who had still neglected to seed teams—that match would take a top team in the country out of contention for a state trophy. The reality was simple: win that dual and the state championship was there for the taking; lose that dual and leave empty handed.

"That first round was the state championship match and everyone knew it," Ramos said. "[Not seeding] the tournament makes it interesting, but you wish they would because you want them to get it right and have that state finals match be the premier match—not a first round match-up. You don't want to have a match-up where a team goes home without a medal that should have earned one. But, that's where it gets tricky."

The captains were sent to the center of the mat and odds and evens were dictated. North had to present first at 145 pounds, and led off with their state champion—North had to show their hand first. Montini countered with their back-up, Elliot Hudson, to not risk losing a match-up between Vince and Gonzalez for the second straight weekend.

Vince went out and looked to set the tone for the team. The senior state champion relished the opportunity to lead off and start the dual in Glenbard's favor. Immediately, he started in on his two-on-one and Elliott backed away and circled out of bounds. This happened three more times before, one minute into the match, Hudson was warned for stalling. On the next start, Vince scored a takedown and, from there, controlled the match.

In the top position, Vince looked to work his arm bar for tilts and turns, but the period ended with him in the lead, 2-0. In the second, Vince chose down, escaped, and snapped to a go-behind. He cut Hudson and scored again. As they went out of bounds and came back to the center of the mat, the Glenbard crowd had begun a chant of, "Let's go Vince! Let's go Vince!"

He again transitioned from his two-on-one, to a snap down, and beat the leg to a go-behind. Then, he cut Hudson. Vince built a strong lead through takedown after takedown and, even though Vince was a pinner, the strategy appeared to be have Vince earn as many points as possible. He dominated on his feet and the crowd knew when he was close to the technical fall and they were yelling, "Two more! Two!" And then, as Vince cut Hudson, "One more, Vince." With the takedown, they shouted in unison, "Two!"

The senior state champion punched his fists in the air as the crowd hollered and applauded; he won by a technical fall in 5:47 and gave North a 5-0 lead. Montini would then answer by bumping their state runner-up to 152 to try and take a match from North.

"We had a few moves that we felt pretty good about," Hahn said. "And the biggest one came in the second match with Corey Hope. Corey was a wrestler that worked hard, listened, and he was the kind of kid that represents the program well. We knew he could be trusted to do his job, but we were not expecting what happened to happen."

Corey Hope was a senior Sectional qualifier and he was given the task of stepping on the mat against a state finalist. His job was to keep the match to a decision and no more.

However, when the match started, one thing was clear: Hope was not in control of the match. With under 00:30 in the opening period, Gonzalez scored a seemingly effortless takedown on Hope and the Bronco fans yelled, "Two!" Almost immediately, Gonzalez cut Hope, pushed down on his head and back and gave Hope a shove. He walked back to the center of the mat with his back turned as Hope stood up, adjusted his head gear, and lowered himself back into his stance.

At that point, Montini fans were seeing that Gonzalez, a state runner-up, would dominate the match. Their cheers became louder—and this was only 00:45 into the first period.

On the Glenbard side, North head coach Mark Hahn was up, screaming at Hope to "Get into position. What are you doing? Tie the elbow and get to your pass!"

As instructions were shouted, Gonzalez took an open high-crotch to his right, Hope sprawled, and Gonzalez transitioned to a duck-under on the other side. Hope sprawled again and scooted his back end out of bounds to avoid another takedown.

Upon returning to the center, and Hahn screaming endlessly for Hope to wrestle according to their strategy, the match would restart. This time, off the tie, Hope found his position and, off an elbow pass, was inside on Gonzalez's right leg—Gonzalez, able to sprawl free, appeared shocked by the attack and that Hope had been in so deep on his leg.

With a new-found confidence, Hope again was in on Gonzalez's legs. They went out of bounds and, on the next series, Gonzalez hit his double, but Hope fended him off with grit on the edge of the mat. Hope had tuned the bout into a match no one had given him a chance to compete in. The first period ended 2-1 in favor of Gonzalez, but Hope was in on his two-on-one and had been able to penetrate off his elbow pass.

Gonzalez opened the second period on bottom and found Hope to be a difficult opponent in the top position. On his first four stand-up attempts in the first 00:45 seconds, Hope returned him to the mat and captured his wrist—Hope was breaking the state runner-up and his energy seemed to be running low as Hope's confidence and strength found life. With each return the Glenbard crowd was enticed to cheer louder, and with each return, "Trap the wrist, drive over it," could be heard from Hope's coaches and teammates.

With a fifth return of Gonzalez and an attempt to put the state runner-up to his back off a wrist and a bar, the North crowd began, "Corey! Corey! Corey!" Gonzalez made his way off the mat; however, on the restart and sixth stand-up, Hope again returned him hard to the mat and remained in control.

The period ended and the score remained 2-1 in favor of Gonzalez; however, Hope was given hope as he chose neutral for the final two minutes.

As the third period began, Hope fired off two shots that drove Gonzalez backwards and off the mat. The "Corey!" chants continued as he attacked and backed Gonzalez off the mat again—that time the referee hit Gonzalez for stalling and the crowd grew louder and more excited than before. Montini fans were seemingly in shock.

Further chants raised in volume and the ties of both wrestlers became offensive. Hope would slide into a bear hug and lock his hands around Gonzalez's body near the mat's edge—the volume from the Glenbard crowd roared as the gasps from the Montini side searched for a breath. Hope stepped out and both wrestlers were called off the mat.

A half-hearted shot by Gonzalez was defended and then Hope reattacked and found himself in on Gonzalez's right leg yet again. But as Hope raised the leg and went for a trip, the athletic Gonzalez was able to fight free. There was about one minute remaining in the match with the score still 2-1.

Off the whistle, Hope fired in on an open double, Gonzalez sprawled, and Hope peeked out on the opposite side, slid behind him, lifted him up, dropped him, and scored a two-point takedown. "TWO!" was echoed in unison throughout the Moline fieldhouse. Hope now led 3-2, briefly, as Gonzalez escaped and the score was tied at 3-3 with a little over one minute remaining.

When the referee restarted the match, Hope again fired in on another double and a scramble began. It ended with Hope trying to sneak behind Gonzalez, but to no avail. A restart would occur back in the center with 00:50 left. As the wresters came to the center, "Let's go, Isaiah," was shouted from one end while, "Come on, Corey!" was the retaliated shout from the other.

Gonzalez quickly went to a shot and Hope defended; Hope reshot,

Gonzalez defended. In the process, Hope fell to his hip, Gonzalez attacked the seemingly in-danger opponent, but Hope found a way to square up, get to his underhook, and came to his feet. Once raised, Gonzalez found himself in on a body lock at the mat's edge, but Hope fought free and out of bounds. Time was running short and the match had major implications on the team score, especially if Hope could pull off the victory.

On the restart, Hope went into a high-crotch and got in deep on Gonzalez with seemingly little effort. Hope scooted and ran his feet and scored the takedown—"TWO!" echoed off the walls.

Hope now led the state runner-up 5-3 and was in the top position and working an arm-bar as the Glenbard fans screamed in excitement. Hope worked to turn Gonzalez, but the match was stopped for a potentially dangerous position with about 00:25 left.

On top, Hope broke Gonzalez down, worked out his wrist and watched the time on the clock expire as he earned an upset win with a 5-3 decision. Hope pumped his fists in the air to the Glenbard crowd and Montini's crowd was seemed stunned by the match's outcome. When the team score was posted on the clock, North had a strong 8-0 lead as the dual headed into 160.

"Corey Hope's match was huge," Ramos said. "We were thinking he would lose by decision or even a major, but he stepped up and won that match. I mean, he stunned Isaiah. Montini was stunned and that match was huge for us. It just showed what a person who was focused on a goal could do."

The next five matches would be the strength of Montini and where Glenbard had to hold it together. At 160, the Broncos' Dan Stelter, a fourth-place finisher, would take a 3-1 decision over Justin Wahrman, a Sectional qualifier; and, at 171, state runner-up Carl Foreside won by a 22-11 major decision over North's Ryan Hope. This brought the team score to an 8-7 lead for Glenbard.

At 189, Glenbard felt they had a chance at a victory—if nothing else, a decision. This was a match that Glenbard was looking to steal. The wrestler, first-year junior Jordan Brooks, was a tall and very strong kid. He was a quick learner and came out during the spring season. He was given a great deal of attention due to his athleticism, commitment, and fallout that occurred at that weight class. The original starter, Alec Pineda, a seasoned wrestler, had quit mid-season and thus Brooks was pushed into the line-up. The talent and coaches around him, mixed with his work ethic, physical strength, and ability to fight for a cradle, however, helped him develop quicker than expected.

In the match, Brooks made first-year wrestler mistakes, but he was still in the match. Headed into the third period, the score was 8-7 in favor of his opponent, Grant Goebel.

At about the 1:20 mark in the third, Goebel was in on a double-leg and the North coaches were yelling, "Bail! Go to your belly." Brooks, however, had a strong grip on Goebel's chin and began yanking it like a chin-whip—he was trying to pull him down as he had been able to do through most of the junior varsity season.

The coaches continued, "Let it go! Get to your belly!" But Brooks persisted. Then Goebel, a much more seasoned wrestler, saw his opening and punched a half in and turned Brooks to his hip. Brooks fought, Goebel adjusted. Brooks fought more, Goebel adjusted. And as Goebel turned Brooks to his back, the Bronco faithful cheers turned into a loud roar of excitement. The fall happened at 5:15—what was to be a decision loss was now doubled in team points. Montini took their first lead, 13-8. Goebel raised himself up over Brooks, clapped his hands in cheer, and screamed out toward the Montini bench as he knew the magnitude of that fall.

At 215 pounds, Montini and North felt the weight class was a swing match. In the end, it would be a 1-0 decision for Montini's Dan Grimes, All-State at 189, over North's Chris VanGundy.

Headed into the heavyweights, North now trailed 16-8 and was up against Garrett Goebel, a 54-1 state champion who dominated the field the previous weekend in Champaign. He faced North's Jeff Jones, a Sectional qualifier and a senior.

Jones, unfortunately, would be the fifty-fifth win for Goebel—it was a fall in 1:30. Goebel came out with a purpose and, though Jones battled, Jones was simply outmatched.

Montini had now opened up a 22-8 lead as the light weights and the heart of North's order was about to step on the mat.

At 103, North's freshman All-State wrestler, Joey Gosinski, came out and reignited the Panthers with a 6-0 win over state qualifier Sam Brody. Brody, who had defeated Gosinski at the Clash, was not counting on the control positions and cradle early in the match. This put Glenbard three points closer as senior Jamie Warczynski faced Montini's Colton Rasche.

Warczynski, a state qualifier, faced a sophomore state qualifier in Rasche. At the Clash Warczynski lost a 9-8 decision—North thought this could be a match that could swing in their favor as both wrestlers were evenly matched. When the final whistle blew, however, the sophomore defeated the senior by a 9-5 decision this time, and Montini reclaimed its margin by fourteen with a 25-11 team score.

What North had believed might happen at 119 turned out to come true. Montini's Benny Marti, a state qualifier at 125, dropped one weight class for the dual. He had wrestled at 119 at the Clash and defeated Varella by an 11-3 major decision. Varella, who needed to keep the match to a decision at worst, gave up another major decision.

Marti added the bonus points for Montini, now up 29-11, as North was left to its final four wrestlers—all members of Murderers' Row.

First up was Tony. The two-time state champion was up against Mark Martin. Martin's job was not to give up the fall, but it was inevitable. Tony came out and controlled position off the whistle, earned a takedown, and worked his butt-wrist.

As Tony pulled and pressured, Martin had two choices: give up his arm, or have Tony rip his shoulder out of his socket. Martin was hit for stalling just as Tony forced his arm up and took a big step over him and planted him on his back. Martin fought, but all he did with each bridge attempt was sink his shoulder blades farther into the mat.

When the referee called the fall, almost simultaneously, Frank, in the corner with Hahn, raised his hand to signal what everyone was cheering about. The fall occurred at the 1:09 mark—this silenced Montini's fans as Tony stood and pointed to his brother. The Montini fans and bench was very much aware of the fire power North was placing on the mat. North now trailed 29-17 with three matches left.

At 130, Glenbard junior state champion Jimmy Chase squared off against state runner-up Jake Gregerson. The match would be a repeat of last weekend's state championship match and Chase, who defeated Gregerson by a 6-5 decision in Champaign, knew he needed something more to close the gap on the team score.

While the match was in control by Chase, he locked up a cradle and turned Gregerson to his back. Unfortunately, there was no fall; however, the points earned added up to a dominant 9-1 major decision for Chase. North trailed 29-21 with two matches left.

Up next for North was senior Geno Capezio. Capezio, a three-time state qualifier and two-time place winner, was facing Montini's Frank Baer, a state qualifier who was two matches away from placing in Champaign.

Capezio knew the bonus point were important to the team cause and, more than anything, Capezio wanted to make the score as close as possible before the final match.

Unfortunately, although Capezio controlled the match, Baer did just enough to not give up the major decision. Capezio earned a 12-6 decision and Montini's lead was cut to a 29-24 margin. However, Montini did hold criteria on falls, two falls to North's one. Therefore, Glenbard had to pin at 140 in order to earn the victory—a technical fall tied the match, but, again, Montini would win on criteria.

To the mat for Glenbard was state runner-up Danny Monaco. For Montini, Alex Saunders.

The match started in Monaco's favor; a takedown in the first twenty seconds and then Monaco looked for North's patented cross-face cradle. However, Saunders, aware of what Monaco was looking for, remained guarded and face down on the mat. He would occasionally bring up his hips, but appeared to have no desire to escape or bring his body fully off the mat.

The crowd from the Glenbard side of the bleachers was yelling throughout the first period, "Stal-ling!" And they were emotionally correct, but technically, at least in that period, Saunders was defending. For Saunders, all he had to do was stay out of Monaco's danger areas and not give up the fall. And, as long as he did not lose by fall, Montini advanced. He knew it, Monaco knew it, both benches knew it, the fans knew, and the officials knew it.

"Saunders was stalling so hard in that first period," Monaco remembered. "He laid flat on that mat for the entire period and was not warned one time. At least hit him [for stalling]!"

Unfortunately, the second period was much like the first. Monaco was in position on top and nearly a turn could be worked. Saunders buried his head, grabbed a wrist, brought his hips up and then immediately down—Monaco and Glenbard was frustrated by the match's direction. However, before the period ended, with about 00:50 remaining, Saunders was hit with his first stalling warning of the match. No position changed, however, and no other points were awarded.

In that final period, almost immediately, Saunders was hit with another stalling warning and Monaco was awarded one point. Once the point was awarded, the Montini boos could be heard; but they knew. The match continued and no other stalling call was made as Monaco attempted to find ways to turn Saunders, and Saunders found ways to stay flat and guarded.

With around 1:30 remaining in the match, the Glenbard faithful were overwhelmed with frustration and they let it be known. "Stal-ling! Stal-ling! Make the fucking call!"

But no such call was made. Saunders stayed covered on the mat and refused to come up for more than a split-second or even raise his head or hips to improve position—he was content and he was not being forced to do more than he was. Smartly, he remained.

Even when Monaco pulled away to give Saunders a chance to work up, he raised up slightly, and fell when Monaco barely pressured him. Monaco restarted in a freestyle start, and Saunders dropped his hip off the whistle and remained flat. At one point even the Montini coaches thought he was going to be hit as they were shaking their heads and covering their mouths with their hands, talking—but they were also content as no danger was being pressured by the referees.

Over the Glenbard bench the fans, elevated, continued their chant down to the mat, "Stal-ling! Stal-ling! Stal-ling!" repeatedly; however, the mat referee, Ron Coit, was never going to take control of the match and make the call. In fact, with about 00:45 to go, Coit talked to Saunders, "Improve, bottom man," and then he motioned.

Frank yelled back at Coit, "Don't talk to him, hit him for stalling!" But, Coit refused. He even motioned for Saunders to work two more additional times without hitting him for stalling—the final time Coit spoke with Saunders came with about 00:20 remaining.

The cheers grew from the Montini crowd as they realized that Coit was not going to hit Saunders for stalling; from the other end, the Glenbard boos came in strong numbers in protest and disbelief that the stalling tactic was endured and Monaco was not awarded for trying to wrestle—of course, it was a matter of perspective.

From North's corner, not only were the fans shouting for the stall call, so were the coaches and wrestlers—everyone in Moline's fieldhouse saw the final seconds unfold. When the whistle blew, Montini's Saunders exploded to his feet and escaped with a 5-1 decision loss to Monaco; and a 29-27 final team score victory for the Broncos. Saunders began the celebration with his coaches and teammates and Monaco remained on his hands and knees, dejected and crying.

"That match was such bullshit," Monaco commented. "He stayed flat on that mat for the entire match and the officials didn't do shit about it. He should have been stalled out. We got screwed because the referee didn't have the balls to make the right call."

Hahn walked over to his bench and gathered his guys to shake hands with the Montini wrestlers and coaching staff.

Montini, for the second season in a row, ended North's season and wrestled on to win the state championship in Illinois' AA division.

Heavy chants of, "Bull-shit! Bull-shit! Bull-shit!" echoed toward the IHSA chairmen and officials and other expletives were exchanged back and forth between Glenbard and Montini fans from across the fieldhouse and out into the parking lot. But it did not matter—North had lost and their season ended.

Tony, for the third season in a row, would not capture a dual team state trophy or medal. North, who ended as the number-ten team in the country, had never even earned a team state trophy.

For Vince, this was his final match in the black and gold and the final match with both his brothers. "I remember us shaking hands with

Montini," Vince said, "sitting down on the mat, putting on my gym shoes, and looking up from that pit in the Moline gymnasium, and I was like, *Holy shit. It's over. That's it. It's done.*"

"How that official never called that kid for stalling is beyond me," Defilippis said. "All of these officials always want to get involved in the match, and then when they should get involved, they are cowards. The way that ended was bullshit. Now, we did lose some matches and gave up bonus points and had chances to earn points and we didn't, but how that ended still doesn't sit right with me. Horrible."

Frank's sentiments were echoed and shared by a variety of wrestlers and coaches, but the final score was the final score.

"We had so many guys wrestle their butts off," Ramos said. "Vince had a big win. We threw Corey Hope out there against a kid who just took second in the state and Hope ends up beating him. We were just hoping he would keep it to a decision and he went out there and kept it close and put himself in position to win the match and he did. And that's what we needed. We needed upsets like that to happen. We gave up two big falls, but then Geno goes out there and had Frank Baer on his back and he should have stuck him.

"I had to go out there and get a pin—and I got a pin. It comes down to the last match, Monaco, Monaco versus Saunders, and we knew Monaco could beat him up, but it was to the point where Monaco had to pin him for us to win it. Saunders just kind of laid there and never came off his belly. That put Danny in a tough situation and he went out there and did the best he could with the situation that was presented. But we lost."

From Hahn's perspective, it was about missed opportunities and giving up the points that they knew they could not afford to lose. "We had opportunities," Hahn said. "But that one hurt. Regardless of how it ended, we gave up big points and you can't do that in championship matches—and that was the state championship match. Did Saunders stall? You bet. But that was what he was sent out there to do. He did his job and we didn't do ours. It's that simple."

The ride home for the team was very somber. A team, so close to making history in an already historic program, replayed their individual matches over and over in their heads.

"It was so hard," Ramos reflected. "I remember going back to the hotel and Coach Hahn not coming out of his room for a little while. We were all emotional. The coaches were emotional, the wrestlers, the parents—it was hard. The bus ride home was silent and it was just something that was hard for everyone to deal with. From such a high the week before of winning state and having three state champs, four guys in the finals, five guys in the semifinals, six All-State wrestler—it was just so rough to have such a down to end the year."

For Tony and Vince, they texted back and forth on the bus—that would be the last time they were ever on the same wrestling team and they knew it.

"It didn't feel real, like it was over," Vince Ramos said. "I think that was hard on Tony—and we never talked about it—but knowing that was possibly the last time we would ever wrestle on the same team together. I know it was hard on me because I would never have Frankie in my corner or Tony as a teammate or my best friends all around me doing what we loved ever again. The whole thing, it was surreal. It didn't feel like it was over, but it was. It just wasn't supposed to end that way."

For Tony, "I think Vince and me thought that maybe there was a chance that we would wrestle on the same team in college," he said. "That was the last time we were ever on the same team again. Our goal was to both win state championships, and we did, and that is one of our best memories together. But my very last memory of us wrestling together was falling short of winning that huge dual meet—and that sucks!"

CHAPTER 29
A NEW LEADER

"That year, really that spring, is when I felt Tony really bought into the program and started to become the leader we needed him to be."

• *Mark Hahn*
Head Coach, Glenbard North High School

FOR TONY, HE HAD ONE MORE OPPORTUNITY AT winning a Dual Team state championship; however, it would be with a very different group of wrestlers—the only returners were Tony and Chase, both state champions, and now sophomore Joey Gosinski, who had placed sixth. The rest of the team would be made up of first year varsity wrestlers, but the program had thrived in that position for many years.

As soon as Awards Night ended, Hahn and Tony had another talk, but it was a different talk. It was not about accolades or awards—Vince Ramos was named the program's Most Outstanding Wrestler that season. Instead, it was about Tony being the kind of leader that would bring the group along with him and help them, collectively, grow as a team. For Tony to accomplish his team goals, he had to take a more proactive role with a group that was dedicated, just varsity inexperienced.

"That year," Hahn said, "really that spring, is when I felt Tony really bought into the program and started to become the leader that we needed him to be. He started grabbing guys and taking them around to tournaments and working with them. That's what we expect our seniors to do."

The response was immediate and positive with Tony and all of the soon-to-be varsity starters.

"My exchanges with Coach Hahn," Ramos said, "were pretty much, 'Hey, I'm going to get you that team state title this year, we're going to get it done. I'm going to find a way to get all of these guys on the same page and lead them to put us in position to win a team state title.' I saw how devastating it was on him and I thought maybe this would be the last year we could do it with some of the guys we had."

For Tony, he started to put his influence on teammates that he felt needed a little bit more of an edge. "I started grabbing guys that you wouldn't think to grab and work with them and try to make them tougher—maybe make their technique a little bit better. We would run in the morning, I would take some to Izzy Style with me. You know, just some of these guys that were going to have to step into the line-up and fill some of the voids that we lost from the great senior class that we had in order to make a run at this state tournament."

As the spring season began, Tony started going to tournaments that he had not participated in previous years and surrounded himself with all of his teammates. He talked with them, watched their matches and helped coach them, and then headed to his own practices after. He was committed to being part of North's first state championship team, and it showed in what he was doing and how the others were responding.

The more Tony was around, the more everyone was around. Other wrestlers were attaching themselves to him, working out with him, traveling and building relationships with him and with one another—by the time Fargo came around, even though many of his teammates did not qualify for the nationals, they were better wrestlers, a closer team, and they were excited about the work that they had put in and the possibilities in front of them.

ONCE FARGO CAME, TONY WAS READY TO CLAIM

the ultimate prize that he had been so close to the season. "I wanted that stop sign so badly that year," Ramos said. "I let it slip away the year before and I felt good going into the tournament."

Throughout his tournament, Tony worked through all of the pairings in his pool and put himself into the final four of his bracket. His semifinal opponent was Ohio's Sam White.

In those semifinals, "I lost to Sam White, and I lost to him that spring, too," Ramos remembered. "He was a tough kid—an Ohio kid. We had a couple of close matches, but he ended up beating me at Fargo. I think that was when they stopped cross-bracketing, I don't remember, but I don't think I had a chance at a cross-over match to see if I could get into the finals. So that was tough after being so close the year before and now I was out of the opportunity for a Fargo title."

After Tony lost to White, he wrestled and finished in the highest placing possible; he took third. To do so, he defeated Iowa's George Ivanon 3-2, 1-0. In the finals, White lost to another wrestler from Ohio, Logan Stieber.

From there on out, Tony focused solely on his senior season and winning his third state championship, as well as "doing anything I had to do to try and win that team championship," Ramos said. "I knew it wouldn't be easy, but I did feel that we could do it with our team with how the state's top teams looked coming back and what we could get done in our room. Coach Hahn was great at getting guys to believe in themselves and getting the most out of them by the season's end. We had a chance, and that was all we needed."

CHAPTER 30
THREE PERCENT

"Tom, I want to be a Hawkeye."

• *Tony Ramos*

ORIGINALLY, TONY HAD NARROWED DOWN HIS college choices to two schools: the University of Iowa and Oklahoma State University. The selection was simple because each head coach was an Olympic gold medalist, and he knew that was his next step. Therefore, his first step had to be finding the right coach and right program that fit him.

At Glenbard North, Tony's head coach, Mark Hahn, had always been a lifelong Iowa fan and always said, "We've never had a wrestler go to Iowa." But, for Tony, appeasing his coach was not his priority—he was looking at style of wrestling and, early on, Oklahoma State looked like a place where he wanted to wrestle, but something just kept pulling him toward Iowa.

"I don't know if it was so much that I wanted to go to Oklahoma State," Ramos said. "It was more or less I wanted the option or opportunity if that's what I wanted. I knew the coaches there were great, the team and the program was solid, and they could compete for a national title. But, at the same time, I was pretty set on Iowa because they had Tom and Terry Brands there—the coaches and the training I was looking for—a great fan base. I just wanted to go to a storied program."

Four days before Tony headed to the University of Iowa for an unofficial visit, Oklahoma State assistant coach Eric Guerrero was in

Tony's home and spoke with him, recruiting him pretty hard. The thing was, Guerrero had Tony leaning toward Oklahoma State—it was pretty much a toss-up at that point. The only thing Tony asked was for them to wait. "We set up a visit to Iowa," Defilippis said. "[And I told Tony to] just wait until we get back from Iowa before you make any decisions. Guerrero agreed [with me] because he had always said that Tony was who they wanted and he didn't want to rush anything."

However, on the day Tony, Frank, his father, and Israel were headed out to Iowa City, Frank received some news that did not sit well with him or Tony.

"Jason Bryant from InterMat called," Defilippis said, "and he knew Tony was interested in going to Oklahoma State. He said, 'Hey, we're running a story on Morrison committing to Oklahoma State. Has Tony made a decision yet?' Well, apparently, Morrison put Oklahoma State's feet to the fire and said, 'I'm going to commit to you guys.' Apparently, Guerrero said, 'Well, we're waiting to hear back from Ramos.' But Morrison forced their hand. I heard he told them, 'Well, if you are waiting for Ramos, then I'm going to commit to Wisconsin.' Obviously, Guerrero couldn't afford to lose them both, so he signed Morrison—and he explained himself on the phone call to me. Business decision, I get it. They run a business."

But, regardless of the decision based on business or not, Tony was not happy with how it all transpired.

"As soon as they told me that they committed to Morrison and that I didn't have to come out for my recruiting trip," Ramos remembered, "I wanted to make a point to them that they got the wrong guy."

On the way to Iowa, Tony recalled, "Izzy kept telling me, 'I don't know what kind of money Tom [Brands] has for you. What if he only has ten percent? What are you going to do?' I told him I didn't know. I said that if I liked it and it was a place where I wanted to be, then I didn't care—that's where I'll go because money is not an issue to me."

"When we walked into Carver, at the top of the bowl," Defilippis said, "[Derek] St. John was there, [Ethen] Lofthouse, [Joey] Trizzino—they are all there with their families. Tony stops at the top of the stairs while everyone else was walking down to the [wrestling] room and I walk over to him."

In that moment, Tony recalled "standing at the top of Carver and I was like, 'Damn, I got to wrestle here.' I had to. Fifteen thousand people fill this place, screaming for me, blowing the roof off of this place; there's no other place that I want to be."

When everybody else was headed down to the wrestling room, Frank went over to his youngest brother. "I asked him, 'Come on, Bubba, what are you doing?' And he stood there, still looking out into Carver and said, 'Everyone's going to scream my name in this place.' I go, 'Slow down.' He turned to me and said, 'Frank, I'm going to school here and everyone's going to scream my name in this arena.' I looked at him and said, 'Let's not put the cart before the horse here, Tony. Let's see what they're saying, let's see what they're offering.'"

Eventually, Tony made his way downstairs and back into the wrestling room. Once that walk through was completed, the next aspect of the tour was to head to the football stadium for the football game. Tom Brands would pick up the recruits and their families after and spend more time with them. That did not sit well with Frank.

"Looking back," Tom Brands said, "I could see when we were heading to the football game something was irritating Frank."

"When we started walking to the football field," Defilippis said, "and Tom [Brands] was handing out everyone's tickets to them, I said, 'Coach, we didn't come here for a fucking football game. We came here to make Tony a Hawkeye.' To which Tom stopped and looked at me and said, 'That's fine with me. Let me drop these guys off and we can go back to my office.'"

Once they returned to Carver and headed into the Tom Brands' office, Frank stopped the head coach in the middle of some talk he was giving about the school and the program. "Coach," Defilippis said, "where are we at with this, financially? Just tell me.' Tom sat back in his chair and started going through some numbers. He was saying to himself, 'Okay, this guy's getting thirty percent, this guy's got forty percent,' and on he went. But I interrupted him and asked where we were at.

"Tom came back," Defilippis continued, "and said, 'Well, I'll be honest with you, Ramos is my third priority right now. I needed a [157 pounder] and we brought in St. John, and Lofthouse is my second priority. I want to give you ten percent,' and I'm thinking, *Did this guy really just say ten percent?* But, I was like, okay it's got to be more than that, he's just saying that. But he goes, 'But all I really have is three percent.'"

Tony, who had been sitting there and listening to the numbers and the offer never skipped a beat, "Okay," Ramos said, "where do I sign?"

In amazement, Tony's father, Al, kicked Tony from under the table and Frank looked to his brother and asked him, "What the fuck are you doing?"

From there, Frank said that Tom Brands was a bit hesitant and told Tony, "You know, maybe you should take some time and talk it over."

But, Tony refused.

"I looked at Tony," Defilippis said, "as if to tell him, 'Yes, let's go talk about this.' But Tony said, 'No. Give me the paperwork. I'm signing.'"

A bewildered father and Frank watched Tony commit. "I couldn't believe it," Defilippis said. "I was stunned. All of the time and money and travel and everything we did, all for three percent. Three percent! I was dumbfounded. But, Tom did say that he would get three percent, 50 percent the next year, and then 40 percent for the rest of his time there. But, to me, 40 percent, I still couldn't believe it. We were looking for a hell of a lot more. But, it was Tony's decision and he made it."

From Tom Brands' point of view, money was an issue, but there were other factors too. "You got to remember," Tom Brands said, "Ramos was not a Fargo champion. He was not a guy winning above his age level where he's making international teams. Really, though, we didn't have the money and that's probably why we weren't recruiting him very hard. But, [Israel] Martinez said we needed to look at him and I went to go watch Ramos work out in an evaluation period. And it was a very physical workout—he was our kind of guy.

"We knew of him and we knew of his drive and we liked that," Tom Brands continued, "but we didn't have much money left. But the way Tony responded, I gathered that once he said he was committed, he was. I know stranger things have happened. But the way that he was, I took his word as a very hard commit. I mean, we got a kid here who wants to be a Hawkeye and, oh yeah, he's pretty tough and, by the way, I watched him slug a guy for forty-five minutes straight and everybody that we know is telling us how tough this kid is. He wanted to be a Hawkeye, but [a three percent scholarship] was all we had at the time to give him."

On the way home, Tony did discuss the decision with his father, his brother, and Israel. However, no matter what any of them said—aside from Israel because he was excited about Tony's decision—Tony did not budge.

"When we got home," Ramos said, "we crunched some numbers and figured out with the scholarship what kind of loans I would have to take out and such. And after we did that, I called Tom that night. I said, 'Tom, I want to be a Hawkeye.' I was pumped up about it, they were pumped up about it. I got a call the next day from my mom because I didn't even tell her. She saw it on InterMat and she was pissed. She said, 'I'm not signing any letter of intent for you.' And I told her, 'I don't care. I'm 18 and I'll do what I want. I don't need your signature. I'm a grown man. I'll make my own decisions and do what I want. I'm not asking you to help me. I'll do it all on my own.' That's how it all went down in Iowa and back at home."

And in that first interaction with Tom Brands, Frank learned and saw what he needed to. "There was no sugar-coating with these guys," Defilippis said. "And I respected the hell out of [Tom Brands] for being so blunt and honest with me. I didn't need a run around. He got to the point and was honest and said the truth about his situation, and I respected that. So I said, 'Great. What about all of the other guys you have here and coming in?' And I'll never forget what he said. He goes, 'The cream will rise to the top, Frank. He's either going to make it, or he ain't. But, if he makes it, he'll be a world and Olympic champion—that's what you guys are telling me you want.'"

Tony would, however, go on one more recruiting trip. "I promised my mom that I would go out to Indiana," he said. "Vince was there, and so was Danny and Geno and Billy—all my friends, really—and they said they would offer me and Vince a full-ride if I went. But, it wasn't for me. It was a time when I had to make a decision that was best for me."

In that, Tony appeased his mother's wishes, but he was set on Iowa and there was no changing his mind once it was made.

CHAPTER 31
ONE LAST TIME THROUGH

"He tried to wrestle after that, but I just started picking him apart and he just injury defaulted. I knew I would see him again in our dual, so I wanted to plant the seed in his head and I think I did that."

• *Tony Ramos*

TONY'S SENIOR SEASON OPENED JUST AS HIS previous three had: undefeated. However, even though he swept his first three opponents that Wednesday night at the Fulk Quad, there was a dual that showed the Panthers where they were at. That season, Minooka High School came in ranked as one of the state's top teams and, on that opening night, they defeated North 47-14. Tony knew that if Glenbard was going to win the state, they were going to have to close that gap and find a way to defeat those top-tier teams.

"After that dual, I remember thinking two things," Ramos said. "One, I didn't think too much of it because we had a lot of our guys out with the football playoffs; but, I also thought, man, this could be a long season. Maybe I over-estimated things a bit and the talent we have. So I knew I had some more work ahead of me, as a leader, to get everyone on the same page."

When the weekend came, Tony once again found himself in the finals of the Conant Tournament. That year, he faced Oak Park-River Forest transfer Chris Dardanes—Dardanes and his brother had transferred in from Fenwick High School that summer.

"I was up like 7-4 or 7-2 and I ankle-picked him and he rolled his ankle a little bit," Ramos recalled. "He tried to wrestle after that, but I just started picking him apart and he just injury defaulted. I knew I would see him again in our dual, so I wanted to plant the seed in his head and I think I did that."

Tony won his bracket, and the team placed fourth behind Oak Park-River Forest, Providence Catholic, and Crystal Lake Central. Tony was undefeated and had scored five falls in his first six matches. But his focus was still helping his teammates grow and improve at a faster rate.

WHEN NOVEMBER TURNED TO DECEMBER, TONY was looking to win his second Ironman title. That year, he refused to drop to 125; instead, he stayed up one weight at 130 pounds as he felt confident in his wrestling and his chances to win another title regardless of what weight he entered.

He won his opening round match by fall in 3:22 over Dustin Scott of Broken Arrow, Oklahoma, and then he claimed a 14-6 win over Parkersburg, West Virginia's, Jordan Nolan. In the quarterfinals, he defeated Blue Mountain, Pennsylvania's, Cortland Choate by a 5-1 decision and, for the second time in three years, Tony was in the semifinals. He had freshman Felipe Martinez of St. Paris Graham; the talk was that Martinez was the next big thing to happen to wrestling.

Tony came out in his grey North singlet and green ankle band with Frank and Coach Hahn in his corner. Martinez, in a black singlet with grey and white piping on the sides, looked to prove his merit against one of the best seniors in the country.

The mat was crowded with people sitting and standing and gossiping and predicting and anticipating the match-up between the up-and-comer and the already-established. The intensity was high, the stakes were high, and then it was time to wrestle.

Within the first twenty seconds, Tony fought himself into a high-crotch to Martinez's right leg. Once he had the leg lifted high, Martinez went from defending Tony with a key lock, to jumping into an Abas roll on Tony's left leg. The roll placed Tony parallel and on the bottom of Martinez, but Tony raised his hips off the mat and looked to come behind as Martinez kept hold of the leg.

As the scramble ensured, Tony stepped over and threw his right leg in and was awarded a two-point takedown as Martinez rolled again, this time out of bounds. The action was fast and funky and, at the forty-second mark, Tony had a 2-0 lead.

Without hesitation, upon their return to the mat's center, Tony wanted to wrestle on his feet and showed the official the neutral sign which gave Martinez an escape point and started both wrestlers back on their feet—the score was now cut in half, 2-1.

Martinez would take an open shot off the whistle; however, Tony defended and worked back into his own tie. Again, on a separation, Martinez took a wild open shot and Tony did not only defend, but reshot into a single on Martinez's left leg. This time, Martinez broke Tony's grip, found himself in a front headlock, and the two held position until a stalemate was called.

When the whistle blew, and Tony moved forward, Martinez started with a shot to Tony's right and then shifted to a shot to Tony's left, but to no avail. The freshman was showing combinations and a fearlessness in his wrestling as Tony was steady and consistently working the head and his ties and taking calculated shots.

Near the end of the first period, Tony drove Martinez off the mat with a double-leg that Martinez was able to defend. Off the restart, Martinez returned the favor with a double of his own; however, he would find himself in deep on Tony, come up, grab a body lock and squeeze as Tony looked to find a way out—there would be none. Martinez drove Tony to his back on the mat's edge as fans were cheering in surprise and the excitement. Some of the voices were encouraging the finish while some were out of concern for the seemingly imminent fall of one of the nation's top wrestlers.

While fighting to pin Tony, Martinez earned a five count and the three near-fall points, but the period ended and Tony survived. Martinez, excited and confident, and now in the lead with a 6-2 score, was walking around with an air of confidence.

When Tony popped up after the period ended, more spectators crowded the mat as Hahn yelled instructions to him. The choice went to Tony and Hahn instructed him to choose bottom.

Before each of the wrestlers were set, the buzz of Martinez catching Tony on his back had spread, and the crowd around the mat had increased dramatically—people just kept funneling in to watch.

Martinez covered Tony's left side and, as Tony stood up, Martinez was able to find his way into a deep spiral ride as he tried to pull Tony into his hips and crab-ride him. Tony, who fought the position, based on all fours and, with Martinez hanging low on his ride, Tony tried to step over, but Martinez's ride was tighter than it appeared and the two went out of bounds.

Off the whistle, again covered on Tony's left, Martinez ran a cross-collar ride and, as Tony came to his feet, Martinez rode him out of bounds again. Tony jumped the next start and was cautioned; Martinez followed and added his own caution prior to the next whistle.

When a clean start was whistled, Tony again found himself on his feet, but Martinez, proving to be a strong rider, made each attempt fail and the action continued with a stand and return until the two wrestled out of bounds.

With about 00:45 to go in the second period, Martinez finally worked his right leg in on Tony and had him flattened on the mat while he worked a pry-half. Tony fought the position, raised his hips, and worked to swim out, but struggled to untangle himself from Martinez. As he continued his fight, Tony jumped into a roll, but Martinez was pressed against him and Martinez was unable to be removed from the ride. But, just as time was expiring, Tony finally fought himself into a flurry to free himself for an escape; however, he was not awarded with a point. The officials agreed that time had expired. The lead remained in Martinez's favor, 6-2.

Coincidentally, though, as the second period wore on, Martinez's conditioning and energy level was lowering. He came up slower and now, as he chose down for the third period, he was slowly working his way to the center for the start of the final period. Tony had no choice but to concede the point and try to win the match on his feet.

As the period started, Tony came forward and Martinez backed away. When Tony secured a tie, he shot in on the freshman's left leg, but Martinez twisted his body and created a scramble that had each chasing the other—Martinez the hip and Tony the leg. Martinez earned another takedown and now lead the match with a controlled 9-2 score.

The struggle continued for Tony as, even though he was working to escape, he could not find a way to unhitch the freshman. Soon, however, Martinez was called for his first stalling call. Off the next restart, Tony stood off the whistle and Martinez tried to once again pull him back down into his hips, but he locked his hands and Tony scored on the illegal hold; he also worked into an escape in the process. The score was now 9-4 in favor of Martinez, but Tony was on the attack and felt as if he was within striking distance.

At the one-minute mark, Tony was in on a low double; however, Martinez locked around Tony's body and fought the position on the edge of the mat. The fight continued and, as Tony was able to reposition and place Martinez on his hip and hooked his top leg, a stalemate was called and the two wrestlers found themselves in the neutral position with about 00:35 left in the match.

Overanxious and in need of a big move, Tony was warned a second time for a caution off an early start. On the restart, Tony attacked, changed levels, and fired in on a high double. He came up to double underhooks as Martinez pressed his hips back, and, as he ran after him looking for a throw, Martinez kept his head low and blocked in good position and found a shot of his own as the over-aggressive Tony continued to step into him.

Tony defended the shot and looked to score defensively, but the time on the clock had expired. Martinez came up, took off his headgear, and pumped his fist. Martinez's hand would be raised and Tony found himself in the consolation bracket for the second time in two years.

"As far as that match went," Ramos said, "I got bear hugged to my back for five in the first and that was that. I knew going into that match, even though I was the one seed, I had a tough draw—Villalonga was on the other side. Felipe Martinez, the word was, he was a freshman phenom—and he was pretty freakin' good. I was a tough senior and he was a freshman, so that was hard for me because I was like, *I just lost to a freshman. What the heck is going on?* It wasn't like the kid I lost to was a slouch, but I had to regroup and refocus and move forward after that knowing I wasn't going to win another Ironman title."

In the wrestle-backs, Tony faced Cody Kelly for the opportunity to wrestle for third. However, Tony was dealt another loss. This time, a 6-4 decision.

"What happened there?" Ramos recalled laughing. "I was winning and I got headlocked—that's what happened there. I had two big matches where two big moves put me in a hole that I had to come back from. All I was really focused on was to not give up big moves, getting a lead and just building on that lead and not relaxing. It just didn't happen."

For the fifth place match, Tony once again wrestled Cortland Choate. The match ended just as their quarterfinal match ended—a 5-1 win for Tony.

GLENBARD HEADED BACK TO ILLINOIS AND

jumped into a three-day stretch of duals that next Thursday, Friday, and Saturday. Tony, still wrestling at 130, won by falls on Thursday and Friday; however, Saturday, he again faced Oak Park-River Forest's Chris Dardanes; this time the score was much closer than the injury default at Conant.

"I felt like that match I wrestled a little tentative," Ramos said. "I kind of got my two takedowns and then just hung out. I probably could've scored a few more points. They probably felt that they were closing the gap, because that's what the talk was, about how, 'Dardanes might be the one to knock Ramos off at the state tournament. He got beat up at Conant, but now it's 5-3. The gap's closing.' When I heard that, it fueled my fire and I needed to start making bigger statements."

Tony won by fall against his next four opponents before the dual team match-up between Glenbard and Carl Sandburg High School. The meet was held over the Christmas break and it was North's final dual before heading up to Rochester, Minnesota, for the Clash VII High School

National Duals.

Tony hoped to face Jon Morrison, who had been coming off of a very successful spring and summer campaign. However, there was some speculation that Sandburg might try to avoid the match-up if possible.

As for Morrison, he was also a senior, like Tony, and had accolades of his own. In 2007, he finished his sophomore campaign as a state runner-up at 103 pounds. The following season he was the Illinois state champion at 119, had an undefeated season that left him 43-0, and earned a second dual team state championship to round out that season.

When he walked into his senior season, his national rank placed him as the number-one wrestler in the country at 125 pounds, as reported by W.I.N. Magazine—Amateur Wrestling News rated him as the number-two wrestler.

That previous summer, 2008. Morrison was a Fargo freestyle national runner-up at 119, after earning a 2007 Fargo national championship. In 2008, he was also named as a second team ASICS All-American wrestler.

The build-up for the match-up was a hot topic on the message boards and within the wrestling community. In the past few seasons, the dual between Carl Sandburg and Glenbard alone was exciting enough to create a following; however, with the anticipation of two of the top wrestlers in the country wrestling, the gymnasium and coverage was going to be even greater.

"I know we had something set up on the coin flip to where, if we won, Sandburg would have to present first at the 130 [pounds]," Ramos said. "I was looking to wrestle that match. When it came around to 130, we had Dalton Boland warming up behind the bench, but made it look like I was going out there so they thought I was going to wrestle 130. They forfeited the match and we sent Boland out there to accept it—now they had to send Morrison on the mat. We knew that they may try and avoid [the match-up], but Coach Hahn had a plan to make sure that it happened."

From the Carl Sandburg point of view, they wanted to wrestle the match. "We absolutely wanted to wrestle that match in the dual," Sandburg Head Coach Eric Siebert said. "That was the only time [Morrison] weighed in at 130 pounds that year. We felt that Jon was a slight underdog, so we felt the more mat time we got against [Ramos], the more it would help our chances down the road."

The coin flip and the match went as Tony had planned—he not only won the match, but he controlled the match as well as feeling that he asserted his supremacy in the process.

"I dominated!" Ramos said. "I took him down and rode him out. Then I rode him out the whole second period. I got my escape in the third, won 3-0, and that was that."

North won the dual 35-21, and Tony felt he left an impression on his greatest high school opponent that season. He also felt he let the state know he was the most dominant wrestlers of the two. Of course, Morrison dropped back down to 125 after the dual and for the remainder of the season. As for Tony, he was dominant and comfortable at 130, even with his two losses.

THE ROAD TRIP UP TO THE CLASH WAS AS SNOWY

and as cold as it had ever been. The winds were gusting and the mini buses that the team drove up were slowed by the icy roads and dart-like snow pelting against the windshields. When the team finally arrived at its hotel, a team meeting took place and Tony, who was weighing in at 130, knew that he may be bumped around for the sake of winning duals.

"I was flexible because I knew I could beat anyone in any weight class and no weight was too big for me," Ramos said. "I was going to wrestle wherever Hahn and the team needed me to go. And I was going to win."

In the opening round, Glenbard wrestled Iowa's Waverly-Shell Rock and the dual began at 215. Tony would be the eighth match as he was bumped up to wrestle 135 to face junior Jake Ballweg.

Ballweg, already a two-time Iowa state finalist and a returning state champion, was ranked number-one in Iowa and twenty-ninth in the country by U.S.A. Wrestling magazine.

When Tony and Ballweg stepped onto the mat, Glenbard was trailing by an 18-9 score. Tony opened up and worked his offense; however, he only scored an 11-5 decision, but he did put the Panthers three points closer, 18-12.

The dual teetered back and forth and came down to 189 pounds. North was trailing 30-25 headed into that match and the dual fell on Chris Wahrman's shoulders. It took the scrappy Wahrman until the halfway mark of the first period to win by fall over Jordan Meier, and North advanced with a 31-30 win.

Next up was the very solid Simley, Minnesota. Glenbard struggled through the dual and Simley went on to win by a 44-14 score; Simley also went on to win the pool. In the process, however, Tony defeated Dan Dick by an 18-8 major decision.

Now wrestling for third place in their pool, North would wrestle Minnesota's St. Michael-Albertville (STMA). For this dual, Tony stayed at 130 and wrestled the highly touted David Thorn. Thorn, who wrestled up to compete against Tony in the dual, was a senior and a three-time state finalist and a two-time state champion coming into the season—just like Tony. Nationally, Thorn ranked seventh, while Tony ranked fourth at

125 pounds.

The match would be all Tony—his strength was too much for Thorn to break past in order to open up a leg attack. Tony won an 8-4 decision. However, the dual went to STMA. It again came down to the final match and Parker Betts would defeat North's Tyler Knutson with a 5-4 decision to give STMA a 30-28 victory.

North would wrestle in the Fourth Place Pool on Day Two. Tony, who was dominant, was looking to close out his career at the Clash undefeated and with a third All-Clash performance.

When the second day came Glenbard would go 2-1 in their pool. They fell to Roseburg, Oregon, 37-23, and then to Don Bosco, Iowa, 28-22. The Panthers won their final dual of the day against Perham, Minnesota, with a 32-28 score. This gave them a fifteenth-place finish in the field of thirty-two.

As for Tony, he finished his day undefeated. He took down Roseburg's Jay Tovey with a 22-9 major decision, and then won by fall over Don Bosco's Jason Mangrich in 5:57. And all of that before ending his career at the Clash with a fall over Perham's Brett Greenwood in 00:49.

His 6-0 record that weekend, and his 24-0 career record at the Clash, earned him All-Clash honors for the third time in his career. He was dominant and in control of his matches and everybody watching saw that.

Soon after he received his award, the team packed up and headed back to their hotel. The night was short as there was much to improve on and an early rise and exit the following morning.

On the way home, at one of the bathroom and snack stops, Tony took it upon himself to have some fun with Coach Hahn.

While Hahn exited the bus, Tony balled up some snow and decided to throw it at his coach. When the snowball burst off Coach Hahn's back, and Hahn turned to see Tony laughing, the race was on.

Hahn, in full Carhartt gear, started to chase Tony through the snow. Tony, only in shorts and a t-shirt, headed toward a snow bank near the woods. Hahn and his coaching staff surrounded Tony and, standing in the snow and shaking, was unsure of where to go next. He could take his punishment, which included some sort of snow penance, or head off into the woods and freeze while the buses left—no one was coming to the senior prankster's rescue.

As fate would have it, Tony, needing to be warmed up, came forth and took some snow down his shirt from Hahn and even some on his head. He would stomp into the food pantry as he worked to remove all of the snowflakes and warm up.

When he came out of the food pantry, he seemed to be up to something else and one of his teammates told Hahn that he was bringing food on the bus. The rule was simple and clear: no food allowed on the bus.

With Hahn waiting for Tony near the door to the bus, Tony had a look of mischief on his face, but there was no food in his hands. Hahn made the assumption and, as the short and t-shirted All-Clash team member walked up the steps and entered the bus, Hahn smacked Tony in the butt and exploded the food he tried to sneak on the road. Laughter broke out and even Tony and Hahn shared a smile as the mood was light and the trip home had a feeling of relaxation. Some of the team goals were accomplished through a number of difficult duals, the team wrestled hard, they were closer, and the second half of the season appeared to have an optimistic vibe about it.

The trip was a success, in that "We went up [to the Clash] to come together as a team, just like we do each year," Ramos said, "and I think we did that. We still had much to work on, and we should have placed higher, but I felt we were all on the same page for the back half of the season."

AS GLENBARD HAD DONE FOR THE PREVIOUS twelve years, they closed out another undefeated conference dual meet season as they headed into the DuPage Valley Conference championships. In that stretch prior to the tournament, Tony won by fall over eight of his final nine opponents. His closest match was against a non-conference opponent in Wisconsin Rapids' Rylan Lubeck, a sophomore who was the number-two ranked wrestler in the state of Wisconsin. Tony won by a 3-2 decision.

When the week of the DuPage Valley Conference championships came around, North was focused on winning its eleventh conference title in a row; however, it would not be easy. After graduating a senior dominated team, and one of the strongest teams in the program's history, it was going to take a collective effort to score big points and win big matches. Still on the heels of North was West Aurora and Naperville Central. And, even though North was able to defeat both schools in their duals, the team race at a tournament was a much different race.

That season, Tony earned the number-one seed at 125 pounds. The team was stronger with him there and another senior, Dalton Boland, in the line-up at 130. However, in contrast to the previous season, there was no debate or coaches' vote in regard to challenging Tony's credentials. For his teammates, only three other wresters earned a number-one seed.

When the tournament began, North did what it traditionally had done; they scored points and dominated the lower weights. Out of the first seven weight classes, North sent six wrestlers into the championship match; they also sent one upper weight wrestler into the finals.

Dan Rios, at 112, started off a string of six consecutive conference champions. A two seed, he took the number-one seed, Adrian Laskero of Wheaton North, into sudden victory and won 6-4. Next up was the returning DVC champion, but two seeded, Joey Gosinski. His match also went into overtime against West Aurora's number-one seeded Miguel Venecia. The match ended with Gosinski earning a takedown and putting Venecia's to his back and holding him for the fall.

The team was two for two in the finals and now Tony was up. He won by fall over his first two opponents: Scott Anderson of Wheaton-Warrenville South, and Jake Dore of Wheaton North. In the finals, he had an old adversary in Josh Zinzer; however, "He really wasn't much of an adversary, and I proved that," Ramos said. Tony claimed the team's third championship with a 9-1 major decision.

At 130 and 135 pounds, Dalton Boland and Jimmy Chase came up victorious. Both were seeded first and wrestled up to their expectations. Boland won by fall over Naperville Central's Josh Tardy in the finals, and Chase earned an 8-3 decision over Spartak Chino of Wheaton-Warrenville South.

When the 140-pound weight class was called for the finals match, it was the number-one seed, West Aurora's Sam Pealstrom, against unseeded North senior Marty Schecht. Schecht, who had only earned a 2-1 season record thus far, had been wrestling junior varsity because he was caught in a position of being behind two state champions in Tony and Chase.

Schecht drew into the number-two seed from Naperville North, Adam Hankin, and defeated him in a wild 13-10 match. In the semifinals, he took on the number-three seed from Wheaton North, Geoff Pevitts, and earned a 6-5 decision to propel him into the finals. Here, in the championship match, Schecht faced Pealstrom. Pealstrom, who won by fall in his first two bouts, would not have as easy a time with Schecht. And, as the match concluded, Schecht won another wild match, this time a 14-12 decision and a sixth individual title for the Panthers.

The only other finalist would be Charleston Soko—he was awarded the number-three seed at 171. After winning by a major decision and a 3-1 decision, he faced Sam Pennisi of Glenbard East in the finals. Pennisi, who had defeated Soko in their dual, was the number-one seed; however, it was Soko with an 8-7 win and a seventh individual title for Glenbard North.

When the tournament ended, North won with a forty-eight point advantage over second place West Aurora. North now extended its conference streak record to eleven championships in a row.

Individually, Tony, now a four-time DVC champion, and only the fourth wrestler in the conference's history to achieve that feat, would take home the Gene Drendel Lower-Weight Outstanding Wrestler award. This was the first year the conference awarded an outstanding wrestler, and they awarded one in the lower weights and one in the upper weights. Tony made or added onto history on three separate occasions that Saturday as both a teammate and as an individual, but it was now time to move onto the Regional. If North was going to have an opportunity to win it first team state championships, they would first have to win their Regional.

CHAPTER 32
THREE OUT OF FOUR

"I like crushing people's dreams. I know that doesn't sound good, but, at the same time, that's what this sport is about. People got dreams and only one person is going to achieve that dream— someone else's dream is going to get crushed."

• *Tony Ramos*

ONCE THE DUPAGE VALLEY CONFERENCE championships ended, it was time for the Illinois state series to begin. For Tony, the week of the Regional was more about the team putting itself in position to qualify for the Dual Team State series. And, in order to qualify for the series, they had to first start by winning their Regional at Elgin High School.

Tony would do his part by pinning his way through the tournament. In the opening round, he defeated Elgin Larkin's Patrick Lipscomb in 3:57; in the semifinals, he dominated Tim Noverini of St. Charles North in 1:55; and, in the finals, Nick Ruffino of St. Charles East was Tony's final victim and the quickest fall of the three—a first period fall in 1:52. With the defeat of Ruffino, Tony earned his fourth individual Regional championship.

In addition to Tony's dominance, the team had another powerful weekend and won the team race with a ninety-point advantage over second place St. Charles East. North crowned six champions and qualified eight wrestlers to the Franklin Park Leyden Individual Sectional.

At the Sectional, Tony received a default win from Hinsdale Central's Terry Ward before winning by fall in 3:02 over senior Jamal Johnson of Skokie Niles West. That win put Tony in the finals for the fourth-straight year and he claimed his fourth and final Sectional title with a 10-4 decision over Stephen Lockhart of Hillside Proviso West.

Tony was not be the only qualifier for Glenbard, however. He was joined by returning state champion, Jimmy Chase, and All-State returner, sophomore Joey Gosinski. Additionally, Dan Rios and Charleston Soko qualified for the Individual State Championships for the first time in their careers.

North's five state qualifiers would be the most qualifiers coming out of the Sectional from any one school.

As a group, the Glenbard wrestlers fared well and, as Tony and the four other qualifiers prepared for the individual state championships, the rest of the team prepared for their dual team Sectional match-up with Hinsdale Central.

THE WEEK OF THE STATE CHAMPIONSHIPS, TONY

started to hear a great deal via word of mouth and through chatrooms that Oak Park-River Forest's Chris Dardanes was going to beat him. This was the talk as he headed into the tournament.

"It seemed like everyone had an opinion about it," Ramos said. "But he hadn't beat me and he wasn't going to beat me."

The way the brackets were aligned at 125, the only time Tony would possibly wrestle Dardanes would be in the semifinals. On the other side of the bracket, and what everyone was truly anticipating, was a finals match-up between Tony and Jon Morrison.

In Tony's opening match of his final high school state tournament, he wrestled Lee Wise from O'Fallon. It took him 00:58 into the second period to defeat Wise by fall and advance into the quarterfinals. When the match-up for the quarterfinals happened, it was Chicago Mt. Carmel's Mike Maggi who squared off and lost to Tony by a technical fall in 6:00.

Tony was now in the semifinals and opposing him was Dardanes. The match-up, itself, was exciting for fans because Tony had heard about how Dardanes was talking about how he was going to defeat him, and how the head coach of OPRF, Mike Powell, had talked about Dardanes being the wrestler who was going to dethrone Tony.

"That was a big match for me," Ramos remembered. "A big match in the fact that all week long and kind of leading up to that [tournament], all I heard was how Chris Dardanes was going to beat me. So, I really wanted to make a statement."

And Tony did just that.

"I remember being up by five, but that was not enough. I got a little tilt in to make sure that I got the major. I got up and looked at [Coach Mike] Powell, put my arms out and was like, 'Eh, I don't know what happened! You guys can keep talking all you want, but it ain't gonna happen.'"

The 10-1 final score was a show of Tony's dominance. Dardanes was pushed into the consolations, and Tony was making his fourth trip into the Grand March and state finals.

IN THE CHAMPIONSHIP, IT WAS THE MARQUEE match-up of the weekend: Ramos versus Morrison. Fans talked about it as they went out to eat or stayed at Assembly Hall to watch the medal matches. Wrestlers were talking about it, as were coaches. Here it was: two state champions, two nationally ranked wrestlers, number-one versus number-two in the state of Illinois, an Iowa committed wrester against an Oklahoma State committed wrestler, Glenbard North and Carl Sandburg, and all for the 125-pound individual state championship.

"The match-up was definitely inevitable," Siebert said. "In my opinion, it was the two best kids in the state—regardless of weight as they combined for seven state final appearances out of a possible eight; that is tough to argue with."

As the finals match neared, Morrison and his coaches had already prepared; they understood the match with Tony would happen. In that, there was not much pressure other than wrestling.

"We felt pretty loose going into the bout," Siebert said. "Jon had already won a state title and could embrace the underdog role with nothing to lose. As for preparation, yes, we put in a ton of time to prepare for the match. We had two goals in mind: Make sure that we can get away [on bottom], and somehow find a way to beat Tony's hands and get to his legs. We knew that Tony wasn't going to leg attack much, but when he did, he was going to make it count."

For Tony, this match was the culmination of four years and a final message.

"So, the whole reason that I went down to 125 [pounds] is because I wanted to prevent Morrison from winning another state title," Ramos said. "That's what I wanted. I made the cut, I made the sacrifice and dropped down—I could've went [130]—and I got the match-up that I wanted. We're in the state finals and I got my chance to end his career on a bad note. And I knew going into that match that I had a huge mental advantage over him—he did not believe that he could beat me. There was something there where he was afraid of me. I didn't just know it, I heard it from people, too. They said that when Morrison heard that I was going down to 125, he wanted to go up to 130."

Based on the last match that they wrestled in their dual, and how Tony controlled the entire match, the thought, to some, was Tony would come out and dominate just as he did against Dardanes. However, that would not be the case—Morrison was a much more talented wrestler and Tony would have to work harder for any points that he was going to score.

Once the opening whistle sounded, both Tony and Morrison came out heavy, banging on each other's head—Morrison was the first to break free of the tie. Tony moved forward after the backward circling, level-changing, and stutter-shot faking Morrison who was not looking to tie up again. In fact, it looked as if Morrison wanted to keep his distance and use his length to his advantage.

The motion was fast and, as Tony tried to work into his ties, Morrison was slick and fast and ever-moving in his stance. When Tony was successful in catching Morrison, Morrison tied up Tony's left wrist as he worked to limit Tony's offense. Tony had attempted two shots, but to no avail. In each attempt there was not much of an opening and the shots were not fully committed attempts. However, 00:45 into the opening period, Morrison took his first fully committed shot—and open double-leg—and got in on Tony's legs. Immediately, Tony defended and hipped into Morrison; Morrison changed over to a single-leg on Tony's left side and pressured him backward as he tried to secure his grip.

Tony, working his left-armed whizzer, worked the position to the mat and the referee called a stalemate with about one minute remaining in the period. Off the whistle, Tony again moved forward and Morrison blocked and faked and, as the two reached the edge of the mat, Tony was in on a shot; however, both wrestlers were out of bounds. For the final 00:45 of the period, Tony increased him level changes, motion, and head taps and ties. In response, Morrison stayed in his stance, tied up Tony's wrists but, more important, on any tie, was able to post with one hand on Tony's opposite triceps or shoulder and then snap and clear out of the tie. Morrison was not looking to give up inside positon and he continued to keep his backside to the edge of the mat as another defense as he looked for his opening.

When the period ended, it was a 0-0 tie. Tony had choice, chose down, and then escaped six seconds into the period. Right away, Tony continued with his high-paced offensive attacks and forward motion; however, when he would finally work into a position to attack, Morrison, hovering on the mat's edge, would snap down and circle back inbounds. He was sticking to his game plan of clearing ties and looking for his opportunity from a distance—he knew he had to make his shot count when it presented itself.

With about 00:30 expired in the second period, Tony fired off an open high-crotch to Morrison's right, but Morrison defended. The contrast of Styles was intriguing: Tony's strong and intense forward pressure with heavy ties to a shot style versus Morrison's more technical, calculated, and open shot style.

The hand fighting and position battle continued and, where Tony was more in control of the match's ties and pace, Morrison had the only committed shot that posed any threat. But, as Tony continued to move forward and Morrison circled back, the referee hit Morrison for a stalling call with 00:30 remaining in the second period as Tony took another shot that backed Morrison off the mat.

Going into the final period, Morrison chose down and Tony, who covered the right side, clamped onto Morrison's right leg, pressured him forward, and hooked Morrison's right ankle. Then, Tony took his right hand over Morrison's head, pulled up on his chin, and cranked it back toward his right side. As Morrison fought the hand, and Tony's hand came off the chin, Morrison hit a stand up and escaped to tie the match, 1-1. With that point, the fans in Assembly Hall cheered as now, in anticipation, the offensive attacks would have to increase.

In the next 00:45, Tony shot Morrison off the mat two more times and continued to pressure forward; Morrison continued to keep his back to the mat's edge. Now, with about 00:45 remaining in regulation, Tony attempted a slide-by that Morrison stepped out of, paused, and reshot an open double on the mat's edge. Tony sprawled, defended, and got into an underhook. Now with wrist control with his right hand and his left-handed underhook, Tony tried to pull Morrison in, but instead drove into Morrison and they went out of bounds.

Back to the center, now with 00:30 remaining, Morrison tied on the head and blocked while Tony pressured into him looking for a shot. As the clock was down to 00:18, and Morrison was back to the mat's edge, Tony attacked and was in on a high-crotch to Morrison's left. Tony would reposition his hands to a double-leg as Morrison tried to sprawl. In that moment, Tony dropped Morrison down to his butt and secured both legs with his hands locked. However, Morrison had Tony's head trapped between his legs and under his chest and he had his hands locked in Tony's crotch. The referees determined that the wrestlers were out of bounds and no takedown was awarded. Defilippis jumped out of his chair and was almost inside of the circle yelling as he spread his arms wide open, and shouted, "How is that not two?" Behind him, Chris Edwards moved out of his chair and looked at the angle from another angle—neither could believe a takedown had not been awarded. In that moment, some of the fans were hollering, "TWO!" throughout the arena, while others combated with their arms waving it off yelling, "No! No takedown!"

The final seconds of regulation ran out with both Tony and Morrison in the middle of the mat not doing much of anything aside from waiting for overtime.

Just three years earlier, as a freshman, Tony went into overtime with the number-two ranked Chris Spangler and would ultimately lose on a sudden victory escape point with eight seconds remaining. Now, again in the state championship match against the number-two ranked wrestler at his weight class, overtime would determine the winner. Against Spangler, Tony let the moment get to him and he did not open up as much as he should have. He shut his offense down and paid the price with a runner-up finish. The next minutes would revel if Tony was going to put himself in position to win by taking chances, or if he was going to keep it close and see how it would play itself out.

Once the whistle started the first overtime period, it was all Tony moving forward on Morrison who was backing up, and Morrison continued to work to control the inside position and block off Tony as needed. To clear Morrison's tie, Tony hit a slide-by with no real attack; however, it did clear his position and allowed a chance to reset himself and work back to his ties.

Tony continued to push his pace and press forward. He would shuck Morrison, Morrison would clear, Tony would take a shot, Morrison would block, and then Morrison would attempt an open double. Tony, in defense, blocked and worked into his front headlock position. Morrison worked backward and Tony countered with a low double-leg of his own on the mat's edge. Morrison would lock around Tony's waist and 00:21 remained as a fresh start was awarded.

Six seconds later, as Tony continued his forward pressure, he hit a sweep single to his left and was in deep on Morrison's right side. Tony would adjust his head to the outside as Morrison hipped in and Tony adjusted his hips, popped them high, lifted Morrison off the mat, and returned him while he drove his shoulder into Morrison's chest as he hit the mat. Morrison, in defense, tried to lock around Tony's body, but Tony was in too tight and, as Tony fought for the points, Frank and Edwards were out of their chairs shouting for the takedown. When the referee confirmed the takedown and the two points, cheers erupted, disappointment murmured, Frank punched his hand in the air via an uppercut, and Tony jumped off of Morrison and circled the mat with three fingers stretching to the ceiling in each hand—he would then work down into a flex pose while facing all of the photographers.

In the foreground would be Tony celebrating and, in the background, Morrison would lie on his back, hands over his face, in defeat. Tony would have his hand raised in Assembly Hall for the third season in a row and then point up to the Glenbard North section of the arena. As he stomped over to his corner, he would viciously come down with a hard slap on Frank's hand and then Edwards' hand. He would exit into the tunnel as a three-time state champion.

The last time that Tony and Morrison wrestled, Tony rode him out. This time, in the state championship, it came down to a takedown with seconds remaining in the first overtime period.

"I didn't want to win 1-0 on a ride out," Ramos said. "I wanted to get a takedown and prove that I could take him down. We get into that match, we go into overtime, I double-leg him, cut across, finish—I had a couple of opportunities to finish earlier in the match, but we kept going out of bounds and he kept kicking out. But this time I made sure that I finished in the center, was solid, got my takedown and just jumped up. I remember just giving a huge flex and screaming out loud and being so pumped up."

"[Tony] was a difficult opponent," Siebert said, "and he presented the same challenges for all of his opponents, not just Jon. He is a tenacious competitor, super strong, huge lungs, unrelenting heavy hands, tough to get away from, and a mentality that always, under any circumstance, finds a way to win. It's hard to think of a scenario in which Tony would not be the favorite in overtime and, in no way is that any sort of knock on Jon Morrison. Jon was in great shape and is tough as nails. But knowing Tony as I did, he is one of the toughest kids I had ever seen both from a physical and a mental standpoint. I really can't recall a wrestler with a bigger knack for winning close bouts. He just always envisions his hand being raised, no matter what the task at hand."

For Tony, his reason for dropping to 125 pounds was more of showmanship, in his opinion.

"I felt that it was kind of my duty to give people that match," Ramos said. "That needed to happen. You know, two state champs going the same weight, both seniors, one going for his third and the other going for his second; it just had to happen. There was no reason to deprive the fans of wrestling [that match] when it could happen. So that's why I felt like I needed to do it. I like crushing people's dreams. I know that doesn't sound good, but, at the same time, that's what this sport is about. People got dreams and only one person is going to achieve that dream—someone else's dream is going to get crushed."

Of course, there was also Oklahoma State choosing Morrison over Tony that fall, and that choice still did not sit well with the future Hawkeye. Therefore, subconsciously, there may have been some internal vengeance as well directed to Oklahoma State.

"That was probably some of it," Ramos admitted. "The recruiting thing was going on and they were recruiting both me and Morrison, and after they told me that they were going to wait on me to come out and visit before they make a commitment to Morrison, they then took his commitment and told me that I didn't need to come out there. I wanted to make a point to them that they made the wrong choice."

After Tony had his hand raised, he was directed off of the mat for his post-match interview. The question first posed to him was: "What was different tonight against Jon Morrison?"

Tony responded dissatisfied with his result: "I wasn't taking many shots—so, I'm not happy. It was a 3-1 match in overtime, that's not how it should be. I got the job done, whatever, [but] I got to go back into the room and work harder."

The next question was in regard to his future at Iowa and remaining in a black and gold singlet.

With a bit of humor, Tony smiled: "I love black and gold—I look good in those colors. I can't wait to get up there. Coach Brands is going to show me a lot, he's going to teach me a lot—a lot that I don't know. He's just someone that, when you get in that room, the intensity level goes up beyond belief."

2009 • IHSA INDIVIDUAL STATE CHAMPIONSHIPS • 125 LB PODIUM
RAMOS STANDS ATOP THE AWARD STAND FOR THE THIRD YEAR IN A ROW
PHOTOGRAPH COURTESY • GLENBARD NORTH WRESTLING • JEFF ELDRIDGE

CHAPTER 33
LAST CHANCE

"I knew it was going to be a tough dual, that we needed every little thing to go our way to get into the finals."

• *Tony Ramos*

THE SUNDAY AFTER TONY HAD WON HIS THIRD state championship, he was back in the Glenbard North wrestling room with his team preparing for their dual on Tuesday night. All season long the team had over-achieved, and they needed one more week of their best wrestling to bring home a team title.

"We were in position to win a team championship," Ramos said. "I truly believed that. Everyone was wrestling at a high level and we just had to get past Hinsdale [Central] and I felt we would be okay."

At the Team Sectional that Tuesday, North had to face a strong opponent in Hinsdale Central—the team many were picking to be able to take North down and bring home their own team trophy.

The dual was wrestled at Villa Park Willowbrook High School. "We knew they had a strong team," head coach Mark Hahn said. "The coaches figured we were evenly matched at probably seven matches each, so we knew it would come down to bonus points and not giving up bonus points. Guys like Tony were going to have to step up if we were going to advance, and we needed some heroes."

When the dual opened at 103, it fed into the strength of North, and ended in the strength of Hinsdale. As figured, the matches were tied at the dual's end; the final score came down to the bonus points.

For North, they earned falls from Wade Hazard at 112 and Dan Rios at 119 before Tony stepped onto the mat at 135. Tony weighed in at 130 and bumped up as needed. The same was true for state champion and three-time medalist Jimmy Chase; he wrestled 140.

Tony scored a technical fall over Alex Orton in 5:16 at 135 and, by the time the dual was down to the final two matches, Glenbard was leading 31-22 and was facing Hinsdale Central's two state medalists at 215 and 285 pounds.

At 215, Hinsdale's sophomore state runner-up, Jack Allen, was wrestling 189-pound freshman Danny Eldridge from North. Eldridge, up a weight class, was given explicit instructions from Hahn. "We told him he could not get pinned," Hahn said. "And if he kept it to a decision that would be a win for us."

In a match that Hinsdale had to have bonus points in for an opportunity to win the dual, Eldridge did enough to keep the match and the dual out of reach. Eldridge kept Allen to a decision victory and, with one match remaining, Glenbard held a 31-25 advantage.

"That match was crazy," Ramos said. "Their head coach was going crazy and [Allen] just couldn't get anything on Eldridge."

When North senior Chris VanGundy took to the mat, he had to wrestle a senior state medalist in Pat Clegg. "Just as we told Eldridge, VanGundy had a job to do: Not give up a fall," Hahn said.

VanGundy adhered to his head coach's words. He held Clegg to a decision and North went on to win 31-28. This qualified them for the team state championships for the ninth time in the past twelve years.

"The guys stepped up big for the team," Ramos said. "Eldridge, who was just a freshman and a weight class lighter, did a great job against their state finalist, and VanGundy did the same. Those guys left it out there for the team and when it came to those matches, you could hear the Hinsdale crowd thinking they had won it. They were wrong. Those guys wrestling how they did, and us other guys scoring bonus points, was the difference."

IN THE OPENING ROUND, NORTH HAD TO FACE

Wheeling High School, and Tony had Luke Smith, a 43-2 sophomore who finished third at the individual state championships at 125 pounds; he lost to Morrison in the semifinals.

When the dual opened at 160 pounds, North had to hold their ground. In the first four weights, they gave up a major decision and two decisions and fell behind 10-3 in their dual. It would be senior heavyweight Chris VanGundy who reset the tone when he won a 10-2 major decision. The next four Glenbard wrestlers followed suit with a fall, two major decisions, and a technical fall. The Panthers were winning the dual 22-

10 by the time Tony stepped on the mat.

"It didn't matter who Wheeling had or what weight I was wrestling, he was going to lose and I was going to score points," Ramos said. And Tony did exactly that. He won a 15-8 decision, and his effort extended the lead to a 25-10 advantage for Glenbard.

Next for North was senior Jimmy Chase, who won by a major decision, while fellow senior, Marty Schecht, won a regular decision to clinch the dual with three matches remaining. Mark Hahn forfeited the final three weights, won the dual, 32-28, and the team set his sights on the highly-touted team picked to win the tournament, Minooka. In the opening dual of the season at the Fulk Quad, Minooka had defeated North 47-14. But that was a different team, and both Glenbard and Minooka knew it.

"I knew it was going to be a tough dual, that we needed every little thing to go our way to get into the finals," Ramos said. "We were where we needed to be. We had a stronger line-up than that first night and our lower-weights would have to earn us bonus points while our upper weights would have to wrestle tough and keep it close."

Glenbard opened the dual with two decision wins and jumped out to a 6-0 team score lead. At 215 and 285 pounds, Minooka returned the favor and the dual was tied, 6-6. Headed into 103, North felt very good about its chances; however, after having a late lead, Brayan Gonzalez gave up a reversal and two near-fall points and lost a devastating 6-4 decision. At 112, North's Rios was also up late in the match and dropped his bout in the final seconds, an 8-7 decision. North was forced to play catch-up with a twelve-point swing in Minooka's favor; those six points were important for North. By the time Tony stepped onto the mat against Minooka's Blake Montella, North trailed 12-9. When Tony exited the mat, after he has scored a technical fall in 5:42, North was back in the lead, 14-12. Tony's match was, thus far, the only match where bonus points were earned.

North then exchanged matches in the next four bouts—they won two and lost two and lead the dual 20-18 as the final two matches at 152 and 160 pounds were left to be wrestled. Unfortunately for Glenbard and Tony, Minooka scored bonus points in each of the final two matches and won the dual 27-20 to advance to the championship.

Tony was visibly upset and could not believe they had lost. They were in position to win and had lost two matches in the final seconds that cost them an opportunity to wrestle for a state championship.

"Those were two huge matches at 103 and 112 pounds, that we needed to win," Ramos said. "If we win them, we win the dual 26-21. But, that goes back to saying we needed everything right to happen to win. We had some little hiccups in the last seconds that made the difference in that dual. I don't think they had more heart, they just won those two matches—they found a way to keep it close and win. Some of their guys came out harder and were ready to go.

"I was so upset with that semifinal loss because I feel we could have beaten Oak Park in the finals and won North's first state championship. It wouldn't have been easy, but on any given day in this sport, anything can happen and it happens at every tournament where someone loses who should have won. We would have had to wrestle the best dual of the season and everyone would have had to wrestle lights out, but that doesn't mean that we weren't capable. But, we lost to Minooka. So, we took third."

After Tony won his next and final match in his high school career, a 15-5 major decision over Edwardsville's Greg Jackson, he went behind the bench and his emotions took over. He cried. He just could not put his head around not winning a team state championship. His father reached over the half wall to console his son, but there was no consoling him—he did not finish his career the way he wanted.

"I broke down after the third place match because I started to reflect upon my career as a whole and all I could think about were the goals that I didn't accomplish and not the great things I had done," Ramos said. "I missed being a four-time state champ by eight seconds. I missed out on winning a team championship by a few points. I only won the Ironman once. I was very upset that I made a promise to Hahn that summer to do everything in my power to make sure that we came away with a state title that year after what had happened the year before, and I let him down. At the time, back then, I felt like I failed him and the team. I missed accomplishing my main goal that season. But, looking back now, I think I set the tone for the guys coming up and the next year they went out and got the job done!

"I just remember after breaking down and getting that all out of my system, just being so happy for the team and the guys that we had. If you look back talent-wise, we may have not been the best team we ever had, especially coming off the guys we had graduated the year prior; but, that was one of the hardest working teams. We really fed off one another and meshed well together—I truly believe that.

"There were so many things that I wanted for myself and for the program that it all came emotionally exploding out of me," Ramos continued. "I think this is what really drove me that summer and leading into college to push even harder to make sure I didn't have those moments where I looked back and said, 'Man, I was so close. What could I have done better?'"

2009 • IHSA DUAL TEAM STATE CHAMPIONSHIPS • THIRD PLACE DUAL
RAMOS SITS AND IS CONSOLED BY HIS FATHER AFTER HIS FINAL MATCH
PHOTOGRAPH COURTESY • GLENBARD NORTH WRESTLING • JEFF ELDRIDGE

CHAPTER 34
SURPRISING EVERYONE ELSE

"I was already in the finals, so those [would be] my first two matches of the day. I had seen [Ramos] before and I knew him from youth tournaments. [My] strategy was the same as always, score early and often."

• *Logan Stieber*
Junior World Team Trials Opponent

AFTER TONY'S HIGH SCHOOL WRESTLING career had ended, he went right back to work because he was going to compete in April at the FILA Junior National Championships. The tournament was held in Las Vegas, Nevada, and he would wrestle in the 60 kg (132.25 pound) weight class. Although he wrestled fairly tough, he placed fifth behind a slew of future All-Americans and national champions.

The winner of the bracket, and named the Outstanding Wrestler of the tournament, was Jordan Oliver of the Gator Wrestling Club. The runner-up was Andrew Long of the Cyclone Wrestling Club and, in third place, from the Hawkeye Wrestling Club, Matt McDonough; McDonough defeated Nick Dardanes of Overtime School of Wrestling who placed fourth.

For Tony, he represented Izzy Style wrestling and he defeated Nate Moore of the Hawkeye Wrestling Club by a 2-1, 1-0 decision for his medal.

After this finish, Tony knew that if he was going to make the Junior World Team, he had to become much more serious about his training and what was important to him. To do that, he needed and sought help from his high school principal, Dr. John Mensik.

GLENBARD NORTH WAS SET TO END ITS SCHOOL

year the first week of June, and graduation was scheduled that first Sunday; however, Tony knew that it was time to move on and prepare for the next two stages of his life: qualifying for the Junior World Team, and establishing residency in Iowa.

For Tony, his classes were pretty much over as senior classes wrapped up by the first or second week of May and, if needed, finals were taken early to ensure all graduation requirements were met and students could walk with their class. Graduation, itself, was not an event that Tony looked forward to; it was simply a formality. What he was looking forward to was the qualifier for the Junior World Team, and he and his parents went in to speak with Dr. Mensik to see about an early graduation.

"I went in and spoke with Dr. Mensik," Ramos recalled, "and told him how I wanted to make the Junior World Team and I wanted to get really serious about it. I told him that I needed to devote all of my time to it and train. I asked him if I could graduate from school a few weeks early so that I could do this. He was great about it. He worked it out with teachers and got it all figured out and I was done with school in mid-April, about three weeks before everyone else so that I could train for a good month solid for the Junior FILAs."

But Tony did not train like a normal high school wrestler for that event. As he had done in the past in regard to his workouts—the extremes—he did the same here.

"I moved in with Izzy," Ramos said, "and we worked out three times a day. This was serious and I approached it that way. I was able to focus on my weight and my wrestling and then it was time to wrestle."

The FILA Junior World Team Trials was held in Colorado Springs, Colorado, from May 18-23, 2009, and Tony had to wrestle and win a mini-tournament and then, if he won that, he would have to wrestle the person who was already waiting in the finals: Logan Stieber.

LOGAN STIEBER WAS NOT ONLY A FOUR-TIME

state champion from Monroeville High School in Monroeville, Ohio, but he also won the Dave Schultz High School Excellence National Award and was the Junior Hodge Trophy recipient.

While in high school, Stieber opened up his freshman campaign winning his first four matches before he suffered his first loss. After he earned a 5-1 record, he never lost the remainder of his high school career—he posted a 184-1 record. His only loss came that freshman year in the finals of the Walsh Ironman where David Taylor of Ohio's St. Paris Graham defeated him in the finals at 103 pounds—that same season

Tony Ramos won the Ironman title at 112 pounds.

When Stieber won his fourth state title, he became only the nineteenth wrestler in the history of the Ohio High School Athletic Association (OHSAA) to accomplish that feat.

Along the way, Stieber had amassed 134 total falls. He was a two-time Cadet and a Junior Fargo Freestyle national champion as well as a Cadet and Junior Greco-Roman national champion. In 2008, Stieber won the FILA Junior national championship and, in 2009, he placed third at the United States Open and fourth at the United States World Team Trials. Due to his WTT finish, that put him in the finals against whomever came out of the mini tournament. He would sit and watch and wait to wrestle. In 2009, Stieber was only a junior in high school.

FOR TONY, HE WON MATCH AFTER MATCH UNTIL

he found himself in the mini-tournament finals against a very familiar opponent—the same opponent he had just faced that past winter at the University of Illinois for the IHSA individual state championship: Jon Morrison.

"At the time," Ramos remembered, "I don't think the Junior Worlds was common for U.S.A. Wrestling—I think it was a newer thing. But I did wrestle Morrison in the finals of the mini tournament and I did that in two periods. I had just beat him a few months back and I was not going to lose to him now. I was still proving the point to Oklahoma State that they made the wrong choice.

"In the finals, the best-of-three series, I had Stieber," Ramos continued. "After I beat Morrison, me and Izzy went back to the hotel to eat and grab a nap. When I woke up, and we started walking back, Izzy turned to me and said, 'We're going to do this—I hope you know that. We're going to shock the world.' And I knew it, too. I had no worries in the world."

As Stieber was sitting out, he had a chance to watch Tony compete. "I was already in the finals," Stieber said, "so those [would be] my first two matches of the day. I had seen [Ramos] before and I knew him from youth tournaments. [My] strategy was the same as always, score early and often."

Israel knew what the match-up would be in the end. "We trained and prepared for that match," he said. "We knew what we were going to get and we were ready for him—I don't think he was ready for us."

When the match started, it opened as everyone expected, until Tony got in on Stieber. "I ended up pinning him in 1:59 and I know people were amazed," Ramos said. "When we came into the second match, I lost the first period 1-0 and I am sure people were thinking the fall was a fluke and Stieber would seal this thing up. But then I won the next period 4-1—I was able to get to my shots and score. And then, in the third, I won 6-0 to close it out. I just dominated the period and no one could believe it. People were saying, 'That guy just beat Stieber.' According to everyone, Stieber isn't supposed to lose. He just doesn't do that. Me and Izzy prepared and now it was time for the Junior Worlds."

As Stieber looked back on that match, "I clearly wasn't [as] ready as he was," he said. "I needed to finish out periods. I knew he was tough before the match and I knew it after. I took away that to be able to win at such a high level, I would need to be one hundred percent focused."

Now that Tony was on the Junior World Team, he trained in Colorado Springs at the Olympic Training Center. However, before any of that was going to happen, he was going to have to purchase a home. To do this, he sent his mom out to Iowa; she would pick his home. As for Tony, he just needed to be near the university and in a quiet place to train and focus.

"My mom actually went out and looked at houses for me so I didn't have to take a break from training," Ramos said. "She would call me, send me pictures, told me what she thought were good options, and she picked me out a duplex in Coralville, Iowa, about three miles away. I could get to Carver in eight minutes—which is all I cared about—and I could get to campus in about ten to twelve minutes. But it was a straight shot down what they call the 'Coralville Strip,' right into Carver-Hawkeye Arena."

Tony purchased his home with the money he was awarded after the car accident he was in as a child. He established residency in Iowa when he closed on the home and moved in on the first of July. From then on, he started his training with the Hawkeye wrestlers as the summer camp sessions began.

THE UNIVERSITY OF IOWA

CHAPTER 35
THE PROGRAM

"I'm more about making the history than remembering it, but I'll tell you what I know."

• *Dan Gable*
Former Head Coach, the University of Iowa
NCAA, World, and Olympic Champion

EVEN THOUGH THE UNIVERSITY OF IOWA OPENED its doors to the public in 1847, it was not until 1911, sixty-four years later, when the collegiate sport of wrestling would be offered at the state's oldest university.

To many who know Iowa wrestling, they know one name: Dan Gable. Dan Gable the 1972 Olympic gold medalist who did not allow one point to be scored on him throughout the Games. Dan Gable the winningest coach in the Iowa wrestling program's history. Dan Gable the coach who won fifteen NCAA championships; nine of those championships in a row. Dan Gable the coach who changed the face of wrestling and continued to modernize the sport.

However, well before Dan Gable was even born, the University of Iowa was growing and building its program.

The first coach in the program's history was Ernest Gustav (E.G.) Schroeder—more affectionately known as "Dad." As a graduate of Simpson College in Iowa—where he participated in athletics, including wrestling—he came to the University of Iowa to study medicine and become involved in coaching.

In his first season, Iowa had its first and only competition against the University of Nebraska—the Hawkeyes lost that dual, 0-3. The following season, Schroeder's team finished with a 1-1 record, defeating

Iowa State 4-0, and again losing to Nebraska 1-2.

It was not until 1913 that Schroeder's program earned a 2-0 record defeating both Iowa State and Nebraska. Schroeder would coach the program from 1911 through 1915 and come back again in 1921 for a one-year stint, going 4-1 in his final season as head of the program. His career coaching totals were 9-3-1; additionally, he served as the university's athletic director from 1937-1947 and, in those eleven years, he led the athletic department out of a financial crisis from the construction of their football stadium and fieldhouse.

Schroeder was a member of the Olympic wrestling committee in 1936, coached varsity tennis from 1923-1937, kept the athletic department moving forward during World War II when pre-flight training programs took over much of Iowa's athletic facilities, and was recognized as the founder of intramural athletics in Iowa.

His impact on the university and sport, not just wrestling, elevated Schroeder to legend status even before his retirement in 1952. The Hawkeye wrestling program, as well as other athletic programs, may not have survived and thrived without his leadership and guidance.

From 1916-1920, head coach Pat Wright kept the team moving forward, but he left with a 3-6-1 career record.

Then, in 1921, for a one-year stint, Schroeder took the program back before Mike Howard was named the next head coach. As Howard took over in 1922, he had no idea that he would become the longest tenured coach in the program's history—his thirty-two-season career is still the longest stretch by an Iowa coach to date. And, according to Dan Gable, "Howard is considered the program's first coach, for some reason. I don't know much about the first two guys, really. I'm more about making the history than remembering it, but I'll tell you what I know. I do know Mike Howard brought more of an understanding of the sport to Iowa than was previously had here."

In 1926, with the inception of the Big Ten Championships, the Hawkeyes placed third and finished the season 5-1 with its only dual meet loss coming to Illinois, 8-9. The sport and the culture was growing under Howard's guidance and, when the NCAA Championships came to be in 1929, Howard's team finished tied for ninth after a tenth place Big Ten finish and a 0-5-1 record.

Despite his lengthy career, Howard never placed better than second at the Big Ten Championships, and he never earned a higher team finish than fifth at the NCAA Championships. His career record ended 93-69-11 and, today, the team's Most Valuable Wrestler award is named after him.

The coach that followed, David McCuskey, would be instrumental in building the program's future. However, early on, his reputation stemmed from the success he had elsewhere in Iowa as a coach.

"I remember McCuskey," Gable said, "from the University of Northern Iowa, which was called State Teacher's College at that time, and he actually won a national title while over there. And, at that time, they were loaded. I mean, they had several three-time national champions during his era and they were just a dynamite team. They were before my time, but I knew about them and that was the program that I was most familiar with because of their success.

"By the time I was in junior high," Gable continued, "McCuskey had left and gone to Iowa. Now, I don't believe that he was a wrestler, but he was one of those guys that got into wrestling and knew how to impact kids and help make them successful."

As Gable entered high school, and continued to wrestle, he attended the University of Iowa summer wrestling camps. "During my sophomore, junior, and senior years," Gable remembered, "when I went to the camps, McCuskey was the coach and I got to know a little bit that way."

Also during the McCuskey era, Gable recalled, "They had some pretty good teams, but really good individuals such as Terry McCann, Gary Kurdelmeir, and Sherwyn Thorson among others."

McCuskey's teams would go on to have a career record of 160-69-7, win two Big Ten Championships in 1958 and 1968, and the highest NCAA Championship finish was in 1962 with a third-place finish. As for individuals, he coached seven national champions.

However, it is what McCuskey did in his later years that set up Iowa's success. According to Gable, "[McCuskey] was a good administrator, [and] he knew how to make the program thrive. In 1968 McCuskey hired Gary Kurdelmeir as an assistant and turned the wrestling room over to him—Kurdelmeir ran the practices. And a change was slowly happening and everyone could see it."

When it was time for McCuskey to retire, he had already positioned Kurdelmeir to take over the program in 1972. However, it was what Kurdelmeir did, prior to taking over, that impacted Iowa wresting and the sport itself.

"In my Olympic year," Gable said, "that [1972] year, McCuskey was stepping down and Kurdelmeir was the assistant coach and he stepped in and wanted to really take the program to a new level. He was a great thinker—they called him 'the Architect'—he's the guy that had the brainstorm to go get me to come to Iowa. He had a plan that he wanted to execute—be better than Iowa State, win a Big Ten championship, and an NCAA championship—and he did it."

As for "the Architect's" plan, it was nothing less than calculated. "How did he get me?" Gable grinned. "He didn't. He got my mom and my dad and all my friends. Then all of a sudden when a timing decision came, and I didn't think I had to make my decision yet, the timing decision was pretty simple.

"He called me up after he had already met me and said, 'Have you thought more about it?' and I said no because he told me that I didn't really have to make my mind up until after the Olympics or close to it. And this was all in March after we had already met at the end of December. He said, 'Well, okay. Take your time.' But, the next day, he called me and said, 'Take it or leave it.'

"He knew the timing was right. He had already done his homework with my mom and dad and all my mom's and dad's friends, and he's already done his homework with my personal friends at Iowa State. And so, when he said that, I hung up and called my mom and dad and they told me to go to Iowa. My response: I got mad at them. I asked, 'Why would you do that? I want to stay at Iowa State. I want to be a Cyclone and help coach there.' So when I hung up with them, I called my friends, and every one of my close friends had already been talked to by Kurdelmeir.

"This guy had already done such a good job of getting everyone close to me to believe that I should go to Iowa—so that's where I went," Gable continued. "I called him back and said, 'I don't have a choice.' It was just like when I went to Iowa State; I didn't have a choice because I was a kid who was influenced by the people who supported me and that's how I made my decisions. The thing was, I was doing too many things day to day, and I didn't want to have to worry about all that stuff. And because I had good mentors, I could trust them.

"It was a great move for the sport, for me moving to Iowa, and all of a sudden we had a great rivalry here with Iowa State. Record crowds were always set and the nation always watched Iowa."

However, what Kurdelmeir did next was what surprised Gable the most—he gave him full control of the wrestling room. "It shocked me that he would turn the keys of the wrestling room over to me when that was his first year as the head coach," Gable said. "He made this my area."

As for Kurdelmeir, he had a variety of areas that he was strong in, but he recognized Gable's strength and knew this was how he was going to accomplish his goals.

"Why did he do it?" Gable reflected. "Because he's a good leader. He knew where I was strong and he let me be strong there. All of a sudden, as a leader, after one month, he goes, 'You know, you've got a lot to learn, but you're better in the room with the kids than I am. So that's your area. You're going to focus on that every day. You're going to line up the workouts every day, you're going to run the practices, and I'm going to do the promotions and line up the recruiting. I'll do the club and meet with the press—I'm going to have you do a lot of this stuff too, but this is your main area.'"

For Kurdelmeir, "His area was promotion," Gable remembered. "His area was loving to talk. His area was creating controversy; like stirring up action and seeing what he could do."

And he knew how to stir up fans and create controversy. He was great at the promotion of big meets and the sport, and he made it a spectacle to see.

In 1971 he stumbled upon a public address announcer named Phil Haddy when Haddy momentarily took over PA duties at a summer tournament. Kurdelmeir would put Haddy on the microphone for the 1972 season and thereafter. He told Haddy to create excitement and be a little crazy—being flamboyant and exciting would not be a tall task. This new style of excitement during matches brought more people in—it became entertainment and show-like.

Additionally, Kurdelmeir mixed up other aspects in the fieldhouse. He had an organ player come in and make noise and made the atmosphere almost inaudible because the guy he had on the organ was not even a good organ player. But it just added more excitement for the fans.

For one dual against Oklahoma, Kurdelmeir brought in all of the mats and put them together. He hated the way Oklahoma wrestled on the edge, so he made a seventy-four foot square and said it was the world's largest mat just so Oklahoma had to wrestle in the middle. The fans loved it and the attention was drawn to Iowa. The next year, the NCAA instituted a rule limiting a mat size to forty-two feet in diameter.

As for putting Gable in charge of the room, again, he knew how to do what was best for the sport and the program.

"He understood that the program would flourish quicker, better, when he puts the right person in the right position of authority," Gable said. "It was that simple. He was very good at that. He did a tremendous job of taking over a program and leading it in a way that had an immediate and profound impact."

Four years later, after he earned two Big Ten championships, two NCAA championships, and crowned six individual NCAA champions, all while compiling an astonishing 51-7-5 dual meet record, he knew it was time to step aside and allow the program to take off under Gable. He had laid the groundwork for the program, and for Gable as a coach.

"With the success we were having at Iowa," Gable remembered, "I was getting calls from all over for head coaching positions. Even my old school, Iowa State, wanted to get me back in some capacity. There was some pressure on him on what he should do. What Kurdelmeir did was what he knew he needed to do to keep Iowa ahead of everyone else. He had the intuition to say, 'We're going to lose this guy unless I move out of the way and give him the program.'"

For Kurdelmeir, he was proud of what he had built; however, he was also not too proud to know how to make the program better.

"He could have kept going for a while longer," Gable said. "But he made the right management move for the program. I'm not sure if it was the right move for him or not, but it was the right move for the program."

WHEN DAN GABLE TOOK OVER THE IOWA

Hawkeye wrestling program in 1977, Kurdelmeir had not only made sure the program was secure, he made sure Gable was ready to be the head coach that he needed to be.

"When I said that Kurdelmeir knew that I had much to work on," Gable commented, "he made sure that I bettered myself in those areas. He knew what he was doing from the start—I truly believe that.

"Aside from putting me in where I was good, he made me go do things that I wasn't good at—like go speak to the local clubs and promote the sport. Or get on the phone and call recruits, or go see recruits—I wasn't good at that kind of thing at that time. I was only good inside of the wrestling room."

However, in the end, "the Architect" had a plan and he followed it through. Due to that, Iowa thrived. In a 2016 interview, upon his retirement from the University of Iowa, former PA announcer and Sports Information Director Phil Haddy commented on how, "Kurdelmeir doesn't get near the credit he deserves for starting the wrestling dynasty at Iowa. Gary started it because he is the one who hired the guy who everyone said was unhireable—Dan Gable. Kurdelmeir was so forward thinking to know that Gable would be good enough to take over as a head coach when he stepped down."

For Gable, now prepped as a recruiter, a speaker and promoter of the sport, and a strong technician in the room with great relationships with the wrestlers, his first order of business was simple: get to work.

As for his style, the Iowa style, Gable said, "I didn't really think about a style. I didn't know the difference. It was just one hard-relentless-knowing-all-the-skills-and-techniques style."

When it came to Gable's influences, he turned no further than his high school and college head coaches.

At Waterloo West High School in Iowa, Bob Siddens was Gable's first major philosophical influence on the sport. "Having had a great high school coach in Coach Siddens," Gable said, "he influenced me more from how you look at each guy instead of looking at the total team. The total team became a total team when looking at each guy and doing what was needed for each guy individually. The other thing he influenced me on was that we didn't dink around in practice. We went six-minute goes after six-minute goes after six-minute goes—if we didn't go six six-minute goes in a practice, on top of all the other stuff, then we probably didn't have a really hard practice. So the work ethic, the amount of competition at practice, really was engraved in me."

Gable would go from Siddens' wrestling room to Dr. Harold Nichols' wrestling room at Iowa State. Nichols, a 1939 NCAA champion for the University of Michigan under legendary coach Cliff Keen, took over the Iowa State wrestling program in 1953 and would turn the Cyclones into a national powerhouse. In his thirty-two years as the head coach, he won six NCAA championships, had thirty-eight individual national champions, and compiled a 456-75-11 record. He was described by *The New York Times* as "one of college wrestling's most successful and respected coaches."

Nichols, who was more than a wrestler, taught his athletes a great deal of independence. This idea of independence came from his time as a wrestler and as a serviceman. As a student-athlete at Michigan, Nichols took time off to serve in the U.S. Army Air Corps in WWII as a pilot; he would reach the rank of Lieutenant. When he returned home from the war, he earned his master's degree from the University of Illinois and then his doctorate at Michigan.

So, for Gable, his transition from hard work with Siddens to hard work with Nichols was not as severe as at it may have been for others.

When Gable entered Iowa State, "I was like, wow, this guy teaches independence," Gable expressed. "He really just showed that the way to get better at wrestling was to wrestle. But, he did it in a way where he made sure there were enough good wrestlers in the room that they were helping their partners and showing them how to get better. We had other coaches who showed the drilling and such, but we didn't do much drilling and such, but we learned to do it on our own.

"But Dr. Nichols taught me a lot about independence. About what you really need once you move on in life—once you become a husband or professional in whatever you do. The same was true for a wrestling match."

When he took over at Iowa, Gable brought what he knew, independence and work ethic, "And," Gable said, "it wasn't for everybody at the beginning. It helped everybody, but only the freshman coming in really jumped on board with this new level of expectation, expertise, or training. Everyone else was pretty much set in their ways.

Well, maybe not everybody, but most of them. And who did I try to influence the most? The freshmen. And once they jumped on board and the older people could see the effect, then they jumped on board."

So even with the successes the program had earned over the years with Kurdelmeir at the helm, Gable wanted to change the mentality even further. "They had a frame of mind that was holding them back," Gable said. "[The older guys] could beat the guys they knew they could beat, but they couldn't beat the guys they knew were better than them or know how to go about beating them. They were tougher against the weaker opponents than the stronger opponents, and that's not how you win. That had to change. We needed to get stronger as the competition got stronger, not weaker."

The key for Gable in changing that mentality was the quality of freshman he had coming into the room. "Once the younger guys were successful," Gable laughed, "the older guys knew one of two things had to happen. [They had to] change and grow and improve; or, stay the same and, who knows how it will end for them."

In raising the level of expectation even higher, and the younger recruits coming in and buying into it immediately, it only took one more season for Iowa to claim its first NCAA championship under Gable. In fact, starting in 1977, Gable and his new mentality and style won nine-consecutive NCAA championships.

However, even though Gable had Iowa accelerating past everyone, he would ultimately stumble upon the second of his two greatest defeats as he looked to win his tenth straight NCAA championship. That defeat occurred in 1987 when everyone was watching, just as his first individual defeat—the first of his two greatest defeats—back in the 1970 NCAA championships had happened.

"What I consider my big athletic-type adversity losses," Gable said, "were my last match in college—because I was undefeated in that style for seven years—and then my big loss was 'Number 10' as a coach going for the tenth-consecutive [NCAA] championship. Because they were so far between, they hit me really hard because I wasn't used to that type of loss."

As for how he dealt with his losses, "I would study and study and study it," Gable said. "And I would learn a lot about what took place within that period of time."

When Gable was a senior at Iowa State, reflecting on his loss to Larry Owings in the championship match, the match that ended Gable's chance to become the first undefeated high school and collegiate wrestling champion, he realized where he had gone wrong.

"When I looked back at it all," Gable said, "it all started back in my junior season at Iowa State. So I went back and analyzed one year. As a coach, when I went back to analyze, I went back five years—I wanted to see who came in in 1982 and who left in 1987. There was a lot to learn and a lot of mistakes made both as an athlete and as a coach. Not that they weren't correctable, but if [the losses] didn't hit me as hard, I may not have gone back to look at them so carefully and learn my lessons as much."

The same process would hold true for some of Gable's most difficult individual losses as a coach. He would struggle with a number of his wrestlers' greatest defeats due to not only the investment each wrestler had made, but also his investment he made in them as a coach. To Gable, each of those losses needed to be reflected upon for clarity and to avoid similar mistakes later in his career with other wrestlers. In consoling his wrestlers after their disastrous defeats, Gable said, "Some of those losses scar those guys a little bit and I don't know if I consoled anybody. I know it takes a while, it did for me, but those losses don't go away. I've never gotten over my loss."

However, Gable knew, more than anything, that the way to help move past these losses was to move forward as quickly as possible to correct the situation.

Just as the back half of the 1970s belonged to Iowa, so did the front half of the 1980s and then all of the 1990s—Iowa wrestling was simply dominant the moment Gable took over. The program set individual and team records with Gable at the helm and, when Gable retired in 1997, he stepped down as the sport's greatest coach.

He had amassed a 355-21-5 dual meet record, collected twenty-one consecutive Big Ten titles with 106 Big Ten individual champions. He also earned fifteen NCAA championships, and helped 152 wrestlers earn All-American honors, with another forty-five claiming individual national championships. From his group of wrestlers, twelve became Olympians—six earned gold, one claimed a silver, and three wrestled to a bronze medal.

The next hire to the program would be a former Hawkeye wrestler. He was a four-time All-American and a three-time NCAA champion who was undefeated his final two seasons. He had amassed an eighty-nine-match winning streak and was named the Most Outstanding Wrestler at the 1984 NCAA championships and, considered by *Amateur Wrestling News*, the "Wrestler of the Decade." He was a current Iowa assistant: Jim Zalesky.

Zalesky had the fortune of being around Gable and the room prior to his head coaching hire. His teams continued where Gable's teams had left off. Hawkeyes won the NCAA championships in 1998, 1999, and 2000; however, there was pressure on the program to release Zalesky following the next six seasons as Iowa only won four Big Ten championships and claimed no team national championships. Likewise, in his final two seasons, Zalesky's teams failed to crown a Big Ten or NCAA champion.

"I think it was pretty tough for him to keep it going actually," Gable said of Zalesky. "I mean, not right at that time [he took over]—there was a lot of horse power there. But I also think because of the fact that things were flowing pretty well right away and he won and he won and he won, it's pretty hard to dissect as well as building the program like that when I came in with Kurdelmeir. Jimmy came in as an athlete when it was already maybe flourishing a little bit, and because things were going really strong that there might have been some things there that he wasn't associated with in maybe the building process to keep it going.

"See, it seems to me, that the only thing I can say is that it's a pressure program and it still is—it hasn't really gone away that much—but it's still a tough job and you've got to use a lot of people around you, but you've got to be the boss and the leader of whoever wants to help. And during Jimmy's time, it seemed, that there were too many guys that were trying to lead the way and he probably needed to nip a few of those guys. You know, you got to know when to put your foot down a little bit."

The Zalesky era came to an end in 2006, one year prior to his contract's expiration date. Iowa was going to move in a new direction, and that direction was Tom Brands—a former three-time national champion for Gable in the early 1990s, and a World and Olympic gold medalist. This hire came with some controversy as, at the time, Brands was the head coach at Virginia Polytechnic Institute and State University in Blacksburg, Virginia, and, with his move, many of his recruits wanted to follow him. In the end, Virginia Tech did not grant a release for the athletes wanting to leave, and any wrestler that followed Brands lost one-year of collegiate eligibility.

TOM BRANDS WAS THE BIG MAN ON CAMPUS from 1990 until he graduated from the University of Iowa in 1993. He claimed All-American status all four years as a Hawkeye, three of those as a national champion—his sophomore, junior, and senior seasons. Internationally, he earned a World freestyle championship, two World Cup gold medals, a gold medal at the 1995 Pan-American Games, four United States national titles, and made four-consecutive United States World or Olympic teams. Additionally, he won the gold medal at 62 kg in the 1996 Olympic Games in Atlanta. Prior to becoming the head coach at Virginia Tech, he had been an Iowa assistant under both Gable and

Zalesky for a combined twelve seasons.

In 2007, after two years as the head coach at Virginia Tech, Brands returned to Iowa and he once again became the big man on campus. The Iowa faithful were confident that he would turn the program back around to its winning ways.

As to why he sought a head coaching position instead of remaining an assistant at Iowa, Brands explained, "Because it's winning. You're in the sport to perform. You're in the sport to impact people. And now, as a head coach, you can pick the people that are loyal to you—and relationships are everything."

Unfortunately, for Brands, he had a few interviews and applied around the Midwest and for a few head coaching positions outside of the area, but nothing was turning out in his favor. That was until he met up with a former Hawkeye at the Olympic Trials that led him to Virginia Tech. As for why he chose Virginia Tech, Brands responded, "It was the only job I could get. I had someone on the inside, Wes Hand. He got me the job at Virginia Tech. Without Wes Hand, I wouldn't even had applied."

The course Brands took in order to become a head coach and then make his way to Iowa stemmed from doing laundry. "[Wes Hand] was talking to me at the Trials that year—the Trials were in Indianapolis, that was 2004—I remember I was going to do laundry, what am I doing laundry for? I was doing laundry for some guys and I walked past this outside cafeteria and there he was and he goes, 'Eh, you going to send your resume in?' I said, 'No, I know how this works.' I was 0-7 on jobs. I'd interviewed a couple times and there were three jobs I didn't even get interviews for and, you know, I was zero for whatever. I told him I wasn't doing this and he said I had to.

"He called me and said, 'If I can get you an interview for sure, will you send your paperwork in?' And I said sure. So the guy called and said they'd interview me for sure, so I sent my work in. We did a phone interview and a half hour later they called me back and told me I had the job. I went out there and took a salary cut—I was an assistant here, I took a salary cut—and I was a head coach at Virginia Tech. And you know why? Because nothing else mattered—money didn't matter. Never."

Regardless of the money, Brands wanted to be a head coach and, if it meant a lifestyle change, he was willing to make the sacrifice, as was his support system at home. "My wife [was] a rock," Brands said. "And I remember sitting in the hotel asking myself what I was doing and I was pouting and whining and she said, 'This is the best day of your life. Shape up.' And she was right."

For the next twenty-two months, Brands was in control of the Hokies who had hired him in an attempt to turn their program around. However, it was not just the program that gained something meaningful.

"Those twenty-two months were great," Brands said. "Best thing I ever did. I learned the world is cruel and if you're going to survive, you have to do it on your own. And you know what? We did. And I say *we* because it was a *we*—Wes Hand and Doug Schwab were my assistant coaches."

In 2005, under Brands, in his first season, the Hokies posted a 16-4 record and placed second at the Athletic Coast Conference (ACC) Championships—he had two individual champions and well as the ACC Wrestler of the Year, Mike Faust, at heavyweight. At the NCAA championships held in St. Louis, Missouri, Brands placed tied for forty-second in his head coaching debut. The Hokies had four qualifiers, but none advanced into the All-American round.

In 2006, his second season, the team plummeted to a 1-16 dual meet record. Brands' Hokies placed fifth at the ACC Championships, claiming three individual champions. That year, at the NCAAs held in Oklahoma City, Oklahoma, his team placed twenty-ninth, a stark improvement from his first season due to individual accomplishments. Brands' two national qualifiers claimed All-American honors—this was Virginia Tech's fifth and sixth All-American in school history dating back to 1921.

With Brands at the helm, the university felt that everything wrestling was moving in the right direction. He and his staff had gone out and recruited a very talented class of young athletes that were to impact not only the following season, but help secure the next four and help put the school on future wrestlers' radars. Unfortunately for the university and a wrestling program that had been up and down and on the brink of just being dropped and looked to be on the rise, Tom Brands announced that he was leaving that spring and would be returning to the University of Iowa to take over its program.

The divorce between the Virginia Tech and Tom Brands was ugly. After Brands departed, reportedly four of the wrestlers immediately wanted to follow him to Iowa. However, Virginia Tech would not release them from their scholarships. The wrestlers petitioned the university to no avail and then went on to sue stating that the university and its athletic director, Jim Weaver, breached the commitment made by the wrestlers when they were recruited that allowed them to transfer without penalty or loss of eligibility. The lawsuit was dismissed in 2006.

Brands was complimentary of the Virginia Tech and its commitment to wrestling and did state that he enjoyed the community and his decision to leave had nothing negative to do with the university or its administration or people. He was, however, displeased with how he felt the wrestlers were being treated after his departure and felt it was the university's way of getting back at him for leaving.

In a phone interview with Brands conducted by writer Mark Viera of the *Washington Post*, Brands stated that, "These kids were wronged. It was done for one reason, and that was to get to me. It hurt me, but it hurt those kids more than me."

However, the university did try to reach an agreement to appease all parties—they wanted the wrestlers to stay one more season under the new coach before being allowed to transfer. Each of the wrestlers refused and, in that, the university held its ground and each of those wrestlers lost one-year of eligibility. When Brands left Virginia Tech, he left its wrestling program in shambles, but his heart was in Iowa and that was where he was headed.

As to why Brands walked away so quickly from a program that gave him the opportunity no other program had granted him, Brands stated, "The [Iowa] job opened. [It was the perfect job] for me. I didn't think it was going to open, especially that quick."

In his mind, Brands had always planned on returning to Iowa; unfortunately, it came at the expense of Virginia Tech and the eligibility of those wrestlers that followed him.

For Brands, he saw the Iowa opportunity open because, "When you're not performing, you better be doing other things right and other things at a high level. And [Iowa was] not performing at a high level—there were a lot of t's that weren't crossed and i's that weren't dotted. And that will get people tired of you real quick. And when your crowds go down and culture and things of that nature, then you got to take a good hard look at what's going on, and that's not the fault of the leadership here, that's just how things were going at the time—not blaming anybody. On the plane ride I asked the guy that picked me up for the interview, 'Was this too soon?' and he said, 'Yes, I think it was a year too soon.'"

Even having arrived one year earlier than maybe expected, Brands was ready to get back to work and rebuild what he loved. In order to do this, he had to sell or rebrand his style or way to the new recruits.

But, according to Brands, "We didn't rebrand it," he said. "We said, 'We're not better than anybody, we're just different. And if you're going to wrestle here, there's a commitment level here that's like no other place.' Not everybody lasted and there were other relationships that didn't last as well. But, you know what, in this business you've got to be tough and part of being tough and developing that toughness is being able to handle tough conversations. And I don't think there's a coach out there that doesn't talk to his guys on a weekly basis, and if there's something off, you arrest it and work on it. I'm not saying it's going to change in that minute, but because you're paying attention you can get ahead of [it].

And loyalty is huge—those people that stayed here. It's either you're here or you're not."

In his twenty-two months as the head of the Hokie program, Brands did learn a great deal about himself as he was about to be in the hot seat of the highest-profiled wrestling job in the county.

As a wrestler and assistant under Gable, Brands understood what being the leader at Iowa meant. "Gable was demanding and hard and he was a leader," Brands said. "He was a boss. Not popular with a lot of people. Remember, it's very lonely at the top and very few people understand the Gable approach. Right now he's revered because he's retired. He has a statue—he's retired. When he was the guy, it was him against the world, and I was his disciple."

In regard to what he gained from being an assistant under Zalesky's leadership, he stated that, "Jimmy, his leadership was—the right word is laissez faire. And that doesn't work because who are you looking at? So what will never leave me is to manage the crisis yourself and make sure that everyone is taken care of—especially the important people in your program."

Therefore, with his knowledge of his past assistantships, as well as his two years in Blacksburg, Brands took the lead at Iowa and preached and coached as his mentor had before him.

When he wrestled for Gable, he learned, "Probably more than anything, independence," Brands stated with certainty, "—probably didn't know I was learning independence. But Gable was always talking about getting the things out of the way in your life that are important. And when I say 'get out of the way' I mean work hard on them." Brands was going to use what he knew worked to be successful, and he was going to do it where he knew he belonged.

In Brands' estimation, the Iowa program was special because it was different from every program out there. "It's different," Brands explained, "because the commitment level on so many levels is higher because of what the fans expect and what the tradition expects—what Gable started and what we're trying to implement and continue. A lot of programs don't talk that way. We try to win a national championship every year. Number one, we do what's best for our individuals, then we do what's best for our team. That's why we're different."

Brands' ways—the Iowa way—proved to be successful. When he took over in 2007, he implemented what he felt was the best way to work along with the help of his assistants.

"When Tom came in," Gable commented, "he brought me back for a year—I think he maybe could have used me for a couple years. But, there were some mistakes being made, maybe, but he's not going to lay down and just not try to correct whatever the possibilities are that he can do better—I know he has that ability."

And, once his recruits from Virginia Tech were eligible, mixed with the talent that was already in the room at Iowa, and everyone had a year under Brands' leadership, Brands led the Hawkeyes to NCAA championships in 2008, 2009, and 2010—he also won the Big Ten championship in those three years.

TOM BRANDS AND HIS HARD-NOSED APPROACH AS

the head coach of the Iowa program was the perfect environment for Tony Ramos. Even before Tony walked into the Iowa room for a workout or a practice as a red shirt freshman in 2009, he was brash, out spoken, and unapologetic. Once he had given his full commitment to Iowa that spring, he had an opportunity to speak with the press and he made a few things very clear: He had no fear and he would wrestle whomever he had to in order to earn the opportunity to be on the mat as the starter. His exact words were published in an article by Andy Hamilton, and then posted in the wrestling room by head coach Tom Brands.

"I'm not going to be scared of anyone," Brands stated that Ramos said in the article. "I'm going to take Doug Schwab and Mike Zadick, and I'm going to go after them; I'm not going to back down. If I do what I want to do, I'm going to get the starting spot, I don't care who's there."

Initially, some of the older wrestlers did not know what to make of Tony—a three-time state champion who committed to the University of Iowa wrestling program was neither uncommon nor imposing. However, it was an eye opener that a young kid who was coming into the program was taking a stand. And, even though some of the guys liked his crass and abrupt forwardness, others wanted to see if he could wrestle as loud as he talked.

In the case of the Iowa coaches, "We loved that," Tom Brands said. "I think some of the guys were maybe rubbed wrong a little bit, but who cares—back it up. [Ramos] called out the best guys in the room; he was ready to take on all comers. We posted it on our board out there. We loved it."

CHAPTER 36
BUILDING RELATIONSHIPS

"...and what separated him from everyone else was his tenacity and his mind—he believes that he can beat anyone, anywhere, and at any time."

• *Terry Brands*
Associate Head Coach, the University of Iowa
Coach, Hawkeye Wrestling Club

ONCE TONY CLOSED ON HIS HOME, BEFORE HE was even unpacked, he was at the University of Iowa's summer camps training and getting ready for the Junior World Championships.

In his first time wrestling with the Iowa guys in the room, he had a small altercation that spoke to who he was going to be as he entered the program.

"The first day that I came into practice and worked out," Ramos remembered, "the first person to grab me was Terry Brands. He probably wanted to see how good I was and to get a feel for me because he didn't really know much about me—he wasn't part of the recruiting process because I committed before they got Terry."

For Terry Brands, he did not know much about Tony, but he was curious. "What I knew about Tony Ramos, initially, was very little," Terry Brands confessed. "I wasn't here yet. I mean, I knew he committed and I knew a little about him, but there was more to learn. You looked at his technical package and the fact that he was a three-time state champion from Illinois, and what separated him from everyone else was his tenacity and his mind—he believes that he can beat anyone, anywhere, and at any time.

"I was able to find out a great deal about him through Internet research. I saw that he was a competitor who wore his emotions on his sleeve and make no bones about that whomever he was facing, he was going to come in and utterly destroy him on the wrestling mat."

The relationship between Tony Ramos and Terry Brands began at the exact same moment in the wrestling room.

"The first workout Ramos had was with Montell Marion," Terry Brands stated. "And I very distinctly remember Montell being extremely frustrated with the practice to the point where things were starting to unravel for him."

Tony also recalled that first practice. "I remember that first practice," Ramos reflected. "We were kind of getting done and Montell Marion showed up and needed someone to go with. And Terry turned to me and said, 'Okay, now you're going with Montell.' Me and Montell were scrapping and Montell didn't like that I wasn't taking a backseat to him. He tried to push me into the weight room [on the other side of the half wall] in the wrestling room. I held my ground and shoved him right back and we got into each other a little bit. It wasn't a fight, but there was scuffling."

At that moment, Terry Brands stepped into the situation and "I told Montell, 'Hey, he's doing the exact same thing that Tsirtsis and you were doing when you came on the scene. And now you want to fight him because of that?' Montell's response to that was very positive. So we got a good response from him and it was a great battle. The issue isn't if Tony got the best of Montell or Montell got the best of Tony, it was the fight and the flurry and hair-flying situation that they both created and they both wanted to get better because neither one of them took a back seat to the other. And that was phenomenal for a freshman to come in and do that, and that was something that we needed to continue. Metcalf brought that into the room, McDonough a little bit, but just that raw ability to be able to step in and compete was attractive."

From Tony's recollection, "I think that's when I became his guy. He liked the fight that I had. He liked that I wasn't going to take a backseat to any of these guys. And that's when I really started to make a name for myself with the program."

Of course, much of Tony being known stemmed from the article that was posted by Tom Brands about Tony's words when he committed. "Basically," Ramos said, "that was the attitude [the coaches] liked. It showed the others that, hey, someone is coming in here and trying to take their spots. Maybe it was to light a fire. But, that was me and that was the attitude they liked, and that was the attitude they looked for."

Different from high school, Tony walked into the Iowa room trying to be a leader in his own way. "Tony came in brash," Terry Brands said of Tony's redshirt season, "but he was fair. He called out guys, but not demeaning them. Early on he had vocal leadership qualities—he was trying to make guys better and if he saw it, he would just say it."

After that initial moment, Tony felt that he and Terry Brands had connected and Terry, in that moment, started working more with Tony in preparation for the Junior World Championships; however, he did have one problem with Tony's ability to fight.

"It wasn't always consistent," Terry Brands stated. "So we had to show him how to build that and, 'Okay, what are you going to do the next time you wrestle him?' The attitude was good, but just the tenacity to not give up anything without a fight. The one thing I did hear about Tony was that he'd do anything you told him and, to a degree, yes. But sometimes he would hit a wall and there was no response. That may have been because he pushed himself to the point where there was nothing left, or if he hit that wall and he was just blank. Was it related to conditioning? Was it related to psyche? Was it related to his diet? Was it related to emotions or energy? In his case, that was the key in figuring that out."

But also in that moment, and in moments after, Terry and Tom Brands knew they could work with Tony because he showed growth in what they were showing him, and he was backing down less and becoming more consistent as the days progressed.

"After that situation with Montell," Ramos said, "Terry took over the reigns—if you will—and started working technique with me and a lot of the freestyle stuff. He just got done training Henry Cejudo and they won a gold medal in the Olympics, and I think he was trying to find another guy that he could mentor into that same role."

Aside from having to stand up for himself, Tony also had to learn how to score all over again. When he came out of Glenbard North, scoring was not a difficult task. Now, in the Iowa room, he was facing a situation that he was not used to.

"The things that stick out to me the most is," Ramos said, "when I first came in was that I was not scoring points on anyone—I just couldn't take anyone down. And the one thing that happens sometimes in college to a young guy who comes in and can't score, is they lose confidence and put their head down—I wasn't going to let that happen.

"I remember wrestling a guy named J.J. Krutsinger, he was a back-up 125 pounder and when I first came in I struggled with him. He was tough, he was a hard wrestler, he was never a starter, but he was a guy who had been in the room and been there for four years who was a hard-nosed Iowa kid wrestling the Iowa style. And when I started competing and a couple months went by, it finally got to the point where I was beating him up and some days he would just walk off the mat.

"What really stuck with me," Ramos said of his progress early on.

"Just seeing my growth from struggling and breaking into the room, to now beating and breaking some of these older guys and beating up some of these lower-tier back-ups. And what helped me the most was experience in the room. Wrestling the experienced and top-level guys and then Terry grabbing me after practice and showing me little things, like move your arm here or grab the leg here. Just being a few inches behind the leg when a guy sprawls on you makes the difference—the small things that you're not aware of or focusing on in high school, but now it's all the little things that matter in college."

That summer and fall would also be the growth of another relationship in Iowa for Tony. Initially, Tony won over Tom Brands with his commitment and brash-nature, he then won over Terry Brands through his fight. Next, Tony would gain an important mentor, friend, role model, and big brother figure in fifth-year senior and Illinois native, Daniel Dennis.

DANIEL DENNIS WAS A FOUR-YEAR STARTER AT

Grant High School in Fox Lake, Illinois, and, while there, built one of the strongest relationships in his life with Ryan Geist, the school's then head wrestling coach.

In 1999, Ryan Geist took over the wrestling program at Grant. In that first year, he coached older brother Charlie Dennis and, through coaching Charlie, he met Daniel and the Dennis family as they were one of the first families he had the opportunity to know.

"When Charlie was wrestling," Geist said, "I remember Daniel running around the bleachers. Charlie had been [wrestling] and Daniel started in the middle school and had some success pretty early on, and I think it just took off from there."

As Dennis entered high school, there was a varsity spot open; however, Daniel was well-undersized for that weight class. And, being undersized in weight, meant that Daniel would probably be over-matched physically as well.

"When Daniel came in as a freshman," Geist remembered, "we had a spot open at 112 pounds. We were pretty thin in the lower weights, but we had a pretty tough 106 pounder in Mike Simmons at the time. Daniel weighed about 100 pounds, but said that he would wrestle 112 for us. Since he was undersized, one of the things that we spoke about was weight lifting and getting him bigger so he could fill that weight class.

"Out of season we lifted four days a week and during season we lifted two days a week and then on Sundays. One thing led to another and Daniel and I ended up making this silly four dollar bet—four was his favorite number and four was my favorite number—and if you ever missed a day, you had to pay the other guy four bucks. We would go an entire year and no one would have paid the other any money."

However, Geist remembered the one time that Dennis did miss a workout, but how Dennis responded spoke to his character as a young man, and Geist never forgot it.

"This is going to sound horrible," Geist said, "but Daniel missed once due to a death in the family. He had to be with his family that Sunday, but he came in, paid the four bucks, and I carried that in my shoe the rest of the year. But that was the commitment he had."

When he came in as a freshman, Dennis was undersized and he had to be mentally tough, physically tough, and very much fearless when he stepped onto the mat.

"Daniel was never afraid of failure," Geist said, "and he got his butt kicked. Even though we were thin in the lower weights, the kids we did have were pretty talented and they took it to Daniel, but he never backed down. In that, he kept getting better because Daniel thrived in that environment. You could just see him growing in leaps and bounds wrestling with those guys. I think also that he didn't want to be the one that wasn't any good, so I think that just drove him even more to try and succeed."

As much as the older wrestlers and wrestlers in general took to Dennis, so did the coaches on staff. "He was hard-working kid," Geist said, "who always wanted to wrestle, always wanted to know more, he doesn't whine, he doesn't complain, and he's always got energy—he was a coach's dream."

What Geist had on his hands was a raw and determined wrestler that he knew he could work with and help grow. So, with all of the struggles Dennis had as a freshman, Geist was able to find his strengths and work to them to help Dennis be successful and more competitive.

"Daniel was initially pretty heavy on his feet," Geist said, "but the one attribute that he did have was he had these huge mitts—these huge hands—so I remember trying to figure out how we could use those more because once he got a hold of you, he was tough.

"So we got the idea by using that two-on-one that Glenbard North was running on us every year. I remember wrestling them and being like, 'Man, that stupid two-on-one is killing us.' And I remember thinking how that would work really well for Daniel and that's what we adapted to for him from freshman to sophomore year. Now he could get his hands on guys, slow them down, and manhandle them because of his strength."

Geist worked with Dennis, and Dennis allowed himself to be coached. He ended his freshman season 14-12, and set his sights on qualifying for the Illinois Freshman and Sophomore State Championships. As he trained, he was working on being more proficient with the two-on-one, and Dennis took his new offense to the qualifier. However, when Dennis did not qualify, he was not turned away from the sport—he embraced it more.

That summer and fall, Dennis was still working out and wrestling and getting better each day. And as he began to grow into his body and learn it better, and his strength was coming around, he had a new wrestling partner enter the room, a freshman who only made him better—Jimmy Kennedy.

Dennis' sophomore campaign was a success. He not only filled out the 112-pound weight class, but he worked himself into one of the state's best wrestlers at his weight.

He won the Sectional championship, earned a first-round bye at the Individual State Championships, and then wrestled himself into the semifinals. Unfortunately, he lost to the eventual state runner-up, Mark Lenkowski of Downers Grove South in overtime, 8-6.

In the wrestle-backs, Dennis defeated Aaron Winning of Bellville Althoff by a 14-3 previous decision—Illinois used walkovers—and then, in the third-place match, he dropped his second match of the tournament to Rockford East's Jordan Kolinski by an 8-4 decision.

Ironically, after taking fourth place at the state championships, Dennis was not certain if he wanted to continue with the sport. Geist, very confused and a bit shocked when heard that, reached out to his wrestler to find out what was going on.

"I remember the conversation that transpired between the two of us when I found out he may not wrestle anymore," Geist said. "He was like, 'Yeah, you know, I think I'm done. My mind is on other things. I want to be a mechanic.' And Daniel liked working on cars and bikes and things and, on top of that, if you want to be good, wrestling is a lot of work. You have to put in time in the off-season—so we talked for a little bit.

"I told him, 'Daniel, you're special. You could be special. You can do things that most people only dream of.' And after we spoke, he came back around and rededicated himself to wrestling."

In regard to what Geist said to Dennis, he had hoped that their relationship would also help push him back onto the mat.

"I think Daniel really respected my opinion," Geist estimated. "And I think this gave him the ability to move forward—he just trusted me. I think he just believed what I told him about him being special and being great if he just got out of his own way and listened to his coaches on what he needed to do. And, after that talk, I think he did that."

In the re-dedication, Dennis came in his junior season as a contender for a state championship. As he did the year before, he once again found himself in the state semifinals against Galesburg High School's Mike Nelson. However, in a very anticlimactic moment, Nelson had to default to Dennis. Dennis was now in the state championship match and would face Kyle Jahn of Bolingbrook.

For the first time, Dennis was in the Grand March—and he deserved to be based on his body of work all season. The dream of being a state champion was one match away. Standing along the mats with the introductions and the music and the atmosphere surrounding him, Dennis remained calm, outwardly, and just appeared to be taking in the moment.

"I was so ecstatic for him," Geist said, "because I know where he came from and what it took to get to this point. I could remember when he was doubting himself in that room, in that office. I remember when he could barely do eleven pull ups and now he could do like seventy. He worked hard and was ready for that moment and we felt he was going to win. There was no doubt in my mind that he was going to win that match."

His teammate, Jimmy Kennedy, won the state championship right in front of him at 106 pounds, and now it was his turn to step on the mat at 125.

The match was rather conservative by both wrestlers once it began. After the first period, the score was tied at 0-0. The second period saw an escape and the third period saw another escape. The score was 1-1 and it appeared the match would go into overtime and, eventually, be won by a wrestler being ridden out by the other. That was until Jahn got in on Dennis' legs.

"I don't remember much about the match," Geist admitted. "But I do remember Kyle Jahn getting in on a shot, posting his head up, his head in the center, and Daniel's feet touching temporarily—it was real quick. We gave a point away and, ultimately, that was the match."

Even though the score read that Jahn won by a 4-1 decision, the match was lost in that moment because it put Dennis in a position where he had to chase the penalty point and, in chasing it, he put himself in bad position trying to score and then gave up a takedown very late into the match.

"We knew Kyle Jahn was on a special mission that season," Geist said, "but we felt Daniel was going to win. So when he lost, it was just devastating."

After the loss, Geist spoke to Dennis and, in that talk, addressed the positives. "I told him, 'Okay, we were here—now we know. Now we'll just win it next year.' It was just that simple."

By the time Daniel was a senior, Grant had become a force in Illinois and the wrestling room was strong. Dennis was able to work out and compete on a daily basis with Jimmy Kennedy, John Deneen, the Barczak brothers, Toby Temple—the team was solid—and Dennis moved up one more weight class to 130.

In the room, Dennis was a leader by example. "He was not a vocal leader, not a rah-rah guy," Geist explained. "He set the example and he really challenged kids through conversations and tried to motivate them that way. I mean, he was so dang tough kids would just look at him and fall in line."

As he had done the previous three years, Dennis once again found himself in the semifinals. This time, it was Wheaton North's Jason Fitzenreider who was currently ranked number five in the state behind Dennis. Dennis would dispel of the Falcon 18-7 and showed the separation between the two. Dennis was now 47-1 on the season, again in the Grand March and, for the final time, in the state championship match. He was down to one opponent and one opportunity to accomplish his goal. For that moment, he would face Kenny Jordan of Chicago Mt. Carmel, a senior with a 37-2 record.

Jordan was a returning state champion from the season before at 119. As a freshman, Jordan placed fourth at 103, losing in the semifinals, but he did not qualify as a sophomore. In his journey to the finals, Jordan won by fall over each of his first three opponents—including a 5:04 fall of the number-one ranked Sean Kinney of Naperville Neuqua Valley in the first round.

When Dennis and Jordan squared off in the state championship match, it was what was expected: a very hard fought match between two very strong and very good wrestlers.

The match was scoreless after the first period. Jordan won the flip and he choose down for the second period—he escaped. The score was 1-0 in Jordan's favor, and Dennis worked into a number of shots for the remainder of the second period, but he could not finish any of them.

As the two seniors headed into the third and final period, Dennis now had the choice. He chose down, looked to escape, and worked to win the match on his feet. However, the opportunity to win the match on his feet never came. Or, maybe it did present itself, but it was never called that way.

"This is frustrating," Geist said. "In the third, we chose down and Daniel looks like he's going to get away, and he momentarily does break away and turns and shoots in right away, Daniel did, and they end up in this long scramble or sprawl and I thought he would get at least one for the escape. Turns out he doesn't even get anything. They put him back down and Kenny runs a nice little triceps ride and is through the crotch and on the wrist and, you know, that's the match…1-0."

Headed into the tunnel, Geist struggled, but no one struggled more than Dennis. Twice he was in grasp of a championship, and twice, truly, one point separated him from winning.

"There was no consoling him," Geist remembered. "I couldn't even console myself. There were a lot of tears in the back of Assembly Hall back there—I felt like I was back in high school when I lost. It hurt so badly because I had known how hard he worked and not to see him smile after his last match was tough."

Originally, the state championships was to be Dennis' last high school tournament. He hoped that his performance and his winning a state championship would attract some college offers; unfortunately, there just was not much there.

"We weren't even going to go to Senior Nationals in Cleveland that year," Geist said, "but Daniel didn't win state. Had he beat Kenny Jordan, he would have got exposure and colleges would have shown some interest. We had some bites from some programs, but we had sent kids [to those programs] and it didn't work out, so I didn't want him going there. So when thinking about what we had to do, we had to go to Senior Nationals and he had to beat some good kids out there to get noticed. The sole purpose of the trip was to get someone to see what we saw in Daniel."

Once out in Cleveland, Ohio, Dennis wrestled hard and he captured the attention of one coach who was scouting and looking for what some consider lost talent that went unnoticed.

"In one of the matches that Daniel won," Geist explained, "someone from Iowa just happened to be watching. Daniel was wrestling a three or four-time state champion from Kansas and he was in this crazy-tough match. He's got this kid who is kicking away from Daniel and Daniel is on his belly and barely hanging onto this kid's foot. The kid keeps kicking and Daniel's arm extends again and again—and he's literally got his fingertips clasped on the end of his foot—and the kid just drops, gives up, and Daniel wins the match in what was the second overtime. It was one of those just exhausting matches."

Excited and drained by the win, and with his forearms burning as his coaches were trying to help him recover before his next match, Iowa's Tim Hartung approached them.

"He came up to us," Geist relived, "and he said, 'That was incredible. What an incredible match. That's definitely the kind of kid we want at Iowa.' The conversations took off from there."

Dennis ended up placing fifth and he walked away with All-American honors and an interest from the University of Iowa.

"Daniel was considering a few schools," Geist said, "and those other schools were offering more [scholarship money] than Iowa. But all I said was, 'Daniel, look, you can go to a place where people love wrestling or a place where people are indifferent about it. I think it's worth a few grand to wrestle in front of people who are going to appreciate you and what you are doing.'"

Dennis considered his coach's words and chose Iowa where he would wrestle under head coach Jim Zalesky. He started as a freshman and, unlike high school, he was physically and mentally strong enough to compete at a high level right away.

"Daniel was fearless that freshman year at Iowa," Geist said. "Just like high school, he was not afraid of failure. He went out there and beat some tough guys and he lost some along the way. He would go out there and he wasn't sacred to try things—sometimes it worked out and sometimes it didn't work—but eventually he figured it out."

As a sophomore, there would be a new head coach, Tom Brands. Dennis redshirted and earned a 13-2 unattached season record. After his sophomore season, and as he entered his redshirt sophomore campaign, now one full year under Tom Brands, he broke his jaw and only wrestled one match, which he won. He would not wrestle competitively until University Nationals in the spring—he would win the title at 60 kg.

Now a redshirt junior, Dennis made the jump that everyone knew he would ultimately make. He placed seventh in the NCAA Championships and ended his season with a 31-6 record. Headed into his final season, Dennis set his sights on a national championship.

AS TONY ENTERED THE IOWA WRESTLING ROOM,

and being so close to Dennis in weight and home geography, they bonded. In many ways, Dennis was as good for Tony as Tony was good for Dennis. The two had very different careers; however, each was always in the hunt for a championship. The only difference was that Tony always won those bigger matches—no matter the opponent or how big the stage was or how bright the lights were, Tony always performed and found a way to win.

In and out of the practice room, Tony looked to Dennis. He saw an Illinois wrestler doing well and he saw someone who worked hard and took an interest in him as well.

"Me and Dennis got attached right away," Ramos said. "He grew attached to the type of wrestling that I was about, and I grew attached to the type of wrestling he was about. He was a mentor of mine and a good role model for me. He was a guy that I hung out with and had seen doing the right things training-wise, going in and getting the extra workouts and practices. Also, he was a guy at the weight class that I was going to step in and fill, so I kind of attached close to him and I attached really close to Terry."

And as Tony trained, Dennis was right there by his side helping him out in any way that he could.

"Dennis and me worked out a lot together," Ramos said. "We would stay after together, get extra workouts in together—drilling and techniques and things. Every time that I could wrestle live with Dennis, we would wrestle live because I needed to get better. I needed to make that jump from high school to college and who better than Dan Dennis to workout with?"

Aside from their time in the room, their relationship outside of the room was just as important to Tony. Ironically, in Coralville, they lived down the street from one another.

"We were pretty much attached," Ramos stated. "He brought me everywhere. I wasn't into the drinking and stuff, but I wasn't going to judge anybody—we all live differently. When it was time to be serious, no one was more serious and committed than Dan Dennis. He did everything right in his training and getting his body ready to compete. I went to his house, he came to my house, and he made sacrifices for me."

That sacrifice took the form of a road trip very early in their relationship where Dennis slept in his car in order to make sure Tony was well cared for when he left for the Olympic Training Center in Colorado Springs, Colorado. Tony was to compete at the Junior World championships, and Dennis wanted to make sure that Tony was not only prepared, but that he was being taken seriously.

"He drove out to the training center," Ramos recalled fondly, "just to make sure that I wasn't getting screwed over and that I had someone working with me at the Junior Camp. He did a lot for me. He stayed in that little car he had and made sure I was getting the right training and partners and getting prepared the right way for the World Championships.

"And he didn't just watch, he worked out with me too. He was kind of like the coach. You see, [Eric] Guerrero [from Oklahoma State University] was the team coach and [Dennis] wanted to make sure that I was being treated the right way—partners and attention and such. Dennis made sure I was not being put with lesser guys the whole time and I was getting what I needed to be successful.

"Even though Guerrero was the coach, Dennis didn't hold back on anything—he didn't care who the coach was. He was going to say what he saw, what he felt, and that's why he came out there. Everyone knows Dennis as a guy who says what's on his mind and that's how he was. If he thought something wasn't right, or if Guerrero wasn't doing the right thing, he just walked up to him and said it."

One issue that came up, that was not Tony-related, was that Dennis kept trying to work out with Jordan Oliver, and Guerrero wouldn't let it happen; there was a bit of a conversation. Tony said that Dennis said,

"You know, you're making Ramos wrestle with all of these big guys, and you won't even let Oliver wrestle with me who is smaller."

In a minor way, an altercation occurred, nothing serious and something that was able to be worked out, but those moments told Tony where Dennis' loyalty and toughness and heart were—and they were with the young and impressionable Tony.

Even before the school year started, Dennis made sure Tony knew his way around campus and that he was comfortable.

"He kind of showed me around and introduced me to people," Ramos said of Dennis. "He helped me get my name out there and, really, he was a good mentor."

TONY HAD NOW FOUND THE WRESTLING STYLE

that he wanted, the coaches that he wanted, and the friend and mentor that he wanted and needed. However, he was missing one more thing—a roommate. As summer progressed, he had some growing pains in this area and it was through the tough-love guidance of Tom Brands that helped shape a better environment for his redshirt freshman.

"The first year, the first guy that lived with me was Paul Donahoe," Ramos said. "He was a wrestler at Nebraska who ultimately got in trouble for some adult picture stuff, went to Edinboro and was [an NCAA] runner-up.

"But," Ramos laughed, "that did not last long at all. Tom was a little nervous that he was moving in with me at first. He was with me for about two weeks and then Tom kind of put the kibosh on that because he didn't like some of the things that were going on.

"They didn't think it was a good idea," Ramos reflected on the living situation, "because—not because of his history and past, he was a good guy—but because they didn't think it would be good to have a college athlete living with a senior level guy with more freedoms who could go out and party and didn't want him doing it around us. They didn't care if he did it on his own time, but don't do it around guys who are underage or bring them along with you."

And all of the things that Tom Brands feared could have happened, would not be given the opportunity to happen. He quickly put an end to that roommate situation.

"So, me, [Daniel] Dennis, Donahoe went out one night," Ramos remembered, "and it wasn't to do anything crazy or anything bad, we were just out at one of the more local bars near Carol Stream, in Addison I think, NOVA, and we were just hanging out and having a good time with Frank and Vince and by the time we got back to Iowa City, I got a call from Izzy that next day.

"He asked me what I was doing and that he was getting calls from Tom and just so I know he's kicking Donahoe out—you know, blah, blah, blah. And I asked Izzy, 'What do you mean? We didn't even do anything. We haven't even done anything.' But Izzy said that Tom said that we went out downtown Chicago and were drinking and getting crazy. I said, 'That's a little stretch from the truth, but I'll call him, I'll talk to him.'

"So, when I called Tom, Tom told me and Donahoe to come in because he wanted to talk to us. We came in, they pretty much told Donahoe that he had to find somewhere else to live and that he wasn't allowed to live with me anymore. Then Tom sat me down to talk and I explained to him, 'Nothing happened. We didn't do anything out of the ordinary. We went to this place that we could all go and just kind of hung out and had a good time.'

"Apparently, Dennis went back and said that Donahoe was going out with us, getting drunk, and not being a good role model. So, Tom told him that he didn't want that going on and they told him to move elsewhere and then they got me two new roommates."

The next two roommates were hand-picked by Tom and Terry Brands for Tony.

"I lived with Lloyd Rogers," Tony said. "A guy that came in from Chattanooga—he knew Terry [Brands] from back in the day and was living with Terry at first—who was a senior level guy who was training. I also had Dave Foxen from Brown University who was grey shirting [or postponing his enrollment in classes until the second term of his freshman year], and working out with the Hawkeye Wrestling Club."

From the standpoint of the Brands brothers, these were two smart guys that they felt were a better and more positive fit for Tony. They all sat and talked and found a way to work it all out within one month of Donahoe's departure. There was an intermittent roommate in there, but he was passing through from living with Brent Metcalf and onto another place.

As the school year was slowly approaching, there was one final social gathering by the wrestlers, and this was where Tony felt he could step up and maybe impress some of the upper-classmen and, maybe, grow his name a little more with them.

CHAPTER 37
A SIX-HOUR DRIVE
FOR A THIRTY-TWO-MINUTE CONVERSATION

"When Tom called, I was a bit concerned. All he said to me was: 'Frank, this is Tom Brands. I will see you in three hours.'"

• *Frank Defilippis*
Ramos' Brother

TONY HAD JUST STARTED TO MAKE POSITIVE progress with Tom and Terry Brands, and he was being recognized as a strong force in the wrestling room by many of his peers on the team. However, Tony was still looking to make an impression that stuck—and an impression he would make. It was still summertime, July, and Tony was still getting to know most of the wrestlers on the team, and he simply just wanted to impress them outside of the room.

What Tony would do was not illegal, it was simply a case of poor judgment and an action that was frowned upon as it did not measure up to what an Iowa athlete should be and what he should be doing with his time and resources.

"We had just finished the University of Iowa summer camps," Ramos explained, "and everyone, afterward, gets together for a good time and hangs out. [Ryan] Morningstar told everyone he was having people over at his house—he lived with Joey Slaton—and I was over at Dennis' house with him and his roommate, Rick Loera.

"So me and Rick Loera were over at his house and, at the time, I had just bought my house—I finally got my settlement from when I got hit by a car—so I had some money, and I thought I was going to be the cool-freshman bigshot, and I was going to order a dancer for the party.

"I told Lorea, 'Hey, I'm going to order a dancer for the party. Don't worry about it. I got it. I'll pay for it—whatever it costs, I got it.' After that, I went online, got a number for one of the companies, and I placed the order. When I got to Morningstar's house, I told him that I ordered a dancer and he was like, 'Okay, cool.' But, at the same time, in his head, he was probably thinking that I was an idiot. But I thought this was college and that stuff would be pretty cool.

"When the dancer showed up," Ramos paused, "this is where things got a little dicey in terms of guys getting in trouble. Nowadays, there's cameras and phones and so many things where you can post things on the Internet in a split second—but we didn't have that yet.

"As soon as the dancer got there, she immediately started doing her thing and she brought a snake with her. So she took out the snake and people started taking pictures with the snake. I was taking pictures with the snake, so did Erickson, Morningstar, and Slaton, I think. Anyway, it wasn't a big deal, but it was fun."

After the party, Tony felt good about himself and felt he had connected with a few of the guys and the night was a success.

NOT A LONG TIME AFTER, TONY'S BROTHER,
Frank, received a phone call from Tom Brands.

"When Tom called, I was a bit concerned," Defilippis said. "All he said to me was: 'Frank, this is Tom Brands. I will see you in three hours.' So I asked him, 'Is something wrong?' And all he said was, 'I'll see you in three hours.' But now I didn't know what to think. I said, 'Do you just want to tell me?' But all Tom said was, 'I'll see you in three hours,' and then he hung up the phone."

When Tom arrived in Carol Stream, both he and Frank went to a local restaurant to talk. Tom stared, shook his head, and Frank said Brands' first words to him were: "I have never had a wrestler who doesn't use drugs or drink cause so much trouble."

Frank was a bit surprised, but not completely surprised. He knew his younger brother and he knew some of the ways that his brother blew off steam and cut loose. So he asked, "What happened?"

According to Frank, "Tom said, 'The seniors were having a party and there were a bunch of pictures. The administration and athletic department saw them and they are not happy. We have to have three of our top wrestlers out for three meets, including the All-Star dual.'"

Frank listened but still did not completely understand Tom's angle because he was talking about seniors and starters on the team—his brother was neither. "What was Tony doing in the pictures?" Defilippis remembered asking. "I know he doesn't drink. And the kid has never done a drug in his whole life."

From there, Frank explained what Tom Brands said to him: "Tom looked right at me and told me, 'That's not the problem. The problem is he makes bad decisions. I brought all of my wrestlers in the room the next day and laid into them. I asked them whose idea was it to invite this girl and then to take those pictures? Here I am thinking a few seniors wanted to cut loose and made some bad choices. They all looked to Tony, and Tony stepped right up and said, 'I did.' And then he kind of smiled about it.'"

"What did he do?" Defilippis asked. "What's the issue?"

Frank continued, "Tom told me: '[Tony] got online and ordered a girl to come to the party. I couldn't believe this freshman did this. I took all of my guys and worked their tails off—toughest workout I could put them through. Then, when they we're all done, I took Tony and put him through another workout. I was going to break him, punish him. But the more I made him do, the more he did. He never said anything—he just kept working. And all it did was upset me more and more.

"'I went over to the treadmill," Defilippis continued as he recreated Brands' dialogue, 'put it on a full incline and put the speed as fast as it could go. I threw him on it and he did it. Half hour straight. I have never had a kid survive that, and I have never gone that extreme with a wrestler either.'"

The story made Frank laugh because he knew his brother's threshold. "Tom," Defilippis said, "I put him through all that shit already. You won't break Tony. When he fucked up in high school, I would throw him on the treadmill and put him through the ringer—he is used to it. That's not going to do it."

Frank then said that Tom Brands told him: "I am telling you that kid wouldn't break—I tried everything."

Thirty-two minutes later, after the story was told and after Frank and Tom Brands spoke, Tom Brands got himself back into his vehicle and drove all the way back to Iowa.

To Tony, with that workout, he had no idea what was going on. He just thought it was another workout. "He put me on the treadmill," Ramos laughed, "but I didn't know it was a punishment at the time. It was afterward when Frankie called me and told me about the whole situation about him coming out to see him. Tom was trying to put me through a workout, but I was used to those workouts from Frankie all throughout high school—sprinting, hill sprints, incline on the treadmill; I was used to all of it. I think he thought he was going to put me on this treadmill and put me through a workout and I'd end up dying or get really tired and break—but that never happened. I was in great shape, I was a tough kid with a tough mind and whatever they told me to do, I was going to do it and I wasn't going to complain about it."

What Tony did not know, and what none of the wrestlers knew, was that someone took those photographs of them at the party, and sent them into the Athletic Director's office. There were going to be some penalties for the actions at the party.

"Apparently," Ramos said, "there were pictures of me, pictures of Erickson, pictures of Morningstar, and Slaton, I think. I mean, all we did was have a good time. It was innocent fun, no harm, but someone sent them into the administration, the Athletic Director, and he was not happy."

But Tony was not initially called in on the issue, he was at his freshman orientation and the Athletic Director, Gary Barta, was speaking to the athletes about rules and proper conduct.

"On my first day at Iowa's orientation," Ramos said, "the A.D. was going over some things about their rules, their three-strike policy that they have and such. Fred Mims [the wrestling sport administrator] called me out at orientation and said, 'You're Ramos, right?' I said, 'Yes.' He said, 'We need to have a talk. I've already got some pictures of you sent to me about some things you did over the summer before you got into school.' In that moment I was like, 'Oh crap!' And that was the first time that I heard this thing was going to be an issue."

When Tom Brands called Tony in, "Tom told me, 'Back in my day, we didn't have to worry about this, it wasn't a big deal, but this is a different time. Everyone has phones, you guys are athletes, and more is expected out of you. You can't be doing these kinds of things because we have to act. Morningstar and Slaton will be suspended for a meet and have to sit out, and you will have to sit out a practice.'

"Since I wasn't competing, there wasn't too much they could do to me because there weren't any meets or anything. But, where I felt bad was Morningstar had to miss the All-Star dual that year. That was part of his suspension—sitting out of that dual and another two dual meets.

"The thing is," Ramos confessed, "none of these guys really did anything—I did it all. I ordered her. I paid for her. I got her to come there. And that was one of the growing experiences where I had to learn to grow up really fast and know that I can't do that kind of stuff and put other people in those positions. It had always been preached to me, but now I saw how high profile athletes are always under a microscope and there's always people watching."

"We had huge ramifications from that party," Tom Brands said. "Ryan Morningstar never sat a match in his career—he's the ironman. He sat two matches; that was a two-match penalty. He wrestled all but two matches in a career because of that. Our A.D. isn't putting up with that.

Times have changed. But I don't think [Tony] really understood. So I sat him down. Some guys need soft talk; well, he needed [something more]."

But Tony had another problem, the guys who were suspended could have retaliated and gone after the redshirt freshman either in the room or in another way; however, they chose not to.

"They weren't happy with me," Ramos said, "but they didn't take anything out on me. They understood that, at the same time, they could have told her to leave, not take pictures with her, things like that. They participated, so I would say that they were good sports, for lack of a better phrase, about taking the punishment and just moving forward."

CHAPTER 38
ON HIS WAY OUT THE DOOR

"I don't know what's going on with you, but you will not be here much longer unless you shape up. The way things are going, you are on your way out the door."

• *Tom Brands*
Head Coach, the University of Iowa
Coach, Hawkeye Wrestling Club

RIGHT BEFORE TONY LEFT FOR THE JUNIOR World Championships in August, he was at camp and received a telephone call from his brother in regard to a conversation he had with Tom Brands.

"Frankie called me," Ramos said, "and told me that Tom was raising my scholarship to forty percent. He said he was impressed and he was excited about the things that I was doing in the room—wrestling with these guys just in the short amount of time I was there. They had some scholarship open up and they raised me from the three percent that I committed to, to forty [percent] for all five years that I was going to be part of the program. That was a big thing for me knowing that I was doing the right things and I was headed in the right direction and the right people were noticing that in me."

When Tony finally arrived in Ankara, Turkey, and weighed in at the 55 kg—the 121-pound—weight class, he was refreshed, excited, and prepared for the 2009 Junior Freestyle World Championships.

Tony's first match-up was against Armenia's Ohan Gikinyan. The score at the end of the first period was 2-2, with Tony being the victor on criteria. In the second period, he would win and advanced with a dominant 3-1 victory. This now pitted Tony against the number-two ranked wrestler in the world at his weight, Rahul Balasaheb Aware of

India.

The match featured a great deal of offense from both wrestlers. In the first period, Tony would score a takedown; however, he would give up a takedown and a quick turn. He lost that first period 3-1. The second period, however, was all Tony, but he was exposed through his aggressiveness. Tony fought for a takedown and, sometimes, was too stubborn in that fight and it took him out of position and a defensive score occurred.

Fortunately, Tony's tenacity and ability to score in quick fashion, gave him the 5-4 victory in the period. Now, with an advancement at stake in the championship pool, it came down to the third period for each wrestler.

When the period opened, the Indian wrestler was quick to attack and put Tony in a hole that was just too difficult to recover from. Tony would lose the period, 6-0, and the match.

Now with a loss, and the likelihood that Aware would not lose to another wrestler in the pool, Tony had to win his next three matches to earn a bronze medal.

In the first match that followed his loss, he won by default over Ivan Anakin of Macedonia. Then, in his next bout, he had Siarhei Yermakou of Belarus. Tony needed all three periods to advance, and it was scored: 2-0, 2-3, 8-2.

Now in the all-important match to reach the bronze medal and make the World Championship stand, Tony had to face a very strong opponent in Azerbaijan's Yashar Aliyev. Unfortunately, Tony was outmatched and lost in two periods: 0-3, 0-1. He did not score and would simply be out freestyled.

When the Junior World Championships was completed, Hassan Rahimi of Iran was the gold medalist—he defeated Aware of India who earned the silver. For the bronze, on each side of the pools, Mikhail Ivanov for Russia would be crowned, as well Azerbaijan's Yashar Aliyev. And, for fifth, Georgia's Vladimer Khinchegashvili and the United States of America's Tony Ramos. Rounding out the field's top ten would be Yerking Areshev of Kazakhstan in seventh, Siarhei Yermakou of Belarus in eighth, Ibrahim Yourulmaz of Turkey in ninth, and, in tenth, Moldova's Vasili Esir.

AS THE SCHOOL YEAR STARTED, AND HIS CLASSES

were underway, Tony was struggling in some of his academic areas because he took a course load that may have been too much, too fast, especially with his intense focus on his wrestling and the time commitments he was giving to his craft.

"My first year," Ramos said, "I went in and was majoring in biology with the thought that I was going to be a doctor. But the transition was harder than I thought it would be. I was in some classes that were pretty tough and I wasn't getting done what I needed to get done. So I needed to figure something out, academically, where I was going to be a successful wrestler, and that took me [a while]."

However, as the school year began so did practices, and Tony found himself in a position that he was not used to since he was three-years-old and in that car accident—injured and unable to participate.

"In my very first workout," Ramos said, "I was working out with [Doug] Schwab and all of a sudden I felt a weird pain in my knee and something was shooting up into my thigh. I went down to the trainer and got checked out, and they told me I had an OCD lesion."

The proper name for the OCD lesion is Osteochondritis Dissecans. It is a joint disorder in which cracks form in the articular cartilage and the underlying subchondral bone. When it occurred, it caused pain and swelling in the affected joint which caught and locked during movement. Even moderate cases required some form of surgery. The surgical treatment consisted of arthroscopic drilling of intact lesions, securing of cartilage flap lesions with pins and screws, drilling and replacement of cartilage plugs, stem cell transplantation, and joint replacement.

After the surgery, the rehabilitation process happened in two phases— immobilization and physical therapy.

"In my case," Ramos explained, "there was a fracture on my kneecap and I actually broke a piece off and it was kind of floating around and I had to get major surgery. They cut open the entire side of my left knee. They had to scope it, go in, and pin it back together. It was like a broken bone and it took about four months to heal and I was out that entire time and was not able to wrestle and not able to compete."

Now removed from the physical aspect of the sport, Tony found himself in a very dark and difficult place emotionally. He was still required to show up to the practices, and he watched from a distance which was very difficult for him.

"I was going to practice and I had to watch every practice," Ramos remembered. "I couldn't do anything because it wasn't like a ligament to where I could do something, it was more like a broken bone. But the reason I think I got so down on myself was that I was watching my teammates and the freshman guys that I was close to going through these crazy workouts where Tom would keep them afterwards when their partners, who were getting ready for competition, were done and pushing them through for an extra hour. And I saw these guys busting their asses and going through that and I could do nothing but sit and watch and it bothered me. It bothered me that I couldn't be out there. It bothered me that I was losing that precious time to where I could have got better. So I think that's why I was so down on myself so much."

The other struggle Tony had was the lack of motivation to go to his classes. Without wrestling, he was crippled in all aspect of his life.

"I was so down on myself at that point," Ramos confessed, "that it affected everything. My grades dropped and they dropped because I wasn't going to class. I didn't go to class from Thanksgiving break all the way until the day of finals. I didn't go to class; I didn't go out. I didn't do much of anything. The only time I went was to take my finals."

Tony had no illusions that he would be able to ace his finals or salvage all of his grades. In that moment, however, he did not care that much for that aspect of his life because the wrestling aspect had been taken away from him. When his grades were reported and he saw them, some new realities started to sink in.

"When I got my grades back for that first semester," Ramos remembered very clearly, "I had a 1.6 grade point average, which is ineligible—you've got to have above a 2.0 to wrestle. I got a call from Tom and he told me to meet him in the wrestling room that night, and I went."

From Tom Brands' point of view, a talk was needed and it was needed quickly. "Tony was a hard worker and very committed," Tom Brands said. "In fact, he was so committed that we needed to talk about the other areas of his life. It wasn't a lack of respect from Tony Ramos. It was more of, I think maybe, how he was raised where he could do a lot of things that a lot of young kids couldn't do and now that continued. Maybe he was thinking now he is more independent than ever and I really don't answer to anybody because I know that I'm pleasing you because I work hard and I'm ultra-committed. But that's not what this is all about, Tony. When we sat down to speak, I had a witness."

There was another person present for the conversation as Tom Brands did not want there to be any confusion. "Yes he did," Ramos said about the talk and the witness. "When I got there Tom sat me down and he had Danny Song there, the strength coach. Tom looked at me and said, 'Song is here because I want another set of ears in the room so if this ever comes up with the administration or A.D., it's not hearsay; there was someone else here who knows what happened.'"

"I took Tony and sat him right [across from me]," Tom Brands explained, "and I pulled my chair right up to him. I was about [six-inches] from his face so that he would not forget. He sat there and I sat here and I talked and looked into his eyes the whole time and I told him, 'I don't know what's going on with you, but you will not be here much longer unless you shape up. The way things are going, you are on your way out the door.' And I said this to him not because I didn't like him, I loved him, but because he needed that.

"I think he started to get mixed up with things," Tom Brands explained. "There was the dancers, his grades, not going to class—which is why his grades were dropping. As a coach, you're saying, 'Well, boys will be boys.' But to what extent and to what expense to the culture? This isn't the culture we're after.

"So, I had this meeting to really explain commitment. Commitment isn't just in here, that's three or four hours. Commitment is a lifestyle. It wasn't that he needed to grow up or mature, he just needed direction. And maybe he needed it from a guy that was a bit more grounded than how Frankie raised him—and that guy was me."

With the conversation and communication now open and honest, Tony needed to speak about his concerns to Tom Brands. Tony wanted to be clear on what he felt was also an important aspect of growing their relationship, from his coach's end, that he needed Tom Brands to respect.

"I looked at Tom," Ramos said, "and I told him, 'I want to be here. I understand what you're saying and I'm going to fix it, but there's one thing that I want you to do that's going to make this situation a lot better. One of things that really bothers me is when something is going wrong, instead of calling me, you are calling my brother or Izzy. Tom, I'm a grown man. I committed to you—I didn't commit to Izzy and I didn't commit to Frankie. If there is a problem, or if you have a problem with me, come to me and we'll talk face to face like men and figure it out.'"

Tom Brands agreed. "And I think that was the turning point between me and Tom in our relationship; the point where we saw eye to eye and understood each other," Ramos said. "I don't know if he was trying to feel Frankie or Izzy out to see how I reacted, or what kind of person I was. I think he went to them to tell them to tell me to straighten up because maybe, initially, he didn't know how to have those conversations with me.

"One of his biggest things was communication. He wanted us to go to him if something was wrong and I wanted the same from him. Neither of us wanted to talk through people, so this made his life a lot easier and it made my life a lot easier. After that talk, me and Tom never had another issue. When he spoke to me, or I spoke to him, even if we didn't like what the other had to say, it was open and honest and there was never confusion.

"What it really came down to," Ramos confessed, "was having that communication and me not pouting about the injuries that I had and being upset that I wasn't able to practice or compete. I needed to do what I could do so that when the time came that I could compete, I was ready to go and go hard and with a clear mind."

With this new understanding, Tony's next semester started with the motivation to prove himself to himself in the classroom and to prove his overall commitment to his coach.

"When the second semester began," Ramos said, "I was on the straight and narrow. I was earning a 3.8 grade point average, and I was eligible because my cumulative was at like a 2.5—it never dropped below. I had some good guidance and started my gen-eds, the classes that ended up leading to my major."

In the classroom, Tony would also find another mentor, this time in the form of a professor.

"One of the classes I took was Educational Psychology with a guy named Mitch Kelly," Ramos remembered. "He was an old wrestler at the University of Iowa who was now a professor, but he was not a professor that was just going to give you a grade. He was a professor that stayed on you, and he knew the situation I put myself in, so he would take extra time to work with me, make sure that I was prepared for class, and things like that. Once I started to learn how to do that from his guidance, I was able to do it in all of my other classes, and with my tutors, to the point where school just became easier for me."

With his eligibility back, Tony looked to compete at the beginning of January; however, in the interim, he needed to make certain that he was taking care of the rehabilitation process and trusting the trainers with what they were asking of him.

"I was doing my rehab at Carver," Ramos said, "with Matt Doyle—he was our old trainer and he was the trainer back when Gable was coaching. He was a great guy who had been around for years; he was a guy that understood wrestling and he got me through it. It was supposed to be a four-month recovery, and I was back in two months."

AS TONY WAS DOING HIS REHABILITATION AND

he was correcting his wrongs in the classroom, he would meet Megan Eskew, a junior volleyball player for the University of Iowa, in the training room as she was rehabilitating her knee after having surgery on her ACL.

One of Tony's friends and teammates, Ryan Morningstar, was hanging around with a volleyball player and Tony asked him about Megan. And even though the two would see each other in the training room, Tony was much more smitten than Megan and he noticed her more than she noticed him.

"Tony and I met at Carver," Megan said. "I was taking a redshirt year [in volleyball] because I tore my ACL and the first day of practice he like broke his knee or something like that. But we both had knee surgery so we were always in the training room rehabbing. The first time I 'talked' to Tony was via Facebook chat. He messaged me and my roommate had told me that he was 'Pesos' [the nickname given to him by Ryan Morningstar] and he was a wrestler. It was just casual conversation. He asked me out on Facebook chat and we met for lunch at Which Wich in Iowa City."

And, for someone who always had something to say, Tony was the antithesis of that person on his date. "I thought [the date] was awkward," Megan said. "I asked a lot of questions just to keep the conversation going. I don't remember much about the conversation except that I thought it was weird that he talked about eating fast food a lot."

As to why Megan kept seeing Tony, "He basically made me keep seeing him," Megan said. "I wasn't dating anyone else at the time. So when he texted to come over and hang out, I would usually say something non-committal like: 'whatever' or 'it's up to you' or 'I'm doing [insert anything], but you can come if you want.' He would always come over.

"He obviously grew on me. My roommate dated a wrestler who was significantly shorter than her through most of high school so she was my voice of reason when the 'Ugh! But he is SO short!' came into play. Also, my friends and teammates loved him because he used to give us rides to and from the bars downtown."

Just as Tony was turning the corner with Megan, he was also turning the corner in the wrestling room and he would soon have his chance to step on a college wrestling mat and compete as an Iowa Hawkeye.

CHAPTER 39
STEPPING ON THE MAT

"I wanted to be the guy. I wanted to be in the Iowa singlet in the middle of Carver and have everyone screaming my name. I wanted to be the guy other guys looked to. This was the experience that I needed to make that next jump."

• Tony Ramos

NOW THAT TONY WAS HEALTHY ON THE MAT AND in the classroom, and he had declared a weight that gave him the opportunity to maintain his health and focus primarily on wrestling, it was time to compete.

"My goal was to be back in time for the Midlands," Ramos said, "but Tom and them didn't think it would be right; just too quick to jump right into the Midlands. But I wanted to wrestle back in front of my home town, big tournament, and really see where I was at with these college guys. The coaches made some choices for me that at first I wasn't really happy about, but in the end it was the best thing for me and probably a smart decision."

Therefore, instead of competing, Tony continued to practice. But Tony still knew he had some mountains to climb in regard to earning the respect of his teammates and the Iowa fans.

"The people in Iowa are funny," Ramos laughed. "They are big wrestling fans, but at the same time they want to see an Iowa guy in the line-up if there's that chance. And when I came in, there was Nate Moore and Tyler Clark. So, at first, I think morale was pulling for those guys and deep down inside they didn't want me in the line-up, but that's just how the Iowa community is. They are really going to pull for one of their own. I wanted to show them that they should cheer for me."

In the wrestling room, Tony knew that the level of competition each day with each wrestler was always at a high. For him, he not only had to match the level of intensity, but he had to surpass it to work past two of Iowa's golden boys.

"We all knew that with Dennis graduating that year, that someone was going to take that spot," Ramos said. "The thing was, I was not going to let any of those guys outwork me—I always did more and I always did extra. I did that because I did not have the same accolades as them coming out of high school. Nate Moore was the number-one recruit coming out of high school and going into college, and Tyler Clark was an All-American who transferred from Iowa State. So I had to do everything extra and do everything I could to make sure that I was giving myself every advantage and opportunity possible.

"We would wrestle together and we would work out together, and I was probably more or less trying to grab these guys to make sure I had kind of a feel for them before live competition. They would not grab me as much, but it wasn't like an everyday thing—I was pretty much going with Montell Marion and [Daniel] Dennis and Matt McDonough more than the other guys. I knew if I could grab those guys, the better guys, they would help me grow and improve and get me to where I wanted to be.

"When I wrestled with Dennis, I really learned position and hand fighting. I also had to learn how to get off bottom because Dennis was pretty tough on top. So, if I wanted to get out, I had to work hard on bottom. He was also a guy who was tough to score on and tough to get to his legs, so I had to learn how to hand fight—he was so strong for his size. Because of that strength, I never felt undersized wrestling those other guys because I always had that feel in the room."

However, even though Tony was from Illinois, and some of the Iowa guys stuck together because they pretty much already knew each other, he never felt as if he did not belong. Of course, having Dennis there, also an Illinoisan, made it all the more comfortable—but the chemistry in the room and between all of the wrestlers was strong.

"The team blended really well," Ramos said, "and I never really felt like an outsider. These are guys that want to wrestle and perform at a high level—to us, this was fun and what we were there to do. The team was focused. However, even still, I knew that I was going to have to go above and beyond to win over the Iowa fans."

In order to do this, Tony turned to Dennis. But he did not turn to him for advice; he turned to him for an example.

"I saw how he worked and carried himself and how he did the right things, and what he did to get where he was," Ramos said. "Dennis was not what many considered the best guy coming out of high school, even though he was right there in every competition— he just never won the big match. But the work he did started to show in college and he worked himself into position to be a national champion. I saw that and I followed that."

Along with Dennis as a set of eyes and hands and a helper for Tony, he also had Terry Brands.

"Terry really took the extra time with me," Ramos recalled, "to do the extra drills, come in for extra lifts. He made me come in at 8 a.m. for drills, working situations, and position. You know, Terry was really good with the single-leg and working his way around the single-leg; one of my best shots was the single-leg. So, through that, the single-leg takedown became my best offensive attack. We meshed really well and that's who I really worked with all of the time for my individual work."

Now that the recovery and rehabilitation time was put in, and he felt physically and emotionally healthy, Tony made his first attempt to get back on the mat in mid-January at the University of Nebraska-Omaha Open. However, he ran into a few problems, and making weight was his greatest issue.

"They wanted me to make [125 pounds]," Ramos said, "and I couldn't get down and I didn't make weight there. From that day on, we made the decision that I was a [133 pounder] and that's where I would be competing."

With a missed tournament, Tony was even more anxious than ever to compete. He would have another chance in Nebraska at the York College Open on January 25, 2010.

When the time finally came for him to wrestle, "I was excited," he said. "This was something that I had seen all of the other redshirt freshman do—go to these open tournaments and compete—it was something that I had been wanting and waiting to do and it kind of ate at me. Now, I finally had a chance. I didn't care where it was at or who it was against, I was going to go out there and wrestle as hard as I could and get the best results that I could."

Tony was given the number-one seed in the tournament and the first opponent he faced in college was Missouri Valley College's Cody Beisel. Tony won by fall in 4:54 and found himself in the semifinals.

His next opponent, this time from Missouri Baptist University, was Gary Brooks. Again, Tony won by fall—this time in 6:20. The same result held true in the finals as he defeated Anton Prater, Brooks' teammate, in similar style, just sooner; a fall in 3:47.

Three matches into his college experience, and he was feeling very good about what he had overcome and where he was at.

"I went out there," Ramos said, "I pinned everybody, got the Outstanding Wrestler of the tournament, and that's how it started. This was something that I had been working my whole life for and here I was, Division I, Iowa Hawkeye, and the opportunity was now a reality. I know it was as an unattached wrestler, but that was the first step in getting where I wanted to be."

Five days later, Tony headed to the Grand View Open in Des Moines, Iowa, which was held at Southeast Polk High School.

He and another Hawkeye, Mark Ballweg, entered at the same weight class. Ballweg was given the first seed, Tony the second. But, open tournaments when Iowa showed up were a little unbalanced.

"They were generally blind draws," Ramos laughed, "unless Iowa was there. The Iowa guy usually got the one seed even if he was unattached because he was from the University of Iowa and then they figured out the rest."

In that tournament, the two Iowa wrestlers were simply split up with age being the determining factor—Ballweg was older. But Tony was concerned more about his performance than his teammate.

"After this tournament," Ramos said, "I would know if I was a top-level college athlete. I knew it in my head already, but I had to prove it."

Tony opened the tournament against an unattached Iowa State wrestler and won by a 12-4 major decision. In his second round of the championship bracket, he defeated Kyle Beebe of Dana by fall in 00:44.

Now in the quarterfinals, he had a formidable opponent in Grand Valley University's Michael Schultz. But Tony continued his dominance with a 14-8 decision before riding out a 9-2 decision in the semifinals over Tom Kelliher who was unattached from the University of Wisconsin.

In the finals, Tony matched up against the older Iowa wrestler entered in the tournament. The match would be Tony's closest thus far, but he notched his eighth-consecutive win, this time by a 4-2 decision.

"When it was all over," Ramos commented. "I put up some convincing results against top guys. In the finals I wrestled Ballweg, who was a redshirt sophomore at the time. He was an older guy, a guy who had already been around wrestling and competing for a couple of years. When I beat him, I saw the results of the work that I had been putting in in the summer paying off, and I was starting to make the jumps competing at the highest levels with some of the best guys."

Tony would go another month before he competed again and, when he did, he did not have to travel very far to do so. The first week of February, in Dubuque, Iowa, he competed in the Loras College Duhawk Open. And, just as he had done in the past two tournaments he entered, he dominated.

When his redshirt season ended, he was 12-0 at 133, had six falls, two major decisions, and four regular decisions. He was now more confident and seeing the fruits of his labor from the time he had put in with Dennis and Terry Brands before, during, and after practices.

"It was more of a young kid and an older class teaching and giving lessons," Terry Brands said of how the Iowa program works. "A guy beats the tar out of you, you respond. If you don't respond, your wrestling is going to remain level or it's going to dip a little bit. If you respond, you're going to get better at a quicker rate. If you're going to fight and not put your head on the mat you're going to get better at a much faster rate. I think what you have in the Iowa room is the philosophy that the older guys beat the living dog out of the younger guys and they see who they are—if they respond, they get better. Tony responded."

FOR THE REMAINDER OF THE COLLEGE SEASON,

Tony worked out with his close friend, neighbor, and mentor, Daniel Dennis, as much as he could.

In the process, Dennis was rounding out his senior season and Tony was gaining valuable experience with a partner who was second to none in the Iowa room when it came to work ethic and a pure willingness to put himself into position to win matches. And, as they had done all season, they put extra workouts in together, hung out together, and confided in one another.

"I trained with Dennis a lot," Ramos said. "I was probably one of his most consistent partners in that final stretch into the Big Tens and the NCAAs. We wrestled probably once or twice a week and I was probably one of the closest guys to him—I know he's close with the older guys, but we were close."

When Daniel Dennis entered the 2010 NCAA Division I National Championships in Omaha, Nebraska, Tony was one of his staunchest supporters.

Two weeks before the NCAA Championships, Dennis wrestled Jayson Ness of Minnesota in the Big Ten Championships and lost by a decisive 9-3 decision in Ann Arbor, Michigan.

Placing second in big tournaments had been something of a burden on Dennis and, now on college's greatest stage, during its most prolific weekend, he had an opportunity to wrestle and be crowned the champion he had come so close to so many times.

Dennis earned the number-two seed and Ness was the number-one seed—if they were to meet, it would be in the finals. First, the preliminary matches had to be won and a match-by-match approach was needed by Dennis to put himself in position for a national championship.

In the opening round, he defeated Kevin Smith of Buffalo State University with a 6-2 decision. He then faced and defeated Kelly Kubec, 8-5, to push himself into the quarterfinals.

The quarterfinal match-up came against another Illinois grown wrestler and former state champion from Naperville North High School, Nick Fanthorpe—an Iowa State Cyclone. In a tightly contested match, Dennis edged the former Huskie 4-3 and found himself in the exact same position he was in during the Big Ten Championships, in a semi-final match against Michigan State's Frank Gomez. At the Big Tens, Dennis, the two seed, defeated the three seed, Gomez, 5-4. However, it was roughly two weeks later and the stakes were much higher.

The score would be tight as each wrestler scored one takedown and earned one escape—no riding time would determine the final score. In overtime, Dennis found himself in position to score on his feet and took the takedown and, with it, a 5-3 overtime victory that catapulted him into the national championship match.

As for who he would wrestle, that match in the upper half of the bracket was still working itself out.

Jordan Oliver form Oklahoma State University and Jayson Ness were knotted in a 0-0 match. Neither wrestler could score a takedown on the other nor could either wrestler escape from beneath his opponent. The same held true into the first overtime: no takedowns; the second overtime, no escapes; and now into the ultimate tiebreaker: one thirty-second period. If the man on bottom escaped, he won; and, if the man on top rode him out, he won. Thirty seconds to escape or thirty seconds to ride for an opportunity to wrestle for the national championship.

Ness had the choice and he chose down even though Oliver rode him out with his cross-wrist rides. In that final overtime; however, Ness was finally able to clear his arm for his stand-up, get to his feet, pop his hips, and battle for his escape and a 1-0 victory when the eleventh minute expired.

When Saturday night came, and the bright lights were shining on a Big Ten national championship match, even though most favored Ness, people knew that Dennis was not only a strong wrester, but also a smart wrestler. People also knew that Dennis had the ability to defeat Ness if he could avoid scrambles and stay in good position.

When the match opened, there were no first-period scores and Dennis chose down to start the second period. Of course, Dennis knew he had to work up and not allow himself to be ridden out or turned like he had been in the Big Ten finals.

Ness remained in the top position until Dennis was able to create a scramble with 00:56 left in the second period. Dennis worked a stand-up and then tried for a switch. He would get dropped to his hip, but he was able to find and grab Ness' right ankle and the scramble began—the scrambles had always favored Ness.

However, Dennis was able to scoot and raise his hips up and came out the back door for a reversal. He earned a 2-0 lead with the score and ultimately erased the riding time Ness had accumulated.

In the third period, Ness chose down and quickly escaped making it a one-point match. Ness would be the aggressor and Dennis was more defensive, but Dennis was wise enough to keep his backside to the center of the mat, wear down on Ness' head in the ties, and kept the Iowa style of being physical, moving forward, and staying in good position. He showed the referee he was working and was not warned with a stalling call due to his forward pressure.

With 1:12 left in the match, Ness took his third shot in the period, but he forced it and it looked as if Dennis was snapping him down at the same time. As soon as Ness shot in, his head hit Dennis' left knee, he hit the mat, Dennis chased the leg, and then ran behind Ness' right side for a 4-1 lead. Immediately, after the takedown, Ness took an injury timeout.

"When Minnesota guys got taken down late in the match and were losing," Tom Brands explained, "they would take that injury timeout to get a fresh start. They put the injury rule in where you get the choice because of Minnesota. Hartung did it three times to Fullhart, Thorn did it to Montell Marion, that's four, and then Ness did it to Dennis."

Now, with 1:07 left in the match, and Dennis holding a 4-1 lead, he was still in control of the match and, per his reputation, he was a smart wrestler who knew position well. Ness had his work cut out for himself if he was to beat Dennis for the third time that season, and he had to do it with the national championship on the line.

The referee set the wrestlers, Ness down, and when the whistle was blown, Ness popped up simultaneously and, within one second, had escaped and brought the match to 4-2.

With 1:06 remaining, a heavy and hard hand fight emerged as both wrestlers were aggressive. One tried to keep position and not give up a score, and the other tried to keep position and find the slightest opening for a takedown.

When the clock was at 00:58, Ness took a shot and Dennis worked his best defensive score, a snap down, and ran behind his opponent's right side—but to no avail. Ness was able to clear his legs and body and returned to his feet.

In the next 00:30, Dennis blocked Ness from the inside as Ness tried an inside trip and made two more shot attempts; however, Dennis was able to keep the pressure forward and that, in itself, was not stalling.

With 00:15 left, and both wrestlers in the middle of the mat, Ness took another wild shot to Dennis' left side—a sweep single; however, this time Ness' head finally found an opening under Dennis' right arm as he put a second move together, a duck under to Dennis' right. Ness now found himself in a body lock position with 00:10 left. He drove into Dennis and Dennis fought like mad to work his hips back. If Dennis gave up the takedown it would go to overtime. If he could fend it off, he would be crowned the national champion.

At 00:08 Ness was finally able to drive Dennis to the mat and Dennis, with double over-hooks on the longer Ness, hit his hips and tried to muscle him over to avoid the takedown. In the process, however, Ness was able to slide his body to the side, shift his weight, and catch Dennis on his back for a near fall count which equated to two back points. With the takedown and near fall, that gave Ness four points in eight seconds and, ultimately, gave him a 6-4 lead, the win, and the national championship.

As soon as the final whistle blew, a great contrast in emotions was seen. Dennis rolled to his back, put his hands over his eyes in disbelief. Dennis was shaken and defeated while, right next to him, Ness was on his knees with his head and hands raised pointing to the heavens and celebrated in utter joy.

When Dennis came to his knees and unsnapped his headgear, he once again lowered his head to the mat, hands on crying eyes, dumbfounded and destroyed in regard to what had just happened in those remaining seconds.

All Tom Brands could do from the corner, hands on his waist, eyes on his fallen Hawkeye, was watch as his Iowa wrestler had found himself out of position twice, and it cost him the coveted national championship.

The Minnesota fans and the Iowa detractors cheered and stomped in celebration of the miracle at 133 pounds. Dennis shook hands with the always well-mannered Ness and took off running into the tunnel.

Two seniors, both fifth-year seniors, had their careers end in very different fashions, and all within the same eight seconds.

Watching in the Iowa section of the arena, surrounded by the black and gold cheers of anticipated celebrations that were now silenced, was Tony. He saw his friend seconds from his dream of glory, all that he had worked for, and watched him fall into ruin, inwardly destroyed by the moment.

After the championships ended and Iowa had claimed the team title, Dennis found himself in pain and confusion, but in that moment Tony was there for him.

"When Dan Dennis lost," Ramos explained, "we were headed to the

Hawk party afterward and I saw him walking there with his head down. I walked up to him and gave him a hug and he stayed there just crying on my shoulder. He was not in good shape. I just stayed embraced and told him, 'Dennis, I love you, you've done great things for me. I can't say that I know what you're going through because I don't—I've never been in that situation—but I feel for you and am here for you if you need anything; you let us know.'"

And as the team returned to Iowa, Dennis' heart would still be in Omaha.

Tony took Dennis' loss personally because he saw the one person who went out his way for him hurting, and Tony was not blind to his individual growth due to Dennis' help. He was there for his friend no matter the situation or time of day or night.

"When I got to Iowa and we connected," Ramos said, "he would call me, bring me into the room for one-on-one training for that extra drilling, that extra feel for position and technique. I was the first person he would call. He was bringing me along and mentoring me which, to me, was above and beyond anything else he could do. He showed me the ropes and the right way to do things, so I was always going to be there for him.

"After we got back [from Omaha] he was not in a good place, not in the right place for a few weeks. I told him to call me and said, 'I'm always home and I'm always sober, so I will always come get you.' I would pick him up from downtown, I would bring him home, and he would just sit in the car and cry and talk to me about things like, 'You can't let this happen to you. I won't let this happen to you. You got to win a national title, you're too good not to. Don't do what I did or you're going to have regrets—you're never going to be okay with it.'

"And seeing him like that pushed me even harder in my training to make sure something like that wouldn't happen to me. I didn't want to feel like that because I'd seen it first-hand."

While Tony listened and tried to console his friend, he found it difficult to bring Dennis around to seeing a future and helping him move past that moment.

"I would try to tell him to look past this," Ramos said. "I was telling him, 'Dennis, I see how tough you are, how strong you are, what you do in the room when me and you practice—you've got to stick with this, you've got to keep going forward. Just imagine yourself at 55 [kg] wrestling, you could be the best guy in the world. You need to think about World and Olympic titles, not this national tournament that's tearing your heart out.'

"I think [through the conversations that we had], that I was a big reason why he tried to go 55 kg and compete and try to make World and Olympic teams."

But, before any of that would happen, Tony would have to get back to training for the upcoming tournament that spring—the ASICS University Nationals.

To be competitive, Tony dropped weight. The weight class that he had not been able to make upon his return from his injury—125 pounds—he not only made, but he went beneath. Tony committed himself and wrestled at 55 kg, 121.25 pounds.

The motivation behind his decision was simple: He wanted to be the best. "I wanted to be the guy," Ramos continued. "I wanted to be in the Iowa singlet in the middle of Carver and have everyone screaming my name. I wanted to be the guy other guys looked to. This was the experience that I needed to make that next jump."

THE ASICS UNIVERSITY NATIONALS HAD ALWAYS

been an important off-season tournament because it gave wrestlers the opportunity to work their international styles—freestyle in Tony's case—and compete against a variety of high-level wrestlers.

All along the way to help Tony prepare would be who had become more of his personal coach, Terry Brands, and a wrestler who had committed himself to helping Tony be successful. That wrestler was Daniel Dennis.

"The things [Dennis] did for me in the wrestling room, I can never pay back," Ramos said. "He was always there for me if I needed a workout, if I needed a partner. He was always pushing me to grow and evolve as a wrestler. Even though he was still struggling with his loss, he never let that take away from him helping me grow and get better."

The nationals that season were held in Akron, Ohio, and Tony felt strong at the weight and had worked himself into the semifinals. He was to face a common opponent, and one that he wanted to make a statement against: Jon Morrison of Oklahoma State University.

Each wrestler took a win in one period of the first two periods, and then were tied at the end of third with no score. In that case, at the time, a ball was pulled out of a bag and the color of the ball gave that wrestler the choice in the clench position. If the position was defended, one wrestler won; if the other wrestler scored a takedown, he won.

"It went to the ball grab," Ramos remembered, "because, at the time, that's what it was and that was basically the luck of the draw. He got the draw, the choice of position, and the takedown."

The loss frustrated Tony for a number of reasons. First off, "Because that was a guy I had beaten and a guy I should never have lost to," Ramos said. "Also, it was a guy that I knew I would be competing against a lot during season, being that he's at Oklahoma State and I'm at Iowa, and we'd probably end up at the same weight class. I wanted to set the tone from the start that nothing's changing from high school. It's going to be all the same, you're going to be the second-best guy always behind me.

"And then I end up losing that match. I felt like I gave him some hope and some confidence for when we wrestle in the future. The other thing that bothered me was that I wanted to show Oklahoma State that they made the wrong choice, they made a mistake. But then I lose that match and they were probably thinking they made the right decision and they ended up on top of that situation."

Morrison went on and lost in the finals to Frank Perrelli of Cornell: 1-2, 1-0, 3-1. Tony earned a third place finish over Shane Youns of Mylan-Sunkist Wrestling Club. The decision was decisive enough, 1-0, 2-0. Now it was back to Iowa as the school year came to a close.

THAT SUMMER WOULD BE DIFFERENT FROM THE

previous season in that Tony now knew the routine, understood what to expect, and committed to the training as a life element. All of those components were vital to his second season at Iowa.

From Terry Brands' point of view, Tony just had to stay the course and continue to focus on improving. "The focus is to always get better and you have to get better at a rate that puts you in contention for the top of the stand," Terry Brands said. "That can mean the Olympics, the Worlds, the NCAAs, that could mean the Big Tens, that could mean winning a match [in a big dual]. You got to become a contender. So every single day that you come to work or to practice, you build to become the best that you can become. So the focus was the same, learn how to become the best wrestler that you could become. If our starter goes down and you're the next guy, then you're going to win the nationals. That kind of mentality."

Unlike the previous summer, Tony had an understanding of the program and the progress.

"That summer," Ramos said, "I was working the camps and at these camps is the time where we do some of our hardest training, so I knew what I was getting into going into camp. But this was also a time where I looked at the new guys coming in, and I remembered what it was like for me coming in and getting beat up, and now I was doing it to these guys. So I was gaining confidence, growing. I was focusing more on getting ready to put myself into a position to make the line-up.

"We knew kind of where I was going to be and what the competition was going to be—the guys at that weight—so I started focusing more on getting better in areas that they were good and where I struggled. This way, when it came time for wrestle-offs, I could compete and I could beat these guys. My mindset also changed to where I knew I was going to have to score tons of points. So, in practice, I would try to score as many points as I could—taking guys down hard, trying to turn them right away and break guys—and that actually helped me when it came down to who they were going to pick to wrestle."

That summer would also be the summer that Daniel Dennis joined the Hawkeye Wrestling Club (HWC) to compete internationally. As part of the HWC, Dennis would work with Tony as he had done the previous season.

"Dennis was there and he was focused on helping me win national titles," Ramos said. "He was helping me get better in the areas where I struggled and giving me good feels and looks. The difference was I was not focusing on him being prepared and helping him get ready; rather, he was helping me and focusing on me being ready."

CHAPTER 40
TAKING OVER THE WEIGHT

"He got better just by how he came in every day and went to work. I also think that there is a reciprocal factor with him: You believe in me, and I will perform for you."

• *Tom Brands*
Head Coach, the University of Iowa
Coach, Hawkeye Wrestling Club

WHEN THE WRESTLING SEASON ARRIVED FOR Tony, and it was time for him to claim what he felt was his—the starting spot at the 133-pound weight class for the University of Iowa—he would have to prove it through a two-match wrestle-off. In the end, after he had defeated his two teammates, his plan and hard work would have all been worth it.

As was customary, the wrestle-offs for the university took place late October or early November, and this was where Tony's new journey would begin.

"It was a four-man bracket," Ramos remembered. "It was between me, Tyler Clark, Nate Moore, and Nick Trizzino. The coaches somewhat seeded it: 1. Moore, 2. Clark, 3. Me, and 4. Trizzino. So Clark and me wrestled."

In the wrestling room, for the wrestle-offs, there was no coaching and no visible clock for the wrestlers—they were expected to wrestle and earn it all on their own and be conscious of the entire match.

"The first match I remember really well," Ramos said. "I had to wrestle Clark and, in the first period, I got a takedown with very short time left in the period. But, since we didn't have a clock or coaching, I ended up cutting him not knowing that there were ten seconds left. That was a huge mistake that could've ended up costing me the match.

"In the second period I chose bottom and gave up a riding point, so we were tied 2-2, but I was winning 2-1 if I could erase that time. In the third period Clark chose down and would escape. I would not be able to erase his rider and I did not score. He won the match 3-2, and letting him go prematurely lost me that match."

For Tony, that wrestle-off had been what he had trained and prepared for—and now it was gone. He had the opportunity he wanted and he was not able to seize it.

"It was very hard on me," Ramos remembered, "because I felt like all of the goals and dreams that I had were now over. That night, Tom called me and told me he was going to have Trizzino and me wrestle-off the next day—this was unusual because they never did backside matches. It was always lose and you're done; but, after that call, I knew right then and there that there was a small chance and I needed to go out that next day and prove that I was ready to compete."

For Tony, his focus had to change—he had an opportunity and he would have to control and dominate his match. "I ended up beating Trizzino in a close match," Ramos said. "But I pretty much controlled it. Then, after the wrestle-offs, there was lots of discussion between us athletes and the staff because there was really no separation, and out of all the matches other than Clark's overtime takedown over Moore, I was the only one to score multiple offensive points. In the coaches' eyes, that was most important."

"There was a dual meet up at Cornell [College in Mt. Vernon, Iowa]," Tom Brands remembered. "We wrestled Cornell and two other schools; we split time there even with Nate Moore, [Ramos, and Clark]. We needed to see how all of them competed—even though those matches didn't mean much from the team score outcome."

Tony stepped on the mat for the first time as a Hawkeye in Mount Vernon, Iowa, on Friday, November 26 against Cornell College. And, even though he had not secured the starting spot, he was excited about finally having the opportunity to wrestle as an Iowa Hawkeye.

"I remember taking a picture of the Hawkeye singlet the night before the duals," Ramos remembered fondly, "and sending it out to my dad and brothers just saying everything we had dreamed of and worked so hard for has finally become a reality. I remembered dreaming of putting that singlet on and competing as a Hawkeye when I was in grade school growing up, and it was finally here."

However, even though the dream came true, Tony knew that he not only had to perform on the mat in reality, but he had to out-perform his other two teammates, Clark and Moore, in order to influence the coaches' decision and earn the role as a starter.

"The day of," Ramos said, "I had to keep my emotions in check because I knew that all my performances would be closely observed as the staff still had a huge decision to make regarding who would be the starter. So, my job was to go out and compete the best way I knew possible and that was scoring lots of points."

Moore would step on the mat first with an opportunity to impress the Iowa staff; in that, Tony would watch and know what he needed to do to outperform and impact the coaches. When the match was over, Moore won a 9-5 decision over Cody Hood of Chattanooga.

"Moore wrestled the first dual," Ramos said. "He only scored a couple of points, so I knew I had to pour it on for the entire seven minutes."

Tony would ultimately step on the mat against Tigue Snider of Cornell—that would be his opportunity. And all Tony wanted was an opportunity.

"The thing about it," Terry Brands said, "was Tony didn't care that we went with [Moore] in one of those duals. It didn't matter to him because in his mind he was going to win the national title. The other guy was like, 'Oh my, gosh, now they're going to wrestle Tony—they took my spot from me.' And I think just that single-minded focus on taking care of business and him believing that 'This is my spot, I'm going to win the nationals and I don't really care what happens in between.' He was set on doing everything he could in his practices and competitions to ensure the opportunity to be atop that stand at the end of the year—and you could see that. And that was the attitude he came to practice with every day."

When Tony walked on the mat for the first time, he simply focused on his goal to dominate the match. And, as the match started, he knew he had to discover ways to score and score over and over, and he did. He would win his very first collegiate match by a 14-5 major decision.

"After the match," Ramos remembered, "I felt great. I felt I competed hard and looked to score points the entire seven minutes. Moore only scored a few points and won, but I personally felt I had the upper hand heading into [the Kauffman-Brand Open in] Omaha where we all were supposed to compete. Unfortunately, that plan blew up rather quickly."

Days before the Kauffman-Brand Open, Tony sustained an injury—a small break in his foot—he was out. Clark, who had been in competition with Moore and Tony, would ultimately break his hand in the first match of the Open when he defeated Ben Cash of Iowa State—then he medically forfeited out of the tournament. Nate Moore seized his opportunity and placed third. However, the Hawkeye staff was still very much on the fence as no clear dominant wrestler had yet emerged at 133.

"It was back and forth, back and forth," Tom Brands said. "But it wasn't back and forth, back and forth late in the season. It was back and forth until December. There was no question [about] the guy who was doing it in [the wrestling room] and the guy who competed the hardest.

"Tony Ramos emerged for one simple fact: It was the way that he trained and the way that he competed," Tom Brands continued. "He wasn't great as a freshman—he was good. There were some other guys in there that basically it came down to who was going to take the spot. He basically built himself into the contender. Mind and body. Spirit and emotion."

Through how he was competing in the room, Tony received the opportunity to step on the mat in a very important dual: Iowa versus Iowa State. To top it off, Tony would also be wrestling his first match in Carver-Hawkeye Arena and in front of the Hawkeye faithful.

"This was my first match ever in Carver-Hawkeye Arena in a big rivalry meet," Ramos said. "I had to go out and show the fans and the rest of the 133-pound field what I had to offer. I still had a broken foot, but it was healed enough and it didn't bother enough to where I couldn't compete. When I was given the green light that I would be wrestling, I didn't care what injury I had because I couldn't take any chances of giving up the spot I felt that I was starting to claim. My goal was to go out and pin my guy or score big bonus points."

Tony earned a 14-5 major decision over Brandon Jones and the Iowa fans rewarded him handsomely with loud cheers and applause. Later that week, Tony went in and watched film with Terry Brands.

"At one point in the match," Ramos said, "I locked up a near side cradle and Terry paused the match, looked at me and said, 'Tom thought he was getting an early Christmas present here.' I wish I would have finished the match right there, but I went on to win and scored multiple times on my feet. Because of this, I kept on getting the nod week in and week out because they saw I had the best upside moving forward, and that upside was points."

From his head coach's point of view, "Probably the thing that put him over the edge was when we threw him in against Iowa State," Tom Brands said. "It was a big dual and we put our best guy in and I never looked back."

But Tom Brands had three solid wrestlers to choose from: Tony, the redshirt freshman; Nate Moore, the sophomore and Iowa City West High School standout; and, Tyler Clark, the junior Iowa State transfer who was an All-American. However, what made Tom Brands so comfortable with Tony stemmed back to the previous year and how he responded to "What we talked about," Tom Brands said. "I didn't ever have to talk about how he trained or how he wrestled or how he competed—that's what made me comfortable."

And after the Iowa State dual, Tony continued to work hard in and out of the room and everyone noticed. "He got better just by how he came in every day and went to work," Tom Brands said. "I also think that there is a reciprocal factor with him: You believe in me, and I will perform for you."

And that was exactly what Tony did in the following two duals. He defeated Josh Harper of Michigan State by a 16-1 technical fall in 5:13, and then defeated an Illinois native, Ryan Jauch, when he downed the Northern Iowa starter by a 12-3 major decision.

The next major showcase for Tony was at the Ken Kraft Midlands Championships in his home state of Illinois, hosted by Northwestern University.

Tony opened his tournament with two convincing wins, a 14-3 major decision over American's Kevin Tao, and a 7-4 decision against Ridge Kiley of Nebraska. However, his next match, his quarterfinal match, was where he needed to standout. He had to face teammate Tyler Clark and he knew that match would leave an impression one way or another.

"This match was big because to me I felt I was solidifying my spot," Ramos said. "Many felt Clark was still the guy and he just hadn't had his chance yet due to his injury. I went out there, got a takedown, escaped on bottom, and won 3-1."

With that win, Tony was one win away from the Midlands finals and making a name for himself while dominating and pushing past the other Iowa wrestlers at his weight.

In the semifinals, Tony had a familiar opponent in B.J. Futrell of Illinois. Futrell, an Illinois high school product from Chicago Mount Carmel, was one-year older than Tony and they wrestled in the same weight class, 103 pounds, during Tony's freshman season—Futrell, a then sophomore, placed fifth in the state while Tony finished as the state runner-up to Chris Spangler.

• • •

After Illinois went to three classes, Futrell won a 2A state championship at 103 pounds as a junior and at 112 pounds as a senior—in that stretch he won eighty-five-consecutive matches without giving up a single offensive point.

Futrell ended his high school career as a six-time All-American in freestyle and Greco-Roman in Fargo and was the national runner-up at the 2008 High School Senior Nationals at 112 pounds. In addition to his production on the mat, in the classroom he was also recognized when he was named to the U.S.A. Wrestling All-Academic Team.

Upon entering the University of Illinois, Futrell started as a true freshman and debuted with a 3-0 record at the ACC/Big Ten Clash. He would end his freshman campaign with a 25-14 record; additionally, he qualified for the 2009 NCAA Championships after a sixth-place finish at the Big Ten Championships. Unfortunately, he did not place.

That April of 2009, Futrell went on to win the ASICS University Nationals at 55 kg and continued his dominance in Greco-Roman. He would defeat Max Nowry of the United States Olympic Education Center 7-0, 4-0.

During the 2009-2010 season, Futrell recorded a 6-1 record before suffering a season-ending shoulder injury. He received a medical hardship waiver and returned for 2011 as a seasoned and confident redshirt sophomore.

• • •

When it came time for Tony and Futrell to wrestle in the semifinals of the Midlands, Tony was confident and ready. Futrell, a much taller and longer wrestler than Tony, gave Tony fits early on in the match. In addition to the points Tony had fallen behind in, he was exposed with his weakness.

"I struggled on bottom this year, bad," Ramos sighed, "which resulted in many big matches becoming losses. I could beat anyone on my feet, but I would let my opponents' slow matches down by riding me on top. I gave up a big lead early against Futrell and battled back; but, in the end, I fell short."

Tony lost his semifinal bout by a 9-6 decision and then had the same struggles against Cal Poly's Flip Novachkov. Tony found himself in a hole early and gave up control of the match when he again could not escape—he lost his first consolation match 10-7.

Now with two losses in the tournament, Tony had one final match, the fifth-place match. He faced another very familiar opponent, and one he already beaten in the tournament—his teammate, Tyler Clark.

Unfortunately, for Tony, he lost to Clark in a 2-1 tie-breaker decision. Now, each wrestler in the Iowa room had a 1-1 record on the other in competition outside of the room, and each knew that head coach Tom Brands put a great deal of stock in real matches and tournament competition when it came down to who would be named the starting wrestler a the weight. So, for Tony, that loss was a difficult one to swallow.

"All of the confidence I had moving forward in keeping the spot was not gone," Ramos remembered, "but it was greatly diminished. I wasn't sure where Tom and the staff were going to go next to pick who would start."

Since Tony could not control who would be chosen, he had to control his response to the situation and how he would improve.

"My big focus turned to mat wrestling," Ramos said. "If I could get to my feet, I was very hard to beat. So we started working a lot there. The discussions from Tom were very positive because, even though I lost, he saw that between all of mine and Clark's matches, I was the only one to score offensive points. Clark wrestled all his matches very close.

"There was a lot of work to be done to get where I wanted to be in March, and I wasn't as far away as the sixth-place finish I took. I gave myself opportunities and chances in every match [to win]."

From the head coach's point of view, "[Ramos] beat Clark," Tom Brands remembered, "and then he lost to him in the tournament. But the way that they wrestled—just how they were going—not really scoring—because that's where Ramos was different [in how he wrestled]. Ramos just worked hard out on the mat. Sometimes he struggled to score points, but he still worked hard and he was trying to score. And he wasn't just trying to strategize to just eke wins out—that's what I liked. His scoring ability we wanted to work on that, had to work on that, but he got better. Wrestling is hard and it's not easy to just score, but he got better."

Tony would earn the nod from his coach for a not-so-competitive dual against Southern Illinois University Edwardsville—he won his match against John Petrov by a 20-5 technical fall in 5:55 and the team won 49-0. However, with that start, Tony knew two certainties that made him shake his head knowing the impact losing to Clark had on the coming weeks: 1. He would be sent to wrestle in the Glen Brand Open; and, 2. He would not be going to Oklahoma State for the dual against the Cowboys.

Not being able to travel for a major dual sparked a conversation between Tony and Tom Brands.

"There was conversation," Ramos said, "and Tom told me he thought it was best if I stayed back and got more matches and tournament experience in Nebraska than traveling with the team. I was frustrated and upset because this was a match I had marked on the calendar and was looking forward to. I didn't question [the coaches] because if I didn't believe in my coaches and trust what they thought was best, then I was in the wrong place. I didn't travel. I went to the Kaufman Brand Open."

The dual, to Tony however, was what was most important. And, even though he believed in his coaches and had a conversation and was given a clear explanation as to why, he did not like it. His attitude as he headed to the Open reflected that sentiment and it showed on the mat in his performances.

Tony opened up the tournament with a fall in 2:00 over Midland's Matt Katusin. In the semifinals he wrestled and defeated Nebraska's Keith Surber with a 5-3 decision. However, on the mat, Tony was not himself.

"I went into this tournament with a terrible attitude," Ramos said. "I was upset that I was not going to Oklahoma State with the team to compete. After my match with Surber, I had to sit down and refocus on why I was sent there by the coaches and that was for more mat time."

After his refocus, Tony wrestled J.J. Krutsinger of Iowa—another wrestler from the same room. Krutsinger was "a very solid 125-pound back-up that we had," Ramos remembered. The match was important to Tony's growth as well because, early on at Iowa, "I struggled with him a lot."

When they stepped onto the mat, the struggle was no more. After he was able to transfer from his anger to his purpose of being sent to the tournament, Tony came into the final match and had a dominating performance. He defeated his teammate by a 17-7 major decision and, more importantly, walked away having learned a few pieces about himself.

"That was a big win for me," Ramos said. "Like I said, I struggled with him when I first got to Iowa, so this showed me how much better I got as the season was progressing. Also, being able to change my mindset and refocus myself with a situation that was fast and not planned gave me confidence that I could always work through anything else that was sudden and not planned."

At the time of the dual between Iowa and Oklahoma State, the Hawkeyes were rated number ten in the country and the Cowboys were number six. The dual opened with Iowa's number-three ranked wrestler Matt McDonough, at 125 pounds, defeating number-eight Jon Morrison, 7-3.

When the 133-pound match came up, Tony missed the opportunity to wrestle the number-one ranked wrestler in the country at his weight class. Instead, it was Tyler Clark who had the opportunity and, when it was all settled, Jordan Oliver defeated Clark handily, 11-4.

The dual would be heavily contested from the corners by both head coaches during every match as they scrapped for every point. The dual came down to the heavyweights. Prior to that match, OSU was winning 15-12 and there had already been three upsets in the dual—Iowa had two of them. At heavyweight, Iowa had the number-twenty ranked wrestler in Blake Rasing stepping on the mat, while the Cowboys had an unranked but solid wrestler in Blake Rosholt in their corner; Rosholt was looking to close out the win in Stillwater.

The match would be deadlocked 1-1 headed into overtime. In the end, the dual resulted in a classic Iowa and Oklahoma State match, as Rasing of Iowa secured the individual win, 3-1, in sudden victory, and tied the dual meet 15-15. That team performance for Iowa also helped them climb two spots in the national ratings.

Tony, though happy for the team's ability to stay with and compete against a strong team, felt that not being in the line-up took away from the team's chances to win. He wanted that match against Oliver and believed he could have helped his team win. From there on out, he had to prove he was the only choice for Tom Brands to turn to for any dual or tournament.

With Cark losing in Stillwater, this gave Tony the opportunity he needed to show his coach his worth—it may have also been his final opportunity so he knew that he had to perform.

His next opponent was again someone Tony had a bit of a past with—Ian Paddock. The dual took place at Carver-Hawkeye Arena and, even though Ohio State was unranked as a team, it was a Big Ten dual. It was in front of the Iowa fans, and it was against Paddock who was currently ranked number fifteen at the weight. The year before, Paddock had made it to the round of twelve at the national tournament—he was one match away from being an All-American.

"[Paddock] was a pretty well-known wrestler at the time around the country," Ramos said. "We grew up wrestling and used to have good battles and I think I usually won most of the matches we competed in."

This match, however, was not like the ones in the past—this was college and wrestlers were passing up other wrestlers based on work ethic and commitment. The importance of the match would show if Tony was making strides and if he was going to impress his coach enough to take over the weight for the remainder of the season.

For Tony, the match-up with Paddock was the fifth match of the night as the dual opened at 184 pounds. When it was time for him to take the mat, Iowa had not yet lost a match—there were two decisions and one major decision before a McDonough fall. Now it was Tony's turn.

The match-up was hard fought on both ends and the intensity ran high. However, when the seven minutes expired, Tony would have his hand raised, a 5-2 decision, and Iowa went into the break with a 5-0 match lead and a 16-0 team score lead.

When Tony returned to the tunnel after his hand was raised, he knew his performance made an impression.

"I think this may have been when I solidified my spot and the questions were basically gone," Ramos said. "This was a guy who was a very solid opponent and who had had some big wins in his career."

Tom Brands felt the same as Tony when it was time to make an objective decision; he put all factors in front of him regarding the direction of the weight class and who would be the starter.

"Even though they were 1-1 in the Midlands," Tom Brands recalled, "and both those guys had a problem with [who started]. They would be like, 'Well, I beat him.' But it's not about you beating him, it's about how you compete. It's about how you train. It's about what you do in [the wrestling room] and how you compete in front of a crowd. It wasn't even close in my mind. So why did I put [Ramos] in? I put him in because he never had a problem with anything in that wrestling room. Never! Commitment."

In addition to the time that Terry Brands was putting in with Tony and the mentoring role that Tom Brands was contributing to Tony's growth and maturation, Daniel Dennis continued to play an important part in Tony's life and wrestling as well.

"Dennis would come in during off-times for my drill sessions with Terry," Ramos said. "He was helping make sure that I was getting the workouts I needed to be at the top of the podium. He was my partner for lots of my individual workouts."

As Tony's workouts progressed and he was growing as a wrestler and a person, his efforts were not going unnoticed. For the remainder of the season, which consisted of the Big Ten dual meet schedule, Tony was named the starter. Along the way, he went undefeated, 6-0, and his closest match was against Andrew Long of Penn State at Rec Hall in University Park. Long had transferred into the Nittany Lion program from Iowa State after he earned a national runner-up finish at 125 pounds the season before.

In that dual at Penn State, Tony used a second-period takedown and a third-period escape to take the 3-2 decision over the returning All-American. The upset marked Tony's arrival.

"The individual win was big for me," Ramos said, "but the dual win was huge for the team. Going into it, the outside world thought there was no chance of us coming out victorious. Even during the broadcast, the announcers, during their pre-match, said that we would need a miracle to win. I remember hearing the crowd disappointed. Then McDonough pinned, and I won, and Montell won—you could feel the energy sucked right out all the fans. It was silent in their gym. We just destroyed them."

The dual ended with number-eight Iowa trumping number-one Penn State, 22-13.

"For me," Ramos added, "it was Long's first match back, but he was the runner-up last season, so I was the underdog in everybody's mind—but not mine. I knew he had no chance of beating me and he never has."

Tony was now 8-0 in dual meets and, along the way, had defeated some high-profile wrestlers, none more so than Long who was ranked number four at the time of the dual.

Aside from now having earned his coach's trust and the role as the starter, Tony headed back home to the Land of Lincoln for the Big Ten Championships.

"I was excited to wrestle in front of a home-town crowd and I expected to win it," Ramos said. "I thought there was a chance of me getting the one seed due to beating Long that year, but I ended up with the three seed behind Long and Graff."

Tony's first match was against the same wrestler he beat just two weeks prior in the team's final Big Ten dual of the season, David Thorn of Minnesota. In the dual, Tony won 7-3; however, this was tournament time and every wrestler was always more prepared with an NCAA berth on the line.

Since Tony had wrestled Thorn recently, he knew what he had to do to secure the win and advance into the semifinals. "I had to score and I knew he would be prepared for my offense from our last dual," Ramos said.

True to his words, the match was extremely close, closer than Tony would have liked, but he pulled out the victory with a late takedown to win the match by a 4-3 decision.

Now in the semifinals, Tony had to wrestle against an opponent he had not wrestled all season due to Wisconsin not being on the Hawkeye dual meet schedule. He had to face Tyler Graff. The match would go into overtime.

"Graff was in many times," Ramos remembered, "but couldn't finish. In the ride-out overtime, there was a very questionable point where many would say I escaped, but it was never called."

Tom Brands remembered that match and the call as well. "He was out," Tom Brands recalled emphatically. "He was out in the overtime and they blew the whistle prematurely. It was a high school referee and I've had trouble with this referee for ten years because he's a high school coach, not a referee—he's a high school coach, and, you know what, if one shoelace is inbounds, you're still wrestling—and he called them out [of bounds] with one foot, there was still one foot one the mat, and Ramos was out. That would have been the match."

The match headed to the second overtime and, "I gave up a takedown and lost 3-1," Ramos said.

Graff headed to the finals where he would lose a decisive 7-3 match against Penn State's Andrew Long, and Tony found himself in the consolations. Tony had expected to be in the finals and win the Big Tens, but he now found himself elsewhere—he had to bounce back.

"When a guy loses," Terry Brands said, "sometimes you have to worry about confidence, you have to worry about some of those things that could pop up in the psyche or mentality or emotions, so we have to see where guys are at and move forward. It was never like that with Tony. It was always just forward."

Tony received a medical forfeit from Paddock and had to face Futrell of Illinois for third. This time, however, there were no bottom position issues and trailing from behind. Tony controlled the match and walked away with a 6-2 decision and a third place finish—this was an automatic bid to the national championships.

"The win against Futrell," Ramos said, "showed how much better I got from beginning of the season at Midlands to now. The win was also a huge confidence boost for me heading into nationals. But, seeing Long win the Big Tens was very frustrating, because I knew I could beat him and that I should have been there. It also played into the final score—we lost the Big Ten title by one point to Penn State and that may have been the deciding factor."

Penn State's 139 to Iowa's 138 team-score margin was the closest team race in the ninety-eight year history of the Big Ten tournament. The loss soured Tony, as well as the coaches, the team, and the Iowa fans. Even though there were many places where that one point could have been earned, it was not. But it was time to move forward to the national tournament and there was no time to look back and wonder *What if?*—it was time to prepare for an individual and team NCAA championship.

As he headed into the two-week stretch before the nationals, Tony assessed his performance. "The Graff match showed me I could compete with the guys considered the best in the weight class," Ramos said. "But it was back to fine-tuning the little details and again, like all season, I had to focus on getting out on bottom which was my weakness and biggest downfall."

When it was time to be back in the wrestling room with Tony, Terry Brands knew exactly how to approach his wrestler. "We had a talk," Terry Brands said, "where I just told him: 'Look, these are the situations that cost you. We've been talking about them ever since you got here to Iowa. Now what are you going to do about it? Are you going to keep making that mistake or are you going to fix it?' And we could have those conversations because we never had a problem with his commitment and we never had a problem with his response."

In preparation, Tony drilled and he drilled and he drilled and he drilled the areas he needed to improve on every day, every workout, and continued to put himself in those positions in order to get better at working out of them. That was the work being put in for the twelve days between the Big Ten Championships and the NCAAs in Philadelphia.

"We drilled," Terry Brands remembered. "And we put him in positions that were going to happen to him—as much as we could foresee—and we just drilled and familiarized those things and honed those areas. It was not as much an emphasis on his opponents as much as it was an emphasis on what he was going to have to do to his opponents."

When it was time to leave for Philadelphia, Tony was comfortable and confident with the work he had put in, and it was now time for him to go and win a national championship.

2011 • DUAL MEET VERSUS IOWA STATE
RAMOS' FIRST MATCH IN CARVER-HAWKEYE ARENA
RAMOS VERSUS BRANDON JONES • RAMOS WON A 14-5 MAJOR DECISION
PHOTOGRAPH COURTESY • UNIVERSITY OF IOWA ATHLETICS

CHAPTER 41
COMING UP SHORT

"A very frustrating match, and a frustrating way to end a season that, if he was going to get beat or knocked out, it was going to be because of that—not opening up and letting guys stay in matches."

• *Terry Brands*
Associate Head Coach, the University of Iowa
Coach, Hawkeye Wrestling Club

WHEN THE NCAAS CAME AROUND, TONY HAD earned the number-six seed. Even though he felt he had a strong draw, he knew the first match would be filled with some excitement and some nerves and he wanted to make certain that he performed well and set a strong tone for his tournament.

"To me," Ramos said, "the seed didn't matter. But my first match was important—always important. I wanted to perform and get that nervousness out of my first NCAAs, and I did."

Tony faced Lehigh's Frank Cagnina in the championship pigtail round and won a 6-3 decision. However, Terry Brands believed the match was much closer than it needed to be.

"In that first match," Terry Brands reflected, "it was too tight. Too tight. So the conversation was, 'Are you going to wrestle?' Because, sometimes, Tony has the tendency to shut down and it can cost him."

In the first championship round, Tony wrestled Oklahoma's Jordan Keller and won by a decisive 8-3 decision.

Now in the second round of the championship side, Tony was aware of not only his opponent, but the difficulties that he would face against Central Michigan's Scott Sentes.

"I knew the third match would be very tough," Ramos said. "If I got through that match, I would have had a match up with Long in the quarterfinals where I felt I was favored because I always gave him troubles and beat him when we competed. But first I had Sentes."

Scott Sentes, as a true freshman, competed in the 2009 NCAA Championships and earned All-American honors by placing seventh at 125 pounds. Then, as a sophomore, in the 2010 NCAA Championships, he lost his opening match in the championship pigtail to Lehigh's Matt Fisk by fall in 3:29. He would lose again and exit the tournament disappointed.

Now more seasoned, Sentes, who was slick on his feet and very tough on top, was looking to make a name for himself as he was also chasing a national title.

As the match opened, Tony tied heavy on Sentes' head and drove forward, pressuring the longer opponent. Sentes, having felt the pressure for the first twenty seconds, used it against Tony as he shrugged him past and came behind. Tony, however, remained on his feet and fought off the position and the takedown and found himself back in the neutral position. Tony applied more pressure on the head and continued pressuring forward.

With about thirty-five seconds expired in the first period, Sentes was hanging on Tony's head with both hands trying to keep his distance. As soon as he broke, Tony was able to snap him down and found himself in his cow-catcher—he would not be able to capitalize as Sentes was able to post and make himself long. Tony then transitioned to his front headlock and tried to beat the leg, but Sentes kept Tony's arm tight, and his length posed a problem on Tony's reach and ability to score. The instructions from the Central Michigan corner was to get Tony off his head, motion, and get to his shots by moving in and out—they did not want the ties which favored Tony.

The head and hand fighting continued as Sentes tried to keep his distance and Tony tried to close the gap. And now, under two minutes, Tony again moved forward and, as Sentes backed and Tony snapped, Tony saw an opening for his high-crotch to Sentes' left side and went for it. Sentes was able to work his leg back and, as Tony reacted to the shot, and Sentes was elongated, Tony snapped him to a front head and had the angle he wanted. He quickly circled and found himself with his left hand in control of Sentes' head and his right arm down to Sentes' calf—his head was positioned in the side and now the scramble was on.

As Tony ran the corner, he may have let go of the leg too soon. Once he unlocked his hands to reach for the waist and come behind, Sentes was able to make himself long again and defeated the position. Tony, still with the pressure on Sentes' head, could not capitalize, and Sentes held out the position for a stalemate.

Sentes would make some half-hearted attempts for a knee pick and snap Tony's head, but he continued backwards as Tony continued forward and attempted two more shots. Sentes, when close to the mat's edge, was sure to circle to the center and then push Tony out of bounds. Tony stomped back to the center of the mat and the pattern of styles continued. With about 00:38 seconds left in the period, Tony snapped, shot a double-leg, and found himself under Sentes. Sentes defended with heavy hips and under-hooked Tony's left side to try and work his legs back and create separation—the stubborn Hawkeye persisted and changed over to a single-leg and drove Sentes out of bounds.

When the period ended 0-0, Tony won the coin flip and chose the down position. Immediately off the whistle, Sentes jumped onto Tony's hips and fought to sink his left leg in—Sentes was successful. Now in his most vulnerable position, and where he had been working to improve, Tony had to find a way off bottom and return to his strength, his feet.

With eleven seconds away from Sentes earning a riding point, the referee stopped the match due to a stalemate on top. This gave Tony time to escape before the riding point was a factor.

Off the whistle, Tony cleared his hips and circled to his right with Sentes draped over his body trying to hang on with a tight tie on the head and the near arm. Tony, with his right hand, reached up for Sentes' head and began positing on it to create more separation; he was now on his feet and simply needed to break the clinch and earn his point.

As he kept circling right, and using his length, Sentes was able to sink his inside leg, his right, between Tony's left leg, now in an Olympic cradle position that stretched Tony out and returned him to the mat with 1:02 left in the period.

Once Sentes fought off Tony's defense, he reclaimed wrist control and worked his legs back in and flattened Tony out—there would be 00:55 left, but Sentes now had the riding advantage.

With every attempt to come up, Sentes remained clamped to Tony's hips, leg in, pressure forward, and defeated the defense. With 00:21 left in the period, another stalemate was called and Tony would have another fresh start to escape.

As the whistle resumed the match, Tony hit an inside leg stand-up with his right leg and Sentes climbed his back and worked his right leg in. Now on his feet, with Sentes on his back and 00:15 left to score an escape, a new fight began.

With Tony blocking off Sentes' left leg and walking forward, he was still trying to free his right leg which Sentes had secured by using his right arm to lock and kept it tight to his body.

At the 00:10 tick, Sentes was called for stalling, but Tony in an opportune position, was given time to earn an escape. The period ended with Sentes still draped over Tony's backside and falling, but still in control of the top position.

When the referee's choice was given to Sentes, he chose bottom and Tony immediately cut him to bring the match back to the feet. On the scoreboard Sentes was up 1-0; however, with a two-minute rider, Tony had to work quickly to erase the riding advantage point—the only way to do this was with a takedown.

About five seconds into the period, Tony found himself defending a quick shot. When he defeated the position, he was now in position to score—the same position from the first period with the front head and calf on the left side of his opponent. Unfortunately, the position did not hold and Sentes kicked back, made himself long, and the two returned to their feet.

While Tony was working shots to score, Sentes was working calculated slaps and half shots and snaps to not put himself in danger, and to also not be hit for a stalling point. Sentes was wrestling with a strategy; Tony was wrestling with an urgency. Then, with 1:20 left in the period, Tony was able to get to his high-crotch on Sentes' right side—the same shot missed earlier.

Tight in on the single-leg with Sentes using a key-lock and his flexibility to defend, Tony circled left on two knees trying to adjust while Sentes followed and kept his forward pressure on Tony—the longer wrestler was also using his left arm to pull Tony's right thigh closer to him to prevent any sort of opportunity for Tony to slide out or come to his feet. A stalemate was called fifteen seconds later and the two wrestlers received a fresh start.

At the one-minute mark, the riding advantage was locked up for Sentes, giving him a 2-0 lead, and Tony's intensity increased. In that, Tony over-committed near the circle's boundary. As that happened, Sentes got in a shot on Tony's left leg. Once Tony felt the lock, he sprawled, but Sentes, much longer, was able to hold the position and keep it tight and safe. Additionally, what made the position so difficult for Tony was Sentes' length did not allow his underhook, in combination with his sprawl, to create enough space to escape. This fight alone used up about twenty seconds that Tony needed. It also showed Sentes was continuing to wrestle and a stalling call was now unlikely. Regardless, Tony still needed to score a takedown; however, he needed the takedown to simply tie the score.

By the time he was able to work back into a shot on the elusive Sentes, there were two seconds on the clock and the match ended with Tony losing a 2-0 decision. Sentes celebrated and enticed the Central Michigan fans by uplifting his hands as he returned to the center of the mat; Tony slowly stood up and threw his ankle bands into the center of the mat, shook Sentes' hand, ran off into the tunnel, and found himself in the wrestle-backs.

"This was a time when not being able to escape cost me the match," Ramos said. "He was long and lanky and anytime I shot, he clamped on to me for stalemates. On top, he was very good."

Terry Brands, however, saw a greater problem than Tony just not being able to get off bottom. "You look at that match," Terry Brands said, "it's a 2-0 match and the question is simple and we talked about it. 'Where are the points at? Well, we have to go back to the day you stepped on campus after the Montell Marion practice. The only way a guy can go with you, Tony, is when you don't open up. The only way. I'm not saying you can't win and I'm not saying you're going to win, but what I'm saying is you're giving your opponent a chance to open the door against you.' And those are the things that happened."

The goal now was to All-American at the highest possible place, and the goal quickly shifted from winning a national championship, to being a third place All-American.

"I needed to go out and storm through the backside [of the bracket] and pick up bonus points to help the team win the title," Ramos said. "That was my new goal since I couldn't win it."

In his first wrestle-back opportunity, Tony scored a 21-4 technical fall over Tyler Small of Kent State. He would then find himself against another Big Ten foe, and someone he would now face for the third consecutive time in a four-week span, Minnesota's David Thorn.

The match was of utter importance because, "This match would get me one match closer to the round of twelve, which was one step closer to All-American honors," Ramos said. "We were very familiar with each other and the score shows a 7-5 overtime win for me, but the score was much closer than the match really was. I was up 5-2 and he escaped, but we ended up in a scramble late in the period and I thought I was giving up back points so I bellied out. This tied the match at 5-5. In overtime, I scored right away and that was the match."

"Look at the match with Thorn," Terry Brands said. "[Tony] did the same thing—he let Thorn stay in the match and eke his way in to tie it. Okay, he won it, but was it really about getting his hand raised? At that point and time it is, but let's go back and then let's go forward in where he struggled and the same thing pops up."

Now in the round of twelve, more famously known as the "Blood Round," Tony's next match determined who would wear the tag of an All-American and who would simply be known as a national qualifier.

Again, Tony would face a much taller opponent and another opponent who was very tough in the top position, Lou Ruggirello from Hofstra University.

Ruggirello was a fifth-year senior in the Hofstra wrestling program; he was a three-time Colonial Athletic Association (CAA) conference champion and three-time NCAA qualifier.

• • •

In the 2008 NCAA Championships, Ruggirello was the sixth seed and won his opening match in a 3-2 tiebreaker over Steve Hromada of Tennessee-Chattanooga. The following championship round, he dropped a 3-1 decision to Navy's Joe Baker. In the wrestle-backs, Ruggirello sounded off three-consecutive falls and found himself in the Blood Round. He faced Nick Fanthorpe from Iowa State.

Once the match began, Fanthorpe was in full control. Ruggirello was eliminated with a 5-1 loss, and he watched Fanthorpe place seventh and earn All-American honors.

In 2009, Ruggirello had wrestled himself into the quarterfinals, only to lose a 6-4 decision to the eventual national champion, Franklin Gomez of Michigan State. In the wrestle-backs, he once again made it into the Blood Round, only to lose 5-2 to the University of Illinois' Jimmy Kennedy.

It would be another year before Ruggirello competed as he would redshirt in 2010 for Hofstra. Two years later, now a fifth-year senior, and after he had won his third CAA conference championship and qualified for the 2011 NCAA Championships, Ruggirello was seeded fifth and, once again, found himself in the quarterfinals. This time he had Tyler Graff, the four seed from Wisconsin. Graff went on to defeat him in a very tight 2-1 match. This put Ruggirello into the wrestle-backs and he waited to see who his next opponent would be.

• • •

When the match between Tony and Thorn was completed, Ruggirello would, for the third year, have another Illinois product in the Blood Round. This would be a very important match in the career of Ruggirello as he was set to graduate and wanted to earn All-American status before he left. Tony, the feisty freshman, was looking to put his own stamp on the tournament and be an All-American for Iowa.

Early on in the match, Tony struggled and was in trouble. "I got in a hole early," Ramos said, "and had given up riding time. I battled back and tied the match 7-7 with thirty seconds remaining. We went out of bounds and I looked to Terry. He told me the choice was mine, so I cut him and looked to score a takedown because I was in and scored so easily the last few times—that was how I worked myself back into the match.

But, as time was expiring, I couldn't get that winning takedown."

Tony lost the match on that escape point, an 8-7 decision. Ruggirello would earn his first trip into the All-American round and place seventh over B.J. Futrell of Illinois. Tony would have to evaluate and avoid what he felt to be a failure as he did not reach his minimal goal of being an All-American.

Back in that tunnel, Terry Brands caught up to his wrestler. "Competitively," Terry Brands said, "he is level-headed after a loss and can evaluate his match. I'm not going to say a good loser, because I know it burns him up, but he was level-headed and that's what made working with him easy. With that approach, we can take that package, evaluate it, and find reasons why—he can do that clearly. He can see the reasons and then ask himself what he has to do to fix it."

Tony reflected on how "In both matches, where it all went wrong for me was bottom. What I realized was I couldn't escape in the big matches and that had to change to be a national champion. I was not happy with my performance at the NCAAs that year. I went there to win it, not to All-American or come one match away. If I wanted to be the best, I knew I had to figure out how to get away on bottom."

"The Ruggirello match was a really frustrating match," Terry Brands remembered, "because of the way he just got the dog ridden out of him. Then, when he decided to get off of bottom, he chose down, and then came up off bottom. Okay, where is it? I know I'm being hard on him, but now he's on his feet and we're cruising and now we're out of time. Very frustrating. A very frustrating match, and a frustrating way to end a season that, if he was going to get beat or knocked out, it was going to be because of that—not opening up and letting guys stay in matches."

Headed into the individual evaluation period after the tournament, Terry Brands discussed with Tony what had to happen. "It's more personal," Terry Brands said, "it's more individual tailored in the spring to what each guy needs to do, so everyone is different. But, everything we do points toward the next NCAA season and the rest of their career and we are talking about that. We are talking about and trying to instill what the psyche of a dominating wrestler looks like. He is learning how to get off the bottom. 'What are we going to do with this bottom position? What are we really going to do about it because it's been a problem and now it cost you when you had a chance to get on the podium? It cost you.' So now we're trying to get that belief to emerge."

When his head coach had time to speak with him, he was just as candid. "I told him," Tom Brands said, "'There's cats to skin. So what are you going to do? Are you still going to be round of twelve, top seven or eight or what? What are we about here? Is this about you being a champion or about you being in the top six, seven, or eight, or twelve?' I mean, twelve is the same as eight really, pretty much—they just don't wrestle it out. And he responded great—he came to work with a purpose."

Tony's work ethic was never an issue, and he went back to the room with a purpose. "I worked daily on bottom position," Ramos said. "I grabbed guys that were bigger and stronger than me to get different feels in that area. I also worked more with Mark Ballweg and Matt McDonough. They were guys that I wrestled with weekly. I was testing myself and grabbing guys like Dennis to push me in the room. Nick Trizzino was the guy I grabbed consistently for drills and he became the guy who prepared me each week for matches. I also grabbed Matt Gurule. He fought during drills and gave me great feels. He was also one of the smallest guys who came in that year and I liked him immediately."

That spring in April, Tony won the FILA Junior National title at 132.5 pounds in Cleveland, Ohio. To do so, he defeated Nick Dardanes in the finals, 1-1, 1-0, and, along the way, he defeated Jason Tsirtsis in the semifinals.

"I don't remember too much about that tournament," Ramos admitted. "But I remember winning it fairly easily. I controlled my matches and was never in danger. This was the first 'Stop Sign' that I had won in my career, so I was pretty pumped because I never won one in Fargo. Also, in that tournament, Stieber took third in the same bracket—he lost to Cody Brewer in the quarterfinals. Regardless, it was a good tournament for me to win with such high level competition in the bracket. It kept my confidence building and rolling in the right direction heading into the summer and into the next year."

That summer, Tony competed at the Junior World Cup in Germany. He went 2-2 and wrestled Toghrul Asgarov of Azerbaijan who had won the Junior Worlds over Logan Stieber that year, 1-1, 6-4, and then went on to win the Olympics the following year in 2012.

"I was in a tight match with him," Ramos said. "And that was when I started to realize that I could not only compete with the best in the U.S.A., but also the best in the world."

Then, as the summer months came to a close, there were not major adjustments happening in Tony's techniques and style; however, two important things did occur for him. The first, "I just needed to make my weakest area one of my strongest," Ramos said. "I needed to not let guys slow down the pace of the match by keeping me on bottom. I was motivated by how devastated I felt walking out of Philly that season and I just kept working on it."

The second major change came in the form of a discussion with Tom

Brands. "Tom had another conversation with me that summer about how forty guys, four guys at each weight, can say they lost in the round of twelve," Ramos remembered, "but only ten can say that they were national champions. That hit me very hard. I wanted to be one of those select few."

2011 • NCAA DIVISION I WRESTLING CHAMPIONSHIPS
133 LB CHAMPIONSHIP PIGTAIL MATCH
RAMOS VERSUS LEHIGH'S CAGNINA • RAMOS WON BY A 6-3 DECISION
PHOTOGRAPH COURTESY • UNIVERSITY OF IOWA ATHLETICS

CHAPTER 42
COMING INTO HIS OWN

"...not only did I beat him handily, but I beat him where he was best. Now I had more confidence, and that was all I needed moving forward."

• Tony Ramos

AT THE OPENING OF THE 2012 SEASON, THE SAME situation still presided over the 133-pound weight class in the Hawkeye wrestling room between Tony Ramos and Tyler Clark in regard to who the starter should be. Even though Tony had been named the starter at the end of the previous season, that did not mean that Clark was going to take a back seat to him and just concede the weight. True to form, there would be a wrestle-off just as there was the season before.

When it was time to wrestle-off, Tony had trained hard, worked on his weaknesses, prepared, was confident, and was ready—but, apparently, he was not ready.

"In that wrestle off," Ramos said, "Clark actually beat me again. I remember just running out of the room so mad and angry because I knew I was better than him and that it shouldn't have happened. And I let it happen again."

Tony had the opportunity to reclaim his pride and the spot as both he and Clark would be competing at the Lindenwood University Joe Parisi Open in St. Charles, Missouri. Again, he knew that Tom Brands put more stock in competition, and he was going to have to make a statement that following week.

While he practiced, and days were leading up to the tournament, "I really focused on where I need to be good to beat Clark," Ramos said, "and that was score the first points on my feet early and beat him at his own game—mat wrestling."

Tony had to work from the bottom half of the bracket and he first defeated Anthony Heneky of Wentworth Military Academy by fall in 2:12, and then he claimed two technical falls: 23-8 over Denny Kleinschrodt of Missouri, and 22-7 over Travis Barroquillo of Indiana Technical. In the semifinals, he faced Iowa Central's Brandon Wright and defeated him with a 17-6 major decision.

Now in the finals against Clark, Tony had his strategy and he had prepared to be better in certain positions to defeat Clark on the mat. "And that's exactly what I did," Ramos explained.

"I went out and scored the first takedown and then I rode him out. In the second period, where I normally would cut to score, I rode him out again. Then, in the third period, because I had secured the rider, he cut me and had to try and take me down on my feet, which I knew he couldn't do."

When the match ended, Tony had secured a dominant 4-1 decision. "That match was huge for me, mentally," Ramos recalled. "But not just for me, for him because not only did I beat him handily, but I beat him where he was best. Now I had more confidence, and that was all I needed moving forward."

The next possible match-up between the two would be at the Midlands Championships at Northwestern University. However, there was still work to be done in between.

After the five wins at Lindenwood, Tony rattled off an additional three more wins before he had a chance to wrestle returning All-American B.J. Futrell from Illinois.

"When I beat B.J. for the first time at the Big Tens my freshman year," Ramos remembered, "I felt something in him when we were competing where I mentally broke him. I realized that if I fought him hard for just long enough, he would eventually just give up. He was going to come out hard and fast, but after I got him to the point where it was a battle and not a wrestling match anymore, he was going to cave.

"Going into this match, it was early in the year and I wanted to make a point. He was ranked high and I went out strong. From the opening whistle I dominated him in every position because I made everything in the match a fight. Coincidentally, it was also right after McDonough lost to Delgado, so I needed to get the energy back in to Carver-Hawkeye crowd—I put even more emphasis on my match and wrestling to make it exciting."

The score would show Tony's growth as he was now separating himself from the pack. He won by a 13-3 major decision and he followed off that performance with a fall against Iowa State and a major decision against the University of Northern Iowa.

Now, it was back to the Midlands Championships in his home state. He entered the tournament 11-0 overall and 6-0 in duals. Up to that point, he had been on a reign of terror. He had recorded three falls, three technical falls, four major decisions, and one regular decision. He earned the number-one seed and had Jose Mendoza of Cal Bakersfield in his opening match.

Mendoza fell to Tony by a technical fall in 5:22, and then Tony did the same to Tigue Snider of Cornell College; however, this was a 21-6 technical fall in 6:58.

Since his Lindenwood win over Clark, Tony's spirits and confidence were high, and that same confidence was what he took into his quarterfinal match against the number-nine seed, and Iowa teammate, Tyler Clark.

"When I had to wrestle Clark at the Midlands," Ramos said, "my goal was to leave no doubt in anyone's mind—Tom and Terry's or Clark's—that the weight was mine."

The final score of the match was a 5-3 decision in favor of Tony, and he handled the match and controlled it from the opening whistle until the end of the match.

Now in the semifinals, Tony had to face Futrell of Illinois again. And, as he had done in the dual, he did again; however, now Tony was widening the gap. The final victory and finals appearance went to Tony in the form of a 6-2 decision.

For the Midlands championship, Tony had to face the number-four ranked wrestler in the country in Devin Carter of Virginia Technical University. Carter, the number-two seed, had scored an opening round fall, a second round major decision, and 11-5 decision in the quarterfinals, and he defeated A.J. Schopp of Edinboro by a 17-7 major decision in the semifinals. Now, he would face Tony, ranked number two in the country, undefeated and seemingly in control of every match that he had wrestled thus far that season.

The opening of the match was filled with many hard ties and snap downs as expected with two wrestlers trying to exert their physical prowess on the other. Tony took two early shots, but they were defended by Carter who appeared to be looking to slow the Hawkeye down with head ties and wrist control.

With a little over two minutes left in the opening period, Tony finally worked into a clean shot and the fight for a takedown was underway. After about a twenty-plus second fight, Tony scored the takedown and then immediately cut Carter for a 2-1 score. Carter would take his first offensive shot with about one minute remaining in the period—the score would remain 2-1 headed into the second.

In the second period Tony had choice and chose down; he escaped within the first five seconds. He now led 3-1 and, control-wise, everything was in his favor. That was until he came in sloppy with his right-handed tie.

Tony reached right and stepped right at the same time, almost carelessly. When he stepped with his right foot, Carter grabbed and dragged his arm past, slid down on the leg, went arm across, and scored a takedown of his own. Now the score was 3-3 and Carter was gaining confidence. As Tony escaped, with little attempt to hold him down by Carter, the score was now 4-3 in Tony's favor.

About halfway through the period, Tony was again in deep on a double-leg; however, he was unable to score the takedown as Carter defeated the position. Momentarily, he was in on Carter's leg again, off a high-crotch, but to no avail.

Carter would take one more shot, Tony another, and the period ended 4-3 in favor of the Hawkeye.

In the third period, Tony did not even try to ride Carter and the escape happened within the first five seconds. The score was now tied up, 4-4, and Carter, all of a sudden, became the aggressor on his feet. The two exchanged shots, but Carter's were more forceful.

With 0:35 left in the match, Tony was in very deep single-leg, brought it up, only to have Carter kick out of it. Tony had control, briefly, but he could not finish.

When overtime began, a seemingly frustrated Tony was hammering in on Carter and looked to score. But, as he was over aggressive on his reach, Carter, with good wrist control, snapped and swept to Tony's right side, sliding down to the ankle and using Tony's forward momentum. Carter then came up with the single and, seconds later, earned the takedown.

Carter would defeat Tony by a 6-4 overtime win and Tony would return to the center of the mat, shove his ankle bands to the mat in disgust, quickly shake Carter's hand, and run off the mat, furious.

"I had huge slip-ups that cost me that title," Ramos said. "I cut him in the first after I scored and then I got lazy. After that, he turned right into me and took a shot and got a quick and easy takedown. Then, in overtime, he hit me in his little drag and scored. I knew I let that match slip away and it hurt deep down. Right after the match, I went in back and did numerous sprints and push-ups because I needed to outwork my competition win or lose to get on top. To me, it helped me get my mind and body over the loss and moving in the right direction of what was next."

That loss would be Tony's first on the season and Terry Brands went back to what he and Tony had spoken about at the end of the previous season about allowing guys to stay in matches. "It's what we already talked about," Terry Brands said. "That's when he gets in trouble."

Tony had an opportunity to bounce back the following week. And, on the seventh day, when the University of Iowa traveled to the University of Indiana for a Big Ten dual, he refocused and defeated Joe Duca by fall in 3:57. The importance of that match was key for Tony's psyche and mentality as he prepared for the following night's dual at Carver-Hawkeye Arena when the number-two rated Oklahoma State University Cowboys rolled into Iowa City. This was a rivalry dual, a fan-favorite dual, and a number-one versus number-two dual. This dual also gave Tony the opportunity he missed out on the previous year, to take on the number-one ranked wrestler at his weight, Jordan Oliver.

CHAPTER 43
THE MAGIC OF CARVER-HAWKEYE ARENA

"The Oliver match was probably the second or third loudest Carver-Hawkeye has ever been."

• *Terry Brands*
Associate Head Coach, the University of Iowa
Coach, Hawkeye Wrestling Club

THE MOST ANTICIPATED DUAL OF THE YOUNG season, to date, took place between two storied programs in front of a sellout crowd at the famed Carver-Hawkeye Arena in Iowa City. The attendance was a staggering 15,400 and that day marked the third largest dual meet crowd in NCAA history.

"The build up and talk was more on the end of Oliver," Ramos said. "He was 10-0 with ten first period falls. But, to me, that meant nothing. People knew I was tough and that I was going to give him everything I had—and let's not forget [the match] was also in Carver-Hawkeye Arena."

In the week leading up to the dual, Terry Brands worked simply on helping Tony improve. "In moving forward," Terry Brands said, "[we] are always working on improving our wrestling and our positioning to be better. But we still want to be familiar with our opponent. I mean, look at what Oliver did to Stieber and how he whizzered down and stepped over and got near fall [points]. You know, we want to be aware of those kinds of things, but we don't focus on them. Our focus is what we are doing to get better."

In addition to the training, there were lighthearted talks between acquaintances. The match-up was attractive for a number of reasons for fans and wrestling experts; however, it was fun for those within the wrestling community as well.

"Izzy called me beforehand," Ramos remembered, "and told me Oliver had told Mark Perry that he was going to take me down, cradle me, let me up, take me down, cradle me, and then pin me. I laughed and told Izzy I would love to see him try."

As Tony's wrestling improved, so did his popularity with the Iowa fans. Very early into the season, the redshirt sophomore was one of the faces of Iowa wrestling and a fan favorite. The fans took to Tony because of his style and the fact that he wrestled with a chip on his shoulder. Plus, he was accessible to the fans.

"I think this started to happen early on that season, but I was more aware of it after the Oliver match," Ramos said. "The fans loved my personality so much. I was great with the kids and fans always taking time after a win or loss to sign autographs and take pictures and it was something they greatly appreciated. I don't think I realized how big I had become and how fast it all happened, but I did see it happening. I had fans excitingly involved in every match I competed in and [gave them] something to look forward to. To me, it was great. I loved being in the spotlight and under the microscope. It made me train harder and stay smart outside of the wrestling room."

Tony had no difficulties speaking to any one single person or the media as a whole about his matches, his wrestling, his training, his opinions, coaches, wrestlers, anything and anybody—he was open, honest, brash, and a great interview. The Iowa fans loved it and gravitated to him because of it. But there was another reason.

"Why did the Iowa fans take to Tony Ramos?" Terry Brands said. "Because he won. He was a winner and he had a knack about him where he could talk and then back it up. It wasn't a situation where he couldn't back up the things that he was saying. He was going to be the best and when it came to those big dual matches, he showed up. One that comes to mind immediately is the Oklahoma State dual against Oliver."

When the night of the dual arrived, the stage was set. In addition to the Tony Ramos and Jordan Oliver match-up, Iowa's eighty-four-consecutive dual meet record, as well as their thirty-eight-consecutive home dual meet record, was on the line. In fact, the last time the Hawkeyes had lost a dual, it was to the Oklahoma State Cowboys four years earlier on January 5, 2008—Iowa was bested 19-14.

So now, in addition to the historic rivalry, topped off with the battle for the top team in the country, the night's headlines were just getting started.

The wrestlers were weighed in, the coaches were in their corners, the teams in their seats or in their warm-up areas, and the fans were eager and in full support of their programs as they flaunted their colors and their critiques on how the entire dual would wrestle out.

As the draw dictated, the heavyweights opened the action and Oklahoma State's second-ranked Alan Gelogaev took the mat against Iowa's redshirt freshman Bobby Telford.

Gelogaev came out with a big throw to Telford's back to open the dual and sent the Cowboy crowd into a frenzy as the Oklahoma State bench erupted in anticipation of the fall; however, Telford fought and recovered to his belly to save the team points. But, by the match's conclusion, the Cowboys' heavyweight, too experienced and athletic, gave his team an early 4-0 lead with a 10-2 major decision.

Next up was the 125-pound weight class, and it was the 2009 NCAA champion and two-time finalist for Iowa, Matt McDonough, against the number-eight ranked Jon Morrison.

McDonough did not disappoint the Iowans there in attendance. He put on a display that enticed the black and gold in the stands as he tied the dual 4-4 with a statement match—he defeated Morrison by a 14-4 major decision and, every time he scored on each of his six takedowns, the Iowa yellow foam Two Takedown finger decorated throughout Carver as echoes of "TWO!" were being hollered in unison.

Now tied, the dual was set to fall into its greatest match-up of the night out of the first three weight classes. It featured number-one ranked Jordan Oliver and number-three ranked Tony Ramos. The anticipation of the match, in conjunction with the crowd's cheers and excitement, were already running high. Once the wrestlers were announced and they reported to the center of the mat, the anticipation and energy was immediately heightened even more.

This would be Oliver's first match back after a small layoff; however, the seasoned defending national champion had already amassed a perfectly impressive 10-0 record. For Tony, already 16-1 with his only loss occurring in the Midlands' finals, he was in his own building, comfortable, and confident.

"Terry kept reminding me before the match that I had to be extremely strong for the first 1:45," Ramos remembered. "If I could survive the first 1:45, then I would be in the match. We both knew that Oliver not making it out of the first period in any of his matches would only play to my advantage. I had the conditioning and strength that not many people had felt in their lifetime. And Oliver was about to feel it."

When Oliver arrived to the center of the mat, Tony's stare was already on the line waiting for him.

The first period was filled with high emotions, high intensity, but no points. Tony tied on the head and looked to wear down Oliver and make the first period difficult on him; likewise, he stayed in good position as Oliver had the power to strike and score from any position either offensively or defensively.

"He came out hard," Ramos said, "and I weathered the storm the first 1:45. He did get to me, but I defended him. The first period ended tied, 0-0. I think this was right about when people started to believe it might happen."

With each snap and circle the crowd anticipated and waited on the edge of their seats. Iowa's mascot, Herky, was mat side pacing and anticipating. Herky slapped his hands and shook his head and looked to the mat and then to the fans and then back to the mat. Iowans, some in their black and gold striped overalls, were bouncing and watching and waiting. And the coaches, both Brands brothers for the Hawkeyes and John Smith for the Cowboys, moved up and down the sides of their mat, coaching and hollering and encouraging and contesting.

The next two periods consisted of position battles as each wrestler scored an escape, but Oliver was hit with two cautions in a series of referee's position. Also in the process, Oliver earned an unofficial point from the top position by generating a riding advantage over Tony. Therefore, in reality, with about 00:36 left in the match, Oliver was winning by an unofficial 2-1 score as long as he could maintain his 1:08 rider.

The score, though close, was not due to an entirely conservative match on either wrestlers' part. There were risks taken by each wrestler and, more than anything else, great defense was executed in the form of sprawls, reattacks, and scrambles. However, through all of the defensive scrambles, none was more impressive than the first of two incredible battles that took place.

In that first scramble, Oliver took a shot and pulled out of it as Tony down blocked and reattacked with a high-crotch. Oliver, seemingly surprised by the reshot and off balance, was able to instinctively secure his key lock defense on his left leg as Tony switched his knees and defeated Oliver's defense and brought the leg up in the air.

In unison with Tony reattacking the leg and Oliver locking down after his stumble, every fan in Carver was on his feet and either screaming or coaching or officiating or watching in disbelief or shock or uncertainty on who would come out of the position. Cameramen were snapping continuous photos and the announcers were in full excitement of the moment. Carver was ignited. There was no lowering the decibels for the remainder of the match—everyone there knew they were in for something special as the two wrestlers, the center of attention, continued to attack their position.

With Tony in tight, just above Oliver's knee, Oliver defended and hopped on one leg. Oliver, who looked to break the hold, attacked Tony's hands and Tony ended up in a hand fight. That battle returned both wrestlers to the mat as Oliver worked to maintain his balance and not give up the takedown.

Again, with Oliver in his key lock, Tony repositioned his knees and again worked to his feet—this time with a more secure lock on Oliver's leg, so secure that, as Oliver tried to defend, Tony held him suspended in the air for a brief moment.

As the position was continually being fought by each wrestler, they worked back to the mat again, neither conceding position nor the fight and, as Tony tried to step over, Oliver looked for a tilt out of the key lock defense. Tony, having felt the tilt, was able to reposition his hips, raise his head and, as he turned back into Oliver, and Oliver's head was now posting on the mat, a takedown seemed imminent.

In that moment, as Tony was turning into Oliver. He was finally able to free his arm with a limp arm drag as Oliver found himself positioned with his head on the mat, his right knee posting away from Tony on the mat, and his left leg caught in between Tony's armpit. There, somehow, Oliver was able to turn his hips as Tony climbed the body and Oliver did the front splits freeing his once collapsed head and body which was now over Tony's head. Underneath, Tony was still working to score around the left leg and Oliver's right hip.

As Tony circled to his left and brought the fight back to their feet, he tripped Oliver with his right foot and Oliver hit the mat. But, upon Oliver hitting the mat, Tony somehow lost his balance. In that stumble, Oliver popped up and turned back into him, now having found his leg free as the wrestlers were back on their feet and in the neutral position.

Herky, along the mat, was in utter disbelief as some Iowa fans had their hands on their heads in amazement that the takedown was not scored. The same was true of the Cowboy fans, except they were ecstatic and boasted about Oliver's athleticism. Each fan knew the magnitude of that position and the possibilities it brought to the match and the dual as a whole.

Now, as the match reached that 00:30 mark in the final period, Tony needed to find another attack. When he shot in and fought his way into Oliver's legs a second time, the stakes were a must score to win or lose the fight and lose the match.

When Tony took his high-crotch to Oliver's right side, he quickly circled and found himself up on his feet. However, unlike the first time, Tony was able to lift the leg and work it to a point where Oliver was forced to hop, off balance, and Tony kicked Oliver's right leg out with his left leg.

As they were both falling toward the out of bounds line, Oliver turned away to kick out and, as he did this, Tony lunged at him perfectly-timed and captured the other leg as they hit the mat and Carver was again on its feet and out of control.

In that same moment, as Tony locked his arms around the ankles and thigh of Oliver, Tom and Terry Brands were right there in front of the action intensely encouraging the official make the call as they pointed and signaled a takedown inbounds. As the referee's two fingers shot up into the air to signal the takedown, Herky jumped up and down along with the thousands of the Iowa faithful who launched their fingers to the sky with an echoed "TWO!"—the arena was loud, and filled with excitement and an upset was brewing.

The points were awarded and the two were called out of bounds; there would be a restart in the middle of the mat. Again, Oliver's rider was at 1:08, so Tony needed to hold him down for nine seconds to secure a 3-1 lead as long as Oliver did not escape.

When the whistle blew with 00:22 remaining in the match, Tony attacked the right ankle on the same side that he covered. Oliver, calm and seemingly patient, fought and ultimately kicked out as the Oklahoma bench was frantically motioning for him to escape. But there was an issue at the table with the correct riding time and that impacted the score.

"After that takedown," Ramos said, "I knew that I had won. All I had to do was ride him out for eight seconds. But, when the whistle blew on the restart, the time keeper ran the riding time clock the wrong way. While this was going on, they had to take a break after Oliver escaped to figure out the clock issue.

"There were maybe six seconds left in the match, but after they came back from the discussion, I looked up and the crowd erupted when the riding time was erased and down to 00:59—no matter what, I was going to win. Of course, John Smith ran over and talked to the refs and, magically, the time got changed to 1:01."

With the escape and the riding advantage, Oliver was awarded two more points and the match went into overtime tied 3-3.

Caught up in the moment, not one person was sitting, not one voice was being unused, and not one camera was being un-shot. No one was purchasing food or using the bathroom or buying a souvenir—the keepsake was the match in front of their eyes.

In the first overtime period, there were no takedowns. The match went to the mat for the thirty-second ride out.

Tony went into the down position to start and Oliver jumped the whistle for his third caution point and that gave Tony the lead, 4-3. When the caution was given, Iowa fans were already signaling the one point before the official was able to motion to the table. The continued cheers only grew louder and louder with each moment.

Oliver would ride Tony out for the thirty-second period and then he chose down. He needed an escape to tie the match and force another overtime. All Tony had to do was ride him out and he would win the match.

As Tony covered and the whistle blew, Tony rode Oliver with all he had—off and on. The fans were frantically screaming and uncontrollably jumping as all were swallowed whole in the moment. When the final seconds ticked, and fans were counting it down, Tony held onto Oliver in the center of the mat. When time expired, Tom Brands punched his fist into the air and Carver's volume had reached a level that it had not heard in a number of years.

When Tony raised himself from Oliver, and Oliver paused on his two knees now conscious of the noise, Tony stood tall and flexed his double rainbow pose and circled so all the fans could see him—it only enticed them to scream even louder when he paused his flex and stared at the Cowboy bench.

"The arena erupted so loud," Ramos said, "that still, to this day, people talk about it being one of the loudest moments ever in Carver-Hawkeye Arena."

In the stands, "It was completely crazy," Megan recalled. "It was such an ecstatic atmosphere that your body would react [to what happened, just] jumping up and down before your mind even knew what was going on. It was such a high."

"The Oliver match," Terry Brands said, "was probably the second or third loudest Carver Hawkeye has ever been. And some could argue that one, [but it was loud]."

Tony recalled, "I was so pumped up and excited that I just accomplished what many people thought to be impossible," he said. "But, in my mind and life, that word 'impossible' does not exist. I believed that I could win and I might have been one of the only people along with four others who truly believed it. I remember even my dad said afterwards, 'I really thought you didn't have a chance.'"

In the win over Oliver, Tony became the first college wrestler to defeat him in two years.

"What stood out to me was the toughness," Terry Brands said. "And then in the end, to be able to put the ride down on him. On their side I know they're thinking, *Okay, we got this.* On our side we're saying, 'I don't think you realize what you've got ahold of here.' You're trying to hold lightning and thunder, and you can't hold onto that. It was one of those things that make Tony Ramos, Tony Ramos, and why he was able to show up for big duals in big ways."

What made Tony exciting for the fans, aside from his wrestling, was the fact that he soaked it all in and shared that with the fans.

"Guys like Tony Ramos wear their emotions on their sleeves," Tom Brands said. "Some guys they win and they run out of the tunnel and you never see them again. Ramos would sit out there and he would bask in the glow. And he loved it. And that's one of the things that was a catalyst for him—was, 'Hey, I get to be the man.' And when it was his time to be the man, he was the man."

Never short on confidence, Tony lived for those moments. "I didn't really see [Ramos' confidence] in the room," Dan Gable said. "I saw it in matches. In the room you need to develop a reputation and carry it through to competitions—so [his confidence] doesn't surprise me."

In Tony's perspective, he was providing a dual personality, depending on who the people in the stands were rooting for. But, either way, he was bringing fans in, making his wrestling exciting, and helping the sport grow.

"People love winners, but people love villains, too," Ramos said. "Either way, they came to an Iowa meet and they're cheering for me or against me—but it gave them something to cheer for. They're like, 'You know, I'm going to this meet and I hope Tony Ramos gets killed. I hate Tony Ramos.' But they're talking about [me], right? Whether you're the hero or whether you're the villain, it doesn't matter. If there were people on every team that had something like that, it doesn't have to be a stare down but their own little thing that they do, people are going to come to see that. And they're going to talk about it. And they're going to ask questions about it. It's going to draw more attention to the sport—it's going to draw more attention to them. We need more, I don't want to say characters, but we need more characters, pretty much, in wrestling."

However, with all of the excitement in that one match, it was still only the third match of the dual. Tony's win gave the Hawkeyes a 7-4 lead heading into Montell Marion's match-up against Josh Kindig.

Marion would win a 9-7 decision and stretch Iowa's team score to a 10-4 lead. However, Oklahoma State would fire back with back-to-back wins by Jamal Parks, an 8-3 decision over Mike Kelly, and Albert White at 157, he won a 7-4 decision over Nick Moore. These two matches tied the dual at 10-10 with four matches remaining.

At 165, Iowa's Mike Evans outscored Dallas Bailey, 5-1, but the Cowboy's Chris Perry evened up the team score at 13-13 with a 3-2 overtime tie-breaker against Ethan Lofthouse.

With two matches left, the Hawkeyes took their first lead as Vinnie

Wagner defeated Chris McNeil, 4-3. This left it up to the 197-pound wrestlers.

In the end, Blake Rosholt of Oklahoma State would outlast Iowa's Grant Gamball, 8-4, and even though the dual was tied at 16-16, criteria dictated who would be the number-one team in college wrestling.

The first criteria was wins, each team had five. The second criteria was falls, neither team scored a fall. But the third criteria did determine the dual. It came down to total match points scored. Oklahoma State scored 54 to Iowa's 51 and they would be awarded the tie-breaker point.

In that, the dual win went to the Cowboys, 17-16, and the Hawkeye dual meet consecutive win streak ended at eighty-four. Additionally, the thirty-eight-consecutive dual meet wins in Carver-Hawkeye Arena also came to a halt.

After the dual, Tom Brands spoke to the media about how, "There are two things we need to address as a team," he said. "One is you have to put unbelievable emphasis on your wrestling. We didn't do that. In some cases we did. The other thing is rolling, falling into positions of the opponent way too much. And it bit us. I would say the same thing if we were the winner of the [tiebreak] criteria."

For Tony, even though he won, he knew there was still work to do. However, the Carver-Hawkeye Arena magic and vision that he had when he walked in on his recruiting trip had now become a reality. The fans were electrified by his match and their intensity echoed throughout the hallowed walls and helped lift Tony's wrestling in such a way that Tony was able to pull the rabbit out of the hat.

That match, though, only marked the halfway point of the season and there was still much to work on as he would face a familiar and talented foe in about a two weeks' time when the Hawkeyes traveled to Ohio State University to wrestle the Buckeyes. Tony, now ranked number-two in the country, would have to face redshirt freshman Logan Stieber who was currently ranked number four. Again, the anticipation was high.

2012 • DUAL MEET VERSUS OKLAHOMA STATE UNIVERSITY AT CARVER
RAMOS TAKES DOWN OLIVER • RAMOS WON A 4-3 OVERTIME DECISION
PHOTOGRAPH COURTESY • UNIVERSITY OF IOWA ATHLETICS

CHAPTER 44
LET IT BEGIN

"It was a good year, but there was a huge road block ahead of me. If I wanted to win that national title, he was a man I was going to have to beat. So, I need to get to work and find a way to do it."

• Tony Ramos

AFTER TONY HAD UPSET THE NUMBER-ONE ranked restler in the country, the team headed to Lincoln, Nebraska, for a Big Ten dual with the number-nine rated Cornhuskers. The team score was never in question and the Hawkeyes handed Nebraska their first dual loss of the season with a 24-9 final score. Tony continued to build on his Oliver win and earned a decision for the Hawkeyes. In the process, he capitalized on three third period takedowns to defeat the number-eighteen ranked Ridge Kelly, 10-3.

Next, the Hawks hosted and defeated the Northwestern Wildcats, 24-13. In the dual, Tony faced another Illinois product in Jameson Oster—Tony won by fall in 2:34. This would be his fifth pin on the season.

For the next two duals, the Hawkeyes faced much more difficult opponents in Ohio State and Penn State—rated seventh and third, respectively—and the duals were away from Carver. Additionally, for the Ohio State dual, Tony would be involved in a match-up that many anticipated. He would face a true freshman and the number-four ranked wrestler in the country at 133, Logan Stieber.

Up to that point, Tony had only suffered one defeat; after, he had dominated and shocked the rest of the field. However, headed into his dual with Stieber, Tony knew where he had to wrestle and where he could not afford to be in order to win. Even though Tony had defeated Stieber the last time they wrestled—the 2009 Junior World Team Trials—he had a quality opponent and he needed to be prepared.

"That first match in Columbus," Ramos said, "was a big match and everyone was looking forward to it. In fact, [my girlfriend] Megan [Eskew] and her dad drove out from Indiana through like five hours of traffic and storms just to come watch."

As Stieber prepared for the match, he also knew he had a tough opponent in Tony and, unlike the last time they wrestled, he would be prepared. "My plan was to take him down and ride him," Stieber said. "I knew that if he had a weak spot at all, it was maybe bottom. So I thought that if it was a close match, a riding point could be the difference. He had just beaten Oliver, so he was ranked ahead of me. I knew it would be a big match."

When the match began, the true freshman immediately took control and Tony found himself in a deficit right away. The Buckeye fans cheered and enticed Stieber to extend his lead, which he did, and Tony suffered an unexplainable 7-0 loss—now his second loss on the season.

"I got beat in every aspect of that match from my feet to the mat," Ramos said. "I knew if I wanted to win, I couldn't let him score at all. After that match, I worked really hard on my defense and improved and focused on defending where he was very good, and that was his single-leg to his cut back. I went over it hundreds of times with Terry and my partner, Trizzino. We also started working religiously on getting out of his claw ride."

There was, however, a greater issue. Even though it was only one match and one loss, there would still be the Big Ten Championships and the NCAAs to wrestle. In that, some were worried that Tony might struggle to win a Big Ten and a national championship if he and Stieber were to share a weight class due to the point differential from their first collegiate encounter.

"When I returned home," Ramos remembered, "I was still working through the match. Megan came over and we started talking—she immediately addressed the match. First, she wasn't too happy with having made that trip due to the performance I had and whatnot."

Megan remembered that "We were sitting in the front row," she said, "and Tony got handled; which is something I hadn't seen before. When he got home, I had more words for him. I like to think I keep Tony grounded; he would probably say that I'm mean. I told him that he needed to get his head out of his butt and that I know how he prepares for every match and that week he was too casual about everything. I had thought he was on a hot streak and getting a little too cocky. He usually ignores me or gives me a hard time about it, and I told him he wasn't the one that had to watch him struggle off his back."

Tony recalled the conversation. "She mocked me and said, 'You were just sitting there—it looked like you were just helpless,' Tony said. "I started laughing like, 'What do you mean?' She goes, 'He just turned you over and you were like, 'Eeeee! I can't do anything.' I was like, 'Are you kidding me right now? You're making fun of me about losing that match?' That was one of the things that stuck with me and why she was so good for me. I knew I had to pick it up or I was coming home and being made fun of by my girlfriend."

Having Megan bring Tony back to reality was a comfort, but to Tony, it was simply one match that he had to move on and learn from. As he had done in the past, he bounced back in his next competitions. He traveled to State College and opened up a 7-2 lead on Frank Martellotti before he locked up a cradle and won by fall in 4:20.

Seven days later, the now number-six rated Hawkeyes welcomed the number-three rated Golden Gophers of Minnesota into Carver for a dual that was decided via bonus points; however, the dual had opened up well in the hands of the Hawks.

After McDonough scored a 7-1 win over top ranked Zach Sanders at 125, Tony faced the very familiar Chris Dardanes. Tony took control of his match in the second period with an escape and a takedown with three seconds left. He gave up a reversal, escaped, and scored on 1:03 riding advantage. Tony took the bout with a 5-2 decision and the Hawkeyes led 6-0.

Iowa's Montell Marion defeated Nick Dardanes before Minnesota's Dylan Ness majored Michael Kelly. This put the Hawks in front 9-4. Nick Moore and Mike Evans ended up being the difference for the Hawks and the dual with a major decision and fall before Minnesota won the final four bouts via one major and three regular decisions. Each team won five matches; however, the fall by Evans, in addition to the major decision by Moore, sealed a 19-17 victory and the Hawkeyes continued to build toward the Big Ten Championships.

Next up for Tony was an opportunity to avenge his loss at the Midlands. He and the team traveled to Ames, Iowa, for the Regional qualifier for the NWCA/Cliff Keen National Duals. They were scheduled to wrestle the number-twenty-three rated Virginia Tech Hokies, and, if they won, they faced the number-sixteen rated team,
Oregon State.

Tony, now ranked number-four at 133, opened up against the number-one ranked Devin Carter of Virginia Tech—Carter had earned his one-ranking after he defeated Tony in December.

"Back at the Midlands," Ramos commented, "I let that [match] get away. I wasn't going to let that happen a second time. Going in, I was confident and I knew that if I dictated my match, there was no way that I was going to lose."

And that was exactly what happened—Tony went out and controlled the match. After a scoreless first period where Tony dictated the tempo, he scored on a second-period takedown. Headed into the third, Tony chose down and earned an escape for the 3-2 decision. The Hawkeyes won the dual by a convincing 31-3 margin.

Headed into their final match against Oregon State for the Regional Championship, the Hawkeyes continued their dominance and defeated the Beavers by a 22-14 score. Tony had a major decision wrapped up against James Roberts, but Tony pushed the match and his opponent and earned a 24-8 technical fall when he turned Roberts for a near fall as time expired.

Tony was back to wrestling aggressively and in control and scoring points in his matches. He would head to Stillwater, Oklahoma, for the National Dual Championships and have two more duals with solid opponents before the Big Tens—including Tony, all three were Illinois high school products and very acquainted. Tony's matches would be against Minnesota's Dardanes and Illinois' Futrell.

In the Minnesota dual, Tony was locked in a 1-1 tie headed into overtime. He not only scored a takedown in overtime to seal it, but he put Dardanes to his back and the score ended in a 6-1 victory.

"[Dardanes] really had me caught up in the hand fight that match," Ramos said. "He was one of the strongest [guys] that I competed against. I spent too much time trying to out hand fight him instead of out wrestling him. I knew I had to correct this."

Even though Tony earned the victory, the team suffered a 16-15 loss and was resigned to the third-place match against Illinois.

When it was time for the match against Futrell, Tony picked up where he left off and scored two takedowns and an escape to secure a 5-2 victory. That was the third time Tony had defeated Futrell in as many matches. As Tony had handled his match, the team handled the dual with a 28-6 performance.

"I think after I lost that first time last year," Ramos said, "I knew I would never lose to Futrell again. He was a strong opponent, but I separated myself from him and a lot of guys—the gap was just too big after that first year. But heading into the Big Tens, my goal was to win it. I had one guy that I had to ultimately beat, and that was Stieber—he got the one seed and I got the two."

THE BIG TEN CHAMPIONSHIPS WERE HELD IN West Lafayette, Indiana, on the campus of Purdue University. Since there was a clear separation of the top two wrestlers in the 133- pound bracket, the finals would be an inevitable match-up between Tony and Stieber.

For Tony, he had an opening round match versus Nebraska's Ridge Kiley; Tony advanced with a 12-2 major decision. In the semifinals, he again faced B.J. Futrell. Again, the distance between the two was too much for Futrell. Tony advanced to his first Big Ten finals with a 6-1 decision.

"With Futrell," Ramos said, "at this point, I knew how to beat him and I knew I was in his head. I went out and, in a very workman-like way, came out on top. He wanted to play the edge, the ref knew it but didn't want to call it, but I've got to finish my takedowns. [I just have to] keep on wrestling, it doesn't matter. If I don't get a shot, [I] have to keep on going back—he's going to break eventually. [He broke] after the first takedown. I knew as soon as I got a takedown it was over."

On the upper half of the bracket, Stieber advanced accordingly. In his opening round he defeated Wisconsin's Shane McQuade by fall in 2:43. In the quarterfinals he defeated Penn State's Frank Martellotti by a 13-2 major decision. And, prior to advancing to the championship match, he scored a 9-6 semifinal decision over Purdue's Cashè Quiroga.

In a post semifinal victory interview, Stieber was asked about his finals match-up with Tony and if he expected anything different from him. "No, it's the same stuff. Same hard-nose attitude. Same. [He's got] a great shot—great condition. It should be fun."

As for Tony, the finals was an opportunity for "redemption," he said. "I'm excited. I can't wait [for the match]."

When the time came for the two to wrestle, the stage was set and, as the match began, Tony scored first on a re-attack. Stieber escaped and scored a takedown of his own on a slide-by and rode Tony out in his belly-claw ride. The period ended with a 3-2 Stieber advantage.

In the second period, Stieber chose down and escaped. He also scored another takedown and rode Tony out for the remainder of the period. The score was 4-2 Stieber, and he would earn the riding time advantage in the process.

For the third period, Tony chose down. However, once he chose down, he was never able to find the neutral position. Stieber rode him out for the entire third period and, when the final whistle sounded and Tony lost, "I was frustrated," Ramos remembered. "When that match ended, I was not ready for it to be over. We are both great competitors, and I wanted to keep on wrestling right then and there and I'm sure he wanted it to continue as well."

In fact, Tony wanted to keep wrestling so much that, once he shook hands with Stieber, he had a few choice words for him.

"I don't remember exactly the words exchanged," Ramos said, "but I do remember it wasn't really anything. We respected each other as competitors, and that was all it was. It was two competitors going hard."

Stieber saw the final moment with Tony the same way. "He's upset, you know, he lost," Stieber said. "But he's tough. He's obviously going to be upset. It's just two competitors—[it was] not a big deal."

The match ended in a 5-2 decision for Logan Stieber, and the true freshman claimed his first Big Ten championship as well as won his second-straight match against Tony.

"It was a tough match," Stieber said. "I knew what was going to happen—he was going to push the pace the whole time. He got the early takedown, but my main goal was to get a takedown in the first period because the last time I wrestled I didn't score until the end. I knew I could maybe ride him if I could take him down, so that was the big thing: Escape. Takedown. Ride out. That was probably the biggest part of the match for me."

For Tony, it was back to the practice room. He knew that in order to win a national championship, he had to beat Stieber. He truly believed he could do it. Of course, he had to work through some of his struggles in the twelve days that led up to the NCAA championships.

"Stieber is a very great position wrestler who was so stingy and hard to score on," Ramos said. "He gave me trouble [at the Big Tens] because his mat wrestling is very good. After I took second, I remember Tom sitting down with me at practice that next week and looking at me and saying, 'These guys don't understand that this isn't a game—this is an all-out fight. And that's what you're going to have to make it to beat this guy.' Going into the NCAAs, that was my attitude. I needed to make it an all-out war where no matter who I wrestled, they just wouldn't be able to hold up."

WHEN THE BRACKETS CAME OUT FOR THE NCAA

championships, Tony found himself seeded third. Ahead of him was the number-one seed, Jordan Oliver, and the number-two seed, Logan Stieber.

"I was a little surprised by the seeding," Ramos admitted. "I beat Oliver and lost to Stieber—I figured I would be second, Jordan third, and that would be my path to the finals. But when I saw [the brackets] I was thought, *Perfect. I know I can beat him.* I just had to take it match by match and then go prove it."

Tony's second national championship, held in St. Louis, Missouri, opened with unseeded Brian Owen of Boise State. The match was controlled by Tony and he scored a 9-2 decision to advance.

"That match I controlled every position," Ramos said. "The only thing that bothered me was not getting the major for the team. I kept the pressure on, but I couldn't get to that final takedown. Other than that, I was advancing and that was important."

In his next match, Tony faced another unseeded wrestler—Aaron Kalil of Navy; however, the match was closer in score.

"Even though I won 3-1, I still feel that I controlled that match," Ramos said. "I scored my takedown, got out on bottom, and held my position."

Now in the quarterfinals, Tony faced the number-eleven seed, Harvard's Steve Keith. Keith, who just came off a big 8-6 victory over the number-six seed, Devin Cater of Virginia Tech, looked to keep his momentum going. The only problem was that Tony was setting his sights on Stieber, and Keith was simply in the way. Tony won by fall in 1:57 and was now in the national semifinals, a guaranteed All-American, and up against the only wrestler between him and the opportunity to win a national championship.

The Friday night match-up in St. Louis would be Tony's greatest match to date and he felt prepared for Stieber mentally and physically. In regard to what he felt he needed to do to win the match, "I had to stay solid and get out on bottom," he said. "As long as I didn't give him long opportunities on top, I would have a chance. And, as Tom said, I needed to make the match a seven-minute fight."

Before the match began, Tony was already out in the middle of the mat, on the starting line, waiting, staring at his opponent. As the referee started the match, the head tie came down hard and strong from Tony; however, Stieber remained calm, cool, and collected as he knew what to expect.

With one minute gone in the first period, each wrestler jockeyed for head and hand position, it was another thirty seconds before either wrestler worked to an advantage. And when that time came, it was Stieber on the first attack.

At the 1:33 mark, Tony had a left-handed underhook and Stieber came down hard, with his left hand and a head snap of his own that freed up enough space for a left-sided sweep single. Once in, the fight against Tony's defense began. Stieber found his hands locked around Tony's right leg, high near the hip; Tony brought his hips in with a strong right-armed whizzer.

As Stieber continued his fight, he worked to his feet and Tony remained tight on the whizzer, balancing on his left hand, with his right arm defending and his right leg being lifted in the air. Soon, however, Tony's defense dropped Stieber back down to the mat and Tony squared up on him—he was working a left-side belly whizzer and looked to break the lock with his right hand. After the total fight, thirty-three seconds later, the stalemate was called and both wrestlers were back on their feet.

The final minute consisted of Tony's right-handed head tie and Stieber's left-handed head tie as the two pressured back and forth. Neither conceded and the first period ended in a 0-0 tie.

On the disc flip, Tony won the choice; however, he deferred and Stieber chose the down position.

Stieber positioned himself set, Tony covered from the right side and, fourteen seconds later, Stieber was up and out with a 1-0 lead. Almost immediately, Tony moved forward as he created pressure and snapped Stieber and took a half shot to Stieber's left leg. Stieber sprawled, kicked his leg back, and fired in on a shot of own. Without hesitation, Tony snapped and re-attacked the re-attack and found himself in on Stieber's left leg—Tony fought to circle as his head was caught between Stieber's legs. Stieber reached around Tony and worked to stay heavy on the body. After a thirteen-second fight, the referee called another stalemate. There was now 1:17 left in the second period and the score remained a 1-0 Stieber advantage. That score never changed as the period came to an end.

In the third period, Tony had the choice and he avoided the bottom position and chose neutral—he put himself in his strongest position. When the wrestlers approached the line and the whistle blew to start the period, Stieber immediately shot in on Tony's right leg and the two began their fight once again. Just as before, Stieber looked to bring Tony's leg up, and, just as before, Tony fought with his right-hand whizzer and balanced himself, pressuring in with his left hand on the mat for balance.

The two continued their position battle and, as Tony saw an opening and pounded into Stieber with his hips, Stieber used that pressure against Tony and took his right leg from the outside to the inside and dropped him into a split position with his legs. Tony fought the position, but Stieber, with an angle, cut off Tony's defense and went behind him for a takedown and a 3-0 lead.

On top, Stieber used his belly-claw ride and Tony worked to come up and find a way back to his feet. When he did come up, Stieber sat him out and turned; however, in the second attempt to do so, Tony dug under Stieber's foot with his right hand, elevated it high, thus dropping Stieber's hip to the mat and lowering his back, as Tony used his left hand as a post. Tony hip-hoisted through for a reversal and, for the first time, found himself in a control position. The Iowa fans called out the "TWO!" points with the referee as Tony kept the pressure on and worked a nearside cradle.

But, once he realized he was not be able to lock up the cradle, Tony cut Stieber for the escape and the match would be a takedown away, 4-2, as neither wrestler had a riding advantage and there was 1:07 remaining in the semifinal bout.

For the next thirty seconds, Tony moved forward and attacked; however, Stieber, with great position and a strong head and hand defense, fended him off. Then, with about 00:28 left, Tony opened up and got in on a sweep single to Stieber's left leg off a head snap—he was now a takedown away from securing a 4-4 tie in the match.

As Tony reached across for the finish, with 00:23 left, Stieber locked around Tony's waist and rolled him through, ended up on top of Tony as each refused to concede their position.

With 00:16 remaining, Tony was sitting on his left hip trying to chase behind Stieber, but Stieber remained locked in tight to Tony's hips and kept his right knee posted in the mat for position. Tony kept trying to cut the corner and he lifted Stieber's leg, but, as he did before, Stieber rolled him through, locked in the crotch for what looked like a cradle attempt off the finish—00:07 left.

Tony then tried to post up as Stieber remained locked: 00:06. Tony raised and tried to swing the single-leg and dropped Stieber's hip as he remained fastened to Tony's back still locked: 00:04. The fight continued but now near the mat's edge: 00:03. Stieber's hip hit the mat, but no finish followed: 00:01. And Stieber, sitting on the mat with Tony coming off his leg, punched his fist in the air as the whistle ended the match and he advanced to the national championship match.

Disappointed, Tony came to his feet, took off his ankle bands, and threw them into the center of the mat from about seven feet away. He stomped to the center, shook hands with Stieber, and overhead the announcer called out, "The Buckeye with the win in the 133-pound semifinal. Your winner, Logan Stieber."

As Tony went to collect himself, Stieber was interviewed. "Every match is different with [Ramos]," Stieber said. "It was a tough match and I'm glad I won. The scramble at the end, I had been working with my coaches a lot on defense and instead of giving up takedowns, I try to roll. It's not super-fundamentally sound, but it's been working a lot and it showed. He didn't choose down last time I wrestled him, so I didn't think he would. But that's to my advantage because it's almost like I'm starting each match 1-0 with him. I knew he was going to push the pace on his feet, so that takedown I scored was really big."

On the top side of the bracket Jordan Oliver defeated the number-four seed, Futrell of Illinois, by an 8-2 decision. Oliver and Stieber would advance to the national championship match and Tony, for the second season in a row, found himself in the wrestle-backs. This time, however, he had already claimed All-American honors—his wrestling, now, would simply determine how high he would stand on the podium.

"I WAS UPSET THAT I DIDN'T WIN," RAMOS SAID.

"But I also felt I competed hard and made it a battle that I knew he didn't want to be in much longer. Unfortunately, in wrestling, there is a time limit and he lasted just long enough. The match ended with me in on a double-leg."

Tom Brands' perspective reflected the toughness of wrestling and how hard the sport is; of course, he did so in a way that placed the responsibility and the ability to create opportunity and use an imagination solely on his wrestler.

"Wrestling is hard," Tom Brands said. "There's always more to give and it's hard. When he was in on Stieber, and Stieber rolls him—most guys roll and they come out and it's going to be neutral—there's my opportunity. Stieber rolls him through and there's a scramble and Ramos is still in there like a dog on a bone and he's coming up, but he got rolled again, and then I think he got flattened out. So, who gives himself two chances like that? Tony Ramos does. Why? Because he's stubborn. But, to beat a guy like Stieber, he had to find a way to give more.

"I'm not saying Ramos didn't work hard, he was a hard worker. He put his time in. I never had a problem with him [in the wrestling room]. Never. But could he give more? We can all give more. But he still had to wrestle. I told him, 'Where do you want to finish now?'"

There would be no time to sulk and Tony knew he had to come back strong and finish third for himself and for his team.

For his first wrestle-back, he had to face a competitor that he was already 1-1 with on the season. He held the only other loss on Tony's record other than the three losses to Stieber: Devin Carter of Virginia Tech.

The match would not be as close the 6-4 overtime loss in the Midlands finals, and it would not be as close as the 3-2 win at the National Duals. Tony came out and dominated with an 8-3 decision.

"Like I said, I knew after the Midlands that I let one get away," Ramos said. "But when I beat him at the [national] duals, and it was a close match, my confidence grew. This time I used what I knew already along with my attitude of making it a fight in all positions. I ended up scoring a lot of points and he knew the first time [when he won, he] was lucky."

With the 8-3 decision over Carter, Tony was now in the third-place match. He would again wrestle Illinois native, Chris Dardanes of Minnesota.

In their Big Ten dual, Tony had been a 5-2 decision winner; however, at the national duals, he won in a 6-1 overtime thriller. Dardanes had closed the gap and Tony knew his position and approach would be the difference in the match.

"This time around," Ramos said, "I didn't get caught up in who could bully who. I created angles and openings off the hand fight and [I] was picking him apart. I was up pretty big and started to coast with about twenty seconds left. I remember going out of bounds and Terry lighting me up about finishing the match the right way. As soon we went back to the center, he shot—this would be the first time I felt and hit my patented cow-catcher. All I needed to do was feel it one time and that feeling was ingrained in my mind and body."

Once Tony turned Dardanes, he stuck him. The official time was 6:50, and that was Tony's eighth fall of season. He earned the bonus points for his team and he claimed a third-place finish at the national championships.

In the tunnel, after he won, he was interviewed. "You're only as good as your last match," Ramos said. "You go out with a loss, you got to sit—especially if you can't do anything in the summer. It's a long way [to have another chance]. Now it's going to be 365 days to wait until next year because I didn't finish with what I wanted.

"[In that Stieber match, I'm] that close to finishing a takedown with time running out to send it into overtime—I got to do it. It's dropping the hip and it's going to haunt me forever because I know I can beat Jordan Oliver. I've done it once; I've done it already. Everyone thinks he's unstoppable—I don't.

"Last year I lost in the round of twelve and sat down [in the tunnel] and watched the finals—I want to wrestle up there. There's nothing bigger than that other than an Olympic title; that's where I want to be."

Stieber would go on to win the national championship with a 4-3 decision over Oliver, and Tony watched from inside the tunnel for a second-straight season.

Tony ended his redshirt sophomore campaign with a 33-4 record. He lost to Carter in the Midlands finals, was 7-0 in duals, 5-2 in Big Ten competition, and 5-1 at the NCAAs.

"It was a good year, but there was a huge road block ahead of me," Ramos said. "If I wanted to win that national title, he was a man I was going to have to beat. So, I needed to get to work and find a way to do it."

That same night, the Ramos family celebrated an All-American; however, Tony called his brother Frank to meet him for a conversation.

"When he came into my room," Defilippis said, "it was one of two really hard moments for me. Tony sat down and I looked at him and he said, 'I did it all right. I don't know why this happens to me.' I looked him in the eye, there was a pause because I had to ask the hard question: 'Did you?' He looked back at me and said, 'I think I did.'"

Frank looked at his younger brother, "This was hard to say because I know he worked hard. 'Well, something was telling me that maybe you did or maybe you didn't somewhere along the way. Maybe it was this or maybe it was that, but you can't leave anything to chance. You only get four chances at this and two of them are gone. You're half way through your career and you feel like it just started.' I knew that feeling. That I understood—it goes fast."

Frank and Tony sat there and talked. "We talked and, he doesn't cry much," Defilippis continued, "but that night, we had a moment."

As for what needed to change, "Nothing needed to change," Ramos said with confidence. "I just needed to keep getting better and believe in the training that I had been doing in my life to get me to where I was at this point. There was nothing out of the norm other than needing to keep improving on bottom and figuring out what it was going to take within myself to beat Stieber."

That spring and summer, "I still trained with the same guys," Ramos said. "Trizzino, Gurule, McDonough—all the same guys. But now I had some fresh blood coming in with some feisty attitudes in Cory Clark and Thomas Gilman. This was great for me because I worked that much harder to always make sure I put it on them so they knew who the big dog was."

ALSO, THAT SUMMER, THERE WOULD BE SOME

internal changes that shocked the wrestlers at Iowa and some of the Iowa fans. Iowa Head Coach Tom Brands and assistant coach Mike Zadick parted ways after the 2012 Olympic Trials. Zadick would leave Iowa and nobody would really understood why.

"I remember Tom pulling me to the side during the Iowa camps [that summer]," Ramos said, "and telling me, 'Hey, I am not hiring Zadick back. We are going to hire Morningstar. What do you think?' I was shocked, but I wasn't going to question him. All I said was, 'If that's what you believe is best, then okay.' Tom addressed a few of us athletes in private before telling Zadick. When he told Zadick, he just grabbed his stuff and left. Then, before practice, Tom informed everyone else on the situation. We all were in disbelief and didn't understand why, and we weren't going to ask. It was a very sore subject; we could all see that."

One of the aspects of Zadick's leaving that confused Tony the most was how well-liked and loyal Zadick was with the team and how he interacted with the wrestlers.

"Zadick had great relationships with the athletes outside of wrestling," Ramos said. "He would have us over to his farm house to help him do things like cut wood or build a fence and spend quality time away from the mat with the guys. Yes, we were still doing some type of work, but it was fun and you could just see how much he cared about us wrestlers.

"Even after Zadick left, he would still call us and ask if we could do favors for him, and I would be willing to bet not one guy ever told him no because, if it was us [asking him], you damn right know he would be doing whatever we needed. Not much was ever said about it, really. The only thing Tom had ever said to me was, 'If you want to keep your job, then you better do it the right way so I don't have to fire you.' I lost a great coach and training partner. Mike Zadick was one of the best coaches I had. He knew a great deal about wrestling and could translate it into teaching very well. No one will ever know the real or exact reason behind the firing of Mike Zadick, but it will go down as one of the biggest shocks to happen in Iowa history."

IN ADDITION TO THE HAWKEYE CHANGES, TONY was about to make a personal change in his own life and ask his girlfriend, Megan Eskew, to marry him. Megan had just graduated from Iowa where she was a four-year letter-winner and earned four All-Big Ten Academic awards for the Hawkeye volleyball program. She was also named a captain and co-most valuable player her senior season; she was now looking to follow her professional dreams.

"Megan always wanted to go back to Chicago, and be a big-time accountant at a big-time firm and that was her dream," Ramos said. "And then she met me and I kind of shut it down. I said, 'Hey, if you leave, or don't stay around, this relationship isn't going to work out. I can't do a long-distance thing, I'm going to be here 24-7. So, it's either you're going to stay here and we'll live together and that's the way it will be, or it's over. And she made a big decision to stick around and be with me and support me and the things I was doing. That was a big sacrifice on her part."

In that, the two officially moved in together and then, "Going into that junior season summer, there was a lot of controversy between Tom and Terry if I should get engaged or not," Ramos continued. "Terry was for it—he loves Megan; he's always loved her—kind of the same reasons why I fell in love with her. He saw what kind of person she was and how dedicated she was to the things she did sports-wise and how she understood [what it takes to compete at a high level].

"But Tom didn't think it was the right thing to do. He called me up and told me we needed to have a talk. We drove around and he explained that there is a time and a place for that kind of stuff and I didn't need to be doing it right now and this and that. But that same day Terry called and told me, 'Hey, you need to go and get married.'

"That's one of those instances," Ramos laughed, "where Tom always says, 'Me and Terry always plan to do the opposite things, don't we?' I was like, 'Yeah, you guys are never on the same page.' But, it eventually came down to what my choice was and I felt in my heart that it was the right thing to do. I don't know if my parents thought it was the right thing to do at the time, but I've made a lot of decisions really fast and things that some people might not have thought were best for me that worked out. I felt it was the right time and she made a major sacrifice by staying with me. So, I felt it was the right thing for me to do to make that next step, make that big decision, and get married and let her know I was ready to be married."

When it was time to propose, "He proposed on the deck of his duplex in Coralville," Megan remembered. "It was the end of July and I was studying for the CPA exam. Tony had just come home from a camp somewhere in Iowa and I was on the back deck getting some fresh air and taking a break from studying. I had left the sliding door open behind me and our Great Dane, Derby, came running out of the sliding door into the yard. Tony came flying into the yard after her. I was a little confused. He wrangled her onto the deck and I saw the ring around her bandana—Tony didn't realize I was outside and the ring was only secured with the Velcro of her bandana, so he thought she was going to lose it in the yard. I had an 'Oh my, gosh!' reaction. I think we both started crying and he asked me to marry him—after I reminded him to get down on one knee."

In that decision, Tony was supported nobly by his coaches, friends, and family. He was going to do what he wanted, regardless. That was Tony; and they appreciated that about him.

• • •

That following fall, before Tony's junior season would begin, he would support Megan and her position as an assistant volleyball coach for the Regina High School Regals. Her team would have a great run throughout their season and playoffs and "Tony agreed to be the mascot at the sendoff pep rally if my team made it to state," Megan explained. "It was that fall that I first found out about him being a mascot when he casually dropped an 'Oh yeah, at mascot camp...' during dinner."

In that, as hard as Tony was working, he was, as he always was, having fun and supporting those he loved when they needed him as well. "That is one of the things about Tony that I think a lot of people don't realize," Defilippis said, "he likes to laugh. He likes to have fun. Wrestling is hard and he needs an outlet—an outlet does not have to be a negative. He does silly things—joking things—that mascot was just another example of Tony having fun and being Tony."

MEGAN RAMOS' INSTAGRAM ACCOUNT
COURTESY • MEGAN RAMOS

CHAPTER 45
OFF TO A FAST START

"I don't know how he feels about me, but I don't like anyone that's at my weight. I don't like anyone that's from a different team. So, is there respect? Yes, there's respect. But, do I like him? No."

• *Tony Ramos*

COMING INTO HIS JUNIOR SEASON, TONY WAS now the face of the Iowa program and the fans and the media and the critics were all looking in his direction as the season was ready to begin for wins, tempo, interviews, and more wins.

As to why Iowa took to Tony Ramos, it was because, "Tony Ramos is a performer," Tom Brands said. "He's fun to watch. He was great for us because he impacted our room. Our fans don't care about anything but winning—they want to see champions. Now, sophomore year he's third, he's an All-American, and he's saying all the right things—you know, he's not shy—and he's got two years left. That's rare."

In regard to Tony being someone people loved to come out and watch, Dan Gable said he was not the only one that was curious to see what the next night brought out of the Hawkeye. "It wasn't only me, it was the people," Gable said. "They come for certain reasons. They come for the interesting character [of the wrestlers] and Tony had that name. Tony had that stare. Tony had that fight. And people in Iowa love that."

When the season opened, the face of Iowa did not disappoint. He strung together a very strong 10-0 run, recording five pins and five major decisions in that stretch. Tony's closest match was against Cody Kievman of Lehigh, 12-3—a nine-point differential. He was dominating and anybody that was in his way was being beaten in such a way that set

Tony apart.

However, Tony's eleventh match of the season was one that he had circled on his calendar since the semifinals of the NCAA championships the year before. The match-up featured the number-one Stieber against Tony who was ranked number two. The dual would be held in Iowa City and Tony was yet to lose at Carver-Hawkeye Arena.

In an interview two days before the dual, Tony spoke about the anticipation of the dual. "It is something I have been looking forward to a lot," Ramos said. "I've been focused on [this match-up] since the end of last year. It's something I knew was going to be around the corner, coming up, so we've been working for it all season long."

However, in response to his preparation and anticipation, the training was, "Not too much different," Ramos said. "[I] have to prepare for every match the same—just a little bit focused more on certain areas or certain techniques that we're trying to fine tune or sharpen up."

In his other match-ups with Stieber, Tony had been close; however, he had not been able to close the deal. He spoke to what he needed to do. "I got to get a takedown, I got to score, I need to ride hard on top, and I got to be able to get out on bottom," Ramos commented. "If [I] want to win a big match like this one, [I] need to get out on bottom and that's something I've been working on.

"We're used to each other, we've wrestled already a lot in college, we wrestled a lot in high school, we wrestled a lot growing up; so, we know what each other is going to bring to the table. But, either way you look at it, it's going to be a match, it's going to be a fight, and whoever wants it more is going to get it."

When asked what makes Stieber such a difficult opponent, Tony commented on how "He's a competitor. He's a gamer. We're both competitors and gamers and one little thing that you do wrong can change the match or the outcome of the match, so you've got to be prepared in every position. You've got to wrestle solid, and you've got to get your offense going."

From Tom Brands' point of view, Tony had to be focused for a full match. "He's going to have to be consistent for seven minutes," Tom Brands said. "And he's going to have to put together some good things that he's done in the [matches prior] and put them all together and keep doing those things for seven minutes in all positions."

When Tom Brands was asked what Tony had done to close the gap on Stieber, he simply stated: "That's a good question and that will be answered [in] forty-eight plus hours from now."

However good the wrestling was between Tony and Stieber, the relationship, when asked in an interview, at least from Tony's point of view, was one of respect, but with a dislike.

"I don't know how he feels about me," Ramos said, "but I don't like anyone that's at my weight. I don't like anyone that's from a different team. So, is there respect? Yes, there's respect. But, do I like him? No. Am I going to go out there and try to put my will on him and break him? Yes. So that's pretty much the kind of relationship that I see between us."

Unfortunately, with all of the buildup and all of the hype leading up to this match, it would never take place. Stieber ended up with a torn hamstring and did not weigh-in for the dual. Instead, Tony faced Kyle Visconti. In that match, Tony used fourteen takedowns and dominated every aspect of the bout to coast to a 30-14 win.

That Sunday, two days after the Ohio State dual, Tony won his twelfth match in a row. This time, it was against Purdue's Danny Sabatello and he scored a 13-4 major decision victory. Tony was wrestling at a high level, he was focused, and he was seven days away from his greatest challenge at the halfway point of the season.

FOR HIS THIRTEENTH MATCH OF THE 2013 season, Tony faced a longtime rival, the number-five ranked wrestler in the country, and a Cowboy, Jon Morrison of Oklahoma State. The dual was held at Gallagher-Iba Arena in Stillwater, Oklahoma, and a combined 5,537 Iowa and Oklahoma State fans attended the historic rivalry; unfortunately, it was not a sellout.

"[The atmosphere] wasn't as crazy as I expected it to be," Ramos said. "The arena wasn't sold out, which surprised me for such a big rivalry, but heading into the match I knew what I had to do to get the job done." The match against Morrison was Tony's first match-up with a ranked opponent, and his first match-up of the season with his longtime nemesis.

"I wanted to go out there and make a statement," Ramos said. "I was excited to finally get the rivalry between me and Morrison back on the map, but I also wanted to show all the people back in Illinois how much better I was and how I had grown in my college career."

When the night opened, the number-two rated Cowboys came out in their orange singlets as the number-four rated Hawkeyes were dressed in their traditional black and gold. There would be a total of fifteen ranked wrestlers walking out onto the mat—at least one ranked wrestler per weight class—and there would be five match-ups those ranked wrestlers.

As the dual opened, Iowa sent the number-one ranked wrestler in the country at 125 pounds, McDonough, out to the mat against Oklahoma State's Eddie Klimara. McDonough won a 10-4 decision and gave Iowa an early 3-0 dual lead.

Even though Tony was focused on his own wrestling and putting himself in position to win a national championship, he was not blind to the top-ranked contenders at his weight class—particularly Morrison. "I had seen the path of Morrison's career and what had been going on at the time," Ramos said. "He had not been at his best and was not the best. He was so up and down and I didn't expect to lose the match; however, I knew he would be very prepared and bring everything that he had."

After McDonough's match ended, Tony was quick to step onto the mat and work his way to the middle. His match-up with Morrison was very much anticipated by the fans as they knew the history and the dislike each possessed for the other.

And, as he had done before, Tony was out to the mat's center, staring and waiting for Morrison to step on the line. When Morrison came forth, and the whistle blew, Tony made the first impression by scoring a first-period takedown. The first period ended 2-1, Tony; however, that would be the only real action that took place. Morrison earned an escape after choosing down and Tony did the same. The match ended in a 3-2 decision win for Tony, his closest thus far on the season, and he was not too pleased with the match.

"I knew I left some points out of the board and the next time we wrestled I would need to widen the gap," Ramos said. "Even though it was not the dominating performance that I wanted, I got the win and it was time to move forward."

Tony moved forward from his match, now 14-0, but the Hawkeyes dropped a 9-0 lead and eventually fell 18-12 in the dual.

The Hawks continued wrestling on the road over the next two weeks. They headed up to Ann Arbor, Michigan, for a dual with the Wolverines and won 33-10; Tony would win by a fall at 2:55 over Rossi Bruno.

Next up, that very Sunday, Iowa headed over to East Lansing, Michigan, for a dual with the Spartans. Both Tony and the Hawkeyes left with big wins under their belts. The team won the dual 27-12, and Tony scored another win by a 15-4 major decision over Brandon Fifield.

The number-four Hawkeyes were rolling; they had one loss so far in dual meets and their greatest test to date would be coming up in the number-three rated University of Minnesota Golden Gophers who were always a very strong dual meet team.

Again, on the road, Tony and company had a strong opponent in their Big Ten rival. Out of the twenty wrestlers that stepped on the mat, eighteen of them were ranked wrestlers in the country. "We knew going into that dual that we were going to have to control our matches and score bonus points," Ramos said.

Tony wrestled number-nine ranked Chris Dardanes, and Tony was looking to provide bonus points for his team. When his match began, he was on the attack. He scored a takedown in each of the three periods; however, he was also unable to finish two takedowns in the final period and only won by an 8-2 decision.

"I needed to do a better job finishing those shots to close out the match for the team," Ramos said. "We knew the dual would be close and I had to do a better job not just dominating the match, but widening that gap to do more for the team. This was just another match in the rivalry between me and Dardanes. I had started to really take it to him every time we competed and this was just another opportunity to show nothing had changed."

In addition to Tony's win over Dardanes, Mark Ballweg, ranked number-nine, defeated the other Dardanes, Nick, 3-1, who was ranked tenth, and that before number ten Dylan Ness of Minnesota took down Michael Kelly, 8-2. The team score was 9-3 Hawkeyes headed into another Iowa hammer, number-one ranked Derek St. John at 157.

St. John took down Danny Zilverberg, 6-2, and pushed the Iowa lead to a 12-3 score before number-eighteen Nick Moore upset Minnesota's number-ten Cody Yohn, 8-2. Up to that point, Iowa had taken five of the first six weight classes and led, 15-3. Unexpectedly, Moore was the last Hawkeye to have his hand raised.

At 174 the Golden Gophers sent their number-two ranked Logan Storley to the mat against number-six Mike Evans. Storley won a 4-3 decision. In the 184 match-up, number-five Kevin Steinhaus was too much for Iowa's number-fourteen Ethen Lofthouse and defeated him, 6-3. The team score was now 15-9 with two matches left. Iowa needed one win to close out the dual; however, number-twelve Scott Schiller and number-two Tony Nelson did not budge as each won by a decision: Schiller had 3-1 sudden victory over number-twenty Nathan Burak, and Nelson scored a 2-1 decision over number-five Bobby Telford.

The dual now came down to criteria. Both teams had won five matches each and there were no bonus points scored. The dual would go to third criteria: total match-points scored. Iowa scored 41 points to Minnesota's 33. In that, the Hawks earned the additional team point for a 16-15 Big Ten dual meet win.

"It's a team win and winning 16-15 is better than not," Tom Brands said. "But, we had a lot of situations we could've controlled [better] and we have room for improvement. Now we go forward and look at Penn State."

Penn State, the number-one rated team in the country, was now headed to Iowa City. As for Tony, he was wrestling at a high level and he looked to continually prove to be the best wrestler in the country at the 133-pound weight class.

Additionally, there were still seven more duals prior to the Big Ten Championships; therefore, Tony had enough time to polish the areas of this wrestling that he needed to hone before the season's end and another match-up with Logan Stieber, this time, most likely, for a Big Ten championship.

2013 • DUAL MEET VERSUS THE UNIVERSITY OF MINNESOTA
RAMOS DEFEATS DARDANES BY AN 8-2 DECISION
PHOTOGRAPH COURTESY • UNIVERSITY OF IOWA ATHLETICS

CHAPTER 46
CARVER'S LOUDEST MOMENT

"That was deafening. That was where the building was shaking. In my opinion, by far the loudest Carver-Hawkeye's ever been."

• *Terry Brands*
Associate Head Coach, the University of Iowa
Coach, Hawkeye Wrestling Club

ON MARCH 30, 2014, K.J. PILCHER, A JOURNALIST for *The Cedar Rapids Gazette* in Iowa, wrote a piece called "Memorable Moments in 100 Years of Hawkeye Wrestling." In his article, the fourth in a five-part series, Pilcher identified one of the loudest moments ever experienced at Carver-Hawkeye Arena. His article read:

> Some consider it the loudest Carver-Hawkeye Area has ever been.
> Brooks Simpson, then a sophomore 190-pounder for the University of Iowa, provided one of the biggest upsets in Hawkeye wrestling history, pinning Iowa State's top-ranked and defending national champion Eric Voelker in a dual on Jan. 16, 1988.
> It sent most of the 13,000 fans into a frenzy and helped fourth-ranked Iowa trump the No. 1 Cyclones, 22-15, and remain unbeaten at Carver-Hawkeye Arena. It also avenged the previous year's national meet, where ISU snapped Iowa's string of nine-straight NCAA titles.
> "I'm very privileged to have been a part of that whole saga," Simpson said. "For me the most meaningful was the fact that it was not just an individual win for me over a solid opponent. It was Iowa beating Iowa State, the team that had taken the title from us the year before."

The Hawkeyes trailed entering the final two matches. Any win by the heavily favored Voelker and the Cyclones seal it.

Simpson, a strong wrestler in the bottom position, hit a side roll, catching Voelker on his back, settling and adjusting before getting the fall in 4:46. Simpson wasn't going to squander the opportunity.

"It was a fight to get him there in a secure position," said Simpson, an NCAA runner-up at 190 in 1990. "Once I secured it, I knew it was just a matter of time before I got the fall."

Fans roared and went crazy.

"The place erupted," former Hawkeye Coach Dan Gable said. "It was exciting."

Simpson's dad stormed the mat and picked up his son. Simpson's father-in-law threw his coat into the air and never saw it again.

"It was pandemonium," Simpson said. "It was more than just celebration. It was kind of chaos."

WHEN NUMBER-ONE PENN STATE ARRIVED IN

Iowa City in that 2013 season to face the now number-three Iowa Hawkeyes, there was more on the line than a simple dual win. The match-up pitted the Big Tens two best teams against one another, as well as showcase two of the top teams in the country that featured sixteen ranked wrestlers at their respective weight classes.

Going into the dual, however, there was much talk and press covering the meet that would take place Friday night in Carver. The meet was sold out, and 15,077 fans would await an opportunity to witness this highlighted dual meet on the schedule.

"There was lots of discussion about how we couldn't keep up with the bonus points that Penn State would put up," Ramos said. "People said they had too many guys that could get falls in the matches and that we would not be able to pin anyone. This bothered me a lot and I made it a personal goal that, no matter what it took, I was going to get six points for us.

"All week long I would be talking to Frankie and my family and it always got brought up. They would tell me, 'You know you need to pin this guy for the team to have a shot at winning, right?' I would just respond with the simple, 'Yes, I will.' I was so confident that I was going to pin him and made myself believe it so much that there was no other option."

Also, that week, Tony's brother Frank made an offer to him if he were to come up big in the dual. Before the dual, Tony had some time with his family and he always utilized it—he loved those moments—they always relaxed him.

"We were at Scheels [a large sports store in the Coral Ridge Mall] and my uncle was there and Frankie and the whole entourage," Ramos said, "and Frankie made a deal with me. He said, 'If you pin [Jordan] Conaway, I'll get you this 9mm,' I was like, 'Okay, no problem.'"

Frank laughed at his youngest brother and said, "Okay. You get the fall and that gun's yours."

So for the first time since high school, there would be an outside incentive, a challenge, set in front of Tony by his brother. When Tony left for Carver-Hawkeye Arena, he was focused on his individual job and the dual.

The first match would be the number-one ranked Matt McDonough versus the number-two ranked Nico Megaludis. The match was as close as a match could get. McDonough would win on an escape as time was running out as Megaludis tried to hang onto McDonough's leg and send the bout into overtime.

The Hawks took a 3-0 dual team lead over the Nittany Lions as the 133-pound match was on deck.

"Before the match," Ramos said, "Terry kept telling me, 'Build the legend. Grow the legend. If there's one incentive for you, it's build your legend.'"

Of course, the building of the legend was more geared toward the fans. "The fans have seen the things [I've] done," Ramos said. "They talk about the Oliver match all the time—give them more things to talk about. Give them greater things to remember from [my] wrestling, [my] abilities, the things I do when I'm on the mat. So I knew going out there and just putting up a major is what people expected, but [I] had to go up and above and beyond that if [I] want to be a legend."

As Tony waited in the center of the mat for his opponent, Jordan Conaway, Terry's words continued to fill his mind. "I was out there and I kept thinking that I couldn't go for a major or a [technical fall]," Ramos said. "I needed to finish it and finish it with a bang. *Grow the legend.* That was replaying in my mind the whole time."

Still hearing Terry Brands' words, Tony intensely waited and stared more intently at Conaway. As the referee and table workers were set and as Conaway, the redshirt freshman who was on a four-match win streak, worked his way to middle of the mat, Tony was now looking daggers through him with each step.

The match would be all Tony as he scored a takedown at the 1:30 mark when he was able to get into Conaway's legs and force a scramble in the middle of the mat. Conaway would escape before Tony added another takedown and was able to build his riding time through the remainder of the first period.

However, with each position Tony was putting himself into, the crowd reacted as if something special was about to happen.

With Tony's lead standing at 4-1, Conaway had the choice in the second period and he chose down—he was granted another escape point. Conaway looked to close the gap on the scoreboard; however, in reality, the 4-2 score was not as close as it appeared.

Twenty seconds into the second period, Tony was again in on another takedown and the crowd stood tall, in suspense, as Tony finished the takedown for a 6-2 lead. Again, Conaway escaped and, again, almost enticed by the crowd's build-up of noise, Tony was in on his leg again.

"I could feel him wearing down," Ramos said. "I was getting in and taking him down and I could feel the energy inside of the arena building with each takedown. I knew it would only be a matter of time before he made a mistake."

After cutting Conaway loose and holding a 6-3 advantage, Tony continually worked for inside position and found himself in control of Conaway's head and arm and snapped him down. In that moment, the Iowa fans sensed it and rose in anticipation—their voices gasped, momentarily, and Tony dug his right arm in and across Conaway's back as his left hand had the chin; the Iowa faithful stretched their necks and cheered. The sound echoed louder than it ever had inside of the arena as Tony reached even further across Conaway's back and locked on his far lat and started to force him over. With each grip and turn, the wave of voices gained more and more momentum until Tony was able to turn Conaway to his back. Then, the place erupted.

Carver-Hawkeye Arena was literally shaking as fans were out of their seats, out of their minds, piling into the aisles for a better view, almost elevated by the moment and unable to control their hands and voices and feet and bodies as Tony pressed Conaway farther into the mat as the Nittany Lion did all he could to fight.

With each crank, cinch, and rotation of Tony's grip, the fans found a way to rise higher and higher, like a tidal wave that was gaining momentum. Conaway was simply in the path as the shadow overhead was growing darker and darker and it appeared to only be a matter of time before he was rendered helpless.

Conaway's efforts to escape continued, but he could not force himself free from Tony's lock. After fighting away from the lock, he altered his fight inward, turning toward Tony as he tried to again belly out—the fall of the giant wave overhead was now slowly collapsing. Tony, stubbornly in tight, dropped his hips and crashed his weight, planting Conaway's shoulder blades into the two-toned black and gold Iowa Hawkeye mat. Conaway was in the unforgiving position of suffocation and ultimate doom; his time had expired as there was nowhere left to turn.

The intensity of the fans now rose to an entirely whole new level, one where the arena was shaking profusely while heavy feet jumped and the screams crushed down to those each section closer to the mat than they started. The sound ultimately carried all the way down until it settled in the mat's center where the inevitable was simply inevitable.

When the referee's hand finally slapped the mat at the 4:23 mark, the noise in Carver-Hawkeye had grown yet again, another entirely new level of insanity. Assistant coach Ryan Morningstar had jumped into the air off the bench with the fall call. Teammates were moving in a frenzy all over and around their seats, and fans were jumping up and down and screaming, some in disbelief, others in a joyous rage of emotion—Carver just kept erupting as the building's foundation was being maximized and put to the ultimate test.

Tony sprang up and flexed to the crowd in utter dominance as Conaway lay washed out in defeat. The cheers continued and, in the center of it all, Tony continued his pose and circled the mat taking it all in—he only broke his flexing to point to his brother.

"The only thing I remember," Ramos said of the moment after the fall, "and I can remember it clear as day, was me jumping up so fast right into the double rainbows. My emotions took over because it was something I told myself and everyone close to me that I was going to do and then I went out there and backed it up.

"All that emotion bottled up into a few split seconds just erupted. I was deaf to the sound in Carver but, again, this was another one of those times where people had told me that was the loudest they ever heard Carver—that the roof could have exploded off the building from the noise."

From the edge of the mat, down in the middle of the noise was the coaching staff, the wrestlers, the cheerleaders, and the fans lucky enough to be mat side and, from down there, the noise was earsplitting. Even Herky was out of his mind with excitement.

"The Oliver match was probably the second or third loudest Carver-Hawkeye's ever been—the [only] debate is whether [or not] the Simpson-Voelker pin was louder," Terry Brands said. "But you can't argue the Penn State pin. That was deafening. That was where the building was shaking. In my opinion, by far the loudest Carver-Hawkeye's ever been."

The referee raised Tony's hand as every fans' arms were also in the air pumping to the sky, chanting and hollering down at him, at the Hawkeyes, at the Nittany Lion fans and wrestlers—Carver had erupted and there was no calming the atmosphere in that moment.

As Tony stomped off the mat and soaked it all in, Terry Brands met him on the mat's edge, yelled into his ear, and sent him off with a right-handed slap on the behind as Tony headed into the tunnel. The legend had grown. When he entered the tunnel, the hysteria of the Hawkeye fans echoed behind him as people were still in awe and appreciation and exhilaration of the moment and continued the cheer.

In a post-match interview by Hawkeye Sports, Hawk Vision Productions, Tony commented how "It was exciting because [I] know [I] did [my] job. They can work to defend something as much as they want, [but] if you just over power them and put your will on them, you'll get what you need to do."

The crowd was ignited and the team felt energized; however, that was still only the second match of the night—there were still eight more bouts to wrestle. The Hawkeyes went up 9-0 in those first two weight classes, but there were still jobs to do in the match-ups that remained.

At 141 pounds, Mark Ballweg kept the momentum rolling in favor of the black and gold. He defeated Bryan Pearsall by a 12-2 major decision. This extended the Iowa lead to 13-0 with some big guns still to come from both line-ups.

In the 149-pound match, Iowa's unranked Brody Grothus faced Penn State's number-eight ranked Andrew Alton. Alton, who needed to stop the PSU bleeding, did just that. He would put his team on the board with an 18-8 major decision. Iowa now led 13-4 with another marquee match-up at 157 pounds.

For the Hawkeyes, they sent their number-one ranked wrestler, Derek St. John to the mat to face Penn State's number-five ranked Dylan Alton. The match was everything it was supposed to be: aggressive, fast, calculated, and close. However, in the end, number-one reigned as St. John scored a 4-3 decision scoring a takedown on the edge of the mat after a twenty-five second scramble. The win added another three points to the Hawkeye's team total headed into the break.

Coming out of the break, the Nittany Lions' number-two ranked David Taylor would lead the comeback for Penn State—he was every bit as dangerous as he was billed to be. He wrestled number-thirteen Nick Moore, but Moore was simply in the way.

The match was Taylor, all Taylor, and nothing but David Taylor. Moore was able to keep it close early on, but the second period featured an array of Taylor tilts and back points and the separation and domination began. Taylor gave his team a well-needed five-point boost with an 18-2 technical fall. Once his score was added into the total, Penn State now trailed 16-9 with three higher ranked wrestlers than Iowa to step onto the mat out of the final four weight classes.

The first would be PSU's 174-pound number-four ranked Matt Brown, and he would face Iowa's number-six ranked Mike Evans, mustache and all. The match would come down to a tight scramble position where Evans battled through Brown's defense and scored a late takedown to take the lead and the win with a 4-3 decision. Evans would pump his arms into the air to further ignite the crowd with his upset victory, and the Hawkeyes increased their lead, 19-9, with three matches left.

At 184 pounds, number-one ranked Ed Ruth of Penn State did all that he could to unranked Grant Gambrall; however, in the end, Gambrall did his duty and simply held Ruth to a 21-10 major decision. This closed the gap for Penn State who now trailed 19-13.

The next match was another where Penn State had the advantage on paper. The number-three ranked Quentin Wright faced Iowa's number-nineteen Nathan Burak. Wright brought the heat, but Burak was able to keep the match close through strong defense and solid positioning. Wright won the match on an 8-3 decision, but Burak kept it close enough for the heavy weight match to determine the winner. If PSU won by a decision, the dual would be tied 19-19; however, with Tony's fall, the Hawkeyes would win on criteria.

When heavyweight Bobby Telford stepped onto the mat in the middle of the 15,077 Carver-Hawkeye crowd, he knew the team needed the win, and so did he.

"It was my third chance [to finish a dual], and against Minnesota and Oklahoma State I was 0-2," Telford said. "It was one of the matches on paper we needed to have. Sometimes we need bonus points, sometimes we just need a win. Either way, I need to be getting my hand raised."

The stage was set for number-six ranked Telford and number-seventeen Jon Gingrich to close out the night. Fortunately, for the Hawkeyes, Telford would leave no doubt and remove any drama from the match as he scored a takedown at the 1:56 mark, rode Gingrich to end the first period, rode out the Nittany Lion for the entire second period, and collected a stall point in the process. Add an escape, a reversal, a takedown, and the rider, and it was a 9-2 decision win and the dual for the Hawkeyes.

Iowa would defeat the number-one Nittany Lions in Carver by a 22-16 score.

"It was a big dual," Tom Brands said in a post-match interview. "We had it highlighted, I'm sure they had it highlighted, but in the grand scheme of things, you have to be ready every week. We had some gutsy performances tonight, but we need to turn it into progress. We're not there yet."

To Tony, that win was not only a message to the critics, it was hope for the Iowa fans. "This showed the rest of the country that we were here to compete and that it wasn't just Penn State and everyone else," Ramos stated. "If we came out and wrestled like each individual was capable at the NCAA tournament, we had a shot at being the team champions. It gave the fans hope heading into Des Moines, Iowa, and it gave us something to build on."

After the dual, Tony had an opportunity to meet actors Ashton Kutcher and Mila Kunis who were in attendance; however, it did not go well as Tony would have liked. "After the match," Ramos explained, "I had the opportunity to meet [them], and they congratulated me on the win and for making [the dual] such an awesome experience. If I could have a do-over in my life, that would be one of them because I sounded like the biggest idiot. I was so star struck. So next time around, I will do a better job."

As Tony left Carver-Hawkeye that night, after he signed autographs and spoke with fans, young and old, he felt like the team was on the right track and his wrestling was moving in the right direction. And when he finally caught up to his brother he reminded him, while laughing, "So how about that 9mm?"

2013 • DUAL MEET VERSUS PENN STATE UNIVERSITY
CARVER-HAWKEYE ARENA'S LOUDEST MOMENT
RAMOS DEFEATS CONAWAY BY FALL AND THEN JUMPS UP FLEXING
PHOTOGRAPH COURTESY • UNIVERSITY OF IOWA ATHLETICS

CHAPTER 47
SEPARATING THE FIELD

"I wanted to make it clear to the field that it was Logan and it was me and that everyone else was fighting for third."

• *Tony Ramos*

WITH THE END OF THE REGULAR SEASON COMING to a close, there were still a few matches to wrestle and techniques to tighten up, but Tony was still on a collision course with Logan Stieber and everyone saw it. Tony, who was still ranked number two with a perfect 17-0 record, with seven by fall, was continuing to focus on not only where he could improve, but where he needed to get better. And, with the Big Ten Championships coming up in just over a month, he needed to fine tune those aspects of his wrestling and continually build over his next six matches.

In the mix of competitors, Tony would have a difficult opponent approaching in Edinboro's A.J. Schopp. Schopp was ranked third directly behind Tony. Additionally, Tony would face a familiar opponent in Minnesota's number-seven ranked Chris Dardanes.

Prior to each of those matches, however, Iowa traveled to Huff Hall in Champaign, Illinois, for a dual Friday night against the Illini. After that, they would return home and host the Cornhuskers of Nebraska on Sunday at Carver-Hawkeye Arena.

In Huff Hall, Tony faced number-ten ranked Daryl Thomas. Thomas, for the first three minutes of the match, held his own and the first period remained scoreless. Thomas' plan of limiting Tony's scoring and keeping him at bay was working.

When the second period began, Tony started in the down position, one of the positions he was working on improving. When the whistle blew and the period began, he not only escaped and scored his point, but he scored a takedown and led 3-0 headed into the third period.

As the third period was well underway, Tony finally found his openings and he exploited Thomas. Tony would score three more takedowns and was working on near fall points when he pressed Thomas' back to the mat and secured the fall at 6:36.

"He came out of his game plan against me and I had to make some adjustments," Ramos commented in a post-match interview. "I could tell he was beginning to wear down and I didn't want to hesitate. I just opened up."

Two days later, the Cornhuskers came into Iowa City with an opportunity for Iowa to claim its fifth Big Ten dual title in the past six seasons. By the time Tony stepped on the mat, the dual was well in hand and he made quick work of Shawn Nagel with a fall in 2:05. This was Tony's ninth fall on the season and his twenty-third consecutive victory in Carver-Hawkeye Area. Next up would be his greatest challenge that season, to date, in Edinboro's A.J. Schopp.

"This was a big match for me," Ramos recalled of the match-up with Schopp. "He was ranked number three and I never wrestled him before—his name was one that was starting to make some noise. I knew he was very good on top and that I needed to get going early against him to not let that factor in."

When Tony and Schopp lined up against each other, the suspense of who was the better wrestler was answered immediately.

"In the first period we got into a flurry where I scored two and two off a takedown to go up 4-0," Ramos remembered. "I finished the period on top and that exchange set the tone for the rest of the match because he didn't have the option of only trying to ride me."

In the second, Schopp chose the top position and Tony extended his lead 6-0 with a reversal. And then, Tony rode him out for the period.

For the final period Tony had choice. He took neutral, added another takedown to his totals, and earned a riding point for not only a 9-0 major decision, his eighth on the season, but for a strong statement that there were only two wrestlers in the 133-pound weight class.

After his win, Tony stood opposite the number-three Schopp and flexed his double rainbow pose which was becoming the pose of choice for the junior Hawkeye.

"I wanted to make it clear to the field that it was Logan and it was me and that everyone else was fighting for third," Ramos said in full and utter confidence.

Tony's dominance continued.

At the NWCA Cliff Keen National Dual Meet Championships, Iowa advanced with a 21-16 win over the number-nine Big Red of Cornell University. Tony, who faced Bricker Dixon, scored five takedowns in the first period, three takedowns in the second, and was working through near fall points before he won by fall in 6:11.

This would pit Iowa against Big Ten rival Minnesota in the semifinals; it also put Tony up against longtime opponent, Chris Dardanes, now ranked number seven.

"Again," Ramos said, "another match with Dardanes, but this time I knew for us to match Minnesota in bonus points for the dual, I would have to go out there and find a way to pin Dardanes. I was up pretty big in the third period and hit a double-leg to his back where I fell into a tight waist and pinned him."

Unfortunately, for Iowa, they dropped the dual, 22-15, and headed to a third-place dual with the number-six rated Missouri Tigers. Tony would receive a forfeit; unfortunately, those six points were still not enough to help the Hawkeyes as they placed fourth with an 18-16 loss in the dual.

"We have work to do, and I'd say the same thing whether we win or lose," said head coach Tom Brands. "We have to move forward. Things are maybe a little bit bizarre right now, and we have to stop going down that path."

But, to Tony, as an individual, there was nothing bizarre about where he was at—his path was clear and it was now coming to another match-up with Stieber. As Tony headed into the Big Ten championships, he was a perfect 23-0 with eleven falls on the season, one technical fall, eight major decisions, two regular decisions, and a forfeit. His junior campaign was indeed something special when the regular season ended, but he was seeking much more. He was looking for his first Big Ten championship, a national championship, and redemption against Stieber along the way.

THE BIG TEN CHAMPIONSHIPS TOOK PLACE AT

the Assembly Hall on the campus of the University of Illinois—an arena that Tony knew very well from his time at Glenbard North. Of course, he had only experienced one loss in the Assembly Hall, and that was his freshman season when he lost in the state championship match. Needless to say, Tony felt at home back in the Land of Lincoln within the confines of the Fighting Illini's orange and navy blue walls.

The 133-pound bracket was one of the most difficult brackets in the tournament as there would be four All-Americans in the bottom half of the bracket, and one All-American in the top half. The Big Ten championships were a mini-national championship tournament for the wrestlers, and the individual and team results always reflected that sentiment.

Tony, the number-two seed, received a pigtail match to open the tournament against Brandon Fifield of Michigan State. He picked up a first period fall, his twelfth, at the 2:08 mark and, as expected, moved forward in the bracket.

In the championship quarterfinal, Tony faced Purdue's number sixteen Cashe' Quiroga. Again, Tony advanced; this time with a 9-5 decision placing him in the semifinals for the third-straight season. For that match-up, he had to wrestle Wisconsin's Tyler Graff; Graff had defeated Tony in the Big Ten semifinals Tony's freshman season, and was also now the number-three ranked wrestler in the country. Between the two, the matches were always close and they always went down to the final moments. In 2011, Tony lost on a controversial no-call. This season, Tony was on a mission and was not going to leave anything to chance.

The match opened up with a three-minute hand fight with no points scored, but the battle for position was evident and each wrestler was looking to create his own opportunities.

In the second and third periods, both Tony and Graff simply exchanged escapes and the match was tied 1-1 with time expiring on both wrestlers. In overtime, however, with about thirty seconds remaining, Graff was the first to attack and he worked into a deep high-crotch on the number-two ranked wrestler in the country. From there, Tony countered and "hit an inside switch, which is a very familiar position for me," Ramos said. "I ended up changing the scoring opportunity to my own and riding him out to move on to the finals for the second time."

In his post-match interview, Tony went through the winning takedown. "He got in deep and I was fighting and fighting," Ramos said, "and, it was something I learned in high school, I hit it a few times, I reached back in, pulled the leg up. Usually, I finish across with a double. But I got my hips back and ran around behind."

This was the closest match that Tony had had since Jon Morrison back in early January, but he was in full control of the Morrison match. Against Graff, he had to keep his composure.

"[I] had to stay calm and reposition," Ramos continued in regard to the Graff match. "A lot of guys there would have panicked—that's one thing that I've noticed with my wrestling, and I think it's brought me over the edge, is even in bad positions [I] can't panic or else [I] won't be able to think [my] way through the match, what's going on, how to finish, how to get out of it—[I] got to stay calm."

In order to stay calm, Tony had to grow in areas of his wrestling.

However, more than anything, his wrestling and his level of experience had allowed him to work through those positions from as far back as his kids' club days.

"When I was little," Ramos reflected in the interview, "my mom would send me to a sports' psychiatrist, probably from when I was six or seven on—I thank her for that a lot—because it definitely makes a difference. I've learned how to self-talk. I've learned how to do it when I'm sleeping. It's actually incredible what that kind of self-talk can do for you."

Tony went on to say that "[I'd thought about that match] for two years. I win that match two years ago and we were Big Ten champs. We lost by a point. So it was something that I wasn't going to let happen again."

Now that Tony had avenged one loss, he was looking to avenge another. "Graff and I always have close matches," Ramos said, "but that win was big for me. He defeated me a few years ago and I was able to get redemption for that loss. Now, it was my chance to get redemption on Logan. We didn't wrestle in the dual at Carver because of his injury, but many people speculated that he didn't want to face me at Carver—nobody did. People always said that Carver was magical and I could do things in that arena that were out of the ordinary."

Excited for the match-up and the opportunity to wrestle Stieber, Tony knew he had to wrestle a complete match against the reigning national champion. When asked what he would have to do better, he simply stated: "Move on bottom."

Even though he had just defeated a strong opponent in Graff who was very good in the top position, Tony was more than aware of how to keep moving. "[I have to keep] kicking," he said. "[I] can't turn into a guy when he's got [my] leg. I got to get out."

When asked if he would take bottom against Stieber, he did not even hesitate. "Yes," Ramos answered. "No question."

On the other side of the tunnel, Logan Stieber was interviewed about the match and about wrestling Tony.

"It's going to be a fun match," Stieber grinned. "Iowa fans are crazy; they're going to be loud, so I'll probably get called for stalling right away—by them. But it's going to be fun. He's awesome, he's had an awesome year, I've had a good year so far; so, hopefully it's a good match and hopefully we put a lot of points up."

Stieber was also questioned about his injury. "I'm back," Stieber stated. "I was out for about a month and it sucked having to watch from the sidelines. But I'm back now and I feel good."

The field was now cleared. It was Stieber. It was Tony. It was number one versus number two. And it was time to wrestle.

2013 • BIG TEN CHAMPIONSHIPS
133 LB CHAMPIONSHIP QUARTERFINAL MATCH
RAMOS DEFEATS QUIROGA BY A 9-5 DECISION
PHOTOGRAPH COURTESY • UNIVERSITY OF IOWA ATHLETICS

CHAPTER 48
THE MONSTER IN HIS CLOSET

"He was tough, always in good position and he always showed up—I don't think he ever had a bad match. I was always excited to wrestle him because I knew it would be a tough match and exciting."

• Logan Stieber
NCAA Champion, Ohio State University

WHEN THE FINAL ROUND OF WRESTLE-BACKS OF the Big Ten championships had completed, Tony watched from the stands and rooted on his Hawkeye teammates. He felt as relaxed and as confident as he could feel, and he was ready for the finals. In fact, while he was sitting up above one of the Iowa trainers who was seated on the floor, he took some water and rained a few drops down with a smile on his face. The trainer, at first confused, looked up, saw Tony, and smiled back. Tony would then head into the tunnel and prepare for the finals.

The Tony and Stieber match featured the two best wrestlers in the country, two wrestlers that were undefeated, and a match everyone had been anticipating since the semifinals of the NCAA championships the year before.

For all of the hype and all of the talk and all of the excitement that surrounded the 133-pound finals match, the time finally arrived and both of the wrestlers, and all of the fans, were ready.

Unfortunately, the match was anything but exciting. The first period consisted of a three-minute hand fight with very little action coming from either wrestler. However, even though the action was not what all were anticipating, it did showcase how strong, defensively, each wrestler was and how difficult it was to create an opening for a scoring opportunity.

"We ended the first period 0-0," Ramos remembered. "I defended a number of scoring positions and this is when I think people started to realize how good my defense was and how hard it was to score on me."

The same, of course, was seen in Stieber as Tony struggled to also work into a scoring position. For the second period, Tony had choice and he would, as he stated, choose down with no hesitation. The test was now. He knew and Stieber knew that this position generally favored Stieber in the past. To Tony, this had been the focus of his training and he had already proven that there was yet to be one wrestler in the country who could hold him down. Now it would be Stieber's turn to see if he could hinder the Hawkeye.

"There was lots of speculation on whether or not I should go neutral," Ramos said. "In the past, he had beaten me from the top position and had a knack for controlling matches in this area. For me, I had been working non-stop on the bottom position and I was confident and comfortable that I would escape."

As Tony set himself, placing his knees behind the line and his hands in the front, securing his base, Stieber covered and every speculation and question out there was about to be answered.

When the whistle blew, it appeared that Stieber would control the position; however, after fifteen seconds had elapsed, Tony had found himself not only on his feet, but off bottom with an escape and a 1-0 lead. The remainder of the period was much like the first—a hard fought struggle for position. The period ended and Stieber would now choose the bottom position.

Stieber would earn his escape, the match was tied, and there would not be much action until late in the third period when Stieber worked himself into a single-leg; unfortunately, for Stieber, Tony battled out of the position and the match went into overtime.

About thirty seconds into the first overtime, Stieber shot in and got to Tony's right side; however, the Hawkeye would whizzer down with his right arm and both wrestlers fought only to find themselves on their feet in that same position. Stieber's lock, however, was high on Tony's leg as Tony tried to break it. But, once he broke Stieber's lock, Stieber was already behind Tony's right hip. Once there, Stieber locked his hands, lifted Tony, and brought him down to the mat with a brief exposure.

When Tony bellied out, Stieber stuck out his tongue to the crowd as a "Two!" echoed throughout the Assembly Hall. Tony quickly collected himself on the mat, belly down, and Stieber pushed off of Tony, flexed his own set of double rainbows, celebrated with his coach, and then returned to the mat's center for his hand to be shook and raised.

In a post-match interview, the national champion and now two-time Big Ten champion, Logan Stieber, spoke to how he was able to defeat

Tony. "I know that he's really picked up his offense this year," Stieber stated, "so I knew I had to stop his offensive shots and I thought I did a very good job of containing his offense. I knew I had to score a takedown and I wanted to get one in regulation, but I couldn't get one. But, in overtime, I was able to get it."

The takedown in overtime marked the second time Stieber had the opportunity to score, and he commented on the difference in those two positions. "I think I was more patient," Stieber said. "I don't know if I was trying to rush it, but I didn't have many shots to score but I knew I could get the leg in."

From Tony's point of view, "I didn't take enough risks in order to give myself real scoring opportunities," he said. "I kept the match close enough to win, but I didn't give myself those big opportunities to make it happen."

However, even in the loss, Tony walked away from the match with some positives. "After that match," Ramos said, "I knew he couldn't beat me in the top and bottom position. I felt like he was starting to get nervous that I was closing the gap more than maybe he was comfortable with. When I spoke to Terry after the match, he just reassured me that we might not have won the match, but we were starting to get to them mentally to where they were going to have to change up their game plan—they didn't want to be in that close of a match."

Terry Brands remembered that very loss in the Big Ten championships and felt that the match was there for the taking; he thought it was a missed opportunity. "There can't be a sometimes when it comes to opportunity in there, there has to be an all-the-time mentality," Terry Brands commented. "So, is my chance to beat him to keep it close and try to win it at the end? Well, I know the skill package that we have—I know the skill package of Tony Ramos. Why do you want to wait? Those are the parts that always confused me. I felt like we waited when we should have been attacking more."

THERE WOULD STILL BE TIME TO IMPROVE before the national championships, and Tony looked to do just that in addition to approaching his matches with a more attack mindset.

"The next time that we would wrestle at the NCAA championships," Ramos said, "I knew I would have to hang it all out there in every position if I was going to win a title."

From Tom Brands' perspective, there was enough time to improve and open up. "We had to keep working on scoring," Tom Brands said. "You know, it was working little things, like strategy and little things that are critical, critical components to [his] wrestling. And just because there's only twelve days between the Big Tens and nationals doesn't mean that Tony Ramos can't get better. Plus, it's a long season. Not for Tony Ramos, but for his opponents. It's long and grueling for those opponents. He's built for this. Plus, the championships were in Iowa. Iowa fans are crazy. But we would have to show up ready to wrestle."

The national championships were held in Des Moines, Iowa, so the Iowa faithful did not have to travel too far to cheer on their Hawkeyes. When the seeds came out, it was no surprise who the number-one and number-two wrestlers were at 133. When the tournament began, it was, once again, another collision course where Tony and Stieber would meet. And the road each took was extremely impressive. Neither left any doubt who deserved to be wrestling in the finals on Saturday night on that stage.

For Stieber, he earned two falls and two technical falls on his way to the finals. He pinned Duke's Brandon Gambucci in 3:00 before he cemented Shelton Mack of Pittsburgh to the mat for a fall in 2:40. In the quarterfinals, he dismantled number-eight Cody Brewer of Oklahoma with a 17-1 technical fall, and then destroyed number-four A.J. Schopp 18-2 in the semifinals.

On the bottom half of the bracket, Tony also scored two falls in the opening rounds. He took down the number-fourteen Nick Wilcox of Bloomsburg in 1:56 and then treated North Carolina's Joseph Ward the same, this time with a fall in 1:07. In the quarterfinals, however, Tony had the number-seven ranked and longtime nemesis, Jon Morrison of Oklahoma State.

"Even though we knew each other very well," Ramos said, "I knew he didn't have a chance and it was going to be the same story as always. I would win, he would lose, and that would be that. In an interview after the match I even said that I didn't know what I had over him, but maybe I was just the monster in his closet."

Before the match started, Tony waited on the starting line, staring at Morrison, who was pacing back and forth, until he was called to the center by the referee.

Off the whistle, the match and the pace was controlled by Tony. With 1:20 left in the first period, Morrison was hit with his first stalling call—Tony's forward pressure and motion had the Cowboy trying to keep up.

There would be no scoring in the first period, but Tony had dominated the position battle. In the second, Tony chose down and, after four exchanges of being returned to the mat and forced out of bounds, he earned his escape with 1:20 left in the period.

Shortly after his escape, Tony also scored his first takedown on the mat's edge and opened up a 3-0 advantage. For the next forty-three seconds, Tony countered and rode Morrison, thus erasing Morrison's

2013 • NCAA DIVISION I WRESTLING CHAMPIONSHIPS
133 LB CHAMPIONSHIP QUARTERFINAL MATCH
RAMOS EXTENDS HIS ARMS AND CELEBRATES HIS 6-1 WIN OVER MORRISON
PHOTOGRAPH COURTESY • UNIVERSITY OF IOWA ATHLETICS

forty seconds of riding time and giving himself a three-second riding advantage. Morrison, who trailed in the match, would choose down in the third.

With 1:16 remaining, there was a stalemate called and then blood time was granted to Morrison. The two wrestlers reset and, after a Morrison escaped with twenty seconds remaining, and a defensive takedown by Tony off a quick Morrison shot, Tony won by a 6-1 decision. After the match, Tony enticed the Oklahoma State and Iowa crowd by having some final words for Morrison. Tony raised his hands to the crowd as if to say, "Now what? He still can't beat me."

The Hawkeye fans erupted in cheers showing their pride in their wrestler while the Cowboy supporters booed and wished ill-will on Tony as he had his hand raised, ran off into the tunnel, and now advanced to the national semifinals for the second-straight season. In the semifinals, Tony faced another Big Ten opponent. This time, it would be Wisconsin's number-three ranked Tyler Graff.

THE MATCH WITH GRAFF WAS CLOSE AND TONY

anticipated that type of match from the get-go. "Tyler is a very solid wrestler who has great game plans," Ramos said. "But, the one thing I knew going into all of my matches with him is that he is always going to mess up somewhere and give me the opening that I need. I found that he couldn't stay solid for the entire seven minutes and there was no way he could hold up to my pace. It wasn't always just against me, but mostly. If you look at his history, he has a track record of mental lapses."

Even with a history of lapses, Graff was the first to score a takedown in the match. "I gave up a takedown early and then a reversal into the second period," Ramos said. "I was down 4-1 and then 4-2 following my escape. He got hit for stalling and stopped wrestling in the second period, so I knew I just had to keep on him and it was going to come."

When the third period came, Tony chose the down position. "I got my escape and kept on moving forward and taking shots," Ramos remembered. "We went out of bounds maybe ten times and they finally hit him for stalling and that tied the match 4-4."

The match went into overtime and there were no takedowns. Tony and Graff then rode each other out and they headed into another overtime period on their feet.

"In the second one-minute overtime," Ramos said, "is where he would have his lapse. He took a bad shot because he knew they might hit him for stalling again, and I just hit an easy go behind for the takedown. I remember as I went around him he just slammed the mat in defeat. I knew right after this I broke him mentally. From that point on, I knew he would never beat me. He blew a 4-1 lead and that was his best chance at defeating me ever again."

So the 133-pound finals were now set. For the second time in two weeks, after not wrestling each other the entire season, Tony and Stieber would square off one more time. This time for the right to claim the title of national champion.

NEITHER WRESTLER EXPECTED ANYTHING BUT A

finals match-up between the two. "I figured that he'd come out of the other side at nationals," Stieber said. "We had been the two most dominant [wrestlers] all year."

Tony, who was currently 0-4 against Stieber in college, wanted to right the ship now in his first NCAA championship finals. That day, Tony and his brother Vince were texting, and Tony told him, "I got nothing to lose tonight. No matter what happens, I will walk off the mat satisfied because I will let it all hang out there."

When Saturday night finally arrived, the stage was set, the match-up was anticipated, and the Hawkeye fans and Buckeye fans were out in full force for what was expected to be an entertaining seven minutes.

After introductions, Tony, as usual, was in the center of the mat staring at and waiting for Stieber. When Stieber approached the middle and the match began, it was not even one second before the offensive attacks began. Stieber, with an open double-leg off the whistle, started it off. Tony, who defended and then worked into a tie position with a left-handed tie, found Stieber combating with his own right-handed tie as each was as aggressive and forceful as possible and refused to willingly back up. Then, about seven seconds after Stieber's first shot, Tony took a shot of his own—Stieber would defend the attempt.

The period featured two of the most aggressive wrestlers in the country opening up their offenses early in the match. Additionally, when they tied up, each dropped his hand like a club on the other's neck fighting for position and openings. The continued battle would be one where each was working forward, and the hand fight was better described as more of a hand and head war with neither backing down nor conceding even the smallest position to the other.

At the 1:46 mark, Stieber took another shot that Tony defended. Immediately after, Tony worked to reach for a two-on-one position, fairly square with Stieber. Stieber reacted by snapping Tony's head with his left hand and then attacking Tony's right side on a low shot where he was able to capture the left leg. In the process of a double-leg, Stieber scored a takedown and now had a 2-0 lead and was in the top position.

In the bottom position, it was whether or not Tony could escape from the crafty top position rider. It took Tony roughly thirty seconds to kick out Stieber's right leg, ankle switch him, turn out, and escape. Once out, Tony jumped over Stieber trying to reattack his leg, and he worked a reattack of his own. However, no points were scored by either wrestler and the two were back to their hand fighting battle on their feet. Stieber had a 2-1 lead with about 1:16 left in an already aggressive, high-paced and energy-filled first period.

The two continued their fight in the mat's center. Stieber, with 00:52 remaining in the first, took a hard left-leg fake and Tony sprawled in reaction; unfortunately, Tony's right hand was posted heavy on the mat and Stieber shrugged that same right arm, hit the corner on Tony and, before Tony could collect himself, Stieber was in on a double from behind, and scored his second takedown of the period, extending his lead, 4-1.

After the takedown, Stieber, in the top position, jumped into his belly-claw ride and Tony would, again, begin to work an escape. Battling, and with 00:35 remaining in the first period, Tony was up to his feet, but he went out of bounds and the two returned to the center of the mat.

Off the restart, there were two consecutive flurries where Tony worked himself up to his feet, but Stieber found his way to Tony's legs and kept him in the down position. With Stieber hanging on to ride through the period, Tony fought his way to the edge and, once he was almost out, Stieber flushed him off the mat. There would be 00:03 left in the period at the time of another restart. There was no change in those final seconds.

"The match started and I gave up an early takedown," Ramos remembered. "But, right away, I noticed [Stieber] wasn't trying to ride me like he did to everyone else. He wasn't crab riding; he was just trying to hang on to me the best he could to add up riding time here and there."

The first period ended in a 4-1 Stieber lead; additionally, Stieber now possessed a 1:10 riding advantage.

In the stands sitting next to one another were Ohio State head coach Tom Ryan, a former Hawkeye and teammate to Iowa head coach Tom Brands, and Tom Brands himself. Neither cornered his finalist; however, that did not take away from their interest and intensity in the match.

For the second period, Stieber had the choice and he chose down. If he could escape within ten seconds, he would still maintain his riding time advantage as well as earn another point for the escape. On the surface, the match score would be 5-1; however, with the rider, Stieber held a 6-1 lead.

Off the whistle, Stieber worked to a tripod and stood up with his outside leg. Tony, in defense, kept his pressure forward with a right-handed tight waist, and then changed off from grabbing the leg and hand-fought with his left as long as he could. When Stieber finally did escape, Tony had reduced the riding advantage to 00:58 seconds; erasing the point.

The score was now 5-1 in favor of Stieber with both wrestlers in the neutral position, and then the flurry happened.

"I can't tell you exactly how the match went," Ramos said, "but I knew at one point I needed three takedowns to win, so I just started firing them off."

Both wrestlers would be circling and vying for position in the center of the mat and, from the open, Stieber fired a double-leg. Tony worked his legs back and his hips down and ended up in his front head position. From there, Stieber came to his feet as Tony continued the heavy pressure from the front head position while looking for his own offensive opportunity.

As Stieber felt comfortable, still in the front head, he took another shot from that position to Tony's right leg, which was back, and Tony, feeling the pressure, sprawled again, finding his front head and then changing over to a left-handed underhook. As Stieber came up, Tony fired in on a high-crotch to Stieber's right leg.

Tony would be in deep and Stieber sunk in a whizzer with his right hand—two seconds later, Tony worked to his feet while Stieber defended, balancing on his left leg.

While he was bent over, Stieber dropped into an Abas roll on Tony' left leg; however, as he jumped into the roll, Tony did not relinquish control of the right leg.

In the process of the roll, Tony stifled the motion and Stieber now found himself on his back, grabbing and trying to work himself free. In that split-second, Tony saw a moment where the Buckeye was exposed with his chest up and his back to the mat. Immediately, Tony dropped to his right knee, still securing the left leg of Stieber and, as Stieber still worked to turn Tony's left leg, Tony collapsed his chest and locked up a nearside cradle. For the first time that season, Stieber gave up a takedown and was now on his back. The arena erupted and there was a grand mix of emotions resonating throughout the arena.

Iowa fans jumped to their feet anticipating the fall of Stieber and a national championship for the Hawkeyes. The Ohio State fans sprung up in concern for their returning national champion and undefeated and seemingly unbeatable Buckeye. Eyes were locked on the mat and whether those eyes were big with fear or big with excitement, all eyes were focused on the moment.

The referee would quickly swipe with his right arm—signaling near-fall exposure, and then he would quickly swipe with his left arm, signaling the same. During this time, Stieber was fighting from his back while Tony worked to maintain his cradle. Stieber found his way back to his chest and, even though the referee had two fingers pressed into the mat with his left hand, which signified a two-point near fall would be awarded, he signaled that the back exposure was back-and-forth, signaling it with his hands and waving it off as such, and, therefore, no points would be awarded.

"When I got to my single-leg," Ramos said, "he tried to roll. I locked up a cradle and got so excited I thought it was over. I saw the ref and heard the ref count two."

In the stands, Tom Brands raised both of his hands yelling, "Two!" with utter excitement. Next to him, Tom Ryan put his hands on his waist in a look of concentrated concern.

As the match continued, Stieber built into a tripod to come to his feet and Tony sunk in his patented cow-catcher as he now tried to bully Stieber back over to his back. Both wrestlers continued to struggle for their own position—one of defense, one of offense—and that struggle lasted about seven seconds before Stieber broke free, earned another point for an escape, and the match was now 6-3 in favor of the Buckeye.

From his seat, Tom Ryan waved his arms across his chest signaling no back points and, at the time of the escape and no awarded back points, Iowa Head Coach Tom Brands left his seat in the stands shouting, "Two near fall!" as he ran toward the stage. He would pause waiting for the call and then jumped around and waited for a late call. When none was given, he took off running to Tony's corner where his brother, Terry Brands, was coaching. From the floor, Tom yelled to Terry, who was up on the stage, "Go up to the table! Terry! Go up to the table! Use the challenge! Use the challenge!" Terry would do just that.

When Terry Brands motioned to the referee on the mat to stop action for a video challenge, the time in the match was down to 00:52 remaining. Terry Brands, as he walked toward the official and the head table, looked sternly at the referee and, with an Iowa style intensity shouted and pointed at him in unison, "You counted two and you know it! You counted two! Back points! Back points!"

When the challenge was made official and the referee asked Terry Brands what they were challenging, he continued his protest, "Back points! Back points!" Terry motioned the count with his right hand to mimic what he saw the referee do.

On ESPN, Quint Kessenich interviewed Tom Brands after he returned from the side of the stage. He asked Tom Brands what he was challenging and the answer was given with wide eyes and a grin, "Near fall," Tom Brands said in excitement. "What did you think?"

The interviewer turned it back to Tom Brands' perspective asking instead what the Hawkeye coach saw. "I saw a two count," Tom Brands said. "He held him. I mean, it's got to be held, but—one count doesn't get it done but two does. We'll see! There's a lot of drama, man."

After the interview with Tom Brands, Tom Ryan was also interviewed by Kessenich in real time in regard to what he saw. "I don't know," Ryan said. "Tough call. We'll see in a minute."

When questioned by Kessenich what would happen if the back points were given and the score would go 6-5, Ryan said, "We got to wrestle. Stay calm, composure—Logan's really composed. He's used to being very composed. Stay composed, keep attacking, building his lead."

Logan Stieber remembered the scramble as, "Ramos got in on a leg and I tried to scramble out. The scramble was crazy. I was on my back and then back up on my feet, and then they challenged it. I didn't think it was back points, but I knew that if there were, I would still be ahead, so I wasn't worried about the outcome."

From Terry Brands' perspective, he recalled how the points should have been awarded. "An official, where he's got two fingers down on the mat, you have an official that, on video, double counts," Terry Brands said. "You have it on film! This is on film. You have pictures with the guy's back flat on the mat—I'm not saying he was pinned—but his back is flat on the mat, what's the amount of time that it's going to take you to be flat on your back and then get off of it? Those were the things that were going through my mind at the time."

For Tony, he was confident of the back points; however, he too had to wait for the review to be looked at and scored as the referee saw fit.

When the review was completed, the referee declared that "The ruling on the mat was confirmed."

The Iowa fans burst out in boos that were mixed with boastful Buckeye cheers. The match score stood at 6-3; Tony was not awarded any points for a near fall count, and wrestling resumed with 00:52 remaining in the second period.

"Till this day I will never say it was a bad call, because that's what they called," Ramos reflected. "But, [the referee] knows in his heart he was wrong. There are pictures and videos showing him holding two fingers on the mat. They said the video review didn't hold up because, as soon as I took him over, Terry jumped up and was in front of the camera angle they had."

When wrestling continued, there was no intensity lost between the two wrestlers. Tony, again, fought for position against Stieber, and Stieber did the same. The heavy ties and pulls and head and hand fights resumed uninterrupted.

Tony fired off another shot that Stieber defended—Tony then found himself in his front head position; again, Stieber made his way back to his feet and, again, Tony worked forward and took another shot—to no avail.

As offensive as Stieber was in the first period and into the start of the second, it appeared that after the flurry, he was being more reactionary to Tony instead of as offensive as he opened.

In the third period, Tony chose the down position. Off the whistle, Stieber, who covered Tony's left side, grabbed Tony's right ankle with his right hand and sunk a tight waist with his left. Tony repositioned himself, Stieber worked to the opposite side; soon, Tony was able to get to his feet, but Stieber returned him. After a twenty-five second battle from bottom, Tony finally escaped. The riding advantage was in Stieber's favor—he had collected 1:10 total—and the score was 6-4, Stieber.

With an intense and animated Terry Brands in his corner, shouting instructions, Tony continued to hand fight and move forward as he tried to find an attack; however, Stieber, difficult to find an opening on, defended. Tony's head snaps and fakes and level changes continued as the junior Hawkeye knew time was closing out on his opportunity for redemption and a national championship; it was all slowly ticking away from him.

Stieber, when the one-minute mark was reached, fired off a shot on Tony, but Tony defended it and looked to reattack—no change in their positions occurred.

The head snaps and fakes and shucks would continue: 00:45.

Level changes, forward pressure, strong head ties remained: 00:30.

And then an opening.

With 00:29 remaining, Stieber took a shot and Tony reattacked—Tony was finally in on Stieber's left leg and the fight was on for a takedown and a chance at overtime.

With his head inside, Tony raised Stieber's right leg and tried to get to his feet. Stieber, hipping in hard and using a left-handed whizzer on Tony's right arm, was doing all he could to keep pressure on Tony's shoulders and force him to the mat. Stieber was winning the battle by not allowing Tony to take full control of the position: 00:15.

In an attempt to score, Tony stepped over Stieber with his right leg, trying to throw his leg in for control. Stieber continued the whizzer and pressure forward: 00:10.

While Tony's leg was high over Stieber's hip, Stieber transferred his weight and Tony countered with a small cartwheel off of him in an attempt to stay connected to the leg. The two faced one another and Tony was still in on Stieber's leg—this time with his head to the outside: 00:05.

Tony transitioned to a nearside cradle attempt, then to a cow-catcher and, as they both came to their feet and Tony was chasing the move, time expired.

For the fifth time Stieber had defeated Tony. Stieber turned to the Ohio State section and pointed with both hands in the air and with his tongue sticking out through a wide smile. He then motioned upwards, repeatedly. With his right hand he shook hands with Tony, had his hand raised as the 2013 133-pound NCAA champion—his second in as many years—and he walked over to the coaches in his corner and participated in a smaller, more humble celebration of a handshake and hug.

"Going into any of my matches [with Ramos]," Stieber said, "I just made sure that I was ready to go. My coaches had me ready and I was never worried. I always just concentrated on me. We had some strategies, like ending periods on top, but my focus was what I did well."

In regard to what ended up being the last time he faced Tony, Stieber did have an appreciation for the matches. "He was tough," Stieber said. "[He was] always in good position and he always showed up—I don't think he ever had a bad match. I was always excited to wrestle him because I knew it would be a tough match and exciting. He's a competitor and he loves to win and that always made the matches exciting."

For Tony, who felt that he left it all on the mat, he was crushed when time expired. "I was devastated," Ramos said, "but I was also okay. It was a weird feeling because I wanted to win so badly. I went out there, put it on the line, competed, and gave myself opportunities to win even after the no near fall call."

When Tony walked back into the tunnel and tried to collect himself, he knew dealing with the loss would be solely on his own shoulders. "There was nothing anyone could say to me at that time," Ramos remembered. "I just had to get over it in my heart and mind and start preparing for the next year—my final year. That would be my final shot at the ultimate dream of becoming an NCAA champion."

When asked about his match-ups with Stieber, Tony was just as complimentary as Stieber was of him. "I appreciated that we went to battle each and every match and how much of a gamer and competitor he was," Ramos admitted. "You had to respect him for that. He kept the fire ignited inside of me. If I were to have beaten him, who knows if that flame I had burning deep down inside of me would have kept going. For him, I was probably the guy that kept him working hard because he knew there was someone out there that he wasn't going to be able to dominate like everyone else. You need—he needs and I need, competitors need—someone like that who is out there to make you better.

"He was a great athlete and wrestler. He was just better than me on those days. There is nothing that I would have changed when I competed.

I am glad we had that rivalry and were able to give fans something to be excited about within the sport of wrestling."

In an interview with FloWrestling, Tony talked more about the relationship aspect and the perception of the two wrestlers.

"People probably think I hate him," Ramos said. "I hate him when we wrestle. I hate him when we're competing. I hate everyone when we're competing. But that's the difference: [Am I] going to be able to separate hating him in life just because he beat [me]? I don't know if I'm going to hate him. I'm not going to love him. I'm not going to probably be friends with him. But, there's a mutual respect."

As for what Tony walked away with, "I figured out the bottom wrestling with him, which is his toughest position," Ramos said. "I wanted to wrestle him. I wanted to prove to everyone that I could beat him—I'm stubborn like that. [When he won his fourth title], I think that really put a cap on my legacy because people realize, 'You know, that's the only person [Ramos] really lost to at the national tournament twice. He lost to Stieber in the semis. He lost to Stieber in the finals.' If you don't count freshman year, that's the only guy I lost to at the national tournament."

In regard to why Tony struggled with Stieber so much, head coach Tom Brands commented, "Stieber's pretty good. When you beat Stieber, you got to beat him and you got to plant him because Stieber will bounce like a ball or he'll roll or he'll scramble or he's funky or he's good on top and he'll ride you and turn you. [That season], he couldn't ride Ramos because Ramos spent hours—hours—on that belly-claw. I remember watching Terry put him in those positions all the time. All the time. And you know what? Stieber couldn't ride him."

Of course, as close as Tony was, there were still aspects that he had to improve on for the following season, and Terry Brands spoke about situational wrestling at such a high level.

"When the matches would get tight with Logan Stieber," Terry Brands said, "and that's usually where Tony would shut down and be very good at not letting guys get to him—his defense. Where a guy is usually skeptical thinking, 'Okay, if I shoot, he might run the corner and cradle me.' Logan Stieber didn't care. He was long, much longer and stronger than he looks. So, when Tony would slap and get in on that leg, Tony would either, if he couldn't back up or break that lock—there was something about Stieber there, a slipperiness or something—he wasn't able to pursue that angle. And he didn't wrestle him in the front headlock enough—that's my opinion. And then the ability to get to Stieber—Stieber's counter offense was very, very good."

Terry Brands continued, "Well, the NCAAs was even a different match from the score. It was a crazy match—a crazy winnable match. You can say what you want about that score, but it was closer than a one-point match. It really was. So it wasn't like he just closed the gap. He did, in my opinion, he did what Iowa wrestling philosophy is, and that is: 'If you get beat, your opponent knows who you are and the next time you take him out. And then the next time you take him out with a bigger margin.' He did that. He just didn't do that in a way that got [his] hand raised. And that was really, again, the communication in going forward into the next season.

"He was good enough to beat Stieber, he just never closed the deal on it. He was good enough to beat Stieber at the Big Tens, and this is hard for me to say because I don't want to read his mind, but did he believe it? Well, if you know Tony Ramos of course he did. So Stieber is just that good still. He's still just that much better than we are. That's what my evaluation was.

"When we got to the NCAAs," Terry Brands concluded, "it was about taking those areas that we need to buckle down on and buckle down. And then, golly, you can't put yourself in a hole like that. You can't do that against a guy like Logan Stieber. And that's really what happened. Even though he came roaring back and even though a dicey call here and maybe a not-so-great call there was maybe the difference in the match, he still got beat and he got beat fair and square. He got beat because he didn't buckle down in the honing areas or the individual part of that season that caught him early. He eliminated some of it, but he didn't eliminate enough of it."

For Tony, that loss in the NCAA finals ended a remarkable and dominant overall season. Even though he came up short of his goals, his mentality put him in position to have a shot at an NCAA championship.

"I had an attitude that year where I just didn't care," Ramos said. "Also, so many things were happening so fast and going so well that the confidence I had just kept rolling over match after match after match. I kept having very good results and putting fear into my upcoming opponents while building my mind and body."

However, with his junior year officially over, and his goals of winning a Big Ten championship and an NCAA championship down to one opportunity, he had to refocus himself and prepare for his final season.

"I had one more opportunity," Ramos said. "I had one more Big Ten tournament and I had one more NCAA tournament. If I didn't make my mark in those two opportunities, then it would be my fault. I could only blame myself."

ALSO THAT SUMMER AS TONY WORKED TO BE A national champion in his final season as Hawkeye, Daniel Dennis would be walking away from Iowa and the Hawkeye Wrestling Club. Tony was sad to see his friend and mentor leave, but he understood it was something Dennis had to do. Tony could see the pain he was in physically and emotionally and knew his friend needed to heal. In that, there relationship would be what it had always been: being there for one another when the time was called upon.

"Our appreciation for each other was never talked about," Ramos said. "It was just understood. I was there for him if he needed anything, I would be there. And if I ever needed anything from him, he would be there for me—that never changed. Dennis and me always looked out for each other. But it was hard on both of us for him to be wrestling at 55 kg because it was just too low of a weight for him. He had a hard time wrestling, he couldn't move. He would come into practice and we would just beat on him because he had nothing left in him—and the same thing happened when it came time for competition. He had nothing left because he spent so much time cutting weight to make 55. It hurt me to see him like that because of how talented I knew he was. I think that was where the decision was made for him to be done and to move on and go to California and live his life his way with climbing and whatnot."

In Tony's estimation, for Dennis to live his own way, he had to be able to go and do whatever he wanted, whenever he wanted. He was not going to be held to one particular place—being mobile was key.

"He made the choice to live out of his truck because he wanted to be mobile and go wherever he wanted, do whatever he wanted to do and not have anything to worry about. He wanted to go explore the world and see what was out there. And that was what he did."

Once Dennis left, Tony had to find comparable partners, but matching Dennis' strength and size and experience would be difficult, if not impossible, to replicate. Tony would, however, grab and work with a number of the guys in the room. Plus, he still had Tom and Terry Brands and a focus to walk out of his senior season undefeated and as a Big Ten and national champion.

2013 • NCAA DIVISION I WRESTLING CHAMPIONSHIPS
133 LB CHAMPIONSHIP MATCH
RAMOS TRIES TO HIT HIS COW-CATCHER ON STIEBER COMING OUT OF A SCRAMBLE
PHOTOGRAPH COURTESY • UNIVERSITY OF IOWA ATHLETICS

CHAPTER 49
SAYING GOODBYE AND MOVING FORWARD

"So I just started waving back at them, smiling, like, 'Hey, see you guys later.'"

• *Tony Ramos*

LEADING INTO THE START OF HIS SENIOR SEASON, Tony heard some rumors about Logan Stieber and how he might not be at 133 pounds that season.

"Earlier that spring, there was talk about how Stieber might go up a weight class," Ramos said. "I had heard some rumblings, but it was more or less speculation, about how Stieber was having some trouble making the weight and, that after the NCAAs, that'd be his last time at the weight and that he would move up [to 141 pounds]."

Once the speculation started, people started talking more and more—and Tony was listening.

"The outside noise about what people were saying didn't really bother me," Ramos said. "The only thing that probably bothered me the most was when people said Stieber was not going to be at 133 anymore, so it opens up the field. I guess it bothered me in the sense that people didn't understand how good I really was. They said, 'Well, Stieber's gone, good. Now Ramos has got a shot.' I felt like I always had a shot even when he was there, but it just never happened."

Once Tony heard a more substantiated claim about where Stieber might be wrestling closer to the opening of the season, he wanted to move up a weight class as well and continue to compete against Stieber.

"At the beginning of the year," Ramos said, "I kind of wanted to chase

Stieber. It was a conflict with me, in my mind; I wanted to go up to 141—I thought maybe it would be better for the team to get Clark and Gilman both in the line-up and then I'll be at 141 pounds and cover one of our weaker areas, and just go from there. One of the bigger things was that I felt that I could beat Stieber. I felt like I was right there plenty of times and I like taking challenges and it was something that I wanted to go after.

"My weight was pretty high when I had to come in—there was certification and the pre-certification I don't think I would have even certified for 133 pounds. Tom saw that and pulled me to the side and said, 'Hey, we got to figure out what's going on here. Either you're going 141 or you're staying at 133, but your weight is out of control for 133.'

"That's when I sat down with him and I sat down with family and we talked about what was best for me, not about me trying to chase after this guy that was considered invincible because nobody had beaten him. I wanted to wrestle him, I wanted to prove that he wasn't [invincible] and that I could [defeat him]. After all of the talks the decision came down to the best decision for me, for my size—for me to wrestle at and compete at 133 pounds."

WITH TONY HAVING MADE HIS DECISION ON which weight class he would compete at, his next move was accepting an invitation to Fairfax, Virginia, for the NWCA All-Star Classic to be held on November 2, 2013. Tony would ultimately wrestle Virginia Tech's Devin Carter, and the two agreed to wrestle an "out of weight class" match-up at 141 pounds. Tony and Carter had a brief history the season before as Carter had defeated Tony in the finals of the Midlands, but Tony then dominated Carter in the national duals and at the NCAA championships. It was a strong addition to the All-Star line-up card, a match-up of two All-Americans; however, this was not the match that Tony and Iowa was looking for at the dual.

"Originally," Ramos said, "Tom [Brands] was trying to get me the match with Stieber that I wanted. One of the compromises [of me wrestling at 133 pounds] was getting me the match with Stieber at the All-Star meet at 141, and that would be my chance at like a national tournament chance or national championship chance instead of chasing after him. So that's what we were working on.

"At first, the NWCA was against it—they didn't want to do it," Ramos recalled. "And then we got a call from them saying that Stieber doesn't want to do it. We said fine, we'll wrestle [undefeated returning NCAA Champion at 141 pounds, Kendric] Maple then. So I was going to go up to 141 and wrestle whoever it was. You know, this All-Star meet thing, people want to see exciting matches, people want to see matches that aren't going to happen during the season and things like that. We were trying to pave the way for that to start becoming a thing.

"We ended up getting a call back from the NWCA saying that Maple and Stieber were going to wrestle each other at 141 and 149. We were pissed about it. We told them it was horseshit because they were stealing our idea—taking it from us and making it work for them. This is when they came back with Carter at 141 and I agreed to it. And what people don't know is that because of weight management criteria, even though we agreed to wrestle 141, I had to weigh in under 136 pounds. I couldn't weigh any more than 136 and Carter could weigh in at 141, so I was giving up a bit of weight."

Regardless of how it all played out, Tony was excited about the opportunity to be involved in the meet and the chance to compete. "I liked wrestling Devin Carter," Ramos continued. "He was a good guy. I think a lot of people thought that I'd be undersized in that match, that I wouldn't be able to counter his leverage and muscle, but I wrestled Carter numerous times and I knew I could wear him out and that extra muscle that he put on was going to slow him down."

Now that Tony was going to wrestle in the dual, his preparation had to be altered slightly from his teammates.

"Training for the All-Star meet is a little bit different," Ramos said. "Usually at that time [of the season] things are much more laid back where we are doing conditioning and just pushing ourselves. For me, we had to do a different plan where I was still going through this pushing phase, but the week before I kind of had to cut back like I was getting ready for mat or tournament preparation while these other guys were still going hard.

"The coaches were great, they really made it work," Ramos remembered. "They understood that this was something that I really wanted to do—we had not participated in the All-Star meet in a few years and I had been asked a few years before—and I went to Tom and said, 'I really want to do this. This is important to me, I want to wrestle in it,' and he made it work."

When the day came and it was time to compete, Tony was on weight and ready.

As he had been accustomed to doing, Tony waited in his stance in the center of the mat staring at Carter, waiting for him to come into the circle and wrestle. When the whistle blew and the match was under way, Tony, in the red All-Star Classic singlet, gave up an early takedown and found himself chasing a 3-1 deficit going into the third period.

When the third period finally came, the match went down to the final thirty seconds before Tony worked into a double-leg attack and then changed it over to a single-leg attack on Carter's right leg. Tony came up, circled left, and Carter tried to jump in between Tony's legs to create a scramble position, but Tony had his leg too tight and dropped his knee down to prevent the scramble situation. In those final twenty-three seconds, Tony would earn a takedown that not only tied the match, but sent the match into overtime.

"Going into that third period," Ramos said, "I think I was down by a couple of points and needed a takedown. I started feeling him break and breathing heavy through his mouth and through his nose and just kept attacking and attacking and pushing and I finally got to my shot and scored."

In overtime, Tony defended a double-leg attack from Carter with his back to the mat's edge, and then hit a reattack double, changed over to a single-leg, this time to Carter's left leg, and scored the takedown to win the match.

Tony got up, flexed his arms in his double rainbow pose, and stomped around as Carter lay on the mat. Carter would eventually get up after Tony's tour around the center of the mat, but he was physically drained. He shook Tony's hand while he took deep breaths, and walked off the mat, hands on hips; Tony ran off the mat, victorious.

"I knew he couldn't keep pace," Ramos said. "He broke and I took advantage. He didn't have anything left. Even after the match he went and lay over in the corner—he was done. He was dead. He was exhausted."

FOR THE HAWKEYES, THEY OPENED THEIR
season as they had normally done, with a confidence builder for the wrestlers. They traveled to the Luther Open in order to work out a few kinks and get back into their routines.

"Every year we usually start with the Iowa City duals or some type of open tournament to get our confidence, build us up, and get us used to that tournament feel for our routine," Ramos said. "Tom [Brands] always said that we needed to have our routine down so that by the middle of the year we know exactly what our routine is and if you have to make minor tweaks, do them early and practice it before the national tournament so once it all matters, there is nothing to chance. Doing this at a lower tournament, it allowed guys to, if they did make a mistake, recover from it."

Tony went 4-0 at the Luther Open with three falls and a major decision in the finals. He then headed to Ames, Iowa, one final time for a dual with the Cyclones. For Tony, ranked number one in the country, he would dismantle Dakota Bauer with a 16-5 major decision. The Hawkeyes would also cruise to a 23-9 dual meet victory as well.

In Tony's four years at Iowa, neither he nor the Hawkeyes ever lost to their instate rivals. Tony reflected on the Iowa and Iowa State rivalry as something special. However, the dual had changed a bit throughout his years at Iowa.

"Being a part of that experience was fun," Ramos said. "But, at the same time, it wasn't what it used to be—it had kind of lost its luster a bit over the years. When I was a freshman, we would go wrestle at Hilton Coliseum and it was packed. Iowa State hadn't been as good over those last few years and the atmosphere kind of went away. I mean, people were showing up, but the stands weren't full; there were a lot of gaps out there.

"But the biggest thing that I remember [my senior season], is getting up and the whole place was just booing me—and you know I'm going to play up to that role. So I just started waving back at them, smiling, like, 'Hey, see you guys later. You'll never have to see me again. Oh, and you never came close.'"

2014 • NWCA ALL-STAR CLASSIC
RAMOS DEFEATS CARTER OF VIRGINIA TECH BY A 5-3 OVERTIME DECISION
PHOTOGRAPH COURTESY • UNIVERSITY OF IOWA ATHLETICS

CHAPTER 50
THE UNEXPECTED

"I knew on his feet that he liked to use his hands—he's a little dangerous in there—but I had to use my hands just like he uses his hands and my hands were a little better today."

• Joe Colon
All-American, the University of Northern Iowa

TONY WAS DOMINATING THE FIELD AS HE HAD done the previous season—he had totaled six falls and two major decisions in his first eight matches; he was also ranked as the number-one wrestler in the country at his weight class. However, there were still a number of skeptics out there who believed that the weight class was still open to a number of different wrestlers. One of those wrestlers that some critics believed had an outside chance of a title, Tony faced in a dual meet in Edinboro, Pennsylvania. He was A.J. Schopp and the number-eight ranked wrestler at the weight class.

Tony had defeated Schopp the season before, Tony's junior season, by a 9-0 major decision—at that time, Schopp was the number-three ranked wrestler behind Tony at number-two.

At the 2012 NCAA championships, the same year that Tony had placed third, the then number-seven ranked Schopp, a freshman, was a national qualifier and lost in the wrestle-backs to Michigan's Zach Stevens missing the All-American round due to that loss. As a sophomore, Schopp was ranked as the number-four wrestler in the country and lived up to his raking as he earned All-American honors for the first time in his career. He ended up losing in the third-place bout to number-three Tyler Graff of Wisconsin by a 6-3 decision.

For the most current match-up with Tony, Schopp and the number-fifteen rated Fighting Scots had the comfort of wrestling in McComb Fieldhouse on the campus of Edinboro University. However, there was very little to indicate that after a 9-0 loss to Tony the season before, that Schopp would have the firepower to answer Tony's ability to widen the gap between opponents the more he wrestled them.

Tony, staring in the middle of the black circled mat surrounded by plaid colors on the outside of the circle with "EDINBORO" stretched across the top of the mat and "FIGHTING SCOTS" across the bottom, waited as Schopp came to the center line for the start of the match.

Senior editor Willie Saylor of FloWrestling wrote a brief article in regard to the match as follows:

> *Schopp was able to score when he high-legged over a Ramos shot early in the first. A scramble ensued that saw Schopp eventually secure both ankles on the edge of the mat. Schopp used his great ability on top to rack up over 1:47 riding time to end the first period.*
>
> *Ramos chose neutral in the second and the period remained scoreless until late. That's when Schopp shot a wrap arm and Ramos eventually countered to tie it at two right at the buzzer.*
>
> *Schopp escaped in the third to make it 3-2 and riding time was erased. With about twenty seconds remaining in the match, Ramos got to rear standing but was unable to convert for points in what would be the deciding sequence and secure Schopp's upset.*
>
> *McComb Fieldhouse was ignited.*

With bagpipes playing at an excitingly absurd level in the background, A.J. Schopp was interviewed after his win by GoBoroAthleticsTV and asked what it was like to earn the victory over the number-one ranked Hawkeye, a wrestler who had had his way with Schopp the last time that they wrestled.

"I wouldn't say he had his way with me," Schopp answered. "It's nice coming up on top, but this isn't the end of the season. I've got to do that again. I've got to do that on top of the big stage, on top of the blue mat in March at nationals. It's great to be able to know that I can do that. I always had that confidence, but getting it done, that's what we're downstairs in the basement training for."

For Tony, he did not feel that much had changed; however, his results were not what he expected them to be, even in his wins early on that season. He knew there was something holding him back.

When it came to Schopp, however, "I knew Schopp was a good scrambler and that he was really good on top," Ramos said. "The first time I wrestled him, my junior year, I was able score a couple takedowns and put up points that first period where the top and bottom didn't matter so he couldn't just hang on, cling on—he actually had to do something. I didn't do that in that first period. I actually gave up a takedown in a scramble and I put myself in a hole from there.

"I go into that third period and I'm down. I had to ride him to reverse and erase riding time, and then I had to cut him and try to get a takedown. Unfortunately, we got into a couple situations where I couldn't finish—I just wasn't sharp. I just wasn't crisp with the things that I was doing. Nothing changed in my training, it was just not going out and performing when it was time to wrestle those matches. More than anything I had a fear of not living up to what I had done the previous year and, not on purpose, I was just too cautious and didn't open up like I should have."

From Terry Brands' point of view, there were no red flags in regard to Tony's performance or major aspects that needed correction. "He was just that good on top," Terry Brands said. "Plus, Ramos gave up a takedown right away, so he was kind of in a tough situation right away. So, he had to eliminate those things in matches. How is a guy taking us down? What is he doing? What are we not doing? What can we do better to get to this guy's lungs, to get to his mind, and to do the things that we need to do to him in order to beat him?"

Coming off the mat, it was easy to see Tony's frustration—in regard to his emotions, he was just as candid in defeat as he was in victory.

"I was upset," Ramos said of his emotions as he walked off the mat. "I knew that the perfect season was over all because I let a match get away from me that I shouldn't have. At the same time, I remember coming off the mat and telling Tom [Brands], 'Two weeks and I'll get my shot again. We'll be at the Midlands and for two more weeks we'll have to listen to people talk about how I won't be able to win a national title and then I'll go out at the Midlands and destroy him like I did last time.'

"I was already moving forward. I wasn't going to sit back and sulk in a loss because that wasn't the goal. The goal wasn't to beat A.J. Schopp at an Edinboro dual meet. The goal was to be a national champion and, at the end of the year, stand at the top of the podium."

For Tony, he continually worked to move forward from his wins and losses. Even though he had always moved on in a fairly healthy manner, he saw a larger picture and how there was something next to prepare for. This loss, seemingly his only real loss outside of Stieber in the past two seasons "was something that was just part of the building process on where I needed to get be," Ramos said. "For me, I knew had to open up and not let the pressure of my goals get in the way of my matches, which wasn't always easy. But, that was what I had to do to work myself back to where I needed to be."

THE FOLLOWING WEEK TONY FOUND HIS confidence back home in Iowa City against Justin Farmer of Buffalo—it would be in the form of a 22-7 technical fall.

"It's exciting after a loss to get back on the winning ways and doing things right," Ramos said. "One of the things we've been talking about was when I was pinning guys I was scoring a lot of points and wearing them out. We're trying to get back to scoring a lot of points and when things open up, take them as they happen."

The following week, however, the number-one Nittany Lions came to Iowa City and Tony knew that he had to keep building as his opponent, Jimmy Gulibon who was ranked number fifteen, was someone he would have to open up on if the team was going to pull off another upset over the top team in the country.

The previous year, Tony created the loudest moment in Carver-Hawkeye Arena history, and there was still a great buzz around Iowa regarding his fall in the Penn State dual. In fact, the buzz was not just around Iowa, but Tony heard about it from his family as well. The season before, Tony was able to win a bet with his brother Frank that won him a 9mm handgun. That current year, the stakes would have to be much higher as a duplication of such a task would be very difficult.

With time off before the dual, Tony, as had become his custom, took those moments for some family time—he said that it relaxed him and he always liked having those closest to him around before he competed.

"Just like the year before," Ramos laughed as he recalled the day, "the whole entourage came down and I was messing with Frankie. I took out the 9mm he had to buy me and I was showing it off. We happened to be out and walked into Scheels, talking to fans and looking around. I looked at Frankie, my Uncle Jerry and Matt were there, and said, 'Hey, Frankie, if you want another pin this year, you're going to have to buy me something else.' He looked at me and was like, 'What do you want, Tony?' I said, 'Well, there's this shotgun I've been looking at.'

"Frankie came back with, 'If you pin Gulibon and win Midlands, I'll buy you the shotgun.' I turned to him and was like, 'No. Forget it. Don't worry about it—whatever. That wasn't what the deal was supposed to be so, no, I'm all right.' He quickly turned and said, 'Okay, if you pin him, then you can have it.'"

When Tony came to the arena, he knew the crowd would be ready. Much had been done to set up that dual meet up between the number-one Penn State Nittany Lions and the number-three Iowa Hawkeyes. Somehow, when the schedule came out, the Big Ten committee did not place that dual on the Big Ten schedule—it almost never happened. It was left to the two head coaches, with the help of their administration, to pull the dual together.

"I think there was a lot of cooperation with a lot of different people," Tom Brands said. "One for sure had to be with Penn State, [Head Coach Cael] Sanderson, and our administration and their administration. [Both had to] work schedules around at Penn State with their schedules—it had to be the right timing and all that—and our schedule had to be the right timing, and you get a date and then you have cooperation between athletics and central campus. It was a big deal to make it happen at prime time and do the things that they did and move the things around that they did."

When Tony was asked about fitting the meet in, he said, "It's good that the coaches worked together to make something happen that the Big Ten screwed up. So, that's exciting that they were able to get together and fix it. You don't see a lot of times when something's wrong getting fixed."

As the crowd walked into Carver-Hawkeye, 13,747 strong were ready to support and cheer on their schools.

After Nico Megaludis defeated Iowa's Thomas Gilman by a 4-1 decision at 125, and gave PSU a 3-0 dual meet lead, Tony raced to the mat before the 133-pound weight class was even called. Tony, in the middle of an onslaught of cheers, waited, on the starting line, for Jimmy Gulibon. Once Gulibon came out, Tony stared and followed him all the way to his start line. The Iowa fans loved every moment.

Off the whistle, Tony was the aggressor and immediately worked to push the pace of the match. He found himself in a snap down position where both he and Gulibon were on their knees and, while Gulibon was looking to use his hands to work back to his feet, Tony used his head and drove straight through Gulibon's hands, into his head, and rammed into him as he dove at his legs and ended on top of him for a takedown on the edge of the mat.

The takedowns would continue and there were even moments of a possible fall within those scrambles. In that, each scramble brought Iowa fans to the edge of their seats and they slowly pushed forward on their toes and raised their chins ready to stand if it happened.

In one moment, Tony was in a front headlock position and, as he chased the leg to his right, he kept digging for his right hand underhook in anticipation of possibly catching Gulibon in a cow-catcher. Unfortunately, Gulibon, aware and protecting his position, continued to scramble. Tony changed off to the leg, chased it, came behind, and scored his two on the takedown.

Gulibon would escape, turn and reattack on Tony, and the same situation would continue: Tony snapped down heavy on the head, looked to beat the leg on his right side, and then, when the cow-catcher was not there—and Tony was digging in transition—he chased the leg and scored the takedown.

The crowd, being teased each time, would come to its feet and the screams would raise with each front headlock position—every fan was locked in on Tony's right arm and where it was going; they wanted and anticipated the fall.

Into the first period, it was a quick 6-2 lead and the energy in Carver grew with each passing second.

"I came out right away with some takedowns and was cutting him," Ramos recalled. "He kept diving in on my legs and I was getting a lot of go behind opportunities. It was more of just a matter of time before I was going to fall into my patented cow-catcher."

In the second period, Gulibon struggled to keep pace with Tony's non-stop motion and movement. Off another front headlock, Tony looked to force his cow-catcher. When the fans saw that position, they scattered on the floor and moved throughout the arena for a better view. Some were coming to their feet, punching their fists, becoming big-eyed and wide-smiled. Others were holding their heads, anticipating a turn, and hoping it would not happen. In the end, Tony again finished behind for another takedown.

Then it happened…again.

Off another front headlock position, Tony found his opening as he circled. His right hand worked in deep enough across Gulibon's far right side, and Tony's right arm locked into position across the back as the slow rotation began. The fight was a struggle as Gulibon was doing all he could to prevent the possible turn, but the energy in Carver gave him no chance.

"When it was happening, I had a flashback of exactly what happened the year before," Ramos said. "I went out there and I was wrestling—and I knew going into that—again, same thing as it was the year before, talking to family, taking to friends, if we wanted to win that dual meet, I had to get a pin—I had to get the fall. I had to repeat what I did last year, send the fans in Carver-Hawkeye Arena in a frenzy and get that atmosphere going so the people following behind me could keep on following.

"When I went out there, I was wrestling—you know [Gulibon] was someone people were talking about; he was a young gun, a PA kid—and I wanted to make a statement that said, 'Hey, this is the big leagues, you're not in high school anymore.'

"As soon as I put my hands on him, I knew—I remember that first takedown. He was kind of on his knees and I blew right through him in a double-leg and his eyes were wide like, 'What just hit me? I'm in for a fight right now.' And after that he was timid and hesitating with everything that he did and things started to open up. I got to my front headlock a couple of times and scored, but I finally got to that underhook on the right side, hit my cow-catcher, and took him over and got the fall. It was just like a replay of what happened the year before. I got up and celebrated and made a shotgun pose to Frankie.

"When I looked at Frankie and kind of gave him the pose [of shooting the shotgun]. He was freakin' happy, but afterwards he was like, 'So how about we just forget this one?' I started laughing and shaking my head and I said, 'No, we're not forgetting this one.' So we went out over to Scheels and picked it up and that was that.

"Even though I got the win, it was still an empty night because we didn't come through as a team and that part sucked. All we hear about is Penn State and they're number one and it's them against everyone else and Iowa can't beat them. I wanted to go out there and shut that up, but it takes more than just one person."

TONY'S SWAGGER WAS BACK IN FULL FORCE. HIS ability to open up and put points on the board and dominate his opponents seemed to find its way back into his offensive arsenal and inner confidence. Next up was the Midlands championships in Evanston, Illinois, and Tony had one final chance to win a major tournament in his home state in front of his family and friends.

As predicted, Tony was the number-two seed to Edinboro's A.J. Schopp. In grand fashion, Schopp advanced to the semifinals with a first-round decision, 6-0, a second-round fall in 4:18, a quarterfinal win, 6-0, and then, in the semifinals, he would wrestle the four seed, Joe Colon, from Northern Iowa.

For Tony, in his opening session, he faced off against a Big Ten opponent from Purdue University, Cashe' Quiroga. Cashe', who had been in and out of the rankings, was a worthy opponent; however, he did not have enough firepower to get to Tony. Tony won with a 13-5 major decision and advanced.

Next up in the championship round was Utah Valley's Chasen Tolbert; however, Tolbert would have little say in the outcome of the match. Tony scored points in bunches and won by a 23-8 technical fall in 6:56. Tony put on a clinic and headed into the quarterfinals against Devon Lotito of Cal Poly.

Again, as he had done in each of the first two rounds, Tony opened up and piled up the points and won decisively with a dominant 14-5 major decision. This would set up a semifinal match against the tournament's number-six seed and a very well-known unattached wrestler, Alan Waters from Missouri.

As nice of a tournament that Waters had put together, his streak stopped with Tony. In a 5-0 decision, the Hawkeye proved that he was not only the best wrestler in that match, but he put to bed any rumors of how Waters' rise to the top would be through the returning national finalist.

"It wasn't that it was a tough match," Ramos said, "as much as it was me controlling it. I got my takedown, rode him out. Got my escape, got a takedown, and rode him out. It really wasn't a big deal. The nice thing was beating him after last year. He beat McDonough and was running his mouth a little bit, and it was one of those things where I wanted to go out and right a wrong to one of our teammates and make all of our fans happy. With him scoring zero points and being pushed in the wrestle-backs, I think I did that."

Now that Tony was in the finals, it was his chance to right another wrong with A.J. Schopp; or at least that was what he thought. On the upper half of the bracket, there would be a small kink in Tony's plan—Schopp did not come out the victor. Schopp fell to Northern Iowa's Joe Colon in a 3-0 match. The revenge on Schopp would have to wait, but the Midlands title was still within reach.

"Going into the [Colon] match," Ramos said, "we knew Colon was good upper body. He had good underhooks and wanted to be in those types of positions. For me, I needed to get to my offense and score without putting myself in areas that favored his strengths."

The match not only featured two contrasting styles, it also featured Iowa versus Northern Iowa. Tony, the first to the middle of the purple Northwestern mat, poised himself in his stance and stared at Colon who walked over to grab his ankle band, picked it up, and walked away. But Tony's eyes stayed focused on him the entire time.

Colon, in the purple singlet with gold trim, would pace back and forth on his side of the mat until it was time to come to the center for the start of the match.

When the whistle blew and the match was underway, Colon would go right to his head ties as did Tony, and the battle for position began. The normally forward-moving Tony would be pushed back by Colon as he was able to sink both of his underhooks into the smaller Hawkeye and drive him backwards and out of bounds.

Tony would be the first back to the center as Colon walked in stride and stepped to the line. The next sequence began with Colon dropping to his hands and right knee, almost trying to get under Tony, and he and

Tony looked to exchange level changes before they ended up in a tie-up position for the second time.

With 2:15 remaining in the first period, Tony worked head taps and level changes to try and work to Colon who was back in a low almost tripod-like stance. However, Colon would hand fight to Tony's head and, in a small flurry of back and forth, Tony would fire underneath Colon's left side. When he did this, Colon down-blocked and trapped Tony's right arm, blocked it, put pressure down on it, and ran to his left as Tony tried to face him. The small flurry ended with Colon scoring a takedown.

The wrestling would continue on the edge of the mat: Colon in the very familiar top position of a cross-collar ride, and Tony working to his standup while Colon transitioned into sinking his right leg in between Tony's legs. The fight worked to the feet and before Tony could work himself free, the two went out of bounds.

On the restart, Colon worked right back into his cross-collar ride and, as Tony worked for his opening and came to his feet, Colon tried to chase and return the Hawkeye to the mat. Tony would escape and level the match by getting back to his feet where he could use his offense to work back into the match.

There was 1:21 left in the period when the two would have another restart.

When action began, Colon worked high on Tony's body as he tried to force his left underhook in under Tony's right arm. Colon attempted this three more times in succession; however, Tony broke away and continually tried to work his offense by getting to Colon's head—he wanted to fatigue him in order to open up his offense and work into his own shots and attacks.

At the 00:38 mark, Tony felt an opening and attempted a double-leg to Colon's left side, Tony's right. Colon, who sprawled his left leg back, also dropped his right elbow to defend against Tony's head getting underneath and to his right side. When he did that, Tony, extended and off balance with his right arm too far drawn-out, staggered and Colon was able to throw his right arm underhook in and pop Tony over to his hip.

Once Tony fell on his right hip and looked to regather his position, he found himself caught on his butt with both of his arms stretched back as supports. Colon would climb the body and take both of Tony's arms as he drove him back and forced him over to his back. As Colon adjusted, and had Tony's chin with his right hand and a deep underhook with his left, the position looked too tight for Tony to fight out of.

Colon then slowly dropped his weight down and Tony, working to fight to his belly, felt Colon pop both legs inside of his and break his supports. As Colon arched his back and Tony had nothing left to bridge on, the mat was slapped and Colon would record the fall at the 2:37 mark.

Tony got up slowly and Colon went to the mat's center and took off his ankle bands. Tony shook Colon's hand and ran off the mat. He would be denied a Midlands championship for the second year in a row and with no more opportunities as a Hawkeye.

The Des Moines Register interviewed Colon after his win; Colon attributed his success in the match to his hand fighting and underhook position. "His hands were heavy, he likes to move, he likes to bounce," Colon said of Tony, "and I knew I had to use my hands and move my feet and I stuck with that. That's how I got that first takedown, using my hands, I snapped him down, went around. Then we got back to our feet and I got back in an underhook and snapped him right back down and got my legs back, he tried to stop it and I just felt it.

"I knew on his feet that he liked to use his hands—he's a little dangerous in there—but I had to use my hands just like he uses his hands and my hands were a little better today."

From Tony's vantage point, "We were only about thirty-seconds into the match, maybe forty-five seconds in and I could feel him starting to wear down. All of his strength, I could feel him getting tired so quickly. You know, I took a bad shot, got in sloppy position and I got taken over to my back and pinned and I was so angry because I knew he could not hold the pace that I was bringing at him for seven minutes.

"I knew right after that match—I went right into the back and my buddy, Zach Pilcher, could tell you exactly how I was. Everything was okay. He walked in the back to come see me and see how I was doing and I was like, 'Hey, don't worry about me. I messed up. That's never going to happen again and that dude will never beat me again.' He knew I was fine because I was calm and collected."

Tom Brands spoke to Tony after the loss, but Tony ended up initiating the conversation. "Tom, look, right there," Ramos said as they watched the video. "You can see that he's tired. He's exhausted and we're only a minute and a half into the match. Tom says, 'I saw that, too. I know. I know he was. He can't hold your pace. He can't wrestle with you. But you have to stay solid.' And that, staying solid, was one of the biggest things I worked on the rest of the year. Staying solid and under control."

With the Midlands over, Tony focused on his techniques and conditioning and fine-tuned the smaller aspects of his wrestling each week as the Hawkeyes would only wrestle in dual meets until the Big Ten championships in March. In fact, aside from Oklahoma State and Lehigh, all of the remaining duals on the schedule weree against Big Ten opponents.

CHAPTER 51
UNDEFEATED IN CARVER

"There is something special about Carver-Hawkeye Arena, and there is something special about our fans, and there is something special about how they reward our guys. Especially when you're doing the job, and the way Ramos competes, he's been able to do the job."

• Tom Brands
Head Coach, the University of Iowa
Coach, Hawkeye Wrestling Club

THE BIG TEN DUAL SCHEDULE STARTED IN Bradley, Illinois, at Bradley-Bourbonnais High School against the number-twenty-one rated Boilermakers from Purdue. Iowa, who had not lost a Big Ten opener in the past fifteen years, was not looking to change anything on that night.

Tony, now ranked number four at his weight, faced Kyle Ayersman. Little would be needed as Tony won an 11-5 decision. Iowa also needed little as they won by a 30-3 dual meet score and recorded their twenty-seventh consecutive dual meet win over the Boilermakers. In the process, Iowa also recorded twenty-five takedowns to Purdue's one in the win. The Hawkeyes would now return to Carver-Hawkeye Arena for a match-up with Michigan State.

When the Spartans walked into the arena, they had no idea they would suffer a 41-0 loss; this would also be Iowa's fourth shut out of an opponent on the season.

Tony won via a fall in 5:25 over Garth Yenter, one of two falls for Iowa, and the Hawkeyes racked up two technical falls, two majors, and four regular decisions to round out the night in front of the 6,661 in attendance. Tony earned his thirtieth-consecutive win at Carver, and now the talks began about if he could achieve being only the third Iowa wrestler, behind Tom Brands and Brent Metcalf, to achieve the feat of being undefeated in Carver-Hawkeye Arena.

However, in order for Tony to remain perfect, he would have to defeat the number-one ranked wrestler at his weight class, Jon Morrison of Oklahoma State. The number-five rated Cowboys were rolling into Iowa City and Morrison, with his ranking, would be looking to add a third career victory over Tony, and one that would prevent him from a perfect career in Carver.

Darren Miller, for *HawkeyeSports.com*, published a piece on the match-up: "Ramos an Underdog?" A portion of the article follows:

> *The Ramos-Morrison rivalry has its roots on mats in the Land of Lincoln. Morrison is from Orland Park, Ill. (Carl Sandburg High School) and Ramos is from Carol Stream, Ill. (Glenbard North). They have gone head-to-head for a decade and Ramos has had his hand raised in all but two of those bouts.*
>
> *Morrison is 83-26 in his college career, 14-0 this season with four wins against ranked opponents. Something void from the three-time NCAA qualifier's resume is a victory against a Hawkeye. He is 0-2 against Matt McDonough and last season was 0-2 against Ramos -- losing 3-2 in the dual at Stillwater, Okla., and 6-1 in the NCAA Championships in Des Moines, Iowa.*
>
> *"I am more aware of what he does because we have wrestled so many times," Ramos said.*
>
> *While Morrison has gone 14 matches this season without a blemish, Ramos has 15 wins with losses to Edinboro's A.J. Schopp (3-2) and Northern Iowa's Joe Colon (fall). Those setbacks have done nothing to shake Ramos's poise. He is still the same Hawkeye who placed third in the nation in 2012 and runner-up in 2013.*
>
> *"Confidence doesn't change, I think I can beat everyone," Ramos said.*

In a storied team rivalry, the match-up could not have been any better for the fans. Between the two historic programs, there was a combined fifty-seven national championships won; coincidentally, no love had been lost between either of the schools before, during, and since those titles had been earned.

For Tony, in two of his last three matches, he had lost to ranked opponents; however, he was more frustrated with the talk than he was with the losses. "I wanted to make a statement," Ramos said. "He was ranked number-one and that's where I should be. I had two slip-ups early in the year, but things were starting to roll and head in the right direction."

In front of the 10,141 in attendance, Tony took the mat in the traditional black Iowa singlet and, as had become expected and what fans had anticipated, he was the first to the middle, dropped into his stance, and stared at Morrison as he prepared, opposite of Tony, in his OSU orange-colored singlet.

When the match began, it was a great deal of hand fighting and control for inside position. Then, at around the 1:30 mark, Tony found an opening and took a shot near the edge of the mat. Morrison would defend; however, Tony had captured the leg and worked back to his feet and he literally dragged Morrison back to the middle as of the mat ass Morrison hopped on one leg. While that happened, the Iowa fans stood on their feet and cheered Tony's control of the situation. As Tony swept out Morrison's left leg with his left leg and he covered for two, the cheers and chants grew louder.

The second period would be more of Tony controlling the match and Morrison looking to work into his offense—but it just was not happening for Morrison.

By the time the third period came around, the match was well in hand by Tony, and he would again work into another single-leg. He brought it up, Morrison looked to defend it with what looked to be an Abas roll, and Tony dropped to his knee and defended the roll. In the process of the drop, Tony saw an opportunity for a fall and slid in a left-handed half and had his sights on locking up a nearside cradle. Once locked up, Morrison was turned to his back and near fall points were awarded to Tony.

The match ended in a convincing 8-2 score and Tony, who was looking to prove a point, would do just that over the number-one ranked Morrison.

Tony got up when the match ended and flexed—this was the second time in three years Tony knocked off a number-one ranked Cowboy in Carver—he also had some words for Morrison.

"At the end of the match I remember Morrison trying to roll and I put him to his back and I was trying to get the fall," Ramos said. "I got up and was like, 'Hey, I'm here and I'm going to be here for a while and I ain't going anywhere. This is my year!' I think he said, 'Okay, we'll see you in March.'"

In a post-match interview, Tony spoke to the critics in typical honest Ramos style. "Coming in here I knew it was going to be a big match," Ramos said. "I just wanted to go out and make a statement because I'm getting tired of hearing people saying I'm off this year. I'm not off. I'm not down. I had a bad match and got caught. Those are two things that happened, but you just keep moving forward."

Tony's record moved to 31-0 in Carver and he was coming down to his final three matches inside an arena filled with such a great history and a number of fond memories for himself, his family, and the Iowa wrestling fans and community.

WHEN THE HOOSIERS CAME TO TOWN, THE

Hawkeyes were not very kind to them. The dual ended in a 38-4 win, and Tony won by fall in 3:27 over Chris Caton—that would be his ninth fall on the season.

For their next Big Ten dual, the Hawkeyes traveled to the Devaney Center in Lincoln, Nebraska, to take on the number-eight rated Cornhuskers. Iowa opened up strong and won three of the first four weight classes. Tony, who scored the only bonus points for either team, recorded a 15-4 major decision over Shawn Nagel. The final score was all Iowa, 22-9, and they were now preparing for a dual with the always tough Minnesota Golden Gophers.

Additionally, over the past few duals, Iowa moved up in the team rankings and earned the number-two rating. Minnesota, who was rated number four, would be coming into Carver-Hawkeye Arena with something of their own to prove.

The dual drew a strong crowd as Minnesota traveled well and Iowa hosted extremely well. The 10,588 witnessed a hard fought dual, and a great deal of match-ups with ranking implications.

When the dual opened with Iowa's number-three ranked Thomas Gilman taking the mat against an unranked opponent in Sam Brancale, it was, unfortunately, the unranked wrestler taking advantage of the match and winning in grand fashion with a fall in 2:03. The Hawkeyes would come out of the gates in a six-point hole instead of a three or four-point advantage. The match at 125 was a possible match-changer as a minimum nine-point swing had just occurred. It would be up to Tony to swing the tide back into the Hawkeyes' favor.

As he took the mat, he faced a very familiar opponent in the number-nine David Thorn. Tony, who had never lost to Thorn, had won close matches and had matches that he completely dominated. For this dual, Tony knew he would have his work cut out for himself in regard to bonus points.

When the match was over, the number-three ranked junior Hawkeye won, but it was only a 6-2 decision. The Golden Gopher lead was cut in half, and Tony totaled his thirty-third-consecutive win at Carver. As number-eleven Josh Dziewa took the mat against number five Chris Dardanes, the Hawkeyes were looking to find ways to close the gap and take control of the dual.

At 141, Dziewa would upset Dardanes and the dual was now tied at 6-6. However, in the 149-pound match-up, Nick Dardanes, ranked number three, defeated Iowa's thirteenth-ranked Brody Grothus, 5-3. Minnesota took back the lead, 9-6.

Iowa's next three wrestlers were three of their strongest in number-two Derek St. John at 157, Nick Moore, ranked number four at 165, and 174-pounder Mike Evans, who was currently ranked number six.

In those three bouts, only Derek St. John would fall. He lost to Dylan Ness, ranked number fourteen, in a 7-4 match. Moore defeated an unranked Danny Zilverberg, 3-2, and Evans scored a 2-1 tie-breaker victory over number-five Logan Storley. Headed into the final three weights, Iowa and Minnesota would again be locked up even at 12-12.

When unranked Sammy Brooks took to the mat at 184, he would lose an 8-6 decision to number-nine Kevin Steinhaus. This meant that a loss for Iowa at 197 could possibly put the dual out of reach. Stepping into the circle for Iowa was number-sixteen Nathan Burak; for the Golden Gophers, number-one Scott Schiller. Unfortunately, for Iowa, there would be no grand upset. Schiller took a 16-5 major decision win and put the 19-12 dual meet out of reach headed into heavyweight.

The final match of the night was now more individual than team as number-three Bobby Telford of Iowa faced number-two Tony Nelson. Telford earned the 3-1 decision win, which was great for Telford; however, as for the team score, the points did not matter.

The matches were split down the middle at five a piece; however, the bonus points at 125 and 197 were the difference.
Minnesota upset Tony's Hawkeyes and head coach Tom Brands was not be pleased with his team's performance.

"This is Big Ten, Division I wrestling," Tom Brands stated unhappily. "We have to be sharper than that. We have to be ready to battle. It's pretty clear that we regressed a little bit as a team, but made strides individually. That's probably how you would sum it up."

Iowa, now rated as the number-three team in the country, would travel to Evanston, Illinois, to face the number-nineteen Northwestern Wildcats. The Hawkeyes would bounce back in grand fashion and won eight of the ten weight classes. The Hawkeyes walked out with a 31-6 thumping of NU and, for Tony, he earned a team-high tenth fall on the season in 5:24 over Dominic Malone.

FOR TONY, HIS NEXT DUAL AGAINST THE VISITING

Michigan Wolverines, rated number eleven, would be his final collegiate match in Carver-Hawkeye Arena. To that point, Tony had compiled a 33-0 record in the building, and he looked to make one more final memory in front of the Hawkeye faithful.

Before Tony even came to Carver-Hawkeye Arena that day, he knew it would emotional. "It was tough," Ramos remembered of the time before the dual. "It was real tough. I knew it would be my last college match, but I knew I would wrestle there again because the 2016 Olympic Trials was going to be there, but, at the same time, that was going to be the last time I put on a black and gold singlet in Carver-Hawkeye Arena, having those fans cheering for me, seeing me put on a show.

"For me, putting on a performance for all of those people, those 14,000-plus fans, who support me and the program, and for those young kids that look up to me, that was what I was going to miss. And the thing I enjoyed the most was after the matches when kids came up to me and wanted an autograph or older people just wanted to talk or take pictures and put a smile on their face; I know it helped make their experience more enjoyable.

"I remember when I was a kid and my dad would take us to the Bears games," Ramos reflected, "and we would go in the back where the players would come out after games and give autographs. There was one time when Brian Urlacher walked by and we asked for his autograph and he acted like we weren't even there. Here we are, five and six-year-old kids and he walked right by us; he pretended like we weren't even there. At that moment my dad told me, 'If you ever get into a place in your life where people look up to you, where people are inspired by you, and they want your autograph, you better stop and take the time to give it to them because that's an honor, that's an opportunity—it's not something that happens to everyone every day.'"

When the meet started, across from Tony was number-nineteen ranked Rossi Bruno. And, as much as Tony wanted to go out with a fall or some big and exciting move, he ended up wrestling a solid match and earned a 6-1 decision win. That win gave Tony win number thirty-four and, as he pulled himself up and had his hand raised for the last time, he was given a standing ovation by the Hawkeye fans as he waved goodbye before running off the Iowa mat and into the tunnel for the final time.

"It was awesome," Ramos said of the sendoff that he received from the 8,358 in attendance. "Just getting a standing ovation in Carver-Hawkeye Arena from all those people was awesome. I heard Tom Brands talk about in meetings about how he wants to see someone get the entire crowd on their feet and keep on clapping and clapping until you run out of that tunnel and he has to come bring us back out so they could clap some more. To me, that was one of those moments."

But, even with the memorable final moment on the mat, Tony was not fully pleased with how it all ended. "After the match," Ramos remembered, "I was mad. I was upset. Not because it was the last time that I was wrestling there, but because I didn't go out there and put on that last show. I didn't go out with my best performance that I could have had. I wanted to pin him. I wanted to go out and dominate. I wanted something more than 6-1 and I felt that I didn't leave the fans with the best lasting memory that I could have."

In response to the media about being undefeated in Carver-Hawkeye Arena, Tony commented openly. "It's not something I was trying to think about all week long, but people keep asking about it. To me, I was trying not to make it a big thing—but it is a big thing. The last person to [go undefeated at home for] four years was Tom [Brands], and three years was [Brent] Metcalf. Those are big shoes to fill; that's a good class of people to be in."

In the same interview, Iowa's head coach reflected on the accomplishment and Tony always providing the fans with some excitement. In return, the fans had always taken to Tony and appreciated his performances in Carver.

Tony would reflect on his achievement and he believed that such a feat was not an easy task. "It is extremely hard to go undefeated at Carver," Ramos commented. "There's only two people who have ever done it for four years. You know [Royce] Alger, [Mark] Ironside, Terry [Brands], some of the greatest that ever went through the program, couldn't even go undefeated in Carver-Hawkeye Arena. And it's not like I didn't wrestle some of the best guys in Carver. I had Jordan Oliver. I wish I would've had the chance to wrestle Stieber there—but they didn't want to take that risk. I've heard people say, 'Ramos and Carver-Hawkeye Arena is like wrestling a guy on steroids.'"

From Tom Brands' perspective, going undefeated in Carver was more prestigious than difficult. "I don't know," Tom Brands thought, "I think it's a badge of honor more than anything. Here's the thing: I think it's relatively easy, especially if you're a guy that likes to please the crowd. You're in your own arena. You're a Hawkeye. When you're a Hawkeye and you wrestle in Carver-Hawkeye Arena, there's no better venue, right? So why not make the most of it?

"How hard is it? I think it's hard to win wrestling matches at a high level. I think it's hard to dominate guys that try to hold points from you. So you got to work hard, just like you got to work hard every match."

That being said, "There is something special about Carver-Hawkeye Arena, and there is something special about our fans, and there is something special about how they reward their guys," Tom Brands reflected. "It's their team and they feel a lot of ownership with that. Especially when you're doing the job, and the way Ramos competes, he's been able to do the job."

THE REMAINDER OF THE REGULAR SEASON
would consist of two more duals: Lehigh and Wisconsin.

In Bethlehem, Pennsylvania, Tony faced and defeated the number-six ranked Mason Beckman. He would do so by scoring a takedown and earning a 3-1 decision.

When it came time to travel to Madison, Wisconsin, Tony was anticipating a match-up with the tough and familiar Tyler Graff. Unfortunately, number-five ranked Graff was held out of his second straight dual with an injury and would only be mat side as Tony chased his stand-in, Matt Cavallaris, all over the mat and scored seven takedowns before finally getting a firm hold on Cavallaris and winning by fall in 6:23.

"I just had to find a different way to get him over," Ramos said. "I was trying to let him stand up, didn't get him, but caught a leg in that allowed me to get a deep arm bar. From there I ran it over and got the fall."

That fall was Tony's team-high eleventh of the season and it helped the Hawkeyes win the dual, 28-10. It also helped give the Hawks a share in the Big Ten dual title with Penn State and Minnesota. This dual team title would be Iowa's sixth in the past seven years.

Also in Wisconsin, the Hawkeyes grasped a comfortable feel with the Kohl Center as the Big Ten championships were to be held there in two weeks. For Tony, that would be his final opportunity at a Big Ten title. As a freshman, he lost to Tyler Graff in the semifinals and placed third. As a sophomore and a junior, he placed second to Logan Stieber. The big question people were asking was: Would this finally be Ramos' year?

CHAPTER 52
CHASING THAT BIG TITLE

"Time doesn't matter to me because I believe in my offense. I'm confident. I believe in my training."

• *Tony Ramos*

BEFORE THE 100TH BIG TEN WRESTLING championship tournament took place, Iowa would have its share of media coverage and Tony, the face of the program, was a topic of interest as his quest for a Big Ten title and a national title was still unresolved and down to the final hours.

During the week leading up to the 2014 Big Ten Championships, Tony was interviewed by *Hawkeye Sports* in regard to his chasing two titles and if there was pressure on him, an urgency, to win now. "Yes, there's a high sense of urgency," Ramos said of winning. "For me there's a few things missing: Big Ten titles and a national championship. I have to take it one step at a time. Right now it's [a] Big Ten championship and then we'll go from there after that."

Going into the tournament, Tony had not lost a conference match all season long. In fact, the only losses he had ever suffered at the hands of a Big Ten opponent was B.J. Futrell at the Midlands and Tyler Graff in the Big Ten tournament as a freshman, and then Logan Stieber as a sophomore and a junior in the Big Ten finals and the NCAA semifinals and national championship match. Other than that, Tony had been pretty much untouchable in what was the most dominant wrestling conference in the country.

At the Big Ten championships, Tony, the one seed, would wrestle the number-eight seed and number-nineteen ranked Rossi Bruno from Michigan. It was roughly three weeks earlier that Bruno had toughed out a 6-1 loss to the number-three ranked Hawkeye at Carver. On this day, however, Tony defeated Rossi by a fall in 1:33—the fall he wanted for his final match in front of the Hawkeye faithful.

That fall for Tony would now total twelve falls on the season, a team high, and advanced him into the championship semifinal round against Cashe' Quiroga of Purdue.

Quiroga, the four seed, was fairly familiar with Tony and his style. As a junior, Tony had defeated defeat Quiroga 9-5 in the quarterfinals of the Big Ten Championships. And, earlier that season, Tony defeated him in the opening round of the Midlands by a 13-5 major decision. Since, Tony had found his groove after the loss to Colon, and everything was headed in the right direction. That was, until the match with Quiroga started.

"I was in a battle," Ramos remembered. "Me and Quiroga had wrestled a couple times, and I beat him good there, but when I came off the mat, I knew there was something there where he made it a point to get up for that match. He wanted to beat me so bad and he came out and he was ready to go and I was just flat."

The first period ended in a 3-3 tie, a takedown and an escape for each wrestler.

In the second period, Tony chose the down position and escaped early on to gain a 4-3 match advantage. There would be no action outside of the escape and a heavy hand fight.

As the third period progressed after a Quiroga escape that tied the match 4-4, Quiroga, who wrestled low off his knees, caught Tony reaching with his left hand and fired in on a double-leg, came up to a body lock position, threw it over, and took Tony down to the mat for a 6-4 lead with 1:15 to go in the match.

Tony, who would work to his feet, fought the hands and broke Quiroga's control and escaped; he was now trailing by one point with about one minute left in the match.

The pressure Tony applied from there earned Quiroga a stalling warning and, with 00:24 left in the match, the two wrestlers went out of bounds and met back in the middle of the mat. Tony, first to the center and set, waited for Quiroga to step to the line. When he did, and the referee resumed the period, Tony immediately took a hard double in unison with the whistle. Quiroga, not prepared for the shot, stumbled backwards and tried to position his hips and legs under him, but Tony locked his hands as he kept driving his knees until he reached his feet and Quiroga had no more fight. Tony lifted the Boilermaker, drove him into the mat, and earned a takedown and a 7-6 lead.

The two wrestled out of bounds with three seconds left and a restart would take place. Off the whistle, Quiroga hit a quick stand-up, but Tony locked on and the match ended with the senior Hawkeye headed to his third Big Ten finals appearance in as many years.

Quiroga, frustrated, removed his headgear with an angry pull of the chin strap and yanked it off his head. When he circled to the center, he removed his ankle bands, shook hands, and flexed downward in disgust with how close he almost was to beating Tony and making his first Big Ten finals.

"Coming back to the center of the mat I knew I had to find a way to win," Ramos said. "As soon as we got back to the center and I heard the whistle blow, I blast doubled him and got my takedown, time ran out, and I won."

Tony commented further in a post-match interview as soon as he exited the mat and entered the tunnel. In typical Tony Ramos style, he was full of confidence. "Twenty-six seconds left you have to go to your go-to shot," Ramos said. "I may not hit it a lot during matches, but I got a double-leg. It was open and I hit it. Once I got my hands on him, I knew I could finish."

It appeared that Quiroga had discovered a kink in Tony's defensive armor. Every time Tony reached, the lower leveled Quiroga fired in a high crotch or double. But Tony answered and figured out a way to defend and keep himself in the match, even with the short time that remained and while he was trailing in the match.

"Time doesn't matter to me because I believe in my offense," Ramos said. "I'm confident. I believe in my training. So, I wasn't too worried. I had to find a way to win and that is what some of the best guys do. They scrap. They find ways to win when they're not feeling the best or not wrestling the best. That's what I did."

From the corner, "That Purdue match was crazy," Terry Brands said. "You have that *Why are we waiting until the bitter end?* But, he is getting his hand raised, so let's just keep moving forward."

On the other side of the bracket in Madison, Wisconsin, the hometown favorite, Badger Tyler Graff—the 27-4 senior who had earned the number-two seed—advanced accordingly.

In his opening round he faced and defeated Penn State's Jimmy Gulibon with an 8-1 decision. In the semifinals, he and the number-three seed, 25-6 senior David Thorn squared off and it was a 9-4 decisive win for Graff, sending him to his second Big Ten finals—his first appearance came three years earlier when he defeated Tony by a 2-1 sudden victory decision in the semifinals before losing to Andrew Long in the finals. This time, however, Graff was prepared to make his mark.

"Graff wrestled great from the very beginning," Badger Head Coach Barry Davis said. "[In the] first match with Jimmy Gulibon, great match, great skill work, but the key is he's been on the offensive the whole tournament. If he can keep this up, he's well on his way here. So, right now, he put himself in position to win a Big Ten championship and tomorrow we'll see what happens. But, if he's moving forward on the legs, then he's got a great shot."

WHEN SATURDAY NIGHT CAME, IT WAS TIME TO
wrestle. The Kohl Center was filled with red and white wearing Badger fans centered on the championship mat while the black and gold Iowa-outfitted fans were packed in just off center.

Tony, who beat Graff to the center of the mat, lowered himself into his stance and stared him down as he was preparing in the corner. Tony, who had wrestled a tight semifinal bout, was looking for his first Big Ten title and would face a strong and more than worthy opponent.

"When I went out there," Ramos said, "I was not letting this Big Ten title slip through my fingers for a third time. I was already a runner-up twice and I knew I was in Graff's head and I knew that he was going to come out and give me everything that he had. But, at the same time, I knew he had that itch in the back of his ear telling him that *Ramos has got something above me*.

"I felt that if I could beat him on top in this match, then going into the national tournament he would know that I beat him everywhere. I beat him on our feet. I beat him on bottom. And now I could beat him on top. That year he blew some of his matches from the bottom position. He was turned or got ridden out by [Joe] Colon and I knew I could take advantage of that position."

When Graff came to the line, he lowered his stance and, as the whistle blew, both he and Tony immediately attacked each other's face and head with their hands. Quick hard pops and slaps and, when it all settled into a tie, the hand fight for inside position began. With continued head snaps and pulls and the wearing down of the other, the match looked to be one of endurance.

As the pressure back and forth continued, and each wrestler was looking for his opening, it would be Tony who would attempt the first offensive move; however, it would be Graff who ended up in the offensive position.

Tony, with Graff moving toward him, pressuring forward, looked to hit his slide-by. Unfortunately, as he went to hit it on Graff's left side, Graff blocked the move and dropped into a head outside single on Tony's right leg. Tony and Graff battled for position as the Badger was looking for the takedown and the Hawkeye was looking to defend the position and break free.

As Tony worked to stuff the head and hip into Graff, Graff lifted Tony's right leg with his head inside—he would reach across with his left arm, change his right arm to the outside and drive and, for a split second, Tony bounced his hip off the mat and hooked a whizzer with his right hand. "TWO!" echoed throughout the Kohl Center as Badger fans wanted the quick score. No score was awarded, however, and the battle for position continued as Graff relocked Tony's right leg.

Once Tony was able to kick his left leg away and work himself back and drop his right knee, he fought with his whizzer and escaped the scoring opportunity for Graff.

The first period ended in a 0-0 score and Tony had the choice in the second. He chose down and, about twenty seconds later, he escaped, was back on his feet, and held a 1-0 lead.

For the remainder of the second period there was a continued hand fight; however, no real offense occurred and, when the period ended, Graff now had his choice and he chose down.

This was the position, the top position, which Tony had wanted. He wanted the opportunity to ride Graff and use the top position to his advantage.

Therefore, when the third period began, it was now a battle of wills, one trying to ride out the position and one trying to tie up the score and move forward in the match. A number of flurries and rolls and tripod stands and returns ensued—the excitement on the ride and possible escapes had people on the edge of their seats. There were moments where Graff looked like he was out or switching control, but Tony always found a way to keep himself in position and maintain control.

One of the exchanges started with Graff attempting a standing switch where he was fighting to turn into Tony while Tony was fighting to re-switch and get his own hips back. As Graff tenaciously hung onto Tony's right leg, the Hawkeye reached over and took hold of the Badger's ankle. In that moment, Graff drove and Tony, falling to his left hip, once again bounced up and defended and kept Graff from scoring.

Graff, however, still had Tony's right leg and now he was switching off to an arm across position before conceding that position and relocking on the leg. The referee would ultimately stalemate the position; however, Tony clocked a continued riding advantage during the entire scramble.

When the match resumed from the referee's position with around 00:50 left, Graff, fighting to get to his feet, found his way to the mat's edge, but Tony fought to keep him inbounds.

As Graff worked from all fours to come up, Tony blocked the legs and, from there, Graff looked to exit the circle. Tony, on two knees, grabbed Graff's left leg with both hands and came to his feet and dragged a kicking Graff back into the circle to keep the riding time advantage advancing and to remain in control of the match.

When Graff was brought back in, he turned into Tony and tried to kick back out toward the out of bounds. In that moment, Tony attacked the legs on the failed kick out and basically ended up in a loose leg lace position as he came back to his feet and, once again, worked to drag Graff back into the circle. Graff, in a backward barrel walk posted on his hands, tried to roll through Tony's legs, but Tony dropped to his knees and Graff was forced back on all fours; he lunged out of bounds with Tony still attached.

Off the final restart, now with 00:19 left in the title match, Graff did get to his feet and dropped back down to one knee—he was looking to have Tony unlock his hands in fear of being called for locked hands. He then rose and dropped again. Each time Tony stayed tight in a parallel position behind Graff and would not be fooled or relinquish his ride. Once the riding time advantage was secured, Tony just let Graff go and the match, on the scoreboard, was a 1-1 tie. However, in reality, with the addition of the 1:30 of riding time, Tony was up 2-1.

Graff, who knew the situation, was now on the offensive with about thirteen seconds left in the match.

With an open shot attempt to Tony's right leg, Graff looked to score. He would be denied.

Graff again snapped and shucked and looked to find a way to Tony's legs—nothing.

While Graff continually made the effort to attack, Tony fought the hands, posted on Graff's face, moved his legs, circled, and kept working to defeat each and every attack. Graff, who was relentless, ran out of time.

As the whistle blew, and the match had ended, Graff had a hold of Tony's right ankle. Tony's arms would go up in victory as he fell backwards to the mat, lie flat on his back and closed his eyes, and then he pumped his fists in triumph. When he finally opened his eyes, and worked to get up, Graff was there to extend his hand. The always gracious Badger helped the Hawkeye to his feet, shook his hand, and walked off the mat in defeat.

Before his hand was raised, Tony pumped his fists in the direction of his family. There would be no flexing, no show, no overjoyed moment of antics. It would simply be relief.

"I had done it," Ramos said of the no-pose and no-flex ending. "I had finally got the first leg to winning a national title, something that had avoided me for the past three years. It was a Big Ten title and that might not be a big thing to people because it's not the national title, but it was big to me. Not a lot of people can say they were Big Ten champions because it's a hard thing to do."

In the corner, Tom Brands clapped his hands as Tony's right hand was raised. In the process, Tony raised his left arm, holding onto his headgear, and spun in a circle to all of the fans.

In the moment of the rotation, the Badger boos came out as the Hawkeye hollers mixed and masked what they could.

As he came off the mat, Tony headed directly to his family. He would see his mom, give her a brief hug, and he walked away as the 2014 Big Ten champion at 133 pounds.

In the end, Tony won in the position that he felt that he needed to dominate. "I guess it's weird that I won riding on top and not getting a takedown, so that might be different for the fans," Ramos commented. "I didn't want it to go to overtime—I wanted to win this one in regulation. [Now] it's more in his head: *He can ride me, he can take me down, I can't score on him—what am I going to do?* He doesn't know what he's going to do at nationals and it's a big thing putting that into his head going into that.

"When it hit zero—I heard the guy on the outside counting ten, nine— and I knew I had to keep wrestling, keep wrestling staying in the center, I couldn't go back. So, a huge weight was lifted. I finally got my name on that side of the wall that you look at every day. That's exciting. Now I just need to add an asterisk up on the other side and do everything I could possibly do here."

In a post-match interview with the *Des Moines Register*, Tony commented on the match and the Wisconsin crowd.

"You know, I know I can ride, I know what he does—he just wants to roll and tripod up," Ramos commented on how he defeated Graff. "If I'm going to ride high like I normally do, yeah, he's going to reverse me like at nationals. So I knew going into it I had to adjust, drop my hips back, ride the ankle, ride the leg. You know, they're going to hit me for stalling, they want to boo, he didn't do a single thing on his feet—I don't care. He backed, he backed, he blocked, put his arm [up]; you know, let them say what they want. I'm the one walking out of here with the title."

However, even though Tony won the title he showed up to win that day, he was not the same Tony Ramos on the mat. Here was a wrestler who had seemingly dominated all but one opponent in the past two years, and he looked flat during the tournament. On the mat, Tony was not the same wrestler. He was not aggressive. In fact, he was the antithesis of the Iowa style. He was tentative. He was cautious. "It's one of those things at the time you don't know," Ramos commented. "But, I know exactly why I looked flat. I hadn't won a Big Ten title yet and I wanted it so bad that I wasn't going to make any mistakes. I was going to wrestle tight and calculated. I was not going to put myself in position to lose. I knew I could win. I knew I could beat anyone. But I wasn't going to take a chance and give someone the opportunity to beat me."

The way Terry Brands saw the match, "I didn't like how the official easily could have called him [for stalling] that second time. I didn't like that. I didn't like how I felt in the corner watching the official and watching our guy. But, he persevered."

When Tony came off the mat, "I was happy for him," Terry Brands said. "Great job getting your hand raised, now let's get to our offense quicker next time. A Big Ten title means that [he's] moving forward at the most critical time in the season that you can move forward."

Unfortunately, for Tony and the Hawkeyes, his Big Ten title was the only title won that weekend for Iowa. And, for the fourth-straight year, Tony was not on a Big Ten championship team. In high school, he had won four conference championships as a teammate, but never a team state title; at Iowa, Tony's teams had never won a Big Ten team title or a national championship. He was down to his final opportunity to win as an individual and as a teammate. There was no next season.

UPON RETURNING TO IOWA, AND WITH THE BIG

Ten Championships now behind him, Tony moved onto the twelve days prior to the NCAA championships. He took time to heal, reflect, and continually worked on improving his wrestling so that he would be able to shine when it now mattered the most, on college wrestling's biggest weekend and on its greatest stage.

Tony earned the number-three seed for the national tournament, and he figured that was where he would end up. Joe Colon of Northern Iowa was given the number-one seed, A.J. Schopp of Edinboro earned the number-two—the only two wrestlers that had beaten Tony that season. Morrison was placed in the four seed and Graff had been given the five. From Tony's perspective, "I figured Morrison would come out of that side. I felt like he was the better wrestler of those guys and he would be in the finals."

However, in regard to his own seed, "I think my seed was probably the worst draw in that tournament. Even compared to the seven and eight seed; I had the worst draw for a three seed in the entire national tournament."

More than anything else though, Tony knew that he would have to focus on his half of the bracket and take the tournament one match at a time.

"When I saw my draw come out," Ramos remembered, "the biggest thing that I had to focus on was not watching the other side of the bracket. I knew that I could get through my side and get out, but it was going to be beating A.J. Schopp in that semifinal and that was where I knew I had to score and keep the match on my feet.

"There was some talk with Tom and Terry about game plan and whether I should take bottom or not, and that was one area where Tom and I butted heads, and Terry and me agreed that I would choose down. I was going to go down, get out, and I was stubborn like that because I thought I could get away from anyone. And Terry believed that I could get away from anyone. But Tom wanted a game plan more of going neutral, not going bottom, and if he goes top, then you are on the mat."

Regardless of the plan, the twelve days that led up to the NCAA championships were about working and modifying areas where Tony needed improvement and where he was strong. The goal was still in place and attainable and the first of two steps to climb had been reached. It was on to Oklahoma City for his final tournament as a Hawkeye.

2014 • BIG TEN WRESTLING CHAMPIONSHIPS
RAMOS STANDS WITH THEN FIANCEE MEGAN ESKEW AFTER WINNING THE BIG TENS
PHOTOGRAPH COURTESY • MEGAN RAMOS

CHAPTER 53
KEEPING IT CLOSE

"The ability to win under those circumstances shows that he was psychologically working on the things that we were talking about. Maybe they didn't show up in the matches, maybe they didn't show up on the scoreboard, but it showed up in the winning category."

• Terry Brands
Associate Head Coach, the University of Iowa
Coach, Hawkeye Wrestling Club

THE 2014 NATIONAL CHAMPIONSHIPS TOOK PLACE at the Chesapeake Energy Arena in Oklahoma City, Oklahoma—Sooner and Cowboy country. For every wrestler who competed, that weekend consisted of one of two emotions: the feeling of success, or the feeling of failure. There was no in-between as every wrestler wanted to win his final match of the tournament. However, that honor was only saved for four individuals per weight, and seven of those wrestlers on the podium would be looking up to one, envious.

For Tony, he commented on the importance of the weekend. "It would mean everything to me right now," Ramos answered in response to how special an NCAA title would be for him to win. "It's the only thing I've got left to do. [I won] a Big Ten title. I've been undefeated in Carver-Hawkeye Arena. I've done all great things that wrestlers have done other than win the big dance, so it would really mean a lot to me to get that title under my belt and I know it'd mean a lot to my family as well bringing that home for everyone [because it is] something we've been working for our whole lives—me, my brother—it'd mean a lot not just to me, but my family, too.

"Growing up I always wanted to wrestle for Iowa; just the history, the coaches. I went there, everyone was always asking, 'Were Tom and Terry Brands really that scary, that mean?' I'm glad I went there. They're great coaches, they're great people. They've taught me a lot. They've taught me how to grow up and how to mature, not just as a wrestler but as a young man. And, I've made a lot of important decisions in my life at Iowa, getting married—I found my wife there—a lot of different things happened. So, I'm excited that I can say that I'm part of the great Iowa wrestling history and tradition and I was there to help build some of it too."

Just as important as the journey had been for Tony at Iowa in regard to his growth and relationships, there was also the question of how he would approach his final challenge of earning a national championship. Some wondered if would he approach it in a strict business manner, others asked if he would enjoy himself along the way and have some fun. "I'm here to have a lot of fun," Ramos answered in regard to business versus fun, "and [handle] a lot of business at the same time. Winning's fun. Winning is the fun part, losing's not fun; [winning is] the fun I'm here to have."

• • •

In the opening round of the championship bracket, Tony faced the number-twentieth ranked wrestler at his weight class, Mack Shelton of Pittsburgh. The match went the distance and Tony would, to the amazement of many, score a takedown near the end of the third period to win a tight 3-1 decision. He was in good position, but he was wrestling very cautiously as he appeared to be holding back and fighting with himself on whether or not to open up during the match.

He would have his hand raised and he would move on to the second round, but there were a number of fans and critics who were concerned or even excited that there may be something wrong with the senior Hawkeye in his last opportunity to stand atop the podium.

In his second match-up in the championship round, Tony faced a tough freshman from the Land of Lincoln, Illinois' Zane Richards, who was ranked fourteenth and who was not concerned with a championship sendoff for the Hawkeye.

Tony had no time against Richards to drop into his stance and give a stare down as Richards was prompt to arrive at the mat's center for the start of the match. However, it would be Tony who was quick to attack and take control of the match early on.

Tony would score early into the first period, Richards escaped, and then escaped again in the second after choosing down. The score was 2-2. Not much long after, a wild scramble ensued where Richards took Tony's offensive position and made it an attack all his own. The two ended up out of bounds and, off the restart with 00:15 left in the second period, Tony fired in a high-crotch to Richards' right leg. Unfortunately, for Tony, Richards' leg was moving back when the shot was taken and Richards had Tony at a disadvantage. When Tony over-extended himself on that shot, Richards ran behind and earned his first takedown of the match with 00:14 left in the period.

Tony quickly escaped five seconds later, earned his point, and trailed 4-3 at the period's end.

To start the third, Tony, who had a twenty-one second riding advantage, chose down. Richards battled hard after Tony escaped and the match, then 4-4, headed into overtime. When the overtime minute began, it was Tony on the attack; however, Richards was not backing down—he was battling for position and working to create an offense.

At 00:41, Richards found his opening and took a high-crotch to Tony's right leg; however, just as Tony had miscalculated earlier, Richards did the same. Tony's reaction extended his leg back before Richards could get in on it; Tony now came down hard into a front-head position. Richards, who was now caught with his head well-over his toes, attempted to work back to the mat's edge. However, in the process, Tony wrenched Richards' chin with his left hand and worked to beat Richards' left leg. In the attempt, Tony had such a strong hold on Richards' chin that, when he chased the leg, he locked up a nearside cradle and scored a two-point takedown on the mat's edge.

The Iowa fans screamed an echoed, "TWO!" and the referee signaled the two as he looked to the mat's assistant referee for confirmation. In that brief conference, Richards sat on the mat and watched, witnessing the call. The two-point call stood and Tony, now in two close matches, again found a way to win and advanced into the quarterfinals. Tony got up, stomped to the center, removed his mouthpiece, had his hand raised, and ran off to the tunnel.

"In his head," Terry Brands discussed, "I think he knew he was going to get his hand raised and I think he rode that line. I think he rode it perfectly. The Pitt match was crazy close and he got the takedown at the end. But the Illinois match was beyond crazy close. And [Richards] is just like Tony. He just doesn't give up; he was a very tenacious competitor and he also didn't believe that he wasn't going to lose. I think Tony knew that and understood that, but he also knew how to beat him.

"When Tony gave up that takedown…holy cow! The ability to win under those circumstances shows that he was psychologically working on the things that we were talking about. Maybe they didn't show up in the matches, maybe they didn't show up on the scoreboard, but it showed up in the winning category."

In regard to why Tony may have been tight in those two rounds or if there was some other factor or a fear that was seeping into his psyche,

Terry Brands stated how he did not think it was fear. "I think it's—," Terry Brands paused, "I think he found that comfortableness, not that you want to be too comfortable—but I think he found that line that was a pathway to victory where he wasn't going to be behind and have to have a scramble with a short time to win.

"But he knew he needed to open up. Even at the Big Tens we knew. Even at Midlands we knew. He knew and when we communicated with him it wasn't like him going, 'Hey, you know what, I'm going to wrestle this thing tight because I know I can win this way.' He knew. He knew that he needed to open up."

Now that he was in the quarterfinals for the third-straight year, Tony found himself up against another tough opponent in Lehigh's Mason Beckman. Thus far, Tony had defeated the number-twenty and the number-fourteen ranked wrestlers, and he now faced the number-six ranked wrestler in his weight class. The only concern was if he was going to open up and distance himself from the competition, or keep it close and suspenseful.

As the referee started the match, Tony came out heavy with his hands and moved forward with purpose. Beckman, who looked like more of a wrestler who wanted to avoid long ties and hand fights with Tony, did not back away from any of the ties and hand fights; instead, he fought and looked to create space from those ties and then fire in on his shots. For the first two-minutes, the more passive Mountain Hawk was stalked by the Hawkeye; however, with 1:00 left in the first period, Beckman had an outside tie on Tony's head with his left hand and, when Tony pressured into him, Beckman hit a low sweep single that had Tony's momentum carry him over the top—the fight was on.

Tony, with a strong defense, used a right-handed whizzer and worked to keep his hips parallel and pressured into Beckman. Beckman, who tried to build up and hit a corner, found it difficult to score. The two battled until they were out of bounds.

The period would continue with ongoing level changes and hand fights and open motion; however, with 00:06 remaining, Beckman hit that same sweep single off that same tie and he caught Tony. Tony turned and found himself falling backward until he hit the mat, bounced up to defend, and time expired. No points were awarded.

In the second period, Tony won the disc flip and chose down; eleven seconds later, he was back on his feet and wrestling in the neutral position with a 1-0 lead. The only real attack occurred with about 1:15 left in the period and it was a slide-by attempt from Tony where he caught Beckman leaning, but he could not capitalize on the motion and movement created off the attack. The period ended 1-0 in favor of Tony and, for the third,

Beckman chose down.

Off the whistle, Beckman created his motion from the bottom position and, off a short sit, he was out, worked to his feet, and the score was knotted at 1-1. Tony held a meaningless four-second riding advantage. The hand fighting worked to the edge of the mat and it led to a shot by Tony. It was countered and reattacked by Beckman and then reattacked with a double by Tony, but both were called out of bounds with 1:31 remaining in the bout.

Tony's pressure continued and, at the one-minute mark, he had Beckman trying to fight back inbounds as the ties and match had begun to seemingly wear on Beckman. On the edge, with his back out of bounds, Beckman fired a shot to Tony's right leg; however, there was not much energy and intensity in the shot. Tony, off his defense, slid down after his down-block to Beckman's left leg and worked to find a way to score. Hanging on, Tony was on both knees and, as he worked up with Beckman stuffing his head and keeping his right foot at bay, Tony gripped tighter as Beckman turned to try and kick free—to no avail. Tony, still on his knees, fought to pull that leg in more as Beckman now tried to square up on the Hawkeye and fight with a whizzer, but Tony was determined; in that moment was Tony's opportunity and he knew it.

Beckman kicked two more times and Tony, tenacious, hung on and, just when it appeared Tony was headed out of bounds too, Beckman turned into him and that small turn in with square hips placed Beckman's own left heel on the mat and gave Tony his opening. With a firm hold with two hands on that ankle, Tony fought and pulled even though Beckman was still kicking and bucking as he tried to escape the hold. Slowly, Tony tugged, repositioned, came up, slowly tugged again, repositioned, and did that until he was far enough inbounds to come to his feet and secure a high single-leg.

Once the high single was secured, Tony literally dragged Beckman back inside of the circle and, as soon as Beckman jumped out toward the out of bounds, Tony changed levels and exploded into him and, with his right hand, secured Beckman's far thigh as Beckman fell to both knees.

The Hawkeye faithful were clear and decisive with a drawn out shout of "TWO!" echoing throughout the Chesapeake Energy Arena. With 00:27 left, Tony had a 3-1 advantage. Tony held the ride and, when the clock finally struck 00:00, Tony, who had one of Beckman's legs, pressured forward and flipped it upward, almost in disgust.

As Beckman pulled off his headgear and sat to his butt, he looked into his corner and realized how close he was to an upset. Tony turned into the mat's center and flexed his patented double rainbow pose; for the third year in a row, he was headed to the semifinals.

"You can't get frustrated," Ramos said in a post-match interview about Beckman in regard to him wrestling on the edge of the mat. "He took more shots, he wrestled a little harder—I mean harder than the other guys I'm wrestling—but obviously my hard pace and hand fighting and getting to that leg won me the match."

When asked about the takedown on the edge of the mat and his patience, Tony said, "I'm comfortable there. I thought I was going to get it by the table, but there's enough room for him to step out and get to the floor, so they had to stop it."

And now, for the third match in a row, although he won, Tony had a close match where the ending could have gone a different direction. In response to why those matches were close, Terry Brands explained that the match-ups were the difference in those outcomes.

"It was just that in those matches," Terry Brands explained, "and when you look at those opponents: Lehigh, the kid's a very, very passive wrestler; Pitt, very strong and elusive wrestler—things that against Tony were perfect storms to beating him. It wasn't like you had a situation where Tony's style was better than the other guy. This guy's style was probably more in favor of beating Tony compared to another guy's style, and you had that BAM! BAM! BAM!"

With each opponent wrestling Tony tight and close, he had to remain calm and focused. "I can't get frustrated [with how they wrestle me or else I'm going to make a mistake," Ramos said. "I've got to stay cool, calm, collective. I can be as frustrated as I want afterwards, but during I've got to stay calm."

On the lower half of his bottom bracket, it was a quarterfinal match-up between A.J. Schopp and number-seven ranked Cashe' Quiroga from Purdue. In the end, it would be the number-two Schopp with a decisive 11-7 victory. Once Tony saw the results, he replied: "Good. I've been waiting for that one for a long time."

Ramos now had the opportunity to right one of the season's wrongs. Again, the greatest concern was if Tony was going to keep pushing the boundaries and allow Schopp to keep a close match, or if he was going to open up and take control of the bout.

"I have to not let him do the funky stuff that he likes to do," Ramos commented on how to beat Schopp.

For the "Schopp match, you had a guy that could ride, and that was always a concern to us with him," Terry Brands said. "But [Ramos] would have to wrestle and just make those positions his positions."

2014 • NCAA DIVISION I WRESTLING CHAMPIONSHIPS
133 LB CHAMPIONSHIP QUARTERFINAL MATCH
RAMOS FLEXES AFTER DEFEATING LEHIGH'S MASON BECKMAN BY A 3-1 DECISION
PHOTOGRAPH COURTESY • UNIVERSITY OF IOWA ATHLETICS

CHAPTER 54
FIGHTING THE SCOT

"It was a hard, explosive, crunching hold—I felt it sitting in the chair when it happened. It was an earthquake."

• *Tom Brands*
Head Coach, the University of Iowa
Coach, Hawkeye Wrestling Club

"**GETTING ON TOP, THAT'S ALWAYS THE PLAN** for me," A.J. Schopp said of his strategy for his semifinal match against Tony Ramos.

From the Iowa perspective, "I wanted to get out to a fast start and control the match," Ramos said.

When the whistle blew, and Schopp circled away from Tony's forward motion, it took about five seconds before Schopp was the one in on a shot to the stalking Hawkeye's right leg.

Tony defended with a whizzer, hipped in hard, and, while Schopp was seemingly coming up with the leg, Tony battled and worked himself out of danger.

A minute later, it would be Schopp again in on Tony's legs; this time on the mat's edge where a scramble ensued. Schopp posted up under Tony and Tony locked Schopp's ankles and continued to put weight on him and looked to not concede a takedown. The positions twisted and turned; however, there would be no takedown as the referee called a stalemate and both wrestlers returned to the center of the mat. The first period ended in a 0-0 tie and, for the second period, Tony, without hesitation, chose down.

In the down position, a position that Tony and Terry Brands were in favor of, but Tom Brands was vehemently against in their strategy conversations, had to now be a position of dominance. And it was, but not for Tony.

For the entire second period, no matter how explosive Tony was, no matter how many restarts occurred, no matter the hand control or body position or hip or stand or sit or anything—no matter what Tony did—the Hawkeye could not and did not shake the Scot from him. In fact, the only time Tony was able to come to his feet without Schopp draped all over him, was when the two-minute second period concluded and Schopp, by rule, had to allow Tony to stand freely.

Tony had been ridden out for the entire period and this now gave Schopp the one-point riding advantage—at least for the moment—and Schopp also had his choice of position for the third and final period of the national semifinals. In the stands, fans were yelling to the Edinboro coaches, "Top! Take top! Ride him out! He can't get off bottom! Top! Top!" as the Fighting Scots fans believed that if Schopp were to choose top and ride out Tony, he had a clear avenue to ride into the finals. However, as fate would have it, Schopp chose neutral and worked to secure the one-point riding advantage and maybe believed that he could extend his lead with a takedown. Or, if nothing else, not be the victim of another late-match takedown, which was Tony's pattern thus far.

When the signal for neutral was given, some of the fans—Edinboro, Iowa, Ramos-haters, and Ramos-adorers—could not believe it. They knew that if Tony was on his feet, and that was where he was most dangerous and most likely to score, he always had a chance to win a match. He had already proven it three times throughout the tournament and now he was being granted, gifted, a fourth opportunity.

Each match throughout the tournament had been consistent for Tony—everyone was trying to keep it close. To that point, Schopp had executed his plan the best.

"We've been training for [guys trying to keep it close and score on me at the end]," Ramos said. "Tom [Brands] talked to me about it— guys are going to wait until the last thirty seconds to try and score on [me] now. They're going to try and keep close and then maybe get one at the end. So it's something I've been aware of and preparing for."

When the third period began, it was now a hand fight and head-grab-and-pull match—these were positions Tony thrived in as he was difficult to wear down and he was very good at wearing down others. However, as the first minute of the period passed, Schopp would now have the riding advantage locked up, a 2-0 lead, 1-0 on the scoreboard, and it was Tony who had to bring the match to Schopp.

In the center of the mat, with 00:51 left in the national championship semifinal, Schopp circled left and snapped off the tie. Tony, who was stalking forward, worked back into his tie as Schopp tied up his wrists, stayed square, and changed over to a two-on-one to Tony's right arm; Tony changed levels and worked to an unsuccessful shot in the process. However, as Tony came up, and Schopp's head was hanging, Tony used his free hand, his left hand, to come up over Schopp's head and crank down in a forced front headlock position.

Schopp, with only 00:47 left to maintain his position in order to advance to his first NCAA finals, stopped moving his feet. Tony, on pure instinct and nothing more, attempted a right-footed foot sweep that, as Schopp lifted his foot, knocked Schopp off balance and forced him to release the two-on-one as he staggered backwards and looked to collect himself. In the process, Tony, who followed the sweep and had his right hand back, moved forward even farther and, as he fell into his front headlock once again, he cranked Schopp's head with his left and attacked Schopp's left leg with his right hand. Tony hit the corner so far that his head was now buried in Schopp's left side and a position battle, one where Tony was known for scoring in, now determined if Schopp or Tony, depending on the winner of the match's final battle, would possibly take the match to overtime, or advance one to the finals.

Tony changed positions from his left arm cinching the head and dropped it to Schopp's left ankle after he had secured the hip with his right arm and positioned himself behind Schopp's leg—he now had leverage over his longer opponent. Schopp responded with a whizzer downward and hard on Tony's right arm that was stretched across the back and that was now forced to Schopp's left shoulder, but Tony did not budge as he fought to keep that position.

As they wrestled to the mat's edge, Tony, still positioned behind the leg and against the left hip, reached up with his left hand, grabbed his right and pulled it into his body, thus crunching Schopp's shoulder into him. In that position, Tony still had Schopp's left leg trapped and, as he was on his feet crunching the shoulder, Schopp's leg was trapped and being bent into that same shoulder as well.

With the Iowa crowd erupting in cheers and amazement and anticipation, and others screaming "No! No! No!" in that moment, Schopp's leg was trapped under Tony's stomach and his shoulder was bent into Tony's chest—Schopp was trapped. Tony then rotated his body and, with 00:33 remaining, sunk Schopp to his back and the eruption of voices became even louder as Tony was conscious to keep one foot inbounds—his head posted out of bounds, his right foot out of bounds, which completed Tony's tripod. While Schopp's back was on the out-of-bounds line, the referee was now signaling a two-point takedown and counting back points in the process.

Schopp would ultimately work his left leg free as flashes from cameras were going off all throughout the arena and more so from the photographers mat side. With his left leg still inbounds, Tony stepped over Schopp with his right, underhooked Schopp's left arm with his right, now parallel and with Schopp's right leg inbounds, looking for the fall.

Tony then stepped and sunk his left leg into a Saturday night ride and, as Schopp tried to bridge and fight off of his back, his shoulder blades were seemingly flat and the only body part keeping the match alive was his own right foot trying to dig into the mat to push himself and Tony fully off the mat—it never happened.

While Schopp was fighting off his back, and Tony was fighting for the fall, Tom Brands, in Tony's corner, was pounding the mat and demanding that the referee call the fall. His hand repeatedly pounded down as he yelled, "He's stuck! He's stuck! Call it!"

The Fighting Scot fought hard enough to not give up the fall that both Tony and Tom Brands were fighting for; however, he did lose the match. When the period concluded and Tony came to his feet, he immediately flexed his patented double rainbow pose over Schopp and held it as he turned in a circle to show himself to the entire arena that was now in a frenzy of cheers and amazement and boos. Tony, who basked in the mat's center with his left hand raised, raised his right hand and loved every second of the moment. When the referee dropped Tony's left arm, Tony turned and took a moment to point to his family and friends in their section, and then he exited the mat and ran off into the tunnel.

The finish was a dominant one, even though the match, as a whole, looked to be slipping away from him. But, in the end, Tony found a way to win and had his hand raised for the fourth-straight time that weekend.

"[That] was a match where, you know what, you got to put the guy down and you got to put him down hard and let's end this thing," Tom Brands said. "[And when Tony did], it was a hard, explosive, crunching hold—I felt it sitting in the chair when it happened. It was an earthquake."

Tony would collect himself in the tunnel, have a small moment of joy, and then head to the media room for his semifinal victory interview. In fact, the first journalist to address Tony stated, "Tony, you didn't waste any time getting here, most guys take a while. It seems like you really want to express yourself right now."

And, with big eyes and a smirk, Tony responded, "I just want to get out of here."

The room had a good laugh as Tony paused and watched them respond to his words, then he completed his thought, "Go get ready for Graff."

Tony first addressed what he felt was the key to his victory. "Circling in front of my single-legs," he stated in response. "Not letting him get to that Jermaine Jones that he likes to do. In my head I was going over it, and I remembered that I could come up and hit a nice cow-catcher on him, and I got into the third period that was exactly what I was looking for. So I knew I could get there. I knew I could do it. He was stuck. He was flat."

Finishing in the top position with his opponent on his back as time expired gave Tony a feeling of dominance, and this was the strong finish that he felt he needed to catapult himself into the finals.

The second question dealt with Tony's confidence and voice. The journalist asked, due to his confidence, if he had to speak a big game before he could go out and perform. Tony's answer was simple: "Nope. Just go out there and do your thing and this is my personality—this is who I am. This is what I love. This is what I live for."

There was a long silence as Tony looked around the room before all of the questions came in at the same time. The one that stood out would be: "Did you feel the clock ticking on you in the match, though?"

"Well, I wasn't too worried about it, I knew I was going to get two," Tony answered in regard to the final minute of the match. "Was I freaking out? Was I panicking? No. When it was getting down to that minute mark, I knew I had to create some type of action. I never used a foot sweep in my life. As soon as I locked my hands I started pulling him in—I heard him screaming—and that's when I knew it was over."

But that win was not just about getting to the finals. Tony also wanted to defeat one of the wrestlers who beat him earlier in the season; a match that Tony felt he let slip away from himself.

"[It feels] awesome," Ramos responded to the question posed about getting revenge on Schopp. "I can't get revenge [on Colon] because Graff won, but [Graff] is someone I beat a couple of times and I'm ready for this final match. I know he's probably been working on some stuff, but I'm real confident going into this."

However, different from the Big Ten match-up between Tony and Graff, "I expect to break it open, score some points," Ramos would say in regard to his expectations of the championship match on Saturday night. "I haven't scored a lot of points this tournament, but I've been getting the job done. Let's go score some points tomorrow night, Saturday night. I'm ready for Saturday night. That's it. I got one more match to go. I'm counting them down. Came here in five and I've got one left."

Tony, no matter how it ended, had now become a three-time All-American and an NCAA finalist for the second season in a row, but now it was time to finish the job he came to Oklahoma City to complete, and that was to win a national championship.

CHAPTER 55
THE KING'S HAT

"That seems to be the word with him is confidence, and he has a unique way of expressing it and a unique way of displaying it. And it's real. That's every day, and he's beautiful for our program."

• Tom Brands
Head Coach, the University of Iowa
Coach, Hawkeye Wrestling Club

BEFORE HE STOMPED ONTO THE WEEKEND'S greatest stage, Tony was in the back room with Tom Brands and his corner coaches, Terry Brands and Ryan Morningstar.

During the 125-pound national championship match, Tony was seated in a chair wearing his gold warm-ups and Iowa hoodie under his black Iowa top. Across his nose, he had on a Breathe Right strip as he looked up and watched moments of the match on a flat-screen television hanging from the ceiling. Tom Brands paced back and forth with his hands in his pants pockets while Terry Brands stood, arms crossed, near a corner watching the same television.

When Tony was ready to gather himself for his match, it was Morningstar who stood behind him, stretched him out, and loosened him up. As his match time came closer and closer, he removed his hoodie and gray long sleeve Team Ramos Iowa t-shirt and pulled up his black Iowa singlet for the final time before putting his t-shirt back on.

Once he felt like he was ready to move closer to the front of the tunnel, he put his headgear on and Terry Brands came up with some final words for the senior Hawkeye. Tony listened and then he snapped his chin strap securely in place for his final collegiate match.

As the arena lights were turned off and Wisconsin's Tyler Graff was introduced, Tony waited to be called wearing nothing but his singlet, headgear, and gray Team Ramos t-shirt. Once Graff reached the center of the mat, the focus turned to Tony. From his entrance, smoke poured out with lights flashing every which way. Then, Tony's introduction sounded off as the announcer proclaimed, "His opponent, wrestling from the green corner, a redshirt senior with a record of 31-2—he is a wrestler from Iowa and a three-time All-American—Tony Ramos."

Camera phones were on and flashes popped off and on and some videos were taken as well. Photographers followed the face of Iowa down the long green carpet that led to his corner of the stage. Once he reached the stairs, Tony stomped to the mat and he was ready to wrestle.

Tony's presence was anticipated by the thousands in attendance who either wanted him to finally capture that elusive national championship that he had been so close to just one season ago, or those who wanted him to fail and fail in an awful and embarrassing manner. As always, there were no in-betweens when it came to a Tony's match—people always seemed to care one way or another.

Once on the stage, Tony removed his t-shirt and reported directly to the middle of the mat for one final stare down as a Hawkeye. That was it. Win or lose, Tony would never wear the Iowa black and gold again.

In the middle of the mat Tony waited in his stance and stared—Graff met him there and stared back into his eyes.

"Graff was kind of moving around a little bit and then stepped up to the middle," Ramos said. "People can't see our eyes. No one can see what we're looking at—they just see what's going on. But as soon as he stepped up, the first place he was looking was down at the mat—and then he decided to look up. He didn't realize that he had already messed up."

When the whistle blew, and the match was underway, it would be an immediate head tie from both wrestlers and a fight for position and control. And, even though there were small moments of opportunities, both wrestlers were very careful not to overextend themselves too much. When the first period came to an end, the score was tied at 0-0.

In the second period, Graff had the first opportunity to score as he chose the down position. Just thirteen days prior at the Big Ten championships, this was where he lost the bout as Tony earned a riding point. However, without applying much pressure or giving too much commitment to the top position, Tony conceded the Graff escape in a mere seven seconds. With just about a full period remaining, the number-three and number-five seeded wrestlers were back in the neutral position.

And, just as there were no real offensive attacks in the first period, the second period mirrored that same sequence. There was no score other than the escape from Graff and he led the championships bout by a 1-0 score as Tony now chose down to start the third period. What had taken

Graff seven seconds to do to start the second, it took Tony two seconds less to open the third.

With his escape, Tony had tied the match 1-1 and, for now, there was no riding advantage for either wrestler. As for any other advantage, there was also none. In that, he score was tied at the end of regulation.

In the first overtime, both wrestlers remained calculated and continually cautious on their feet. There were no real attempts to score and the match headed into a second overtime period.

Tony had his choice to start, and he chose the down position. The down position. The position that had haunted Tony a few times in his past. The position where, even though he had been able to escape on Stieber when it mattered, had also shown signs of weakness against Schopp. If there was a weakness, this position was it for Tony. However, confident in what he not only needed to do, but what he had to do, he had no reservations about the fact that he would escape.

When the whistle blew, Tony moved. Graff countered and there were no immediate signs of an escape. Again, Tony fought and turned and stood and worked to create motion and movement and separation—no escape. Attempt after attempt was thwarted off by Graff and, when the first thirty-second period had ended, Tony had not been able to escape. Graff, now, simply needed an escape and to fend off Tony's attacks. Tony, however, needed to ride Graff out and force another overtime period—he had already proven that he was capable of riding out the four-time All-American just about two weeks ago in Graff's home arena. He would now have to do it again.

When Graff set himself for the second thirty-second period, the outcome came down to one simple question: would Tony be able to ride Graff out, or would he release him and then try to win the match on his feet?

Tony would cover and, off the whistle, Tony grabbed Graff's inside ankle, Graff's right, as he also grabbed a tight waist with his left as the Badger looked to stand. Tony, who fought to keep position, found himself on his knees as Graff found his way to his feet; however, Tony still had control of Graff's right foot and knew his national championship depended on him hanging onto it.

Graff turned again to kick free, but Tony was latched onto his ankle like a dog on a bone and then came to his own feet. From there, Graff looked to roll; however, as he did, Tony defended the Abas roll as Graff reached under and took hold of Tony's left leg. A scramble looked like it was about to happen, which was what Graff was initiating and hoping would earn him the escape, but it did just the opposite.

With Graff still clinging to Tony's leg, Morningstar, in his chair, was intently watching it all unfold while Terry Brands was jumping out of his chair and waving his arms while Tony sunk his hips, cinched Graff's right ankle closer to his right armpit and, while his leg was over Graff's body in a perpendicular position, grabbed Graff's right arm just under the bicep and pulled him into him to expose his back as the referee worked through a three count on the near fall exposure. The Iowa fans were going crazy in their seats.

As Graff fought off his back, Terry Brands continued to jump and excitedly work his way back to where Morningstar was, passed his chair, and then celebrated as Morningstar grabbed his arms and tried to keep him in the corner—this would not be possible. Just outside the center of the mat facing the head table, Tony remained tight on Graff's right leg and worked it out to a high single as Graff continually kicked to find a way to free his leg. Tony would be awarded the two points and, with 00:16 left, and Graff, with a look of frustration, was in desperate need of an escape or a reversal.

Once Graff saw the two points awarded, he punched the mat with his right hand as Tony collapsed down on him and continued controlling the ankle. Tony would also climb and claim a tight waist. Both wrestlers were down on the mat and Graff was doing all he could to get out of bounds for a fresh start; Tony worked opposite of Graff to keep the clock running.

As Graff had his hands on the mat and mule kicked, Tony tied up both of his legs as Terry Brands and Ryan Morningstar jumped up and celebrated by pushing each other in pure bliss. Terry Brands pointed and yelled as time expired and Tony, still on his knees on the mat's edge, raised his hands in triumph.

Brands pointed to his senior national champion and Tony raised his body and pointed to the section of the arena where his family and friends were sitting, cheering, hugging, and soaking up the same moment of victory. Deb Ramos hugged Megan, both crying, and Tony himself fell to his knees, arms raised tall, eyes closed, and then fell back to the mat.

Thirteen days earlier, Tony had no typical flex and pose and planned celebration—his emotions had taken over. This moment was the same. There was no flex and there was no pose—there was just a natural emotion coming out that was unplanned and unprepared.

As the announcer pronounced Tony the national champion, there would be a challenge from the Wisconsin corner on the back points awarded.

Terry Brands, all over the situation called out to the referees as they reviewed the call. "Hey, [Pat] Fitzgerald never misses a call!" Terry Brands yelled at the head table. "I remember saying that and Fitzgerald gave me a wink. And [Fitzgerald] doesn't miss a call—he was at his best that year. It was the right call. It was the right call on Tony's part, too.

"Graff," Terry Brands paused, "you knew he was going to roll. I think [Graff] did just enough to stay in there to beat him in the end; meaning, on his feet, shutting it down, taking it to overtime and then riding him out, and now all [he had] to do is get away. That's what Graff's thinking. I mean, the match is over in Graff's mind—that's what I saw. But that's not what I saw with our guy. Again, you know what I was thinking: *You guys are looking awful comfy over there. You got no idea what you're ahead of because I know what's coming.* [It didn't matter how much time was left], he's going to find a way to win."

So, when Tony pulled back Graff's arm and scored on the quick tilt, "It wasn't a surprise," Terry Brands reacted. "It was elation. Tony knew what was coming—we all knew what was coming. You know, he set it up, dropped down, set him up and came through the zone—twenty, nineteen [seconds] to go—you know it's coming, right? And really, if you look at it from the Iowa point of view, or the objective point of view, it was the only choice that Graff had; otherwise, we're going to another minute overtime and we're grinding on your head and pushing you backwards. Are you going to go another minute or minute thirty where you got to get off the bottom and now you got to hold him down again? He had to [roll]. He had to go for it.

"And that was the beauty of it. It was vintage Tony Ramos in the fact that he forced the guy to wrestle where he wanted him to wrestle. Maybe it didn't work on his feet with the matches before that—maybe these guys had these great plans, even though they had no chance to beat him because all they wanted to do was keep it close. And, ultimately, that was the way that we won. Because it comes to the point where a guy has no choice. And that's where Tony, in vintage Ramos style, put Graff. He had no chance to win the match when it really came down to it."

Of course, there was still the moment of truth. One season ago, no back points were awarded to Tony and those were also two points that Terry Brands thought were undisputable. Tony, Terry Brands, Iowa, and the arena had to wait in anticipation of the verdict regardless of what they saw or what they thought they saw.

When Fitzgerald came to the center of the mat with the call, he said, "Upon further review, the ruling on the mat is confirmed."

With those words, Tony, again, raised both of his hands and then extended his right hand over to Graff as the two shook.

Once the handshake was complete, Graff walked off the mat, almost in disbelief, and Tony extended his pointer fingers in the air from both hands as Fitzgerald raised Tony's left arm while Tony mirrored that with his right. He circled around the mat and proudly proclaimed himself the 2014 NCAA 133-pound national champion.

Immediately, Tony darted off of the mat, jumped down from the stage, and made a mad dash to his family in the front row. Once there, he jumped up to the elevated seats and was pulled up and hugged by his family and friends. He brother Frank put a black hat on Tony's head that read, in gold lettering, "NCAA CHAMP."

Tom Brands headed into the tunnel and, once released from the grips of his family, Tony sprinted to the back tunnel. There, he caught up to Tom Brands, walking with his hands in his pockets, proud. Tony, without Brands seeing him, jumped onto his coach's back and clasped his arms around him. Tom smiled and Tony released his embrace as they walked to the back of the room.

In the process, someone shouted, "T-Ram, 133 national champion!" It echoed in the tunnel.

As Tony was followed by many and congratulated on being a champion. Graff, on the other side of the arena, was with his coaches; he felt the defeat Tony had felt the season before.

Graff's emotions flowed out of his body as he walked with his coaches following him. His hands were on his hips as his eyes were closed. In utter disappointment, and possibly disbelief, he walked until he had cleared the hallway and found a place, no particular place, where he dropped to the cold cement, placed his warm-ups on the floor, rested his back up against the cinder-blocked wall, and bowed his head between his knees. This would only be for a moment as he covered his head with his warm-up top before falling to his left, now lying on the cold, emotionless floor in tears as his final opportunity to win a national championship had slipped away from him forever.

The difference one year and two points in the other direction made on the emotions of two wrestlers was profound.

Although there were some who said that Tony was lucky and that he caught a break, Dan Gable disagreed. "To me," Gable said in regard to Tony earning the two-point near fall off Graff's roll, "that's making your break. Making your luck. And I wasn't down on [Ramos] because he had been doing that all through the tournament and the tournament before that and in those last dual meets. So, it wasn't like, 'What's new?' Hey, he was good enough to win it because he showed it in all of the close ones. But, I still think he was better than what he showed during his senior year, and he was still the national champion. That tells you something about how good Tony Ramos was."

WHEN TERRY BRANDS FINALLY HAD A MOMENT

with his wrestler, "The first thing he said to me," Terry Brands remembered, "was when he came out and he was walking in that Ramos walk, and he goes with big eyes and his arms opened wide, 'You shouldn't roll when you're in there. We've been talking about that.' It was a job well done and a feeling of satisfaction that we came to the tournament and accomplished what we set out to accomplish."

Tony was then shuttled into the interview room, NCAA CHAMP hat and all. He still had his singlet on and he would remove the strip from his nose as he was announced to the media: "From the University of Iowa, your national champion, Tony Ramos."

The first question posed to Tony commented on him finally accomplishing this goal. Tony smiled, tooth missing, "It's awesome. I'm excited. I can't wait to get out of here, go take that drug test, and celebrate with my family. Get my bracket and go home and put it on the wall."

The second question focused on his running to his family and if it was planned. "Oh yeah," Ramos said still smiling, shaking his head forward. "You always have something planned. They're the closest people to me other than the wrestling team, Tom and Terry, the other coaches, and I wanted to see them as quick as I could."

And then, the obvious was addressed. "Tony, you may be the first NCAA champion to come in here with a national champion hat. Whose idea was that?" the journalist asked with a laugh.

Tony laughed in response, "My brother's got ideas for everything. I didn't even know he had it. He just put it on my head when I was over there. It's pretty cool though."

Even though the mood was light and Tony was goodhearted and good-natured in his responses, it all became serious when he was asked about the stare down at the start of the match. Immediately, his playful tone became more serious and reflective as he spoke about how Graff actually looked down and that was when Tony said that he knew he was in Graff's head.

Publicly, Tony was asked about the close matches throughout, and he stated with confidence that he won a national title and that equated to wrestling up to his capabilities. That was enough to get the job done, and that was all that mattered up to that point.

When he reflected further, there were still a few pieces that he knew and felt confident about. One of those was Graff's decision in the tiebreaker to create a scramble.

"I knew he was going to roll," Ramos said. "Did I expect him to roll when I was on the single-leg? Probably not as much. I thought maybe he would try and kick away. And then he did. I was like, you know what, I just have to catch this arm, lean back—I know I'm not going to get a five count—but I can get a quick two count and the match is over.

"I ended up riding him out and I think that was one of the coolest moments that I had and heard the ref counting six, five, four—[I] hear him counting down and I see Terry and Morningstar jumping up in the corner and I looked at them and started smiling and shaking my head like, 'We did it. We finally did it. Let's let this five-seconds run out and we can go and celebrate.'

"You do everything that you do for this moment. But, if I had a chance to go back and do it all again, I wouldn't wrestle that same tournament. You'd see a different guy out there wrestling, having a lot more fun, not being so tense. The other thing is that it builds [my] confidence because [I] didn't wrestle my best and I still had a chance to win. I didn't wrestle my best at the national tournament and I still won the national tournament, that means [I'm] pretty freakin' good."

The reality, however, was that Tony was afraid of losing a match, any match that tournament; therefore, he kept everything close and believed that he could come away with a win in any situation.

"I did not think [my senior season] was my best wrestling-wise because I started to see the season as a clock," Ramos admitted. "Instead of going out there with no worries or free, it was always in the back of my mind: *This is the last chance, don't screw it up.* The NCAA has a set clock on you to win a national title and that's four years or five, if you redshirt. Time is something that if you let it get to you and play with your mind it can be catastrophic. I didn't let it ruin my season, but I did let it control how I competed and how I went about preparing for the next year. I wouldn't say I didn't prepare right or [didn't] work my butt off that following summer because I did. I will say that when it came to competitions I was too cautious and afraid to make a mistake that could be detrimental.

"I'll tell you exactly what happened at that tournament: I wrestled so tight because I didn't want to lose. I didn't want to feel that pain [of losing in the finals] again. But, at the same time, I wrestled enough where when I needed to score, I scored."

Tony continued, "I wrestled mistake free, pretty much, and it got the job done. But, if I had to wrestle the tournament again, I wouldn't want to win it like that. A lot of people ask me, 'Is that how you should do it? Wrestle mistake free? Do you just do enough to win?' No. Dominate everyone.

"My training was all the same. I was training just as hard, I was doing all of the same things that got me to where I was; it was just going out there and not actually opening up. I would go out and be tight—everything was slowed down. I made sure everything was calculated. There had to be a clear opening before I would allow myself to attack and the previous year I would just get in fire fights and flurries and I would just attack.

"It wasn't a lack of urgency," Ramos commented, "it was more a fear of not living up to what I had done the previous year. I had so many expectations and I dominated so much that year before that I wanted to keep doing it. But, at the same time, that thought was always in my head and held me back from opening up a little bit more in my matches because I wanted to win everything and get that national title so bad that it affected everything else that entire year."

Regardless of how he wrestled, he accomplished his goal. And, as Tom Brands walked down the hall, he was interviewed about Tony while wearing an NCAA CHAMP hat of his own. A journalist commented on how good he looked in it.

"I'll tell you what, it feels good," Tom Brands smiled. "I kept saying he's the king; I had to go back and get the king's hat."

In regard to his senior Hawkeye's confidence and how he openly wore it, Tom Brands was very complimentary. "That seems to be the word with him is confidence, and he has a unique way of expressing it and a unique way of displaying it," Tom Brands said. "And it's real. That's every day, and he's beautiful for our program."

2014 • NCAA DIVISION I WRESTLING CHAMPIONSHIPS
RAMOS STANDS WITH THEN FIANCEE MEGAN ESKEW, AND HIS FATHER AND MOTHER
PHOTOGRAPH COURTESY • TONY AND MEGAN RAMOS

2014 • NCAA DIVISION I WRESTLING CHAMPIONSHIPS
RAMOS SMILES IN HIS "NCAA CHAMP" HAT AS HE ADDRESSES THE MEDIA
PHOTOGRAPH COURTESY • TC LIFONTI

THE HAWKEYE WRESTLING CLUB

CHAPTER 56
THE TIME IS NOW

"You don't have to make up your mind now. Think about it—one hundred and twenty-five and a half [pounds] on an overnight weigh-in; 57 kg on an overnight weigh-in. It's tailor-made for you."

• *Terry Brands*
Associate Head Coach, the University of Iowa
Coach, Hawkeye Wrestling Club

ORIGINALLY, TONY RAMOS HAD PLANNED ON taking some time off after his national championship; however, the actual amount of time off was always in question.

Terry Brands was one of the first people to sit down with Tony and discuss the opportunity in front of him, and he did it three days after Tony was crowned an NCAA champion.

"The way I remember it," Terry Brands said, "is that he said he was done with wrestling. He sat in my office and told me, 'I'm probably going to go to Arizona State and coach.' Those were his words verbatim."

On hearing this, Terry Brands was simply surprised, particularly since there had been the major change in the Olympic weights just one year ago in 2013.

"I couldn't believe it," Terry Brands remembered. "When I asked him why, Tony said that he didn't think he could make the weight. I told him, 'You know they changed the weight and that weight class is perfect for you, right? You don't have to make up your mind now. Think about it—one hundred and twenty-five and a half [pounds] on an overnight weigh-in; 57 kg on an overnight weigh-in. It's tailor-made for you.'"

It took a few days for Tony to sit back and consider all aspects of the move as he contemplated all of his options. And when those few days passed, and Tony had the opportunity to speak with his fiancée and family, he had decided to put off coaching full-time and keep competing. "At first," Ramos remembered, "I wanted to just jump into coaching because making the cut to 57 kg was something that I just wasn't willing to do."

The first voice of encouragement came from Tony's fiancée, Megan Eskew. "Tony was watching the U.S. Open," Megan said, "and I could tell he was itching to compete. I told him to wrestle in the Trials, but he said we already scheduled our wedding shower on that day and he didn't think Tom would let him compete that season. I told him to talk to Tom and wrestle in the Trials. It was a pretty simple conversation. I knew he wanted to and when I told him to, that sealed the deal."

After that conversation, Tony spoke with Terry Brands. "Terry really pushed for it," said Ramos. "He told me that, 'This is the weight I used to wrestle, I've done this and I know how to do this. We're the same size.' And then I saw guys my size wrestle at the U.S. Open and be able to compete. After that, it was a no-brainer."

Tom Brands said, "I don't think he was planning on wrestling until he saw the U.S. Open and realized that, 'Hey, I can go with these guys.' For me, I was like, 'Why did your confidence waiver at that next level?' But he had to see it and once he saw it, now he's back, he's the old Tony Ramos—his confidence is right back up there. I remember talking to him when I was in Vegas—I don't know if I called him or he called me or missed a call or it was a text, but the communication was, 'I can beat these guys. I'm going.' And there was enough time—he hadn't eaten himself out of shape yet and there was enough time for the trials to get it done."

As Tony saw it, if he was going to dive into this, he needed to revisit the conversation with Megan and validate her support. However, she did more than support his decision as, "She sat me down," Ramos laughed. "She told me that she knew what it would take and what the sacrifices would be. At the time, she was willing to put aspects of our relationship on the back burner for training and me being gone for a long time. So she knew what she was getting into; but, at the same time, she also knew what I needed to do."

In the end, "With support of family and talking with coaches, they made it possible and helped me see that it was possible," Ramos revealed. And when he realized that it was a possibility, "I walked into Tom's office and told him I wanted to train for the trials. After that, I never looked back."

ONE YEAR EARLIER, DECEMBER 17, 2013, THE FILA
Technical Commission announced the weight class changes for men's freestyle wrestling. These weight class alterations would take place for

the 2016 Olympic Games in Rio de Janeiro, Brazil. According to FILA, its Technical Commission worked with the federation's Medical Commission, Scientific Commission, Referee Commission, and Athletes' Commission to form the basis of these changes. Therefore, at the start of 2014, there would now only be six official freestyle weight classes for the men: 57, 65, 74, 86, 97, and 125—all weights in kilograms.

In having made these changes, the sport now lost two vital weight classes, 61 and 70 kilograms, for the Olympics; however, FILA would continue to include these in all other official FILA competitions such as World and Continental Championships, World Cups, and Golden Grand Prix events.

Losing these two weight classes created a number of difficult decisions for athletes in regard to where they would wrestle or if they would continue to wrestle. Since the 57 kg class would be the lowest weight, wrestlers either had to cut a significant amount of weight or bump up, essentially, two weight classes to 65 kg. The same would be true for the loss of the 70 kg weight class.

Therefore, the gap in the lower and lower-middle weight classes created a number of immediate problems for a large percentage of top-level American athletes—surely it did the same in other competing countries as well. Either way, by 2016, everyone had to adjust. The changes were set and that was that.

The given chart shows a better depiction of the current weight-class system by FILA approved prior to the 2016 Olympic Games.

Olympic Weight Category	57 kg	125.5 pounds
Non-Olympic Weight Category	61 kg	134.5 pounds
Olympic Weight Category	65 kg	143.3 pounds
Non-Olympic Weight Category	70 kg	154.3 pounds
Olympic Weight Category	74 kg	163.0 pounds
Olympic Weight Category	86 kg	189.6 pounds
Olympic Weight Category	97 kg	213.9 pounds
Olympic Weight Category	125 kg	275.6 pounds

Up until 1996 at the Atlanta Games in the United States of America, wrestling had ten total weight classes. By 2000, at the Sydney Games in Australia, the freestyle division had been stripped of two weight classes dropping it to a total of eight. Then, in 2004, with the addition of the women's freestyle team for the Games held in Athens, Greece, the men's freestyle team totaled seven weight classes as the women were introduced to the Olympic Games with four weight classes. The same held true for the 2012 Olympics in London, England; however, for the current 2016 Olympic Games, the men and the women would meet with equality—each having six weight classes.

In an ESPN Associated Press release in December of 2013, FILA ruled to cut the men's divisions from seven to six weight classes so they could add two women's weight classes to ensure a 6-6-6 split among the three disciplines. FILA president Nenad Lalovic then went on and added how, "We want to make changes that make the sport better. If we need to change, we will. Our goal is to be excellent in everything we do."

The move was critiqued due to taking away weights instead of enriching the sport more. The addition to the women's division was not the issue, the issue was why subtract weights from the other divisions in the process. To clarify, wrestling was actually reduced to two fewer weight classes with the addition of another discipline—the sport went from 10-10 in men's freestyle and Greco-Roman, to six men's freestyle, six men's Greco-Roman, and six women's freestyle: 6-6-6. Thus, there was now 18 combined weight classes instead of the original 20, and that now with an added discipline.

As an ambassador for the sport of wrestling, Dan Gable said, "We better have two more weights by the time 2020 comes. We had 20 with two teams, now we have 18 with three teams, but that's also our fault. We never had anyone on the [International Olympic Committee] before. I believe this is the first time in the history. I mean, we just haven't been doing our homework. If we want a good sport and have the opportunity to add more weight classes, we have to have more authority to do more of the politics with the right people. And we have to have that authoritative respect—and we have not had that for a long time. Things won't change in a day or two, but I think we're finally moving in the right direction, but let's hope we're moving quickly enough to get more weight classes by 2020 because it's ridiculous that we have twenty-five pounds per weight class. But let me tell you, the rest of the world, that's not a wrestler, except maybe judo, they don't understand the weight difference. They don't understand it. Until you wrestle and can feel that weight difference, you won't know that. The bottom line is, we have to get them educated and become more authoritative and in a respective way."

However, as for 2016, the weight classes had been set and wrestlers had to adjust in a manner that each felt suited him best.

FOR TONY, WHO HAD WRESTLED ALL FOUR YEARS at 133 pounds for the University of Iowa, and who had always been adamant about not cutting weight because he simply hated to do it, he now found himself in the politics of FILA if he wanted to compete professionally and internationally. For Tony, to compete at the level he wanted to and to be able to achieve his dream of winning an Olympic gold medal, the cut would not only be difficult, it would be necessary—in the back of his mind, he knew that.

The rest, of course, was seemingly simple. Since he had already established a strong trust and relationship with his coaches, Tom and Terry Brands, particularly Terry Brands, and Terry coached the Hawkeye Wrestling Club, it was an easy transition.

"Me and Terry were really close," Ramos stated, "and I felt that he could get me where I wanted to be. Terry was always working with me and I had the best relationship with him, so I wanted to stay there because I knew with him I would be most successful. Once we sat down and figured out pay and negotiated things, we settled and were able to move forward."

As far as what was special about Terry Brands as a person and as a coach, Tony said that, "Me and Terry really understand each other and it's easy to share how we feel. Sometimes what he might say and what I might say, we might not agree, but we understand it and we never judge each other. He is kind of like a father to me, but also like a brother, too. I can go to him to talk or for anything. He took me under his wing and he took my wife in and my son in and the relationships that we have is special. And I think that comes through when he is coaching me. If I lose, he feels just as bad as I do. And, when I win, no one is more proud."

In the end, Tony's decision simply dealt with possible regret. "Even if it doesn't work out for me," Ramos said, "at least I gave it a chance and I can't say, 'What if?'"

Therefore, the only place for Tony to train in a healthy environment with the men who have supported him and helped him grow and become as successful as he was, was with Terry and Tom Brands and where he felt the most comfortable, confident, and secure: Iowa.

THE HAWKEYE WRESTLING CLUB WAS FOUNDED in 1973 by then head coach Gary Kurdelmeir and assistant coach Dan Gable. The financial backing of the club came from Roy Carver, an Iowa philanthropist who was chairman and founder of Bandag Inc., a tire-retreading material with operations in ninety countries.

"It was another one of [Kurdelmeir's ideas]," Gable remembered.

"Now, he might have got the idea from Iowa State, because Iowa State's coach Nichols had former athletes staying around and training with the athletes—that made a big difference. I'm sure he followed [the idea of the club] pretty close. He saw the effect that guys had on some of the athletes even if they weren't or were training for the Olympics, or even after, they'd keep them around locally and they'd wanted to come back to practice."

In regard to how the club itself was implemented, Gable said, "I think he wanted to follow a system that was doing very well and stay with it and beat it—and he did it."

Of course, there was the issue of money and trying to find a way, a creative way, to entice the wrestlers to stay in the area. "Unlike most people," Gable stated, "[Kurdelmeir] had one huge donor so he could get an easy start. [He] didn't have to go out and sell the club. He only had one guy to sell it to and he was already on board—and that was Roy Carver."

Since Carver's wealth was always shrouded in intrigue, and he was always ready and willing to help the University of Iowa as Iowa was where his roots were from, the sales pitch would simply need to show something new and something exciting. Therefore, when Kurdelmeir approached Carver about the HWC, he knew Carver would not only be intrigued by it, but on board and ready to help.

As for Carver's impact on the club, the first issue that Kurdelmeir had to handle was Carver's excitement about the concept of bringing the club idea to Iowa. "Obviously, [Kurdelmeir] had to calm Carver down a little bit," Gable laughed, "and keep him within his limits. I mean, Carver just pulled out his checkbook and would say, 'What's it going to take? I got a big check here for you. Just say a number and I'll write it.'"

Initially, though, Kurdelmeir wanted Carver excited because he could help make this concept happen financially. "But, after the fact," Gable said, "[Kurdelmeir] had to tell Carver he couldn't do that kind of stuff."

And Kurdelmeir orchestrated the organization of the club perfectly because, by the time he had to tell Carver that he could not just run around with his checkbook open, Carver had already done enough to stabilize the Hawkeye Wrestling Club at the University of Iowa.

When Gable reflected on Carver's ways of throwing money around, he was not critical in a negative way by any means. "That was the way Carver knew," Gable said. "He was the head of a big company and he knew that if you are going to hire people, then you have to give them good opportunities to get those people to come here. Carver was good with the business aspect and Kurdelmeir knew how to handle [Carver]—he knew how to handle me, too."

However, through all of the changes that the club had undergone through the years, one basic piece of business had never changed: there were no written contracts.

The club was predicated on its word—the word of the athlete to train and compete at Iowa and the word of the coaches to coach and help the wrestler athletically and financially.

For current head coach, Tom Brands, when he competed for the HWC in the mid-1990s, the club simply made sense for him and what he wanted to do. "The way that I was wired ever since I was a little kid," Tom Brands said, "the Olympics was the pinnacle. I'm not sure I would have went anywhere [else] anyway."

In Tom Brand's perspective, "The Hawkeye Wrestling Club was basically the genius of having a great program; meaning, the best people stick around to train—they don't go other places to train. Or, they have a reason and a means to stick around and train—they don't have to go out into the work force. They can just stay around and train and compete."

However, over time, there were obstacles that, depending on the athlete and his situation, the club could only offer so much. And, even though the club and the support was growing, there were still necessities required to maintain the interest and draw of Iowa's elite.

"At that time," Tom Brands said, "the Hawkeye Wrestling Club didn't provide a whole lot in terms of dollars; but, if you were good enough, other clubs around the country would pick you up. And then the great thing at that time that was starting to be pioneered was wrestle for Foxcatcher [in Pennsylvania], stay in Iowa City. And that was a win-win. They paid us a monthly stipend to train and score points for them at the national tournaments and to wear their colors, their singlets and their uniforms, but we could stay right here and train. Even if that hadn't opened up, I'm not sure I would have left here just because of the experience I had. There was no way I was going to leave where my teeth were cut."

But, over time, as wrestling had grown and evolved into a sport where other training centers were opened and options became available, the HWC had to continually evolve to keep pace with. In that, being able to keep wrestlers around becomes the issue.

"The Hawkeye Wrestling Club's important," Tom Brands said, "because there's a lot of different places to go now. Regional training centers have exploded, there's big money people in five or six or seven programs that are single-handedly funding and trying to pull the best guys to their clubs. We're able to do that because of the relationships that we have with these guys when they graduate and we've got to raise money—it's competitive."

At the forefront of recognizing the competitive market, Tom Brands and the club, in 2008, needed to make a sudden change in order to make itself even more available for Iowa's strongest prospects. That season, Tom Brands identified the talent that was around him and had the foresight to analyze the potential growth of the club and where they needed to grow to stay ahead of the curve.

"We knew that we had to raise money to stay competitive," Tom Brands admitted. "In 2008, we started looking at our budget, we started looking at the class that was coming out in 2010—Metcalf, Dennis, Morningstar, Ericson, Kenny, Slaton, Borschel. Those are all names of guys coming out of that class and what are we going to do if they all want to compete internationally? Well, they're going to get poached out of here."

Therefore, to be able to sustain their future growth, Tom Brands knew that the club could not afford to wait and be ill-prepared to keep those athletes around when their collegiate eligibility expired.

"I had the foresight, not the brains," Tom Brands stated, "but the foresight to say, 'Hey, we've got to wrap this thing up.' And so we slowly got a group of businessmen in the corridor here that really went to work and really understood what the challenge was—money. We went from a $40,000 to $50,000 budget and maybe one big donor, to over $200,000 and three or four big donors and a lot of fundraisers. Had we waited until 2010, we would have been behind in what the genius of Gable's philosophy was being the Hawkeye Wrestling Club—and really Kurdelmeir—and that is to keep your best guys around to help your team."

From there, the growth of the club has been a continued process as the times and athletes are ever-changing. "Even over the years," Tom Brands admitted, "the club has had to keep evolving. Athletes have become needier, probably, from finances. I'll say that some things have changed a little bit, but the philosophy behind the club has remained the same."

The club's philosophy states: "Since its inception in 1973, the focus of the Hawkeye Wrestling Club has always been to provide the training, coaching, and resources necessary to help our athletes pursue their dreams of becoming World and Olympic Champions. The money raised through the HWC goes directly to benefit the athletes helping with living expenses, training and traveling needs. Maybe the most important aspect of the HWC is its pursuit in trying to get the best post-collegiate athletes to train with the HWC together in Iowa City to attain the ultimate prize in wrestling... World and Olympic gold medals."

Prior to the 2016 United States Olympic Team Trials, the Hawkeye Wrestling Club had produced 16 Olympic qualifiers and eight medals—

four gold, one silver, and three bronze.

WHEN IT CAME TIME FOR TONY TO COMMIT TO
the Hawkeye Wrestling Club, the same style of contract that was used in 1973 remained the same style of contract in 2014—it was a verbal contract based on trust and a commitment to one another.

"The contract," Frank Defilippis said, "was verbal. It was an agreement between Tom, me, and Tony. We had a dollar figure in mind when we went to the table, and Tom actually did better than that. And when I asked Tom to put it to paper, he said, 'My word is paper. Don't you trust me?' I said, 'Yeah, coach, we trust you.'"

The way Tom Brands expressed the HWC contract for Tony, or any wrestler, was that, "It's [by our] word. We commit a stipend to them and my word is good."

For Tony and Frank, that word was enough. As for the details of the contract, each wrestler received his own stipend; however, nothing was disclosed as to what Tony or any other HWC member received. As would be expected, over time, stipends increased with the growth of the club and costs of living.

For Tony, he was exiting the University of Iowa with about $75,000 in student loans and his contract had to be enough to support not only his loan payments, but also his ability to support his soon-to-be family.

Initially, before Tony decided to continue wrestling, "There were some misunderstandings there," Tom Brands said. "I think he worried a little bit about how he was going to be taken care of—he had student debt and this and that—but we're focused. We're not talking in the middle of his senior year about there being a spot for him—we think that's implied. But I did learn something because I think if he would have heard that [we had a coaching spot for him], I think he probably may have been more of a Hawkeye and really wonder if he was going to stay here—I think he would have been here.

"But the other thing is that he is motivated by things that I'm not motivated by," Tom Brands continued. "So he saw, 'Hey, I'm a national champion, now I'm a big name and things are opening up to where I can get coaching, I can coach anywhere I want.' I'll put it this way: There's a lot of people calling. So he might be thinking, 'I can go and make some good money.'"

However, for Tony, unlike maybe some other wrestlers in other programs who were the face of their program and won a national championship, he was never on a full-ride scholarship. Over his five-year career at Iowa, going from his redshirt freshman year scholarship of three-percent, he was then bumped to forty percent for his first year after the

Junior World Championships, and then for his final four years as well—all at forty percent. However, he incurred debt that he was very conscious about that needed to be repaid, and that was a major concern for Tony.

"Here you have the face of Iowa wrestling," Defilippis said. "Wherever you walked there were posters with Tony all over them. Billboards along the roads, oversized posters plastered in the bookstore. And [the coaching staff] didn't even consider taking care of him. There have been worse wrestlers in that program who received more [scholarship] money than Tony—that's ridiculous. So, going in, we had to make sure Tony was taken care of because Tony would never ask Tom for a bump. But, when you went to Iowa, it was clear people were coming to see [Tony]. The least they could've done was taken care of his senior year."

In that, Tony's HWC contract was very important. That and the fact that he was to be married that same year and wanted to be able to support his wife and future family.

"Tony does not really plan and think everything through," Defilippis admitted with a grin. "He was getting married, he wanted to have a kid—all along the way he had no idea how he was going to pay for it—and with a Theater Arts degree. He had always been a fly-by-the-seat-of-his-pants kind of guy. He's confident in his work ethic that he can figure something out. Now, he needed to be more secure because it was about Tony and Megan, not just Tony."

IN PLANNING FOR THE WEDDING, TONY RELIED

heavily on Megan. The two were engaged going into Tony's junior season, but the plan was to wed after he graduated from Iowa because the original plan was that Tony would not be competing that summer.

"When I wanted to get married, it was a pretty crazy-time," Ramos said. "I went to Tom and told him I wanted to get married. I went to Terry and told him I wanted to get married. Tom didn't think it was the best idea in the world. He wanted me to wait until after I was done with school, [he said,] 'You don't need these kinds of distractions; are you going to be able to balance both of this?'

"That night I got a call from Terry. 'Hey, you got to get married. Marry her now. Do it. You're ready.' I was like, *Aw gosh! What do I do? One's telling me not to, the other's telling me to get married.*"

But, for Tom Brands, it was not that he did not like Megan, quite the contrary—"I love Megan," Tom Brands said. "She is very smart and she's a strong person with a strong personality—and that's probably good for Tony; she keeps him grounded. But, there were some things that concerned me, and the wedding was one of them. When you talk to him,

'I can handle it. I can handle anything. I shut that stuff off when I come in here.' But I was concerned. He was a different wrestler. He was tighter. The scores weren't as wide-gaped. He had to work harder and eke some things out and that's maybe why you're vulnerable.

"That ain't my style—getting married in the middle of this whole thing. Especially being as involved in the planning as much as he was. People are wired differently, and I'm not passing judgement on him. There were things that concerned us."

As for Tony, he was going to do what he always did; he was going to do what he wanted, regardless. "I had to do what was best for me," Ramos said. "I feel I have made a lot of rash or quick decisions that have turned out great for me, and this was one of them. She's just like me, except she's a girl. She's competitive, she's got a lot of drive."

The engagement worked through Tony's first national title and now into his training as he attempted to make his first World Team. Megan helped Tony with his schedule and eating habits, but, maybe more importantly, she also provided a toughness and understanding for what Tony was about to undertake that helped ease his mind.

"Megan was a big push for me competing," Ramos said. "To me, I didn't think I could make the weight—I thought that slot was impossible. I was ready to move onto the next thing in my career, but she had told me, 'I will help you. We'll make sure you're on the right plan and we'll get you what you need.' She was really dedicated to helping me do that and that gave me what I needed to go in and talk to Terry."

As Tony trained for the World Team Trials, he was doing his best to balance everything that was going on in his life, and he had Megan there, by his side, helping in any way that she could.

Since the wedding was planned around the idea that Tony would not be competing, dates were reserved, plans were made, and Tony, on the day of the World Team Trials, had to be away from his future bride who was attending their wedding shower back in Iowa. While Megan would be opening gifts and exchanging pleasantries with family and friends, Tony would be fighting for the opportunity to represent the United States on domestic and foreign soil.

2013 • ENGAGEMENT PHOTOGRAPH FOR TONY AND MEGAN
PHOTOGRAPH COURTESY • TONY AND MEGAN RAMOS

CHAPTER 57
BRANDING THE MODERN WRESTLER

"Unconsciously, I guess I had always been building and branding myself. But I really began to take it seriously the day after I won my national championship."

• *Tony Ramos*

JUST AS THE MOST SUCCESSFUL AND HIGH-profile wrestlers were graduating from college, their unconscious branding of themselves had already been taking place while they were still in college and they were just being themselves.

Twitter, more than any other social media outlet, had quickly allowed fans of all ages and other interested parties to watch, follow, and interact with their heroes and anti-heroes and teams and clubs instantaneously. And the platform was growing among all age groups and at a rapid pace.

Wrestling, for the first time, even though there had been magazines and websites, was more mainstream to its own audience and had a platform that reached its growing community instantaneously.

Also for the first time, young wrestlers and fans had more access to their interests than ever before in regard to current status, thoughts, and gear. Wrestlers who had graduated, the best in the country, were in position to now be endorsed via their popularity—like other professional athletes.

Slowly, but then all at once, products and company endorsements came pouring in and were providing these modern wrestlers with a different lifestyle than those wrestlers who came before them.

The positive: Wrestlers could specifically train and not have to move around and jump into the work force and fight for time to train and compete at the same time. As for the drawback: More possible distractions.

"The positives," Tom Brands said, "is that these guys are being paid to just train—to just wrestle. That is one less burden and distraction."

Dan Gable agreed with Tom Brands' sentiments. He said, "If it's done in a way that you don't know that it's done—fine. But, if you actively get out into too much, unless you're a proven stud, I guess it could hurt. But, there are a lot of reasons a match is lost—are you going to point your finger at that stuff? The only thing you can't do is let it get in the way of what will make that promotion the very best. The promotion will be the very best when the wrestling is at its very best because you are at your very best in what you are capable of doing. It can't be a stumbling block.

"It may take a little bit away," Gable continued, "but it is more in line with how each guy's personality is. Dave Schultz, for example, would go up to his competitors and put his arms around them ahead of time and then go out there and try to break their arms minutes later. But it depends on who you are. For me as a coach, and for me as an athlete—I just keep my distance. I like that mystique. Now, from a promotion standpoint, it is good [for the sport]. Less mystique, but more exposure."

In that, as more and more wrestlers had become more and more accessible, and fans could reach out and businesses were capitalizing on these wrestlers and their names—their brands—one core argument raised was that the purity of the sport was in jeopardy. On the athlete's side, "It gives us the same opportunity as other athletes to be professionals," Ramos said. "Because we are professionals. This is our livelihood; how we support our families. Why shouldn't we help pave the way for the next generation of wrestlers where they can have it easier than we did? It has to start somewhere and I'm proud to be at the forefront of the movement."

For wrestlers like Tony Ramos, David Taylor, Kyle Dake, and a variety of others, their marketing plans were already modern and in place just because of their age and exposure to social media—it was not foreign to them. However, it was Jordan Burroughs who had paved the way for all of these guys only a few years before. And, once other wrestlers saw what Burroughs was able to do, and companies saw the impact of the market and the loyalty that wrestlers had to those who helped their sport, offers were coming in and everyone was looking for the next contract and opportunity.

IN 2010, MICHAEL DISABATO AND CAGE FIGHTER approached and signed who they believed to be wrestling's next most high-profile athlete, Jordan Burroughs—and they were right. As soon as

Burroughs graduated from the University of Nebraska, his rumored contract was about $12,000 per year—that is $1,000 per month plus royalties; and Burroughs would seemingly do very well with his royalty share. Regardless, with that contract, Burroughs became the first United States *amateur* wrestler to make wrestling *professional* in the sense where he could exclusively train and wrestle instead of having to hold a side job or live overly moderately with a humble stipend distributed through a wrestling club. Burroughs would pave the way as the athlete, and DiSabato as the promoter, were very progressive in their thinking to help the sport of wrestling grow.

In 2013, after winning his fourth NCAA championship at a fourth different weight class, Cornell University standout Kyle Dake was rumored to receive a hefty contract from Cage Fighter. This offer and contract would make future offers much more substantial as, once this occurred, ASICS turned and offered a pretty lucrative contract to Jordan Burroughs after he won the World Championships, and Adidas brought their money to the table with David Taylor. Now, all of that being said, the companies were financially backing the wrestlers, but the wrestlers, and there were more, were also branding themselves via social media outlets. This cooperative effort helped to market the wrestlers and it only made the companies more transparent to the wrestling market as it opened up their publicity and product as well—no media outlet had been more imperative for this new-aged wrestler market than Twitter.

FOR TONY, HIS BRAND WAS BUILDING AS HE WAS going through college and, at its inception, it was simply a young man on his phone speaking his mind and posting his interests. Due to his popularity, Tony had a strong following on Twitter at the right time, and being savvy with his social media outlets did not hurt his soon-to-come endorsements as he was promoting himself daily. Also, for Tony, his outspoken nature only drew more attention to him. And, people, agreeing or disagreeing, were following and helping his popularity and, at times, notoriety, for his brand.

"Unconsciously, I guess I had always been building and branding myself," Ramos said. "But I really began to take it serious the day after I won my national championship. I knew that sponsors and money and stuff like that were available and I knew people were going to call. The difference for me was I had a support system who understood business and marketing and things like that and know how to make money. So, I was guided in the right direction that was best for me as a wrestler and financially for my family. I was able to let [Frank] work and not have me jump at the first [offer].

"With Taylor building his brand, me building my brand, and all of us coming out of college at the same time, we were able to feed off of each other, I guess in a way where this company is giving this guy this much and going back and forth. This way, athletes were getting what they should be getting and not these dirt cheap contracts that strap guys into bad deals just because someone was throwing money at us. We were making these companies finally open up their checkbooks and paying these athletes what they deserve. In this, I think we are paving the road for these younger kids coming out of college and we are starting to build money lines for them."

From these moves, the conversations among the top-tier wrestlers appeared to stem around agents and types of contracts and how they were protecting themselves—it was slowly becoming the business of professional wrestling and, even though mistakes were made, as it happens at the onset of any new venture—wrestlers were exposed and aware via the Internet and a variety of media outlets in ways that had never existed before in sport—particularly wrestling.

Being exposed to all of the marketing and seeing how everything was being handled and how it turned out, better decisions and contracts were now being negotiated. "Where past wrestlers had made their mistakes," Ramos commented, "the newer-age wresters had seen those mistakes and were taking a closer look at the contract for its validity and seeing what they could and couldn't do."

The learning curve was sharp and fast, and everyone was trying to adapt and overcome what some saw as bad contracts.

"More than anything," Ramos explained, "we were all learning about contracts and language. We were better at seeing what we can and can't do and things like that where some of the wrestlers before us maybe didn't understand it all and got into legal trouble. And then, some of these companies try to strong-arm guys because they're paying out the money, but we learned to understand our contracts and call them out when they tried to make claims on what we could and couldn't do.

"When they would say we couldn't go with another company, we knew what we had. It was more like, 'Hey, we can go out and get an apparel contract because you don't have that right in our contract. You have this so I can go somewhere else for [that].' And they didn't like that we were educated and that we understood these things."

From the Iowa perspective, going back to Dan Gable, endorsements were something that wrestlers earned via titles, not simply given on popularity. This influence may have been the basis to Tony's philosophies—at least in regard to shoe contracts.

"It's different now," Gable said. "I don't think anybody had this kind of thing going [until recently]. In fact, I had to pay $500 to go to the Olympics because I did a camp and they paid me $500. I never even knew it, but the Olympic people, or whomever it was, contacted my dad and he paid the $500 or they weren't going to allow me to wrestle. He told me a year after the Olympics that he had to do this. So, it's a different ballgame. [We] didn't have a lot of those things to worry about—and that doesn't mean you have to worry about them, you just have to set them up. You just can't let it get in the way."

From Tom Brands' perspective, he had a personal joke with Tony in regard to some of his endorsements and contracts. "I always complimented him on how he made $100,000 and never won a match," Tom Brands smiled.

"What's different?" Tom Brands asked. "What's different is that now it's a job. When I graduated from college, all I had to do was train. That was it. I think it's great what these guys are doing [with the social media], it just ain't my style. I don't begrudge any of them for what they're doing because it's the world we live in. But it can't be a distraction. Used the right way, it's great—I love technology. It just can't be a distraction and get in the way of what's important."

Terry Brands held the same opinion as his brother Tom. "What some of this [funding] has done is changed maybe the focus of some guys. It's a change in culture where some guys think: *Okay, I arrived. Now pay me.* I mean, there was never any time off. The number one goal was Olympic gold. There was no time off for hunting or going to Alaska or Hawaii. [The thought process] was: *I can't take time off because the best guys in the world aren't taking time off and I need to stay ahead of them.* So, it's good for the sport because it creates that interest, but it may give guys the wrong impression about what it means to have arrived.

"If you win the Worlds and the Olympics," Terry Brands continued, "the marketing is done. Is that too old school? But, I'm not against it— I'm not against any of it. What I'm against is the excessive pursuit of building myself into a household name when I'm a wrestling guy and I'm a purist. My whole hang up on this is that these guys are spending a whole lot of time here, when they can be spending that time on their wrestling. Win the Olympics and all of these problems go away. The shoes, the shirts, the whatever it is you're trying to do—win the Olympics and everything that you are trying to do with your promotions goes away. And, if you want to do it, have someone on board to do it for you."

For Tony, and a number of other wrestlers, the new generation of professional wrestlers had arrived, and they were marketing their endorsements and themselves in ways both the wrestling world and the advertising world was still very much new to understanding. This was not to say that the old way of earning endorsements was unjust in its principle. It was a shift in culture and the fast-paced technology now brought fast-paced money, and everyone was trying to cash in.

In fact, some of it was so fast that even the companies were fighting for legalities over contracts and items that they believed they could hold some of the wrestlers to; each day brought something new.

For Tony, one of his greatest contract debates came from ASICS when he signed with Flips/Under Armor. "When the whole Flips/ Under Armor thing started to happen," Ramos admitted, "ASICS was not happy with me. They tried saying they were a competitor and this and that and we pulled up the contract. Well, the contract had me for shoes only and since Under Armor doesn't make wrestling shoes, it's hard for them to be a competitor. All of a sudden, after they said it was okay to go out and get apparel deals with Cliff Keen; they didn't like that a bigger company like Under Armor wanted us for apparel."

However, at the onset of it all, Tony did a great deal of his promotional work on his own. "When it came to the shirts," Ramos said, "I did most of it all on my own. I came up with the designs and had a guy on the team draw them up. Jeret Chiri was the artist working on them. I would get them back, ask him to alter this or that, and then I would pay him a few hundred bucks him for the work and what I felt he earned. He never gave me a price, but I didn't want handouts, I didn't want anything for free."

Additionally, for Tony, his Hawkeye connections were vast and that also opened up help from an alumnus of the Iowa program and two-time national champion who had a company. "I also got a lot of help from Mark Ironside and his company, Ironside Apparel [and Promotions, Inc.]," Ramos said. "He helped with designing stuff and did a lot in the beginning stages for me. He gave me a boost with online sales and gave me an online store. He did all of the shipping and all of the stocking. He took his fee on it, but I was still getting my quarterly paychecks and royalties and things like that."

Therefore, in the beginning, for Tony, it truly was a matter of Hawkeyes helping Hawkeyes. However, as Tony's popularity grew, so did his brand. "Unfortunately," Ramos said, "as my brand grew, I had to expand—I needed to get bigger. We still did some work with Ironside, not as much, but Nike was starting to come around and wanted to work with us—not sign a deal, but work with us with apparel and things like that. I was starting to think it over and, at the same time, I was building my own website and had my own online store on it and I was shipping things from my house and doing all of the inventory on my own. As that started to get more and more successful, which was when Flips stepped in and negotiating began.

"They started asking what I was making in sales, and they said that if they could get me a big enough contract, then they would take over all of it and I wouldn't have to worry about anything. So we worked out a deal with Flips and now I don't do anything with sales. They send me designs and ask me what I want and what I need and they take care of it all. It freed me up to just train and I couldn't be more appreciative of Flips and Ironside and everyone that helped me get to this point."

With the t-shirts came the fans now wearing the T-RAM brand and asking for autographs and, for Tony, it was an incredible experience.

"The first time I saw one of my shirts on a kid," Ramos recalled, "it was awesome. When we were kids we'd buy all of these football jerseys and things like that and wear them around and now there are kids out there supporting wrestling—whether it's Team Ramos or Magic Man, [David Taylor's company]—and it's cool. It's a great feeling to see that support and love from the younger and older generations."

Of course, with the brand comes the responsibility to live up to the brand and be what the brand represented. However, for Tony, he never considered it a responsibility—he earned all of this being himself and he was going to remain himself. Likewise, what many people neglected to realize about Tony was the approachability with him. Just as he had done in college, signing every autograph for every child who waited, he was the same now as a professional.

"I was never going to just walk away from a kid," Ramos said. "I didn't make myself more available—I just lived my life like I always did. But I never denied anyone because I know what that feels like. I am happy to sign anything or talk for a few minutes—these are the people that are supporting me and it is my obligation to give back to them and show that appreciation. So when I have that chance, I do what I can to do it."

As Tony's outspokenness helped build his name, he would go even further and take those opinions public and engage in what was considered "Twitter Wars" with other wrestlers in regard to issues like contracts or just wrestling talk in general.

One such instance came when 2004 and 2008 Olympian Daniel Cormier was offered a wrestling shoe contract in 2014 after making the move, along with the University of Missouri's four-time NCAA finalist and two-time NCAA national champion Ben Askren, to the sport of Mixed Martial Arts. Tony weighed in on the issue, stating, via Twitter, that Cormier, who did not "make weight" at the 2008 games in Beijing, China, was therefore undeserving of a shoe contract. Cormier, who was hospitalized when his body shut down from trying to make weight, was unable to compete. Tony did not care and he made that very apparent.

Tony commented on how Cormier was not a gold medalist, and because he missed weight that was even more of a reason for him to not be deserving of a shoe contract.

Those comments by Tony opened a tumultuous blend of comments. First, Ben Askren joined the conversation and took the standpoint of the modern wrestler embracing the new opportunities being given to him. Askren's stance was one of reinvesting in the wrestler and the sport and that such a movement was positive for wrestling and the sport's growth.

Askren and Tony battled back and forth on the issue; however, many would side with the claim that it would only benefit the sport. Tony, who never backed down from his stance, spoke about how he could have signed a shoe contract, but that he did not feel it was right without a medal. And, when other wrestlers and their parents or families jumped into the debate over not having a medal and having a shoe, Tony held firm to his stance stating that they did not deserve one.

"There's some truth in what Tony is saying," Terry Brands defended. "But that's just Tony Ramos being Tony Ramos."

For Tony, he was positioned on his opinions and he was going to hold firm to his beliefs, and there had been no distractions. To others, at times, they may have felt he was being short-sighted or maybe just reacting more quickly than he was thinking or he was led into his belief system due to being from Iowa. Regardless, attention was drawn to him and his name and his opinions and, due to instances like that, his brand was continually growing. Right or wrong, his presence and name and opinions enticed conversation—his voice mattered, his voice marketed; those who loved him and those who despised him were talking about him, and that only helped his promotion.

CHAPTER 58
MAKING A STATEMENT

"It's always wrestle your best match. And our best match is what we do best. For Ramos, that is applying pressure and being relatively relaxed because his confidence is everything."

• *Tom Brands*
Head Coach, the University of Iowa
Coach, Hawkeye Wrestling Club

"**WHEN YOU TALK ABOUT TONY RAMOS, YOU'RE** talking about a unique competitor," Tom Brands commented. "It doesn't mean that he's going to win, it doesn't mean that he's automatically going to do well. But it's exciting. It's exciting."

Entering the Unites States 2014 World Team Trials in Madison, Wisconsin, roughly two months removed from winning his first NCAA Championship, Tony Ramos entered the tournament at the 57 kg weight class—that was the first time he would make the weight, and he would earn the number-four seed in his weight's bracket.

Tony, who wrestled out of the Hawkeye Wrestling Club, also represented the Titan Mercury Wrestling Club, as well as his other sponsors who were helping to financially support and allow him to solely train and focus on making the United States World Team.

One of the biggest questions occupying many of the critics was if Tony would be able to make the transition from folkstyle to freestyle. Of course, what many people failed to remember was that Tony placed fifth in the Junior Freestyle World Championships back in 2009, as well as in Fargo. He had wrestled freestyle before and there was not too much concern on the issue of the stylistic change or adaptation. To both Tony and his coaches, wrestling was wrestling.

"All that changes," Terry Brands explained, "is that now you're talking about beating the cheap tilts, the chest locks off leg attacks. You're talking about defending a gut. You're talking about defending an ankle lace. We're showing him a couple of things on top—but he was already very good at his ankle lace off his single. So, you're talking technical details from a freestyle-oriented point of view.

"But, it's really control the center of the mat and score points—it's the same. Now add your philosophy to it. Now add your technical package to it. Now add your mental toughness and emotional stability to that and let's see what you got. And that's where we were—he was the best right away."

Of course, Tony had just come off a year of not only having great success, but one where he was defeating top-notch opponents.

"When you win," Terry Brands explained, "it makes it a little bit easier to move forward. Coming off that NCAA championship and just knowing that he ran the tables in the NCAAs—and there's some guys in that NCAA tournament that have a lot more fire power than the guys that he would have to wrestle in the trials—helps the process. Add that he's down eight pounds to that, so he's going to be that much bigger. So, everything from a confidence point of view made sense to him. That would be my take on it."

Now, as Tony took the mat for the first time as a professional, a number of questions would be answered, and they would be answered almost immediately in regard to if he was ready.

IN THE FIRST COMPETITION OF HIS NEW JOIRNEY,

Tony faced the number-five seed, Danny Mitcheff from Lorain, Ohio, a member of the Northeast Ohio Regional Training Center (NEORTC). Tony, in the quarterfinal match, against his first domestic competition, won a 9-5 decision.

Now in the semifinals, Tony had the number-one seed, Angel Escobedo, who had a remarkable resume entering the tournament.

• • •

Escobedo was a four-time Indiana high school state champion where he compiled a 223-1 record—his only loss came to another Glenbard North wrestler, Joe Gomez, in the finals of the Hoffman Estates Conant tournament. In 2002, Escobedo was a FILA Cadet freestyle national champion.

At the University of Indiana, Escobedo was a three-time Big Ten champion as well as a four-time All-American. In 2007, he placed fourth at the NCAAs and also participated in the Junior World Championships— he did not place. As a sophomore, he would be an NCAA national champion. In the 2009 season, he placed fifth; and, in 2010, as a senior, he placed third.

Immediately after his college competition days ended, Escobedo jumped directly into freestyle and the international scene where he opened with two runner-up finishes—one at the U.S. Open and the other at the World Team Trials. He would, however, win the University World Team Trials and place third in the Heydar Aliyev Golden Grand Prix.

In 2011, Escobedo became a New York Athletic Club (NYAC) International Open champion and, again, placed second at the Olympic Test Event.

As he continued to grow in his new discipline, he placed second at the Ziolkowski International and fourth at the NYAC International; both competitions were in 2012.

And then, in 2013, Escobedo placed fifth at the World Championships, second at the Sargsyan International, and, once again domestically, second at the United States World Team Trials.

• • •

Entering his match with Tony, Escobedo's experience and resume were obvious advantages. However, for Tony, he had nothing to lose coming directly out of college and now competing against the best wrestlers that the United States had to offer.

When the match opened, Tony, in his blue HWC singlet and his matching blue socks, attacked and moved forward immediately into Escobedo off the whistle and brought the fight to him—his flair was still engrossed in that Iowa dominant-forward-wear-down-the-opponent style that brought him a great deal of success.

In the first period, there was much hand fighting and Tony was the aggressor with shots taken and inside position being held.

With one minute remaining in the first period, Escobedo was placed on the shot clock and, after thirty seconds, Tony was awarded one point for Escobedo's inability to score. The remainder of the period consisted of hand fighting, level changes, and fakes—a great deal of motion and not a great deal of aggressive offense.

Ramos entered the break with a 1-0 lead.

As the second period began, Tony moved forward right off the whistle and was in on Escobedo's left leg. After a twenty-second fight to elevate the leg, and then another ten-second fight to work a finish, Tony settled for a push-out point by walking Escobedo off the mat. He now led, 2-0.

The next two minutes were a continued hand fight and Tony staying in a good low stance, not being placed out of position. Escobedo moved into quick fakes and level changes and a few slide-by attempts; however, none of those opened Tony up.

When the second period ended, Tony found himself with a 2-0 victory and in the mini tournament finals against the number-two seed, Nico Megaludis, a product of Pennsylvania wrestling.

• • •

In high school, Megaludis wrestled to a career record of 170-1, his only loss coming as a freshman in the state championships where he wrestled back and placed third. After winning the next three Pennsylvania state championships, he moved on to Pennsylvania State University and competed for the Nittany Lions.

As a true freshman in 2012, Megaludis wrestled at 125 pounds and earned a 28-8 record with a fifth place finish at the Big Ten championships. However, it was his run at the national championships that put him on the map as he avenged a total of four regular season losses in two bouts on his way to upset after upset of higher-ranked opponents. In the end, he reached the national championship match, but he fell to Iowa's Matt McDonough by a 4-1 decision.

In 2013, as a true sophomore, his record improved to 28-4, and he would, once again, qualify for the national championships—this time with a third place finish at the Big Ten championships. He wrestled back after he dropped his semi-final match to the University of Illinois' Jesse Delgado.

At the NCAA championships, Megaludis earned the number-four seed and wrestled to national runner-up honors. Again, he lost to Delgado, just as he had done two weeks prior—this time it was by a 7-4 decision.

Before competing in the 2014 World Team Trials, Megaludis, then a true junior, earned a runner-up finish at the Big Ten championships and, for the third year in a row, claimed All-American honors—this time with a third place finish at the NCAAs.

• • •

Megaludis, the number-two seed as he entered the Trials, walked onto the mat in his blue singlet, with his blue socks, and blue ASICS shoes to match, only to already find the red singleted and socked Tony Ramos at the line and in his stance waiting for him. As had been custom for Tony, he stared at his opponent and followed Megaludis with his eyes as Megaludis walked to and fro.

As the match began, both wrestlers paused and then attacked immediately, hammering the other's head while they ended up in a heavy tie—this aggressive, high-paced tempo never tapered.

With a little over a minute used in the first period, Megaludis gained position first, attacking Tony's right leg off a low ankle pick. Even though Megaludis was in on the shot, Tony defended and the score remained notched at 0-0.

At the halfway point in the first period, Tony pounded Megaludis down into a front headlock position and put himself in an opportune position to score. He worked to his right before he quickly transitioned to his left—Megaludis countered with a desperate reach with his right hand to save giving up the takedown. As Tony battled to score, Megaludis found a way for his hands to lock and stalemated the scoring opportunity; however, in place, was a newly instituted FILA rule where an "almost takedown" granted the offensive wrestler one point. Tony took the point and the 1-0 lead with just over one minute remaining in the period.

The remainder of the period was heavy hands and hard fought hand and head positions, back and forth, with great energy and aggressiveness by both wrestlers.

When the break was over, and Tony stomped back to the middle of the mat. The second period began and, within seconds, Megaludis was on the attack taking a shot. Tony defended with a down-block and found himself again in a front head position. He did not score.

From here, shots—open doubles, high-crotches, snaps and pass-by attempts—were fired by both wrestlers while quick reactions, head position, and strong defense, along with exceptional mat awareness, did not allow the other to score. The match was only more exciting with each passing second.

Megaludis' only true scoring opportunity came with about 1:28 to go. He was able to work through Tony's head and hand defense as Tony moved his own right elbow outwardly instead of keeping inside position and control; Megaludis dropped into a low snatch of Tony's right ankle. Unfortunately, for Megaludis, Tony's hips also dropped heavy and squared up on his attempt, as well as keeping wrist control with his right and a whizzer with his left. In that, Megaludis' chance for a takedown was fended off successfully.

Tony went forward and won the mini-tournament against Megaludis by the narrow 1-0 margin. However, that one point was enough to put Tony into the finals against the U.S. Open champion and 2012 Olympian, Sam Hazewinkel.

After the Megaludis win, Tony was interviewed about his match-up with Megaludis and also having to face Hazewinkel in the finals. In typical Tony Ramos fashion, the interview did not disappoint.

As soon as the microphone was put in front of him, Tony was adamant about making it clear that it is "Time to make room for the new guys, the young guys," he said. He went on to criticize his opponents by stating that they—Simmons, Hazewinkel, and Escobedo—"Are satisfied with winning a medal. If you think I'm going overseas and just bringing home a bronze or silver and be satisfied, you're wrong—it's about winning gold, it's not just about winning a medal. You got to want it all."

Tony's brash nature and raw emotion was nothing new to wrestling fans and followers of Iowa or Tony; however, it was new to the older, more experienced wrestlers who were much more reserved and calculated in their media responses.

To that point, Tony had only earned the right to wrestle Hazewinkel in the finals—he had not defeated him. That match was to come later in the evening.

When asked why he made the cut to 57 kg, Tony's response was simple: "Why wait? Go win the world title now. There's no reason to wait."

As for how he viewed the change from folkstyle to freestyle, he was extremely confident because, "Wrestling on my feet, that's where I'm best," Ramos said. "My defense is awesome. I'm just good there."

In response to his match against Nico Megaludis, Tony continued to display his bravado when he stated that the smaller weight wrestlers are not equipped to handle the bigger weight wrestlers cutting down. "A lot of people think those twenty-five pounders can compete at thirty-three," Ramos commented. "They're tough, but we're a little bit bigger. We're fast, we're a lot stronger—it's a different ballgame up there."

In answering why he was successful, Tony commented on his strengths. "Wrestling on my feet, that's where I'm best," Ramos said. "I mean, my defense is awesome. I got taken down one time today, the rest of the points scored were push outs. I'd rather give up one than two, right? [My defense is just good]. I'm just good there—I'm good in every position."

As Tony answered a few more pieces, he was posed with a question in regard to Hazewinkel and the strategy he needed to defeat him. This time, more conservative, but with no less confidence, Tony stated that he needed to do the "Same thing I've been doing all tournament—scoring points, wrestling hard. He doesn't like to go to the legs a lot; he's more of a defensive guy. So I'm going to have to get to him and score."

While he may have been new to the international scene, Tony was not new to speaking his feelings or allowing himself to be exposed—good or bad—in people's eyes as he spoke from his gut. He had no problem letting his feelings be known. In that, Tony was dangerous because he felt, for him, it was an all or nothing venture.

"I've got nothing to lose," Ramos confessed. "I'm trying to make a name for myself. But, in reality, there's a lot to lose, too, because you're losing your chance at a world title, you're losing your chance at a lot of stuff. I want to make a statement—make that Ramos name a household name."

Tony continued with his rant in regard to his mindset about his final match-up that evening with Hazewinkel. "I'm done seeing these old guys wrestling," Ramos stated. "They've had their chances."

That evening in Wisconsin, Tony would have his chance. Cornering him continued to be one of the men he put his faith and trust into during his time at Iowa, Terry Brands. His other corner man would be the longtime HWC coach and supporter, Mike Duroe.

"When you look at the guys he beat," Terry Brands said, "Mitcheff, Escobedo, and Megaludis, it was business as usual for us. Now we were on to Hazewinkel."

SAM HAZEWINKEL REPRESENTED THE UNITED

States during the 2012 Olympic Games at 55 kg in London, England. Since then, the 55 kg weight class had been inundated with Hazewinkel's presence at nearly every major competition in freestyle and Greco-Roman. Even though he did not always walk away with a gold medal, he was always a fan favorite and a wrestler his competitors had to watch out for.

• • •

Hazewinkel's background was just as impressive. Coming from a National Wrestling Hall of Fame family, his exposure to the sport was early and often. His father, Dave, and his uncle, Jim, twin brothers, were members of the 1968 and 1972 United States Greco-Roman Olympic teams; in addition, they each represented the United States on four other World Teams making them the Greco-Roman representatives in their respective weight classes for six consecutive years.

Hazewinkel's father was the first American to win two World medals in Greco-Roman wrestling—he won a bronze in 1969 and a silver in 1970.

As for Hazewinkel himself, he was a three-time Florida state champion, earning a 140-0 record for Pensacola Christian Academy. He was also a Junior Greco-Roman national champion in 2002. That summer, he also entered into the United States World Team Trials; he placed fifth in Greco-Roman.

During that time, Hazewinkel had already committed to attend the University of Oklahoma. As a Sooner, he became a four-time All-American; his highest finish was as a runner-up in 2007 after finishing third in each of his first three seasons.

While competing at Oklahoma, Hazewinkel wrestled both freestyle and Greco-Roman outside of his collegiate seasons. However, when it came to the World Team Trials, he focused in on his strongest style, Greco-Roman. In 2004, he placed third at the Olympic Team Trials after placing third at the U.S. Open. In 2005, he bettered his performance—he won the U.S. Open and placed second at the World Team Trials.

In 2006, Hazewinkel qualified for the World Team Trials with a third-place finish at the U.S. Open, but fell short of his goal, once again, losing in the finals and placing second.

In 2007 and 2008, Hazewinkel would be competitive and placed high in all of his entered tournaments, but he was not earning the right to represent the United States and he decided to make a change. In 2009, he competed almost evenly between freestyle and Greco-Roman, and this time he placed third at the World Team Trials in Greco-Roman, and that was enough for him to alter his style and focus to freestyle.

In 2010, he earned an eighth-place finish in the U.S. Open; however, in 2011, Hazewinkel broke through. He won the U.S. Open, placed second at both the Pan-American Games and the United States World Team Trials, and also finished second at the Hargobind International. And, although he was not the number-one representative for the United States, he was now in position to make his move going into an Olympic year.

In 2012, Hazewinkel's hard work all came together and his move to freestyle proved just. At 55 kg, he won gold at the Pan-American Games and, for the first time in his career, he won the United States Olympic Team Trials. In London, unfortunately, his dream of winning a medal would be unfulfilled. He ended the Games ranked seventeenth in the world, but it did not deter him from continuing to compete and chase his dream of making another Olympic team and winning a gold medal.

In 2013, however, he placed third at the World Team Trials in freestyle. He once again earned a U.S. Open championship in 2014, but he came up short in the finals of the World Team Trials and placed second in both freestyle and Greco-Roman. He would continually be regarded as one of America's top athletes in each style; however, it was not until 2016, the next Olympic year, which he would once again wrestle in the United States World Team Trials. By May, he had the number-one ranking for Untied States Senior Men's Freestyle at the new Olympic weight, 57 kg. Andrew Hochstrasser was ranked second, followed by Angel Escobedo, Danny Mitcheff, and Tyler Graff.

THEREFORE, AS TONY PREPARED FOR HIS MATCH-up with Hazewinkel, he knew that he was stepping onto the mat with not only a veteran and a well-accomplished and well-respected wrestler, but he was going to be up against a very talented and knowledgeable wrestler in two styles—and one with an extensive background in Greco-Roman. Tony and his coaches knew that they had to be conscious of where

Hazewinkel was most dangerous, in upper-body positions, and that he was very defensive. However, Tony also knew what he had to do in order to win—he had to bring the match to Hazewinkel.

"I knew that I just had to go out there and wrestle my match," Ramos said. "Just like I had done the whole tournament already. I wasn't going to sit back and see what happened; I was going to do what I do and attack and score and keep putting the pressure on him."

Additionally, due to Hazewinkel's defensive nature, Tony knew he had to make his attacks count in order to score points and make his first United States World Team. But, more than anything, Tony just had to wrestle his match and put himself in position to wrestle that match successfully.

"When we finished with Megaludis," Tom Brands explained, "it's not like, 'Okay, now you're done with Megaludis so now erase that and let's get a new game plan.' It's always wrestle your best match. And our best match is what we do best. For Ramos, that is applying pressure and being relatively relaxed because his confidence is everything."

In the first match in a best-of-three series, Tony wore a blue singlet with his blue socks and was ready to wrestle. He was already in the center of the mat with his stare down in full focus as Hazewinkel, in red, and one who enjoyed the center stage as much as Tony, was not yet ready to relinquish control of what he felt was his weight class. As he stepped on the mat, Hazewinkel was seemingly neither intrigued nor intimidated by the newcomer's stare.

Almost immediately, when the match began, Tony tied on the head and worked to control Hazewinkel's left hand. It was obvious that Tony was going to wrestle his style of wearing his opponent down; however, he was also going to work to control Hazewinkel's upper-body attempts in the process.

For the first minute, both wrestlers worked into ties and level changes and looked to defeat the other's hands in order to score; however, neither would be successful as the other's motion and defense was stingy and strong.

At the 2:07 mark, Hazewinkel was called for a passivity warning and the call was confirmed. Off the restart, Hazewinkel took a low single attempt to Tony's right ankle; however, he did not score. The ties and hand fighting continued until the 1:41 mark—Tony was also hit with a passivity warning in that time.

Off another restart, Hazewinkel fired in on a shot that Tony blocked before firing back on a reattack. Neither wrestler came close to scoring, let alone getting to his opponent's legs, but each knew that one of the two would be called for passivity if no scoring was going to take place. In that, each knew he had to open up and put the other on the defensive.

With half of the period gone, Tony was in his tie, stepped in deep on a high-crotch to Hazewinkel's right leg—enough to make him sprawl and put his chest well over his feet—and, as Tony backed out of the attempt, he stuffed the over-extended former Olympian and hit a sweep to his own right side. Now in on Hazewinkel's leg, he circled to raise the leg into the air as the one-time Sooner looked to defend.

Fortunately, for Tony, he was able to quickly raise the ankle and keep Hazewinkel off balance as he crowded him and came behind Hazewinkel. Now on his hands and feet, Hazewinkel looked to fight the takedown by not dropping any of his four supporting points to the mat.

On top, Tony had a cross-collar tie and continued to work into a spiral ride on the edge of the mat, but Hazewinkel defended it magnificently. It was not until Tony circled his motion, and Hazewinkel split his legs apart that Tony would drop to Hazewinkel's left leg, block off on his right knee, crowd him, and bring Hazewinkel's ankles together as he locked up a leg lace.

Once the lace was locked, Tony drove his feet and took Hazewinkel through for not just one turn, but for two as they went off of the mat. Tony now had a 4-0 lead in the first period of the best-of-three match-up with 1:06 remaining in the first period.

Tony would get up, stomp back to the center of the mat, and wait for Hazewinkel to stand up and work his way back to the center. For the next thirty seconds, Hazewinkel controlled the center of the mat, but he could not find an opening to attack. As this happened, Hazewinkel began to look a little frustrated with the newcomer and his head pops and head ties were coming down with a noticeable aggression, but Tony remained strong in the ties and created enough movement to keep Hazewinkel guessing.

Headed into the break, Tony kept his 4-0 lead as he received instructions from Terry Brands while Mike Duroe toweled him off. When Terry Brands was done speaking, Duroe had a few words and then slapped Tony in the head before he headed out for the final three minutes of the first match.

Tony stomped back to the mat's center and was there waiting when Hazewinkel arrived. When the whistle blew, the two would tie on the other's head as clock started to tick down.

The first thirty seconds consisted of a great many head ties and upper body positions and level changes. Hazewinkel controlled the center of the mat with his back to it; Tony, more-or-less on the outside of the center, did not over penetrate or commit, but remained in a strong stance, still fighting for position.

With forty-five seconds gone, Tony was instructed by the referee to initiate action. And as one minute was about to expire, Hazewinkel attacked off of a head tie. While Tony was looking for a two-on-one tie on his left, Hazewinkel's right, Hazewinkel back tripped Tony's left leg with his right and then dropped down into a single-leg position. The fight ensued on the mat.

Hazewinkel, in on the leg, now had to defeat Tony's defense. With his hips parallel, and Hazewinkel's right leg still over the top of Tony's left, Tony looked to lock up an Olympic cradle. The fight for position down on the mat lasted about twenty-five seconds before both wrestlers came to their feet—no points either way were awarded.

The next forty seconds consisted of Hazewinkel working to get past Tony's head and hand position, but he would not be able to. No matter how he tried to lock up, tie on Tony's head, work to lower his level to shoot under him, he just could not find an opening.

With 00:20 to go, Hazewinkel came down with hard and heavy ties on Tony's head—to no avail.

With 00:10 remaining in the first match, Hazewinkel again tried to work to a throw position, but he could not get inside position. Tony circled and, with time expiring, continued to circle back and block until the first match in a best-of-three was complete. Tony won a 4-0 decision.

In utter frustration, Hazewinkel would give Tony a final shove well after the whistle blew, but he would have to stand in the mat's center, with his left hand down, watching Tony's right hand raised and circled to both sides of the mats as he heard the Iowa fans cheer.

The two would jog across the mat and shake the hands of the other referees and then Tony marched off the mat as he and Hazewinkel would now prepare for the second match in their best-of-three series.

WHEN IT WAS TIME TO REINTRODUCE THE TWO

finalists at 57 kg, the lights were lowered, the World Team Trials entrance crowded with smoke and a smaller light show was in full force. Out of one entrance came Sam Hazewinkel. Green lights flashed, smoke rose, and out from the dark and into the light he would walk, suited up in his blue singlet. He would walk to the mat's side, walk and then run up the stairs, and then loosen his arms as Tony was already on the mat, suited in his red singlet with matching red socks waiting for him, staring at him. Tony's eyes followed Hazewinkel across the mat as he positioned himself in his stance, still following Hazewinkel and never breaking focus.

When the referee came to start the match, Tony remained in his stance looking at Hazewinkel. Once the referee and Hazewinkel looked to the head table for permission to begin the match, and it was confirmed, it was time to wrestle.

The two shook hands and the series was now into match number two. The level of intensity was already intensified. For Tony, if he won, he would be the World Team Member for the Unites States of America. For Hazewinkel, he needed to win to push a third match to give himself a second opportunity to wrestle for a spot as the United States World Team Member.

As the match began, both wrestlers were moving well, changing levels, and looking for their own position. In this, Hazewinkel was looking to attack from the upper body ties where he was strongest. Once in on Tony's arm, Hazewinkel was feisty with his two-on-one and wrist control. Tony worked to defend, and would, but Hazewinkel, remaining centered, was forcing the position and trying, seemingly, to be the first to score for the period.

When the first minute of the first period expired, it was Tony who was warned for passivity.

After that verbal warning, Tony now worked to control the center of the mat. He dictated the ties and the position on Hazewinkel and, as he changed his tie from his right hand to his left, and gave a snap on Hazewinkel's head, Tony used that momentum and fired in on a high-crotch to Hazewinkel's right side.

Hazewinkel rotated his hips in defense and looked to turn the corner, but Tony was in deep. As Hazewinkel turned, Tony was able to duck his head under Hazewinkel's right leg and, from there, lifted Hazewinkel up into the air. Hazewinkel would be looking to level his hips off as he anticipated Tony throwing him over for four. When Tony tried though, with great kinesthetic awareness, Hazewinkel did not go—he kept his hips down and created a scramble. Tony was, however, awarded one point for the appreciation of the lift, but Hazewinkel took his defensive position and turned it into an offensive position. He was now in on Tony's legs, came out the backdoor, and battled Tony to the mat to earn what appeared to be a takedown, but was awarded as a reversal. Since Tony was credited with the correct throw, though he scored no exposure points, Hazewinkel could only earn a reversal from the position the two ended up in. The match would be confirmed and tied, 1-1, as the referee restarted both wrestlers back on their feet.

When the match resumed, Hazewinkel worked back to his tie positions. To combat, Tony kept his levels moving and worked to control the inside position. However, Hazewinkel was fighting for the same position and, with 00:45 left, it was a tug-fest on each other's head as the physicality of the match began to pick up.

With 00:31 left in the first period, Hazewinkel received his first passivity call. Off the whistle, he took a quick shot; again, Tony defended and reattacked in on Hazewinkel's left leg.

As Tony climbed the leg, slowly, and Hazewinkel sat to his butt, Tony was awarded with the takedown. With Hazewinkel's arms wrapped high and tight around Tony's chest, Tony rocked him over for what appeared to be another two-point exposure. However, the exposure was not confirmed and Tony was simply awarded for the takedown. He now had a 3-1 advantage and the period ended with Tony having Hazewinkel in a front headlock. He stomped over to his corner where Terry Brands gave instructions with a focused intensity as Mike Duroe toweled him off. Staring into each other's eyes, Terry Brands and Tony were communicating on a number of levels.

Tony knew that he was three minutes away from representing the United States of America on the World Team, and Terry Brands knew his wrestler had to keep his focus, his position, and his offense if he was to win the period. Once Terry Brands had said what he needed to, Mike Duroe offered his input as Terry Brands now toweled Tony off. And, as each wrestler was called to report back to the center of the mat, Terry Brands yelled a few more instructions at Tony as he tramped back to the center of the mat.

The period opened with Tony tying hard on Hazewinkel's head, and with Tony having a two-point advantage over the former Olympian.

The first minute of the second period consisted of Tony looking to keep attacking his low single or high crotch, and Hazewinkel still working to defeat Tony's head and hand defense to get to his ties.

At the halfway point, Hazewinkel took more of an offensive mindset in having to find a way to open Tony up. He took a heavy hand tie on Tony's left and continually pulled and pulled until he circled and worked to a snap down. Tony, who re-tied, suddenly felt Hazewinkel drop low into a sweep single to his left leg. Tony then sprawled and extended his body and found himself in a front head. Hazewinkel, who appeared to want to avoid that position, backed out and, as he came to his feet and worked backward, he discovered Tony was now in on a low-ankle double-leg off a re-attack. Tony's seamless transition put him on Hazewinkel's legs and caught him off guard and off balance. The move dropped Hazewinkel backward and to his hip; Tony climbed up and earned a takedown.

The two wrestled out of bounds and Tony now led the match, 5-1, with 1:24 remaining in the second period of the second match.

From the HWC corner, Terry Brands was furious about the no-call, and let it be known. In that prior sequence, he felt Tony deserved four-points for the move as Hazewinkel's back was, he felt, exposed off the low double. In this, Terry Brands continued to scream and ridiculed the referee to the point where the referee started the match, stopped the match, reached into his pocket, and issued a warning, via a yellow card, to the corner. When the warning was issued, Terry Brands continued to coach over the warning and clapped his hands emphatically urging Tony on.

Hazewinkel now had no other choice but to open up and take some chances. He would have to find a way to either take Tony down and turn him, or hit a four-point throw to force criteria in his direction. His chances would be limited, so they had to count.

At the one-minute mark, Hazewinkel went to his strength, upper body, and, as Tony stepped to him, Hazewinkel fired off an arm throw. Tony, in defense, rotated his hips and no points were awarded in the attempt other than a proper-throw point. The match was now a three-point difference; 5-2, in favor of Tony. Time was running out for the reigning World Team Member.

With 00:45 remaining, Tony continually looked to control the tie and keep inside position. Hazewinkel was able to keep his back centered, but still struggled to gain inside position. Unable to break through, Hazewinkel dropped to a boot-scoot to his left, but Tony defended, and with 00:30 left and a three-point lead, Tony continued his hand fight and inside control to fend off Hazewinkel.

With a heavy hand on Hazewinkel's right side, Hazewinkel would re-tie over Tony's hand, pull, and then take a long sweep single to Tony's right. Hazewinkel was in on the leg and found his opening; he would now have Tony off balance as he was in on the ankle.

Off the shot, and in a stumble, Tony dropped his knee and pressured his hip into Hazewinkel as Hazewinkel worked to circle behind and score. In the fight, Tony was able to reach back to his right ankle with his right hand and defend with a key lock. Hazewinkel, understanding the position, brought up his back leg; however, in the process, Tony applied his front weight on Hazewinkel's hand and controlled the wrist on the mat—Hazewinkel's right wrist was cemented in resilite.

Fighting to free up his position, Hazewinkel circled back and found himself on his feet with Tony's leg; however, Tony was not conceding the position; there was 00:09 left in the match. With 00:07 left, Hazewinkel swiped across at Tony's left leg with his left and knocked Tony down to the mat. Tony protected his back and kicked as Hazewinkel stayed locked on his leg; however, Tony sprung back up. In the process, Hazewinkel was awarded two-points for the takedown, but Tony was able to work his leg free, circle out, and time expired.

Tony raised both of his hands high with the number-one finger pointing on each, and Terry Brands jumped onto the stage and positioned himself inside the circle as he pointed at Tony and intensely congratulated his wrestler who won the 5-4 match, took the best-of-three series, and now earned the opportunity to represent the United States of America on the World Team.

As he continued to celebrate, Tony walked directly toward Terry Brands, embraced him in a hug, turned around, posed his double-rainbow flex, and then returned to the center of the mat for his hand to be officially raised as the winner.

Hazewinkel, gracious in defeat, shook the referee's hand, Tony's hand, and then stood and watched Tony's right hand raised for the second time. Tony lifted his left arm in unison and again pointed his pointer finger to the sky to signify he was in fact the number-one wrestler in America at 57 kg. The Iowa fans in attendance loved it.

After the match ended, Tony was interviewed by a variety of wrestling media outlets. He was first questioned on the changeover in styles after not wrestling freestyle for a long period of time.

"Wrestling is wrestling," Ramos said without hesitation. "It doesn't matter the style, it's about scoring points. I'm best on my feet and that's what this is, so who cares about the rules? You find a way to win."

When asked about the difference in his series with Hazewinkel, his answer was simple: "Wrestle hard."

Having won the mini-tournament and then having won the series, "That was the easy way," Ramos explained. "I love wrestling. I love competing. He got to sit out, oh well. Maybe I had an advantage because I had been wrestling. He might not have [had] the right warm-up. So I don't think it makes a difference if you sit out or not."

When Tony walked away, he had the confidence that he needed moving forward. From Tom Brands' point of view, he felt there was no one, that day, who would have been able to defeat Tony. Tony came in confident, wrestled confidently, and answered a number of questions about his ability to adapt. Likewise, when facing a seasoned veteran in Hazewinkel, he met the challenge and dominated the match, regardless of Hazewinkel's experience in freestyle and Greco-Roman wrestling.

"We knew Hazewinkel was Greco a little bit this and that," Tom Brands said, "but I think it was well in hand. I think our mentality won the day and I don't think Hazewinkel could beat us in a thousand years. Not Tony Ramos."

While Tony had just completed competing in the his first United States World Team Trials, his fiancée, Megan, was at their wedding shower, meeting with family, opening gifts, and waiting to hear updates on how her husband-to-be was doing.

"I remember calling her afterwards," Ramos said, "and saying, 'I did it. We're going to Uzbekistan.' We were both so freakin' excited. I knew that I was going to [win the tournament] even beforehand because I sent a care package with my mom to the shower. I wrapped up some things in this embroidered red, white, and blue suitcase. It said 'Team Ramos' and it had Megan's name on it and inside of it was a couple of items. There was a book and a note. In the note I wrote, 'Here are some things that you'll need when we go over to Uzbekistan.'"

"It was very sweet and I was very surprised that he could pull it off without me knowing," Megan said. "It was the most thoughtful gift—like a book I had briefly looked at in the book store and said I wanted to read along with a heartfelt letter. It was emotional because of the thought he put into it especially knowing it was killing me to not be able to go to the tournament with him."

"From what I heard, the entire place was in tears," Ramos said. "As Megan was opening it, my aunt was reading it. But she was that confident in me as well that I was going to do it. She told me from day one that I was going to do it."

CHAPTER 59
THE FOURTH OF JULY IN CANADA

"We keep making progress. It's not like, 'Okay, now we got another set of data and let's change.' It's more like we explain where we need to tweak and how to [be at our best] for the World Championships."

• Tom Brands
Head Wrestling Coach, the University of Iowa
Coach, Hawkeye Wrestling Club

FOR TONY RAMOS, 2014 WAS A VARIETY OF NEW and exciting experiences. He had won a Big Ten title and a national title; he was now the 57 kg representative for the United States World Team, and he was getting married. All along the way his support group, which consisted mainly of his family, Megan, Tom and Terry Brands, and friends continually supported and encouraged him. However, with all of the planning taking place, and the wedding coming up, Tony's schedule had to be adjusted so that he could incorporate some competitions in order to better prepare him for the World Championships and work through some of the areas where he needed to improve.

It was decided that since Tony was going to be getting married on July 19, he would attend the Canada Cup over the Fourth of July holiday weekend and compete.

"They wanted me to get in one [international tournament]," Ramos explained. "That was the plan. I couldn't go to Baku and the Pan-Am's because my wedding's right in the middle of it, so we found something. It might be coming up quicker than I wanted it to but, who cares? Let's get out there and get some mat time. But not just mat time, let's go out there and get a gold medal."

This would be the first time Tony had to make the cut to 57 kg in a timelier manner. Between the Trials and the Canada Cup, there would be about four weeks to prepare and progressively work down his weight. In the process of the cut, Tony experienced some up and down moments; however, he was able to be where he was comfortable the night before weigh-ins.

"It was good," Terry Brands remembered of Tony having to make his cut for the first time internationally. "I was there with him on that one. Those plus-two [kg allowances] are a little different. It was when he wasn't as disciplined when that weight cut reared its ugly head."

Unfortunately, even though Tony was within striking distance of his allowance, he ran into a small problem at the facility he was working out at in Canada—they did not want him to sweat on the equipment.

"It was actually a weird deal," Terry Brands remembered, "because they didn't want him to sweat on the machines, so he had to go into an air conditioned room and work out really hard. It was really weird. You're in a foreign country—you're in Canada—and they're just different. Their mentality was different. But he got it down and that was good."

On July 5, 2014, the 57 kg weight class would wrestle in the Canada Cup in Guelph, Canada. Tony, who would have his first international opponent since 2009 at the Junior World Championships, opened with Sam Jagas of the Brock Wrestling Club located in Canada.

Tony came out in typical Ramos fashion. He had his matching Titan Mercury Wrestling singlet color-coded with his socks and made quick work of Jagas. He won by a 10-0 technical superiority.

In the quarterfinals, for his next match, he had Germany's Marcel Ewald, a German National Team member since 2003. Ewald, a carpenter by trade, was a very seasoned freestyle wrestler. Now, at the age of 31, he was looking to add to his steady career of accomplishments. From 2002 through 2013, Ewald had claimed eight championships, some fifth and a third-place finishes, and an eleventh-place finish at the 2003 World Championships; additionally, he was coming off an eleventh-place finish at the 2013 World Cup.

Suited up in his red singlet with yellow piping, Tony coordinated his red socks with yellow accents, and was out in the center of the mat waiting for the German to step to the line.

When both wrestlers were set, and the whistle blew, both Tony and Ewald came out with heavy hands and ties on each other's head. Tony fought for his right-hand head tie, while Ewald tied over Tony's right with his left hand and looked to create motion from there with his free hand hand fighting. From Tony's corner, Terry Brands was shouting, "Move your hands! Nothing on your head—work inside! Nothing on your head! Don't give up your left side! Protect your left side!"

After a minute of each working to control the center and assert his own position over the other, the referee stopped the match and invited each to engage—he encouraged more action.

When action resumed, it would be about thirty more seconds before someone made a move—it was Ewald who fired off the first attempt. Off a tie and break and tie and break, Ewald lowered his level and looked to hit an open high-crotch to Tony's right side. In an immediate down-block, Tony defended and transitioned into his front headlock. From here, Tony reattacked by chasing the left leg of Ewald and cinching his head by way of the chin in the process. And, as he hit the corner, he hooked Ewald's left ankle and came out on top as the German conceded the two points and now looked to fight out of parterre. There would be no turn and both wrestlers would be brought back to their feet.

Again, Terry Brands' instructions echoed the same sentiment he had been shouting out to Tony before, "Protect your left side! You control your left side! Work that head! Work that head down!"

The heavy barrage of head ties and heavy hands continued as Ewald worked his best to position himself past Tony's defense, but he struggled. As the first period was coming to a close, Ewald looked to transition into possible ties and upper-body positions; however, Tony circled himself free or blocked accordingly. The first period ended with Tony holding a 2-0 lead.

In the HWC corner was Terry Brands and he was instructing his wrestler on snapping off the head and working into his shot. Terry Brands wanted Tony to open up and be more aggressive by working into his offensive shots.

After the break, Tony was the first of the two wrestlers back to the mat's center. When Ewald came, and the match's second period was whistled live, Tony faked and looked to attempt shots, but he did not fire any off or commit to anything early on.

Terry Brands remained relentless in his instructions. "Inside!" he yelled. "Inside! Pull the head and hook! Come hard to that single!" Soon, Tony found himself being warned for passivity and, ultimately, he was placed on the shot clock. Terry Brands was not happy with this call.

"We had been working two offensive leg attacks to zero!" Terry Brands openly protested to the referees. "You guys get in on the match!"

With thirty seconds to score, and even though his motion was more fluent and he would fire off two high-crotches, Tony neither put himself in danger nor scored—Ewald was awarded one point. The match was now a 2-1 score in the American's favor with about 00:30 remaining in the bout.

Patient and in control, Tony never panicked. He stayed in poised and in the middle of the circle as Ewald worked to find an opening on the young international wrestler. However, as the period was closing, Ewald become very aggressive and he was now looking to force a score so badly that he began to wrestle in an erratic pattern in an attempt to change levels, fire in on a shot, and attack the head. Out of all his movements, with Tony in more of a defensive mode, Ewald was suddenly in on Tony's right leg.

Ewald went from the mat to his feet; Tony posted and stuffed his head and did all that he could in order to return his leg to the mat in an effort to break free and not give up a takedown. The fight persisted and Tony found himself trying to defend via a key lock; unfortunately, it would not hold and Ewald limped his arm out and scored a two-point takedown with no time remaining in the match.

Tony, not satisfied, immediately got up, looked to Terry Brands, and motioned for him to throw the challenge cube in order to contest the takedown points awarded as time had expired.

The German paced around the mat and talked to his coaches during the review. Meanwhile, the American stayed in the center of the mat before moving toward Terry Brands as each was awaiting the final decision after the video review. In time, Terry Brands walked over to the table.

When the final decision was declared, each wrestler was called back to the center of the mat. As the referee grabbed each wrestler's wrist, and no points were awarded, it was Tony's hand that was raised in victory. He was now on to the semifinals.

In his semifinal bout, Tony faced a 22-year-old by the name of Steven Takahashi from Canada. Takahashi, who had earlier placed third at the Brazil Cup in November but failed to place at the Dave Schultz Memorial in late January, was wrestling well and the match-up was between two younger competitors who were looking to make a name for themselves.

The match opened with Tony coming down hard with his right hand on Takahashi's head, but Takahashi turned that position into an arm-throw attempt. He was not able to put Tony in danger, but he was seemingly prepared for the American.

Takahashi's hands appeared to be as heavy as Tony's hands to open the match; however, as Tony took a shot, he was soon warned for being passive. Terry Brands came out of his chair, walked the mat's circle, and declared, "Red just took a shot!"

The referee walked over to Terry Brands and politely told him to return to his chair. "Sit down, coach, please," the referee said as he walked toward him, "Sit down."

Terry Brands motioned to the table judge, but the table judge had no interest in what he was saying. The match continued and a series of level changes and shots, from Tony, occurred; however, Tony, in the red singlet, was hit once again for passivity. When the whistle stopped the match, Tony was placed on the shot clock. Terry Brands, utterly amazed, stood up and clapped, mockingly, and motioned his hand in a circle as if to say, "Just roll the clock."

Tony worked to two open shots and stayed heavy on the head; however, after the thirty seconds expired, it was a caution red, one point blue. Takahashi now had an early 1-0 lead.

With the match being restarted after the awarded points, Tony stayed heavy on his fakes and ties and, as blue was being directed to open up, Tony fired in on a double. He was not able to commit his hips farther inside before Takahashi was able to defend. However, as Takahashi came out of the double, Tony transitioned into a reattack—a sweep single to Takahashi's left leg.

As Tony circled the leg out, battled, and climbed the hip and earned his first takedown of the match, the score was 2-1. Tony was in the top position and looked for a turn.

The first period ended with Tony half-heartedly trying to lock up a leg lace. He came up, walked over to his corner where Terry Brands was waiting for him with a towel and some finer details.

Opening the second period, the head ties and shrugs and passes continued, as well as the upper body ties from Takahashi, but Tony worked himself out of a tie and into a high-crotch on Takahashi's right leg. There was no takedown as Tony could not finish and the two would restart in the neutral position.

When the whistle blew, it was once again the aggressive American who reattacked from a two-on-one inside trip attempt from Takahashi that was not very secure. Tony tried to run the corner and, as he circled with his front head, he discovered Takahashi's right leg, snatched it up, and continued his circle up to his feet.

Once Tony had Takahashi's leg up in the air, he circled back and hit a strong trip that caught Takahashi off guard and sent the Canadian's back flat and hard to the mat. The crowd gave an appreciative gasp in the moment of impact, and Tony was awarded a four-point score and now possessed a 6-1 lead.

With Tony securing a five-point lead, and about 1:30 left in the match, Takahashi had to find a position where he could maybe gather some high-point moves in high-percentage upper-body positions. The drawback would be if he could not find his way into those positions, then he may be in danger of being scored on. Initially, he tried to forcefully punch in his underhook, but Tony blocked accordingly with tight elbows and good head position. When he gathered position, it was very short-lived as Tony circled out and repositioned; Takahashi was in an uphill battle.

As the clock approached the 00:30 mark in time that remained in the match, and Tony took a stronghold of Takahashi's head and kept it buried—it appeared as if the weight on the Canadian's head was much too much to work through and earn a reasonable position for a throw. But as he backed out, and stepped back in, and fought for some, any type of lock or throwing position, he would have no such luck as Tony kept moving and blocking and securing his position and victory. With time almost expired, Takahashi stepped in one more time; however, this time Tony did not block, he dropped to a single-leg instead and worked to a quick finish—Takahashi simply conceded the takedown in disappointment. For the takedown, Tony did not receive any points, but he won the match by a 6-1 decision.

Takahashi would remain on the mat, on his knees, with his head and elbows on the mat—exhausted and overwhelmed by his defeat from the American. When he finally did come to his feet, he shook Tony's hand, the referee's hand, and then walked off with his hands on his waist. Tony exited triumphantly and now prepared for his finals match.

For his final's match-up, Tony had to face Dillion Williams of Canada. The 22-year-old wrestled out of Team Impact Wrestling Club and was nicknamed "The Human Highlight Reel."

In 2012, Williams had won a bronze medal at the Junior Pan-American Championships competing at 60 kg in the freestyle division. In 2013 and 2014, Williams would represent the University of Alberta, the Golden Bears, and win back-to-back silver medals at the Canadian Interuniversity Sport (CIS) Championships.

When it was time to wrestle, Tony came to the mat in his bright blue HWC singlet with yellow piping and, as always, his matching socks. Across from him would be the much longer Williams bouncing up and down while Tony, in his stance with his hands on his knees, looked up staring at his taller opponent—Williams just looked over Tony, to the right, left, and never made eye contact.

Both wrestlers were young and full of a fearless fire that could be seen as they advanced into the championships match. Likewise, it was a match-up that many were excited about as both had explosive offenses and quick reattacks from their defense. As the referee came to the middle of the mat to begin the match, it started out as a position battle where Tony had to try and find a way to work his hands on the taller Canadian and close the gap.

For Williams, he opened his offense by looking to work his two-on-one ties on Tony's left arm. In this, Tony blocked and circled while he received clear instructions from his corner to simply attack. Tony, as per his style, weighed heavy on his opponent's head and looked to wear him down and, at the same time, find an opening to work himself into an attack. After each tie, and during each tie, Terry Brands demanded Tony take a shot.

"It's open!" Terry Brands hollered from the corner as Tony circled out of a snap or from having pressure on Williams' head. "It's open now!"

However, contradictory to what Terry Brands wanted, Tony looked to wear on the head of Williams and work to find the opening that he felt more comfortable with. One-minute passed before either wrestler found an opening that appealed to him. As fate would have it, Tony would be the first to commit.

Tony found his opening in the form of an open single to Williams' right leg. Williams, who fought to extend his long body and kick, found the tenacious hold on his ankle too tight to buck out of. As Tony worked to climb the hip, Williams worked to the mat's edge, circling on two hands and one leg, as Tony dove and locked up a double, which drove him to the mat. Williams nearly jumped out of bounds in defense, but no points were awarded.

Terry Brands was again up and out of his chair, infuriated. "Fleeing the hold!" Terry Brands exclaimed. "He's going to the edge! He's going to the edge!"

The match continued in spite of the protests and Terry Brands would be asked twice to sit back down in his chair. From there, there were a great many level changes and fake shots motioned; however, no one was committing to an all-out shot. When Williams decided to finally take an honest shot in an attempt to score, it came off a hand fight where his arms would get crossed. From there, Tony reattacked by snapping the longer opponent's head down with his left hand a split second before he took a sweep single to Williams' left side. Tony was in deep on the leg and the fight for position was on.

Tony, who would be able to circle up to his feet and circle out the leg, earned a takedown as he tripped Williams to the mat and jumped directly to Williams' midsection and locked up a gut wrench. No attempt would be made for the turn, but Tony took a 2-0 lead before heading back to the center of the mat.

"Hands down, move your feet," Terry Brands dictated to Tony from the corner. "You can go again! Score quick! Score fast!"

As Terry Brands was saying these words, Williams penetrated in on an open double-leg attack. Tony, who would be able to get his hips back, defended, but the crowd came alive with the attempt against the American. And that was how the period would end.

When Tony stomped over to his corner, Terry Brands was there, alone,

THE FOURTH OF JULY IN CANADA

to towel him off and instruct him. Tony, focused on his coach's words, took it all in before heading back to the center.

On the restart, the message being communicated to Tony was to push his opponent and, as Williams took a half-hearted shot, Tony would, again, reattack and find himself in deep on Williams' left leg. As he did before, Tony circled out and back, but this time they went off the mat and Tony simply earned a push-out point. He now held a 3-0 advantage over the Canadian.

It was not much longer before Williams became anxious and took another ill-timed open shot. Tony defended, reattacked, and again scored. The match score extended 5-0 in favor of Tony with about 1:45 remaining in the match.

Tony continued to circle and defend and score off of Williams' wild and desperate attacks.

This time, "Build with pressure," would be Terry Brand's mantra dictated from the HWC corner. Tony, strong in the front headlock position, scored again and kept the pressure on Williams and maintained his inside position the entire time.

Tony scored one more takedown off a reattack and he earned an 11-0 technical superiority. He would have his left hand raised as the winner, earn a gold medal, and he won his first international tournament of his young career.

"I had a good showing and got my first taste of international wrestling," Ramos said. "But even though I won the tournament and wanted to let it be known that I was here and I was ready to make a statement on the world scene, I had a close match with the German and I knew I needed to get better at tightening down at the end of matches and closing matches out. I did a good job in my other matches with scoring points and staying in my stance and offense, but there was work to do. Terry and me talked and coming home with gold was good, but we talked about getting quicker takedowns in situations and putting matches away so guys weren't able to hang around."

Terry Brands agreed with Tony's assessment. In no way had the young American fully arrived in such a way where he was simply dominating all positions. There were some validation in the victories in what Tony had done north of the border, but there was work to be done as he was still in positions that were not comfortable for either Terry or Tom Brands to see their wrestler in, especially when he did not need to be in those positions.

"It's always easier to move forward after a victory, but there wasn't much validation because there was a guy in on his leg, taking him down with no time left," Terry Brands said of Tony's arriving on the world scene and dominating. "So the validation was, 'You know what? You haven't arrived yet.' This was from a coaching point of view and he knew it. That [Ewald] match was way, way too close and then Tony destroyed the guy in the finals. It's too close—the same things we had been talking about and they're still there. We have to wipe them out. We have to widen that gap. We have to be in on guys. You're ahead by a point with how much time left? Put a nail in the coffin. Get that takedown and let's get this thing over with. Instead of him being in on you when you're ahead by a takedown and by a takedown you lose."

From Tom Brands' perspective, and he had been unable to make the trip, he saw it as another opportunity to improve and continually progress.

"We keep making progress," Tom Brands said of the process after the win. "It's not like, 'Okay, now we got another set of data and let's change.' It's more like we explain where to tweak and how to [be at our best] for the World Championships."

And the World Championships were now on Tony's radar. So far, in 2014, he had been undefeated and he was yet to lose domestically. Also, internationally, Tony was newly 4-0 in competition. The World Championships, however, would bring the best out, and this was what Tony was waiting and looking forward to. He wanted to prove himself among the world's most talented wrestlers.

CHAPTER 60
ADJUSTING TO THE WORLD

"So I was at one of my darkest places, but it was very hard for me to be mad and selfish once I found that out."

• *Tony Ramos*

WHILE TONY WAS PREPARING FOR THE 2014 World Championships in Tashkent, Uzbekistan, his first World Championships, he was riding an unbeaten streak that stretched back to the second half of his collegiate season that included his Big Ten and NCAA championships, his winning the United States World Team Trials, and then the Canada Cup. "My confidence was high and I always feel good going into my competitions because I believe in the work that I put in," Ramos said. "The World Championships were no different. I was there to wrestle and I was there to win. My mindset was clear and focused and I felt very good about where I was at with everything."

Tony's first World Championship experience would draw him against Mongolia's Ghenadie Tulbea; however, after weigh-ins, and the brackets are based on the weigh-ins, Tony's draw changed. He would now wrestle Mongolia's Bekhbayar Erdenebat instead. The 22-year-old Mongolian, who was ranked seventh in the world and who was also a 2012 Junior World Champion and placed ninth at the World Championships in 2013, would come in with the same grit and fire for the 23-year-old Hawkeye graduate.

Tony came to his mat in his red U.S.A.-issued singlet with white piping and coordinated red socks. He waited, in his stance, in the center of the mat, staring at Erdenebat as he came to the mat's center. When

Erdenebat dropped into his stance, both he and Tony were now staring at each other and the only break in the contest was when the referee came over to check their skin and knee slips, and shake their hands. Tony, however, did not look away—Erdenebat would acknowledge the referee and then look back at Tony.

Once the whistle was blown and Tony started circling left and changing his levels, not much time passed before the two locked onto the other. Erdenebat looked to tie up the American with a two-on-one to Tony's left side. The hold was ultimately broken by the referee after no offense was being used out of it.

Off the restart, Tony continued with his level changes; however, as he reached with his left hand, Erdenebat attacked with a sweep single to Tony's left side and worked to bring the leg into the air. Tony battled his hip in, leg down, broke the lock around his leg, and circled back in on the edge of the mat. He now looked to score as a flurry took place between the two wrestlers trying to find an opening on the other. Erdenebat would come down into a front head as a result and both wrestlers, down on their knees, and would end up out of bounds with no points being awarded to either wrestler even though one of the three officials motioned with his scoring paddle for a pushout in favor of the Mongolian. The other table official would call the mat official over for clarification, but he would hold to his vantage point that both were out while on their knees—a white paddle was confirmed, a 0-0 score would be the result, and the two started neutral in the center of the mat.

When the match resumed, Tony came down heavy on Erdenebat's head, changed his levels, and Erdenebat, ultimately, did the same and worked to a low shot that was off the mark, but it created some separation.

The ties ensued and each time the American tied heavy with his left hand, the Mongolian over tied with his right and looked for hand position with his left. In the process, Erdenebat was hit with the first passivity call and that changed the tempo of the match.

Once the two wrestlers restarted, Erdenebat came out more aggressively than he had already been. Tony looked to tie the head with his right hand as Erdenebat lowered levels and looked to get in on a high-crotch to Tony's right side. There would be no success in his attempt, but it triggered a flurry of action. Coming back into one another, Tony again tied heavy with his right, Erdenebat snapped off at seemingly the same time Tony was attempting to motion to Erdenebat's right. This snap brought Tony down to his knees with his head down for only a moment. In that brief moment, however, Erdenebat transitioned from a front headlock to, as Tony was coming up, a low ankle single-leg to Tony's right foot. This caught the American off guard and off balance.

Tony, trying to collect himself, stepped over Erdenebat's attack and looked to defend a low single, but Erdenebat captured the left ankle in the progress and received a two-point takedown for his efforts. Tony based out and looked to defend from the parterre position. Erdenebat lazily worked a lace, transitioned to a minimally attempted gut, and then worked his leg in on Tony's right side with no intention other than stretching the American out and killing some time in that position. The position would be halted by the referee and each returned to his feet. Erdenebat now held a 2-0 advantage over Tony with about 1:50 remaining in the first period.

Now with the lead, Erdenebat became much more defensive as Tony had to work his ties and position to try to defeat the Mongolian's head and hand defense. After an assault of ties and reties, the referee stopped the match as Tony had blood on his forehead that needed to be attended to. This break in the action gave Erdenebat time to breathe and regather himself for the final minute of the period. Tony, as well as his corner, was not pleased with the stoppage of the match for the blood; however, there was also nothing that they could do about it.

While Tony was being attended to, after a fairly long delay where the cleanup took place, Terry Brands was up on the stage giving Tony direction and instruction on how to work into his attacks. Terry Brands' body language showed his coaching intensity, investment, and his ability to communicate to his wrestler about his own position as well as Erdenebat's.

As the match resumed, Tony came out looking to attack the head and work into his high-crotch on Erdenebat's right side. His levels and motion were quickly delivered and steady, but Erdenebat was content to stay square and fend off the positions being brought to him.

Erdenebat would, however, see a quick opening on Tony and shoot in under Tony's tie. He would not penetrate far enough to capture the leg, but it would give Tony a chance to lock up his front head and a chance to beat the leg with a reattack opportunity. The position failed, but Tony's level of motion and movement was now much greater than Erdenebat's and, little by little, Tony was taking over control of the match tempo as he continued to wear on the head and neck of Erdenebat.

With the pressure of Tony moving forward, Erdenebat attempted another shot to his left. Tony, who felt the shot, circled and came behind as Erdenebat circled to his feet. There would be no takedown or any points awarded, but the match was seemingly swinging into Tony's favor as the Mongolian was doing all he could to keep Tony's pressure off his head and block any attack.

The period would end ten seconds later and, with the whistle, Tony executed one good additional tug on Erdenebat's head before stomping over to his corner for the break.

Terry Brands spoke to Tony while Bruce Burnett toweled him off. Team U.S.A.'s trainer worked on Tony's head, but it would be Terry Brands that would capture Tony's attention and focus in the small time between periods. Tony, who had not capitalized on two scoring opportunities, trailed 0-2 as he headed into the final period of the match. The referee came and escorted Tony back to the center of the mat and both waited for the Mongolian who took an additional fifteen seconds after the allotted time to come back to the mat's center to be checked by the referee before the second period began. However, Erdenebat, who already had an extended break, was sent back to his corner to be toweled off some more. Terry Brands was not pleased with the stall tactic to get more time to breathe. "Come on!" Terry Brands hollered. "He's fine! Make him wrestle!"

There would be another additional fifteen seconds giving the Mongolian a full-minute rest from action. And then, the referee walked over to Tony's corner for clarification on some issue and this provided more time while Tony waited, in the middle, for wrestling to resume.

When the final period was finally underway, Tony would come out heavy on Erdenebat's head and, seconds later, was finally in on his high-crotch to his opponent's right leg. Erdenebat, very slick in his defense, rolled and looked to expose Tony in the process. There would be no exposure as Tony kept his chest high, but a small scramble took place until Tony was able to come out behind Erdenebat on the mat's edge, throw in his right leg, pry half Erdenebat, and score what appeared to be a two-point exposure as the mat judge signaled two-points and one of the table judges confirmed the exposure with his paddle.

Tony would relentlessly crank the position on Erdenebat's right side torqueing the arm to the head, and turned Erdenebat for another two-points that the mat judge signaled, accordingly; however, no other paddles were raised by the mat judges. The action continued and, unfortunately, in the process, Tony would be riding too high in his position and Erdenebat came up and took Tony's head and crotch and flipped him in a vertical position scoring a four-point throw in the process; the call was confirmed. That move now put Erdenebat on top and in position to turn Tony again; it also gave the Mongolian a 6-2 lead on the scoreboard; however, Tony had had two turns and believed the score should have read 6-4.

In the background, an American coach was yelling, "Challenge that! Challenge that!"

At the 3:57 mark, with 2:03 remaining in the period, the United States challenged the score when Terry Brands threw the red cube into the center

ADJUSTING TO THE WORLD

of the mat. But, while the match was still being wrestled, the referee came over and threw the cube back at Terry Brands in Tony's corner as if to not allow the challenge. In response and in obvious objection, Terry Brands caught the cube thrown at him, wound up, and heaved the cube back across the mat in the direction of the referee in protest to the protest not being acknowledged. At the 4:15 mark, the referee stopped the match to instruct the wrestlers about their finger locks, but he continually ignored the protest and Terry Brands.

The red cube remained off to the side of the mat as Tony, still wrestling, was working to score on two separate attacks. Off one of the attacks, Erdenebat reattacked, got to Tony's leg and pushed him out of bounds, near the red cube, for another point. The score was now 7-2 Erdenebat, and there was 4:43 on the clock—leaving 1:17 remaining—and the red American protest cube simply remained on the mat in between the stopped action and the scoreboard. It was still being ignored.

Tony would beat the Mongolian back to the center, wait for him, and when the match resumed, Tony immediately worked on Erdenebat's head and tried to force his front head position. Erdenebat, in clear exhaustion, took an ill-advised leg attack on Tony and Tony came around for the two-point takedown. The score now read 7-4 on the score board as the Mongolian clammed up in the bottom position before the match was stopped and each of the two wrestlers were brought back to their feet.

Attempt after attempt by Tony would be blocked as Erdenebat was simply looking to hang on. The Mongolian was tired and worn and doing all that he could to block and prevent any penetration from the American. But Tony did get back in on Erdenebat's legs.

Once in, Tony's body would be flat with Erdenebat on top of him, but he fought to gather his base, post up, tried to capture his opponent's left arm with his right while keeping a hold on Erdenebat's right leg, and flipped him over looking to score points. Erdenebat, with just enough left in him, cartwheeled through the air and did not have his back exposed in the process. Time expired.

The final score would be 7-4, Erdenebat, and Tony now had to wait to see if he would have an opportunity for a wrestle back in the repechage. Unfortunately, even though Erdenebat would defeat India's Rahul Balasaheb Aware, 9-8, and Bulgria's Mehmed Feraim, 4-0, he would fall in the semifinals to Georgia's Vladimer Khinchegashvili, 6-3, thus eliminating Tony from the competition.

Tony's first World Championships and he was one match and done. He was devastated.

"It's rough," Ramos would comment of his being eliminated from the tournament after one match. "It was my first World Championship—my dad came out and my wife came out—I was upset. I was real upset. I felt like I had let everyone down and made them come out here for nothing. It was one match and then it was over. It was hard. It was a tough pill for me to swallow because, like I said, I felt like I let everyone down. But, at the same time, I saw where I needed to get better. I was pretty close. I was right there with some of the best—a guy who was wrestling for the bronze medal—so there was some reassurance at the same time. But, it was still a lot of mixed emotions because it was like, *I did all this for one match and I'm away from home, my family, and I sacrificed all this for nothing.* International is different. It's one and done.

"When Terry and me spoke, he talked to me about what he's gone through. Terry's been one and done at tournaments before. So, he and Tom just tried to keep my mind going in the right direction. 'What are we going to do for next year? How are we going to get better? How are we going to improve?' It's not over, there's a World Championship every year—and that was the same time that Megan told me that she was pregnant. So I was at one of my darkest places, but it was very hard for me to be mad and selfish once I found out."

From Terry Brands' point of view, he did see some positives in the match and in his wrestler's style.

"I think the [most important thing we saw] in the Erdenebat match was that the collegiate carries over," Terry Brands said. "Look where we scored. We got a [U.S.A.] coaching staff that is about, 'You can't win unless you do it this way.' That's not true. That's not true. You can win by wrestling with your personality, your style, you just have to have a set of fundamentals you understand. All of a sudden when he got behind and then had to go—and he ended up figuring out how to get a takedown and slapping in the leg and turned him and then he got into a situation where he's turning him again—it's a funny call. Those guys haven't seen that before. But he wasn't in control, so there had to be maybe more refinement there. Number one: why you coming from behind there? Number two: why you making me throw the cube? Number three: you know the guy is going to be in on you—and you know [Ramos] doesn't have good athleticism when his leg is off the mat, so you can't let the leg come up in the air. That's what I'm thinking. Very, very close match."

Terry Brands continued, "I remember the U.S.A. coaching staff saying, 'Oh, this is going to be so easy because he has Aware next.' But they didn't really know who Aware was and I'm going, 'Ramos, you wrestled Aware.' And Ramos goes, 'Yeah, I wrestled him in the Junior Worlds—that's who I lost to.' Aware was a Junior World medalist and our staff was saying, 'Beat Erdenebat and you're going to the finals.' I'm saying, 'No, that's not the message you give him.' So there's that and we're in camp and where is Tony best with a single-leg? Locked, right? They were telling him to post his hand—things that we had to argue with that made no sense to me. Having guys do those things weighs on guys and makes them doubt instead of being confident [in what they do well]. So I think he learned—he scrapped it out with one of the best guys in the world."

Regardless of the philosophies and comments made or protests being ignored, the match was there for Tony to take and he was unable to capitalize.

"He probably shouldn't have been rolling around," Tom Brands critiqued. "He should have iced the position. I remember him in there and he should have nailed the position—there was no need to roll around once he had the score. He should have just got on him and not made more of what isn't there, especially Tony Ramos because that's where he gets in trouble when he goes out of familiar territory.

"The conversations we had were more of anchoring the positions for me," Tom Brands continued in regard to what Tony needed to do better in that opening match versus Erdenebat. "It was like, when you have a chance to anchor a score, get the sure thing. Don't flop around and certainly know the characteristic of you-score-first. He gets that first score and he's still as stingy as he is; it's a whole different ballgame."

When the World Championships ended, Tony had a very bad taste in his mouth. In that moment, though, he also had news that his wife was pregnant and expecting their first child. The trip was bittersweet, but Tony now had to get back into the wrestling room and prepare for the World Club Cup Championships—he had about one and one half months to fine tune his techniques and work to ice those positions that Tom and Terry Brands felt were the difference makers in his wrestling.

THE 2014 WORLD CLUB CUP CHAMPIONSHIPS

were held in Jouybar, Iran, November 27 and 28. However, before that, Tony would compete in a Global Wrestling Championship match on November 22 as almost a warm-up for the event. The event was held at Cornell University and would pit the Titan Mercury Wrestling Club against the Finger Lakes Wrestling Club. Matches featured Kyle Dake versus Andrew Howe, Tyrell Fortune versus Tervel Dlagnev, and Tony Ramos versus Sam Hazewinkel. All matches were considered a "Super Match" as each bout would be a fifteen-minute bout. In addition, there would be a $30,000 purse to the winners.

In a Global Wrestling Championship promotion, Hazewinkel commented on his opportunity to wrestle: "To come out here, to Ithaca, and wrestle in a match like this—a Super Match—this is what I dream about."

Tony also commented and spoke about the prize money involved: "I'm excited about the money. It's one of the biggest purses in wrestling. I'm going to go out there and do everything that I got to do to walk away with that."

For Tony, the money was the difference in this match as his life was about to change. "A $30,000 split was on the line and I had a baby coming that I knew about but nobody else knew about," Ramos admitted. "Megan and me weren't telling anyone at the time because it was so early—so that money would go to starting a nursery and moving in that direction.

"I had already wrestled [Hazewinkel] before, but this match length was going to be longer, much longer. It was going to be a 15-minute match. I knew that he was older and that I could wear him out, so it was something that I was pretty excited to have the opportunity to do simply due to the fact that Titan Mercury and Global Wrestling wanted me to come out and compete for that kind of money."

Regardless of Hazewinkel's age, he was still a very accomplished wrestler and someone who was still a high-level competitor. For Tony, and his coaches, the focus was on improving and wrestling hard and preparing for his next competition.

"I was coming off a long break," Ramos explained, "and they wanted to do this before we left for Iran as kind of a warm-up—getting us to compete again. But, there were still things that I needed to work on, get my shape better, get my weight under control we were wrestling at 135, but I was struggling to get down to my competition weight—so there was work to do."

In regard to the timing of the event, or events like this one, Terry Brands believed that it was good for the athlete and for the sport if it fit into the training. "[These events] have to make sense in the schedule," Terry Brands commented, "and that was the biggest animal to skin. When they do make sense, I am all for them. It is a great way to put a lot of money in their pockets for an event like that, and it is great for the arena, awesome visibility—the spectrum of it—and it is fun for the fans and good for the sport. If it doesn't fit the schedule, you don't go. But this did."

For the Global Wrestling Championships, it fit into the schedule and was about one week before the World Cups in Iran; it would give Tony an opportunity to compete before he had to face some of the best in the world. It also gave him the momentum he needed to work through some of the weight issues he was having at the time.

Once he weighed in, and had the twenty-four-hour grace period, his weight would generally work itself back up to 145 pounds; this was

Tony's natural walk-around weight.

"In college," Ramos explained, "I wrestled 133 and I would walk around at 139 to 140 pounds, and that was where my body was used to competing at. In the short amount of time that I was training, I put on more muscle mass. I'm not tall, but I'm kind of stocky and, I'm not going to say that I have the best diet—I like to enjoy things—I like to enjoy the fun foods and things like that. But, it was definitely a lifestyle change that I needed to make to get my body down to 125.5 pounds the right way."

In regard to diet and Tony's weight, having this event early allowed him to work his weight, try to control his weight, but also gave him some motivation in the process to have control prior to Iran. When it came to the match, "Who's going to win a nine or twelve or fifteen-minute match?" Terry Brands questioned. "We are. We're always going to win those matches."

And that was what Tony did. He battled and wore down Hazewinkel and the final score was 10-0. Neither Tony nor Hazewinkel scored in the first round. In the second round, Tony scored a takedown with about thirty seconds remaining and took a 2-0 lead. The third round was scoreless even though both wresters had opportunities to finish attacks but could not. In the fourth period, Tony scored two additional takedowns before hitting a low single-leg takedown and two-point ankle lace in the fifth round.

For the win, Tony was awarded the flyweight championship belt with his victory along with $7,500. He would now have some money to start his child's nursery, and he would be headed to Iran for the World Club Cup Championships.

But, to Terry Brands, he still had some concerns with how Tony was performing. "I am taking that information back," Terry Brands explained, "and I am thinking how we still don't understand the pieces of international wrestling that is going to put us at the top. You got to score points.

"The Iranians and the Russians know what they have to do to win, and they do that. They ride that line [of scoring and not being scored upon] very well. We have to attack more and score and put the pressure on them."

Terry Brands took his concerns back to Tony and they worked and prepared for Tony's matches in Iran.

THE OPENING ROUND OF THE WORLD CLUB CUP
Championships placed the United States Titan Mercury Wrestling Club, positioned in Pool B, against the Arabic Army of Syria.

Not only would Tony defeat his opponent, Ali Miras Khaled, by fall, but the Titan Mercury Team would not lose a match in their opening round. They would score an 8-0 victory and move on in their pool.

The United States then faced Team Manzandaran of Iran. This was not Iran's strongest team, who was in Pool A on the other side of the bracket, but Team Manzandaran members were still tough-willed Iranian wrestlers. Tony faced and defeated Reza Atri by fall, and Titan Mercury would again advance, this time with a 4-4 tie, but with a 20-15 differential in classification points.

Now in the finals of their pool, Titan Mercury wrestled Azerbaijan Gomzik Cho 2. Tony had a very strong opponent in Namik Sordomzada who was a very competent and accomplished wrestler. Tony would claim a 3-2 victory and the United States, with a 6-2 match differential, advanced into the semifinals against China's Union Wrestling.

Titan Mercury would once again dominate the competition, winning by an 8-0 margin, and Tony's efforts reflected that same domination as he defeated Qi Mu De, 7-2. Tony was now 4-0 on the day and he would face Iran's Hassan Rahimi in the finals of the World Club Cup Championships that evening.

This would not be the first time that these two had met. Tony and Rahimi already knew each other from the 2009 Junior World Championships when Tony placed fifth; Rahimi was the gold medalist. Rahimi had defeated Rahul Balasaheb Aware from India for the top spot in the world. Aware, who Tony was one match away from wrestling at the 2014 World Championships, was Tony's first loss in the 2009 championships. He defeated Tony 3-1, 4-5, 6-0. Therefore, even though there was an ocean and five years between them, they were not unfamiliar with the other.

To date, Rahimi, who was coming off a bronze medal at the 2014 World Championships, would be the most accomplished wrestler that Tony would wrestle to date. In 2009, Rahimi took a bronze at the Asian Championships in Pattaya, Thailand, and he won the gold at the 2010 Military World Championships. In 2011, at the World Championships in Istanbul, Turkey, he took another bronze before winning a gold at the Asian Championships in 2012 in Gumi, South Korea. He followed up his second gold with a third gold at the 2013 World Championships in Budapest, Hungary. And, of course, Rahimi placed above Tony at the 2014 World Championships when he won a bronze medal in Tashkent, Uzbekistan.

For Tony, this was his opportunity to wrestle one of the best wrestlers in the world and prove his worth.

"The atmosphere was awesome," Ramos remembered. "It was the

first time as a member of Team U.S.A. that I got to compete in a dual setting where we're training next to each other, competing together, working out all the time—it was great. We had early success and then in the finals I had Rahimi who I knew would be a tough match."

Unfortunately, for Tony, Rahimi would not only win the match, but he would do so in a dominating fashion. Tony would fall to the number-three ranked wrestler in the world, 9-0.

"The understanding of what it takes to win at that level just wasn't there," Terry Brands stated. "That was what we needed to work on."

Additionally, Titan Mercury took a loss and the silver as they fell 6-2 in matches.

For Tony, there was much to improve upon as he headed home to train for the 2015 season which opened with what was nicknamed as the "Toughest Tournament in the World," the Golden Grand Prix Ivan Yarygin Memorial International.

"THE YARYGIN IS IMPORTANT BECAUSE YOU have the travel adversity," Terry Brands explained. "You have the time zone adversity. You have the sleep deprivation adversity. You have the food and comforts of home adversities. The word is 'acclimation.' You know, people think of acclimations as time zones—I don't. I think of acclimation as it embodies the entire living process. What's it like here in the U.S. and then what's it going to be like in Russia? And that Krasnoyarsk, Russia, trip is the hardest. That weather is extremely harsh. The time zones couldn't be any worse—you're ten to thirteen times zones…crazy, crazy stuff.

"To go there and compete. To go there and weigh-in and compete, and to be competitive, it shows you where your mindset is. None of [those adversities] matter when you step on the mat and that's why you go there to not focus on that but to focus on how to win and get better and to move forward. You're in a situation where you're learning how to be very, very good under extreme duress."

For Tony, his first Yarygin would be as kind to him as his first World Championships. This would also be the first time that Tony would not have Terry or Tom Brands in his corner. And, as Terry Brands had stated, there were a number of adversities that made this more difficult than any other tournament. Not having his coaches mat side for the first time in his adult career would be another adversity for Tony to overcome because of the trust and confidence he has when they are with him.

"We know the travel is bad," Ramos echoed, "and it is one of the toughest tournaments with not just the best competition, but you're traveling thirty hours around the world with all of these flights just to head to an uncomfortable environment. But, at the same time, you've got to be able to compete and that is why Terry and Tom send us there.

"You've got the best competition there. You've got very knowledgeable fans, and it's not a—I'm not saying it's not a beautiful place—but it's not a fun area to be in because it is so cold, it is so far away, and the travel is not ideal and the hotels—all foreign hotels are the worst. We get these tiny little beds with these very thin mattresses—everything is small and cramped. It is just like on television when you see those Euro-style apartments. It is exactly what it's like.

"The food is pretty much the same things every day," Ramos continued. "You better bring something that you like or buy something that you are going to be able to eat. Even when we were over in Iran it was rice and lamb or goat or whatever they had every single day. The soup was called borscht—there are not many options. But, the one nice thing about Krasnoyarsk was they had an American restaurant right next to the hotel. So, if you really need to not stray too far from the American culture, you can head out over there and grab some burgers and things like that.

"When you go to practice, you have about a ten-minute walk down to the school. The schools are just like big wrestling schools with four or five different rooms with hundreds of kids in and out all day long. They're just practicing and learning about wrestling. The biggest thing about the Russians is they don't teach the young kids how to wrestle, they teach them more about finishes and using their bodies and tumbling and things like that before they teach them how to wrestle.

"But the atmosphere is cool. The kids want to come up and take pictures with us and say hi or try to communicate as best they can. They don't get to see the top Americans all the time, so it is special for them, too."

When his draw came out, Tony's bracket consisted of forty-six wrestlers and, in his first match, he faced Russia's silver medalist from the 2013 Junior World Championships, Ismail Musukayev, who was also a 2014 Intercontinental Cup champion.

Tony fell behind 4-0 at the end of the first period and, when the match was concluded, it was a 10-0 technical superiority for Musukayev. Tony would have to wait, as he did in the World Championships, to see if he qualified for the repechage. Once Musukayev wrestled to a finals appearance, Tony now had the opportunity to wrestle to a bronze medal. He would, of course, have to win three matches to do that.

In his first match of the repechage, Tony wrestled Russia's Viktor Rassadin who lost to Musukayev in the second round. At the end of the first period, Tony was chasing one point and trailed, 3-2. However, the second period would distance the two as Tony dominated the first two minutes of the three-minute period. Unfortunately, Tony put himself into the lead before he gave up position late in the match and lost an 8-4 decision. He would be eliminated from the tournament.

Rassadin would lose to another Russian, Artyom Gebekov, 8-7, and Gebekov would lose 2-1 to Mongolia's Bekhbayar Erdenebat for the bronze medal. For the other bronze, Mongolia's Tcogtbaator Damdinbazar won a 3-0 decision over Russia's N'urgun Skryabin. In the finals, Musukayev earned a silver medal, losing to Viktor Lebedev of Russian, 7-1.

"In that first match," Ramos said, "Musukayev got me pretty good. In that second match, to get back into the wrestle-backs, I was winning and I blew it when I tried sitting on the lead and allowing him to hang around. You know, that's where I learned when Terry spoke to me when I got back, he said, 'You tried to [ride out the win] in that match against Germany and you did it again. We need to fix this now.' But that is up to me to fix mentally. I have to go get another score or control the match better. I went down and got in on the leg and I tried to just hang on to the single-leg and I ended up getting crotch-lifted.

Tony finished his tournament ranked 31 out of 46, and it also left a very bad taste in his mouth. Luckily, for him, the team was headed to Paris for a competition before returning back home. However, initially, Tony was not planning on competing, but he needed to prove something to himself.

"Terry wasn't out there at that time," Ramos said. "It was Bill Zadick and we were going to head over to Paris that next week to compete in the Golden Grand Prix there. Zadick and me didn't really talk too much about the Yarygin; it was more about getting ready for the next competition and a few little things that I could've done better like finishing matches and getting to my offense and not leaving it up to the ref. But, I was anxious to get back on the mat and compete because I know I should have finished better."

ONCE IN PARIS, TONY HAD A DECISION TO MAKE:
57 kg or 61 kg. "After the Yarygin, I got pretty big," Ramos explained. "We had a two kilogram allowance, but I buckled down mentally and got the weight off and it came off pretty easily because I just made weight the week before and I felt good."

In the opening round, Tony received a bye. In the quarterfinals, he faced France's Youssoup Deliev and won by fall in 00:50. This would put him in the semifinals where he would face off against Canada's John Pineda.

Tony, who was looking to improve from his shortcomings a week ago in Krasnoyarsk, was able to control the match and secure his 4-1 victory. He was now in the finals and secured himself a medal.

In the finals of the Grand Prix, Tony wrestled Adamma Diatta from the Republic of Senegal. The 27-year-old from West Africa was a 2008 FILA African Champion and that qualified him to wrestle in the 2008 Summer Olympics in Beijing, China. He would defeat Cuba's Yowlys Bonne of Cuba in the first round of those Olympic Games; however, in the round of sixteen, he fell to Japan's Tomohiro Matsunaga. This placed Diatta in the repechage and he exited his Olympic experience after a loss to Turkey's Sezar Akgul.

Now, seven years later, he was still a top competitor at 57 kg for his country as he had totaled four more African Championships, even though he missed qualifying his country for the 2012 London Olympic Summer Games. Since then, however, he had been wrestling some his best wrestling throughout his career, and he now had the young American in the final of the Paris Grand Prix.

Tony was dressed in a red singlet while the taller, longer Diatta was in blue. The match opened with a heavy hand fight for control and head position. The battle of hands and heads, as well as level changes continued just past the first minute of the match's first period with the only two attempted shots coming from Diatta; however, all of the pressure and forward motion and movement was coming from Tony. In that, Diatta was warned first for passivity at the 1:05 mark.

Even with the warning, Diatta's offense did not pick up. Tony, however, continued to apply his pressure and, of the two shots he took, he had one viable attempt that came up short. At the 1:47 mark, Diatta was again warned and now placed on the shot clock. That did, of course, open up his aggressiveness as he worked to try and use his height on Tony by fighting for his right-side and then his left-side underhook. Unfortunately for Diatta, Tony was sure to always block and clear the tie and work to reattack; in those moments, each wrestler tried to attack out of creating a flurry of some sort. When the thirty seconds expired, Tony was awarded the period's first point and he took a 1-0 lead.

Now trailing by a point, the West African worked to pull and tie even heavier and harder on Tony's head. Accustomed to the hand and head fight, Tony held his position and battled back in his own style of pulling and creating motion while blocking and looking for an opportunity to attack the legs.

With six seconds remaining in the first period, Diatta took an ill-advised shot only to find Tony in on one of his own off a reattack. Tony attacked the corner, brought Diatta's left leg up as he tried to defend with a whizzer, and Tony continued his chase of the far leg. Diatta would extend his body as much as he could and, fortunately for Diatta, he had the benefit of time running out before Tony had earned the takedown.

Going into the break, the American led, 1-0.

When the break ended, Tony was the first wrestler back to the center of the mat and his pressure and forward movement set the tone for the rest of the match. Diatta, not to be undone, immediately battled back into Tony off the whistle and tried to tie up his hands. Ten seconds later, Diatta attempted a shot that would fail and Tony followed it into a single-leg of his own on Diatta's left leg. Diatta struggled to make his body long as he dropped his foot to the mat and fought Tony's grip, but Tony, tenaciously fighting for position, refused to break his hold. The two battled until they ended up out of bounds. Tony was awarded with a two-point takedown as Diatta fell out of bounds and Tony, still inbounds, gained control behind his hips.

The match now resumed with Tony up, 3-0; however, Diatta's corner threw in the challenge cube—a stuffed minion dressed in a blue cape—as they felt the wrestlers were both out of bounds well before the takedown occurred.

After the review, Tony was awarded only one point for Diatta going out of bounds first, prior to the takedown; Tony held a 2-0 lead with 2:37 remaining in the match.

The aggression of the wrestlers only heightened and, after a Tony reattack off a Diatta fake, Diatta now found his opportunity to score when Tony was in on his legs. Defensively, Diatta sprawled and knocked Tony down and over to his left hip. Diatta raced to chase behind Tony as Tony spun counter clockwise and, eventually, worked himself out of danger and out of Diatta's grips. No points were awarded as there were now two minutes left in the match.

Fifteen seconds later, Tony was in on a double-leg that drove Diatta off the mat in defense and scored him another point. Tony now led the former Olympian, 3-0. With the lead on the scoreboard, Tony now controlled the center of the mat as Diatta wanted to, again, use his underhooks and he banged heavy on the American's head and worked to punch his position into his advantage—it never happened. Tony was circling and applying his own pressure and, in the process, caught Diatta off guard and pushed him out for another point as time expired.

In one week, Tony was able to turn the tables. At the Yarygin, Tony faced criticism and doubt by some due to his inability to advance accordingly. Now, a week later, Tony had reset the criticism, but still knew he had to be more confident and consistent.

"I think the difference was that I did a better job of believing in my offense more and going out and putting up some points," Ramos said. "I had some tough matches there. The kid from Canada was their top guy and the guy in the finals from Senegal, he was their top guy and one of the top guys in the world. I went out there and even though it was a 4-0 match, it was four times that I was in on the legs going out of bounds. I should have finished those and it should have been an 8-0 match. So, I was attacking and going out there and doing the right things to win."

Tony now won his first tournament overseas and, in return, would return home with a ranking of number-nineteen in the world. "It was nice to see that ranking because it's nice to know that my training and hard work is recognized," Ramos said. "But, I was like, 'Nineteen? I don't want to be nineteen. I better get to work. I want to be on top.' I mean, it gave me some incentive because I like to prove people wrong, so it was more of one of those things where I had to come in and work harder because I know I'm better than nineteen. So, seeing that kind of [ranking] puts that kind of emotion into my training and into my head and into my body."

Once state side, and settled back in Iowa, Tony jumped right back into his training as he was preparing for his next competition.

CHAPTER 61
MAKING IT ALL FIT THE SCHEDULE

"Tom is just as big of a role as Terry. I think it's comforting to see both of them in my corner—familiar faces and two guys who I know have my back and my best interests. Each one is just as important as the other."

• *Tony Ramos*

WHEN TONY RETURNED TO CARVER-HAWKEYE Arena for his training, he was welcomed by an old friend who had come back home to help the Hawkeye Wrestling Club members train, as well as step on the mat one more time.

Daniel Dennis, who had been away for about two years, where he spent time climbing, camping, and coaching, was back home. When he left Iowa in 2013, he was exhausted and his body needed time to heal. That was when he packed up his vehicle and headed west—far away from the wrestling room and some on his toughest defeats.

"We're in a sport, a game essentially," Dennis said in a *Sports Illustrated* article written by Richard O'Brien, "but it's more than that for people who really put a lot into it. That was my world crumbling. I had invested so much in it. I was so committed and so determined and having that in the palm of your hand and then have it slip away. It was terrible."

Dennis continued to discuss the toll wrestling had taken on his body as well. "My body was beat up, my mind was beat up," Dennis said. O'Brien would then go on in the article to explain how Dennis had suffered from chronic back pain, and a neck injury had rendered his left arm periodically numb and unresponsive—in Dennis' words, "a fraction of what it was."

Dennis spoke about how his routine had changed from his training days in Iowa; in fact, it was the exact opposite of the routine and the pounding that his body endured throughout his training.

"We'd get up in the morning and we'd hike to where we were going to climb," Dennis explained, "and we'd climb all day and then come back, eat dinner, and have a beer. There might be a fire, maybe the group camping next to you would have a guitar and you'd get together and play till three in the morning."

In that time, Dennis was isolated by choice and he would often find himself in an area where his cell phone rarely gathered service. However, when the phone would reconnect, he often found his voicemail inundated with messages from friends and teammates and coaches asking him when he would return to Iowa and start training again. Dennis said that he never took the calls seriously and that he was content with where he was and what he was doing. His body was healing and he was not feeling defeated or beaten down. He was given new life and he was enjoying his days and his opportunities for reflection.

For money, Dennis worked the occasional wrestling camp and, as he worked his way out to California, he took up a job as a roofer and coached at a local high school in the evening.

In 2014, Dennis' father died of a brain tumor. When O'Brien spoke with Dennis' mother, Jane, she had communicated to her son that his father would have loved to see him come back and wrestle. As a result of that conversation with his mother, Dennis decided to come back and wrestle in one more tournament.

With the support he received from his friends in Iowa and in California, he headed back to Iowa City for that one more competition—the U.S. Open.

When he arrived, he was mostly working with Brent Metcalf and Tony Ramos, but enjoying the process more than worrying about the process. In fact, once he was in the room, he had a weight that was lifted off him and he was more carefree and open. The time away had been a positive change for Dennis.

For Tony, having Dennis in the room became, once again, a great advantage to him. "It's awesome having [Dennis] around," Ramos said to Ross Bartachek in an interview with *IA Wrestle*. "He gives you feels and puts you in positions that not many guys are very good at."

As far as Tony knew, Dennis was back to help him and Metcalf train and, from what was communicated to him, Dennis would be around for about one year to wrestle 61 kg, and that would be that.

"For me, personally," Ramos explained, "he is one of the best assets in the room because he does a lot of things that the top contenders at my weight do and he makes me better in those positions."

In the given time that Tony would have with Dennis, at least for that one year, he was excited to have his friend and supporter back—especially when he saw him in the room for the first time. He knew Dennis would help make him a more complete wrestler and give him great looks and feels that he would not get from some of the younger guys.

In that, Dennis would be training for the U.S. Open at 61 kg, and Tony would be preparing for a major AGON event in Iowa entitled: "AGON V, Iowa against the World." AGON was a professional amateur wrestling event by where the wrestling was real and the winners were awarded with small purses of prize money. The idea behind AGON was to promote the sport of wrestling and help wrestlers earn money in the process.

THE AGON EVENT WAS TO FEATURE FORMER

Olympic gold medalist, Henry Cejudo, a one-time protégé of Terry Brands, against Tony Ramos, the up and coming protégé of Terry Brands. The match was to highlight a man who had achieved the American Dream and another who was still looking to capture his own dreams.

The location, the timing of the event, the undercard, and the promotion all fit into Tony's schedule; he had the full support of Tom and Terry Brands as he underwent a match that put a spotlight on him, the Hawkeye Wrestling Club, and the sport of wrestling. In agreeing to the match, Tony knew the magnitude of what it meant for him as far as showing people that he was now the guy and all of the talk could stop about what America needed to be doing at 57 kg.

"That match was very big for me because of the fact that everyone wanted Henry to come back in 2016," Ramos said. "All I kept hearing people say was that the U.S. had not had a medalist since Henry and he needs to come back. So, not only in that sense was it big for me, but it was big for me because it was Terry's old protégé and we were always compared—and we will always be compared. So I really wanted to go out there and I really wanted to prove a point."

• • •

The credentials that came along with Henry Cejudo were more than impressive. He was a four-time state champion, two in Arizona and two in Colorado, an ASICS National High School Wrestler of the Year recipient in 2006, a fifth-place finisher in 2005 at the Junior World Championships, and a runner-up in 2006. Also, as a senior in high school, he placed second in the United States World Team Trials after he won the U.S. Open and the Pan-American Championships.

Out of high school, Cejudo simply trained at the Olympic Training

Center in Colorado Springs, Colorado. In 2007 he was the United States World Team Trials champion. He won the Pan-American Games again, won the U.S. Open, placed fifth at the Kiev Invitational, placed second at the Takhti Cup in Iran, and placed third at the Yarygin. He would, however, not place at the World Championships.

In 2008, Cejudo's stock rose dramatically. Even though he only placed second at the U.S. Open, he wrestled on and won the United States Olympic Team Trials. From there, he won a third Pan-American championship, and became the youngest wrestler in American history to win an Olympic gold medal.

After his gold medal performance in 2008, Cejudo took some time off. However, in 2012, he decided that he wanted to return to wrestling and worked to capture a second Olympic gold. At the United States Olympic Team Trials held in Carver-Hawkeye Arena, however, he placed second to Nick Simmons. After his match he retired from wrestling. In doing so, he removed his wrestling shoes and threw them into the Carver-Hawkeye stands while receiving a grand ovation from those in attendance.

In 2013, Cejudo made the move to Mixed Martial Arts (MMA) and that was his focus until he agreed to compete against Tony in the AGON event to be held in Cedar Rapids, Iowa.

• • •

In a promotional video, Tony talked about the event: "I've always wanted an opportunity to wrestle with Cejudo. He's a 2008 Olympic gold medalist—he's done what I want to do. It's something I've been waiting a long time for; it's finally here and I'm excited for it. Everyone knows that if it wasn't really for Terry, he might not have that Olympic gold medal. Now Terry's with me, he's in my corner—he knows everything that Cejudo has, so I'm going to be well-prepared. I'm ready to go for the match. He's been taking a long time off of wrestling. You know, wrestling is not just a sport you can pick up. You can't just jump in and out of it. You can't just pick up a match in 2015 and think it's going to work out for you.

"I think my style's going to give him problems and my strength and my size. I also have Luke Eustice who was one of the last Americans to beat Cejudo. I've got the Hawkeye Wrestling Club. I've got Bret Metcalf. I've got world-class wrestlers every day that I'm competing with and I've got something that he's not getting right now. I'm going to be ready to go—he better be focused. I'm looking to go into battle for six-minutes and I'm looking to put him in retirement for good."

After, Tony would address the event as a whole. "They're talking about this is Iowa versus the world," Ramos said, "which I think is awesome. It's great that it's in one of the best wrestling communities, wrestling states in the world. I think this is a really unique event. It's going to be a good show. I'm excited."

Henry Cejudo would be interviewed by Takedown Wrestling and he addressed his participation in the event and Tony as an opponent.

"What I know about Tony is, it's going to be six minutes of intensity," Cejudo commented. "He's going to come out and collar tie me, he's going to go out there and wrestle—front headlock. Like you said it's the 'Iowa Style' of wrestling where they want to control the head, control the hand fighting to get their angles to shoot. I think my style matches up pretty well with any style pretty much because I can adjust to certain styles, to certain people. I'm looking forward to it."

As to why he accepted the bout with the financially healthy living that he was making in MMA, he felt it was a good way to help promote wrestling. "I was asked to go out there and put the sport of wrestling on the map," Cejudo explained, "and to me this is part of putting to sport on the map. Wrestling is such a great event like AGON V. Wrestling is more of an art than any other sport because it takes two tough people that need to become creative to defeat each other with a certain style of grappling rather than having so many different components. So I think having events like AGON V and promoting wrestling at its highest is only good for our sport."

Tony also spoke to Tony Hager and Takedown Wrestling about promoting the AGON V event. Hager addressed a few wrestling issues and then asked Tony what he felt his strengths would be against the former Olympic gold medalist.

"I think size-wise we're the same," Ramos answered. "I know one of Cejudo's biggest strengths when he was back competing is he was way bigger than everyone—he was a big 55 [kg] guy. I'm a big 57 [kg]. We're going to be about the same. I think I'm stronger and I have been training wrestling longer now—you can't just take time off and hope to come back and that it's going to work out for you. He came back in 2012 and ended up losing to Simmons. He took more time off, now he's trying to come back in 2015—so I've got some strength there. And another one is I got Terry in my corner. Terry Brands was his coach. He knows everything about Cejudo and I'm going to have the best game plan or the best inside knowledge anyone's ever had going into competition against him."

From where Terry Brands stood, he saw "An Olympic champion there and a guy that's coming in on a contract to do one thing and that's to win one stinkin' wrestling match and that's it. You have the new Olympic gold medal wannabe wrestling somebody who'd been there, done that.

So it's kind of like the old and the new and it's coming together and it's in Iowa City and it's somebody that I coached—I spent a lot of time with both of those guys."

In regard to having coached Cejudo, Terry Brands was very direct in what Tony should expect: pressure. "I told Tony that he's going to keep coming no matter what the score," Terry Brands said. "And he will throw things at you that you've never seen before, and when you think you're safe, you're not. And that's exactly what happened."

SB Nation covered the event and RossWB wrote this in his article about the event when it came to the Tony and Cejudo match:

Ramos produced the most thrilling win of the night, taking down former Olympic gold medalist Henry Cejudo 12-8 in an absolute barnburner of a match. Ramos fell behind early, 2-0, then got a takedown to tie things up right at the end of the first period. He gave up a 4-point throw early in the second period and went down 6-2, but managed to score points of his own during the scramble and things sat at 8-4 Cejudo when the dust settled. Things did not look good for our favorite stare down artist. Then things got really exciting. Ramos got to Cejudo's legs and scored another takedown to cut the deficit to 8-6 before Cejudo had to take a brief injury stoppage with 45 seconds left. When the action resumed, Ramos was on the attack and he finished by locking up a cradle and taking Cejudo to this back as time expired. He didn't get the fall, but he did get a 12-8 win in front of a raucous pro-Iowa crowd.

"I was down four with a four-point criteria against me, but there were two minutes left to wrestle," Ramos said of his match in the closing moments. "I knew that I had time and I knew that I could score points fast. I got to him a few times, but I gave up a few points by not being solid on my finishes, so I just kept attacking and eventually things opened up at the end of the match. I got a takedown and in my head I was like, *You still got to score again, so lock something up and go for it.* I kept attacking and that cradle opened up."

In typical Tony Ramos fashion, after he scored six points in the final twenty seconds, and topped it off with a cradle as time expired, he popped up in celebration before his signature double rainbows made an appearance out of pure excitement. Running toward him on the stage and lifting him up in the process was his brother, Frank, and, not far behind was Tom Brands. After Frank released Tony and continued his own celebration, Tony turned toward Tom Brands and slapped his hand down hard before Brands hugged and lifted his wrestler. Tony circled the mat, arms outstretched and his head shaking up and down.

"The outstretched arms was just a response to all of the critics who keep saying that I can't do it," Ramos explained, "and I did it again. It was more of a 'Why-you-going-to-keep-doubting-me?' pose. I've proven my success."

When it was over, Tony made his way to the center of the mat and had his hand raised.

"Tony's comeback in the end was awesome!" Tom Brands exclaimed. "He's a wrestler and wrestlers wrestle and wrestlers love pressure and wrestlers thrive and wrestlers aren't denied and I literally lost my mind and don't even remember how I got on the stage. It was a pure joy for me."

From Terry Brands' vantage point, Tony walked away with exactly what he needed to take that next step.

"His determination and his ability to be able to understand that he was in dire straits trouble and what is he going to do about it," Terry Brands said of the turning point in the match for Tony. "And what I think he learned in that match—kind of a self-taught wrestler— was that he got back in a similar situation and then forced the guy to get [where he wanted him], like the Graff match, and that caused him to get that final two and two and then ultimately ending up in that cradle. But ultimately that was the difference. He forced [Cejudo] to do something that he didn't want to do. The frustrating thing there is, when you talk about that and you communicate that to him, he never drew that connection to his other wrestling. It's almost like he had more to prove to beat the Olympic champion than a no-name Russian halfway across the world. For me, it doesn't matter because they're all the same. They're just another guy that you got to take out."

Even with the slight frustration with Tony, Terry Brands also acknowledged what a match like that does for Tony so close to the World Championships.

"A match like that," Terry Brands expressed, "will keep you sharp. But what's your approach to it? What's your mentality going into that? My motivation is that this is going to get you better for the Trials. So that's the only reason why I was in on it. The money doesn't matter, all that matters is if [the competition] fits into your schedule. Is taking a match going to help me be the best world beater and be at my best to contend for a World and Olympic gold medal? Period. That's it."

The issue of wrestling and money was the only difference in the relationship between Terry and Tom Brands and Tony. As for everything else, the workouts, the attitude, and the end goal, it was all the same. The match, even though it did put money in Tony's pocket, was also a well-timed competition that helped prepare him for his next step, the World

Cup Championships.

AFTER DEFEATING CEJUDO, TONY NOW HAD A solid competition and positive match under his belt, as well as his weight down early to where it was more manageable and healthy, heading into the World Cup Championships in Los Angeles, California. The championships brought the world's top teams together—different from the Club Cup Championships because the only affiliation that mattered was one's country. The wrestling event would be held in a basketball Mecca: the Los Angeles Forum.

The United States brought in a team of the current World Team members to compete, and Tony would be outspoken about the importance of American attendance at the event.

"If you're from America," Ramos would say, "you should be here. It doesn't matter if you're a wrestling fan or not."

For the Americans, they opened their dual competition against Cuba. For Tony, who led things off for Team U.S.A., he had to wrestle Yowlys Bonne. Bonne, who had been on the international circuit since 2002 when he won the Junior Pan-American Championships in both freestyle and Greco-Roman, made an immediate splash upon entering. Now, as a 32-year-old decorated wrestler, with a 2014 World Championship bronze medal recently under his belt, he faced the young and upcoming American who was looking to continually grow his name.

In the opening period, Tony scored the first point due to getting in on a solid single-leg attack and, after having had Bonne hop around on one foot for quite some time, earned a pushout point when he could not finish his single. And, even though Tony could not return Bonne to the mat for a takedown, he was able to take advantage of his position with the pushout. Unfortunately, for the remainder of the period, Tony was defending Bonne's offensive attacks even though neither scored offensively or defensively.

In the second period, Tony went up 2-0 with another pushout before he was put on the shot clock for blocking and not opening up. In the process, Tony again attacked and found himself in on Bonne's leg; unfortunately, this time, Bonne created back exposure with a tip and then worked into position where Tony found himself cradled up and on his back—Bonne would ultimately win by fall.

Tony acknowledged his error in his attack; however, he did not agree with some of the critics' arguments that he should not have been attacking. He was up 2-0 and on the shot clock. He could have conceded the one point by not attacking and still held a 2-1 lead with 1:16 in the match; however, that was not how Tony approached the situation. He approached the shot clock as an opportunity to close out the match.

"You got to wrestle every position, every second of the match and staying solid," Ramos said of his loss to Bonne. "I got off my corner on that single-leg, got in a flurry—it cost me the match."

One journalist asked Tony if maybe in a situation where he did not need to force the issue if forcing the issue was the right philosophy.

"I never worry about [when to finish a takedown and when I should give it up to stay out of danger]," Ramos commented in regard to his decision-making process. "I feel like I got the best single-leg in the world. I finish on a lot of guys. If I don't finish, I'm trying to find that edge and at least get the pushout point. So that's more my strategy. Start taking him to the edge where he's got to worry about now giving up two or one, but either way I'm scoring a point. Always try to score. If it doesn't happen, it doesn't happen.

"You know, I probably could've gotten to Cuba six or seven more times, and I even put myself in position, even if I didn't come out of that scramble, where I wasn't totally out of the match. I was down two takedowns. That's how I got to look at it."

Unfortunately, no matter how he looked at it, Tony allowed a match against a high-powered quality opponent to get away from him. Team U.S.A., however, did not allow the same to happen to them as they went on to defeat Cuba by a 6-2 score in order to advance to the second round of pool competition.

In Round Two, the United States wrestled against Russia. Tony, who again led off for the stars and stripes, this time defeated his opponent, Omak Syuryun, 4-2. This ended up being a big win for Tony as Syuryun had been wrestling at a high level. He had just come off a runner-up finish at the Dave Schultz Memorial—he lost to Tyler Graff in the finals—and he had a strong showing at the Yarygin. Additionally, he had placed in the top two at every entered tournament prior to the 2015 Yarygin; in the 2014 Yarygin, he placed fifth.

As for what Tony did better in that match compared to his last, "The difference was staying solid in every position," Ramos said. "Staying on the corner, staying on the attack, staying on the offense.

"[In the] first period I gave up a little slide-by," Ramos commented on how the match had started for him. "[But] I felt the guy wearing. He was breathing real hard after the first period. So, I was excited to get a win after that first match where I gave up a big lead. Two points may not be a big lead, but I felt I controlled that match until that last scramble."

Even though the United States and Russia would split matches, four each, Team U.S.A. had criteria on technical points and advanced to the finals against Iran.

For the final dual of their pool, and the chance to go to the finals at stake, the U.S. and Tony opened up against Mongolia's Damdinbazar who was coming off a gold medal performance out of a field of twenty-four competitors at the President Cup of Buryatia Republic and a fifth place finish at the 2015 Yarygin. He was also ranked tenth in the world in the current rankings.

"He was in good position," Ramos said of the difficulty he had scoring on Damdinbazar. "He kept knee-tricking me, I got to him a few times. I stayed in good position and wrestled hard."

It was not until the second period when Tony scored his one point; still, he did not waiver from his philosophy of attacking even after it cost him the match against Bonne.

In the end, it was the American with a 1-1 decision over the seasoned Mongolian.

"Keep wrestling," Ramos would answer of his strategy. "They're going to try and hit you for [passivity] and one, so just stay in the center, control the mat, and get position."

The win helped Team U.S.A. score early and put them on a roll.

"I'll probably get a lot of crap for saying this," Ramos confessed, "but if the individual does [his job], the team will take care of the rest. So I want to go out there and score as many points as I can. I really wasn't worried about the team, even though the team factors into it, but I've got to set myself up for best position for the World Championships. You know, make a statement to these guys, let them know who I am—that guy felt me, he felt me get to him, now I've just got to finish."

In regard to his next match, Tony had a good feeling on who his opponent would be. "I'm pretty sure I know who I'm going to have," Ramos would say with a smile, "and I've wrestled him before. I'm pretty sure I'm going to have Rahimi—World Champ 2013—I'm ready to go. I'm excited. I live for those moments."

When the finals began, and it was the United States versus Iran, the sound of the crowd was dominated by the Iranian horns and hollers—almost as if the Americans were wrestling in Iran.

However, when the whistle was blown, it was all about what was in front of Tony, and that was the opportunity to avenge a loss and make a statement.

The first thirty seconds of the match was more of a feeling out period by both wrestlers as they changed levels and posted on each other's heads with their own hands. The referee stopped the match and warned each to stay out of the face of his opponent.

As the match resumed, Tom Brands could be heard yelling instructions to Tony. "Work that head," Tom Brands coached. "Fast feet! Head up!"

The following thirty seconds were nothing more than head ties and position battles. When the referee stopped the match at the one-minute mark, it was Tony who was cautioned to work.

The match went another thirty seconds with heavy hands and good motion before a wrestler found an opening on his opponent and, in that moment, Rahimi was in on Tony's left leg off a sweep single.

Tony defended in a whizzer and worked to fight the hands of the Iranian, but as he placed more pressure on the whizzer, Rahimi limped his right arm free, sending Tony and his weight forward; he then chased the leg and tackled Tony from behind for a two-point takedown. Rahimi, with 1:15 remaining in the first period, took a 2-0 lead.

Once back to their feet, and a fresh start, the whistle blew and Rahimi attacked Tony's head, poking the American in the eye and knocking his contact out. The referee stopped the match and told Rahimi to stay out of the face; Rahimi made a motion of apology to Tony by gently reaching his hand out toward Tony and then patting the back of Tony's head as he passed.

Off the restart, and now with one minute remaining in the first period, the head ties came down much harder and the snaps became more vicious. Each fired off his own shots, but to no avail. Then, with nineteen seconds remaining, Rahimi tried a super duck on Tony, but Tony blocked before he reattacked and finally was in on the former World Champion's left leg.

A fight for position intensified as Tony tried to secure the leg, but Rahimi was not willing to concede any more of that position than he had already given up. With an onslaught of pressure and heavy hips, Rahimi freed himself and the two, suddenly, were back to banging on each other's heads and looking for one final opening. The period ended with Rahimi leading, 2-0.

Coming back to the center of the mat for the start of the second and final period, the Iranian horns and cheers, now mixed with some American bravado, also intensified as the gravity of the opening bout in the championship dual was exciting, closely contested, and still anyone's match. Besides, on American soil, Tony always found a way to win big matches.

The posting on the heads, as well as the heavy ties, ensued. Tony would also take three attacks on Rahimi within the first thirty-five seconds. None of his attacks were enough to get him inside, but it did set the tone enough to have Rahimi placed on the shot clock fifty-one seconds into the period.

When Rahimi forced a shot under Tony in that shot-clock period, Tony defended and, now with an underhook and the chin in a front headlock position, looked for his cow-catcher. Unfortunately, Tony would not be able to position his hips behind the arms or gather a strong enough hold and Rahimi, well versed in all positions—Rahimi cleared the hold and ultimately conceded the one point to Tony. The score was now 2-1 in favor of Rahimi with 1:38 remaining in the match.

As the referee restarted the bout, the head ties came down heavy, and, all of a sudden, off a change in head position from one side to the other, Rahimi swept in on Tony's right leg; the Iranian cheers grew in volume as Rahimi was in position to score yet again.

Tony, in defense, stuffed the head inside of him, hit the corner, brought the single down to the mat, and was now trying to hit the corner and step over his opponent. As the two hit the mat and Tony was looking to be in scoring position, the American fans let themselves be heard. Once Ramos hooked Rahimi's right ankle, an eruption of "TWO!" echoed throughout the Forum.

There would be no takedown called as the referee kept his hands out signaling "no score" as Rahimi now crowded back into Tony and dropped Tony's right hip to the mat—Rahimi was pushing him backwards and near the circle's edge.

Once Rahimi felt in control, he leaned back and was awarded a two-point exposure of Tony. Tony, now with his right leg across Rahimi's hip and on his butt, took his right hand and latched onto Rahimi's chin and cranked it to the right while using an underhook on the left side. Tony wrenched the position and, as the referee signaled a two-point exposure for him, the Americans in the crowd, again, echoed another "TWO!"

The match would be stopped, however, in the middle of Tony having a figure four around Rahimi's body while cranking his head over in a pry half and exposing him for a second time. The two wrestlers were not out of bounds, but the match was stopped as Rahimi was being turned with 1:06 remaining. There was no second set of points for an exposure and, on the score board, it showed Rahimi with a 4-3 lead.

Both Tony and Rahimi believed they deserved more points than what they were awarded, or at least felt the other did not deserve what he was granted. When they came to their feet, each wrestler was protesting to his corner his own account of what he felt the score should be. Tony, bleeding from his right ear, appeared to want the challenge cube to be thrown in and motioned a few times for this to happen—Tom Brands obliged his wrestler.

While the sequence was being reviewed, each wrestler was gathering further instruction from his coach and, as they had done the entire match, the Iranian horns continued to sound in support of their wrestler.

When the challenge decision came back, it was in favor of Rahimi—the Iranians again came to life in the Forum. Tony, due to the lost challenge, was penalized one point and Rahimi now held a 5-3 advantage with 1:06 remaining in the match.

Off the start, Tony was the aggressor and it appeared that Rahimi was wrestling in a purely defensive style—now backing up and changing levels instead of circling to control the center of the mat. Rahimi would be warned repeatedly, "Contact. Blue, contact. Contact. Blue, action," but he would remain at a distance.

At 5:15, with forty-five seconds remaining, Rahimi was hit with a caution and one, and it would be confirmed. The score was now 5-4, Rahimi, and Tony had to continue his pressure and find an opening and an angle to score.

With the match down to its final twenty-eight seconds, Tony remained on the offensive and, after a missed shot and a defensive block of Rahimi, Tony fired off a high-crotch to his left, had it blocked, fired in on a double, and both men came up to their feet in an over-under position. Rahimi, who dropped his arm and kept his attack at Tony's hip, pressured Tony backward and, in the process, earned a pushout point to now increase his lead 6-4 with twenty-four seconds remaining. The Iranian horns blew up again and Tony, who could still win the match with a takedown and thus criteria, still had time to score as each wrestler worked his way back to the middle of the mat.

Right off the whistle, Tony took a quick shot, which Rahimi defended, and Tony only moved forward and took attempt after attempt. He would not get to Rahimi's legs, but Rahimi would again be cautioned and Tony earned another point off of the confirmation. The score was now 6-5, Rahimi, as the closing seconds were fast approaching.

The match ended with Rahimi holding Tony in a front headlock and, due to the noise level in the Forum, neither wrestler could hear the final horn or whistle; in that, the two kept wrestling. The referee had to go over and break them apart with his hands and the two got up pushing each other. Rahimi had blood on the right side of his cheek, probably from Tony's ear, and there was tension.

When they came to the middle for the winner's hand to be raised, Rahimi motioned that the score was wrong, crossed over the referee, pushed Tony in the chest, and pointed at the scoreboard. He had his corner throw in the blue challenge block, he then picked it up, crossed paths with Tony again and pushed him, and went over to the table. On the scoreboard, it read that it was a 5-5 tie; Rahimi had criteria.

The score was reviewed and corrected, and when Rahimi's hand was raised, the Iranian horns again sounded as vociferous cries ran through the Forum.

After the loss, as best he could, Tony addressed what had happened in the fury of confusion with the points on the edge of the mat.

"I don't know what happened," Ramos commented in regard to the match. "They said we went out of bounds, but I thought I had two back. But the thing is, even if it was, I still got to find a way to get to the legs. I scored off one of his attacks—kind of the same mistake I made against Mongolia—driving him forward and pulling him back on top of me, which makes it look like I'm exposed. So I've got to fix that. I wrestled him earlier this year at the Club World Cups and I think I got either [beat by a technical superiority] or lost 10-1, so I'm making progress.

"I feel like I can beat him; I feel like I belong out there. That's the guy you got to beat if you want to win a World Championship. He's won the World Championships; I think he took second or third in the Olympics. He took third again this year in the World Championships. He's always up top, he's got a couple medals. To do what I want to do I got to get through him and close that gap. I closed it a lot, I think, but I got to get over the hump."

In regard to the pushing and shoving, "We wrestle hard and things get intense," Ramos said of the extra-curricular moments during the match. "He kept wrestling [so] I was going to keep wrestling. He was trying to grab me under my chin in there and squeezing my neck—that kind of little stuff they like to do that you can't see. I'm not going to stop. I'm not just going to sit there and take it.

"The first time I wrestled him, he kept getting to my right leg, single-legs," Ramos would say of learning during the match and from his previous match-ups with Rahimi. "I wasn't circling out of front headlocks and, as the match was going on, I felt like I was clearing those positions better and actually firing off more attacks than last time."

Tony exited the World Cup Championships with a 2-2 performance and earned a silver medal as Iran defeated Team U.S.A. five matches to three.

In regard as to his struggles with Rahimi, "It's a hard thing to really explain," Ramos said of his up and down performances on the mat. "International wrestling you're not wrestling every weekend, so there's not a lot of consistent competition. Because of that, maybe it's harder to stay consistent. I think that is one of the things the Americans struggle with. But these foreigners, they're wrestling every weekend at different things. They're wrestling in leagues, they're wrestling in tournaments—they have the opportunities. For us it's harder because we do have to go overseas for everything, pretty much."

However, even with the lack of steady consistency, Tony did feel that he was strong in some areas. "My defense was pretty good," Ramos said. "I knew that if I got to the legs, that I could finish, but it's the actual getting to the leg and getting past these foreigners who have that Eastern European wrestling stance, or more of a lazy or laid back attitude, where I have to improve."

As for Tom Brands' evaluation of Tony's performance, he felt that his pupil needed to manage the matches better and go through his progression with more of an imagination.

"Look, they're good wrestlers," Tom Brands said plainly. "When you wrestle the Europeans you have to manage two things. One is what they're trying to do—you have to manage that in their wrestling. If you don't do that, then you're too far behind and when your strong wrestling comes on in the end, it's too late. The other thing is, you have to have certain things that you do that get to this guy that renders him or makes him ineffective earlier in the match. Hand fighting. Set-up. Head position. BOOM! I get to my attack—I don't piddle nick around. I come up and throw him out of bounds for one. Who cares if I get one? We try to get two and then in the process of getting two we end up losing four. Come up and get one! BOOM! Okay, 1-0. It's still early in the match, he's still dangerous but manage it. Manage it with your head fighting. Mange it with your hand fighting. Manage it with your set-ups. Manage it! Go up through the zone, BOOM! He kicks out, so what, stay in there. It's 1-0 still, but now I'm taxing him. Now he's got to come. I feel it because now the pressure's on him. He's a competitor, too.

"[American wrestlers] struggle because we don't have an imagination a lot of times. The imagination is: *What's this guy doing to me and how's that leading to what's he going to do to me?* That's my imagination. And then the other imagination is: *This guy really wants it pretty bad and he's the best in the world and my imagination has to go beyond anything I've ever felt in that wrestling room in college or any other opponent that I've had.* These guys want to win. They have a desire, and I have to have an imagination. These guys make hundreds of thousands of dollars by winning wrestling matches.

"I got an imagination that: *This guy is trying to beat me and he's the number-one guy in the world. And I've beaten him before, but that didn't mean anything to him because it was rinky-dink. This is for all the marbles! This is for the World Championship!* This is why it means something to them! My imagination should be: *This is the World Championship.* This is where they're the best. They don't care about a [silly] money challenge that didn't mean anything but $5,000 or $8,000 if I won! They're going to win the worlds because it's $100,000 U.S. And they're going to win the Olympics because it's $1,000,000 U.S. That's my imagination—I ain't going to let him do that! That's what I mean."

For Tony, he had to manage his matches better—and he was well aware of that. As for coming into his matches with a greater imagination, that had to now be seen through his matches from that match forward if he was now going to pass those top-tier wrestlers.

NEXT ON TONY'S SCHEDULE WAS THE ASICS

United States Senior Nationals at the beginning of May in Las Vegas, Nevada. Tony, who had not competed in the U.S. Open the previous year, now had an opportunity to show, domestically, that the weight class was his and his to give up when he was ready.

Since Tony was the number-one wrestler in the land, he earned the number-one seed in a field of 31 competitors. However, during the week leading up to the tournament, Tony faced a setback.

"I don't think a lot of people know this," Ramos explained, "but I wasn't going to wrestle in the U.S. Open. I had gotten injured two or three days before competition—a herniated disc in my neck. While we were wrestling, drilling, at the end of practice, a heavyweight fell on my neck—Jason Burak landed right on top of me when I was coming up with my head. I had shooting pains going down my arms and I couldn't even finish practice. I couldn't wrestle. I couldn't even grab anything.

"When I went in and they told me about the herniated disc. I had to go get an injection because they said that I opened up just enough space to pinch the nerves. Unfortunately, the injection they gave me wasn't coming around as fast as we thought it would, but Terry still wanted me to make weight. He's a genius. He had me on the plan that, 'You have to make weight even if you're not going to wrestle because your body has to be used to it.'"

Terry Brands remembered, "We left for the U.S. Open and he's not going. We didn't call U.S.A. Wrestling—we didn't tell them—because we never do that until the bitter end. At the weigh-in I'll go find [Bruce] Burnett and say, 'Hey, Tony's not coming.' So, we're there and I wake up the day of weigh-ins and he calls me out of the blue."

"I called Terry," Ramos said, "and I told him, 'My neck's good. I'm ready to go.' He was already out in Vegas, so there I was jumping on a plane."

"Now, we knew it was going to be that way," Terry Brands said of the healing process. "We just didn't know if it was going to be in time or not because sometimes those adjustments don't always set in as fast—but his did."

"After weigh-ins I felt great," Ramos said of his neck. "I was ready to compete. It was comforting knowing that my body could go through that injury and recovery so quickly because, psychologically, I knew that I would always be ready to go mentally and physically."

His first two matches were 11-0 technical superiorities over lesser experienced opponents. In those opening rounds he defeated Britain Longmire of Swisher Shooters and then Allen High School's Cruz Merritt.

In the third round, Tony faced Nick Simmons of the Sunkist Kids. Simmons, who had been all over the freestyle scene since 2009 and was well-respected in the wrestling community, as well as a member of the United States National Team in men's freestyle for nearly a decade, was a top contender in the eyes of many fans. However, it would be the former Hawkeye over the former Michigan State Spartan by a 4-0 decision. Tony advanced.

In the semifinals, Tony had a match-up that the wrestling community was excited about as Joe Colon was the last American wrestler to defeat Tony. For Colon, he was looking for some more of that magic.

During their match, Colon was the first to score off a mishap by Tony. Off a fake, Tony left his right leg open and Colon fired in on a low single and turned his attack into a two-point takedown. Colon then worked his lock into a gut wrench and drove high and hard to his right side and, with Tony defending, ran his feet until he rolled Tony through for another two-points, this time with the exposure. Colon was quickly up 4-0 with only thirty-four seconds gone in the first period.

From Colon's corner, his coach, Doug Schwab, a former Hawkeye and current head coach for Northern Iowa University, could be heard cheering and screaming against his alma mater as he coached. His focus was coaching Colon to defeat Tony's wrists and his head position.

With 1:03 left in the first period, following a reattack from Tony, Colon was placed on the shot clock. Ten seconds later, Tony was in on his high-crotch and, after a twenty-second fight, he earned the takedown on Colon. Immediately after that takedown, Tony hit a trapped arm gut wrench of his own and tied the match, 4-4.

The first period ended that way and, as each wrestler went to his corner, the second period would determine who would make the finals.

Colon came out looking to attack off his underhooks; however, Tony defended accordingly. From Colon's corner, Schwab was instructing him to get to his double underhook position in order to attack Tony's body.

With less than one minute remaining, and Tony leading on criteria, Colon had to score. With Colon's momentum and leverage coming forward hard on Tony, Tony would use that position to his advantage as he hit a sweep single to Colon's left leg, brought it off the mat, and ultimately scored another two points with 00:24 remaining.

The referee stopped the match and brought both wrestlers to their feet for the final 00:16.

Off the whistle, Colon attempted two open double-leg attacks—he did get into Tony's right leg with his second attack. In that sequence, Tony brought his foot back down to the mat and hipped in and defended the single, but Colon now came up into his left side underhook and kept the pressure forward in the final 00:08.

Tony was able to block and defend with his head and right hand as Colon chased him in those final seconds. Colon did not score.

When the match ended, Tony turned first to the crowd and made a motion of wiping his hands clean by raising his right, dropping his left, and then working his hands in an up and down manner as if to clean them off. Then, Tony turned to Schwab over in Colon's corner and made the gesture that he broke his wrestler by cracking an imaginary stick nice and slow as if to accentuate the break.

Schwab responded in that moment on the mat side looking at Tony: "He's a tough guy. Big tough guy."

Tony had his hand raised and now entered the finals. In response to his match, "He caught me off guard on a fake," Ramos said in giving up the early points to Colon. "That's sometimes where I'll get caught—I'll fake and leave my foot there and people drop to it. So I made that adjustment. The only thing he has are underhooks. He wanted to go upper body, you saw it at the end and he wanted to go upper-body with that trip. I knew what was coming. I was ready."

For Tony, he was looking to keep improving in that match and just keep wrestling well. However, he did have an ulterior motive being that his last American loss was to Colon.

"All I can say about that match [at the Midlands]," Ramos said, "is that it's been a year and a half wait and it's not my fault. He's never made it [back to the finals of a tournament]. I was just glad that he was able to win and meet up with me so I can put an end to all the talk. He's been running his mouth non-stop. Schwab's been running his mouth non-stop. That's why I looked at Schwab and told him, 'Broke. It's over. Quiet your mouth. You got lucky one time and caught me.' I've beat everyone so far and I've got one more guy to go. I just wanted to make a point that this is my weight class and it's going to be my weight class until I'm ready to give it up."

It was now onto the finals against Andrew Hochstrasser. Hochstrasser, who either pinned or recorded a technical superiority over each of his first four opponents, which included a fall in 2:40 over Tony's teammate and number-two seed Matt McDonough, was coming in with some momentum of his own.

"He's really solid," Hochstrasser said about his match-up with Tony in the finals. "He really likes the reshot, so when I attack I'm going to make them crisp and plan to beat him."

From Tony's perspective, he also felt that he had a good feel for his opponent. "I know Hochstrasser is a defensive wrestler," Ramos said. "You get to your shots, you got to come up fast, [and] you finish hard. So I'm ready to go. I have to [open him up with] fakes get my angle and move my feet."

When Tony came to the mat, he was dressed in his red HWC singlet and Hochstrasser was in the blue TMWC.

Tony came out with his levels and front head attempts, but Hochstrasser blocked each accordingly. From each position, Tony remained offensive and looked to score via attacks and reattacks. At the forty-seven second mark of the first period, Hochstrasser was hit with his second passivity and was now on the shot clock. As time pressed, Hochstrasser could not work past Tony's head and hand defense; however, he did not feel any panic or become desperate enough to come out of his strategy. Tony was awarded one point at the conclusion of the shot clock and, as the first period ended, Tony was up, 1-0.

As the second period began, Tony continued to work his levels and heavy hands, but Hochstrasser was on the attack and created his own motion as he worked to score. After twenty-six seconds had passed in the period, Tony was immediately placed on the shot clock by the referee.

Regardless of the clock, Tony remained in his ties and elbow passes and levels and shots, and Hochstrasser defended. As the shot clock expired, he conceded the point and now, on criteria, was losing as Hochstrasser was the last to score. For Tony, he now had to find an attack and had 2:05 to make that attack equate to points.

From Hochstrasser's corner, his coach was yelling for him to "Create angles. Get to those angles."

To that point in the match, the defense for each of the wrestlers had been impeccable. However, in the coming seconds, it would be Hochstrasser to be the first to have a strong opportunity to score.

As Tony stepped heavy with his right, and then again while moving forward, Hochstrasser fired a shot in on Tony's right leg, lifted it into the air, and a position battle ensued. Tony, who immediately whizzered and pressed his hip into Hochstrasser's hold, working to break his grip, was able to bring his leg down and step his foot back. Once out, Tony came forward and Hochstrasser snapped him hard to the mat and passed him by, chasing him. In reaction, Tony slid to his left side and then passed Hochstrasser by in the process of the retie. There was now 1:40 left in the period with criteria still in favor of Hochstrasser.

With 1:14 remaining, Tony, for the second time, found himself in on a shot to Hochstrasser's right leg. The first time, in the first period, Tony could not finish. In this, his second time in on the leg, Hochstrasser would again hip down on him while Tony, on all fours and with his head between Hochstrasser's legs, fought for a finish and points. As Tony worked to come out the backdoor, Hochstrasser, as he defended earlier, attacked Tony's ankles and tried to gain position. When Hochstrasser, who was longer, was able to pull his hips in and up, he turned into Tony and, not looking to give up any more than two, Tony conceded the takedown in the tangled position and bellied out. This takedown gave Hochstrasser a 3-1 advantage with just under one minute remaining in the match.

Once on their feet, with 00:49 remaining and Hochstrasser leading 3-1 and scoring his last points off Tony's attack, Tony needed to finish a shot in order to earn criteria and the win. Once back on their feet, Tony immediately pressured forward and positioned himself into a left-handed underhook. Hochstrasser, who was clamping down on that underhook with his right arm, worked to control Tony's wrist with his left hand. However, in the process of blocking, Hochstrasser, feeling the weight of Tony's pressure, paused on his feet and, in the process of not being active, soon found Tony in on a sweep single to his left side. Fortunately, for Hochstrasser, he defended the shot, but Tony fired in another, this time a double-leg with 00:29 remaining.

Off the mat, Tony brought Hochstrasser's right leg up into the air, but Hochstrasser turned his hip away, jumped down to the mat—appearing to concede the takedown—but posted his four supporting points and kept his knees and elbows off the mat without giving up the takedown; they were near the mat's edge. As the clock stopped with 00:19 remaining in the match, Tony received one point for Hochstrasser fleeing the mat and now trailed 3-2 as both wrestlers were brought to their feet and to the center of the mat for a restart.

In the corner, Terry Brands was yelling, "TWO! He posted down." And when only one point was awarded, Terry screamed, "No! No! No! No!" He repeated this on and on and looked over at the referee at the table, walked over and gave a stern look of disapproval at him and the other referees for not awarding a takedown instead. Emphatically, Terry Brands hollered out to Tony, with short time remaining, "Again!"

Off the start, Tony looked to hit his high-crotch and, even though he made it in deep, Hochstrasser kicked out of the threat as 00:12 remained.

Immediately reattacking, Tony shot in another double-leg and, in deep for the third time, found Hochstrasser draped over him and locking around his waist. Tony, with his head underneath and between Hochstrasser's legs, found himself in a post-up position with the clock at 00:06.

Within the next second, Tony lifted high and popped Hochstrasser's legs over him, exposing his back and, with 00:02 left, earned a four-point move and a 6-3 lead. As time expired, Tony hung onto Hochstrasser's legs and earned the coveted national championship plaque—known more widely as the "Stop Sign" as the plaque is shaped in an octagon.

Terry Brands leapt onto the stage with both hands raised in the air, fists clenched with the challenge brick being strangled in one hand, and just screamed enthusiastically.

At the same time that the match ended, the blue challenge cube was thrown in protest to the confirmed four-point move. Tony, however, stood, circled the mat, and, with his arms spread out wide open, enticed the crowd by curling his fingers in and out as if to say, "Give it to me. Let's hear it."

Even though the call went to review, it was not overturned. With the loss of the challenge, Tony earned another point and the match ended in a 7-3 decision for the former Hawkeye.

After the match, Tony was interviewed by U.S.A. Wrestling.

"When we went out of bounds," Ramos explained in regard to the final moments of the match, "there was like fifteen seconds left. I knew I had to get somewhere. I knew he was going to crawl over the top. If I could hook an arm or expose him, that's all I needed.

"I wrestled the whole match. He did one thing, one scramble, but I know how freestyle works—they're going to put you on the clock no matter what—so I had to go out there and wrestle."

When asked by another journalist about the championships Tony referenced his shortcomings in the past at the nationals.

"I never won [a freestyle national championship] when I was in grade school," Ramos shared. "So all you kids that go to Fargo and never brought home a Stop Sign, don't ever stop believing in your dreams. I got one of these when I was in college, but nothing is as important as this one right here."

The next question shifted from being the young gun to being the target. "It's awesome," Ramos said of other wrestlers gearing up to defeat him. "I beat everyone. Who else is there? I said it earlier, this is my spot. When I'm ready to give it up, I'll give it up."

A journalist then asked Tony about the final moments of that match when he was trailing and if he panicked when he saw that time was running out. "You can't panic!" Ramos exclaimed. "If you panic, you can't think. If you panic, you can't wrestle the situation. You can panic after the match. You can swear, whatever you want to say, up and down the wall after the match when you're done. But you can't panic when you're out there."

When it was all said and done, Tony was not only able to win, he was able to do so in grand fashion. Not only did he have to fight through difficult positions, but he had to also fight through his injured neck.

"I think being injured made me a little more focused and attentive to my positions," Ramos said of his awareness on the mat. "I was more tuned in when Terry was screaming, 'Get him off your head! Don't let him hang on your head! Get him off your head!' I was more conscious of keeping guys off my head and clearing ties just so my neck wasn't getting pulled."

Terry Brands agreed with Tony's sentiments about being more focused due to his injury. He also believed that the injury gave him two options—but there was really only one option. "I know that when the chips are against you, that's when you fight the hardest," Terry Brands said. "Or sometimes maybe it's not the hardest, but you still fight—so you persevere."

And that was exactly what Tony did; he persevered. "He got on a plane," Terry Brands explained, "showed up, made weight, and won the U.S. Open. Vintage Tony Ramos."

When the match was over, Tony exited in the typical Iowa way—running back into the tunnel—but that one moment would be much different from others. One child caught Tony's ears and asked him for an autograph. Tony stopped, removed the very singlet that he just wore during his U.S. Open victory, signed it, and give it to that young fan.

"I was a little kid, too, and had people I looked up to," Ramos said of his gift. "Why not give him my singlet? It's gonna mean more to him than for me to bring it home. So I decided to take it off, sign it, and give it to him. Hopefully it made his day and maybe his year."

• • •

Also wrestling in the U.S. Open would be Daniel Dennis. He followed through on his commitment to compete one more time. However, after finishing fourth at 61 kg, losing to 2012 Olympic bronze medalist Coleman Scott for third, after only having had trained for six weeks, he was beginning to hear words of encouragement from some of his peers and coaches about continuing to compete.

In addition to the positive reinforcement that Dennis was receiving, he appeared to have the wrestling bug biting at him again. So much so that he agreed to wrestle at the Spanish Grand Prix in July. This gave him a new focus, and it kept him in the room to continually work on his craft, as well as continue to work with Tony and give him looks and feels that he needed to mature more quickly.

ON MAY 21, TONY WRESTLED IN THE BEAT THE Streets "Salsa in the Square" match-up in New York's Times Square. He wrestled Yowlys Bonne of Cuba, the same Bonne that defeated him at the World Cup Championships just forty days earlier, a match that had Tony winning until a flurry at the end caught him on his back and cost him a win against the time-tested and decorated Cuban.

Now, in the middle of the city that never sleeps with a mat in the middle of Time Square raised on a platform, there could be redemption. Off the mats traffic lights were reflected as they were changing in and out of unison. Rush hour transportation backed up and bumper to bumper car horns blared while people filled the streets and sidewalks that were also covered with exhaust, vendors, and all walks of life from all over the world. Tony was working toward his second
World Championship appearance, which was only twenty-four days away and this match would give him an idea of where he was at.

When the match began, with the lights reflecting off the mat from tail lights and electronic billboards all around mirrored advertisements as people crowded the edges for a look at the excitement, Tony and Bonne would come out banging on each other's head like two lumberjacks with axes hammering down to split wood. The match was stopped nine seconds in and the referee addressed the aggressive nature with each wrestler.

The next forty-five seconds consisted of heavy hands and levels; however, at the 2:10 mark, Bonne hit a duck under to Tony's right side and lifted him high into the air. Tony, who worked to defend the position, was unable to recover from the quick pop of Bonne's hips and bellied out mid-air in order to only concede a two-point takedown and no more.

Bonne then worked out of the parterre position and, with his hands locked in a reverse lift position down by Tony's hips, he hopped to Tony's left, then right, rotated and lifted Tony into the air, and executed a reverse lock throw with a four-point exposure. Tony fought his position until he was brought back to his feet with 1:32 remaining in the first period; he trailed, 6-0.

The match resumed and another ten seconds would pass before Tony was in on a shot of his own. He attacked Bonne's right leg, pulled him up and into the center of the mat; he had Bonne's foot resting on his right shoulder as the Cuban balanced on his left foot and fought Tony's hands to keep distance from a trip and a takedown. Tony worked for about the next twenty-seven seconds to return him to the mat; however, he was unable to earn a takedown or pushout, and the referee broke the position and reset the wrestlers back on their feet with 00:45 remaining in the first period.

Handing fighting, level changes, and an inside fight for position rounded out the first period; however, as time expired, Bonne had Tony caught in a fireman's carry and exposed his back as he took him over. Fortunately, for Tony, no points were awarded, and the period ended with him trailing the Cuban, 6-0.

Tony headed to his corner and Terry Brands instructed him accordingly. The interaction would be brief as Tony was motioned back to the mat's center. Bonne, however, spent an extended period in his corner as Tony anxiously awaited the restart.

As the second period began, Tony was pushing a high tempo while Bonne was casually moving on the mat—Tony knew that it was his responsibility to force the action. He did. In the first 1:30 of the period, he fired off three shots to Bonne's zero. At the 1:45 mark, Bonne was warned to be more active; however, his demeanor and ability to move forward never changed. When Tony took his fourth shot of the period with 1:20 remaining, he got to Bonne's right leg and lifted it off the mat.

Bonne, with a right-hand overhook and a left-hand underhook, tried to throw Tony over in defense. Both wrestlers ended up on the mat, with neither relinquishing position, but no points were awarded either way. Bonne stayed elongated in the splits and Tony, still stubbornly on the right leg, lifted Bonne's leg high and worked for a trip—Tony had to settle for the pushout. The score was now 6-1 and there was 00:52 remaining.

Bonne walked back to the center of the mat seemingly exhausted. When the whistle blew, he was soon signaled for passivity, but the call was white paddled—no score confirmed so no points were awarded—and then, in the process, Tony was again in deep on a double-leg and quickly changed to a single on Bonne's right leg. As Tony pressured up, Bonne would once again underhook and grab Tony by the chin, flip him over for a four-point exposure, and now have a nine-point lead, 10-1, as Tony came to his feet with the leg and tried to pop his hips for a takedown—Bonne defended. The position did not change and, as Tony worked to bring Bonne's leg to the outside, both wrestlers seemingly paused as they fought for their position. Bonne, now for a third time, threw Tony over with the same counter throw. Those four points ended the match with a 14-1 technical superiority win for Bonne.

The match did not end with the result that either Tony or Terry Brands was looking for, but it was time to head back to the room and tweak his positions and situational wrestling, as well as hone his strengths. The World Team Trials were next and there were some areas to cement prior to the competition.

GOING INTO HIS SECOND WORLD TEAM TRIALS, and coming off his U.S. Open win, Tony had the opportunity to sit back and watch the competition in the mini-tournament as he, the reigning World Team representative for the United States, only had to wrestle in the finals through a best-of-three series.

"It didn't matter to me who I would face in the finals," Ramos said. "The weight was mine and no one was going to change that."

As fate would have it, Tony watched Joe Colon win the mini tournament as he went on an impressive run defeating Matt McDonough and Angel Escobedo. Colon, after his loss to Tony in the previous year's WTT, had been expressing his desire to defeat him now and take over the 57 kg weight class. For Colon, an opportunity to make the World Team and knock off Tony a second time would be on the line. For Tony, an opportunity to put an end to all of the talking for good, was enough of a motivator.

In the finals, though, once it came to the best of three series, it was all Tony Ramos. In the first match, Tony defeated his nemesis with a 6-0 shutout. He led 4-0 with time expiring in the match when Colon took a shot only to have Tony reattack the position and score a final takedown with no time remaining on the clock. After, Tony came to his feet and again made the motion to the crowd of wiping his hands clean of Colon with an aggressive and exaggerated up and down wiping of his hands.

There were some cheers and there were some boos in response to Tony's actions. After the match, Tony went to Colon's corner and shook Doug Schwab's hand before exiting the mat with a 1-0 lead in the championship series.

When it came time for the second match, it was again all Tony Ramos. This time it was a 3-1 decision over Colon and that would give Tony a second opportunity to represent the United States on the World Team.

"I'm training to beat the best guys in the world," Ramos said in an interview after his match. "I'm not training to beat Colon, to beat Escobedo, McDonough, Graff, whoever's there in the finals. So I think that's what's going to separate me this year from what I was doing last year just coming off an NCAA tournament and kind of jumping right into this."

Tony also addressed a question pertaining to his confidence, or overconfidence. "People might call it cocky," Ramos responded, "but I'm confident in myself so I don't care what they say. I'm going to be in Vegas, I'm going for a medal, and if they don't want to cheer for me, I don't care."

• • •

At the 61 kg weight class, Daniel Dennis placed second to now three-time World Team member Reece Humphrey. One month later, Dennis traveled to Spain and claimed the Spanish Grand Prix gold medal at 61 kg; this was his first international medal since joining the National Team. Conversely, it appeared as if Dennis, who was originally only coming back for one match and to work in the room with Tony and Metcalf, was executing a more long-term plan, though nothing was, at least to Tony, verbalized by anyone. Tony, thinking something might be up with Dennis coming back and maybe dropping to 57 kg, no longer trained with Dennis from the Spanish Grand Prix forward.

"I told Terry that I wasn't going to bring Dennis along as my partner for the World Championships," Ramos said of a possible situation with both former Hawkeyes at 57 kg.

When word reached Tom Brands in regard to Tony's decision to not take Dennis as his partner, Defilippis commented that, "Tom made Tony take Dennis. He said it had to do with team spirit." Either way, Dennis traveled with the club; however, he only worked with Metcalf. Tony kept his distance from Dennis, even though nothing had been formally communicated.

THE 2015 WORLD CHAMPIONSHIPS WERE IN LAS

Vegas, and, when the draws were released in the bracket of 44 competitors at the 57 kg weight class, the number-seventeen ranked wrestler in the world, Tony Ramos, saw his draw and knew that, eventually, he would have to face Rahimi if he was going to make the semifinals. In that, Tony first had to defeat two opponents before he could even think about the Iranian who had bested him the last two times that they had wrestled. But Tony was, as he always was, confident.

"You got to control your destiny," Ramos said of his draw. "If I win this, I'm going to go through everyone, I'm going to beat everyone. So, [I] got to control what [I] can control and not leave it up to someone else."

Having the World Championships in America provided Tony with some comfort; however, he sought further comfort in asking both of his coaches, Tom and Terry Brands, to corner him throughout the tournament.

"Tom is just as big of a role as Terry," Ramos stated in response to where each of the coaches fit into his comfort level. "He's not always in my corner, but in the room he's talking to me, telling me things, and we're working on things—he runs some of our practices. I told Tom and Terry that I wanted them both in my corner for the World Championships—and they both were. You can't have two coaches in the corner in freestyle, but at the break two coaches can come out. So Terry is the one doing the talking and Tom comes up with him and kind of towels me off and is just like, 'Hey, watch this,' or, 'Do this,' during the break. I think it's comforting to see both of them in my corner—familiar faces and two guys who I know have my back and my best interests. Each one is just as important as the other."

In his first match at the championships, Tony faced Colombia's Wber Eucli Cuero Munoz; Tony handled Munoz with ease and won a 10-1 technical superiority.

With his win and advancement to the Round of 32, Tony then faced Makhmudjon Shavkatov of Uzbekistan. Although he did not have as much ease in winning the bout, he claimed a 3-3 decision victory and headed into the Round of 16. Tony would now square off against Hassan Sab Rahimi of Iran—the number-four ranked wrestler in the world and the 2013 World Champion.

Tony, who had faced Rahimi at the World Cup in 2014, and lost a 6-5 decision, now had an opportunity, on the grandest of wrestling stages and on American soil, to return the favor. Unfortunately, in a tight quarterfinal match-up with time running out and the score tied 1-1, and with Tony having criteria, Tony would lose 3-1.

"I was trying to win the match," Ramos would say of having Rahimi beat on criteria and also having him on the shot clock, and then losing in the final seconds trying to hit a tip. "I was trying to end it there. I was in good position. I was in one of those times where you got to be smart. I just slipped, I slipped off him—we're sweaty, we're wet—and it stings. It stings a lot. It's not a good feeling."

In the repechage, Tony faced Belarus' Asadulla Lachinau who had lost to Rahimi in a 7-0 decision prior to Rahimi defeating Tony.

In that repechage match, and the opportunity to wrestle back for a bronze, Tony lost a 7-1 decision. Ten minutes later, Tony addressed the media regarding his exit from the World Championships, and he did the interview without hesitation—as he had always done.

"It's part of the job," Ramos said of answering the media's questions after a heartbreaking loss. "You know, this is a job, this is [my] profession. It really pisses me off when the announcers and people say 'amateur wrestling'—this isn't amateur, this is professional. You look at the NFL, you look at [the] NHL, NBA, after those guys lose, have heartbreaking losses—Super Bowls, NBA titles—where are they right after that? They're at the podium, they're answering their questions, they're doing their job, and this is part of my job."

In regard to his repechage match, he was chasing early and was eventually just looking to find ways to score.

"I was trying to get whatever I could," Ramos said of trying to score points off any takedown in those final moments of the match. "Singles. High-crotches. He wrestles a really European style where he's lazy, hands down—it's hard to get under those guys, but [I have] to find ways.

"[I learned that I have to] score points and you're going to win. Wrestle tough every match. Nothing different. Nothing that [I] already don't know. When guys come here it's a different ballgame. It doesn't matter what happened throughout the year; this is the World Championships.

"[I would rate my performance here at the World Championships as] maybe a five or a six. I mean, I didn't get what I wanted, but I won a few matches. I got back on that backside, I battled hard with the guy I think is going to win the tournament, so I got to get over that hump and win that match. I got to wrestle like I did those first three matches: smart, great position, and getting to my offense. That second match I was out of position a lot; I let him get to my legs a lot—just doing dumb things that I wasn't doing earlier in the day. So, I just got to wrestle great throughout the whole tournament."

The loss stuck with and stung Tony; however, it did expose aspects of his wrestling that he could improve upon, and would need to improve upon in order to give himself the best opportunity to chase his dreams of being an Olympic champion. When he looked at his loss, and took the emotion out of it, it had value.

"It's just going to show me where I need to get better," Ramos answered regarding what he had learned. "That last match really exposed when I fake I let guys get in on me a lot, so I've got to get better at it. Blocking that re-shot, and re-shooting back on them. When I fake I can't be on my heels, I've got to be on my toes. It's something we've been working on a lot since last year when I've been doing it; that's how I lost to Mongolia. But I'm old and it's really hard to break a bad habit, so I really got to get over that."

• • •

While Tony was training for the World Club Cup Championships, his former training partner and Hawkeye Wrestling Club teammate, Daniel Dennis, wrestled in the Bill Farrell Memorial International—and he did so at the 57 kg weight class.

This was the first time Dennis wrestled at 57 kg and he placed third behind Tyler Graff, the champion, and Zachary Sanders. With this shift from 61 kg to 57 kg, there began a small murmur of voices in the wrestling room and, ultimately, within the wrestling community in regard to what his presence may mean to the weight class.

Additionally, it opened up Tony's eyes to the possibility of a situation with him and Dennis wrestling at the same weight class. Tony was still frustrated because "Even though all of this appeared to be going on, Tom was not communicating to me that Dennis would be wrestling at 57 kg for the Trials. But, at that point, I was only working with Thomas Gilman and Cory Clark. I stopped drilling with Dennis long before because things felt off. [Clark and Gilman] were great partners and I was getting good feels and looks from them, so I didn't think my training was suffering other than not getting all of the attention as the number-one guy in the room."

"A bit before the world championships," Terry Brands explained, "that was when they stopped working out together. I wouldn't have wrestled Dennis either—but that's me. But the fact that he's there, you're aware, you see, you have an extensive time frame, a full year where you're watching this guy. The pressure should not be a negative thing for veterans. For me, it could only benefit him.

"When I was training Tony, I wasn't like, *I'm going to beat Dennis.* But [Dennis] got kind of distant with me [that] last year because he misinterpreted what I was saying to him after the U.S. Open. I said, 'You are on a different path because of where you're at with your physical shape; you have to build your shape more—it was a true statement. It was actually a healthy thing to say because it showed I cared about his development.

"And then Dennis said the same thing that Ramos said, he said that 'Terry is coaching Tony to beat me.' And I heard about it and I grabbed Dennis—I mean I grabbed him—'Hey, what's this? You said that I'm training Tony to beat you? I'm training Tony to get on the Olympic team. You really think I'm training Tony to beat you?' Then he said, 'No, no— it was a misunderstanding.' I was so hot. I said, 'Okay, if it's a misunderstanding then we're going to talk about it after practice.'

"We went our separate ways and then that night I called him and we hashed it out. He said, 'Well, you know, I watched you doing this…' I go, 'Dennis, your face doesn't even cross my mind when I talk to Tony. What crosses my mind is if Tony's going to open up and attack. I'm coaching Tony Ramos to be the best guy in the world, and if he beats you because of that then I have no hard feelings at all and I don't really care what you feel about me.' So, this wasn't something that was just unique to Tony, but I think Daniel dealt with it at a way more stable rate.

"[As for a promise about cornering Tony,] according to Tony, that is what Tom told him. That was not something [Tom] told me about or that I knew about. But everyone knew Dennis was dropping [to 57]—how can you not know? How can you not know?"

AT THE WORLD CUP CLUB CHAMPIONSHIPS IN Tehran, Iran, Tony earned earn a 3-1 record as the Titan Mercury Wrestling Club would, again, take the silver losing to Iran's powerhouse club, Bimeh-Razi, in the gold medal match by a 7-1 score.

Tony won his first three matches: a 6-4 decision over Khashalov Afhgan, a Cadet World silver medalist and Cadet European Champion, from Azerbaijan ATA Spor in the opening dual of pool competition; a 10-0 technical superiority over Brazil CBW's Uziel Correa Junior; and a 6-6 criteria decision over future 2016 Olympian Garnik Mnatsakanyan of Armenia Tashir. In the finals, Tony dropped a 4-1 decision to 2015 World Champion Vladimir Khinchigashvili of Iran.

• • •

Also wrestling for Titan Mercury at the Club Cup Championships was Daniel Dennis. Dennis, who was wrestling at 61 kg for the tournament, and compiled a 2-2 record. Along the way, Dennis was preparing to compete in the U.S. Senior National Championships at 57 kg in less than one month. The Hawkeye Wrestling Club was now, seemingly, cornering the field at 57 kg, and people were not only noticing, but they were talking.

• • •

However, around the time Tony had chosen not to drill with Dennis anymore, he had also communicated with his wife, Megan, about how uncomfortable he was with the training situation he now found himself in. Tony even went as far as discussing leaving Iowa and going to train elsewhere. Megan, in response, was more practical about their situation in regard to stability.

"I remember he mentioned [leaving Iowa and training somewhere else] in November prior to the trials and then seriously again in the beginning of January," Megan said. "He told me we needed to leave and that he didn't want to train [in Iowa] anymore. I already was committed to working February [through] May for hours I was already paid for, and I refused to move anywhere with no income and a baby and without a solid lead on where to go."

But Megan also addressed Tony's training concerns in her discussion with him, but she may not have recognize all of his frustrations at the same time. "I told him Tom and Terry are the best people he could be training with and to trust them," Megan reasoned in regard to staying in Iowa. "I was working seventy-plus hours and if I wasn't working or sleeping, I was spending time with AJ. [Being so busy,] I didn't realize how much he was bothered by the situation."

After speaking with Megan, Tony would conceal his feelings and agree to stay in Iowa City and train through the Olympic Trials. Up next on his schedule was the Yarygin—a tournament that worked with or worked over a wrestler's mentality on being uncomfortable. The location, in conjunction with a number of other factors, forced one to acclimate to his surroundings if he was going to be successful, or defeat him for being distracted and not focusing on task that was right in front of him. Tony would have much to work through in Krasnoyarsk.

CHAPTER 62
THE ELEPHANT IN THE ROOM

"At least being treated with some professionalism and honesty and respect would have given me the option to leave and go train somewhere else or stay. He gave no options because he lied—and maybe that's the way he wanted it."

• *Tony Ramos*

AS TONY HEADED INTO THE FINAL STRETCH OF competitions and workouts before the Unites States Olympic Trials, just five months away, he, as well as Daniel Dennis and Terry Brands, were asked in a FloWrestling interview, conducted by FLO's premium producer and wrestling fanatic, Mark Bader, to weigh in on the dynamics of the Hawkeye Wrestling Club wrestling room as both Tony and Dennis trained in the same room, with the same coaches, for the same right to represent the United States of America in the 2016 Olympic Games in Rio de Janeiro—and at the same weight class. In the end, only one wrestler would be able to be represent his country, and he would have to earn it in Iowa and under the roof of Carver-Hawkeye Arena, an arena where both had created a number of memories and had been embraced and loved by the Iowa faithful.

On the surface, each wrestler answered modestly and with due respect to his competitor and friend; however, to Tony, this issue of Dennis being in the same room and being coached by the same coaches with nothing being openly communicated had still been weighing on him greatly.

ON JANUARY 27, 2016, WHILE THE U.S. TOOK SOME wrestlers to Krasnoyarsk, Russia, to compete in the Ivan Yarygin Grand Prix, Bader's interview expressed each wrestler's public stance on the situation in the Hawkeye Wrestling Club regarding two top-tier athletes at the same weight, for the same club, competing for the same spot on the United States Olympic Wrestling Team.

The Tony Ramos interview was dubbed: "Elephant in the Room." In this short interview, Bader asked Tony his position on the dynamic of both he and Dennis training in the same club and, more intimately, in the same room.

In response, Tony alluded to the notion that he had thought about the situation, but that Bader's question, a tough question and a good question, was "a loaded question no matter how you ask," Ramos said. "I think me and Dennis do a good job of trying not to make it awkward or uncomfortable. But, at the same time, you know, it is a big elephant in the room. It's going to be an awkward situation come [the] Olympic Trials when we do wrestle. Who's going to be in whose corner? Who's going to coach who? Things like that are questions that have been running through both our heads, but that haven't really been discussed much with anyone. So, those are things like that you think about, but at the same time you can't let be that big of a distraction because you got to focus on yourself and be selfish sometimes."

In the Daniel Dennis interview, the title takes on a different tone and reads: "From the Trailer to the Trials." In that segment, Bader touches upon what Dennis had gone through when he walked away and why and how he returned. When Bader asked a similar question to Dennis about the club and room dynamic, Dennis approached the relationship aspect first.

"My relationship with Tony," Dennis paused, "—he took over the weight class when I graduated, obviously. He did a great job. We know each other well. We've known each other well. He's a kid that I went out to Colorado Springs to be his training partner. We have a long history, a long past—and it's positive. We're in the same room now and I'm focused—we're at different ages and different points—where I'm focused on what I think is going to help me best and he's focused on what he thinks is going to help him best. So, we have the same goal. We're on maybe a little bit different tracks, pretty parallel, I think, but a little different tracks to get there, but it's good—it's a healthy room. There's no spite. So, it's a good environment to be in."

In each of those video interviews, there was no comment or look or interpretation that showed any notion of malice or resentment for the other's presence. In fact, each addressed his greatest concern with the ultimate goal of focusing on the self and being prepared as an individual when it was time to wrestle.

When Bader spoke with Terry Brands, his ideas conceptualized a culmination of what each wrestler had referred to; however, he did make a statement in regard to who may corner each wrestler—though it was mere speculation and nothing more by Iowa's associate head coach as there had been no indication of any formal conversations.

"The situation with Dan Dennis and Tony Ramos in our room is a good situation for us—selfishly, as a program," Terry Brands said. "From their perspective, I think that they know that they are going to collide or there is a possibility of it. You never know, but there's a possibility of it and it does heighten their training."

As Bader probed further into the idea of there being a possible issue in regard to both wrestlers training side-by-side, Terry noted that he did not "think there's an elephant in the room as maybe some people think. I think it's a healthy thing. And it's certainly a healthy thing if both of them are approaching it the right way. If one is like, 'Well, what the heck, you know—whatever,' then there is going to be that nag in the back of your mind that's negative, and that's dangerous—that's what you don't want. You want to eliminate that. You want to be feeling really, really good that I can walk into the room and I can see what my opponent is doing every day—I'm doing more; if it's me. It'd be like me training in the same room with [Alireza] Dabir or [Kendall] Cross or whatever, you know? It would be like that. It would be a situation where as hard as I work, I would even visualize where they're at in their workouts when they're not there—now I'm seeing it. So maybe it's even more of an advantage for me."

In this, Terry took the position of such a dynamic being an advantage to both Tony and Dennis as he looked at how he might take the situation or use the situation if he were in that position.

As Bader inquired about the coaching dynamic if the wrestlers did end up having to wrestle the other, Terry was very candid in his interpretation of a situation that had not yet been discussed.

"I think that there's an understanding there," Terry said. "We haven't talked about it. But, from my perspective as a coach, both guys will be taken care of and, more than likely, I will be in Tony Ramos' corner. I've been with him and, when Daniel left, it kind of opened up my relationship with Tony a little bit more. It doesn't mean that I don't have a relationship with Daniel or I have a better relationship with Tony—I wouldn't say that's the case. What I would say is that, as a program, and maybe the individual coach who knows how to slap him on the rear end and push him out on the mat—Tom would be the guy that handles Daniel and I would be the guy that handles Tony. And that's without talking to anybody about it; that's just the feel."

And, in those feelings, publicly, all looked well and healthy with the club. Both wrestlers were focused and careful in what they said and all looked as if the Iowa way was strong and moving forward in a direction of dominating the 57 kg field.

HOWEVER, ACCORDING TO TONY, A PHONE conversation with his brother Frank did take place with coach Tom Brands that positioned both Tom and Terry Brands in Tony's corner throughout the Trials—including if a possible match-up between Tony and Dennis occurred.

According to Tony and Frank, there were two specific conversations that Frank and Tom Brands had regarding the issue with Dennis at 57 kg—Terry Brands was not present for either conversation.

Frank claimed that the first conversation was over the phone after Tom Brands found out Tony did not want him coaching in his corner anymore. The second conversation happened at a hotel in Evanston, Illinois, during the Midlands Championships.

"Once we were getting word that Dennis was dropping [to 57 kg]," Defilippis said, "the first phone call I made was to Terry Brands."

According to Frank, "Terry's response was, 'You don't even have to have this call, you know where I'm at. But I see where you're at.' And I told him that if Tom is going to be coaching Dennis, then I don't want him coaching Tony and neither does [Tony]. And that's what stemmed the call from Tom."

When Frank picked up Tom Brand's phone call, Tom, according to Frank said that "Tom heard of Tony's dislike for the situation, and Tom said it came to him through the biggest mouth on the team. He was upset that Tony didn't want him coaching him. But, over and over, he reiterated that, 'Tony is my guy and I have his back.' I said I didn't want to have any of these issues from here on out—I want it out of the way now."

From Tom Brands' perspective, "I remember talking to Frankie, and he went cold on me for a while—so I knew that he knew. He's like, 'My dad's worried. Where is this coming from?' And I'm like why are we playing these games? I [said], 'What do you mean where is this coming from?'" After that statement, Brands gave no further insight to the remainder of the conversation with Frank.

As for Frank, he commented on how Tom Brands had said very little to him. "All he said to me," Frank recalled, "was that Tony should not be worrying about this—Tony is his guy. That was when I told Tom that hearing about this should have come from him."

When asked to provide further depth and details on that specific conversation with Frank, Tom Brands paused and responded with, "Here's the thing: every one of our guys, we take care of them to the best of their ability—every one of them. To the best of THEIR ability, not mine. And... there was never a question of my loyalty—never. And sometimes in this sport when things get crowded, the best case scenario happens. That's the way it went."

No further elaboration to the conversation was provided.

Frank and Tony were not happy with how the conversation ended; however, they took Tom Brands at what they say he communicated to them as his word. As for Tony, he said, "All I wanted was clarity. I had no reason not to believe him. He knew that I was not happy with the situation and he made it clear to me and Frank that he would corner me. After he said that, I believed all would be okay."

In addition to his training for the Olympic Trials, Tony was beginning to think about his life after competing more seriously now that he had a family to support, and he was now more aware in regard to how his decisions impacted his family. Coming into 2016, Tony started setting his sights on a future in coaching for when his competition days ended. And, as the days passed by, Tony felt he was not going to be hired on staff at Iowa, and he may be missing opportunities to coach elsewhere.

"Tony told me," Defilippis said, "that he didn't want to be stuck after the Trials and all of the jobs were taken. He doesn't want to have that problem—he wants to get out of [Iowa] soon. Tony told me, 'They're never going to put us on staff—no one here is getting on staff.'"

Therefore, Tony had some worries about how he was going to provide for his family and where he would be as he moved forward.

Additionally, although he was the same Tony Ramos on the surface, he was dealing with a number of issues internally that were simply eating away at him. The conversations about the cornering issues calmed him some, but he was still uneasy with the situation.

In regard to what Frank was looking for, it was simple: honesty. "I would rather Tom sat me down," he explained, "and said, 'Listen, this is what's best for the team, and that is my responsibility. My responsibility is not to Tony Ramos, my responsibility is to the University of Iowa wrestling team.' I could've lived with that. Don't tell me a lie. Don't feed me a line. We sat together in a hotel room in Evanston and he looked into my eyes and said, 'I will put my money and my loyalty where my mouth is. There is no one I want more on that Olympic team more than Tony Ramos. And, if that match is to ever happen, I will be in Tony's corner, toweling him down while Terry takes the lead—just like I am at the World Championships.'"

But, to Tony, this was where he felt many of the problems began to take shape. "This is where all of the controversy started," Ramos said. "Dennis came back in 2015 and it was supposed to be a one-year thing where he came back to wrestle 61 [kg] and to help me and Metcalf train and get better because he was a great partner for us. It was never the plan of him going down to 57 [kg] in 2016 and stay—even in some of his articles and interviews he states that."

Dennis did speak publically about how and why he came back to Iowa. "It's always in the back of your mind," Dennis said of competing. "I didn't plan on coming back to competing. I didn't have any urge to continue competing but, at the same time, I'm always looking and watching what's going on in the wrestling world. And consciously or subconsciously you're going to be comparing yourself and how do you match up with this guy, how do I match up with this guy, and it's something that is in you and I don't think it's ever going to go away. So, there's always going to be that in the back of my head, but I didn't picture myself coming back to wrestle.

"And I didn't plan on it at all," Dennis reiterated, "I got talked into it. And there was one morning [Ryan] Morningstar called me and we were talking and he started nagging at me again and Royce [Alger] had been on me for a while, and it was just a lot and it was like all right screw you guys, just shut up, I'll wrestle at one thing and that was the [U.S.] Open and one thing led to another and that led to another and then you're traveling to Russia, Siberia, cold as hell—I didn't plan on this two years ago."

As for what prompted the drop, Tony felt that Dennis "Had a good run at the World Team Trials—he takes second and I'm starting to realize now that [Dennis dropping to 57 kg] might happen. So, I tell Terry, 'Hey, I'm not taking Dennis this year as my training partner because I don't want to give him any advantages of feeling me out going forward toward an Olympic year.' And Terry said he totally understands and that we'd figure something else out, and Metcalf would be with Dennis."

From what Tony and Terry Brands had discussed, Terry followed through on his word and, through the training of the 2015 World Championships, Tony did not have Dennis as his training partner; Metcalf did. In fact, at that time, Dennis was making a decision to move out to Virginia Tech in Blacksburg, Virginia, to either just coach or train and coach with former Hawkeye Mike Zadick and Derek St. John.

Terry Brands' perspective saw the situation as where was the best training situation for Daniel Dennis from Dennis' perspective.

"He was going to come back and wrestle for Titan Mercury," Terry Brands said. "Royce [Alger] talked him back into it—Royce takes full credit for that—and he was going to wrestle 61 [kg] and he was going to be the guy. He came back, he did that, he qualified for the Trials in 2015—I think he was fourth—so he got that bid and he lost in the finals of the Trials to Reece Humphrey. So he's done, and now people are saying, 'You're right there. You can do this. You're the guy.' So he's going to go down [to 57 kg]. You know he's going down—I knew he's going down.

"So, it was about him finding a place to train. Well, Virginia Tech called and he was going to go there and Tom intervened. He was like, 'That's crazy, man; you're a Hawkeye. You've been here your whole life—why would you leave? Why would you go there to train? If you're going to compete, come here and compete.' And so, after weeks, or a month, he came to the conclusion, after visiting there and seeing how they actual are, and it wasn't as green as he thought, yeah, this is where [he's] comfortable—[he] can win here. So, he took our offer."

When Dennis did take the offer from the club, Tony found out about it while at lunch. "We were having lunch with an old roommate and HWC member," Megan said, "and he told us at lunch that Dennis was coming back to Iowa City to train—that he had been set to head out to Virginia Tech but Tom made him a monetary offer he couldn't refuse. I was pretty mad at that point because it took a lot of negotiating with Tom to get a reasonable salary for Tony and the amount that Dennis was getting was [allegedly] more than Tony's salary. Tony was more quiet about it, but I could tell it upset him."

Frank had his own opinion on what had happened. "When [Dennis] left," Defilippis said, "he was gone. He was going to coach and be on Virginia Tech's staff. But Tom couldn't bear losing St. John, Zadick, and Dennis all to Virginia Tech."

From Tony's point of view, "[Dennis] was headed out to Virginia Tech and was going with Zadick and St. John—he was gone. Tom Brands hears he's gone and bends over backwards to [keep] Dennis in the Hawkeye Wrestling Club [and] stay in Iowa City because he can't lose three Hawkeyes to Virginia Tech."

From where Tom Brands stood, "[We have] a continuing relationship [with our wrestlers]. I don't know the conversation [with Dennis about staying at the club and dropping to 57 kg], even if there was a specific one. I know there are six weight classes in an Olympic year and [Dennis is] not a 65-kilo guy—he's a 57-kilo guy."

However, for Tony, "All I heard was that Dennis was staying and he wasn't going to Virginia Tech anymore," Ramos said. "He was going to stay and train for the Olympic Trials. It wasn't until after that I started hearing more to the story from people who were on the other side or who were very close to the other side. They told me about how when Dennis was on his way out and Tom had called him and asked him what he was getting offered [at Virginia Tech] and [allegedly] said, 'Please stay.'"

Therefore, once Tony started hearing more and more from others in regard to Tom Brands and Dennis, the words and promises that Tony believed that Tom Brands gave him, began to unravel in his mind and slowly started affecting his relationship with Tom Brands and impacting his wrestling.

But, Tom Brands said the situation in regard to Dennis choosing to stay in Iowa did not happen the way Tony had heard. "What is Tony's best chance of making that team?" Tom Brands asked. "Go where you need to go. I didn't say, 'Stay here'—I never told [Tony] that. Go where you need to go—I hope it's here. Same with Dennis. Go where you need to go—[Dennis] comes here."

Unfortunately, for Tony, when he physically distanced himself from where he felt the issue was, in Iowa City, the issue still followed him all the way to the Golden Grand Prix Ivan Yarygin. It was there, in Russia, where Tony had a conversation with another HWC member, Brent Metcalf, which, once again, ignited an issue that Tony thought was put to bed.

"Me and Metcalf were talking at the Yarygin," Ramos said, "and Metcalf said, 'Well, how do you feel about [Dennis going 57 kg]?' I said, 'How would you feel if they brought in Jordan Oliver to train right next to you and coached him to beat you? How would you feel?'"

After that conversation with Metcalf, word quickly reached Tom Brands about Tony's further unhappiness. "Me and Tom did have private conversations," Ramos said. "It was right after the Yarygin tournament, Tom had heard that there had been some rumblings on my end from one of the athletes and he approached me and asked if he needed to walk on egg shells around me."

"He was on a stationary bike in the room," Tom Brands said of the conversation. "I went up to him and hid my face, laughing at him, looked at him, hid my face—the whole thing was silly—and then he said, 'What's going on here?' So I walked up behind him on the aerodyne and starting talking to him. I said, 'What's going on here? This ain't you. You've been a straight-shooter your whole life.'"

At that, Tony said, "'What are you talking about?' to where [Tom] said, 'Well, I heard some things.' So I said, 'Okay, what'd you hear? Let's talk about it.'—I've always been straight forward with Tom and when I'm not happy, we talk about it. He said, 'I heard you're not happy with the situation with Dennis.' And I told him straight out: 'Tom, I like being your guy and I've been the guy for two years. I don't think it was fair you guys did this to me in an Olympic year bringing in what's going to be the guy I'm going to have to wrestle in the finals.'"

To Tony, he felt there was only one other wrestler in the country that could challenge him for the Olympic spot. "I knew that I would face Dennis in the finals," Ramos said. "To me, he was the next best guy at the weight that I would have to compete against. And I am fine with that, just not training in the same room by the same coaches who have promised to train me and focus on me—he left. True, he is a Hawk, but he left—I never left."

In response to Tony's frustrations, Tony commented on how Tom Brands told him that "It would be a good thing [to have Dennis in the room] because I could see what he's doing and this and that. But when I am training, I am not watching [Dennis], I am focusing on me. But, all I said was, 'Tom, I'm just letting you know how I feel about it.' When I said that, Tom proceeded to tell me, 'You know who we want on that team. You're our guy. We want you on the team. We have your back one hundred percent and I will be in your corner just like the World Championships. Terry will coach you and I'll come out and towel you off and Dennis will be on his own—I don't know what he's going to do.'"

Due to the relationship that Tony and Tom Brands had over the past seven years, Tony revealed, "Of course I believed him. I was frustrated, but if that's what he told me. Why shouldn't I believe him?"

When the conversation was over, Tom Brands knew how Tony felt in regard to the Dennis situation. "He let me know he wasn't happy," Tom Brands said. As for a resolution, "There's no resolution," Tom Brands stated. "We're in the middle of it."

In that, Tony would have to handle the situation as best he could both physically and emotionally. Tom Brands and Terry Brands would also have to continue to work with the situation knowing Tony's uncomfortableness, but also staying true to Dennis as a member of the club who had Olympic dreams of his own.

Additionally, while the conversation with Tom Brands was happening, Terry Brands had looked over and seen the interaction. After a while, according to Tony, when Tony and Tom were done speaking, Terry approached Tony.

"Terry came up to me," Ramos remembered, "and he said, 'Hey, I just talked to Tom and he said you're uncomfortable and don't feel good about [Dennis] being here. You know, I told Tom not to bring him back from day one. I told him that 'Dennis was out of here, he's leaving—why are you going to do this? Me and you were not comfortable when Gable wanted to bring back guys to our weight class, at least Gable talked to us about it.' Since Terry has always had my back, and I felt really good about Terry being there and advocating for me, I again had no reason not to trust Tom. I knew Terry supported me, and I believed Tom's words."

However, even though Tony had Terry Brands in his corner, he was very clear about wanting to always be the guy for Tom Brands as well. This may have played a bit on Tony's emotions and mental state as well over the course of the next few months. And, although he had Terry Brands training him and was secure in that, he was missing out on also receiving what he had always had and taken comfort and confidence in, Tom Brands' attention and coaching.

As the days wore on, the situation with Tom Brands became more awkward for Tony and he felt the same was also true for Dennis. "It started to get very weird and uncomfortable," Ramos said. "[Dennis and I] would walk by each other and not say a word—just look [at each other], and things like that."

There were no split practices where Tony or Dennis had both Tom and Terry Brands coaching him, and there was no dual coaching—the room and the coaches were divided in regard to who they were working with. However, even though the coaches were working with certain individuals, the club's overall goal of making everyone better each day and giving each wrestler an opportunity to be an Olympian was still intact.

"I had Terry in my corner," Ramos said. "And he was really the only one I felt was truly in my corner. Duroe had coached me before with Terry and Tom, but Duroe started working with Dennis. Then they threw Morningstar in my corner to work with Terry, but Morningstar is one of the people that recruited Dennis back here calling him non-stop begging him to come back with Royce Alger. So why Morningstar and not Duroe? Or, better yet, why not Tom like he promised? It's little things like this as the Trials got closer that I started to learn more about how this all happened. And this is not what I should have to be dealing with.

"I literally said this to [Tom] when we had our talk," Ramos confessed. "I told him that 'You talk a lot about eliminating distractions so you can be free and this and that, [but] you put the biggest distraction in the room training next to me every day.'"

And even if there were distractions for Dennis, Tony did not see them. But Tony felt distracted when he went into the room to workout.

"The thing that bothered me the most about it," Ramos said, "and this is where it's hard I think for the average fan who is still stuck in the mindset that we're amateurs—we're professional athletes. This is our job. This is our life. This isn't just something you play around with. I would have probably taken this a lot better had Tom treated me like a professional and said, 'Hey, we're gonna bring in Dennis at the same weight—how do you feel about it?' From there, we could have talked about it and then he should've said, 'Well, I don't care how you feel about it. This is what we are doing—end of conversation.' At least being treated with some professionalism and honesty and respect would have given me the option to leave and go train somewhere else or stay. He gave no options because he lied—and maybe that's the way he wanted it. He gave me the lines: 'You're our guy. We want you. We're in your corner one hundred percent; screw whoever else is there.' But he lied. He never offered me that courtesy after seven years. Tom Brands did what was best for Tom Brands, not the athletes."

Speculation leads one to consider how two men who are known for their open and candid demeanor had such a difficult time communicating with one another in regard to one moment that comes around every four years, a moment where one of them earned a gold medal for the United States in 1996, and one who was looking to win a gold for the United States in 2016.

For Tony, there was the pressure of being the number-one ranked wrestler in the United States at 57 kg and he had never lost to a domestic opponent. Add into the equation that wrestling had become his profession and how he used that lifestyle to support his family. A loss or missed opportunity to make the Olympic team and not medal or earn more for his family was a great deal of pressure to put on himself. Unlike Dennis, Tony had a wife and son—so, from a support standpoint, the stakes were much higher in Tony's mind and there was much more to lose from where he was wrestling.

For Tom Brands, the Iowa Hawkeyes had not won a national title since 2010; additionally, the Hawkeye Wrestling Club did not qualify a wrestler for the Olympics in 2012. Skepticism would critique that Tom Brands possibly had to put the club in the best position possible to secure an Olympian.

From Tony's standpoint, he did not know if there was pressure on Tom Brands or if Tom Brands felt pressure at all for having an Olympian come out of the club. "[Tom] could be feeling pressure, trying to stack the deck to make sure that he had someone on that team," Ramos said. "Maybe he feels pressure from the HWC Board—it could be something like that, I don't know. I can't speak for Tom. But, at the same time, we are professional athletes and things need to be handled better in a professional situation."

In regard to the program, Tom Brands felt that having Tony and Dennis was the "Best case scenario. It was the best case scenario [having both of those guys in the room]. And I don't [feel pressure]. I feel absolute joy when our guys accomplish what they set out to accomplish. What good does it do if we don't have anyone on the team—in 2012 we didn't and that ain't a whole lot of fun. My approach is the same, it doesn't change from collegiate to international wrestling. Is it important to our program? Yes. But it's the next step that's most important."

Regardless of what people were saying or feeling, Terry Brands made it clear, "There were no ulterior motives."

From there, unfortunately, the confusions and miscommunications would continue over the next few months. On the surface, all seemed to have been resolved; however, in reality, Tony felt he was dealing with too many uncertainties and distractions and was now not receiving the focus, attention, and coaching from Tom Brands, one of the two men he trusted more than anyone else in the Hawkeye program, to do right by him and help him accomplish his goals. It was, of course, Tom Brands that Tony came to Iowa to wrestle for and not having him now, when he felt that he needed him the most, hurt him. Unfortunately, Tony was internalizing his confusions and uncomfortableness and still went to work each day as focused as he could be, and with the intent of doing everything he could to secure his spot on the 2016 United States Olympic wrestling team. In order to do so, his next duty would be qualifying the 57 kg weight for the U.S. at the Pan-American Games.

CHAPTER 63
QUALIFYING THE WEIGHT

"I'm not going to say that there was pressure, but when I got that match over with, there was so much relief because I'd gotten the weight qualified and I only had one more focus, and that was to make the Olympic team."

• *Tony Ramos*

HEADED INTO THE PAN-AMERICAN OLYMPIC Qualifier in Frisco, Texas, Tony had one more opportunity to qualify his weight prior to the United States Olympic Team Trials.

In Tony's opening bout, he faced Jefferson Mayea Figueroa of Ecuador. It only took Tony twenty-five seconds to advance into the semifinals. Mayea took a shot, paused on his knees, tried to fire in another shot, and Tony was waiting for him. Off the second shot, Tony down blocked, sunk in his arm to the far side and locked across the back, took the chin, and hit his patented cow-catcher.

"It actually was something that we saw on tape," Ramos laughed. "Duroe came up to me the night before and said, 'This guy is going to shoot, stay on his knees, and dive in again.' So I looked at him and said, 'I can catch him in my cow-catcher then.' After I said that, Duroe kind of just laughed at me like, 'No way,' and that's exactly what happened. The guy shot, stayed on his knees, tried to dive in again, and I whipped him right over. After the match, I walked right over to Duroe and said, 'Hey, I told you I was going to cow-catcher him.' He just laughed."

For his semifinal bout, Tony had Venezuela's Pedro Mejias Rodriguez, a former Central American and Caribbean Games gold medalist, as well as a former South American Games and Juegos Deportivos Bolivarianos champion.

During the match, Tony scored a takedown and then ran off five-straight ankle laces to catapult himself into the finals with a 13-2 technical superiority.

"I knew this match was huge," Ramos expressed. "And not just huge in the sense that it qualified the weight, but that I wouldn't have to go anywhere after the Trials and make scratch weight to have to qualify the weight for Rio. I'm not going to say that there was pressure, but when I got that match over with, there was so much relief because I'd gotten the weight qualified and I only had one more focus, and that was to make the Olympic team."

As for his opponent, Tony knew he was different from other Venezuela wrestlers. "We knew he was good," Ramos said of Rodriguez. "He wasn't like some of the other Venezuela wrestlers where it's going to be a walk in the park. He had kind of done some damage on the world scene and been around for a while but, at the same time, we knew that he wasn't very good on bottom and if we got on top, we could expose that."

Once Tony was in the position that he knew he could expose, he knew the score and "I thought, *Okay, I need about five of these*," Ramos said. "So, I took advantage of what I had. I locked up that leg lace and that was the end of the match there. When I hit the last one, it was a huge sigh of relief. The weight was now qualified, the mission was to qualify the weight here. It's done."

Not only was qualifying the weight a relief, but qualifying it on American soil also made it easier. "Doing it in Texas was much more comforting," Ramos said. "It was much easier than having to travel to some Third World county and having to deal with all of the uncomfortable things that go with that travel."

From his coach's point of view, "The feeling [of qualifying the weight] was good," Terry Brands said. "But the feeling of accomplishment is, 'What's next now? The weight's qualified. You did your job to that degree, now what's next?—a Pan-Am title.'"

For now, the mission was accomplished, but there was more to do. Tony still had one more match. For the finals, he had an all-too familiar face in Yowlys Bonne Rodriguez of Cuba.

"We got Bonne," Terry Brands said of the finals match-up. "By the way, we are 0-2 against him. This is a guy that pinned him, so now let's see this thing carry forward and move forward in a positive direction headed into the Trials. Before the match, [Ramos] was like, 'I'm on top of this. I got him. I understand this and that. I'm good.'"

The match-up would be anti-climactic to the tournament that Tony had strung together. Bonne not only won the match, he dominated the match. Tony fell to the Cuban by a 10-0 technical superiority.

"I don't know if I wasn't that focused," Ramos reflected. "But, at the same time, we knew this guy was good. I had a lot of people telling me I needed to stay out of this position and stay out of that position or out of here, so I was more focused on staying away from what he did instead of going out there and actually doing what I do.

"I think that's why the first time I wrestled him, I had the best results—I was wrestling my style and not worried about his areas. I didn't know everything he had, I just went out there and did what I did. To beat that guy, that's what I've got to do."

From the corner, "The match was tight," Terry Brands commented, "and then da-da-da-da-da-da-da-da. If you take the American result, yes, he's on the team. But, if you take the international result, he's not a World Champion and that's what he wanted. I'm not saying I'm disappointed in him, he's disappointed, and so I've got to do everything I can to help him get there."

When Terry Brands spoke to Tony back in Iowa City, he claimed that Tony said that he was okay after the loss. "This was the tough part on me," Terry Brands recalled, "because he said he felt good. He told me, 'I feel good about the match.' That was his comment, and that's not characteristic of him. And I'm thinking, *10-0, how do you feel good about that?* When we got back we talked and he felt he did a few good things. So, this was another one of those things that came up that didn't make sense. This isn't Tony. This isn't Tony. This isn't what you were like."

In regard to what Terry Brands was looking for in the final stretch before the Trials, he wanted improvement. "So we're looking for the progress," Terry Brands said. "We're not looking for the 0-0, we're looking for the points and the matches where he's scoring points. And where did that go and why is that not coming out? Why aren't we building from that? These are all the questions that this coach was having."

Tony would now focus all of his attention on his training for the United States Olympic Team Trials. He worked out with Clark and Gilman and, along the way, he picked up a private trainer and set his schedule to accomplish his next goal of being an Olympic qualifier so that he could fulfill his dream of being an Olympic champion. The next time he stepped on the mat, it would be back in Iowa City in Carver-Hawkeye Arena—the building he had never lost in.

CHAPTER 64
EXCITED AND AGITATED

"There's a lot of energy that I got put toward this, a lot that I want to go out and prove—so I am excited."

• *Tony Ramos*

THE WEEK OF THE TRIALS, THE HWC OPENED ITS doors for outside interviews. Each of the HWC's wrestlers were met by the press and interviewed.

As Tony was approached and asked what it meant to be back at Carver-Hawkeye Arena for competition, he smiled and stated, "I'm pretty excited. I'm pumped up, I know that. It's one of those things where I'm trying to focus more on the process right now instead of getting caught up in all the excitement and what's about to transpire from this weekend."

Originally, even though Tony was not certain which Olympics he would train for, he had been exposed to the idea long ago that he could be an Olympian, and he trained to achieve that dream. Now, a few days away, his dream was on the cusp of becoming a reality.

When Tony began wrestling, he almost lost it just as quickly when he was hit by that car. His work ethic and journey, with its ups and downs, had all been a piece of his process to achieving his ultimate goal of being and Olympian and winning a gold medal. The process continued from his days at Villa-Lombard, to Izzy Style, into Glenbard North High School, going on to the University of Iowa, and finally wrestling for the Hawkeye Wrestling Club. All of his work and time and commitment to the sport now came down to one day.

"This weekend," Ramos said in an interview, "[we have] the

opportunity to go out there and achieve goals and dreams that you have set since you were a little kid or once you realized that this was a possibility, and I think some people might get caught up or carried away in that emotion. So, like I said, I'm just trying to embrace the process, go back and think about things from where I came from and what I've been doing and just try to keep me calm and focused and really in tune with what I need to do to make this possible and make that trip down to Rio in August."

And with the opportunity to achieve dreams, Tony, who spoke about not trying to become wrapped up in it all, did take some time to reflect and explain nervousness versus excitement. He said he was, "Not really [nervous], I know I'm getting excited. Somedays you're sitting there thinking and asking yourself questions and thinking about things like— you know I wanted to call my dad the other day and ask him, 'Hey, when you first put me in wrestling, did you think that this was ever possible? You know, when did you really think there was a chance I could be representing the U.S.A. on the Olympic team?'"

Even with the excitement of doing something only six wrestlers in the United States had the opportunity to do, Tony addressed the process he went through and how "It's different in a lot of different ways," he said. "You're not wrestling every weekend, you got to be able to balance your training and your off-time and your on-time. It's more monthly or every other couple months you're competing, so it's a lot of ups and downs and a lot of different peaking times."

In the midst of all of the serious questions, however, there were moments of lightheartedness from Tony that showed a more calm and relaxed person in the middle of it all. One reporter asked him about his record at Carvery-Hawkeye Arena, and how he had never lost there. Tony gave a big smile and shook his head. "It's been brought up," Ramos laughed with a grin, "and that's not the only record that's been brought up. It's been brought up that I haven't lost to an American since 2013. So, there's a lot of those kind of little things going around, those types of stats. I know Metcalf was undefeated in Carver going into 2012 and it didn't end up going his way, I don't want that to happen to me. I want to keep it clean. Tom's even joked about who would win if me and him were to wrestle off after everyone was gone because he's the only other guy who's undefeated in Carver-Hawkeye Arena."

And even though Tony had the home mat advantage of Carver and the Iowa faithful in his corner, he also believed he was at an advantage because, "I'm sleeping in my own bed. I'm in my own environment and doing things I'm used to doing every single day. There's nothing that's going to change for me."

Tony's interview ended the same way Dennis' interview ended and, answering questions about their relationship and how the room had been up to this point. Each wrestler answered in a respectful and appreciative tone toward his teammate and friend. There was a respect for who the other person was—and there was no denying that their time together in college was dear to each of them.

AT THE OLYMPIC TRIALS PRESS CONFERENCE ON

the Friday night of the Trials, two days before Tony was to take to the mat, he was asked about what he felt in regard to who other wrestlers and media outlets or journalists had picked to win and why. Tony was not the favorite to many reporters and wrestling syndicates. His response: "It blows my mind actually," a surprised Ramos said.

When the interview continued, Tony was very eager to point out, "I have only heard one person actually pick me to win. But, you know…it's whatever. People can say I don't score a lot of points and this and that, but people don't score a lot of points on me either. I put myself in chances to win every match I wrestle. And I don't think I give myself a chance to lose every match either because you have to score a point on me to lose. And if I'm not giving up points, how am I going to lose the match? The other thing is, I haven't lost, like I said, domestically. People just see what they want to see, they don't see the [technical] fall that I had or the twenty-second pin at the [Pan American] Games, they only see the four-point match or the two-point match. There's a lot of energy that I got put toward this, a lot that I want to go out and prove—so I am excited."

For the remainder of the night, Tony headed back to his home, settled in with his family, rested, and prepared for his weigh-in on Saturday. After Tony made weight, he slowly put fluids back into his body, ate, and worked to help his body recover as quickly as possible. In addition to his own concerns, he also followed Saturday's Trials as teammates Brent Metcalf and Bobby Telford were in their pursuit of an Olympic berth. He wanted to support them even if he was not there watching them.

By Saturday night, Metcalf and Telford were eliminated from the tournament—Tony and Dennis were now Iowa's final hopes of sending an Olympian to the Games that were simply 127 days away. In less than twenty-four hours, Iowa would know the fate of its two sons, and if one of them would bring an Olympic qualifier back to the Hawkeye state.

CHAPTER 65
THE TRIALS' TRIALS

"That's just Ramos being Ramos. In tight matches, he's clutch. He finds ways to win; and that's what champions do."

• Ryan Morningstar
Assistant Coach, the University of Iowa
HWC Coach

NOBODY STOMPS INTO CARVER-HAWKEYE ARENA like Tony Ramos—and the Hawkeye faithful gave him the return ovation that he deserved.

As soon as Tony's head was visible in the tunnel, the place slowly and then, as more people saw him, suddenly erupted with cheers. The Iowans began to stand, take notice, and when match number forty-nine was called to Mat Four and his name was finally called, Tony began his patented stomp from the tunnel to the far side of Carver, and the cheers only became more deafening with each step.

The Iowa fans stood, trying to gather a clear view of Tony as they peered their heads around others in front of them—he had never lost in Carver and they were conscious of that feat. They also knew this first match was important for the face of Iowa, for the Hawkeye Wrestling Club and for the Olympic hopeful, and they let him know that he had their unwavering support.

Of course, also in Carver that night, were Tony's ardent critics and adversaries. For every ten that cheered in favor of him, there was one who opposed him. One such fan had cupped his hands to his mouth and yelled, "I hope you lose, Ramos! You're terrible! I can't fucking stand you!" And then he looked around and nodded his head with a smile of defiance. However, the black and gold drowned out such shouts and, when acknowledged, it only enticed them to cheer louder.

One younger person was so preoccupied with his phone that he had been looking down and then suddenly noticed the decibel level had risen. He turned to a man in overalls next to him and questioned, "Why is everyone standing? What happened?"

The man shot a look of disdain as if to say, 'Why are you even here?' and responded, while he continued to clap his hands, "Tony Ramos just entered Carver. Now get up and show some respect."

And as the stomp to Mat Four continued amongst the hollers and hisses, and children reaching out with their pens and programs and headgears and shoes for an autograph as people took pictures with their cameras and phones, Tony, focused and all business, eventually made his way up the stairs and onto his mat. The music in Carver turned to "We Built This City" by Jefferson Starship. The hope for many of the fans in Iowa City would not be a rendition of the song where a rebellion against the establishment would commence after the six minutes had concluded. The fans were, however, anticipating a Hawkeye advancement into the semifinals and, ultimately, on the 2016 Olympic Team.

BEFORE NASHON GARRETT ARRIVED TO MAT

Four, Tony was already waiting there in his red Titan Mercury Wrestling Club singlet, pacing in his silver prototype Omniflex-Attack™ 2 ASICS. In Tony's corner was Terry Brands and behind him, simply watching from a distance, was Tom Brands.

There was no in-his-stance-stare-down from the mat's center, but Tony faced Garrett's corner and watched him work his way up the steps and then onto the mat. When Garrett arrived to the mat in his blue singlet and with his head coach from Cornell, Rob Koll, and assistant, Mike Grey, on the floor, Tony followed him, walked to the center of the mat, dropped into his stance, and was ready to wrestle.

Garrett, the 2016 NCAA champion at 133 pounds, was picked by many of the critics to defeat Tony. His length, mixed with his athleticism and explosive double-leg gave many experts all the firepower of doubt that they needed to print or speak words of defeat for the reigning U.S. World Team Member.

"Freestyle is all about explosion and quickness and speed," Garrett said. "Those are the things that I'm good at. It's more heightened in this style. Defensively and offensively, everything that I do is heightened in freestyle. I have more chances to earn more points for the dynamic things that I do."

As for Tony, he acknowledged Garrett's strengths; however, he saw the match-up more in his favor. "He has an explosive double-leg," Ramos said. "But I'm confident in what I do well and that's what I have to do well—apply pressure, move forward, and defend. When my opportunity opens, I capitalize. He will have to go a full [six-minute match] with me. And a long match with my pressure favors me."

And Tony was not alone in his perspective. Although there were many who saw Garrett as the obvious choice of advancement over Tony, the former Hawkeye had his passionate supporters. "I'm not going to mention any names on who said this," Ramos said, "but they asked him how [he thought] Garrett will do at the Olympic Trials. He said, 'He's gonna do good, but once Ramos gets his hands on him, it's a different story—he's never felt power like that.' [Garrett did feel that power] when we wrestled in Arizona and I think that's in the back of his head. I think he remembers what that feels like. I'm not worried about any of those guys."

However, once both wrestlers were in the center of the mat, none of the critics or articles or tweets or video interviews or expert match analysis mattered—the match, all by itself, would be decided the outcome the old fashioned way: it would have to be wrestled for a winner to be declared.

Off the whistle, Tony immediately moved forward looking to work the head and neck of his taller opponent with his left hand—Garrett backed and circled away looking to stay out of Tony's ties. While Garrett was backing up and leading a heavy left leg with quick level fakes, he appeared to be setting Tony up to take a long and heavy stride that he could capitalize on with his open double-leg attack.

Thirty seconds into the match, Garrett would find an attack. While backing up with Tony chasing forward, Garrett dropped levels and snapped Tony's head down with his right hand before penetrating in on a deep double-leg that lifted Tony off the mat and brought him down just outside the center of the mat. Garrett was awarded the takedown; however, after his points were awarded, Garrett seemed content with his 2-0 lead as he did not attempt a turn in the top position. With the sound of the referee's whistle, both wrestlers were placed back on their feet and the match restarted.

Again, Tony moved forward and Garrett moved backwards. And, as Tony was working on Garrett's head and neck, Garrett was using his length to keep Tony at bay by repeatedly posting on his face. After a number of face shots, the referee stopped the match and instructed Garrett to stay out of the face and engage.

From Tony's corner, Terry Brands was yelling, "You can't wait, Tony Ramos! Go! Go!" Likewise, from the stands, Frank could be heard screaming, "Your offense, Tone. Get to your offense!"

Once the match continued, Tony stayed forward and Garrett backed and circled and tried to tie up Tony's hands in order to defeat his ties. With the period at its halfway point, Tony continued forward with short steps and his right hand down to protect his lead leg; however, Garrett, as he did a minute earlier, dropped levels and fired in as Tony paused his foot and stopped moving.

Garrett was in deep on Tony's right leg; however, Tony was able to keep Garrett up high and control the defense. To combat Tony, Garrett took the leg and backed Tony out of bounds for a 3-0 lead.

Again, Tony moved forward after Garrett, and Garrett backed and circled off of the whistle. Then, about ten seconds after that push out, Garrett took a double that Tony was able to down block and defend. The hand fight continued as Garrett kept tying up Tony's wrists.

At the 00:54 mark, Tony took his first shot off a head snap—a sweep single. Garrett circled away from it; it was non-threatening and ineffective. For the remainder of the period Terry Brands hollered for Tony to create action and, as time expired, Tony took a high-level double after the period's conclusion and ran and dropped Garrett to his back. Some of the Garrett fans were not too pleased with the finish after the whistle.

As each wrestler returned to his respective corner, there was thirty seconds to regroup. For Tony, Terry Brands offered coaching as Ryan Morningstar toweled him off. Tom Brands remained on the floor, in the background, watching and supporting.

When the second period began, and Tony trailed 0-3, he would, four seconds in, take his second shot of the match. He chased as Garrett backed up and looked to work a two-on-one to tie Tony up. The two changed positions with wrists and inside control and Tony made another shot attempt. In the process, Garrett was again warned to stay out of the face with his hands as he had posted off Tony's face to break contact.

From Tony's corner, Terry Brands continued to encourage his wrestler as he yelled to him, "Do not wait! Get to him!"

For the first forty-five seconds of the second period, Tony had been the aggressor and continued to move forward. As Garrett had continued to back up and circle, he was warned to keep contact and then he was hit with his first passivity warning.

At the two-minute mark, Tony was in on a high-crotch to Garrett's right; however, Garrett defended and pushed Tony off. Still, Tony moved forward and, as he did, and as Garrett backed up, Garrett changed levels and fired off another double. With his hands low, Tony brought Garrett's chest back up with double underhooks.

With 1:47 remaining in the match, and Garrett leading 3-0, Garrett was now warned for passivity and placed on the shot clock by the referee; the call would be confirmed by the other two referees.

In a more conscious effort, Garrett did not move back as much; however, he circled back and, once again, took a nice quick shot to work in on Tony's right leg fifteen seconds into the thirty-second shot clock window.

Garrett used his length to keep his hands locked, and Tony defended with a whizzer on his right side to battle the position. Even still, Garrett was able to create a lift and elevated Tony off the mat, but Tony, with his whizzer still in tight, hipped in and, almost as if doing a cartwheel with his bottom half, squared up his hips and then, upon return, was able to run the corner on Garrett and take a single-leg of his own.

Tony elevated the captured leg, in on his own offense now, tripped Garrett for the takedown, and covered. With the called two and the two confirmed, the Iowa fans rose to their feet and their voices were heard. Almost immediately, Garrett sprung up and Tony pushed him out of bounds; however, there was no one-point pushout call here as Garrett made his way to his feet and then fell to the mat out of bounds. It was never signaled by the referee and, therefore, never paddled by the judge or mat chairman. However, in Tony's corner, Terry Brands felt this was a missed point and passionately exclaimed for it: "Where's the one? Come on!"

With his takedown, Tony brought the match to within one point, now trailing 3-2, and Iowa fans were hoping for something special—they knew Tony had a knack for finding ways to win matches. There was only 1:14 left in the match for Tony to work into his offense and score in order to win and advance into the semifinals.

Immediately, off the restart, as he had done the entire match, Tony moved forward and Garrett backed up off the whistle. Still, Terry Brands remained relentless on Tony, pounding the mat and screaming, "Don't wait!"

Tony continued to chase the retreating and circling Garrett. With each tie Tony grabbed, Garrett posted away. Then, with 00:49 remaining, Garrett took a straight-on double that Tony was able to defend with his underhook. As for Garrett, he hung onto Tony's wrists and was holding them inside to limit Tony's offense. In this position, the referee once again warned Garrett to open up, which led to Garrett breaking the hold.

From there, Garrett continued to back up as Tony moved forward. With 00:24 remaining, Tony attempted another shot that Garrett hipped down to defend and circled out of; unfortunately, Garrett was warned again by the referee to remain in contact and not be passive—this was his third warning.

Now, with 00:23 remaining in the match, Tony needed a solid attack to pull off the win. Again, he moved forward on the whistle and immediately took a shot on Garrett, which Garrett defended by posting and pushing away. Two seconds later, Tony took another shot; it was defended. Then another shot; it too was defended—but each defense ended with Garrett posting on Tony's head and circling back and away, not keeping contact in an offensive form.

For this, Garret was hit for a caution and one and, in the background, behind his brother, Tom Brands was clapping repeatedly with his hands over his head in excitement and agreement. Also with that point, the match was now tied at 3-3. But, this not only equaled the match, it also gave Tony criteria with only 00:13 left.

From the stands of Carver-Hawkeye, the fans could be seen or heard hollering in cheers, hissing in disgust, or shocked and speechless with wide eyes watching.

When the whistle blew, and with an angry Rob Koll in Garrett's corner, Tony now circled and backed up for the first time as Garrett aggressively moved forward. However, throughout the remaining seconds, Garrett did not take an open double until there were about six seconds remaining. In defense, Tony went double underhooks and sprawled back. While Garrett was content in that position, Tony, not content, ran the corner, locked up a cradle and, as time expired, put Garrett to his back—no points were awarded; however, Morningstar was looking for two points for either a takedown or exposure; Terry Brands was looking for both sets of points.

As the clock notched zeroes all the way across, Tony did a summersault out of the cradle and stood up with his arms open and looked to the crowd as Carver erupted with a mixture of cheers and boos. Garrett remained momentarily on his knees and on the mat in disbelief; his coaches were enraged at the call. But Tony, Tony basked in the celebration and circled the mat with his arms outstretched. A few steps into his pose, he made eye contact with Koll in Garrett's corner and made the break sign with his hands. Koll responded by wafting Tony off with his right hand as he gave a look of abhorrence and walked away.

As Tony had his hand raised, his skeptics jumped on their social media to broadcast their disagreement with the caution and one call, while his supporters retorted through posting pictures with captions that praised Tony's aggressive-forward style and how he pushed Garrett and wrestled a very smart and technical match.

When Tony exited the stage, HWC member, Daniel Dennis, stepped up for his quarterfinal match at 57 kg. Tony would be followed by Terry Brands and, once Ryan Morningstar left, Tom Brands cornered and spoke with Daniel Dennis, along with Coach Mike Duroe, right before his match began.

For Tony, as he ran toward the tunnel, amidst the noises, he stopped and signed some autographs for the young fans in the front row. After that, he exited to the standing ovation that was a mix of congratulations, obscenities, and those still in awe of the match.

The match itself was criticized by many for Tony not doing anything the entire time. The match was also critiqued for Garrett continually backing up and not engaging, making it difficult for Tony to work into an offense. No matter how the match was seen, prior to the tournament, a warning was given to each wrestler and coach about how the caution and one would be called.

Terry Brands echoed what was communicated to everyone beforehand when the referees spoke. He said that, "The officials told us before the tournament that if you're running and you're avoiding contact, we're going to stop the match and warn you—the next one's going to be a point and a caution. So everybody in the tournament knew that was going to happen. And they stopped the match with thirty or so to go or whatever—they had every justification to call that at the end that put him ahead."

In response to that caution and one call being called an "Iowa Call," Terry Brands simply stated, "It was the right call. It was just another situation of Tony being Tony and putting himself and giving himself an opportunity to win the match—so that magic is still there."

Additionally, Terry Brands felt that the referees left points on the mat for Tony as well. "When Tony took Garrett down and [then Garrett came up] and Tony ran him out of bounds, that should've been another point," Terry Brands pointed out. "At the end of the match when Tony hit the corner and locked up that cradle and turned him, that should have been two more, at least. So I don't want to hear about a close match."

As far as the strategy was concerned, "You know [the double] is coming," Terry Brands stressed. "You know that situation is going to be there. The key is to down block and, even though we want to be offensive, we know Garrett is going to get a shot off—and then [Tony can] run that corner down and score."

And that was what Tony did. He took advantage of his ability to defend well and then work into his own shot off hitting the corner.

"We have worked on that position for countless hours," Terry Brands said of working a defense against such an offense. "We've had him bounce off his butt and give up no takedowns. We've had him in positions where guys start in locked and his hands are up and then we have the guy drive in on a double—he has been in there so many times in practice because it's going to happen at some point, right? So we worked it and worked it and it paid off to help win that match. Regardless to what people say, Tony still figured it out and won the match—he just has to not let those matches be so close."

From Tony's point of view, "He hit me with that double once and I felt it—anyone could see he was trying to hit it, he tried it four more times and it kind of warmed me up for that Coleman [Scott] match. He got a few doubles but never finished, I got off of them.

"He got the shot clock and the push out—to be honest, I thought he was on the shot clock in the first period, I thought they hit him twice, but it was only once. But in that Nashon match, I needed to stay calm and know I can get to my offense when I needed to score. That's another thing [everyone says] is that I can't score when I need to score. And when it comes time to score, who's the one scoring—who's winning the matches?"

By the end of the match, Tony worked to his offense and tried to get in on Garrett to score. "He got one take down and ran and ran and ran and ran," Ramos remembered. "The ref told him in the beginning of second period, he said, 'He's been chasing you this whole match, I'm going to hit you.' He warned him. And I also felt like I was chasing him the whole match, so I wasn't surprised. I just had to keep trying to get to him; [I] had to try to get to him."

But once that caution and one was awarded, "I wasn't trying to get the takedown," Tony said. "I knew I was going to win so I stayed in good position."

Staying in good position and winning the position battle and not giving up points but scoring them had been Tony's modus operandi for the past two years. "That's just Ramos being Ramos," assistant coach Ryan Morningstar said. "In tight matches, he's clutch. That's been his career. He blows guys out and against the top level guys, he finds ways to win; and that's what champions do."

In regard to the point awarded to Tony, Morningstar stated, "The referee warned [Garrett], 'Stay in there, you got to stay in there or I'm gonna hit you,' and that's what happened—he got hit. [Ramos] was all over him. That's a difficult match-up for Ramos, a guy that's explosive like that and he got it done that first match. You're at the Olympic Trials, get your hand raised, and that's what he did."

Tony's hand being raised and a thirty-fifth consecutive win inside Carver-Hawkeye Arena, now squared him off in the semifinals against former Cowboy, current North Carolina Tar Heel head coach, and former Olympian, Coleman Scott.

**2016 • UNITED STATES OLYMPIC TEAM TRIALS
57 KG CHAMPIONSHIP QUARTERFINAL MATCH
RAMOS DEFENDS GARRETT'S DOUBLE-LEG • RAMOS WON A 3-3 CRITERIA DECISION
PHOTOGRAPH COURTESY • UNIVERSITY OF IOWA ATHLETICS**

COLEMAN SCOTT WAS THE OLYMPIC BRONZE

medalist at 60 kg in the 2012 London Games. His resume, long and prestigious, consisted of his being a three-time Pennsylvania Interscholastic Athletic Association (PIAA) state champion for Waynesburg Central High School who posted a career record of 156-12. He would move on to Oklahoma State University where he became a four-time All-American, including an eighth, a fifth, and a national runner-up, before finally earning a national championship in 2008. Scott then wrestled onto the national and international scene and placed in a number of tournaments, domestically and foreign; however, he never claimed a championship. In return, though, he had gained a great amount of experience and growth in his craft until his breakout season in 2012.

In 2012, as the tournaments and qualifiers began, Scott would win the Dave Schultz Memorial Invitational, the United States Olympic Team Trials, and then earn a bronze medal in London.

Soon after one more season of competition, Scott took an assistant coaching position at the University of North Carolina and, one year later in 2015, took over as the Tar Heel head wrestling coach. He trained his wrestlers during the day, and then continued to train as an individual in the evening. After placing third in the United States Open in 2016, a qualifier for the Olympic Trials, Scott was ready to give his Olympic dream one last chance.

Coming into the United States Olympic Trials, Scott, who trained through the Sunkist Wrestling Club, earned the fourth seed and received an opening round bye—he awaited the winner between Joe Colon and Obenson Blanc, each of the Titan Mercury Wrestling Club. Colon would win the match by a 14-10 decision and Scott would face him.

In Scott's quarterfinal match with Colon, Scott would be forced to fight off a low single twenty seconds into the match. Once back to their feet, no more heavy action occurred for another thirty-four seconds.

With 2:06 left in the first period, Scott lowered his level and blasted into his patented open double-leg—he drove Colon to his butt for a two-point takedown, but, Colon, locked tight around Scott's chest, tilted and exposed Scott for two-points of his own. With 1:48 in the first period, the referee brought them both to their feet and the score was tied, 2-2.

As the wrestling resumed, Scott immediately worked his levels and fakes while Colon worked to stay lower than his taller and lengthier opponent in order to help defend Scott's double-leg—this also to helped Colon work to his low single attack.

Suddenly, with 00:45 left in the first period, Scott took another double-leg that was fended off by Colon. Once defended, and as Colon brought

Scott up with double underhooks, Colon worked a throw that Scott fought. In that process, a throw occurred that appeared to be initiated by Scott in a defensive position to earn the exposure; however, Colon was awarded the two-points for the takedown and then, as they came to their feet, Colon remained in the double underhook position. Ultimately, Scott did get Colon to the mat and received one point for the reversal. This now gave Colon a 4-3 lead with 00:24 left.

When the referee stopped to bring both wrestlers to their feet. Scott's corner—which consisted of Kenny Monday and Kendall Cross, both Olympic gold medalists—threw in the challenge brick to contest the awarded points.

After the challenge, Scott was awarded the two points and Colon was also awarded two points, the match was tied 4-4, but Scott was ahead on criteria as he scored last.

The first period ended that way.

When the second period began, Colon became offensive off the whistle. Scott, who was still working his levels, however, was more apt to work into head ties and seemed more defensive.

Then, with 2:01 left in the match, Scott faked an ankle pick to Colon's right side and found an opening in the form of a high-crotch to Colon's left side in full transition—Scott scored beautifully and now led, 6-4.

In the top position, Scott worked from Colon's waist down to his leg lace and turned Colon for another two-points. Then, masterfully, Scott circled to put Colon's back in toward the center of the mat and hit a second leg lace for an additional two-points. Again, with great mat awareness, Scott made certain he had more room and hit two more leg laces for four more points. Those laces were enough to score Scott enough points for a 14-4 technical superiority and the match was terminated with 1:29 left.

Coleman Scott won, advanced, and now faced Tony in the semifinals at 57 kg.

ONCE AGAIN, AS TONY WAS CALLED TO HIS

competition mat, this time Mat Three, the Iowa faithful continued with grand support for their most famed son in recent years as they stood and cheered.

Tony, in his red TMWC singlet, stood atop the stage and watched as Coleman Scott made his way to the mat. As he had done with Garrett, Tony did not take his eyes off Scott as he climbed the stairs, walked onto the mat, and was checked by the referee. Scott, who was walked to the middle by the referee, had not made eye contact with Tony and warmed-up at the top of the circle while Tony danced his warm-up in the middle—the former Hawkeye watched every move of the former Cowboy.

And, as the mat was being cleaned by one of the medical staff personnel, Scott paced back and forth and Tony's eyes just followed him back and forth. Once the mat was declared ready to wrestle, Scott met Tony, waiting in the middle, they shook hands, the whistle blew, and Scott posted his arm as Tony moved forward.

Scott's reach was impressive. His body, formally that of a 60 kg wrestler, tall and lengthy, posed a challenge for Tony. Of course, Tony had just faced the same challenge with Garrett, as well as many of his opponents where he had to find a way to close the gap to score points. Similarly, like Garrett, Scott utilized his distance and modeled that John-Smith-Oklahoma-State style of strong level changes, quick fakes, and well-timed, calculated, and selected offensive shots.

Initially, Scott was able to use his distance and his right hand to post on Tony's head and keep him at bay.

With 00:23 into the period, Scott fired off his first double; however, Tony defended and blocked with an underhook before he worked his head tie. Scott also worked himself free and got back to his heavy, quick footed right leg with fakes and level changes.

The referee would stop the match once and warn Scott for passivity, and, on the restart, Tony worked to a low percentage high-crotch shot that Scott easily defended. Two more times the match was stopped by the referee as he spoke to each of the wrestlers and warned Tony for passivity in each of those stoppages. With that third break in the period, this one with 1:44 left, Tony was placed on the shot clock.

Near the end of the shot clock, Scott took an open double on Tony, but Tony defended it by catching him in double underhooks; however, Scott, who would not earn a takedown, did earn one point for Tony's inability to score in the mandated thirty seconds. That one point for the shot clock violation gave Scott a 1-0 lead with 00:57 left in the period.

For the remainder of the period, there would be a great deal of motion and level changing by Scott, much of Tony working to close the gap between the two wrestlers, and when the two would tie, hammers clubbed down on the other's neck.

Then, as Tony was looking to gain a two-on-one for wrist control, Scott changed his level, Tony at the same time stepped in, and Scott took a sharp open double that drove Tony backward, giving him little opportunity to stop the momentum—Scott shot Tony off of the mat and he was awarded another point for a 2-0 lead with 00:07 left in period one.

In the seconds that remained, Tony took one more shot, to no avail, and, at the period's end, Scott gave a good forearm down on Tony's head. Each walked away to his respected corner.

Scott stepped to his coaches, Monday and Cross, and for Tony, once again, Terry Brands spoke to him while Morningstar toweled him. Just off the stage, located at the bottom of the steps, listening to what Tony was being coached to do and what to stay away from, was Tom Brands. When Terry walked back down to the corner, Tom moved back and resumed his position as an invested spectator.

Back in the center, the referee started the period and Tony immediately fired an open high-crotch to Scott's right leg—Scott turned and stepped out of it.

What appeared to be different this period was that Tony was in on ties and that gap was closing. Scott, who for the first period kept distance and used his length and short fakes and quick levels, had turned to hard ties and hand fighting from the inside.

For the opening minute, each wrestler displayed heavy hands and hard chops on their opponent's neck—a more physical match was transpiring as the final period was working to its halfway point.

With 1:46 remaining, Scott, after being warned for passivity, took a strong double-leg attack and switched over to a single-leg on Tony's right side. Tony, strong in his defensive position, was holding Scott off until Scott was able to clear his hips and pressure in. Scott then lifted Tony and put him in danger; but, when Scott went to finish with a slap of the head and left-footed sweep, Scott missed as Tony's leg was not where Scott expected it to be—Carver's magic had created an illusion.

Scott, out of position, fell to his right hip, Tony kicked out and caught Scott for a takedown, and the match was now tied 2-2 with Tony in the top position and with 1:30 left in the match. With the two-point score and the last to score, compared to Scott's two one-point scores, Tony held criteria if the match were to end in a 2-2 tie.

Now, with 1:16 left, Scott had to score in order to claim the victory. For Tony, he had to either score or fend off any attacks in order to advance to the Trial's championship match.

Immediately off the whistle, both wrestlers looked to physically pound the other's head in a tie position; however, as Scott looked to come out of it, Tony, with 1:07 remaining, took a low, sweeping single on Scott, climbed the leg, and scored another two points for the takedown. He now had a commanding 4-2 lead. In the process of the takedown being scored by the mat judge, once the points were confirmed, the Iowa crowd erupted knowing Tony was seconds closer to a finals appearance and one match closer to Rio.

At the 00:47 mark, the referee stopped the match and brought Tony and Scott to their feet. However, in the process, Scott motioned toward his head and, in Tony's corner, Terry Brands was jumping up and down, kneeling on top of the stage momentarily, yelling for Tony to keep moving, attack, and not slow down.

Unfortunately, for Tony, the match was stopped for Scott. Tony walked over to Terry Brands who was passionately coaching Tony to be smart and keep moving, Terry pointed to his own head to communicate to Tony to be smart. Tony nodded to his animated coach whose final motivational words as Tony went back to the middle of the mat was, "Let's go!" Tony knew what that meant.

Once the match was re-started, the communication from Scott's corner being yelled was, "Don't wait! Don't wait!" And, as he tied with Tony and untied, Tony appeared to be more complacent in the mat's center and was appearing to simply play defense. Tony did place his back to the outside of the circle and danced side to side for roughly ten seconds until he referee stopped the match at 00:17 to warn him for passivity and to engage.

Scott came down hard off the whistle, once again with his left hand and, as Tony looked to take off the tie, Scott hit a shrug and passed Tony by. When Tony's momentum carried him forward, Scott came behind him with 00:06 left. In the continuation, Scott looked to expose Tony by pulling him backward, but no exposure occurred. Scott stayed in a gut wrench position until time ran out.

With his takedown Scott had tied the match at 4-4, and he had also scored the last points. With that criteria, the blue paddles were raised to represent the winning wrestler.

Immediately, Scott jumped up and pumped his fists in excitement— he was headed into the championship match. As the Tony Ramos haters stood and cheered, and many of the Iowa crowd was stunned by the winner, Scott walked and screamed with his arms wide open.

Tony, however, as he walked back to the center, was speaking with the referee as he went to shake Tony's hand—Tony did not shake hand as he protested the call, as did Terry Brands in his corner.

What Tony and Terry Brands knew that the announcers and the referee on the mat, as well as some of the people in Carver-Hawkeye did not realize, was that Tony actually had criteria over Scott.

"From where I was sitting," Terry Brands said, "they raised the blue paddle and I was [yelling], 'No! No!' like crazy because the criteria was clearly in our favor. So I was trying to figure out was up the official's sleeve or U.S.A. Wrestling's sleeve that they're going to let this guy get off the mat and then I won't be able to protest it after the hand's been raised—that's the protocol. So I was trying to communicate that waving my arms and yelling, 'No! No!' But Tony knew. He's smart. You saw him motioning to the officials."

And with raised fingers signaling a European two with his thumb and pointer finger, Tony walked to the table and explained the criteria to the table. He looked at the table judge and said, as clearly as possible with his mouthpiece still in, "I've got two 2s." In the process, he raised both of his hands to indicate a two-point and two-point score. This same explanation could be heard by many of the knowledgeable fans around the mat and inside Carver while others protested that Scott scored last and that was criteria.

As the referee came from the center for confirmation, he learned what Tony already knew. Tony's two two-point moves (2+2) gave him criteria over Scott's two one-point moves and one two-point move (1+1+2). The totals were the same, but Tony had earned the higher scored points.

When Tony walked backward to the center of the circle, chest out and arms wide to his side, the confirmation was given in the form of a raised red paddle. And, as Scott questioned what had just happened, seemingly unaware of criteria, Tony outstretched his arms and circled the middle of the mat making certain every person, in every seat, from every vantage point in Carver, saw him. The Iowans and Tony Ramos supporters erupted with cheers while the Tony Ramos opposition yelled foul play and homer officiating.

With his arms wide, and as fans rose from the seats and cheered, Tony went into his patented double rainbow flex before flexing downward and pacing the mat and stomping before he slapped himself twice in the chest—Carver-Hawkeye Arena only became louder, as usually happened with big match Tony Ramos wins.

"That's Tony—whatever," Terry Brands said of the celebrating. "The celebratory stuff and the personality shows through—it's raw. I don't think it's anything scripted or premeditated. I love it."

Cheers soon simmered and boos erupted and then cheers raised again as the referee explained criteria to Coleman Scott and, seemingly, all of Carver-Hawkeye Arena.

"We knew he had criteria," Ryan Morningstar said. "Even the officials didn't know that he had criteria. [But] Ramos is a smart wrestler and he knew exactly what he had to do to win and that takedown was huge against Scott. I mean, that second takedown, that's what the best guys do. He could have rested, he was winning, he could have rested, [but] he went out and got another takedown. That's just Tony Ramos. He's a competitor and he's going to get it done."

Tony came to the mat's center and met Scott—Scott, soon realizing criteria, shook Tony's hand and the two embraced in a hug and exchanged words in a respectful and complimentary way.

After Tony's hand was raised, and his name was announced as the winner, the two would once again embrace. For Tony, there were no further celebratory gestures. He humbly walked over and shook hands with Scott's corner, Monday and Cross, and then returned to the stairs in his corner. While Tony was coming down, he passed the next wrestler up on the mat, Daniel Dennis. Coming down the stairs, Tom Brands slapped Tony's hand as he was positioned in Dennis' corner for his semifinal match.

Tony ran back to the tunnel and collected himself and, there to greet him, was the media; Tony was now 36-0 inside of Carver.

Before a question could be asked, Tony went into his rant on how he felt he had been treated by the media. He stated: "All I got to say to everyone is: You guys picked Scott, you picked Graff, you picked Nashon, you picked Dennis. I'm not surprised. Who else you want me to take out?"

It had appeared, even from his pre-Trials interview, that Tony was upset with how the media was choosing the other wrestlers over him. He had obviously taken in what was being said about himself, his opponents, and that was his first opportunity to shout back—and he shouted back with confidence.

As to his answer when asked why it had been taking so long for him to work into his offense and score points, Tony declared, "These guys are smart, they're experienced; I'm looking for the right opportunities to try and make more happen. This is the Olympic Trials, you make one mistake and it's over."

And, to his point, Tony had been calculated, schooled in the criteria, and knew how to win. It may not have looked pretty or flashy to many, but he continued to advance in the tournament and, in the end, just like during his NCAA championship run, that was all that mattered.

In regard to the 15,000 screaming Hawkeye fans, Tony acknowledged with a big smile on his face that it was, "Awesome, just like being back home. I've had a lot of big wins at Carver; that's another big one."

After the match Tony and Scott had appeared to exchange words with one another. Tony, not one to hold back or be short with answers to the media, explained the interaction. "I told Coleman after the match, 'Hey, great match. If you're done with your career, you've had a great one.' He told me, 'It's up to you now. Just go out there and win it.'"

Tony defeating an Olympic bronze medalist was a major victory. He had again defeated a top contender at his weight, this time against an opponent with Olympic merit, and it only helped his confidence going into his final match. "[My confidence] is high," Ramos commented. "I've got to win two more tonight. Two to go and then I'm going to Rio."

But, until then, Tony was going to "Go see my family, hang out with my son—cannot wait to see that little guy. Get some food and come back and be ready for tonight."

From his coach's point of view, "He scored," Terry Brands said, "and then what did he do right away? He scored again—that was the difference in the match. It was classical wrestling in a really, really, really tough match, and that's how you win. And I remember Tom when we came up to the office, he was like, 'Brilliant. Brilliant wrestling. That's how you do it—that's how you win world championships, just like that.' And I couldn't agree with him more because that's how you win. You score, and then you score again and neutralize what [one might think] is a winning takedown."

But, Terry Brands felt that he noticed something off in Tony, and after that match ended he sought to understand what he felt was wrong. "I went up to Tony," Terry Brands explained, "after the match I'm asking him, 'What's wrong with you?' And I swear I thought he said, 'I got a burner—a stinger.' But I asked him and he said, 'I didn't say that.' But I knew something was wrong—but he wasn't saying anything."

And even though Tony showed no outward signs of something being wrong, and he stated that he was not injured when asked, Terry Brands still felt, in his gut feeling, that something was not right. However, with the win and advancement into the finals, and Tony indicating that he was fine, Terry Brands did not press the issue.

ON THE BOTTOM HALF OF THE 57 KG BRACKET, Hawkeye Wrestling Club member and former University of Iowa teammate Daniel Dennis was positioned as the third seed in the tournament. He had won the United States Open in Las Vegas at 57 kg with a 10-0 technical superiority over former Olympian Sam Hazewinkel, this one year after placing second at the World Team Trials at 61 kg.

In the opening round, just as the number-one seed, Tony Ramos, and the number-two seed, Tyler Graff, received, Dennis also had a bye into the quarterfinals. From Dennis' position, he awaited the winner between Missouri Wrestling Foundation's Alan Waters, the 2016 Dave Schultz Memorial International champion, and Erkin Tadzhimetov, a fourth-place finisher at the United States Open wrestling out of Orem, Utah, and for the New York Athletic Club.

Waters won a 10-3 decision and Dennis had to wrestle him in the quarterfinals. When that match came, Dennis, upon entering Carver-Hawkeye Arena for the first time in a very long time, was greeted by all of Iowa in a warm and inviting manner. The cheers were loud and the HWC supporters knew a finals match-up might be imminent between Dennis and Tony; in fact, many were hoping for this as it would ensure a Hawkeye on the Olympic team. But, more importantly, the fans saw one of their sons back on the mat, and they embraced him with an ovation of unbridled support.

As the match took place, Dennis had it well in hand. He ended up winning by a 9-2 decision and he was one match and one very difficult opponent away from an appearance in the finals and an opportunity to earn a trip to the Rio Olympic Games. The opponent that stood in his way was the number-two seed in the tournament from the New York Athletic Club and a wrestler who had defeated him pretty handedly nearly five months earlier, Tyler Graff.

The last time that Dennis and Graff had wrestled, it was in the semifinals of the Bill Farrell Open in Hempstead, New York, and the match ended a mere 00:37 into the first period.

Off the whistle, Graff took a high-crotch to Dennis' right leg and then, once on top, dropped to a leg lace that Dennis defended. Once he defended, Graff then worked up and trapped Dennis' left arm. Once the trapped arm gut wrench was secured by Graff, he turned Dennis three consecutive times for an 8-0 lead. When they were whistled to stop by the referee, Dennis was hit with a caution and one and that additional point was awarded to Graff—this within 00:24 of the first period.

As soon as the match resumed—it was stopped for some blood clean up—Graff started in the top position and locked up one more gut wrench, driving and scoring on Dennis' right side, for an 11-0 technical superiority less than a minute into the match.

With the experience and result of that last match, Dennis knew he had a formidable opponent on his hands in Graff, and Graff knew that just because he scored quickly and what appeared to be an easy victory back in early November, Dennis was a very strong and shilled opponent; one he would have to tactically plan for and work to defeat.

Dennis commented on what he knew he needed to do to come out as the victor against Graff. "Not get lazy," Dennis said. "Graff's a competitor and he comes out and wrestles hard as hell. He beats a lot of people on coming out hard and people not ready for it. He did that to me in New York and the match lasted, shit, twenty seconds maybe. Not long. I don't want to say he caught me but, in my mind, he caught me.

"I feel like I'm a better wrestler than that," Dennis continued. "Not getting lazy is big and important and knowing his game plan. His game plan is to come out, get ahead big and then either put the match away fast or ride off that. And knowing that you gotta make adjustments obviously after the first time you get your ass kicked by a guy, so try and make those adjustments."

The match opened and stretched itself in Graff's favor. He took a 2-0 score on Dennis and both wrestlers remained aggressive as each fought for position—Graff looked to extend his lead while Dennis looked to tie and, possibly, put himself in position to take the lead. Dennis eventually had his opening.

Still trailing late into the second period, Dennis scored on a takedown and, after that, he was in his strongest position: top. As soon as he had his hands locked and his gut wrench secured, Dennis drove and turned Graff not once, but twice—and the hollers in Carver echoed all around. This would put the score at 6-2 with time running out. Graff worked to try and force his offense, but Dennis stayed in good position, worked to continue control of the match's pace with his ties, and never placed himself in any danger.

In the end, Dennis came out on top with a 6-2 decision, a standing ovation from those in the black and gold as his hand was raised and as he exited the floor. The Hawkeyes were now guaranteed an Olympian.

After his semifinal victory, he asked about how he was able to give himself the advantage in the match. "I got a pretty good gut and it's four points if you can [turn] them twice," Dennis said. "As soon as [I] get on top, if I can lock up the gut, I feel good about synching up. That was the only chance I had on top. I wish I would have given myself more opportunities to get on top, but you take what you can get and capitalize on what position you're in at the moment. I was up on top, locked it up tight as hell, and I got points out of it."

With a 6-2 lead, Dennis was next questioned with how his style changed with the lead and what his mindset was with the four-point cushion. "Just awareness of now," Dennis stated. "I'm obviously looking to score, but I'm not looking to control position obviously not do anything reckless, do anything stupid like I've done in the past and try to control everything after you're in the driver seat and you don't want to give that up—keep there and keep in control of the match and control the pace and then control the position."

In the end, regardless as to how his first two matches went, there was still one more match. And this one match, the finals match, would be a best-of-three series and it would be the opportunity to wrestle not only the number-one ranked wrestler in the United States of America at his weight class, but also his HWC teammate, a friend, and someone he had a past with.

For the Iowans, it would be Hawkeye versus Hawkeye in Iowa City, center stage in Carver-Hawkeye Arena—they would have their Olympian. As for the media, they would have a great story no matter how it worked out. And, for the skeptics, it would be one more person that they felt would be the one to take Tony Ramos down.

"We both did our job on getting to the finals," Dennis said, "and I think that's what people who are looking at this weight are probably excited to watch that match-up. For people who are looking forward to that match, that's probably one of the bigger match-ups they want to see."

When Dennis had been asked about him and Tony, and both were asked about the situation a great deal, Dennis always and respectfully brought up Tony's accolades in comparison to his own. However, accolades aside, Dennis had been in a number of those same positions as Tony with one small difference: Tony Ramos had won those big matches.

Dennis' former high school head wrestling coach, Ryan Geist, described the two wrestlers and their careers as very similar with different outcomes. "Realistically," Geist explained, "I know it didn't happen this way. But realistically, all the accomplishments that Tony had, could have been Daniel's. [Daniel] could have been a two-time state champion, he could have been an NCAA champion—he was so close on all those fronts and it easily could have gone the other way in any of those matches, but it didn't and that's just the way it is.

"For Tony," Geist continued, "a lot of those things came out because he won those matches—he was good enough to win those matches and he won them. You have two kids pairing off in the finals who are good enough to win this title, and it's been talked about the accomplishments that Tony had and how he was a more decorated wrestler, but they're equal opponents—no doubt about it. Even in their successes—although one got the first place and one got the second place—they were on the same playing field the whole time. A lot of people don't recognize that they were, but they were. And with those one-point matches, it just so happened that Daniel was on the short end of those."

In regard to Dennis' impressions of Tony and that specific match-up and the fact that they trained alongside each other, Dennis said: "I don't know the last time we wrestled live competitively. It's been probably awhile. I'll expect—he doesn't want to lose, I don't want to lose. You're going to have two guys out there who want to make a name for themselves and who want to do well.

"He's a competitor, his first two matches showed it; coming back in amazing fashion and scoring when he needs to. He's a competitor—I know that—he knows I'm a competitor. It's not like he's a Russian and I kind of think I know a little bit about him—I mean, we know each other. That's a kid I helped a long, long time ago. And vice versa, he helped me as a by-product."

But, regardless of the past, this was the match-up Dennis wanted because it would now truly allow him to know where he was. "He's got a lot going for him," Dennis said. "He's the big man on campus right now and that's not in debate—he is. I want to dethrone him."

As for how Dennis felt going into the final match-up, he appeared calm. "I'm confident," Dennis said. "If I can just wrestle where I'm good, I'm comfortable on who I wrestle. As long as I feel good, I like my odds."

CHAPTER 66
OUT TO DINNER

"He wasn't wrestling a teammate. He was wrestling an opponent that stood in the way of his goals, and it was off-putting to see them eating together."

• *Megan Ramos*
Tony Ramos' Wife

EVEN BEFORE TONY WAS ABLE TO GATHER himself and his belongings after his semifinal victory, he met with a reporter directly after his match in the tunnel. In that interview would be the first time that Tony would learn about who would be in his corner and who would be in Dennis' corner during the finals. At that moment, the cornering issue that Tony felt that he addressed, and took Tom Brands on his word with so that it was a non-issue, was now an issue.

If there was a change to what they had spoken about, Tony had expected to hear it directly from Tom Brands—but he had not expected a change based on his previous conversation with Tom months earlier and now he heard about it from a reporter.

"There was no conversation, verbally," Ramos said, "about Tom not cornering me. The only conversation we had was the one we had in January where Tom said to me, 'You're our guy. Terry's going to coach you. I'm going to come out and towel you off and be in your corner. Dennis will be on his own.' Then I see on Twitter that Tom had told Andy Hamilton [a sports reporter for *The Des Moines Register*] and Tony Hager [of *Takedown Wrestling*] and others [in media] that it would be Terry and Morningstar in [my corner] and Duroe and Tom in Dennis' [corner]. And that's where it all started."

Tony would finish his interview and then head off to take a shower.

After his shower, Tony received a text from Frank. The conversation via text message was as follows:

> FROM: ANTHONY RAMOS   10 APRIL 2016 . 12:25 PM
>
> "Tom told me when we had that talk that he would not be in Dennis' corner. Well, that was a lie."

> FROM: FRANK DEFILIPPIS   10 APRIL 2016 . 12:26 PM
>
> "Yeah it was. I'll deal with that after you win and re-attack Dennis to death."

> FROM: ANTHONY RAMOS   10 APRIL 2016 . 12:27 PM
>
> "You see, he said it will be Terry and Morningstar with me and him and Duroe with Dennis."

> FROM: FRANK DEFILIPPIS   10 APRIL 2016 . 12:28 PM
>
> "Everyone saw."

> FROM: ANTHONY RAMOS   10 APRIL 2016 . 12:31 PM
>
> "I know, it's just he tells you bullshit."

> FROM: ANTHONY RAMOS   10 APRIL 2016 . 12:32 PM
>
> "Whoever wants to go eat, we're going to Monica's. I just showered."

> FROM: FRANK DEFILIPPIS   10 APRIL 2016 . 12:28 PM
>
> "At Games, don't have him in your corner either now—doesn't matter. Terry is your coach anyways."

> FROM: FRANK DEFILIPPIS   10 APRIL 2016 . 12:30 PM
>
> "Everyone is here. Do you want everyone to go eat? We're ready."

> FROM: FRANK DEFILIPPIS   10 APRIL 2016 . 12:32 PM
>
> "I will have words with him after."

> FROM: ANTHONY RAMOS   10 APRIL 2016 . 12:35 PM
>
> "You leave yet?"

> FROM: FRANK DEFILIPPIS   10 APRIL 2016 . 12:35 PM
>
> "Just left."

"When we went to Monica's for dinner," Defilippis said, "and we walked in, there was Morningstar—who's supposed to be Tony's coach—sitting next to Daniel Dennis eating dinner."

Tony and his family and friends stayed and ate regardless; however, it was the topic of conversation at lunch.

"I accidently might have been the one to make it an issue," Megan Ramos said. "I just saw them eating and I thought it was so strange. I get that they were teammates, but you would never see Morningstar eating with Logan Stieber before a match, for example—and to Tony, it's the same thing. He wasn't wrestling a teammate. He was wrestling an opponent that stood in the way of his goals, and it was off-putting to see them eating together. I think I said, 'I hope Morningstar wants you to win.'"

But, in that moment, Megan would not be the only voice that echoed concern—ultimately, to Tony's family and friends, it became an awkward meal and some sarcasm followed their time together.

To Tony, however, it was just uncomfortable—but he tried to mask his emotions as one more distraction, he felt, was now placed in front of him hours before the biggest match of his life.

Regardless of who was where, Frank said, "I told Tony it can't be a concern. We will address it when it's over. Focus on Dennis, beat his ass, and when it's over, we'll address it."

Unfortunately, Frank believed that no matter what he said to his brother, it was too difficult to reel him back in after witnessing that.

"After seeing that," Defilippis said, "his head was fucked. There was no reason for that at all. Morningstar did Dennis' weight cut with him. He was staying in a hotel [with Dennis] and going to dinner with him through the whole Trials; yet, he's in Tony's corner?—I don't get it. It doesn't add up."

When Terry Brands addressed the dinner situation, he said that Tony had made too much it. "No question [it was a bigger deal than it needed to be]," Terry Brands said, "mentally he is so far away from where he needs to be right now—it's really amazing that he won those first two bouts. I was out to eat with Frankie and Tony and Pilcher the night before after the weigh-ins. Daniel Dennis can say the same thing about me. But [if Ramos believed Morningstar was against him] it's simply not true; it's an imagination."

From Tony's perspective, however, it was very different because of how Terry went about interacting with Dennis and him. "When I walked into Monica's," Ramos said, "there was Dennis sitting and eating with Duroe and Morningstar—I couldn't believe the situation. What Terry did a good job of all week, I think, was that he would eat with me, not Dennis, and not put himself or Dennis in those situations."

Ryan Morningstar addressed the dinner conflict when asked the following day on Monday, April 13, in an interview with Tony Hager of *IA Wrestle* for the podcast "Potentially Dangerous." "If I would have known that Ramos—," Morningstar paused, "I didn't think Ramos would think anything of it. If I knew it was going to be an issue, there is no way I would have put myself in a situation that would make him upset. I just didn't think that would bug him. It never even crossed my mind, to be honest.

"Ramos left with his crew, he had, I don't know, ten to twelve people with him and went out to eat," Morningstar continued. "[Tom] Brands said, 'Hey, Dennis doesn't have anybody to go eat with. Take him to go get something to eat, then take him back to the hotel.' Right as I was leaving, Duroe came running up out of Carver, jumped in, in the car, we took him to eat and then I took him back to the hotel to relax—so it never crossed my mind that it was going to upset him. I never—it just never crossed my mind that he would get upset about that, I guess.

"It wasn't like we were sitting down plotting the match," Morningstar continued. "We were strictly eating and being in a relaxed environment where—I don't even know how much we even really talked about wrestling. We were hanging out—it was relaxing."

However, to Tony and his family and friends, Morningstar's time and relaxation with Dennis was a contradiction to Tony's best interests; he did not make Tony's time before the finals relaxing.

This was the coach that was named to corner Tony, via Twitter, and he had yet to contact or speak to Tony; now, he was out with Tony's competition.

Even though the dinner may have been innocent and something Morningstar never second guessed as a problem, there was a continued lack of communication in Tony's eyes by the staff. This situation that made Tony uneasy, was simply perpetuating a hostility and confusion to a problem that was not sitting well with him due to the conversations Tony and Frank claimed to have had with Tom Brands. Now, each situation that Tony felt was addressed and put to rest, was playing out completely different on this one day, his most important day.

Tony believed that the entire process was being handled poorly. To Tony, Tom Brands' actions had become a distraction—and the one thing Tony made clear was that "Hawkeye wrestlers are told over and over to remove distractions from their lives and their routines."

Unfortunately, and unknowingly, to Ryan Morningstar, his making Dennis comfortable, did the opposite to Tony.

"I tried to block it out as much as I could," Ramos said. "But the situation, for me, before the finals, was uncomfortable. Even when I got back to Carver, no one had communicated anything to me [verbally about who would be in my corner]."

CHAPTER 67
IT TOOK A HAWKEYE TO BEAT A HAWKEYE

"Get your hands where you want them and you got to get to him. You got to get to him. You don't have to be crazy here, but you got to get to him."

• *Terry Brands*
Associate Head Coach, the University of Iowa
Coach, Hawkeye Wrestling Club

ENTERING CARVER FOR THE FINALS AND THE right to represent the United States of American at the 57 kg weight class for the 2016 Olympic Games in Rio de Janeiro, Brazil, Tony stomped to the center mat when his name was announced and cheers from the Iowans followed.

As he arrived, he stood in his red TMWC singlet, serious and anxious at the same time, and he looked at his opponent across from him also warming up. On the surface, Tony appeared focused on the presence of the situation. The opponent, just feet across from him was a man that was an Iowa teammate, a mentor, friend, training partner, HWC teammate, and now a momentary adversary—Daniel Dennis. They knew each other well as people, and they knew each other well stylistically as wrestlers.

Dennis, across the circle from Tony, stood in his plain blue U.S.A. singlet and was serious and nonchalant all at the same time. He squatted, looked around him, and appeared to also be focused and understood the magnitude of the situation.

For the first time, Carver-Hawkeye Arena was split. Here were two of its favorite sons wrestling for the right to be *the Hawkeye* to represent their love and passion for the sport at the sport's most elite level in just under four months.

The crowd, regardless of loyalties, had chosen sides and everyone was interested in the outcome of this particular match. For those who loved Tony or Dennis, the choice was easy—the same was true for those who held a strong disdain for one. However, even for the casual fan or follower with no stake, everyone had an interest in someone—and everyone had an opinion on who would win the best-of-three series and why, but only one former Hawkeye would be crowned champion.

As for the coaching staff, it was divided, physically, for the match. In Tony's corner, Terry Brands coached up against the raised floor. For Dennis, Mike Duroe coached up against the raised floor. Behind that same raised floor, centered, were two chairs and two more Iowa coaches: Ryan Morningstar and Tom Brands. Neither would coach from the corner, it appeared, when the match began. Morningstar was in the seat near Tony's corner, while Tom Brands sat in the seat closest to Dennis' corner.

The excitement was high and Iowa City was focused on the first match as each of the wrestlers came to the center of the circle, as directed by the referee, for the weekend's most anticipated match-up: Hawkeye *versus* Hawkeye.

When the whistle blew, and AC/DC's "Back in Black" was playing throughout the arena from the speakers above the mats, some were standing, some were sitting, but all were watching. As for what was happening on the mat, it was two styles and two men and one possible outcome. Someone would win, someone would lose—a trip to Rio would have to be earned.

Off the start, both Tony and Dennis stepped forward and tied down hard on the other's head looking to begin the wear-down process—Iowa style versus Iowa Style.

However, according to John Smith, former two-time Olympic gold medalist, who was commentating the match, he believed that it was indeed a match-up of two very different styles.

"This is going to be a different match-up," Smith said, "these guys wrestle differently. I think Dennis has got the capability of throws—I've got a chance to watch him in several matches and wrestled overseas, I've been real impressed with him. Ramos is about position. Position, position, position. He's patient, he's won two matches today by criteria—3-3, 4-4. He beat two outstanding people."

The head ties and snaps from Tony persisted, and a two-on-one tie from Dennis was where his position was being fought from. With just eighteen seconds into the match, Dennis took the first shot, a head snap to a high-crotch to Tony's right leg, which Tony circled away from. Then with 00:31 expired, Tony was given his first warning to open up from the referee, who had already spoken to him during the match. "Red, action," the referee said as Tony held a two-on-one wrist tie on Dennis' right hand as Dennis tried to raise Tony's levels.

The warning stopped the match and, once it began, within the next five seconds, Dennis took a second shot—the same high-crotch off the head snap as the first attempt. Dennis would, for a third time, take the same shot selection at the 00:55 mark in the first period. However, as the match continued, Dennis was next to be cautioned by the referee to open up as well and create an offense.

With the continued head ties as Dennis worked for his two-on-one ties and Tony worked to change his levels, neither Tony nor Dennis could position past their opponent's defense for a clean opening in order to be successful on a high percentage shot.

At the halfway point in the first period—with 1:26 left in the period, and by rule—the referee had to place one of the wrestlers on the shot clock. In that, Tony was given his second caution and placed in a position where he had thirty seconds to score or concede one point to Dennis.

Once on the shot clock, and the re-start of the match, Tony came in for his left-handed head tie, and Dennis defended with his right hand over the tie and his hand under Tony's chin, near the throat, to block.

Out of Tony's corner, as Tony snapped Dennis down hard, Terry Brands could be heard yelling, "Keep wrestling there!" he screamed. "Get to the legs! Create your angles! Your ties!"

When the thirty seconds ended, Tony was content with the head snaps, levels, and position he was in—he neither panicked nor did he seem worried about the one-point lead Dennis now had.

From their seats, as the match was being wrestled, Tom Brands and Ryan Morningstar were talking to each other while their two HWC wrestlers were competing in front of them.

For the remainder of the period, there would be a great back and forth struggle for position in order to reach the other's body for an opportunity to score—Dennis would, again, take two more shots, blocked by Tony, but not shots that were truly open for a possible score. However, his attacks, even his half-shots, gave him an advantage over Tony's zero attempts.

When the first period ended, Dennis was up 1-0 and Tom Brands rose from his chair and walked up on the mat to towel off Dennis—Morningstar walked up and toweled Tony.

At the start of the second period, more head-ties came before Dennis worked to a quick drag to another half-shot to keep the offensive advantage in the referee's eyes in his favor. However, Tony would maintain his offense and continue to work Dennis' head and arms and try to find his opening—to no avail.

After the first thirty seconds of the second period had expired, Tony was again placed on the shot clock. And, just as the first time, Dennis was able to defend and keep his position. Now, with two-minutes left in the match, Dennis held a 2-0 advantage over the two-time World Team member.

With 1:27 remaining in the match, Tony took his first shot, a sweep to Dennis' left side. Dennis defended and continually looked for his two-on-one offense.

As each wrestler continued to fight for his own position, the referee stopped the match, with 1:20 left, and put Dennis on the shot clock. And, just as Tony had done, Dennis remained steady to his offense and did not place himself in a poor or vulnerable position.

When the shot clock ended, Tony earned his first point and now, with 00:59 left in the first of a best-of-three series, the score would be 2-1 in Dennis' favor.

Tony would chase a bit and found himself in a football lock on Dennis' head, working for his front head position, and then he transitioned into a second shot in the period with 00:38 left. He reached Dennis' left leg on his attack; however, Dennis, strong in defending that position, worked to his front head—his strongest position—but Tony was able to clear the position and came back to his feet unscathed but also without a finish.

The action and levels and motion picked up in the final 00:15, and Tony found himself forcing that football tie out of his front head position on his feet. Unfortunately, for him, he was unable to create an angle to score. He then attacked Dennis' left leg with 00:09 remaining, looking for some final second drama that he had become accustomed to, but he did not score. Tony then fired in on a double-leg, but Dennis defended, and time expired.

Dennis won the first match, 2-1, handing Tony his first loss in Carver-Hawkeye Arena. The two shook hands, Dennis had his hand raised, and Dennis took the series lead, 1-0.

Tony would run off into the tunnel, collect himself, and start preparing himself mentally for the second match—a match he would have to win if he was to become an Olympian.

AFTER THE END OF THE FIRST MATCH, TONY MET

with Terry Brands in a back area of Carver and Terry Brands knew something was off; however, he did not know what was wrong. "I asked him, 'What's wrong, man?'" Terry recalled. "But [Tony] kept telling me everything was fine—and it clearly wasn't."

In reality, there was much on Tony's mind. First, "People can say that Tom wasn't in Dennis' corner," Ramos said, "but he was. You can have

2016 • UNITED STATES OLYMPIC TEAM TRIALS
57 KG CHAMPIONSHIP MATCH ONE
RAMOS WALKS OFF THE MAT AS DENNIS' HAND IS RAISED
DENNIS WON A 2-1 DECISION IN THE FIRST OF A BEST-OF-THREE SERIES
PHOTOGRAPH COURTESY • UNIVERSITY OF IOWA ATHLETICS

two coaches, but only one coach can be mat side—the other can towel off and coach during the thirty-second break. And that's what Tom did. It didn't matter where he sat, he was in Dennis' corner. As for if I wanted Morningstar in my corner after I saw him [eating dinner with Dennis], I never had the conversation with Terry about it because I didn't feel it was the right time to be thinking and talking about that considering the situation. But, after the fact, Terry said that I should have said something to him and then he could have been four hours ahead of [the situation]."

In regard to others communicating to help Tony's situation, "Terry was pissed at me for not telling him about dinner and Morningstar and finding about how who is corning who and when," Defilippis said. "He said if he knew he could've done more to help get Tony more mentally prepared. But I told him, 'How do you not know? How do *you* not know? Don't give me this you don't know who's in his corner. This is your program just as much as it is Tom's. You guys are running a business together—this is a business.' And no one even talked with Tony about it. Not once."

In regard to the actual wrestling of the first match, there was much hesitation on each wrestlers' parts.

"We have both trained so much with each other, even though for a whole year we didn't train together, not much changes," Ramos said. "We just fine tune things. We know [where the other is] good. He was my training partner in 2014 in Uzbekistan and all we worked on is where I wasn't good—they would put him in those positions on me. So he was very familiar with me. And one of the big things we worked on, because we knew he had a good gut wrench, [Tom] would throw him on top of me to work my gut wrench defense—and positions [I struggled with]. So, I was cautious, and I think he was too, and [that first match] came down to the shot clock violations."

As for what Tony needed to do during the second match, "Get to your set-ups," Terry Brands told him. "Get your hands where you want them and you got to get to him. You got to get to him. You got to get to him. You don't have to be crazy here, but you got to get to him. Do not let the officials settle this match."

In that communication, Tony knew that he had to change and he took Terry Brands' words to heart. "Terry told me," Ramos said, "he said, 'You got his front headlock, you got out of it—you know that's where he's best—now, we got to keep attacking and stay off that shot clock. Whatever you're doing and they caution to put you on the shot clock, you got to change right then and there. You can't wait until they put you on the clock this next match. You can't give up two shot clocks.' So, that was the thing, to go out in that next match and wrestle the whole match the way I did the last thirty or forty-seconds of the first match."

Terry Brands addressed the mentality and problem solving that Tony needed to have his hand raised at the conclusion of the second match. "I think it's a combination of [not wanting to make a mistake in the first match and not getting out of position]," Terry Brands said. "I think that you have to solve those problems on the mat. That's why you spend a lifetime learning how to score a single-leg. That's why you spend a lifetime learning how to get into situations that can win [you] the match like [he] did with Coleman Scott—you're talking about an Olympic bronze medalist right there that he beat. These are things that you solve during matches."

WHEN THE SECOND MATCH WAS CALLED, THE Hawkeyes in the stands stood and cheered. Many were anticipating a more open and action-filled match after the feel-out first match where Dennis was victorious.

For the second match in the series, Tony was suited up in his blue TMWC singlet and paced the full length of the mat as Dennis warmed up in his plain red U.S.A. singlet, and paced in his corner. Once Dennis came to the center to shake the referee's hand, and then Tony's hand, the match would open much differently than the first. Overhead, the speakers would be playing "Eye of the Tiger" by Survivor and, soon enough, Carver would either see a third match between the two former Hawkeyes or see an Olympian crowned.

In the first second of the match's opening whistle, Tony took a quick fake and then fired in on a shot to Dennis' left side. Dennis defended and ended up in his strongest position, his front headlock—this was a place that Tony and Terry Brands knew that Tony wanted to avoid. However, Tony also knew that, regardless of Dennis' positions, he had to work into his offense and put the pace of the match in his control.

And, as Dennis looked to bounce and score from that front head, Tony was able to circle out, clear the position, and return to his feet—all of this in a mere six seconds into match number two.

Once on his feet, Tony attacked again; first with his fakes, then his hands, and then he worked himself into his football lock front head as he looked to work Dennis down to the mat—this was also where Tony usually found his cow-catcher. Dennis, knowing the position, worked into an area where he was very comfortable, his two-on-one. This allowed him to defeat the lock and work out of Tony's tie. However, neither Tony nor Dennis budged on their lock and tie, and the referee had to stop the action in order to resume action. At that point, the first twenty-two seconds had been all Tony's action and forward progression to score.

Tony had wanted to come out aggressive, and that was what he was doing.

"Those were rushed shots," Terry Brands said. "They were shots that were—I guess objectively looking back on it—the first one he cleared the front headlock, so [he] was probably thinking, 'Okay.' But you don't do it that way either, and he knows, he knows that's not a situation you rush into."

When the whistle blew, Tony stayed aggressive. While leaning forward with heavy hand pressure on Dennis, Dennis used it against Tony and snapped him into a front headlock position. Again, this was a very strong position for Dennis; but, it was also a position Tony had successfully defended the first two times he found himself there.

Dennis snapped Tony and tried to beat the corner, but Tony blocked and defended. Dennis snapped again, and the chase was on. Both men were circling and, as Tony raised his right arm to block Dennis' spin, Dennis kept moving and moving and moving and ultimately found himself with a takedown, a 2-0 lead, and in his most dangerous position: top.

In each of his first two matches, Dennis found ways to win through his gut wrench. He felt this was his most dominating move and a position that he was very confident and secure in. As for Tony, he knew Dennis knew this position not only well, but also very well on him from when they trained together—Tony would have to defend what he knew was inevitable.

With forty-five seconds elapsed in the first period, Dennis locked up his gut wrench and, on Tony's right side, squeezed and brought his knee under Tony's right hip, giving him leverage as he drove his feet and looked to score on a turn. While Dennis was going over, Tony was able to post his right hand and looked as if he might be able to pop his hips free and trap Dennis underneath him; however, Dennis stayed in his lock, did not panic, and rolled Tony through for a two-point turn. Dennis now had a 4-0 lead and he remained in the top position with his gut wrench still locked and a split crowd that cheered in surprise as everyone was on the edge of his seat.

Tony did work his hip flat as Dennis remained in his butterfly grip and, once again, and this time to Tony's left side, Dennis kicked his left leg under Tony's body, giving him leverage and, in the process, was able to lift Tony's hips off the mat as he went for a second gut wrench. Tony, this time with his right hand, was able to grab Dennis' left knee and, with his right hand, posted, held Dennis for what looked to be a strong defense as Dennis pumped once and then twice and then a third time. The third time was the charm for Dennis and he had enough to pop Tony over for another two-point turn—Dennis now led 6-0 and was still in the top position.

"Defend the gut!" Terry Brands commented in regard to the position. "[Tony needed to get his] hips down, turn in. Especially after the first one. Stop it! Is Dennis' gut that good? Maybe it is. But where's Tony's defense?"

The two momentarily paused as Tony went into his defense, but Tony raised his hips instead of dropping them. Dennis, still locked tight around Tony, went for another gut wrench that turned into three consecutive turns in the middle of a loud and half-excited-and-half-shocked crowd that was surprised how it came to an end.

The match would be terminated at the 1:04 mark in the first period with the technical superiority—a 10-0 win for Dennis and the opportunity for him to represent the United States of America in the Olympic Games in Rio de Janeiro, Brazil, come August.

As Tony was released from Dennis' grip, he paused on his knees, as if to catch his breath and to take a moment, and he appeared to realize what had just happened—he was devastated.

With Carver going wild, Tony rose and stomped to the middle of the mat. Dennis, who also rose, walked to the middle as well, and for only the second match in Carver-Hawkeye Arena out of thirty-eight total matches, and for the second time in less than an hour, Tony would not have his hand raised. Of course, this final loss was the more difficult of the two as it ended his dream of being a 2016 Olympian.

When the referee grabbed Tony's hand and shook it, Tony was already trying to exit the mat—he pulled and motioned to leave, but the referee held onto his wrist. Ultimately, after the turn, the referee allowed Tony to break away and, as Dennis' hand was being raised in triumph to the Hawkeye cheers of an Olympian in Iowa City, Tony raced off the mat, onto the floor, and into the tunnel in defeat and utter confusion of how it all ended in this manner.

2016 • UNITED STATES OLYMPIC TEAM TRIALS
57 KG CHAMPIONSHIP MATCH TWO
RAMOS CATCHES HIS BREATH AFTER DENNIS' FINAL GUT WRENCH
DENNIS WON THE BEST-OF-THREE SERIES WITH A 10-0 TECHNICAL SUPERIORITY
PHOTOGRAPH COURTESY • UNIVERSITY OF IOWA ATHLETICS

CHAPTER 68
THE BLOWOUT

"It wasn't about eating with Dennis. It wasn't about being in the corner. It was about an environment that you guys were creating and not even trying to hide."

• *Tony Ramos*

AFTER THE LOSS TO DANIEL DENNIS IN THE finals of the Olympic Trials to represent the United States of America in the 2016 Rio de Janeiro Olympic Games, Tony Ramos did what he had not done since he was in his kids' club days.

"When I exited the floor," Ramos said, "it was everything that I had worked for my whole life just crushed. It was rough. I didn't know really what to do. They tried to grab me for a drug test right away and I told the guy, 'I ain't taking no fucking drug test.' But I knew I had to if I wanted to wrestle the next cycle or it's a four-year ban. But I just wanted to be left alone."

And as he had positioned himself underneath the stairs in order to place himself away from everyone and unloaded his feelings and confusions, he desperately tried to wrap his head around what had just happened, but his emotions were just too much.

"I went back in the stairwell," Ramos remembered, "I was where no one could see me and the only one there was Terry—at least that I know of or could see. I was trying to hide as much as I could. Terry was in just as much pain as I was and no one really said anything, he just kind of let me have my space."

As Tony stated, behind him, as had always been the case in good and difficult times, was Terry Brands. When Terry caught up to Tony, "He was underneath the stairs," Terry said. "I went there and he was there for maybe five, six, seven minutes. And then he left and I followed him. Then he went into the locker room and I followed him in the locker room. We did not have a conversation—not at that point—there was nothing I could say."

IN 1996, TERRY BRANDS DEALT WITH A SIMILAR
type of defeat at the Olympic Trials in Spokane, Washington. Terry, a then World Champion, lost to Kendall Cross in a best-of-three match scenario. Terry won the first match handily, and then lost the final two matches. When the third match concluded, Terry fell to the mat in disbelief, crawled forward, and realized that his chance at an Olympic gold medal in the 1996 Atlanta Games that year was over.

When he exited mat side, he left the area and went off—out the doors of the building and just continued to walk away. It took his brother, Tom, to physically restrain and gather him outside before his coach, Dan Gable, arrived to console his wrestler.

"Did he say anything to me?" Terry reflected, "I don't remember anything in that moment. He was there and he never left my side—that I remember. Was it enough just having my coach there? I don't know—yes...no—it wasn't [enough] for me. There wasn't anything that was enough, or there was everything that was too much. I did not accomplish what I set out to do. There was no consoling me. We never really talked. He knows—I know."

Gable remembers Terry's loss as, "One of the most gut-wrenching losses in my career," he said. "I don't think I ever saw a guy act like that. That was hard. Terry's loss was so extreme. In that moment, there wasn't anything I said. But later that night we probably had more of a conversation, but I don't think he probably heard a lot of what I said. It was too quick. Too quick."

For Gable, from his own experience of having lost back in the 1970 NCAA finals to Larry Owings, he understood the importance of the coach just being by his side. Gable was a senior at Iowa State University, where instead of winning a record third-consecutive NCAA championship and going undefeated throughout his high school and college careers, he had lost his final match. In that loss, his coach was there for him as well.

"My coach was always there for me," Gable said. "He just wasn't one of those coaches that didn't think I needed [to be consoled]. But my assistant coach, Les Anderson, just a few years ago before he died, actually came up to me and apologized—he wanted to take some credit for that loss and he had never really sat down next to me and talked to me about it. I told him that he didn't need to because everybody in the arena thought I was going to win—except for Owings, maybe his coach. I was even out of my game plan for winning because I was doing everything to promote the sport, but you don't do that until after you wrestle. My focus wasn't good—so it was mostly my fault. It would have been nice if the coach said, 'Don't do this. Be careful for this.' But, everyone had too much confidence in me, including myself."

When Gable addressed the Hawkeye match-up, he believed, "The difference between Dennis and Ramos," Gable said, "was probably confidence. I think Dennis was pretty confident. I think Ramos was like strategically confident. And maybe Dennis a little bit too—knowing maybe I can get him down or something like that. If it wasn't for that gut wrench, I think it would have been a tight match."

In each situation, each wrestler, Terry Brands or Dan Gable or Tony Ramos, there was something missing that day or something added that day that took their focus off just slightly—and each reacted in his own way. For Terry Brands, there was maybe an added stubbornness and possible over-confidence; reaction: physically removing himself. For Gable, it was not preparing correctly for his match and simply being over-confident as he was more involved with promoting the sport than focusing on his match; reaction: self-reflection. For Tony, it was the distraction of not having *his* coaches, in *his* corner, coaching *him*; reaction: words.

Regardless, for each loss, there was an opponent that was more prepared, confident, and focused. In their defeat, there was a reaction—immediate or postponed. And, in that moment, each coach, closest to his wrestler, remained by his wrestler's side.

For Tony, there too was distraction and a loss of focus and an opponent who was relaxed and centered and confident in his match-up. And by his side was Terry Brands. Tony's coach. Tony's friend. Tony's mentor. But there was also, in that moment, nothing to say to help Tony's situation—he had lost everything that he had worked for and there were no words to ease that pain.

On the other side, there was Tony's other confidant, Tom Brands, who was not physically in his corner as he had been since Tony entered Iowa and the HWC. And, from Tony's memory, "I don't remember Tom being there at all [after I lost to Dennis]. I did not see him or talk to him."

In his greatest defeat, one of the two men Tony had given everything he had to, was not there to support or console him—Tony felt abandoned. However, Tom Brands remembered it differently as he claimed that he did go to Tony after his defeat. "I did not talk to him," Tom Brands said. "But I made sure I put my hands on him—which I do every time. And he was at his locker and Terry was there and [Tony] was busy. I don't know if he had a drug test, but he was hurrying up with some things; I rubbed his head. [But] there was nothing to say—he [was] distraught."

At the same time Terry Brands was with Tony, Frank had found his way down into the tunnel of Carver, located his youngest brother's vicinity, but kept his distance. But, in that moment, Frank was not looking for his brother, he was looking for Tom Brands—the man he said lied to him and his brother.

Frank remembers that after his youngest brother had just lost his dream to be an Olympian, he came down into the tunnel as quickly as he could and started asking everyone where Tom Brands was. When asked how long before he spoke with Tom Brands, Frank responded, "How long does it take to get down five flights of stairs? At first Mike Duroe saw me and I said, 'Don't you touch me. Don't touch me—go get Tom—you know why I'm here.' And he went and got Tom and we left to talk."

The problem that Frank had was that "Tony's a grown man," Defilippis said. "There was nothing that I could do to make it better—I'd only make it worse [emotionally] if I'd gone to him. He saw me when he was walking out of the locker room with the drug test guy following him and he saw me going into the locker room. So he knew what was going on."

"When I heard that Frankie was looking for me," Tom Brands said, "I was like, 'Oh good, where is he?'"

AFTER MIKE DUROE BROUGHT DEFILIPPIS TO

Tom Brands, back by the wrestling offices in Carver, the interaction on what had transpired between the two began in the waiting room.

"When he got to the [waiting room]," Tom Brands said, "I said, 'Come on [into my office].' But Frankie said, 'I don't need to go in there, coach!' [So] I just sat [in one of the chairs in the waiting room] and he stood up and vented."

As for Frank's communication, it was an attack in anger as to what had just happened to his youngest brother and how he felt the situation was handled. Frank was emotional and hurt and, "I started pointing in his face," Defilippis said. "And I said to him, 'You are a stone-cold liar. I am not one of your nineteen-year-old impressionable kids that that works with. I am thirty-five-years-old. I am an adult. And I know what you said to me. You told me you would be in Tony's corner.'"

Frank continued, "And then [Tom Brands] said, 'Frank, I am in his corner. I'm in his corner for life.' And that right there set me off. That's when I said to him, 'What are you, a fucking life coach or a wrestling coach? Tell me what's going on.' But he had no answers for me. He just sat there."

Then Frank said Tom Brands told him, "Dennis is a Hawkeye, Frank. He's a Hawkeye, too." But that did not sit well with Frank.

"That was the first time in all of our conversations that he said that to me," Defilippis stated. "So I asked him if he knew what a real man does. A man says, '[Frank,] you might not like this, but this is what's best for my program and my number-one priority is the Iowa Hawkeyes. And what my guys get out of Dennis being in the room is immeasurable. So I have to have him here. It's just the way it's going to be.' The only reason he didn't do that is because he, A: He didn't think the match was going to happen; or, B: He didn't [care]. So he told us what we wanted to hear and then goes back on his word later because maybe he rethought it or—I don't what it is. But don't say something as a man, as the head coach, because it's all going to come back on you. Everything. Not one person there doesn't know he lied about it. Not one person. But they won't say anything because they don't have the balls—they're afraid.

"I told him, 'The difference between me and the 15,000 other people up there talking shit about you is that I'm saying it to your face. At the end of the day you have to own what you did.'"

Although Tom Brands said that he did not remember all the details of the conversation with Frank, he did say that he knew Frank was angered and that there was not much to say to comfort him, so he mostly listened. "It wasn't a fight—what am I going to do, fight with him?" Tom Brands said. "Verbally spar with him? I know how he feels. I know what he's got invested. I know how much he loves Tony. But I'm also not going to stand by and [let him] tell me that, you know, that things happened that didn't happen. I mean, there's no way that I gave up on Tony Ramos or didn't support him or wasn't in his corner or whatever—I mean there's just no way."

When asked if that was the accusation made by Frank in their conversation specifically the promise to corner Tony, Tom Brands replied, "I don't even know."

With some added moments of spoken anger and spells of silence in the conversation, Frank commented how "Tom kept going back to saying, 'I am in his corner, Frank. I'm in his corner for life.'"

In addition to what Frank claimed he was promised by Tom Brands, what Frank saw also bothered him in regard to how Tom Brands responded to both Tony and Dennis being called to the mat.

"When Tony walked out," Defilippis said, "he walked out with Terry and Morningstar. When Dennis walked out, he walked out with Tom, and Tom was in his corner and smacked him five in the corner and then went back and sat in his seat. Don't give me [that], *that's* in somebody's corner. Period. Tom said, 'I sat neutral.' Really? In between periods,

Tom was toweling down Dennis and giving him instructions—the match is all over, anyone can watch what happened. So don't tell me you're in his corner for life. You're not."

While Frank and Tom and Terry Brands stood outside the office, according to Frank, "[Tom Brands] asked me what I wanted to do. I said, 'Tom, what I want to do and what I'm going to are two different things. You just shattered my brother's dreams. His life—up to this point, this is his life. He's got a child and, on top of it, I know what I've gone through with the kid—you don't want to know how I feel.'"

At that moment, Frank said that Terry Brands stepped into the situation. Frank's emotions were very high and Tom Brands was allowing him to vent. But Terry Brands needed to intervene because nothing was going to change—the match was over. "Terry said," according to Defilippis, "'Well, he lied to you. What do you keep doing here, Frank? He lied to you. Just walk away.' And he was right—so I walked away. Because, now, it was time to move on."

From the point of view of Tom Brands, who did not share the content of the interaction, he said that he felt the conversation was a good one even though it was very emotional. "It was a very good conversation," Tom Brands said, "because, when it ended, it was open-ended. [But] I didn't feel good about anything—Tony Ramos just got beat off the Olympic team 2016. I didn't feel good about anything. I felt good that [the conversation] was open-ended."

When Frank left, he still did not have the answers he wanted, but, "[Tom] knew exactly where I stood when I was done talking with him," Defilippis said. "And [Tom knew] exactly where Tony stood."

For Frank and Tom and Terry Brands, there was a strong investment in Tony as a wrestler as well as a person. And even though a Hawkeye was on the Olympic team, it did not sit well with either Frank or Tom or Terry that Tony's dream of being an Olympian in 2016 was gone. Tony was hurt. Frank was hurt. Tom and Terry were hurt. Emotions were high on all ends and there were no words or actions to comfort anyone. All that was left to do was move forward, and each would do so in his own way.

CHAPTER 69
THE BETRAYAL

"My issue is not with Dan Dennis. My issue is with Tom Brands and how everything was handled."

• *Tony Ramos*

EVEN THOUGH TONY HAD YET TO TAKE HIS DRUG test, and it was about two hours since his match, Tony was still trying to gather himself as much as he could; still trying to wrap his head around the situation. "[In that time], I had been texting back and forth with Megan," Ramos said. "It was tough."

What made the situation even more difficult for Tony was that when he and Megan were texting, she wanted to take some of the blame for him staying in Iowa City when he wanted to leave. Originally, when Tony had heard about Dennis staying to train, he wanted to leave—that was what sparked the conversations with Tom Brands. But, to Tony, once Tom communicated to him that he had nothing to worry about, and Tony took him at his word, Tony chose to stay. He still felt uncomfortable, but his wife and Frank assured him that with Terry in his corner and training him, maybe that would not be the best time to uproot his family and training facility.

"When she texted me, she said, 'This is my fault.' And I told her, 'This is not your fault. It was my decision. I stayed.' But I know she was hurting just like I was. She invested a lot as well."

Megan, emotional, wanted to be there, physically, for Tony, but she could not at that moment. "First of all," Megan explained, "[Tony] told me he wouldn't be around for a while because he wasn't able to complete his drug test yet. Second, he told me he wanted to let loose in his interview and asked my permission. I said, 'Go ahead.' I'm usually the voice of reason, but I couldn't keep it together emotionally after the match."

Not many people were left in Carver-Hawkeye Arena when Tony was ready to leave, but he still needed to complete his drug test. Afterward, when he came out of the drug test room, Terry Brands, Frank, and one of Tony's best friends, Zach Pilcher, were right there waiting for him. This was the first opportunity Terry had to physically console Tony. Again, there was nothing to say, just an embrace. "When Tony walked out of the drug test room," Defilippis said, "he and Terry just hugged. Terry had been through the same thing and there was nothing that I could offer to that, so I walked away."

"He came up after drug testing," Terry Brands commented, "and I said, 'You got to keep your head up, man.' And he hung onto me for about five minutes. I don't really remember from there."

But, after that moment, Tony was asked to head into the media room. To Tony, he already knew what was on his mind and what he felt that he had to do.

"I knew it was going to get brought up," Ramos said. "I had told my wife ahead of time that I—she felt the same way the whole time. I was asked to go do a press conference and, at first, I wasn't sure if I wanted to do it; but, at the same time, I felt it was my obligation as a professional athlete. You don't see people who just lost the Super Bowl turn down interviews—not the good ones—just because they're hurt. I've still got to do that because it's part of the job. So I told them that I would do it. When I spoke with Megan, I told her that I wasn't going to hold anything back. I'm going to tell them exactly how I feel. And she said, 'You do what you got to do. I support you one hundred percent.'"

THE INTERVIEW IMMEDIATELY TOOK ON A LIFE

of its own. "The first question was, 'How do you feel right now?'" Ramos remembered. "I opened up with, 'I lost. I own that. I'm not blaming anyone for this and that, but this is how I feel.' And I went on with how I felt betrayed with this and that and the only thing people saw was me trying to make excuses. I don't think I was making excuses. Right from the beginning I said I own the loss—I lost. The loss is on me and no one else because I was the only one out there."

This was the Tony Ramos interview with a variety of reporters asking him questions:

REPORTER   "Tony, do you think maybe you can describe your emotions and feelings right now?"

TONY RAMOS	"Um, I guess the biggest thing for me right now that I'm feeling, um, you know I'm not trying to put the blame on anyone for the loss—you know, that's on me; I was the one out there wrestling. But I feel like this whole situation between me and Dennis was handled, I guess, not in the best way. Um, you know, I was lied to a couple of times. I was stabbed in the back. I feel like I was loyal to a fault to coaches and athletes and the things that I've seen and, right now, the first thing I'm thinking is I need to move on and get out of this program."
REPORTER	"Can you elaborate on that?"
TONY RAMOS	"Uh, yeah. I know, you know, I'm not going to hold anything back. Um, I was told by Tom Brands over two months ago that he would not be in Dan Dennis' corner, and him and Terry would corner me. Um, we had the conversation, right away I see Tom Brands is going to be in Dan Dennis' corner from the media, from Twitter. Um, you know, then they have Ryan Morningstar in my corner. Well, I go out to eat, Ryan Morningstar is sitting at a table and eating dinner with Dan Dennis. You know, that's just things that probably shouldn't be handled like that in that situation. Um, you know, Dennis was on his way out of here, going to Virginia Tech, and Tom bent over backwards to bring him back. You know, why would you do that to your top athlete who's number one on the ladder right now and put him in that situation? Um, but that's life, that's things you deal with. You know, Terry Brands, he's the man. The whole time he was by my side, the whole time he agreed with how I felt. Um, at the same time, you want me to elaborate more, just go look at the comments from the HWC members. Go look at the comments from Ryan Morningstar. I don't think there was one person in this program, other than Terry Brands, that really wanted to see me win that match."
REPORTER	"And I guess I need to go watch that HWC, can you maybe elaborate?"
TONY RAMOS	"Yeah, I mean, you know, just go look at the comments made by Brent Metcalf saying that Dan

Dennis is the Donald Trump. You know, at first he was just throwing his hat in the ring, and now he's the number-one guy. And this was before, months before, we had even wrestled or knew it was going to happen. You know, things like that. But, it's whatever."

REPORTER "It's obviously a unique situation with you guys. Looking back, you know, what should the coaches have done? How should they have handled—"

TONY RAMOS "—They should never have brought him in. Terry Brands agreed with me on that, too. You know, he said, when we had this conversation, when they never approached me, they never asked me how I was going to feel about it. Two months into it, three months into it, right after the Yarygin, they had heard some rumblings that I wasn't okay with what was going on. Tom came to talk to me and that's when it was established that, you know, he was not going to coach Dennis, he was going to be in my corner. Um, obviously, that didn't happen. You know, he even told my brother that he was going to put his money where his mouth was and his loyalty where his mouth was and—I see where it's at now.

REPORTER "Why weren't you okay with [Dennis] coming back?"

TONY RAMOS "Um, would you be okay with someone coming back if you were the top guy and you had the top coaches working with you and they're bringing a guy in at your weight class who's going to meet, who you know you're going to compete with in the finals? [Pause] Not at all. I don't think anyone would be. Would Brent Metcalf be okay training next to Frank Molinaro every day? Would Jordan Burroughs be okay with having Kyle Dake or David Taylor in the room with him every day?"

REPORTER "What was the difference between that though and say, McDonough, when you had that situation?"

TONY RAMOS "McDonough was here, he didn't leave. McDonough wasn't on his way out. Um, they didn't have to go and beg McDonough to come back."

REPORTER	"What was it, I mean, what was it, something, I guess, that affected you or bothered you in the training situation, him being there?"
TONY RAMOS	"Yeah, it did. And there were talks between me and my wife of leaving in the middle of the season. And she kind of asked me to stick it out; I stuck it out. But, uh, you know, now it's time; I need to get out of here."
REPORTER	"Any, I know it's early, any idea where you'd maybe want to go?"
TONY RAMOS	"I don't know what's next yet. I don't know if I'm going to keep competing. I don't know what I'm going to do yet."
REPORTER	"If you don't keep competing, what—what direction, could you consider coaching, fighting?"
TONY RAMOS	"I'm going to find a coaching job and I'm going to freakin' find a way to beat, you know, whoever I can."

• • •

When Tony exited the media room, it was already after the medal ceremony. "I think the media was glad they stuck around and got the interview," Ramos said. "As soon as I said that I needed to leave and that I was betrayed, everyone's eyes were huge. They were like, 'Wow, what just happened?'"

With the exiting of the media room and the instantaneousness of modern news and social media, Tony knew exactly, in that moment, how all types of people felt—Iowa supporters, Iowa haters, diehard fans, casual fans, everyone and anyone with a phone or a computer and an open opinion on the matter discussed the interview.

"I knew what people were saying on social media," Ramos said. "I check that stuff all the time. I knew they wouldn't like it and I understand why they don't like it because they're worried about how it will impact recruiting and how it's going to affect the program. And it's the same people who are [upset with me] are the same people who are saying Tom Brands needs to be fired and that there needs to be a change. Then I come out and say the situation I was in and they now need to look to the leadership about what is going on instead of getting on me and how I'm going to impact the program with this. Maybe there's a problem already going on."

When asked if Tony understood that maybe the HWC supporters and alumni and fans of the program felt betrayed, he responded with how, "I think they feel betrayed because I brought the issue out in public. Me and Tom had talked privately on the Dennis situation numerous times and I tried to handle it privately—[Frank and I] tried to handle it privately. And, honestly, it didn't work—I was lied to. So, it had to go public. I don't regret anything I said because it was all true."

However, the greatest misconception that Tony felt was out there was that he did not support Dennis. "Dennis is the guy at the weight," Ramos said. "He beat me and I own that loss—I said that. I hope he wins gold. But people see or hear about that interview and say that I took the night away from him—that's not what I was doing. I was asked how I felt and I told them how I felt. My issue is not with Dan Dennis. My issue is with Tom Brands and how everything was handled."

• • •

For Terry Brands, even though he understood where Tony was coming from in regard to his frustrations with Daniel Dennis and how he was brought back into the Iowa room, he did not fully agree with the end result.

"From my perspective," Terry Brands said, "from my perspective, personally, objectively—not having a conversation with Tony, not having a conversation with Daniel—is [training in the same room] only makes them both better. It's a very, very dicey environment, it's a very, very high-octane environment, and it's going to make you a tougher, make you a better, a stronger person.

"The things that I agree with [Tony on] weren't that [the spot was his]—it was never his. The conversation was never, 'Daniel should never had come back because you should get all the coaching'—heck no. No way. I would never say that. But I do understand what he's saying. Daniel left. He left. 'So, now, what are you going to do?' is the message.

"I understand what you're doing. I understand what you're saying, Tony, but it's still not yours whether Daniel goes to Virginia Tech or retires or comes to Iowa—the spot is not yours. It's that sense of entitlement that is getting [him] into trouble and making it hard and harder and harder for [him] to not only win the world championships, but even to win the Trials. So that's the part that's tough on me. I do—I do see what he's saying—I do agree with what he says. I understand what he says. I don't agree with the solution he took. I just don't. Tony is not an excuse maker—that's not Tony. He's never been that way. I have seen him own losses, big losses, while at Iowa. This isn't Tony. Looking back, I think he pressure-cooked himself right out of the entire tournament."

WHILE THE RAMOS INTERVIEW WAS TAKING place, Tom Brands had no idea what was going on in the media room and what Tony Ramos was discussing. In fact, it was the University of Iowa's Sports Information Director (S.I.D.), Chris Brewer, who went to Tom Brands and let him know that there was a situation with the interview and the media was waiting to hear from him for a response to what Tony had said.

"I didn't see the interview," Tom Brands said. "I was told about it by our S.I.D., and there was a host of people waiting for me for a response. I had no context. So as the interview questions came, I got more context, except for what Brewer briefed me on."

This was the Tom Brands interview with a variety of reporters asking him questions:

REPORTER   "Coach, have you spoken with Tony Ramos since his loss?"

TOM BRANDS   "I have not spoken to Tony Ramos. I, uh, have spoken with his brother. Um, I was in proximity to Tony Ramos and put my hands on his head—uh, he's not feeling very good, right? Because you put your life into something and it doesn't go your way—we're all competitors here."

REPORTER   "He seemed, um, I guess upset in his interview with the [Dennis] situation here and how it was handled and—and who was going to coach who—I guess, when was that stuff discussed amongst you guys about if this happened, who would be where?"

TOM BRANDS   "Uh, this is a situation that I am just aware of his comments—first of all. Second of all, um, corner, when you corner a guy, you're not in his corner for his matches, you're in his corner for his life. I've been in that guy's corner since the day he walked onto campus. Have been and always will be."

REPORTER   "Um, when did you discuss who would be in the corner physically in the wrestling match? If it happened?"

TOM BRANDS   "It was discussed that I would be in his corner, and I was."

REPORTER   "Tony said that he was lied to."

TOM BRANDS   "How was he lied to?"

REPORTER   "About the corner situation."

TOM BRANDS	"I don't see it that way. Here's what I see: I see two guys after the same thin. They're both Hawkeyes, they're both vital to our program [and] because of the Hawkeye Wrestling Club they've had opportunities to pursue something that's the pinnacle of the sport, and when you're talking about things that maybe, um, unravel a little bit, um, maybe it's easy to go the sour grape route. All right, maybe that's easy. Um, when you're accusing someone of lying and-and-and-and things that are not true, um, you know I have a hard time, uh, believing that's true. When, since day one, when that guy walked on campus, he's been my guy. Just like every other guy upstairs in that wrestling room—eligibility or members of the Hawkeye Wrestling Club, we give our soul to those guys equally. And, you know what, there's—there's a lot to be said for you get what you earn—that's been thrown around a lot with the *Terry* video—and, you know what, you do get what you earned. And the bottom line is we had two guys at the weight and I am very happy for Dan Dennis and I am down about Tony Ramos. I'm as down about Tony Ramos as I am about Brent Metcalf. And if Tony Ramos wins that wrestling match, then I am extremely happy for Tony Ramos and I am as down about Dan Dennis as I am about Brent Metcalf. And it's really that simple."
REPORTER	"When did you, or anyone at Iowa, first contact Dan and, you know, try to maybe ask him to come back and wrestle? Or, how did it come about?"
TOM BRANDS	"Dan Dennis, when he left the program, he has made several—and I said this when I was walking through the mix zone—he has made several trips to Iowa City. He's not a stranger here. He's my guy, all right. He's a Hawkeye. And, uh, whether he went to California or wherever he ends up, he's our guy and he was welcome in our room on hundred percent. And, uh, we-we tried to get him here full-time several times and, uh, you know he just felt like it was something that he had to do to get into coaching and then he got committed and started developing relationships, like coaches do—it was hard for him to leave California. All right, you know what? Every four years there's the Olympic

	Games, and 2016 came around and he had an opportunity."
REPORTER	"Do you think, for Tony, the proximity to losing is, uh, the emotions are so raw that's contributing to the, his comments a little bit?"
TOM BRANDS	"I can't speak for him, but I know he's hurting. But I don't know what reasons there are for that, that—that's not, um, something that I focus on. I focus on the message to Tony Ramos is, is come talk to me. All right, I haven't even talked to him—I got ambushed. I got ambushed here. But I'm calm and I'm cool because the message is, is that, you know what? I'm in your corner. You know, it's more about being in the corner of a match, it's about being, you know, with you every step of the way. I mean I, when I think of Tony Ramos, I don't think of, you know, the Rio—Rio 2016 Trials. I think of, I mean a whole host of emotions come in and it's—it's about development and the things that he should be really proud about."
REPORTER	"He said that he's moving on. He's done here. Do you think that—that this is salvageable?"
TOM BRANDS	"It's salvageable from a relationship point of view because I don't give up. Um, but, you know, this is not the first time that I've heard that he would like to go and coach closer to the Chicago-area. So, it's not the first time I've heard that. He's a valuable commodity as a coach and there's programs out there. Tony Ramos is good with kids. He's good with—with his coaching. He's good with mentorship. And that's one of the reasons why when—when—when our guys graduate, and they're at that level, not all of them stick around. There's a reason why they don't stick around, and there's a reason why the ones stick around, it's because we make it easy for them to stick around. He was an asset to us. He's a mentor. He's a big part of our program. We call it an extension of our coaching staff. The NCAA rules say they are not coaches, they can't be coaches, but they can still be an extension of our coaching staff just because they're rubbing elbows with our eligible guys every day. That's the genius of the

	Hawkeye Wrestling Club and that's the genius of these clubs around the country. And you know who pioneered that? The University of Iowa, with Roy Carver and Gary Kurdelmeir and Dan Gable. That's who pioneered that. This isn't something where, you know, we're the, you know we're leading the charge—there's—there's a serious competition out there for getting guys like Dan Dennis and Tony Ramos. So, no, it's not surprising to me that, um, he would be looking to better his family in a professional coaching position."
REPORTER	"How about Dan Dennis? I mean, what can you say about him? His story?"
TOM BRANDS	"I said it in the mix zone, I don't remember seeing you there, Mike."
REPORTER	"I'm sorry?"
TOM BRANDS	"But the one thing I said, is—I'm just calling you by name so people know that we know each other, we got a good relationship right?—Um, the one thing I said is he lives his life how he wants to live it and that's something that a lot of people gravitate toward. People like that, you know, when you can say what you want to say and, uh, you're unfiltered, and then you can go live how you want to live. And you know what? It's not a sympathy thing, it's a choice by him and that's what I love about it. And you know what? We all march to the beat of a different drummer. And, uh, you know, those two guys are opposites, and I've talked about that as well. Tony Ramos is motivated by what Dan Dennis isn't. Dan Dennis is motivated by things that Tony Ramos isn't. But both those guys helped our program, and there's no—there's no—uh, no way around that when you look at the results, the results of our guys at those two guys' particular weight class. And I'm talking specifically Cory Clark and Thomas Gilman. And then Brandon Sorensen and on up the line-up because mentorship spreads."
REPORTER	"Tony seemed to say that other athletes in the Hawkeye Wrestling Club, other coaches, maybe favored Dennis at times as well, that Terry was the one that was kind of on

TOM BRANDS	"I don't see anything like that. I know that our coaches—here's the great thing about having the Hawkeye Wrestling Club, is—is you got elite athletes and there's not forty elite athletes in there—there's, in our case there's five and one of them had double knee surgery. All right? And so we had four guys in this tournament. And what happens is our coaches, they gravitate toward certain guys. And Terry's responsibility became Metcalf and Ramos. My responsibility was more Telford and Dennis—and then Morningstar factors into it. And-uh, you know, and—and then [Ben] Berhow obviously with the relationship with Telford being a heavyweight. You know, he—he was with Telford. Um, you know, um, there's a lot of things that just slide into place there."
REPORTER	"Would you like Tony Ramos to stay here and keep training and competing here?"
TOM BRANDS	"Tony Ramos has an open door—and he knows that. And that's maybe my emotion and appeal, but, hey, I'm not going to talk to Tony Ramos through this dog-gone press conference. I'm answering your questions because Chris Brewer came up with an ambush and here I am. I mean..."
REPORTER	"Just one question: Learning all this, when will you reach out to Tony?"
TOM BRANDS	"Um, I'll reach out to him as soon as possible—when I walk upstairs and I get my phone, wherever it is, it's not here. Um, I spoke to his brother. This, you know, being upset, it's competitive, competitive thing we do here—extremely competitive and extremely personal. So, but, you know, let's move on."

• • •

After the Tom Brands interview, the social media world starting weighing in on his responses. Some were supportive of what Tom Brands said and took to heart his explanations and circled some of their criticism of Tony around the "sour grape" comment and how Tony was a sore loser.

When Megan started sifting through some of the comments about Tony, she was simply hurt and had some feeling of guilt.

"I tried not to let it bother me," Megan said, "but I did—I cried a lot. I wanted to protect Tony the best that I could. I felt really guilty because I didn't realize how bad things were mentally for him until it was too late and that we really should have left or at least Tony should have went and trained somewhere else."

Others took to Tony's defense stating that the Tom Brands interview made the coach look guilty of lying, and that his evasiveness to the question of cornering Tony by use of the metaphor, "I was in his corner," was ridiculous.

From the perspective of Dan Gable, there were two issues worth being discussed: First, he addressed the issue of cornering and the impact a coach can have on a match; and, second, the lack of communication.

"All the controversy afterwards," Gable said, "for me, was like: there's two sides. I always say there's two sides. I don't very seldom ever see something that's one-sided—I just don't. I always think that one side causes the other side to do something—like in marriages, all kinds."

On the issue of cornering a wrestler, "If you are going out there and you think a coach is going to win the match for you," Gable said, "you're crazy. I didn't care who was in the corner but, you know what, when it came down to the Olympics, first round, the guy actually saved my match because he was really good in the corner. The guy knew what to do, immediately, and then gave me the advice I needed to win the match. So, even though I had the mentality that I don't care who's in my corner, it can make a difference in key situations having the right guy."

And no matter how the situation was handled, Gable knew every coach was different and that coach had to handle situations his own way. That being said, Gable was clear that communication was the key, regardless of what one feels that another person should already know based on what was going on around him. Everything needs to be addressed. However, Gable also knows everyone handles situations differently.

"I look at me and I look at Tom and Terry and we're all different," Gable said. "We all operate on different tunes. Just because I think handling a situation one way isn't necessarily how they should handle it. That's how I'd handle it. But other people might say, 'You should know. I shouldn't have to tell you that.' That's why I think there could have been more communication ahead of time because these are kids. Even though they're adults, they're still kids."

After the Tony Ramos interview happened, Gable, now one of the sport's greatest promoters, did see the light through the dark cloud being cast in Iowa City.

"I would have liked to not see this happen," Gable said, "even though it kept us in the news. From a [Coach Gary] Kurdelmeir point of view, any promotion is good, whether good or bad. Personally, I like to prevent those negatives. But, the Brands, they have their own way of thinking. Tony Ramos has his own way of thinking. And what Tony thought might have been true might not have been true. But unless you actually had a pow-wow, and everybody knows exactly what is going to happen, there's things that happen that aren't planned. As much as I love things to be one-sided, if there are two parties that need to be informed and updated for prevention, then I think that should be the case."

And as Gable reflected on communication and how lessons had to be learned sometimes, he reflected back on one of the most difficult times in his life and how his lack of communication, in his mind, was the cause of his older sister's death.

"I mean, I go back to my sophomore year of high school," Gable reflected, "and I was walking with my neighbor and he said all of these nasty things about my sister and I never said a word about it to anybody—and then he killed her a month later. If I'd a just walked into my house and said something to my mother or father she might still be alive."

The lesson Gable took away from this moment was one of communication and getting back on his feet. "I couldn't let it ruin my life," he said, "but I can sure take on the responsibility of doing the best I can from now on to make sure that communication is out to the people I care about. So you've got to learn some tough lessons sometimes. I'm sure the coaches are learning some lessons from what's taken place and I'm sure Tony's probably learning some lessons—maybe regretting some things. I mean, it's a pretty emotional time. But, at the same time, maybe he's focusing on the wrong part. Maybe the focus should've been elsewhere. But, good conversation leads to good communication which leads to good preparation and eliminates some of these crazy times."

When Tom Brands left the media room, he said he was also working to communicate and understand what had just happened. "I tried to call both Tony and Frank," Tom Brands stated. "They didn't pick up."

As for Tony, "Frankie kind of got [Tony] together," Terry Brands said, "and I told [Tony's brother] Vince he had to stay the night with him. Frankie said they had to get going and I told him he had to stay the night with him. And after they left, I walked into an ambush in the office."

CHAPTER 70
OUT FOR BLOOD, OUT FOR A BURRITO

"I finally felt relieved that the stress that I was under was gone after that press conference, and getting all of that off my chest."

• *Tony Ramos*

BY THE TIME TERRY BRANDS RETURNED TO HIS office in Carver-Hawkeye Arena, the two interviews—neither of which he had seen or heard—had spread like a wild fire and caught up with him there.

"When I got to the office," Terry Brands explained, "everyone was swearing—saying this and that about Tony—and I said, 'Wait, wait, wait—what's going on?' And Metcalf takes out his phone and points it at me and says, 'Show you what your boy just said.' I said, 'Who?' Metcalf shook his phone, 'Ramos.' I shook my head and said, 'I've seen and heard worse from your best friend, buddy.' As soon as I said that, Metcalf got a little scowl on his face and I said, 'Get that phone away from me before I bust you and the phone.'"

After that exchange with Metcalf, Terry Brands walked into his office and, "Then a couple other guys walked by and they were on their cell phones," Terry Brands remembered. "And they were just growling up and down—and I was just ambushed. I had no idea what had happened. So I get in my car—and I'm emotionally spent—I'm going home at this point and time. I get halfway home and I start putting it together: This guy just went on a rant. So, I called Frank and said, 'Hey, where are you?' Frank said, 'I'm at Tony's.' Then I asked him if he was spending the night and I said, 'I'm coming over right now.'"

In the time Terry Brands had to deal with the wrestlers in his office, and even more Hawkeyes who saw or heard or who were texted highlights of Tony's interview and were out for blood, Tony and Frank were out for a burrito at Panchero's. "It was late," Ramos said, "it was all that was open, and I like burritos."

While at Panchero's, Frank's phone had been ringing and text messages were coming in non-stop. When Frank finally opened his phone, as he waited for his burrito, he was reading text messages from friends, family, current and former Hawkeyes, and even Hawkeye legends.

"After I read four or five of the texts," Defilippis said, "I turned to Tony and asked him, 'Hey, did you really say all of those things?'"

Tony looked up and said, "It's the truth. If they can't handle it, it's not my problem. I didn't lie, he did."

When Tony and Frank arrived back at Tony's home, there were two things that happened that had never happened before: Tony had never lost when he returned from wrestling at Carver; and, Tony's son A.J. was up.

"When I got home," Ramos said, "A.J. wasn't sleeping, he was awake—which was crazy because it was late at night and he is usually in bed by seven. Megan said that he was crying and wouldn't go back to bed. I walk into the room and there he is sitting up on the bed and it was just a big release to see him and hold him and kind of have him there to comfort. It was good to see my wife, too. But, at the same time, I felt relieved—I finally felt relieved that the stress that I was under was gone after that press conference, and getting all of that off my chest."

Once Tony was able to put his son to bed, the wives stayed upstairs while Tony and Frank ate downstairs and occasionally spoke to one another.

It would be some time before Terry Brands walked into Tony's home. He was at the house, but he was in the driveway as he had to speak to a few former Hawkeyes.

"As I was driving home," Terry Brands recalled, "and I live way out, about seven miles outside of Iowa City and I was three miles from my house and I live on the other side of Tony, I turn around and now I know what's going on. I had not seen the video, but I knew that this guy had just said something that has somebody stirred up and I called a few guys. How I remember it is that both guys were adamant that what he did was unforgivable, and I was adamant about how there is no difference what [some former Hawkeyes do] to us every single day and what Tony did to us in the heat of the moment where Flo[Wrestling] stuck a microphone in his face and took advantage of a guy—which, that's not really true because [Tony] is still accountable. And Tony hasn't been accountable and that's the thing that [upsets] me the most.

"So I go: 'You know what, why don't you actually be proactive and instead of making an enemy? Why don't [you] reach out to this guy? Why don't you reach out and say, 'Hey, I want to know what's going through your head? Let's meet. Let's meet in two or three days when your head clears because I want to know why you feel this way about me.' By the grace of God, [Luke] Eustice actually reached out and sent a text to Tony when I was at Tony's house, and Tony said, 'Eustice just texted me and wants to meet with me.' I just had tremendous joy going through my heart and I was like, *Finally! Someone finally understands that he's a Hawkeye. He's a HAWKEYE and we're going to reach out and keep him as one of us.* He went through a tough time. We just got to get him to own the loss. We got to get him to be accountable, and we just got to get him to go back to his roots and everything's going to be okay.

"Then I get a call from [Royce] Alger, and he wants [Tony] dead. Dead. Not shot dead, but 'He's dead to me.' And I got Royce because, by the end, he was like, 'I'm glad I called you. I see what you're saying.' It was a forty-five minute conversation with Alger, and I was sitting in Tony's driveway to get him to realize that this is a Hawkeye. 'This is no different than this thing that this other guy that you think is so grand and glorious and [speaks poorly about] me and Tom daily, and the program, and wants to take Thomas Gilman's head off with Joey Dance every single day that he's around him. I know what's going on. I know the psychology of it—I'm paranoid that way. It's no different. But because you don't vibe with Tony, and because you're close with this other guy, you're going to be done with Tony, but you're not going to be done with this guy? You guys are so unstable. You guys are so one-sided and subjective that it's not even reasonable for me to sit here and have a conversation with you. It's no different. IT'S NO DIFFERENT!'"

When Terry Brands finally went into Tony's home, he found his wrestler, his friend, hurting and sat down next to him and just listened. "He said things like, 'How do you get through it?' Terry Brands said. "He said things like, 'Yeah, yeah, I know…' And then he'd be like, 'Why? Why? Why? Why? How does this happen?' And then it would be confusion and just the things that you would expect."

Terry Brands sat and listened and spoke when appropriate. As he talked, he felt that he was able to hone in on the right aspects of the moment that Tony needed to hear. He responded to Tony's questions and felt as if he was bringing him around, but each time he came close to having Tony, there was an interruption."

Upstairs, Megan was doing her best to stay out of the conversation, but she was still very emotional and curious as she was just as broken down by the situation as Tony was. "[Frank's wife] Beatrice was with me in the kitchen," Megan said, "and Terry and Frankie were with Tony in the living room. I wasn't part of the conversation and I was trying not to eavesdrop. I was just relayed bits and pieces afterwards."

Throughout his talk with Tony, Terry Brands felt that he was making progress in having Tony come around to him even though the loss and the situation was still very fresh and he was still very emotional about how the last few months had transpired.

"So this is all going on and these guys are coming my way," Terry Brands said. "And the only guy who didn't get it, at the end, was Frankie. He kept interrupting, 'Yeah, but…' And I would get Tony there and Frankie would be up in the kitchen where I couldn't see him over the balcony, and I'm telling Tony, 'You got to own it. You got to be accountable. You got to go back to your roots. Time will heal this—whether you leave or not, whether my brother's a liar or not, I understand what you're saying. You want to leave, that's the best thing for you, I'm in support of you and I'll help you do anything I can to help you go wherever it is you want to go. You want to stay, I'll help you.'"

What Tony took to heart was, "When me and Terry talked, he agreed with me and told me that this was betrayal at the highest level. It's his brother and he told his brother not to bring [Dennis] in and not to do this, but no one will understand the situation or why it's betrayal at the highest level unless they were in it and have competed at that level. And then he told me what's next. But, I couldn't, 'I've got to get out of here. I can't stay here.' Terry told me, 'I knew when it was time for me to leave and if you got to go, I agree with you, go. I'm going to help you wherever you are and along the way. If you ever need anything, if you want to come and train—things like that. And then he told me, 'You got to find peace. You find peace in your family. You find peace in the Bible. You got to do what you got to do to find peace on a daily basis. If you need someone to talk to, you can always call me.'"

CHAPTER 71
MONDAY MORNING

"When I woke up, I felt relieved. I felt free and like I got a fresh start."

• *Tony Ramos*

BY THE TIME TONY WOKE UP MONDAY MORNING, he had clarity and a simple reminder of life's bigger picture. "When I woke up, I felt relieved," Ramos said. "I felt free and like I got a fresh start. And as soon as I saw A.J., he brought me back to reality. There he was with big eyes, smiling, and it was refreshing—I was still dad. No matter what happens, my family is always going to love me. I'm always going to be their hero in their eyes."

As for the second part of Tony's morning, this free and fresh perspective was also providing new opportunities. "When I checked my phone," Ramos commented, "[the day] just kept getting better and better because my phone was ringing non-stop. Coaches calling, kids asking where I'm going to end up saying, 'Hey, where you going? We want to know what's going on.' It felt like there was still a lot of support. I was even getting text messages from former Hawkeye athletes."

Also on that Monday, Frank was working to create some new and positive opportunities for his brother as well.

"I DIDN'T SLEEP ALL NIGHT," DEFILIPPIS SAID. "I spent all night trying to figure out the best place for Tony. I got in my car at 7:00 a.m. and headed back to Chicago with an idea."

In Frank's mind, there was one place where Tony could not only thrive, but he could also learn a great deal and grow in his wrestling. On top of that, one of Frank's greatest concerns was helping Tony solidify a place where could work, build his resume, and raise his family.

And the more and more he thought about it, he thought of one place, with one wrestler, where Tony and his family could thrive—but he was not sure how the conversation would go because Tony had just defeated that person the day before in the semifinals of the Olympic Trials in Iowa City.

According to Frank, the phone conversation went like this:

DEFILIPPIS	"Coleman Scott, Frank Defilippis, Tony Ramos' older brother. I just want to say that I've been a long-time fan, and I have a couple of questions if you have a minute."
COLEMAN SCOTT	"Of course I got a minute. Thank you."
DEFILIPPIS	"Are you done competing?"
COLEMAN SCOTT	"Frank, I'm with my wife and kids right now, I'm headed to Giordano's pizza. I'm done, man. I'm a head coach, I gave it one last go—that's it."
DEFILIPPIS	"Is there a spot at North Carolina for Tony? We're weighing out our options."
COLEMAN SCOTT	"Is this serious?"
DEFILIPPIS	"Absolutely."

"Once I told him that it was serious," Defilippis said, "we set up a time to meet. I got back to my house, showered and got dressed for work, and by 1:00 p.m., on no sleep, I was at the O'Hare Giordano's having lunch with Coleman Scott, his wife, and two kids—and I thought it all through, too.

"There was no better fit that I could think of. The other thing was, Coleman is strong where Tony struggles, and where Tony is strong Coleman struggles. They won't be in competition anymore, and Coleman will be his coach.

"At first, yes, I wanted Tony to stay in Iowa—but he couldn't. Terry left Iowa before and did his thing; Tom left Iowa for Virginia Tech—so Tony was going to do what he had to do and I was going to help him. There is still some respect there [with Tom Brands] because of what he did for him while he was there—and you have to respect that, but there's no trust [right now]. So, will Tony end up back in Iowa? Who knows—my guess is it's not likely if Tom's there—but anything is possible."

In regard to North Carolina, Frank made it clear that there would have to be some stipulations—business-wise—to make this new opportunity attractive to Tony and his family as well. His brother needed a paid position on staff because Tony wanted to start building his resume, and he wanted stability.

Coleman had to make some phone calls, go back to North Carolina and figure some way to piece it all together, and then call Frank back.

When Coleman returned Frank's call to discuss the finer details, Frank gave two numbers to the Tar Heel Wrestling Club. The first number would be what Tony needed, and the second number would be a number Tony would like to have. The club gave Tony what he would like to have.

With Tony now on board, and Coleman Scott a product of Oklahoma State University, pieces were beginning to fall into place for North Carolina to now attract newer recruits, and to also build on their club like their alma maters had.

"What I like most about this situation," Defilippis said, "Coleman's young, aggressive, and he gets it. He understands the roots where these new kids are coming from, and so does Tony. Tony's timing and when he graduated and where he was at, couldn't have been better—sometimes you get lucky. I mean, he's good, but he got a little lucky, too; the timing was there."

In regard to how Frank felt about Coleman after his conversation, "I can't say enough about him as a man," Defilippis said, "because I don't know if I could have [hired Tony] after having just wrestled [and lost to] Tony the day before, and I told him the same thing."

THE FOLLOWING DAY, TUESDAY, TONY WENT into surgery for an out-patient procedure—this had been planned regardless of the outcome on Sunday. "I had a tear in my knee that I needed to get fixed," Ramos said.

And as he pondered where he was going to be going from that point forward, he found his position difficult. By placing second at the Olympic Trials, Tony was now the alternate to the 57 kg weight class, the class he had represented the U.S. at the senior world level for the past two years.

"You know," Ramos said and paused, "it's tough for me to want to play that alternate role. So I think I need to decide where me and my family are going to end up first, and then figure out if I want to be in that role as the alternate. I'll probably stay in some decent shape, but I don't know—I think I need some time to let my mind heal and my body heal and maybe just start getting ready for 2017."

In tandem with Tony's plan to work and train, he also had the task of making certain his family was in good hands. "I'm looking at this thing from all angles," Ramos said. "As a father, a husband, and if I want to keep competing, what's going to give me the best opportunities and what's going to help me succeed? I'm looking at the fact that I want to coach next year—maybe be a volunteer to where I can go in and work with guys and help that program work to be a powerhouse. But, most importantly, my family has to feel comfortable and they have to feel welcomed—click with the wives and with the people they're going to be surrounded by. Megan is big with family and she likes family close by, so if we end up not in the Midwest, it's going to be hard for her, so she's got to feel comfortable."

Through it all, the entire journey, Tony was reminded of a number of important pieces to his life and where his life was at in that moment.

"People have been reminding me," Ramos said, "that when one door closes, there's opportunities that open up that can be blessings in disguise to make [me] a better athlete for competition and a better person to move forward in life. I really do appreciate all of the support that I am getting from everyone. I am sure a lot of people think that it is all hate, but the supporters, they're not going to go on the message boards, they're doing it by emailing me, messaging me, calling me. So there's just as much support as there is backlash."

Frank runs Tony's website where he receives his requests for camps and appearances, which he looks through, and forwards over to his youngest brother for consideration. "There was an overwhelming amount of support for Tony from people," Defilippis said. "People have this stigma about Iowa wrestlers. There's a stigma about them that if you go there, you fall into it by default. People don't realize [Tony's] a good kid. They think he's some jag-off that stares at people—like a punk. He's a good kid. He's never been in a street fight in his life—he doesn't drink, he doesn't do drugs, he's never in trouble—the [stare] is just what works for him; it's how he turns on his lights to go to work. That's all. If you don't like it, you don't have to—he's the furthest thing from a jag-off.

"But he's caught in that stigma, that Iowa way," Defilippis continued. "And most those kids there, they are all good kids. They wrestle hard. They work hard. They are in a good place. They love to wrestle and compete—that's what's fun for those guys. They just happen to do it in Iowa and have been successful. But people see them as mean and they don't shake hands and they are jerks and robots and no one's having fun—nothing could be further from the truth. I can't tell you how many times a kid or parent or anyone who meets Tony, or any Iowa wrestler, says to me, 'Man, we didn't think he was going to be that nice.' I get that all the time. All the time! After [Tony] lost, I can't tell you how many emails we got in support and wanted to say something to comfort him. They know who he really is. And that comes with stardom, too—not everyone's going to like you. But he sticks to who he is pretty well—he is who he is."

Frank concluded, "And even though I'm not happy with how it all ended, Tom and Terry Brands get a lot of the credit for Tony and his success. Tony could not have done it all without them and I don't think Tony would have been as successful somewhere else. Those guys helped make Tony who he is and we will never forget that."

ONCE TONY AND TOM BRANDS HAD A MOMENT TO speak to one another, it was brief. "It was about a minute and a half," Tom Brands remembered. "It was pretty much, 'I love you.' A hug. Then, 'Goodbye.'

"He came in and said, 'I want you to know, it's over,'" Tom Brands said as he revisited that final conversation. "And I said, 'I get the first word. You get the last word. I'll always be in your corner and I love you.' He got up and said something, I probably said something, we hugged, and he left."

As for Tony's feelings about Iowa, he said "Iowa will always be a very special place for me. I grew up there, met my wife there, and have a lot of great memories there. But it was time to move on."

ON APRIL 27, 2016, TONY RAMOS ACCEPTED A volunteer coaching position at the University of North Carolina where he would be trading in his black and gold—the first time since fourth grade—and putting on the Carolina blue and white.

"Coleman and me have two totally different perspectives on things," Ramos said, "but he is strong where I am weak and I am strong where he is weak—together we are looking to do great things here. I am real excited for this next chapter in my life."

THE TAR HEEL WRESTLING CLUB

2016 • UNITED STATES OLYMPIC TEAM TRIALS
57 KG CHAMPIONSHIP SEMIFINAL MATCH
RAMOS AND SCOTT SHARE A MOMENT AFTER THEIR MATCH
PHOTOGRAPH COURTESY • UNIVERSITY OF IOWA ATHLETICS

BIBLIOGRAPHY

49 North Wrestling. (2014, July 8). *2014 Canada Cup: 57 kg Tony Ramos (USA) vs. Steven Takahashi (CAN)* [Video file]. Retrieved 2016, from https://www.youtube.com/watch?v=v6Q3z8ZhjIY&t=6s

49 North Wrestling. (2014, July 8). *2014 Canada Cup: 57 kg Tony Ramos (USA) vs. Steven Takahashi (CAN)* [Video file]. Retrieved 2016, from https://www.youtube.com/watch?v=v6Q3z8ZhjIY

49 North Wrestling. (2014, July 9). *2014 Canada Cup: 57 kg Final Dillon Williams (CAN) vs. Tony Ramos (USA)* [Video file]. Retrieved 2016, from https://www.youtube.com/watch? v=g2-xvpu Qfsk

Abbott, G. (2014, November 21). So, exactly what is the Global Wrestling Championships, which launches Nov. 22 in Ithaca, N.Y.?? Retrieved 2016, from http://www.teamusa.org/ USA-Wrestling/Features/2014/November/21/Update-on-the-Global-Wrestling-champion ships?fb_comment_id=754824921255813_75633598443 8040#f 250ea403678288

Abbott, G. (2014, November 22). Dake, Dlagnev, Ramos win championship belts in first Global Wrestling Championships. Retrieved 2016, from http://www.teamusa.org/usa-wrestling /features/2014/november/22/dake-dlagnev-ramos-win-global-wrestling-championships-belts

Abbott, G. (2015, January 31). Ramos wins gold, Metcalf gets a bronze at Grand Prix of Paris. Retrieved 2016, from http://www.teamusa.org/USA-Wrestling/Features/2015/January /31/ Ramos-wins-Grand-Prix-of-Paris-Metcalf-gets-bronze

Abbott, G. (2015, July 11). UPDATE: USA wins seven golds and 17 medals in all styles at Grand Prix of Spain. Retrieved 2016, from http://www.teamusa.org/USA-Wrestling /Features/ 2015/July/11/USA-wins-seven-golds-at-Grand-Prix-of-Spain

Abbott, G. (2016, March 5). Ramos, Dlagnev qualify USA at their weights with semifinal wins at Pan American Olympic Qualifier in Texas. Retrieved 2016, from http://www.teamusa. org/ USA-Wrestling/Features/2016/March/05/Ramos-Dlagnev-qualify-their-weights-for-Olympics-with-semifinal-wins

Askren, B. (2014, April 22). Why Cage Fighter Mike is good for wrestling. Retrieved from Askren Wrestling Academy: BLOG: https://awawisconsin.com/why-cage-fighter-mike-is-good-for-wrestling/

Associated Press. (2013, December 17). FILA announces new weight classes. Retrieved 2016, from http://www.espn.com/olympics/wrestling/story/_/id/10153107/wrestling-drop-2-weight classes -rio-games

Bader, M. (2011, December 5). *133 lbs match Tony Ramos Iowa vs. Shayden Terukina Iowa State* [Video file]. Retrieved 2016, from http://www.flowrestling.org/video/527000-133-lbs-match-tony-ramos-iowa-vs-shayden-terukina-iowa-state#.WR3UOmgrKUk

Bader, M. (2011, December 5). *Tom Brands, Derek St. John and Tony Ramos* [Video file]. Retrieved 2016, from http://www.flowrestling.org/video/527199-tom-brands-derek-st-john-and-tony-ramos#.WR3T4WgrKUk

Bader, M. (2012, March 4). *133 lbs finals Tony Ramos Iowa vs. Logan Stieber Ohio State* [Video file]. Retrieved 2016, from http://www.flowrestling.org/video/616587-133-lbs-finals-tony-ramos-iowa-vs-logan-stieber-ohio-state#.WR2XVGjyuUk

Bader, M. (2013, March 10). *Logan Stieber body locks Tony Ramos in overtime* [Video file]. Retrieved 2016, from http://www.flowrestling.org/video/699672-logan-stieber-body-locks-tony-ramos-in-overtime#.WR2Xx2grKUk

Bader, M. (2013, October 8). *Tony Ramos The IOWA Way* [Video file]. Retrieved 2016, from http://ww w.flowrestling.org/video/721819-tony-ramos-the-iowa-way#. WR3vBWgr KUk

BIBLIOGRAPHY

Bader, M. (2015, March 29). *Elephant in the room* [Video file]. Retrieved 2016, from http://www.flowrestling.org/video/942449-elephant-in-the-room#.WR3PL2grKUkBader, M. (2015, March 29). *From the Trailer to the Trials* [Video file]. Retrieved 2016, from http://www.flowrestling.org/video/942439-from-the-trailer-to-the-trials#.WR3pS2grKUk

Bader, M. (2015, March 29). *In this Corner* [Video file]. Retrieved 2016, from http://www.flowrestling.org/video/942451-in-this-corner#.WR3OeWgrKUk

Bader, M. (2015, March 29). *Trailer 2 Trials* [Video file]. Retrieved 2016, from http://www.flowrestling.org/video/942450-trailer-2-trials#.WR3O0mgrKUk

Bader, M. (2016, January 30). *57kg r1, Tony Ramos, USA vs Grigoriev, Russia* [Video file]. Retrieved 2016, from http://www.flowrestling.org/video/904241-57kg-r1-tony-ramos-usa-vs-grigoriev-russia#.WR3PrGgrKUl

Bader, M. (2016, January 30). *57kg r2, Tony Ramos, USA vs Syurun, Russia* [Video file]. Retrieved 2016, from http://www.flowrestling.org/video/904311-57kg-r2-tony-ramos-usa-vs-syurun-russia#.WR3QCWgrKUl

Bartachek, R. (2015, January 31). Ramos wins Paris Grand Prix title. Retrieved 2016, from https://iawrestle.com/2015/01/31/ramos-wins-paris-grand-prix-title/

Bartachek, R. (2015, May 20). Beat the Streets Preview: Salsa in the Square. Retrieved 2016, from https://iawrestle.com/2015/05/20/beat-the-streets-preview-salsa-in-the-square/

Bartachek, R. (2015, June 2). Tony Ramos – "It Was Only a Matter of Time". Retrieved 2016, from https://iawrestle.com/2015/06/02/tony-ramos-it-was-only-a-matter-of-time/

Bartachek, R. (2015, June 13). Ramos Earns Spot on Second World Team. Retrieved 2016, from https://iawrestle.com/2015/06/13/ramos-earns-spot-on-second-world-team/

Bartachek, R. (2015, July 12). Dennis Wins Gold in Spain. Retrieved 2016, from https://iawrestle.com/2015/07/12/dennis-wins-gold-in-spain/

Bartachek, R. (2015, September 14). *Tony Ramos Video Interview after World Championships* [Video file]. Retrieved 2016, from https://iawrestle.com/2015/09/14/tony-ramos-video-interview-after-world-championships/

Bartachek, R. (2015, November 4). Dan Dennis to make 57 KG Debut at Bill Farrell. Retrieved 2016, from https://iawrestle.com/2015/11/04/dan-dennis-to-make-57-kg-debut-at-bill-farrell/

Bartachek, R. (2015, December 20). *HWC's Dennis wins national title* [Video file]. Retrieved 2016, from https://iawrestle.com/2015/12/20/hwcs-dennis-wins-national-title/

Bartachek, R. (2016, January 29). HWC's Dennis and Ramos struggle in USA's first day at Yarygin. Retrieved 2016, from https://iawrestle.com/2016/01/29/hwcs-dennis-and-ramos-struggle-in-usas-first-day-at-yarygin/

Bartachek, R. (2016, March 7). Ramos takes Silver at Pan American Olympic Qualifier – Qualifies weight for Rio. Retrieved 2016, from https://iawrestle.com/2016/03/07/ramos-takes-silver-at-pan-american-olympic-qualifier-qualifies-weight-for-rio/

Bartachek, R. (2016, April 10). *Tom Brands talks Dennis vs Ramos* [Video file]. Retrieved 2016, from https://iawrestle.com/2016/04/10/tom-brands-talks-dennis-vs-ramos/

batupload. (2014, July 8). *2014 CAN CUP SR FS 57kg Tony Ramos (USA) vs Dillon Williams (Impact)* [Video file]. Retrieved 2016, from ttps://www.youtube.com/watch?v=sApVtdQzX0A

batupload. (2014, July 10). *TONY RAMOS (USA) Wins 2014 FS 57kg FILA CANADA CUP* [Video file]. Retrieved 2016, from https://www.youtube.com/watch?v=IfuxA2KcgrY

batupload. (2014, July 11). *2014 CAN CUP SR FS 57kg Tony Ramos (USA) vs Marcel Ewald (Ger)* [Video file]. Retrieved 2016, from https://www.youtube.com/watch?v=_2Dr_hyxcjE

BIBLIOGRAPHY

Big Ten Network. (2013, February 1). *Penn State at Iowa - Wrestling Highlights* [Video file]. Retrieved 2016, from https://www.youtube.com/watch?v=RjY7fGRBGLI

Biography: Hassan Rahimi. (2016). Retrieved 2016, from https://www.revolvy.com/main/index. php?s=Hassan%20Rahimi&item_type=topic

Biography: Marcel Ewald. (2016). Retrieved 2016, from https://www.world-of-wrestling.com/marcel-ewald

Biography: Steven Takahashi. (2016). Retrieved 2016, from Wrestling Canada Lutte website: https://wrestling.ca/athlete/steven-takahashi

Brands, T. (2016, May 4). Personal interview.

Brands, T. (2016, May 16). Personal interview.

Bratke, K. (2015, May 8). *He's Been Running His Mouth* [Video file]. Retrieved 2016, from http://www.flowrestling.org/video/769417-hes-been-running-his-mouth#.WR3BSWgrKUk

Bryant, J. (2015, April 13). With Raucous Support in Los Angeles, Iran Tops Host United States to Win Freestyle World Cup. Retrieved 2016, from https://unitedworl dwrestling.org/article /with-raucous-support-in-los-angeles-iran-tops-host-united-states-to-win-freestyle-world-cup

Bugos, J.T. (2010, December 6). Ramos becomes 'the man' at 133. Retrieved 2016, from The Daily Iowan website: http://dailyiowan.com/2010/12/06/Sports/20354.html

Bugos, J.T. (2010, December 6). *Ramos rocking Carver: Tony Ramos is becoming 'the man' at 133*. Retrieved 2016, from http://dailyiowan.lib.uiowa.edu/DI/2010/di2010-12-06.pdf

Bush, J. (1994, January 30). Glenbard North crosses threshold to DVC title. *Daily Herald*.

Canadian Olympic Committee. (2016). Biography: Dylan Williams. Retrieved 2016, from Canadian Olympic Team Official Website: http://olympic.ca/team-canada/dylan-williams/

Capezio, G. (2016, February 4). Personal interview.

Cherry, J. (2015, February 23). Personal interview.

Cindy Sentes. (2013, October 3). *NCAA D1 2011 Scotti Sentes, CMU vs Tony Ramos, Iowa* [Video file]. Retrieved 2016, from https://www.youtube.com/watch?v=lCTuxO9uB-A

Considine, J. (2015, November 8). Personal interview.

Cooper, C. (2013, July 9). *2013 Iowa Hawkeye Wrestling Highlight* [Video file]. Retrieved 2016, from http://www.flowrestling.org/video/717116-2013-iowa-hawkeye-wrestling-highlight#. WR2dcGgrKUl

The Daily Iowan. (2014, March 9). *Tony Ramos on winning his first Big Ten championship* [Video file]. Retrieved 2016, from https://www.youtube.com/watch?v=rNtEkfZmWe4

The Daily Iowan. (2016, April 10). *Tom Brands responds to Tony Ramos* [Video file]. Retrieved 2016, from https://www.youtube.com/watch?v=aIGAkrlqTpo

Darren, M. (2014, January 8). Wrestling: Ramos an Underdog? Retrieved 2016, from http://www.hawkeyesports.com/news/2014/1/8/Ramos_an_Underdog_.aspx?path=wrestling

Defilippis, F. (2015, October 8). Personal interview.

Defilippis, F. (2016, May 19). Personal interview.

diweb. (2006, April 5). *Tom Brands named Iowa Wrestling Coach* [Video file]. Retrieved 2016, from https://www.youtube.com/watch?v=l93JykiC3E4

DMRegister. (2013, February 1). *Iowa coach Tom Brands after beating Penn State* [Video file]. Retrieved 2016, from https://www.youtube.com/watch?v=72yfu_aSB2A

DMRegister. (2013, February 1). *Iowa coach Tom Brands after beating Penn State* [Video file]. Retrieved 2016, from https://www.youtube.com/watch?v=72yfu_aSB2A&t=25s

BIBLIOGRAPHY

DMRegister. (2013, February 1). *Tony Ramos after the Penn State dual* [Video file]. Retrieved 2016, from https://www.youtube.com/watch?v=K2PeNEzqX6E

DMRegister. (2013, March 10). *Tony Ramos: I've got to get to my offense quicker* [Video file]. Retrieved 2016, from https://www.youtube.com/watch?v=8OCQVCt7Bv4

DMRegister. (2016, September 23). *Joe Colon reaches Midlands finals at 133* [Video file]. Retrieved 2016, from https://www.youtube.com/watch?v=YiJJbLUXNSY

DMRegister. (2016, September 23). *Midlands champion Joe Colon* [Video file]. Retrieved 2016, from https://www.youtube.com/watch?v=erFTU1T9s9k

DMRegister. (2016, September 23). *Tom Brands on Tony Ramos* [Video file]. Retrieved 2016, from https://www.youtube.com/watch?v=aJGgnMV3DLE

DMRegister. (2016, September 23). *Tony Ramos: 'I wanted to make a statement'* [Video file]. Retrieved 2016, from https://www.youtube.com/watch?v=ceQni9eZY1E

DMRegister. (2016, September 23). Tony Ramos lifts 'huge weight' off shoulders at Big Ten finals [Video file]. Retrieved 2016, from https://www.youtube.com/watch?v=QUmi1OvrdyA

EasternIowaWrestling. (2013, September 14). *Terry Brands - Imagination* [Video file]. Retrieved 2016, from https://www.youtube.com/watch?v=fv6O557N4mM

Edwards, C. (2016, January 3). Personal interview.

Fickel, D. (2006, October 22). *Best 2007 High School Juniors*. Retrieved 2016, from USA Wrestling Magazine website: http://www.eteamz.com/kyusawrestling/files/Best2007HighSchoolJuniors.pdf

Fickel, D. (2015). Wrestling USA Magazine National High School Records and Rankings. Retrieved 2016, from http://www.wrestlingusa.com/high-school/records-and-rankings.html

Floreani, M. (2010, March 19). *Daniel Dennis on being in the Finals* [Video file]. Retrieved 2016, from http://www.flowrestling.org/video/319560-daniel-dennis-on-being-in-the-finals#.WR3pE2grKUl

Fulk, B. (2015, June 12). Personal interview.

Gable, D. (2016, May 16). Personal interview.

Geist, R. (2016, April 28). Personal interview.

GLBLMedia Sports. (2014, January 10). *141 Carter vs Ramos - 2013 NWCA All Star Classic* [Video file]. Retrieved 2016, from https://www.youtube.com/watch?v=1oms NDWRoAc

GoBoroAthleticsTV. (2013, December 5). *A.J. Schopp on His Victory over #1 Tony Ramos of Iowa* [Video file]. Retrieved 2016, from https://www.youtube.com/watch?v=kpYR3vrZzOU

GoBoroAthleticsTV. (2013, December 15). *Wrestling: Edinboro vs. Iowa* [Video file]. Retrieved 2016, from https://www.youtube.com/watch?v=31p0CPnUfbo

Goodwin, C. (2013, December 6). Iowa squeaks by Edinboro, 22-19. Retrieved 2016, from http://www.dailyiowan.com/2013/12/06/Sports/35939.html

Goodwin, C. (2014, March 10). Iowa's Ramos claims first conference crown. Retrieved 2016, from http://www.dailyiowan.com/2014/03/10/Sports/37004.html

Goodwin, C. (2014, March 14). *'The Stare' still hungry* [Video file]. Retrieved 2016, from http://www.dailyiowan.com/2014/03/14/Metro/37107.html

grappler1999. (2003, February 12). *2009 Illinois Tony Ramos vs. Jon Morrison for the state champ* [Video file]. Retrieved 2016, from https://www.youtube.com/watch?v=uhpq3rGYLOw

BIBLIOGRAPHY

Greddy NOva. (2016, April 14). *2016 Olympic Team Trials Wrestling 57kg Finals - Tony Ramos vs Dan Dennis Match 1* [Video file]. Retrieved 2016, from https://www.youtube.com/watch?v=T5S7-Wix1a4

Hager, T. (2014, February 27). Senior Day: Reflections on Iowa Wrestling's Senior Class. Retrieved 2016, from https://iawrestle.com/2014/02/27/senior-day-reflections-on-iowa-wrestlings-senior-class/

Hager, T. (2015, June 17). Tony Ramos and Brent Metcalf featured on Takedown Wrestling. Retrieved 2016, from https://iawrestle.com/2015/06/17/tony-ramos-and-brent-metcalf-featured-on-takedown-wrestling/

Hager, T. (2015, November 27). TITAN MERCURY WC FALLS TO POWERFUL BIMEH-RAZI TEAM IN FINALS OF WORLD WRESTLING CLUBS CUP IN IRAN. Retrieved 2016, from http://takedownwrestle.com/wrestling-news/titan-mercury-wc-falls-to-powerful-bimeh-razi-team-in-finals-of-world-wrestling-clubs-cup-in-iran/

Hager, T. (2016, January 26). *Daniel Dennis on going to Yarygin, his return to mats and Olympic quest* [Video file]. Retrieved 2016, from https://iawrestle.com/2016/01/26/daniel-dennis-on-going-to-yarygin-his-return-to-mats-and-olympic-quest/

Hager, T. (Producer), Bartachek, R., & Ryder, N. (2016, April 13). *Potentially Dangerous *special* with Ryan Morningstar* [Podcast]. Retrieved 2016, from https://iawrestle.com/2016/04/13/ potentially -dangerous-special-with-ryan-morningstar/

Hahn, M. (2015, December 20). Personal interview.

Hamilton, A. (2014, September 6). Tom Brands on Tony Ramos [Video file]. Retrieved 2016, from http://www.desmoinesregister.com/videos/sports/college/iowa/wrestling/2014/09/05/9998979/

Hamilton, A. (2014, September 8). Ramos drops opening-round bout at World Championships. Retrieved 2016, from http://www.desmoinesregister.com/story/sports/college/Iowa/wrestling /2014/09 /08/tony-ramos-world-championships-tashkent-uzbekistan/15270019/

Hamilton, A. (2015, September 6). Endorsement influx a game-changer for USA Wrestling. Retrieved 2016, from http://www.desmoinesregister.com/story/sports/2015/09/06/usa-wrestling-world-championships-wrestlers-cashing-more-than-ever-business-deals/71730844/

Hamilton, A. (2016, February 29). Grand View dismisses Andrew Long after rule violation. Retrieved 2016, from http://www.desmoinesregister.com/story/sports/2016/02/29 /college-wrestling-grand-view-dismisses-andrew-long/81128280/

Hamilton, A. (2016, April 8). Ex-Hawkeye, Olympic hopeful has quite a tale to tell. Retrieved 2016, from http://www.hawkcentral.com/story/sports/college/iowa/wrestling/2016/04/08/olympic-trials-daniel-dennis-returns-to-wrestling-after-two-year-layoff/82786998/

Hardy, P. (2016, April 4). *Former Iowa wrestler Daniel Dennis talks about his break from the sport* [Video file]. Retrieved 2016, from https://www.youtube.com/watch?v=yEjHYbh7ooI

Hassan Rahimi Videos. (2016). Retrieved 2016, from https://www.revolvy.com/topic/Hassan+Rahimi&stype=videos

Hawk Central. (2015, April 4). Ramos stuns Olympic champ [Video file]. Retrieved 2016, from http://www.hawkcentral.com/videos/sports/college/iowa/wrestling/2015/04/04/25284375/

Hawkeye Sports. (2011, March 19). 2010-11 UNIVERSITY OF IOWA WRESTLING INDIVIDUAL MATCH-BY-MATCH RESULTS: Tony Ramos. Retrieved 2016, from http://sidearm.sites.s3. amazonaws.com/hawkeyesports.com/documents/2016/6/30/1011 _ stats _4_.pdf?id=11481

BIBLIOGRAPHY

Hawkeye Sports. (2012, January 7). Wrestling: Tie Goes to the Cowboys. Retrieved 2016, from http://www.hawkeyesports.com/news/2012/1/7/Tie_Goes_to_the_Cowboys.aspx

Hawkeye Sports. (2012, January 20). Wrestling: Hawkeyes Fall at Ohio State. Retrieved 2016, from http://www.hawkeyesports.com/news/2012/1/20/Hawkeyes_Fall_at_Ohio_State.aspx

Hawkeye Sports. (2012, March 19). *2011-12 UNIVERSITY OF IOWA WRESTLING INDIVIDUAL MATCH-BY-MATCH RESULTS: Tony Ramos*. Retrieved 2016, from http://sidearm.sites.s3.amazonaws.com/hawkeyesports.com/documents/2012/3/19/season_stats_final.pdf

Hawkeye Sports. (2012). *2012 Volleyball Media Guide*. Retrieved from http://www.hawkeyesports.com/documents/2012/8/27/2012vbmediaguide.pdf

Hawkeye Sports. (2013, January 4). Wrestling: Hawkeyes over Buckeyes, 22-9. Retrieved 2016, from http://www.hawkeyesports.com/news/2013/1/4/Hawkeyes_Over_Buckeyes_22_9.aspx

Hawkeye Sports. (2013, January 13). Wrestling: Hawkeyes Unable to Finish in Stillwater. Retrieved 2016, from http://www.hawkeyesports.com/news/2013/1/13/Hawkeyes_Unable_to_Finish_in_Stillwater.aspx

Hawkeye Sports. (2013, January 26). Wrestling: Iowa tops Minnesota, 16-15. Retrieved 2016, from http://www.hawkeyesports.com/news/2013/1/26/Iowa_tops_Minnesota_16_15.aspx

Hawkeye Sports. (2013, February 1). Wrestling: Big Wins, Close Wins Lead Iowa over Penn State. Retrieved 2016, from http://www.hawkeyesports.com/news/2013/2/1/Big_Wins_Close_Wins_Lead_Iowa_over_Penn_State.aspx

Hawkeye Sports. (2013, February 10). Wrestling: Hawkeyes Win B1G Dual Title. Retrieved 2016, from http://www.hawkeyesports.com/news/2013/2/10/Hawkeyes_Win_B1G_Dual_Title.aspx

Hawkeye Sports. (2013, February 16). Wrestling: Bonus Points Lead Iowa past Edinboro, 31-6. Retrieved 2016, from http://www.hawkeyesports.com/news/2013/2/16/Bonus_Points_Lead_Iowa_past_Edinboro_31_6.aspx

Hawkeye Sports. (2013, February 22). Wrestling: Hawkeyes Advance with Bonus Points. Retrieved 2016, from http://www.hawkeyesports.com/news/2013/2/22/Hawkeyes_Advance_with_Bonus_Points.aspx

Hawkeye Sports. (2013, February 23). Wrestling: Hawkeyes Fall to Missouri at NWCA Duals. Retrieved 2016, from http://www.flowrestling.org/video/701764-logan-stieber-two-for-two#.WR2aoGgrKUk

Hawkeye Sports. (2013, March 9). Wrestling: 4 Hawkeyes Advance to Finals. Retrieved 2016, from http://www.hawkeyesports.com/news/2013/3/9/4_HawkeyesAdvance_to_Finals.aspx

Hawkeye Sports. (2013, March 25). *2012-13 UNIVERSITY OF IOWA WRESTLING INDIVIDUAL MATCH-BY-MATCH RESULTS: Tony Ramos*. Retrieved 2016, from http://sidearm.sites.s3.amazonaws.com/hawkeyesports.com/documents/2013/3/25/season_stats_final.pdf

Hawkeye Sports. (2013, December 12). Wrestling: Hawkeye Go Big 1-10, Top Buffalo 46-0. Retrieved 2016, from http://www.hawkeyesports.com/news/2013/12/12/Hawkeye_Go_Big_1_10_Top_Buffalo_46_0.aspx

Hawkeye Sports. (2014, January 3). Wrestling: Hawkeyes Win 16th Straight Big Ten Opener. Retrieved 2016, from http://www.hawkeyesports.com/news/2014/1/3/Hawkeyes_Win_16th_Straight_Big_Ten_Opener.aspx

BIBLIOGRAPHY

Hawkeye Sports. (2014, January 4). Wrestling: Hawkeyes Sweep Spartans, 41-0. Retrieved 2016, from http://www.hawkeyesports.com/news/2014/1/4/Hawkeyes_Sweep_Spartans_41_0.aspx

Hawkeye Sports. (2014, January 10). Wrestling: No. 3 Hawkeyes top No. 5 Oklahoma State, 24-6. Retrieved 2016, from http://www.hawkeyesports.com/news/2014/1/10/No_3_Hawkeyes_top_No_5_Oklahoma_State_24_6.aspx

Hawkeye Sports. (2014, January 25). Wrestling: No. 2 Hawkeyes fall to No. 4 Gophers, 19-15. Retrieved 2016, from http://www.hawkeyesports.com/news/2014/1/25/No_2_Hawkeyes_fall_to_No_4_Gophers_19_15.aspx

Hawkeye Sports. (2014, January 31). Wrestling: No. 3 Hawkeyes top No. 19 Wildcats, 31-6. Retrieved 2016, from http://www.hawkeyesports.com/news/2014/1/31/No_3_Hawkeyes_top_No_19_Wildcats_31_6.aspx

Hawkeye Sports. (2014, February 9). Wrestling: Seniors say Goodbye, Iowa tops Michigan, 26-6. Retrieved 2016, from http://www.hawkeyesports.com/news/2014/2/9/Seniors_say_Goodbye_Iowa_tops_Michigan_26_6.aspx

Hawkeye Sports. (2014, February 14). Wrestling: Hawkeyes Roll Past Lehigh, 31-6. Retrieved 2016, from http://www.hawkeyesports.com/news/2014/2/14/Hawk eyes_Roll_Past_Lehigh_31_6.aspx

Hawkeye Sports. (2014, February 23). Wrestling: Iowa tops Wisconsin, earns share of B1G title. Retrieved 2016, from http://www.hawkeyesports.com/news/2014/2/23/Iowa_tops_Wisconsin_earns_share_of_B1G_title.aspx

Hawkeye Sports. (2014, March 8). Wrestling: 5 Hawkeyes Move on to B1G Championship Round. Retrieved 2016, from http://www.hawkeyesports.com/news/2014/3/8/5_Hawkeyes_Move_on_to_B1G_Championship_Round.aspx

Hawkeye Sports. (2014, March 8). Wrestling: 7 Hawkeyes Advance to Semis of B1G Championships. Retrieved 2016, from http://www.hawkeyesports.com/news/2014/3/8/7_Hawkeyes_Advance_to_Semis_of_B1G_Championships.aspx

Hawkeye Sports. (2014, March 22). *2013-14 UNIVERSITY OF IOWA WRESTLING INDIVIDUAL MATCH-BY-MATCH RESULTS: Tony Ramos*. Retrieved 2016, from http://sidearm.sites.s3.amazonaws.com/hawkeyesports.com/documents/20 14/3/28/season_stats_final.pdf

Hawkeye Sports. (2015). *ALL-TIME RESULTS: Iowa Wrestling*. Retrieved 2016, from http://grfx.cstv.com/photos/schools/iowa/sports/m-wrestl/auto_pdf/alltimeresult s.pdf

Hawkeye Sports. (2015). Biography: Tony Ramos. Retrieved 2016, from http://www.hawkeye sports.com/roster.aspx?rp_id=1238

Holland, D. (2016, March 22). Personal interview.

Holland, S. (2016, June 24). Personal interview.

Holmes, R. (2015, September 12). *Tony Ramos Takes World's Performance in Stride* [Video file]. Retrieved 2016, from http://www.flowrestling.org/video/794452-tony-ramos-takes-worlds-performance-in-stride#.WR287GgrKUl

Illinois Athletics. (2016). Biography: B.J. Futrell. Retrieved 2016, from http://www.fightingillini.com/roster.aspx?rp_id=1589

Illinois Matmen. (2007, February 7). Illinois Best Weekly Class AA Rankings. Retrieved 2016, from http://illinoismatmen.com/aa_rankings_2007.html

Inductee: The Hazewinkel Family. (2011). Retrieved 2016, from http://nwhof.org/blog/dg-inductees/the-hazewinkel-family/

intermatwrestle. (2015, April 12). *Tony Ramos after winning against Mongolia 2015 World Cup* [Video file]. Retrieved 2016, from https://www.youtube.com/watch?v=pUTh_x8LTTo

BIBLIOGRAPHY

Iowa Hawkeyes. (2013, January 2). *Tom Brands interview: Jan. 2, 2013* [Video file]. Retrieved 2016, from https://www.youtube.com/watch?v=nJP8Yxal7-8

Iowa Hawkeyes. (2013, January 2). *Tony Ramos interview* [Video file]. Retrieved 2016, from https://www.youtube.com/watch?v=8s2-K6m57Fk

Iowa Hawkeyes. (2013, February 12). *Tom Brands, Matt McDnough, and Tony Ramos on Olympic Wrestling* [Video file]. Retrieved 2016, from https://www.youtube.com/watch?v=arer3bQobG0

Iowa Hawkeyes. (2013, November 4). *Tony Ramos vs. Devin Carter - 11.2.13* [Video file]. Retrieved 2016, from https://www.youtube.com/watch?v=Qw6rmeiwBMI

Iowa Hawkeyes. (2013, December 17). *Iowa Wrestling Prepares for Penn State - 12.17.13* [Video file]. Retrieved 2016, from https://www.youtube.com/watch?v=Q7hhbkldn0o

Iowa Hawkeyes. (2013, December 21). *Iowa - Penn State Wrestling - 12.21.13* [Video file]. Retrieved 2016, from https://www.youtube.com/watch?v=fJ2lXouetJM

Iowa Hawkeyes. (2014, March 5). *Iowa Wrestling Heads to 2014 B1G Championships* [Video file]. Retrieved 2016, from https://www.youtube.com/watch?v=eaTr1A2k10I

Iowa Hawkeyes. (2014, March 8). *B1G Wrestling Session 2 - Iowa Hawkeye Highlights* [Video file]. Retrieved 2016, from https://www.youtube.com/watch?v=mxqfMV1JxoU

Iowa Hawkeyes. (2014, March 9). *Tony Ramos wins 133-pound Big Ten title* [Video file]. Retrieved 2016, from https://www.youtube.com/watch?v=02r7CvLm5QU&t=15s

Iowa Hawkeyes. (2014, March 9). *Tony Ramos wins 133-pound Big Ten title* [Video file]. Retrieved 2016, from https://www.youtube.com/watch?v=02r7CvLm5QU

Iowa Hawkeyes. (2015, April 4). Iowa crowd erupts for *Ramos*. [Video file]. Retrieved 2016, from http://www.hawkcentral.com/videos/sports/college/iowa/wrestling/2015/04/04/25284297/

Kersey, J. (2014, March 19). NCAA Wrestling Championships: Q&A with Iowa's Tony Ramos. Retrieved 2016, from The Oklahoman website: http://newsok.com /article/3944943

Lalovic, N. (2013, December 17). FILA announces new Olympic and non-Olympic weight classes and rule changes. Retrieved 2016, from http://www.teamusa.org/USA-Wrestling/Features/ 2013/December /17/FILA-announces-new-weight classes

Levins, M. (2014, January 10). Tony Ramos, If Looks Could . . . Retrieved 2016, from https://www.thepredicament.com/2014/01/tony-ramos-looks/

Levins, M. (2016, January 29). The Final Call for Iowa's Haddy. Retrieved 2016, from https://www.thepredicament.com/2016/01/final-call-iowas-haddy/

Levins, M. (2016, April 7). Daniel Dennis continues down the road. Retrieved 2016, from https://www.thepredicament.com/2016/04/daniel-dennis-continues-road/

Louwagie, S. (2011, January 21). *For wrestlers, 133 up for grabs*. Retrieved 2016, from http://dailyiowan.lib.uiowa.edu/DI/2011/di2011-01-21.pdf

Louwagie, S. (2012, November 30). Ramos, Hawkeye wrestling look to "prove a point" against Iowa State. Retrieved 2016, from http://www.dailyiowan.com/2012/11/3 0/Sports/31072.html

Martinez, I. (2016, February 19). Personal interview.

May, W. (2015, September 3). World Championships Special: Freestyle Rankings. Retrieved 2016, from https://unitedworldwrestling.org/article/world-championships-special-freestyle-rankings

Miller, D. (2014, January 8). Wrestling: Ramos an Underdog? Retrieved 2016, from http://www.hawkeyesports.com/news/2014/1/8/Ramos_an_Underdog_.aspx?path=wrestling

BIBLIOGRAPHY

Miller, Z. (2008, December 7). *130lbs Felipe Martinez (St. Paris Graham) VS Tony Ramos (Glenbard North) Seminfinal* [Video file]. Retrieved 2016, from http://www.flowrestling.org/video/89876-130lbs-felipe-martinez-st-paris-graham-vs-tony-ramos-glenbard-north-seminfinal#.WR2W2WjyuUk

Minnesota State High School League. (1994). Retrieved 2016, from Minnesota State High School League website: http://mshsl.org/mshsl/showstate.asp?actnum=424

Monaco, D. (2015, December 28). Personal interview.

Morgan, J. (2015, September 12). Rough day for Tony Ramos at wrestling world championships. Retrieved 2016, from http://www.hawkcentral.com/story/sports/college/iowa/wrestling/2015/09/12/tony-ramos-world-championships-wrestling-iowa-hawkeyes/72178906/

National Registry for Wrestling. (2015, September 5). *Interview with Tony Ramos, 2015 USA Wrestling World Team Member at 57 kg* [Video file]. Retrieved 2016, from https://www.youtube.com/watch?v=1tPBdo_cRoI

New York Times. (1981, June 18). ROY J. CARVER 71; IOWA BUSINESSMAN. Retrieved from http://www.nytimes.com/1981/06/18/obituaries/roy-j-carver-71-iowa-businessman.html

nin01994. (2013, March 31). *2013 NCAA wrestling championships 133 Quarter-final* [Video file]. Retrieved 2016, from https://www.youtube.com/watch?v=FaSXwzdVqzA

NsideSports. (2014, March 27). *Tony Ramos Press Conference* [Video file]. Retrieved 2016, from https://www.youtube.com/watch?v=maQF5pJOnH4

NWCAONLINE. (2013, November 5). *Iowa's Tony Ramos Talks Win Over Devin Carter in All-Star Classic* [Video file]. Retrieved 2016, from https://www.youtube.com/watch?v=1cuCIkGrD6U

O'Brien, R. (2016, August 19). U.S. wrestler Daniel Dennis's unusual journey carries him to Rio Olympics. Retrieved 2016, from https://www.si.com/olympics/2016/08/19/daniel-dennis-usa-wrestling-rio-olympics-comeback

OhioWrestlingSite.com. (2006, December 8). Taylor/Stieber showdown highlights Walsh Ironman. Retrieved 2016, from http://intermatwrestle.com/articles/1917

Pilcher, K.J. (2010, March 4). Memorable moments in the 100 years of Hawkeye wrestling. Retrieved 2016, from http://www.thegazette.com/2010/03/04/memorable-moments-in-the-100-years-of-hawkeye-wrestling

Pilcher, K.J. (2014, March 21). Sweet revenge for Ramos in semifinal win: Ramos reaches 133-pound finals. Retrieved 2016, from http://www.thegazette.com/2014/03/21/sweet-revenge-for-ramos

Pilcher, K.J. (2015, June 13). Ramos retains U.S. World team spot: Hawkeye Wrestling Club member sweeps former Panther Colon in finals. Retrieved 2016, from http://www.thegazette.com/subject/sports/ramos-retains-us-world-team-spot-20150613

PSU Sports. (2013, February 1). Wrestling: NITTANY LION WRESTLERS DROP CLOSE 22-16 DUAL AT IOWA. Retrieved 2016, from http://www.gopsusports.com/sports/m-wrestl/recaps/020113aab.html

PSU Sports. (2016). Biography: Nico Megaludis. Retrieved 2016, from http://www.gopsusports.com/sports/m-wrestl/mtt/nico_megaludis_771153.html

Pyles, C. (2014, March 21). *Ramos Ready For Graff* [Video file]. Retrieved 2016, from http://www.flowrestling.org/video/740150-ramos-ready-for-Graff#.WR2nYWgrKUk

Pyles, C. (2015, May 10). 57kg Finals Tony Ramos (HWC) vs. Andrew Hochstrasser (TMWC) [Video file]. Retrieved 2016, from http://www.flowrestling.org/video/769643-57kg-finals-tony-ramos-hwc-vs-andrew-hochstrasser-tmwc#.WR2-02grKUk

BIBLIOGRAPHY

Pyles, C. (2015, May 21). *57kg Match Tony Ramos (USA) vs. Yowlys Rodriguez (CUBA)* [Video file]. Retrieved 2016, from http://www.flowrestling.org/video/770319-57kg-match-tony-ramos-usa-vs-yowlys-rodriguez-cuba#.WR2-fGgrKUl

Pyles, C. (2016, April 13). *Tony Ramos vs Nahshon Garrett At 2016 Olympic Trials* [Video file]. Retrieved 2016, from http://www.flowrestling.org/article/40979-tony-ramos-vs-nahshon-garrett-at-2016-olympic-trials#.WR3utmgrKUk

R., M. (2014, March 22). 2014 NCAA Wrestling Championships results: Semifinals winners and finals match-ups. Retrieved 2016, from http://www.sbnation.com/2014/3/22/5535294/2014-ncaa-wrestling-championships-results-semifinals-winners-David-Taylor-Iowa-Penn-State

Ramos, A. (2015, October 15). Personal interview.

Ramos, A. (2016, April 13). Personal interview.

Ramos, A. (2016, June 25). Personal interview.

Ramos, A. (2016, July 16). Personal interview.

Ramos, A. (2016, August 18). Personal interview.

Ramos, A. [Team Ramos]. (2015, March 29). *AGON Interview* [Video file]. Retrieved 2016, from https://www.youtube.com/watch?v=x1p-1kfLq-U

Ramos, D. (2015, November 9). Personal interview.

Ramos, M. (2017, July 26). Personal interview.

Ramos, V. (2015, August 22). Personal interview.

Reedy, J. (2006, April 7). Brands' departure leaves Va. Tech wrestling with a tough decision. Retrieved 2016, from http://pilotonline.com/sports/brands-departure-leaves-va-tech-wrestling-with-a-tough-decision/article_94fb7504-43e5-52dd-9c0b-4c948c45fb9a.html

Reyes, R. (2016, April 10). *Daniel Dennis is an Olympian!!!* [Video file]. Retrieved 2016, from https://www.youtube.com/watch?v=rI053CALJFw

RossWB. (2014, May 31). TONY RAMOS WINS SPOT ON U.S. WORLD TEAM. Retrieved 2016, from SB Nation website: http://www.blackheartgoldpants.com /wrestling/2014/5/31/5768562/tony-ramos-wins-spot-on-u-s-world-team

RossWB. (2014, September 9). TONY RAMOS, BRENT METCALF FAIL TO MEDAL AT WORLD CHAMPIONSHIPS: Dreams die painfully in Tashkent. Retrieved 2016, from SB Nation website: http://www.blackheartgoldpants.com/wrestling /2014/9/9/6128155/tony-ramos-brent-metcalf-2014-fila-world-championships

RossWB. (2015, April 6). IOWA BEATS THE WORLD AT AGON V. Retrieved 2016, from SB Nation website: http://www.blackheartgoldpants.com/wrestling/ 2015/4/6/8343701 /iowa-vs-the-world-agon-v-results-brent-metcalf-aaron-pico-tony-ramos-henry-cejudo

RossWB. (2015, June 15). TONY RAMOS, BRENT METCALF WIN AT WORLD TEAM TRIALS: 3 The United States team competing at the World Championships will have a distinct Iowa flavor -- again. Retrieved from SB Nation website: http://www.black heartgoldpants.com/wrestling/2015/6/15/8779627 /tony-ramos-brent-metcalf-win-at-world-team-trials

Ruettiger, M. (2016, April 2). Personal interview.

Ruggiano, J. (2015, May 19). U.S. OPEN CHAMPION TONY RAMOS GIVES THE SINGLET OFF OF HIS BACK. Retrieved 2016, from http://tmwc1.com/2015/05/u-s-open-champion-tony-ramos-gives-the-singlet-off-of-his-back/

RussVenti94. (2012, March 18). *2012 NCAA Wrestling Championships "133 Semifinals"* [Video file]. Retrieved 2016, from https://www.youtube.com/watch?v=ICiwS_AjjH4

BIBLIOGRAPHY

Saylor, W. (2013, December 5). Schopp Wins Battle, Hawkeyes Win War. Retrieved 2016, from http://www.flowrestling.org/article/23707-schopp-wins-battle-hawkeyes-win-war#.WR2ir2grKUk

Saylor, W. (2014, March 20). *Tony Ramos (Iowa) vs. Zane Richards (Illinois)* [Video file]. Retrieved 2016, from http://www.flowrestling.org/video/739880-tony-ramos-iowa-vs-zane-richards-illinois#.WR2uzGgrKUk

Saylor, W. (2014, March 22). *133lbs semifinal Tony Ramos (Iowa) vs AJ Schopp (Edinboro)* [Video file]. Retrieved 2016, from FloWrestling website: http://www.flowrestling.org/video/740133-133lbs-semifinal-tony-ramos-iowa-vs-aj-schopp-edinboro#.WRyy8mjyuUk

Saylor, W. (2014, May 31). *57kg Finals Nico Megaludis (PA) vs. Tony Ramos (IL)* [Video file]. Retrieved 2016, from http://www.flowrestling.org/video/746458-57kg-finals-nico-megaludis-pa-vs-tony-ramos-il#.WR3vTmgrKUk

Saylor, W. (2015, May 8). *57kg Semifinals Anthony Ramos (Titan Mercury Wrestling Club) vs. Joe Colon (Titan Mercury Wrestling Club)* [Video file]. Retrieved 2016, from http://www.flowrestling.org/video /769416-57kg-semifinals-anthony-ramos-titan-mercury-wrestling-club-vs-joe-colon-titan-mercury-wrestling-club#.WR2_XmgrKUm

Saylor, W. (2015, May 21). Beat the Streets Results. Retrieved 2016, from http://www.flowrestling.org/article/31637-beat-the-streets-results#.WR2_6GgrKUl

Saylor, W. (2015, December 20). *Dan Dennis Adjusts To 57 Just Fine* [Video file]. Retrieved 2016, from http://www.flowrestling.org/video/816866-dan-dennis-adjusts-to-57-justfine#.WR3ph2g rKUk

Schultz, M. (2016, January 25). Personal interview.

Sesker, C. (2014, August 14). World Championships preview in freestyle wrestling at 57 kg. Retrieved 2016, from http://www.teamusa.org/usa-wrestling/features/2014/august/14/world-championships-preview-in-freestyle-wrestling-at-57-kg

Sesker, C. (2015, November 22). Two-time World Team member Tony Ramos set to compete for Titan Mercury team at World Wrestling Clubs Cup in Iran. Retrieved 2016, from https://www.thepredicament.com/2015/11/two-time-world-team-member-tony-ramos-set-to-compete-for-titan-mercury-team-at-world-wrestling-clubs-cup-in-iran/

Sesker, C. (2015, December 21). Daniel Dennis beats 2 Olympians, wins U.S. Nationals. Retrieved 2016, from https://www.thepredicament.com/2015/12/daniel-dennis-beats-2-olympians-wins-u-s-nationals/

Siebert, E. (2016, October 18). Personal interview.

Smith, E. [Earl Smith]. (2014, November 25). D1CW Video Vault X-2007 Illinois State Finals Tony Ramos vs Adam Sheley [Video file]. Retrieved 2016, from https://www.youtube.com/ watch ?v=Ygqi-aLoSWw

Staff Report. (2014, March 22). Ramos earns long-awaited title as Hawkeyes finish fourth. Retrieved 2016, from http://qctimes.com/sports/wrestling/college/big-10/iowa/ramos-earns-long-awaited-title-as-hawkeyes-finish-fourth/article_d8500ffe-da19-5cf8-8967-26d0da2733d7.html

Steen, A. (2016, August 8). Adama Diatta - Senegal Five Wrestlers to Root for in Rio. Retrieved 2016, from http://news.theopenmat.com/international-wrestling/five-wrestlers-root-rio/58789

Stieber, L. (2016, August 29). Personal interview.

Takedown Wrestling. (2015, April 1). *Takedown Wrestling: Henry Cejudo* [Video file]. Retrieved 2016, from https://www.youtube.com/watch?v=QD-2NxkCsos

Takedown Wrestling. (2015, April 1). *Takedown Wrestling: Tony Ramos* [Video file]. Retrieved 2016, from https://www.youtube.com/watch?v=g-3qfPDGtoY

BIBLIOGRAPHY

Takedown Wrestling. (2015, April 1). *Takedown Wrestling: Tony Ramos* [Video file]. Retrieved 2016, from https://www.youtube.com/watch?v=g-3qfPDGtoY&t=17s

Takedown Wrestling. (2016, April 10). *Dan Dennis wins two straight against Tony Ramos* [Video file]. Retrieved 2016, from https://www.youtube.com/watch?v=RC90wMVYg70

Takedown Wrestling. (2016, April 15). *Takedown Wrestling - Dan Dennis* [Video file]. Retrieved 2016, from https://www.youtube.com/watch?v=GLcsMpq 5f8k&feature=youtu.be

Tavakolian, H. [Hooman D. Tavakolian], H. D. (2014, December 1). *JouyBar, Iran November 2014 - 57kg Tony Ramos vs. Hassan Rahimi* [Video file]. Retrieved 2016, from https://www. you tube.com/watch?v=spU16DqRGl8

Team USA. (2016, April 10). *Olympic Wrestling Trials | Tony Ramos vs Coleman Scott | Full Match* [Video file]. Retrieved 2016, from https://www.youtube.com /watch?v=3oCffnsyIww

Team USA. (2016, April 10). *Olympic Wrestling Trials | Tony Ramos vs Daniel Dennis, Match 2 | Full Match* [Video file]. Retrieved 2016, from https://www.youtube.com/ watch?v=-gXvW7 96FBo

Team USA. (2016, April 10). *Olympic Wrestling Trials | Tony Ramos vs Nashon Garrett | Full Match* [Video file]. Retrieved 2016, from https://www.youtube.com/watch?v =OEtcIhmjTWY

Titan Mercury Wrestling Club. (2014, November 13). *Global Wrestling Championships Live Nov 22 via GFL.TV* [Video file]. Retrieved 2016, from https://www.youtube.com/watch?v= WakMB hSHq70

United World Wrestling. (2015, February 1). F*inal - Freestyle Wrestling 57 kg - RAMOS (USA) vs DIATTA (SEN) 2015 Grand Prix of Paris* [Video file]. Retrieved 2016, from https://www.youtube.com/watch?v=nrDxVl_RrRE

United World Wrestling. (2015, April 11). *Round 1 FS - 57 kg: Yowlys BONNE RODRIGUEZ (CUB) df. Tony RAMOS (USA) by FALL, 4-2* [Video file]. Retrieved 2016, from https://www.youtube.com/watch?v=ObDo0AfNCTw

United World Wrestling. (2015, April 12). *57 kg - Hassan RAHIMI (IRI) df. Tony RAMOS (USA), 6-6* [Video file]. Retrieved 2016, from https://www.youtube.com/watch?v=c Gksw-aORdY &t=602s

United World Wrestling. (2015, April 12). *57 kg - Hassan RAHIMI (IRI) df. Tony RAMOS (USA), 6-6* [Video file]. Retrieved 2016, from https://www.youtube.com/watch?v= cGksw-aORdY &t=217s

University of Michigan. (2016). Wrestling Bio - Eric Grajales. Retrieved 2016, from http://www.mgoblue. com/sports/m-wrestl/mtt/eric_grajales_498820.html

USA Wrestling. (2009, March 23). *Anthony Ramos dec Jon Morrison - FILA Jr WTT freestyle Challenge finals at 55 kg* [Video file]. Retrieved 2016, from https://www. youtube. com/watch?v=beLOClnzA3g

USA Wrestling. (2009, May 23). *Interview with 55 kg FILA Jr WTT freestyle champion Tony Ramos* [Video file]. Retrieved 2016, from https://www.youtube.com/watch ?v=yv8 e9BLaPDY

USA Wrestling. (2009, August 9). *55 kg Freestyle: Tony Ramos (USA) dec. Ohan Gikinyan (Armenia)* [Video file]. Retrieved 2016, from https://www.youtube.com/watch? v=fjGhHa w_HJU

USA Wrestling. (2011, April 11). *FILA JR FS Final 60kg - Tony Ramos vs. Nick Dardanes* [Video file]. Retrieved 2016, from https://www.youtube.com/watch?v=3yJ4CI4_XbU

BIBLIOGRAPHY

USA Wrestling. (2011, April 11). *FILA JR FS Semifinal 60kg - Tony Ramos vs. Jason Tsirtsis* [Video file]. Retrieved 2016, from https://www.youtube.com/watch?v=8aWml-RAmI4

USA Wrestling. (2012, March 3). *Iowa's Tony Ramos after his Big Ten semifinal win* [Video file]. Retrieved 2016, from https://www.youtube.com/watch?v=Tb590jEiGrE

USA Wrestling. (2012, March 4). *Big Ten champion Logan Stieber of Ohio State* [Video file]. Retrieved 2016, from https://www.youtube.com/watch?v=WMjlbJn-D0s

USA Wrestling. (2012, March 17). *3rd place at 133 pounds Tony Ramos of Iowa* [Video file]. Retrieved 2016, from https://www.youtube.com/watch?v=Cu2-P9tmxes

USA Wrestling. (2013, March 9). *Iowa's Tony Ramos after his semifinal win at Big Tens* [Video file]. Retrieved 2016, from https://www.youtube.com/watch?v=i5prTkgxGMM

USA Wrestling. (2013, March 9). *Ohio State's Logan Stieber after Big Ten semifinals* [Video file]. Retrieved 2016, from https://www.youtube.com/watch?v=pcKOM2KsoFw

USA Wrestling. (2013, March 10). *Big Ten champion Logan Stieber of Ohio State* [Video file]. Retrieved 2016, from https://www.youtube.com/watch?v=43A0nLuU8dg

USA Wrestling. (2013, March 16). *133-pound semifinal winner Logan Stieber of Ohio State* [Video file]. Retrieved 2016, from https://www.youtube.com/watch?v=H4yWxEtwfGA

USA Wrestling. (2013, March 22). *Tony Ramos Iowa after 133 lbs semifinal win* [Video file]. Retrieved 2016, from https://www.youtube.com/watch?v=A4id7ik7CYE

USA Wrestling. (2013, March 22). *Tony Ramos (Iowa) after quarterfinal win at 133 lbs. at NCAAs* [Video file]. Retrieved 2016, from https://www.youtube.com/ watch?v=y5notTDdtmM

USA Wrestling. (2013, March 23). *Logan Stieber (Ohio State) after 133 lbs NCAA finals victory* [Video file]. Retrieved 2016, from https://www.youtube.com/watch ?v=jK8oSagiCdI

USA Wrestling. (2013, December 21). *Iowa's Tony Ramos after winning by fall against Penn State* [Video file]. Retrieved 2016, from https://www.youtube.com/watch ?v=fTEewiIRfU8

USA Wrestling. (2014, March 20). *A.J. Schopp (Edinboro) after 133 lbs. Round of 16 NCAAs victory* [Video file]. Retrieved 2016, from https://www.youtube.com/watch? v=hU09Q8DJL9U

USA Wrestling. (2014, March 21). *Tony Ramos (Iowa) after 133 lbs. NCAA quarterfinals victory* [Video file]. Retrieved 2016, from https://www.youtube.com/watch?v=EEx-mpoLoYk

USA Wrestling. (2014, March 21). *Tony Ramos (Iowa) after 133 lbs. NCAA quarterfinals victory* [Video file]. Retrieved 2016, from https://www.youtube.com/watch?v=EEx-mpoLoYk&t=16s

USA Wrestling. (2014, March 21). *Tony Ramos (Iowa) after 133 lbs. NCAA semifinals victory* [Video file]. Retrieved 2016, from https://www.youtube.com/watch?v =0egcshtrYEc

USA Wrestling. (2014, March 21). *Tyler Graff (Wisconsin) after 133 lbs. NCAA semifinals victory* [Video file]. Retrieved 2016, from https://www.youtube.com/watch ?v=0q1ejVqH1vI

USA Wrestling. (2014, March 22). *Iowa Head Coach Tom Brands after team finished 4th at 2014 NCAA Championships* [Video file]. Retrieved 2016, from https://www.youtube.com /watch? v=4iQ_olYyUQM

USA Wrestling. (2014, May). USA WRESTLING SENIOR MEN'S FREESTYLE RANKINGS - MAY 2014. Retrieved 2016, from http://www.teamusa.org/USA-Wrestling/Rankings /US-Senior-Rankings/FS/Individual/2014/May/28/USA-Mens-Freestyle-Ranking-May-2014

BIBLIOGRAPHY

USA Wrestling. (2014, May 19). Big 10 *Champion Tony Ramos prior to 2014 NCAA Championships* [Video file]. Retrieved 2016, from https://www.youtube.com/watch?v=g1siqON8E1w

USA Wrestling. (2014, May 22). Tony *Ramos (Iowa) 2014 NCAA Champion at 133 pounds* [Video file]. Retrieved 2016, from https://www.youtube.com/watch?v=U7itj8zXn_k

USA Wrestling. (2014, May 30). Seeds for six weight classes set for U.S. World Team Trials in Madison, Wis. on Saturday. Retrieved 2016, from http://www.teamusa.org/USA-Wrestling/Features/2014/May/30/Seeds-announced-for-day-one-of-World-Team-Trials

USA Wrestling. (2014, May 31). *Tony Ramos, 57 kg World Team Trials freestyle champion* [Video file]. Retrieved 2016, from https://www.youtube.com/watch?v=-sQLdVR--I4

USA Wrestling. (2014, May 31). *Tony Ramos, World Team Trials 57 kg Challenge Tournament winner* [Video file]. Retrieved 2016, from https://www.youtube.com/watch?v=hhQRF12Dn4g

USA Wrestling. (2014, June 4). *57 KG - Angel Escobedo vs. Tony Ramos* [Video file]. Retrieved 2016, from https://www.youtube.com/watch?v=wRHeGbgE0ME

USA Wrestling. (2014, June 4). *57 KG Finals (2 of 2) - Tony Ramos vs. Sam Hazewinkel* [Video file]. Retrieved 2016, from https://www.youtube.com/watch?v=Z7mYGipe1tg

USA Wrestling. (2014, June 4). *57 KG - Tony Ramos vs. Nico Megaludis* [Video file]. Retrieved 2016, from https://www.youtube.com/watch?v=JfKv9mFFbZM

USA Wrestling. (2014, June 23). *Tony Ramos excited for first World Team opportunity* [Video file]. Retrieved 2016, from https://www.youtube.com/watch?v=N8jJ4nImBac

USA Wrestling. (2014, August 13). *Tony Ramos looking to dominate his way to a World Championship in 2014* [Video file]. Retrieved 2016, from https://www.youtube.com/watch?v=Cs7ytYkeDaE

USA Wrestling. (2014, September 8). 57 KG Round 1 - *Tony Ramos (USA) vs Bekhbayar Erdenebat (MGL)* [Video file]. Retrieved 2016, from https://www.youtube.com/watch?v=gmrQVeO-Mjs

USA Wrestling. (2014, October 23). T*ony Ramos on first Worlds experience, training with Iowa and future plans* [Video file]. Retrieved 2016, from https://www.youtube.com/watch?v=FWW8a7Se0y8

USA Wrestling. (2015, February 21). *Tony Ramos on Russia, Paris, World Cup and becoming a new dad* [Video file]. Retrieved 2016, from https://www.youtube.com/watch?v=9mQhQqJQTak

USA Wrestling. (2015, April 11). *Tony Ramos (USA) after win over Russia in 2015 FS World Cup* [Video file]. Retrieved 2016, from https://www.youtube.com/watch?v=Y2ornyqRyq0

USA Wrestling. (2015, April 12). *Tony Ramos (USA) after loss to Rahimi (IRI), 2015 FS World Cup* [Video file]. Retrieved 2016, from https://www.youtube.com/watch?v=-Xd2BNyFXBQ

USA Wrestling. (2015, May 8). *Andrew Hochstrasser, 57 kg freestyle Semis winner at U.S. Open* [Video file]. Retrieved 2016, from https://www.youtube.com/watch?v=tl6Mhz1uNPs

USA Wrestling. (2015, May 9). *Tony Ramos, 57 kg freestyle Champion at 2015 U.S. Open* [Video file]. Retrieved 2016, from https://www.youtube.com/watch?v=1chQ565tBq0

USA Wrestling. (2015, June 13). *Joe Colon after WTT Challenge Tournament win at 57 kg* [Video file]. Retrieved 2016, from https://www.youtube.com/watch?v=EnVsfmZu4rY

USA Wrestling. (2015, June 13). *Tony Ramos, World Team Trials Champion at 57 kg* [Video file]. Retrieved 2016, from https://www.youtube.com/watch?v=lCLiwRmni6A

BIBLIOGRAPHY

USA Wrestling. (2015, June 14). *Daniel Dennis, WTT Challenge Tournament 61 kg winner* [Video file]. Retrieved 2016, from https://www.youtube.com/watch?v=yOucXNU-n58

USA Wrestling. (2015, June 18). *57kg Finals (1 of 2), Joe Colon, Titan Mercury WC vs Anthony Ramos, Titan Mercury WC* [Video file]. Retrieved 2016, from https://www. youtube.com /watch?v= Ai1CWcXmCCk

USA Wrestling. (2015, June 18). *57kg Finals (2 of 2), Anthony Ramos, Titan Mercury WC vs Joe Colon, Titan Mercury WC* [Video file]. Retrieved 2016, from https://www. youtube .com/ watch?v= KRpYBLNWcLE

USA Wrestling. (2015, June 28). *Tony Ramos at World Team Training Camp at OTC* [Video file]. Retrieved 2016, from https://www.youtube.com/watch?v=NJMMfwaCdhU

USA Wrestling. (2015, December 19). *Daniel Dennis, 2015 U.S. Senior Nationals champion at 57 kg* [Video file]. Retrieved 2016, from https://www.youtube.com/watch? v=C72S_PjR Tfc

USA Wrestling. (2016). Biography: Angel Escobedo. Retrieved 2016, from http://www.team usa.org/USA-Wrestling/Athlete-Bios/ES/Angel-Escobedo

USA Wrestling. (2016). Biography: Coleman Scott. Retrieved 2016, from http://www.teamusa .org/usa-wrestling/athlete-bios/sc/coleman-scott

USA Wrestling. (2016). Biography: SAM HAZEWINKEL. Retrieved 2016, from http://www. teamusa.org /usa-wrestling/athletes/Sam-Hazewinkel

USA Wrestling. (2016). USA Wrestling tournament results. Retrieved 2016, from http://www .teamusa.org /usa-wrestling/results

USA Wrestling. (2016, January 21). *Daniel Dennis on going to Yarygin, his return to mats and Olympic quest* [Video file]. Retrieved 2016, from https://www.youtube.com/watch? v=8B kbOGPD9RU

USA Wrestling. (2016, January 21). *World Team member Tony Ramos on going to Yarygin and Olympic year ahead* [Video file]. Retrieved 2016, from https://www.youtube.com /watch? v=eHrXLz1TZGA

USA Wrestling. (2016, March 5). *Tony Ramos (USA) after 57 kg semis win at Pan Am Olympic Qualifier* [Video file]. Retrieved 2016, from https://www.youtube.com /watch?v=MVsmg 5P3e6c

USA Wrestling. (2016, April 4). *HWC's Dennis, Metcalf, Telford, Louive, Ramos talk about Olympic Trials* [Video file]. Retrieved 2016, from https://www.youtube.com /watch?v= d_sEzFMjnYI

USA Wrestling. (2016, April 8). *Tony Ramos after Olympic Trials Press Conference* [Video file]. Retrieved 2016, from https://www.youtube.com/watch?v=QZzyK3LkMqc

USA Wrestling. (2016, April 10). *Daniel Dennis wins 2016 U.S. Olympic Team Trials at 57 kg* [Video file]. Retrieved 2016, from https://www.youtube.com/watch ?v=_0bXETpi0uE

USA Wrestling. (2016, April 10). *Tony Ramos after Olympic Trials semis win at 57 kg* [Video file]. Retrieved 2016, from https://www.youtube.com/watch?v=jSqhz6eb-oY

USA Wrestling. (2016, June 11). *Tony Ramos (USA) after win over Azerbaijan at Freestyle World Cup* [Video file]. Retrieved 2016, from https://www.youtube.com/watch? v=yw6nhuFvWWU

USA Wrestling. (2016, June 11). *Tony Ramos (USA) after win over India at Freestyle World Cup* [Video file]. Retrieved 2016, from https://www.youtube.com/watch? v=SWkiN zwJJMM

Vakulskas, B. (2013, March 23). *Tony Ramos, 3-23-13* [Video file]. Retrieved 2016, from https:// www.youtube.com/watch?v=wgARFSFBVkU

BIBLIOGRAPHY

Vakulskas, B. (2013, March 23). *Tony Ramos, 3-23-13* [Video file]. Retrieved 2016, from https://www.youtube.com/watch?v=wgARFSFBVkU&t=47s

Velliquette, N. (2014, March 21). *133 Quater Finals: Ramos (IOWA) vs. Beckman (LEH)* [Video file]. Retrieved 2016, from http://www.flowrestling.org/video/740119-133-quater-finals-ramos-iowa-vs-beckman-leh#.WR2rc2grKUk

Velliquette, N. (2014, March 21). *133 Semi Finals: Ramos (Iowa) vs. Schopp (Edinboro)* [Video file]. Retrieved 2016, from http://www.flowrestling.org/video/740134-133-semifinals-ramos-iowa-vs-schopp-edinboro#.WR2vM2grKUk

Velliquette, N. (2014, March 25). *133lbs Finals: Ramos (Iowa) vs. Graff (Wisconsin)* [Video file]. Retrieved 2016, from http://www.flowrestling.org/video/740818-133lbs-finals-ramos-iowa-vs-Graff-wisconsin#.WR2xOmgrKUk

Velliquette, N. (2014, May 13). *RAMOS (Ep. 1.)* [Video file]. Retrieved 2016, from http://www.flowrestling.org/video/745287-ramos-ep-1#.WR3RB2grKUk

Velliquette, N. (2014, May 20). *RAMOS (Ep 2.)* [Video file]. Retrieved 2016, from http://www.flowrestling.org/video/745532-ramos-ep-2#.WR2nBWgrKUl

Viera, M. (2010, February 6). Virginia Tech wrestling bounces back from brink of extinction. Retrieved 2016, from http://www.washingtonpost.com/wp-dyn/content/article/2010/02/05/AR2010020503959.html

WIAA: Tournament Series Results. (1999). Retrieved 2016, from Wisconsin Interscholastic Athletic Association website: https://www.wiaawi.org/Sports/Wrestling/StateResultsArchive.aspx

Wikipedia. (2014, September 8). 2014 World Wrestling Championships – Men's freestyle 57 kg. Retrieved 2016, from https://en.wikipedia.org/wiki/2014_World_Wrestling_Championships_%E2%80%93_Men's_freestyle_57_kg

Wikipedia. (2016). Biography: Adama Diata. Retrieved 2016, from https://en.wikipedia.org/wiki/Adama_Diatta

Wikipedia. (2017, March 22). Biography: Harold Nichols. Retrieved from https://en.wikipedia.org/wiki/Harold_Nichols

Wikipedia. (2016). Henry Carlos Cejudo. Retrieved 2016, from https://en.wikipedia.org/wiki/Henry_Cejudo

Wikipedia. (2016). 2015 Wrestling World Cup - Men's freestyle. Retrieved 2016, from https://en.wikipedia.org/wiki/2015_Wrestling_World_Cup_-_Men's_freestyle

Wikipedia. (2016, May 9). Biography: E. G. Schroeder. Retrieved 2016, from https://en.wikipedia.org/wiki/E._G._Schroeder

Williamson, J. (2013, March 23). *Logan Stieber Two for Two* [Video file]. Retrieved 2016, from http://www.flowrestling.org/video/701764-logan-stieber-two-for-two#.WR2aoGgrKUk

Wilson, N. (2016, April 9). Chico's Garrett wrestles for spot on Olympic team. Retrieved 2016, from http://www.chicoer.com/article/NA/20160409/SPORTS/160409729

Wisconsin Badgers. (2013, March 22). *Wisconsin Wrestling: Barry Davis on Tyler Graff and Day 2* [Video file]. Retrieved 2016, from https://www.youtube.com/watch?v=tRWy-od70ic

Wisconsin Rapids Wrestling. (1998). Retrieved 2016, from Rapids Wrestling website: http://www.wisconsinrapids.com/wrestling/scheduleresults.html

Wisconsin Wrestling Rankings Archive - 2006-2007 Final Individual. (2006). Retrieved 2016, from Wisconsin Wrestling Online website: http://www.wiwrestling.com/archive0607individual.htm

WrestlingStats.com (Ed.). (n.d.). NCAA Wrestling Tournament Bracket Sheets. Retrieved 2016, from Wrestling Stats website: http://www.wrestlingstats.com/ncaa/brackets.htm

BIBLIOGRAPHY

Yetzer, N. (2012, January 18). *Carter v Ramos* [Video file]. Retrieved 2016, from http://www.flowrestling.org/video/574870-carter-v-ramos#.WR3X5mgrKUk

2007 • TONY RAMOS AS THE GLENBARD NORTH PANTHER MASCOT
TONY WAVES THE SCHOOL FLAG AT THE HOMECOMING FOOTBALL GAME
PHOTOGRAPH COURTESY • GLENBARD NORTH HIGH SCHOOL YEARBOOK